The Historical Jesus Question

'Tis a pious account, cried my father, but not philosophical—there is more religion in it than sound science.

Laurence Sterne, *Tristram Shandy*

THE HISTORICAL JESUS QUESTION

The Challenge of History
to Religious Authority

Gregory W. Dawes

Westminster John Knox Press
LOUISVILLE
LONDON • LEIDEN

Book design by Sharon Adams
Cover design by PAZ Design Group
Cover Illustration by Kurt Scholz

First edition
Published by Westminster John Knox Press
Louisville, Kentucky

A Deo title

This book is printed on acid-free paper that meets the American National Standards Institute Z39.48 standard. ∞

PRINTED IN THE UNITED STATES OF AMERICA

01 02 03 04 05 06 07 08 09 10 — 10 9 8 7 6 5 4 3 2 1

Library of Congress Cataloging-in-Publication Data

Dawes, Gregory W.
    The historical Jesus question : the challenge of history to religious authority / Gregory W. Dawes.—1st ed.
       p. cm.
    Includes bibliographical references and index.
    ISBN 0-664-22458-X
    1. Jesus Christ—Historicity—History of doctrines. I. Title.

BT303.2 .D38 2001
232.9'08'09—dc21   2001032583

Contents

Preface

The present work is intended as a companion to my recently published anthology entitled *The Historical Jesus Quest,* although I hope that it will also be useful in its own right. In compiling the anthology I was faced with the task of selecting eleven authors whose work would illustrate important developments in the earliest stages of the historical Jesus discussion. The authors chosen covered a spectrum of views and a considerable period of time, from the pioneering work of Benedict Spinoza in the seventeenth century to the cautious reopening of the question by Ernst Käsemann in the mid-twentieth. The anthology did include some introductory comments, setting the work of the authors chosen in its wider intellectual context. However, the format did not allow for a satisfactory discussion of the issues that were raised. The present work is intended to remedy that defect, by offering a series of extended studies. Their aim is not that of summarizing the exegetical and historical conclusions at which these scholars arrived. (There are plenty of works that offer excellent summaries of those conclusions.) Rather, my intention is a broader one. I am interested in exploring the challenge of historical knowledge to religious authority, a challenge that first emerged in the educated circles of seventeenth-century Europe and of which the historical Jesus question is merely the most obvious expression.

For the historical Jesus question, while interesting on its own terms, is still more interesting when it is regarded as expressive of this major change in religious attitudes. In the introductory chapter I have tried to describe this change, using Hans Frei's phrase "the great reversal." For an increasing number of educated Europeans, the Bible ceased to be the framework of all knowledge. Instead it became merely one object of study among others, to be fitted into a framework of knowledge derived from outside of itself. This represented an unprecedented challenge to biblical authority, in which historical knowledge came to be pitted against Christian faith and the Bible lost its claims to uniqueness. The theological response to this challenge is the subject of this book. I am interested in the various ways in which theologians attempted to defend biblical authority, either by accepting the challenges of history or by reaffirming Christian claims in defiance of historical knowledge. I believe that this story will be of interest not just to students of theology, but to a much wider audience. For it not only offers an insight into the problems facing educated Christians in an increasingly secular modern Europe. It also illustrates the difficulties facing any claim to ethical or religious authority in the modern world.

When the idea arose of writing a volume to accompany my anthology, it soon became clear that it would be necessary to make a further selection. For not all the authors whose work was included in the earlier work deal with these underlying issues. (One thinks, for example, of William Wrede, whose interests were historical and exegetical rather than theological.) Even when they do deal with the theological issues, there is a some duplication in the answers they give. (The conclusions of Johannes Weiss, for instance, are recapitulated in the work of Albert Schweitzer, and the reflections of Martin Kähler are taken up and developed in the work of the "dialectical theologians.") For this reason I decided to choose just seven authors from the original eleven. Given that the separation between historical and religious perspectives had already occurred, these authors represent the most significant attempts to reconcile the warring partners or (in some cases) to formalize the divorce. There have, of course, been more recent attempts to reconcile historical and religious claims. For this reason the last chapter will go beyond the anthology in order to examine the work of Wolfhart Pannenberg, adding an eighth author to our list. While still more names could have been added, the work of these authors may be regarded as foundational. The theologians of our own time live in their shadow.

The introductory chapter deals with the earliest modern challenges to biblical authority, which I locate in the mid-seventeenth century. That chapter will attempt to identify the factors that brought about this revolution in human thought and will examine some examples of its religious impact. After these preliminary remarks, chapter 1 studies the work of the first of our major authors, Benedict Spinoza. For it is Spinoza who outlines the program historical criticism would follow for the next three hundred years. The next chapter discusses the work of David Friedrich Strauss, whose scepticism (at least in the early stage of his career) is coupled with a desire to salvage the religious meaning of the Christian story by deployment of the category of "myth." This, too, I will suggest, set a pattern that continues to the present day. The third chapter deals with the challenge of apocalyptic thought in the work of Albert Schweitzer, which both highlights the difference between Jesus' world and ours and suggests what aspects of his message may be reappropriated today. The following chapter deals with the work of the theologian who took most seriously the challenges posed by the "great reversal" of the seventeenth and eighteenth centuries, namely Ernst Troeltsch. In the following two chapters I discuss the "dialectical theology" of Karl Barth and Rudolf

Bultmann, both of whom reject many of the assumptions on which the historical Jesus quest had been based. United in their rejection, they go on to offer different ways of reaffirming the primacy of the biblical story in a world in which that story seems no longer credible. The final study focuses on the thought of two more recent thinkers, both of whom are reacting—albeit in different ways—to the work of Barth and Bultmann. The first of these is Ernst Käsemann, whose 1953 essay accepted many of the criticisms made by the dialectical theologians. But it also cautiously reopened the historical Jesus quest, leading to a renewal of the discussion that Barth and Bultmann had attempted to bring to a halt. The second of our more recent thinkers is Wolfhart Pannenberg, whose reaction to the dialectical theology is much more thoroughgoing. For Pannenberg—like Troeltsch before him—attempts to develop a consistently historical theology. The conclusion evaluates the answers given and poses the question of what options, if any, remain open to the theologian today.

At the beginning of their study of the development of seventeenth-century scientific thought, Stephen Toulmin and Jane Goodfield write: "Anyone who embarks on a work of historical synthesis and interpretation . . . inevitably places himself much in the debt of scholars by whose devoted work he profits." I am very conscious of this debt, especially when it comes to identifying the critical shift in mentality that characterizes the seventeenth century. Although I have tried to become acquainted with some of the more important works of this period, the footnotes to that section betray my reliance on the scholarship of others. With regard to the authors whose work is discussed in the studies which follow, my problem is somewhat reversed. Here I have relied as much as possible on a firsthand acquaintance with the primary sources. As a result, I am uncomfortably aware of the vast body of secondary literature with which I have not been able to interact. I suspect that few of my conclusions will come as a surprise to those who have studied these thinkers in depth. However, given the importance of the topic, there is no harm in surveying the field afresh. This fresh survey has also enabled me to build up a cumulative argument in support of the conclusion found in the final chapter. Whatever one makes of that conclusion, I hope the book will give the student some appreciation of the work of these pioneers. Each has taken the challenges of modernity very seriously and—whatever position we ourselves adopt—there is much we can learn from their attempts.

There is a further problem with which the author of a book like this is faced. In an ideal world, the work of these scholars would not be studied in isolation from the social and political context of their time. The question of historical context is particularly important when one is attempting to understand the dialectical theologians, namely Karl Barth and Rudolf Bultmann. For while their theology is comprehensible in its own terms, it must also be seen as a response to the needs of their age. If it were not for the First World War and the readiness of liberal theologians to support the German war policy, something like the dialectical theology *may* eventually have emerged, but perhaps in quite a different form. However, it is impossible to do justice to these matters here. For this reason I have deliberately refrained from making any comment on the social and political context in which these theologians wrote. The only comments of this type are to be found in the introductory chapter, which tries to set the scene for the book as a whole. All I can do is to alert the reader to this fact and to urge her to bear it in mind.

I am grateful to Dr. David Ward of the University of Otago's Department of Philosophy for reading and commenting on a draft version of chapter 1. Professor Alistair Fox of the Division of Humanities provided much-appreciated assistance by way of research grants. Our head of department, Associate Professor Paul Trebilco, allowed me to reorganize my teaching, so as to free up some time for the completion of the project. My colleague Dr. Ivor Davidson provided much-needed guidance as I penetrated the labyrinth of modern theology, although he will probably be among the first to take issue with my conclusions. I am grateful to the librarians of the University of Otago and of the Hewitson Library, Knox College for their assistance. Dr. David Orton in his role as editor for both Deo Publishing and Westminster John Knox Press has been very supportive of the venture, even when he must have wondered what form it would eventually take. Finally, no acknowledgments would be complete without mentioning Kristin, who lived with the book day and night, at considerable cost to herself, and who is probably sick to death of hearing the words, "Listen to this! It's *really interesting.*"

To end this preface, I would like to offer some further words of advice to the reader. I hope the present work will be accessible to a general audience and that such readers will not be discouraged by the large number of footnotes. Those who simply ignore this scholarly apparatus will miss nothing essential to the argumentation of the book. Those who are interested may wish to note that I use the abbreviation "cf." (Latin *confer* 'compare') not in its more technical sense, but—in the absence of a direct quotation—either to indicate the sources of my ideas or to offer supporting evidence. With regard to my sources, I have relied upon translations of the key works wherever these were available, going back to the original language only where this seemed necessary to defend a particular interpretation. Where important texts were not available in English, I have supplied my own translations, but I have included the original language in the footnotes, for the reader who is able and willing to consult it. The format is a bit unwieldy, but once again my intention was to leave the body of the work as free as possible of scholarly encumbrances, while making it possible for my colleagues to check my claims.

With regard to the reading of the book, I confess that it has grown to a length far in excess of what I originally intended. However, I hope that this, too, will not be an impediment to the general reader. First of all, each essay is intended to be comprehensible on its own terms. Together they offer a cumulative argument, which is spelt out in the conclusion, but the reader who dissents from my conclusion may still find the individual studies helpful. If a reader wishes to read just one or two chapters, I would encourage her also to read the introduction, which sets the scene for the later discussions and to which reference is made throughout. Secondly, I have arranged the material under topics. While this does make for a degree of repetition, it also means that the reader may take a "cross-section" of the work by judicious use of the subject index and the chapter subheadings. If she wishes to focus on, for example, the understanding of history or the question of miracles, then she may simply turn to the relevant section of each chapter. For a fuller understanding, of course, it will be necessary to read the book as a whole. Ideally, the book will make itself redundant by leading the reader back to the work of the great scholars to which it makes reference. If it does this, it will have amply justified both its existence and its length.

Introduction

The Challenge of the Seventeenth Century

The European races . . . up to our own times . . .
have been living upon the accumulated capital of ideas
provided for them by the genius of the seventeenth century.
Alfred North Whitehead

It is a perilous task to attempt to trace the origins of a major change in human thought. Yet to fail to do so would be to attribute too much to the genius of individual thinkers and to neglect the context in which they worked. The scholars we are about to study altered forever the attitude of educated Europeans towards the Bible. But those attitudes had begun to change before the first of our authors, Benedict Spinoza, put pen to paper. This changed view of the Bible was, of course, neither sudden nor universal. Nonetheless, those who put forward these ideas were influential figures, and it soon became necessary for Christian thinkers to grapple with the issues they raised. What was this change in attitude towards the Bible, and why did it occur? This is the question to which this introductory chapter will be devoted.

My suggestion is that five major cultural movements contributed to the rise of modern biblical criticism.[1] These five movements, individually and

---

[1] There is nothing very original in these suggestions, which closely resemble those put forward by, for instance, the historian Klaus Scholder in *The Birth of Modern Critical Theology: Origins and Problems of Biblical Criticism in the Seventeenth Century* (1966), translated by John Bowden (London: SCM, 1990). But it is good that we should be reminded of the seriousness of the seventeenth-century challenge to religious authority. Incidentally, I have not followed up Scholder's suggestion (26–45) that the Socinian controversy represents the emergence of reason as an independent force in matters of faith, a development that led inexorably (even against the intentions of its exponents) to the criticism of scripture. I am not entirely convinced by this argument, but, in any case, the developments Scholder mentions could be understood as yet another example of the reaction to religious controversy, a matter discussed in section two of the present chapter. While Scholder also ends his study (cf. ibid., 110–42) with a discussion of the work of René Descartes (1596–1650), my discussion is broader, focusing on the redefinition of the task of explanation that is associated with the rise of modern science. For a more detailed study of the crisis of biblical authority in England and of the deist response to this crisis, the reader may wish to consult Henning Graf Reventlow's magisterial work *The Authority of the Bible and the Rise of the Modern World* (1980), translated by John Bowden (London: SCM, 1984).

collectively, offered a dramatic challenge to the taken-for-granted Christian view of biblical authority. In doing so, they set the scene for the rise of the question of the historical Jesus. A first influence was a new sense of historical distance, which took the form of a growing awareness of the diversity of human cultures over time. This new sense of history begins to develop long before the time of Spinoza, but its influence can be traced in both his work and that of his contemporaries. A second factor was a disillusionment with religious controversy, which has its roots in the conflicts of the sixteenth and early seventeenth centuries. A third influence was the new astronomy of Copernicus and Galileo, which offered a very direct challenge to the biblical worldview. A fourth factor is represented by the voyages of discovery, which greatly expanded the European view of human history. A fifth and last cultural change was a new sense of what constituted a reliable claim to knowledge, which was closely related to the emergence of the natural sciences. The impact of all these movements on seventeenth-century thought was profound. Indeed their echoes are still being heard today. The authors who are the subject of this book either accepted these changes, reinterpreting their faith accordingly, or found some way of shielding their faith from the new knowledge of the age.

1. A New Sense of the Past

Renaissance Humanism

A first cultural shift is one that predates the seventeenth century but deserves at least a passing mention, since it continued to be of importance as that century dawned. It is the growing sense of the distance between the present and the past. This sense of the past is already evident in the sixteenth century—it is, for instance, taken for granted by the Protestant Reformers[2]—but at that time it was a relatively recent development. It is true that, in tracing the history of European thought, it is easy to exaggerate the contrast between Middle Ages and the Renaissance. Much recent scholarship has reminded us how deeply rooted in the medieval period are the developments that we think of as "modern."[3] Nonetheless, the evidence suggests that our modern sense of

[2]Peter Burke, *The Renaissance Sense of the Past* (London: Edward Arnold, 1969), 40.
[3]Cf. Brian P. Copenhaver and Charles B. Schmitt, *Renaissance Philosophy*, A History of Western Philosophy 3, Opus (Oxford: Oxford University Press, 1992), 3–4. These authors note the artificiality of our modern division between the medieval and the Renaissance worlds, while agreeing (332 et passim) that a new sense of history began to emerge about this time.

history dates back no further than the Renaissance, that is to say, the fifteenth century in Italy and the sixteenth and early seventeenth centuries elsewhere.[4]

A leading exponent of this idea is the historian Peter Burke. Burke suggests that this new sense of the past embraced at least three factors. The first is what he calls "the sense of anachronism":[5] the realization that the world inhabited by our forebears was not necessarily the same as our own. While medieval thinkers were certainly aware that the world of the past was in some respects different from that of the present, in Burke's words, "they did not take the difference very seriously."[6] The second factor is a new attention to evidence, coupled with the realization that not all historical sources are equally reliable. In other words, with the Renaissance we witness the emergence of what we now call "historical criticism": the evaluation of historical sources for accuracy and the reconstruction of the past in the light of this evaluation. The third factor is an interest in historical explanation, more precisely an interest in what Burke describes as "middle-range explanations."[7] Whereas medieval authors understood history by appeal to either the motives of individuals or the (revealed) purposes of God, Renaissance authors were interested in intermediate forces. They focused on tendencies and recurring patterns that could be understood by observation and analysis. In all three ways, Burke argues, the sense of the past we find in Renaissance thinkers differs from that which is commonly found during the medieval period.[8]

Burke's claims have been given further support by the legal studies of Donald R. Kelley. For Kelley, too, the humanist tradition of the Renaissance marks a significant shift in our understanding of the past. Many thinkers of this period were struck by the distance between their world and that of the documents they studied. As a result of this, they were aware of the difficulty of gaining access to that world and representing it accurately.[9] As Kelley writes,

> medieval authors had possessed a 'sense of history' to the extent that they distinguished it formally from annals and substantially from poetry and insisted on its narrative and truthful character, but they showed little awareness of perspective or the scholarly problems of gaining access to 'antiquity'.

[4]Cf. Burke, *The Renaissance Sense of the Past,* 1.
[5]Ibid.
[6]Ibid.
[7]Ibid., 77.
[8]For a similar view, see Margaret T. Hodgen, *Early Anthropology in the Sixteenth and Seventeenth Centuries* (Philadelphia: University of Pennsylvania Press, 1964), 34.
[9]Cf. Donald R. Kelley, *Foundations of Modern Historical Scholarship: Language, Law, and History in the French Renaissance* (New York: Columbia University Press, 1970), 23–24.

> They were indeed conscious of Christian tradition and various formulae
> of cultural change . . . but they lacked the self-conscious, self-confident,
> self-promoting curiosity of Petrarch and his humanist successors.[10]

Kelley points out that the emergence of a historical consciousness during the Renaissance was closely related to the development of philology.
Philology sought to understanding the past by way of the editing, translation, and interpretation of ancient texts.[11] A key figure here is Lorenzo
Valla (1407–57), whose exposure of the "Donation of Constantine" as a
medieval forgery would become a powerful symbol of the iconoclastic
power of this new science.[12] Kelley also notes that it was this interest in
history (rather than metaphysics) which led Renaissance humanists to be
suspicious of the allegorical reading of texts,[13] a suspicion picked up and
developed by the Protestant Reformers.[14] This last development should
not, of course, be overstated. For Renaissance philosophers did continue
to employ allegorical explanations, which were common in, for instance,
the interpretations of Plato written by Marsilio Ficino (1433–99).[15]

The Study of the New Testament

The impact of this new historical consciousness on the study of the New
Testament has been documented by Jerry H. Bentley. Indeed Bentley
argues that it is the humanist scholars of the Renaissance who should be
regarded as the founders of modern biblical criticism.[16] Influenced by
"the revival of Greek learning, the emergence of philological criticism,
and the invention of printing,"[17] these scholars set about assembling
New Testament manuscripts, developing principles of textual criticism
and, most significantly, understanding the New Testament as the product

---

[10]Donald R. Kelley, "The Theory of History," in *The Cambridge History of Renaissance
Philosophy*, edited by Charles B. Schmitt and Quentin Skinner (Cambridge: Cambridge
University Press, 1988), 747.

[11]Cf. Kelley, *Foundations of Modern Historical Scholarship*, 19–21.

[12]Cf. ibid., 38. Burke (*The Renaissance Sense of the Past*, 55) notes that the "Donation
of Constantine" was "suddenly seen to be a forgery" by at least three Renaissance scholars, acting independently, a fact that merely illustrates how widespread the new awareness
of history was.

[13]Kelley, *Foundations of Modern Historical Scholarship*, 22 (see also 31: "In general, for
Valla as for most humanists, it was the letter and not the spirit that gave life").

[14]Cf. T. H. L. Parker, *Calvin's Old Testament Commentaries* (Edinburgh: T. & T. Clark,
1986), 70–72, 76–77.

[15]Cf. Copenhaver and Schmitt, *Renaissance Philosophy*, 155–56.

[16]Cf. Jerry H. Bentley, *Humanists and Holy Writ: New Testament Scholarship in the
Renaissance* (Princeton, N.J.: Princeton University Press, 1983), 3.

[17]Ibid., 15.

of an age different from their own.[18] Setting the results of their textual study over against the dogmatic use of scripture, the humanists not only prepared the way for the Reformation, but also set the scene for a thoroughly historical method of biblical interpretation.[19] Lorenzo Valla himself turned his hand to the textual criticism of the New Testament and called into question the accuracy of the ancient Latin translation known as the Vulgate, which formed the basis of medieval theological discussion.[20] However the most influential figure in this field is the famous Desiderius Erasmus (ca. 1469–1536), whose edition of the Greek New Testament was to become the *textus receptus* (received text) that was to be so influential in later centuries.[21] Erasmus's philological study also had its theological implications, leading him, too, to criticize the Vulgate. For instance, in translating Luke 1:28 (χαῖρε, κεχαριτωμένη; "Greetings, most favored one") Erasmus pointed out that one should not read into this verse the medieval discussions of the doctrine of "grace," as the traditional *Ave gratia plena* (Hail, full of grace) might lead one to do.[22] More dangerously still, he read the phrase ἐφ' ᾧ ~ in Romans 5:12 in a causal sense ("because"; Latin *quatenus*) rather than as a relative (the Vulgate's *in quo*; "in whom"). This apparently minor change risked undermining a key biblical proof text for the doctrine of original sin.[23] Much more could be said on the impact of renaissance humanism on biblical scholarship. But it should already be clear that—long before the seventeenth century began—new ways of interpreting the Bible were already being explored. The earliest writers we will study would build on those foundations.

2. The Effect of Religious Controversy

The Wars of Religion

Turning to the seventeenth century itself, we may note a second influence on the attitude of educated Europeans towards the Bible. This factor deserves closer scrutiny, since it brings us very close to the time of Benedict Spinoza, the first of the authors to be studied in the chapters that follow. This second influence is that of the conflict between Catholic and Protestant Christians, which so devastated Europe in the

[18]Cf. ibid., 215–17.
[19]Cf. ibid., 218.
[20]Cf. ibid., 32–69.
[21]Cf. Bruce M. Metzger, *The Text of the New Testament,* 2d edition (Oxford: Clarendon Press, 1968), 106.
[22]Cf. Bentley, *Humanists and Holy Writ,* 169–70.
[23]Cf. ibid., 170–72.

century after the Reformation and which reached its climax during the Thirty Years War (1618–48). While religion was only one of the factors contributing to that conflict, the fact that it was waged in the name of religion gave it a symbolic significance that endures to our own day. In the minds of many European intellectuals, the war not only showed that appeals to religious authority were contradictory, since each side claimed divine guidance; it also showed that dependence on religious authority led to irreconcilable conflicts and bloodshed. For such thinkers, in other words, the wars of religion called into question the authority not just of the churches but also of the Bible. While some thinkers went so far as to reject religion altogether, it was more common to appeal to reason rather than revelation, in support of a "natural religion" that would have no need of the authority of the Christian scriptures.

The Deist Option: Edward Herbert

A clear illustration of these tendencies is to be found in the work of Edward Herbert (Lord Herbert of Cherbury, ca. 1583–1648), often regarded as the founder of English deism.[24] While various of Herbert's writings could be chosen, a useful starting point is the work entitled *De Religione Laici* (On the religion of a layman), published in 1645. Herbert begins this treatise by describing the problem of competing religious claims, which are so often accompanied by dogmatism and intolerance.[25] Herbert is clearly appalled by the consequences of these exclusive religious claims. For instance, at one point he writes:

> Because . . . the schoolmen every one, clad in whatever gown or robe, have allowed no religion to be adorned with any but their own faith and their own miracles . . . , if they banish every doctrine which does not enter by this gate, and if finally they keep the keys for themselves and themselves alone, good God! what tyranny they will introduce! Especially when they boast their own church so incapable of error that almost no dogma may be rejected, or even softened, without danger of anathema, not to say at the peril of one's life.[26]

[24]On Herbert's relationship to deism, see Reventlow, *The Authority of the Bible and the Rise of the Modern World,* 185–86, and Peter Harrison's *"Religion" and the Religions in the English Enlightenment* (Cambridge: Cambridge University Press, 1990), 61–62. Chapter 3 of the latter work provides a helpful overview of Herbert's writings.

[25]Harold R. Hutcheson (*Lord Herbert of Cherbury's* De Religione Laici [New Haven, Conn. Yale University Press, 1944], 61–62 et passim) argues that early deism, in particular, was motivated by both "indignation at the barbarity of religious persecution" and scepticism of the possibility of certainty in matters religious.

[26]Edward Herbert, *De Religione Laici,* in Harold R. Hutcheson, *Lord Herbert of Cherbury's* De Religione Laici (New Haven, Conn.:Yale University Press, 1944), 119.

Given these competing claims to religious authority, Herbert continues, the ordinary layperson (*Viator* the "Wayfarer") is left in doubt as to the path of salvation.[27] For not only are these different religious authorities in conflict, but there is no clear way of deciding between them, unless we ourselves have received a revelation from God.[28] How then shall the ordinary person make progress? Herbert's suggestion is that we search out and live by certain basic religious convictions, convictions that transcend the divisions of religious communities.[29] These traditions are accessible to reason alone; they do not require appeals to authority. As he writes, "those truths . . . that flourish everywhere, and always will flourish, are not confined by the limits of any one religion. For they are divinely inscribed in the understanding itself, and are subject to no traditions written or unwritten."[30] For Herbert these "catholic" (in the sense of universal) truths can be reduced to five: "1. That there is some supreme divinity. 2. That this divinity ought to be worshipped. 3. That virtue joined with piety is the best method of divine worship. 4. That we should return to our right selves from sins. 5. That reward or punishment is bestowed after this life is finished."[31] Because these truths have been "engraved on the human mind by God,"[32] they are universally acknowledged.[33]

The challenge to traditional theological claims is clear. For Herbert's argument is not a rejection of religion, but an insistence that only human reason can lead to truth in religious matters. As he writes, "we must either submit to the leadership of Reason or wander in endless labyrinths."[34] Interestingly, this insistence is itself theologically grounded. For Herbert argues that reason can yield truth in religious matters because God has left signs of his truth in creation and in the history of human religions.[35] In other words, Herbert's confidence in the power of human reason is based on what we might call a theology of providence.[36] His understanding of providence extends the history of revelation

---

[27]Ibid., 87.

[28]Cf. ibid., 129.

[29]Ibid., 89.

[30]Ibid.

[31]Ibid., 129.

[32]Ibid.

[33]Peter Harrison (*"Religion" and the Religions in the English Enlightenment*, 65–73) describes the way in which Herbert's five truths first appear in his 1624 work *De Veritate*, in the context of an epistemology: such truths arise from a "Natural Instinct" implanted in us by God, which offers the most secure form of access to truth.

[34]Herbert, *De Religione Laici*, 121.

[35]Cf. ibid., 103 et passim.

[36]For a more precise description of Herbert's understanding of providence, see Reventlow, *The Authority of the Bible and the Rise of the Modern World*, 188.

well beyond the biblical framework, both chronologically and geographically.[37] The providence of God is a universal providence, embracing the
whole history of humanity.[38] For this reason, the truths yielded by Herbert's "natural theology" do not depend on any particular revelation or
any particular set of religious authorities. They may be *confirmed* by these
particular revelations, but they can be *known* without reference to them.
In fact, Herbert argues that all claims to religious authority are to be
judged by their conformity to these independently accessible truths.

More specifically, Herbert's work offers a clear challenge to the
authority of the Bible, even if this is hedged about by apparently orthodox qualifications. As we have just seen, Herbert's theology of providence extends salvation history beyond the biblical framework. This is
already a significant departure from Jewish and Christian tradition.
However, his work also contains a more direct challenge to biblical
authority, one more closely related to the rise of historical criticism. For
Herbert argues that we should not accept any account of past events
uncritically. Theologically he justifies this scepticism by distinguishing
(in a rather arbitrary manner) between two types of faith: faith in past
events and faith in the future action of God. The second of these, faith as
related to the future, "proceeds from the highest faculty of the soul";[39] it
is what relates us to God. Faith as related to past events, on the other
hand, is less reliable: it "depends chiefly on human authority, and has reference to some epoch, and is more or less probable, according to circumstances."[40] It follows that this second type of faith is subject to some
important qualifications.

In particular, when the Wayfarer is faced with accounts of past events,
he ought not place his faith too quickly in what is narrated. For the
trustworthiness of such histories depends on a number of factors. In particular, it depends on whether their authors were eyewitnesses of the
events narrated and on the history of their transmission. More particularly, the Wayfarer must be careful not to accept accounts in which the
authors recount matters that seem beyond human comprehension.[41]
Miracles, too, are—it seems—to be regarded with suspicion, for Herbert
notes that little credence can be given to reports of things which
are "extravagant" and "repugnant to the universal nature of things."[42]

---

[37]Cf. J. Samuel Preus, *Explaining Religion: Criticism and Theory from Bodin to Freud*
(New Haven, Conn.: Yale University Press, 1987), 38.
[38]Cf. Herbert, *De Religione Laici,* 125.
[39]Ibid., 91.
[40]Ibid.
[41]Cf. ibid., 93.
[42]Ibid.

Finally, Herbert notes that writers of histories are greatly liable to error. Their own stupidity or superstition may lead them astray, their own deeply felt convictions may distort their accounts, or they may deliberately falsify what they are writing in order to flatter their hearers. The possibility of deception is particularly great in religious matters. As Herbert writes, "you will find scarcely any who are not inclined to credulity when religious worship is forwarded by it."[43] At the best of times, therefore, knowledge drawn from such sources is unreliable. There is what Herbert calls "an enormous gulf" between knowledge one has arrived at by personal experience and knowledge that is arrived at by faith in historical narratives.[44]

So far, of course, Herbert has made no comment about the Bible, at least not in so many words. But he goes on to do so, and his remarks indicate to what extent he has broken with traditional Christian attitudes. First of all, Herbert implicitly consigns the Bible to a general category of "sacred books," the contents of which must be critically examined before being accepted.

> When the Wayfarer, therefore, amid diverse churches and groups which have cried up the word of God for their exclusive advantage, takes in hand their Sacred Book (whatever its name), he should observe . . . what is considered appropriate to right Reason—to a just conformation of the faculties, that is—and what to Faith regarding the past, so that he may decide about each one separately.[45]

Herbert immediately points out that the Bible occupies a special position, at least for the people of Europe: "Our European will find conspicuous above the rest, both in antiquity and in extraordinary authority, the Sacred Scriptures communicated to the Jews, and by them to the Gentiles."[46] But from the point of view of traditional Christian attitudes the damage is already done. Indeed, while Herbert urges assent to the truth of the biblical narratives, he does so only on condition that a certain freedom of judgment be left with the individual. An act of discernment is required, and the right to make that discernment must be safeguarded: no religious institution may arrogate that judgment to itself. For not everything in scripture is worthy of being described as "the Word of God." As Herbert writes, not only does the Bible contain "the words . . .

[43]Ibid.
[44]Ibid., 95.
[45]Ibid., 97–99.
[46]Ibid., 99.

of villains, women,[47] beasts, nay of the devil himself," but the apostles and prophets themselves speak "in human fashion."[48] The reader will not be surprised to discover that the teaching that merits the name "Word of God" corresponds to Herbert's five "catholic truths." Indeed Herbert argues that other matters were included in the Bible only so that these truths might be more clearly expressed and encouraged.[49] Once again, therefore, it is only these "catholic truths" that the Wayfarer is encouraged to accept and observe.

It could be said that Herbert was not a profound thinker, but he was an influential one.[50] His value for our study is to illustrate how the scandal of religious conflict—as well as the broadening horizons of the European world—could lead to a radical questioning of biblical authority. Not only does Herbert illustrate the tendencies of the age in which he lives, but he anticipates by some twenty-five years many of the ideas about the Bible that would be put forward in a more systematic way by Benedict Spinoza.

3. The New Astronomy

The Challenge to Biblical Authority

A third influence on attitudes to the Bible was the rise of the new astronomy and its associated cosmology. For this cosmology quickly came into conflict with both the biblical picture of the universe and that which enjoyed the authority of Aristotle (384–22 B.C.E.).[51] The most immediate challenge was the heliocentric cosmology set forth by Nicolaus Copernicus (1473–1543), which called into question the accepted picture of a geocentric world. While the new astronomy had enormous implications for religion in general, our immediate concern is to note its impact on attitudes to the Bible. (The key text here is Josh. 10:12–14, which suggests that the sun revolved around the earth, not vice versa.[52])

[47]Herbert's translator and editor here notes (99, n.12): "One would like to credit Herbert here with at least sardonic laughter, but that, I am afraid, would have been beyond the range of his humor."

[48]Herbert, *De Religione Laici,* 99–101.

[49]Cf. ibid., 101.

[50]Cf. Preus, *Explaining Religion,* 25.

[51]Although both the authority of scripture and that of Aristotle were at stake, the principal issue seems to have been the interpretation of the Bible. For a discussion, see Ernan McMullin, "Galileo on Science and Scripture," in *The Cambridge Companion to Galileo,* 271–72.

[52]See, for instance, Scholder, *The Birth of Modern Critical Theology,* 47. Among the achievements of Joseph Smith, the nineteenth-century founder of the Church of the Latter-day Saints, was the "discovery" of an ancient scriptural text, *The Book of Mormon,* which corrects the biblical cosmology (cf. *The Book of Mormon:* Helaman 12:15).

By overturning the taken-for-granted biblical cosmology, the new astronomy contributed to the process of undermining—or at least limiting the scope of—biblical authority.

As witnesses to this fact, we may turn to the work of two of the great pioneers themselves, namely Johann Kepler (1571–1630) and Galileo Galilei (1564–1642). To a reader of our own time, it may seem strange to find astronomers discussing matters of biblical interpretation. For we are inclined to regard these as quite distinct fields of knowledge. But as we will see, this distinction is itself partly the work of Kepler and Galileo: in their day it was by no means as clear. Given the close association of astronomy and theology, Kepler and Galileo could hardly avoid discussing the relationship of their work to the Bible. In doing so, they are keen to suggest that the new cosmology of Copernicus is not fatal to the cause of biblical authority. They are anxious to portray themselves as devout Christians, and there is no need to doubt their sincerity. Yet in defending biblical authority, both thinkers urge a rethinking of its limits. What they defend is not scriptural authority *tout court,* but scriptural authority *in matters religious.* In other matters, they suggest, the Bible is fallible or—at the very least—an unreliable source of knowledge.

Johann Kepler

Kepler's brief discussion is found in the introduction to his *Astronomia Nova* (1609) and may be summed up in three propositions. The first point Kepler makes is that before we set about interpreting the biblical texts, we should attempt to discern the *intention* of the biblical writers. What exactly were they trying to achieve? The second point follows immediately from the first: what the biblical writers were trying to achieve—Kepler insists—was the transmission of a religious message. Their aim, in other words, was religious and moral rather than cosmological. His third point is that, in conveying its religious and moral message, the Bible makes use of what he calls "the common idiom."[53] In other words, the Bible adapts its message to the general understanding of the world found among its readers. As an example of such adaptation, Kepler cites Psalm 19, which apparently speaks of the movement of the sun. Here, Kepler argues, the psalmist is actually speaking (in a hidden way) of the incarnation of the Son of God and of the spread of the gospel. But he does so by speaking of the sun coming forth "like a bridegroom from his tent." Because the psalmist has employed this everyday manner of expression, his words might appear to be in conflict with the Copernican view of a stationary sun. Yet if these three interpretative principles are taken into account and the psalm is read allegorically in

[53]Kepler, *New Astronomy,* 60.

the light of its religious message, the apparent conflict with Copernican cosmology disappears.[54] Kepler argues that the same may be said of the much-to-be-debated passage in Joshua. This, too, needs to be understood as an accommodation of the divine message to our everyday under-standing of the world. As Kepler writes, when Joshua commands the sun to stand still, he

> was simply praying that the mountains not remove the sunlight from him, which prayer he expressed in words conforming to the sense of sight. . . . For if someone had admonished him that the sun doesn't really move against the valley of Aijalon, but only appears to do so, wouldn't Joshua have exclaimed that he only asked for the day to be lengthened, however that might be done?[55]

In response to Joshua's prayer, God—who understood what he meant—stopped the motion of the earth, so that it *appeared* as though the sun stood still. Kepler goes on to reject the idea that the Bible contains infor-mation about the structure of the universe. He insists that this is not the purpose for which the Bible was written. Those who think it was, he writes, should "regard the Holy Spirit as a divine messenger, and refrain from wantonly dragging Him into physics class."[56] What about the authority of "the saints" or—as we might say—of Christian tradition? What role has this to play in the interpretation of the Bible? Here again, Kepler sets clear limits on religious claims. For he distinguishes between theology and (natural) philosophy, or—as we would say—between the-ology and science, and suggests that religious authority is limited to the-ological matters. In other words, while in religious matters one may appeal to religious authority, in scientific matters the supreme rule ought to be the authority of reason.[57] Kepler concludes by noting that the holiness of ancient and modern Christian writers is not affected by their astronomical ignorance and that true piety is in any case to be found in respect for the truth.

Galileo Galilei

Kepler's remarks already impose clear limits on biblical authority. But a still clearer statement of these limits can be found in Galileo's *Letter to the Grand Duchess Christina* (1615), in which the great pioneer sets out his views on biblical interpretation. Galileo begins by arguing that it is his

---

[54]Cf. ibid., 61.
[55]Ibid.
[56]Ibid., 62.
[57]Cf. ibid., 66.

opponents who have misunderstood biblical authority, by illegitimately extending its scope. Worse still, they have done so in a way that is contrary to the sense of the Bible and the intentions of its earliest interpreters.[58] The problem here, as Galileo sees it, is that his opponents wish to invoke scriptural authority in support of scientific matters, that is to say, in support of what he calls "purely physical conclusions which are not matters of faith."[59] Galileo concedes that one must accept what we would call the inerrancy of the Bible. As he writes, "it is most pious to say and most prudent to take for granted that Holy Scripture can never lie, as long as its true meaning has been grasped."[60] But this apparently pious acceptance of biblical authority is immediately qualified. We must indeed accept the *true* meaning of the Bible, but we should not assume that the true meaning of the Bible is identical with the "literal meaning" of its words.[61] For if the intended meaning of the Bible were its *literal* meaning, Galileo argues, then we would be forced to admit that the Bible teaches many things that are foolish and heretical, such as the corporeality of God.

If the Bible is indeed holy scripture, whose authority is to be accepted devoutly, then why is this act of discernment necessary? Why does the Bible contain propositions that, when taken literally, are evident falsehoods? Galileo argues that it is because of the accommodation of the sacred scriptures to human weakness. When the scriptures teach what *appear* to be mistaken propositions, they are merely reflecting the common human manner of speaking. As Galileo writes, these matters "were expressed by the sacred writers in such a way as to accommodate the capacities of the very unrefined and undisciplined masses."[62] Now if the Bible adapts its message to human weakness when speaking of the very nature of God, then we have every reason to expect that its descriptions of the universe will be similarly adapted.[63] It follows that in scientific matters one should begin with the authority of human reason and interpret scripture in the light of its findings. Only in this way can we arrive at the true meaning of the Bible.

What are the principles to which Galileo is appealing in this discussion? The first is one that we have already noted in Kepler's work: the

---

[58]Cf. Galileo, "Letter to the Grand Duchess Christina," in *The Galileo Affair: A Documentary History*, translated and edited by Maurice A. Finocchiaro, California Studies in the History of Science (Berkeley, Calif.: University of California Press, 1989), 90. This volume is henceforth cited as *GA*.

[59]Ibid.

[60]*GA*, 92.

[61]Ibid.

[62]Ibid.

[63]Cf. *GA*, 92–93.

long-accepted principle of "accommodation." God has spoken to human
beings in terms they can easily understand, rather than in terms that are
philosophically or scientifically precise. However, there is a second principle in Galileo's argument. For like Kepler, Galileo is attempting to limit
the scope of biblical authority. We see this idea expressed in the witty
remark he attributes to Cardinal Baronius, that "the intention of the
Holy Spirit is to teach us how one goes to heaven, not how heaven
goes."[64] It is more clearly expressed in Galileo's letter of 1613 to his close
friend, the Benedictine priest Benedetto Castelli (1578–1643), where
Galileo insists that the role of sacred scripture is to teach those religious
truths that *cannot* be arrived at by natural reason.[65] Galileo is appealing
here to what modern students of science and religion would call "the
principle of independence,"[66] which keeps scientific and religious claims
apart. According to this view, science and religion do not come into
conflict, for they deal with different aspects of reality. Galileo attempts to
establish this principle of independence by imposing strict limits on biblical authority.[67] Biblical authority, he argues, is to be exercised only in
matters that are inaccessible to human reason. It follows from this principle that one should not invoke the Bible in opposition to at least the
demonstrated findings of natural science.

Much more could be said about Galileo's argument. It could be
argued, for instance, that his principle of independence is theologically
problematic.[68] His argument also suffers from internal weaknesses, for
Galileo does not hold to this principle consistently.[69] (He concedes that
where the findings of the natural sciences are *not* yet demonstrated, the
Bible is to be preferred, a concession that undermines his earlier statements by suggesting that their subject matter may indeed overlap.) However, there is no need to discuss the viability of Galileo's exegetical

[64]*GA*, 96.
[65]Cf. Galileo, "Letter to Castelli," in *GA*, 51. The relevant passage can also be found
in Richard J. Blackwell, *Galileo, Bellarmine, and the Bible* (Notre Dame, Ind.: University of
Notre Dame Press, 1991), 198.
[66]Marcello Pera, "The God of Theologians and the God of Astronomers: An Apology
of Bellarmine," in *The Cambridge Companion to Galileo*, 374–76.
[67]Cf. McMullin, "Galileo on Science and Scripture," 298.
[68]Cf. Blackwell, *Galileo, Bellarmine, and the Bible*, 67, n.26; Pera, "The God of Theologians and the God of Astronomers," 380–85. Pera (373–74) paraphrases Galileo's view
as "factual statements . . . have no salvation value," whereas Cardinal Bellarmine's view
was that there is "factual knowledge" in the Bible that is essentially related to salvation
and that therefore "cannot be revised." My own view is that Bellarmine's position seems
the only one compatible with Christian orthodoxy, although appeals to Galileo's position
remain a popular way of avoiding conflicts between science and religion.
[69]Cf. McMullin, "Galileo on Science and Scripture," 314–19. For an attempt to reconcile Galileo's principles, see Blackwell, *Galileo, Bellarmine, and the Bible*, 78–82.

principles or the consistency of his arguments. All I need note here is Galileo's attempt to limit biblical authority. Where there is a clear conflict between the literal sense of a biblical passage and the secure findings of the new astronomy, Galileo is in no doubt that the new astronomy is to be preferred. In these cases, the Bible should be reinterpreted accordingly.[70]

Now it is true that, in arguing for such a limitation, Galileo is claiming to have ancient authority on his side. After all, he begins his discussion by citing Augustine (354–430 C.E.) and interlaces his own comments with quotations from the same church father.[71] At this point, however, we would be unwise to take Galileo at his word.[72] He claims that his limitation of biblical authority involved no break with Christian tradition, but this claim deserves closer scrutiny. Is Galileo correct in invoking Christian tradition? Or does his approach to the Bible represent a break with traditional Christian attitudes?

This is not an easy question to answer. For when it comes to the limits of biblical authority, Christian tradition is deeply ambiguous. As late as the sixteenth century, we find contrasting attitudes. On the one hand, the great reformer John Calvin (1509–64) could follow Augustine in arguing that "the Holy Spirit had no intention to teach astronomy."[73] On the other hand, his predecessor Martin Luther (1483–1546) could casually dismiss the Copernican theory by reference to the book of Joshua ("I believe Sacred Scripture, since Joshua commanded the sun to stand [still] and not the earth").[74] In doing so, Luther echoed a widely

---

[70]Galileo is not prepared to go as far as Spinoza, some sixty years later, and to affirm that the biblical authors may have been simply mistaken. Indeed, his argument assumes the divine inspiration of scripture, which would seem to exclude simple error. The doctrine of "accommodation" is what enabled him to avoid taking this more radical step. To this extent Galileo belongs to a long tradition that resolved apparent conflicts between accepted truth and biblical statement by reinterpreting the Bible. Spinoza would attack this tradition in the person of the medieval Jewish exegete Moses Maimonides (see chapter 1).

[71]Galileo, "Letter to the Grand Duchess Christina" *GA*, 87–88 (see also 94–95, 96, 101, 105, 110–11, 115). One of the tragic ironies of this discussion is that, 350 years later, the assembled bishops of the church that condemned Galileo's views would quote one of the same passages from Augustine (*De Genesi ad litteram* 2.9.20) in support of a similar restriction on the authority of scripture (see the second Vatican Council's "Dogmatic Constitution on Divine Revelation" [*Dei Verbum*], §11, n.32).

[72]Cf. Scholder, *The Birth of Modern Critical Theology*, 46; McMullin, "Galileo on Science and Scripture," 306.

[73]Cited in McMullin, "Galileo on Science and Scripture," 301.

[74]Martin Luther, "Tischreden" §4638, in *D. Martin Luthers Werke kritische Gesamtausgabe* (Weimarer Ausgabe; Weimar: Hermann Böhlaus Nachfolger, 1916), *Tischreden* 4:412–13 (*ego credo sacrae Scripturae, nam Iosua iussit solem stare, non terram*). See also Scholder, *The Birth of Modern Critical Theology*, 47.

held conviction that the Bible was reliable in matters that (we might say) are not strictly religious.[75] Indeed Augustine himself does not speak with a single voice. For Augustine will frequently appeal to the Bible to decide what we would call scientific matters, even in the same commentary in which he enunciates the "principle of limitation" to which Galileo appeals.[76] (It seems that Augustine is caught between an instinctive Christian reverence for the Bible and a desire to defend it against Manichaean claims that it is clearly mistaken in matters of fact.) To take but one instance, Augustine defends the biblical claim that there exist "waters above the heavens" (Gen. 1:7) against those who argue that the existence of water in such a place is physically impossible. After discussing how this *might* in fact be possible, Augustine notes that—whatever mechanism one may postulate—there is no doubt that such waters exist. As he writes, "whatever the nature of that water and whatever the manner of its being there, we must not doubt that it does exist in that place. The authority of Scripture in this matter is greater than all human ingenuity."[77] In other words, when Christians before Galileo discussed these issues, they may have accepted a weak form of the principle of independence (the Bible is *primarily* about faith and morals). But they also countered it with a strong sense of biblical authority, even in matters that might seem to have little relevance to salvation. There were clear limits to the restrictions that could be placed on the Bible's authority.[78] It was Galileo's tragedy to have overstepped these limits.

[75]Despite the remark cited above, Calvin was also capable of casually dismissing the Copernican theory, which he apparently attacks as a mere product of human perversity (cf. John Hedley Brooke, *Science and Religion: Some Historical Perspectives,* Cambridge History of Science [Cambridge: Cambridge University Press, 1991], 96–97).

[76]Cf. McMullin, "Galileo on Science and Scripture," 298. See also his "How Should Cosmology Relate to Theology?" in *The Sciences and Theology in the Twentieth Century,* edited by A. R. Peacocke (Stocksfield: Oriel Press [Routledge & Kegan Paul], 1981), 18–25.

[77]Cf. Augustine, *De Genesi ad litteram libri duodecim* (401 C.E.), 2.5.9; English translation: *The Literal Meaning of Genesis,* translated by John Hammond Taylor, S.J.; Ancient Christian Writers 41 (New York: Newman, 1982), 1:52. For Augustine on what we have called "the principle of limitation," see *De Genesi ad litteram* 2.9.20; *The Literal Meaning of Genesis,* 1:59.

[78]The challenge of the Protestant Reformation and its aftermath merely hardened the official Roman Catholic attitude. Well before the Galileo affair, Cardinal Bellarmine had developed what Blackwell calls a *de dicto* principle of scriptural authority, which may be regarded as a very strict interpretation of the Council of Trent. He argued that, though there are many things in the Bible "which of themselves do not pertain to the faith, that is, which were not written because it is necessary to believe them," nonetheless, "it is necessary to believe them because they are written" (cited in Blackwell, *Galileo, Bellarmine, and the Bible,* 32 and 105). Their authority comes not from the sacred character of the matters of which they speak (*ex parte objecti*) but from the authority of the speaker (*ex parte dicentis*). See also McMullin, "Galileo on Science and Scripture," 282–83.

4. The Voyages of Discovery

The Framework of History

We come now to a fourth influence on attitudes towards the Bible. This was the broadening effect of the voyages of discovery, which opened up both the Americas and the lands of the Pacific to European knowledge. For these voyages were accompanied by, and themselves encouraged, a great curiosity about the diversity of human habits and customs. That diversity was greater than anyone in Europe had hitherto believed.[79] As new peoples were discovered and their geographic distribution charted, the question arose of their origins. How were they related to the biblical picture of the beginnings of history? In particular, could they be fitted into the relatively restricted framework of the descendants of Noah? (On the basis of the biblical account of the flood, all present-day inhabitants of the earth must be descended from Noah.) While many attempts were made to answer this question, they soon became increasingly forced. It was not long before a new framework of universal history emerged that swallowed up that of the Bible.[80] In Margaret Hodgen's words, "as geographical knowledge, combined with Biblical criticism, began its work upon the intimate fabric of the Book of Genesis, the unrevised sacred history no longer seem inviolate or universally satisfying."[81]

Men before Adam: Isaac de la Peyrère

The clearest witness to this shift is the appearance in 1655 of a work called *Praeadamitae* (translated into English as *Men before Adam*), written by Isaac de la Peyrère (1594-1676).[82] In this book La Peyrère argued that Adam was not the ancestor of the whole human race but only of the Jewish people, and that human beings had existed on many parts of the earth before Adam. While his work drew on internal scriptural evidence, it also referred to both ancient chronicles and the recent discoveries by

[79]Cf. Hodgen, *Early Anthropology*, 208.

[80]Cf. Brooke, *Science and Religion*, 170.

[81]Hodgen, *Early Anthropology*, 230. The Book of Mormon is (among other things) a most interesting nineteenth-century attempt to fit the North American Indians into the biblical framework. It should be noted that Joseph Smith's was not the only such attempt in nineteenth-century North America and that these nineteenth-century attempts were themselves part of a tradition dating back to the sixteenth and early seventeenth centuries (see R. H. Popkin, "The Development of Religious Scepticism and the Influence of Isaac la Peyrère's Pre-Adamism and Bible Criticism," in *Classical Influences on European Culture A.D. 1500–1700: Proceedings of an International Conference Held at King's College, Cambridge, April 1974,* edited by R. R. Bolgar [Cambridge: Cambridge University Press, 1976], 273–74).

[82]Cf. Scholder, *The Birth of Modern Critical Theology*, 67.

European explorers.[83] Even on the first page of his work la Peyrère
refers to "ancient Chaldaean [Babylonian] calculations" and "the earliest
documents from Egypt, Ethiopia and Scythia,"[84] as well as the existence
of what he calls the "newly discovered parts of the earth, and those
unknown regions to which Dutchmen have recently sailed."[85] (The last
is probably a reference to the South Pacific voyages of Abel Tasman.[86])
What these ancient writers and records suggest, he argues, is that the
earth has been inhabited for much longer than the usual interpretation
of the biblical record allows.[87] This conclusion is reinforced by the historical records of the newly discovered peoples.[88] La Peyrère refers to
the attempts that had already been made to fit these peoples into the
framework of the biblical history. For various scholars had tried to trace
their ancestry to peoples who were already known. La Peyrère rejects
this strategy as implausible.[89] He insists that the existence of these peoples is explicable only if we assume that there existed human beings
before Adam.

This bold speculation about the origins of the human race involves,
of course, a radical reinterpretation of the Bible. In the course of this
reinterpretation, la Peyrère anticipates the source criticism of later centuries.[90] He even attempts a naturalistic reinterpretation of some of the

[83]Cf. David Rice McKee, "Isaac de la Peyrère, a Precursor of Eighteenth-Century
Critical Deists," in *Publications of the Modern Language Association of America* 59 (1944): 468,
and Popkin, "The Development of Religious Scepticism," 276 et passim.

[84]As Popkin points out ("The Development of Religious Scepticism," 273, 276–78),
la Peyrère could draw upon collections of classical texts and of Babylonian and Egyptian
sources that his immediate predecessors had compiled. Thus the knowledge on which he
draws to question the biblical framework is a product, not just of the voyages of discovery, but of the humanist revival of classical learning.

[85]Isaac de la Peyrère, *Praeadamitae sive Exercitatio super versibus duodecimo, decimotertio et
decimoquarto capitis quinti Epistolae D. Pauli ad Romanos quibus inducuntur Primi Homines ante
Adamum conditi* (Amsterdam: Louis & Daniel Elzevier, 1655; originally published without
the name of either author or printer, so the name of the publisher is conjectural), "Systema," 1 ("Prooemium"): *tum ex antiquissimis Chaldaeorum rationibus: tum ex vetustissimis
Aegyptiorum, Aethiopum, et Scytharum monumentis: tum ex nupere detectis terrenae machinae part-
ibus: tum et ex regionibus illis incognitis, ad quos novissime percrebuit navigando pervenisse Batavos.*
The reader may wish to note that the work is divided into an exegetical section (Exercitatio) and a much longer discussion (Systema Theologicum ex Prae-Adamitarum hypoth-
esi). The key passages are also cited in Scholder, *The Birth of Modern Critical Theology,* 83.

[86]Cf. Scholder, *The Birth of Modern Critical Theology,* 164, n.82.

[87]Cf. la Peyrère, *Praeadamitae,* "Systema," 3.5–6 (pp. 129–43).

[88]Ibid., 3.7 (p. 149).

[89]See, for instance, ibid., 4.14 (pp. 235–39) on the native inhabitants of the Americas.

[90]For instance, he notes (ibid., 4.1 [pp. 171–73]) that many biblical texts seem to be
put together from earlier sources, and in particular calls into question the Mosaic author-
ship of the Pentateuch.

biblical miracles.[91] As an example of his reinterpretation, we might take the story of the flood, which—he argues—affected not the whole earth but Palestine alone.[92] While defending his interpretation of Genesis 7:19, which speaks of the flood, la Peyrère calls upon Deuteronomy 2:25 ("This day I will begin to put the dread and fear of you upon the peoples everywhere under heaven"). He points out that the final phrase of that verse can hardly be understood as referring to the whole earth *as we now know it*. It, too, must refer only to Palestine. "*Everywhere under heaven,*" he writes, "is here to be understood as that [part of the heavens] which overlooks the Holy Land. For God did not put the dread of the Jewish name at that time on the peoples who live under the Chinese, or the American, or the Australian heaven, or that of Greenland."[93]

No more than Kepler or Galileo does la Peyrère claim to be attacking the authority of the Bible. On the contrary! For in several places he speaks of his work as a work of "reconciliation." He is attempting to reconcile (*conciliare*) not only the differing biblical texts with each other, but also the Bible as a whole with the new knowledge of his time. For instance, he argues that if we accept there existed human beings before Adam

> the history of Genesis appears much clearer: it is reconciled with itself. It is reconciled similarly in a marvellous manner with all profane documents, whether ancient or more recent; think [for example] of the Babylonian, the Egyptian, the Scythian and the Chinese. The earliest creation of things, which is expounded in the first chapter [of Genesis] is reconciled with the Mexican people, whom Columbus reached not long ago. The same [account] is reconciled with those people of the South and the North who are not yet known [to us]. All of these [peoples], along with those of the first and oldest creation of those things, which are narrated in the first chapter of Genesis, were probably created with the earth itself in every land and were not generated from Adam.[94]

[91]See, for instance, his reinterpretation of Josh. 10:12–14 in "Systema," 4.5 (pp. 194–99).

[92]Cf. ibid. 4.7 (pp. 202–7).

[93]Ibid., 4.7 (p. 206): *Omne coelum hoc loco intelligendum, quod imminebat terrae sanctae. Neque enim terrorem Iudaici nominis immittebat Deus tunc temporis in populis qui habitabant sub coelo, vel Sinensi, vel Americano, vel Australi, vel Groenlandico.*

[94]La Peyrère, *Praeadamitae,* "Exercitatio," chap. 8 (p. 19): *clarior multo apparet historia Geneseos. Conciliator eadem cum seipsa. Conciliatur item miris modis cum monumentis omnibus profanis, sive antiquis sive recentioribus; Chaldaeis puta, Aegyptiis, Scythiis et Sinensibus. Conciliatur vetustissima rerum creatio, quae exponitur capite primo, cum hominibus Mexicanis quos non ita diu Columbus penetravit. Conciliatur eadem cum hominibus illis Australibus et Septentrionalibus, qui nondum cogniti sunt. Quos omnes, sicut et illos primae et vetustissimae creationis rerum, quae enarrantur cap. I. Geneseos; probabile est creatos fuisse cum terra ipsa in terris omnibus, neque ab Adamo propagatos.*

Most importantly of all, through this reinterpretation of the Bible "faith is reconciled with right reason."[95] La Peyrère goes on to suggest that his reinterpretation of the Bible can even serve the cause of the Christian faith. For it removes obstacles to belief among intelligent people.

> Thus if the Babylonians themselves were to come, or those most ancient astronomers, masters of the calculations of the course of the stars—composed and put together (as they say) hundreds of thousands of years before—if the ancient chroniclers of the Egyptians were to come, with the primaeval dynasties of their kings, if Aristotle himself were to come, if along with Aristotle there were to come Chinese, perhaps outstanding philosophers and chroniclers, or if at some time there are found wise men among those unknown [peoples] of the South or the North, who—like the Chinese, Egyptians, and Babylonians—have their histories handed down and known for many myriads of years, on the basis [of this reinterpretation] all of these could freely accept the Genesis account and gladly become Christians.[96]

His contemporaries, needless to say, were not convinced. Despite the considerable success of the book, churchmen were unanimous in their condemnation, and in Paris the Parliament ordered that the book be burned by the public hangman.[97] La Peyrère was imprisoned for six months and released only on condition that he retract his views.[98] He did so, soon converting to Roman Catholicism.[99] Like Galileo, la Peyrère had discovered that there were clear limits within which biblical authority could be questioned, even in the name of a much-needed reinterpretation.

It would be easy to pour scorn on the theologians and churchmen who condemned la Peyrère's theory. However, in retrospect we can see

[95]Ibid.: *conciliatur fides cum recta ratione.*

[96]Ibid., chap. 26 (p. 51): *Itaque si venerint Chaldaei ipsi, vetustissimi illi Astronomi, penes quos erant rationes cursus syderum, a multis retro centenis annorum millibus (ut aiunt) compositae et confectae: si venerint antiquissimi Aegyptorum Chronologi, cum antiquissimus Regorum suorum dynastiis: si venerit Aristoteles ipse: si venerint cum Aristotele Sinenses, philosophi et chronologi fortassean eximii: vel si qui olim reperientur sagaces apud Australes et Septentrionales incognitos: quibus, sicut et Sinensibus, Aegyptiis, et Chaldaeis, suae sibi sint epochae, a pluribus annorum myriadibus traditae et cognitae: Accipiant ultro illi omnes ex positione hac historiam Geneseos, et fiant lubentius Christiani.*

[97]Cf. McKee, "Isaac de la Peyrère," 458.

[98]Ibid.

[99]As McKee points out (ibid., 458–60), it is unclear to what extent these retractions were sincere, and there is some evidence that he continued to hold these views in private, even corresponding on the topic with Richard Simon (1638–1712), another founder of modern biblical study.

that their instincts may have been correct.[100] For while this conflict was not as dramatic as that over the new astronomy, it was in the long run more destructive of biblical authority. The problem was that, even if it could be argued that the scriptures were not a "textbook of mathematics and physics," they were certainly "a historical textbook."[101] Richard Popkin points out that, as early as the second century, Christian apologists had refuted pagan ideas of the antiquity of the world by reference to the Bible.[102] Indeed in the early fifth century Augustine sees these ideas as such a threat that he devotes two chapters of *The City of God* to their refutation.[103] In chapter 11 of book 12 Augustine dismisses what he calls

> certain wholly untruthful writings which purport to contain the history of many thousands of years of time. For we compute from the sacred writings that six thousand years have not passed since the creation of man. Hence the writings which make reference to far more thousands of years than there have been are vain, and contain no trustworthy authority on the subject.[104]

Although Augustine also argues from discrepancies in the pagan chronologies, his ultimate appeal is to the authority of the Bible. For Augustine, there can be no doubting the biblical chronology.[105] For the truth of the biblical history is guaranteed by the fulfillment of biblical prophecy in Christian times. In chapter 40 of book 18, Augustine again appeals to biblical authority in historical matters. Here he rejects the pagan claim that Egyptian astrology may be up to 100,000 years old. He does so for the very simple reason that it is at variance with what he calls "the truth of the Divine Scriptures," which tell us that "six thousand years have not yet elapsed since the creation of the first man."[106]

The same attitude of confidence in the biblical record as history can be found among writers closer to the time of La Peyrère. The Protestant

---

[100]It is a sign of the difficulties that lie ahead that la Peyrère must spend a large part of his treatise trying to reconcile his new interpretation with the traditional doctrine of original sin. For a helpful summary, see McKee, "Isaac de la Peyrère," 460–61.

[101]Scholder, *The Birth of Modern Critical Theology*, 68. On the assumption that the Bible was a reliable source of historical knowledge, see also Peter Harrison, *"Religion" and the Religions in the English Enlightenment*, 99.

[102]Popkin, "The Development of Religious Scepticism," 272.

[103]Ibid.

[104]Augustine, *The City of God Against the Pagans,* translated by R. W. Dyson, Cambridge Texts in the History of Political Thought (Cambridge: Cambridge University Press, 1998), 12.11 (p. 512).

[105]Ibid., 12.11 (p. 513).

[106]Cf. ibid., 18.40 (pp. 878–79).

Reformers, for instance, had great confidence in the historical reliability of the Bible,[107] and in this respect they were merely following a long Christian tradition. Martin Luther, for instance, wrote that in matters of chronology his policy was to produce his calculations "primarily from Holy Scripture. For on this we can and should truly rely, and with constant faith."[108] From earliest times, therefore, Christian writers had been fitting historical knowledge into a framework—whether of six or seven great ages or of six millennia—that was ultimately derived from the Bible.[109] At first the new interest in history deriving from renaissance humanism merely strengthened this interest in biblical history.[110] But by the time of la Peyrère, the new knowledge was breaking the biblical framework apart. For European thinkers were faced with new peoples, of whom the Bible said nothing, and with ancient civilizations whose records called into question the reliability of the biblical account.

Christianity among the Religions
There was another development that flowed from the expanded geographical and cultural knowledge of the early seventeenth century. It deserves at least a brief mention here, since it will prove to be a key theme in the work of the authors whom we are later to study. The newly discovered diversity of human beings brought with it a new sense of human *religious* diversity, and this diversity proved to be bewildering. As Margaret Hodgen writes, "the sum of religions, sects, rituals, gods, and idols known to any well-informed Christian during this period was disconcerting and overwhelming."[111] It soon became clear that the existence of ancient religious traditions outside of the biblical framework could no longer be ignored.[112] This changed perspective is evident as early as 1645, once again in the *De Religione Laici* of Edward Herbert. For Herbert begins his work by noting that

> many faiths or religions, clearly, exist or once existed in various countries and ages, and certainly there is not one of them that the lawgivers have not pronounced to be as it were divinely ordained, so that the Wayfarer finds one in Europe, another in Africa, and in Asia, still another in the very

[107]Cf. Scholder, *The Birth of Modern Critical Theology*, 68.
[108]Cited in Scholder, *The Birth of Modern Critical Theology*, 58.
[109]Cf. Scholder, *The Birth of Modern Critical Theology*, 69.
[110]Cf. ibid., 71.
[111]Hodgen, *Early Anthropology*, 215.
[112]The biblical framework could be stretched to accommodate Islam, albeit as a Christian heresy. Cf. Norman Daniel, *Islam and the West: The Making of an Image* (1960; Oxford: Oneworld, 1993), 209–13.

Indies. Indeed, I have scarcely anywhere offered arguments drawn from the land of my birth, for Asia boasts its extraordinary philosophers, apostles, and teachers; Africa its penetrating geniuses and exalted theologians; India its gymnosophist, Brahmans, Banjami, and Bongi;[113] Europe its own illustrious and distinguished spirits.[114]

Confronted with this new evidence of religious diversity, at least some scholars began to regard even Christianity as one religion among others, no longer able to be exempted, by a kind of theological fiat, from the history of religion.[115] We have already seen that the work of Herbert illustrates this process. While he assumes that the Bible contains a divine revelation, he is quick to put it in the same category as other "sacred books." It is easy to see the direction in which such a discussion could—and would—go. For later writers would abandon Herbert's belief in divine providence. They would understand this succession of faiths as nothing other than a product of human history and culture. (One thinks of David Hume's "natural history of religion."[116]) Once placed in the context of a history of religions, even Christianity could be subject to naturalistic forms of explanation. At the time Herbert wrote, these developments lay in the future, but they are clearly foreshadowed in the seventeenth century.[117]

5. The Limits of Reliable Knowledge

The Limits of Explanation
A final influence on the interpretation of the Bible in the seventeenth century is a little harder to describe and to document. It may be described as a redefinition of the nature of explanation, with a corresponding redefinition of what we might call "reliable knowledge." These are deliberately vague terms, broad enough to encompass a number of related, but not identical, developments, whose impact on the Bible can be traced in the seventeenth century. The first of these developments had

[113]Herbert's *Baniamos* may be a corruption of *Banianos,* but to what group his *Bongos* refers is entirely unclear (cf. *De Religione Laici,* 87, n.3).

[114]Herbert, *De Religione Laici,* 87.

[115]The process is traced and extensively documented in J. Samuel Preus's *Explaining Religion.*

[116]Cf. David Hume, "The Natural History of Religion" (1757), in *Principal Writings on Religion,* Oxford World's Classics (Oxford: Oxford University Press, 1993), 134–96.

[117]They did not lie very far in the future, as Peter Harrison points out. The final chapter of his *"Religion" and the Religions in the English Enlightenment* (130–72) shows that later natural histories of religion are firmly rooted in seventeenth-century developments, including the work of Herbert (cf. 161–62).

a particular impact on the dominant style of biblical interpretation. Medieval writers had followed the Fathers of the church in assuming that the biblical text could yield several levels of meaning. As a work that came from God it could be expected to contain hidden mysteries. In the words of one early Christian writer, the Bible contains "an infinite forest of senses."[118] For this reason the Old Testament and the New could be read together and the meaning of the New Testament could be found "hidden" in the Old. As confidence in the divine authority of the scriptures faded, so did confidence in its figurative interpretation. (This confidence had already been shaken by the criticisms of the Protestant Reformers and of some humanists.[119]) The Bible was soon widely considered to have only one, literal meaning, rather than an infinite range of possible interpretations.

A second development, however, is more characteristic of modernity and affects attitudes towards the Bible only indirectly. This may be described as a new interest in "the causes of things," accompanied by a restriction of the sense of the word "cause." Aristotle and his medieval interpreters had held to a very broad sense of the term "cause" and thus to a very broad sense of "explanation." In its classical definition, this view held that there were four types of cause: efficient, material, formal, and final.[120] (If a sculptor were creating a statue, for instance, the movement of the chisel could be described as the efficient cause, the stone as the material cause, the plan of the statue in the sculptor's mind as formal cause, and the purpose for which he was completing the work as the final cause.) However, the new interest in causality which emerges in the seventeenth century reduced explanation (in effect) to matters of efficient causality. It particularly rejected teleological explanations, which describe the world in terms of final causality, or purpose.[121] What is interesting is that this rejection occurs across the field of early modern philosophy, so that it is shared by philosophers who might otherwise appear to have little in common.

---

[118]The phrase (*infinita sensuum silva*) comes from Jerome (ca. 342–420 C.E.), cited in Henri de Lubac, *Medieval Exegesis,* vol. 1, *The Four Senses of Scripture* (1959), translated by Mark Sebanc (Grand Rapids: Eerdmans, 1998), 75. For Thomas Aquinas's discussion, see his *Summa Theologiae,* 1a.1.10.

[119]Cf. Parker, *Calvin's Old Testament Commentaries,* 70.

[120]Cf. Aristotle, *Physics* 2.3 (194b17–195a3) and 2.7 (198a14–198b8), in *The Complete Works of Aristotle: The Revised Oxford Translation,* edited by Jonathan Barnes, Bollingen Series 71, 2 (Princeton, N.J.: Princeton University Press, 1984), 1:332–33, 338–39; and *Metaphysics* 1.3 (983a24–984b22) and 5.2 (1013a24–1014a24), in ibid., vol. 2, pp. 1555–57, 1600–1601.

[121]For Aristotle's defense of teleological explanations, see his *Physics* 2.8 (198b10–199b30), in *The Complete Works of Aristotle,* 1:339–41.

Francis Bacon

In the empiricist tradition, a key figure in the rejection of teleology is the great pioneer of scientific method, Francis Bacon (1521–1626). In his *Of the Dignity and Advancement of Learning,* Bacon divides the search for the causes of the natural world into two disciplines, namely, physics and metaphysics.[122] Aristotle's four causes are parceled out between these two disciplines: physics "inquires and handles the Material and Efficient Causes," metaphysics "the Formal and Final."[123] While Bacon speaks highly of metaphysics (in principle), he also notes that the study of formal causes is often fruitless. For this reason he suggests it be put off until such time as a careful study of the natural world has been completed.[124] Teleological explanations, too, are rigorously excluded from the field of physics.

> For the handling of final causes in physics has driven away and overthrown the diligent inquiry of physical causes, and made men to stay upon these specious and shadowy causes, without actively pressing the inquiry of those which are really and truly physical; to the great arrest and prejudice of science. . . . For to introduce such causes as these, "that the hairs of the eyelids are for a quickset and fence about the sight"; or "that the firmness of the skins and hides of living creatures is to defend them from the extremities of heat and cold"; . . . and the like, is a proper inquiry in Metaphysic, but in Physic it is impertinent. Nay, as I was going to say, these discoursing causes . . . have in fact hindered the voyage and progress of the sciences.[125]

[122]Cf. Francis Bacon, "Of the Dignity and Advancement of Learning" (*De Dignitate et Augmentis Scientiarum* [1623]), 3.4, (translated in *The Works of Francis Bacon,* edited by James Spedding, Robert Leslie Ellis, and Douglas Denon Heath [London: Longmans & Co., 1875], 4:346). This is an expanded and revised version, in Latin, of a work that Bacon wrote and published in English in 1605, entitled *The Advancement of Learning.*

[123]Ibid.

[124]Cf. ibid., 360–61.

[125]Ibid., 363. Bacon's examples do not seem so objectionable today, accustomed as we are to what appear to be teleological explanations in those sciences that deal with the structure of plants and animals ("plants contain chlorophyll so that they can photosynthesize" or "polar bears are white so that they cannot be seen"). These explanations have an apparently teleological form because they deal with living organisms, which gradually adapt to their environment, and within which the functioning of the part is related to the functioning of the whole. However, these are not in fact teleological explanations (in the strict sense of the word), but rather a shorthand way of referring to the causal influence of past events (i.e., the formation of the organism or natural selection). (Cf. W. V. Quine and J. S. Ullian, *The Web of Belief,* 2d edition [New York: Random House, 1978], 117–18.) The only areas of science in which teleological explanations do continue to be used are those dealing with human and animal behavior, since both humans and animals can be said to "perceive, remember, recognise kinds, learn, believe and want" (Andrew Woodfield, *Teleology* [Cambridge: Cambridge University Press, 1976], 166) and are therefore capable of acting purposefully. Nonetheless this is very different from attributing purposeful action to inanimate objects or the world as a whole.

This leads Bacon to the colorful claim that "the inquisition of Final Causes is barren, and like a virgin consecrated to God produces nothing."[126] While Bacon does not so much reject teleological explanations as relegate them to metaphysics, it is worth noting that even his metaphysics leaves little room for such enquiries. Indeed commentators have noted that when discussing metaphysics, Bacon both redefines what he means by "formal" causality and effectively ignores final causes.[127] As one author writes, for Bacon metaphysics is little more than "the most general part of what might otherwise be called physics."[128] While there is no doubt that Bacon's "new method" greatly increased the efficiency and reliability of our search for knowledge, it did so by arguing (in effect) that certain types of knowledge are simply unattainable.

René Descartes

The rejection of teleological explanations is equally marked in the rationalist philosophy of René Descartes. When discussing "the principles of human knowledge" in part 1 of his *Principles of Philosophy* (1644/47), Descartes argues against the search for final causes. Human enquiry, he insists, should be limited to the exploration of efficient causality. Interestingly, Descartes supports this restriction with an apparently pious appeal to the limits of human knowledge. To search for final causes is presumptuous, since it assumes that we can know the mind of God. As he writes,

> concerning natural things, we shall not undertake any reasonings from the end which God or nature set Himself in creating these things, {and we shall entirely reject from our Philosophy the search for final causes}: because we ought not to presume so much of ourselves as to think that we are the confidants of His intentions. But, considering Him as the efficient cause of all things, we shall see what the natural enlightenment with which He endowed us reveals must be concluded (concerning those of His effects which appear to our senses), from those of His attributes of which He willed that we should have some notion.[129]

[126]Bacon, "Of the Dignity and Advancement of Learning," 3.5 (in *The Works of Francis Bacon,* 365).

[127]Cf. Anthony Quinton, *Bacon,* Past Masters (Oxford: Oxford University Press, 1980), 44–46; Frederick Copleston, *A History of Philosophy,* vol. 3, part 2, Image Books (Garden City, N.Y.: Doubleday, 1963), 106–12.

[128]Copleston, *A History of Philosophy,* vol. 3, part 2, 108.

[129]René Descartes, *Principles of Philosophy* (1644/47), translated by Valentine Rodger Miller and Reese P. Miller, Synthese Historical Library 24 (Dordrecht: D. Reidel, 1983), part 1, prop. 28 (p. 14). The material within brackets ({}) is taken from the 1647 French edition.

A similar dismissal of enquiry into final causes is found in Descartes's "Fourth Meditation" (ca. 1641), where he writes: "I consider the customary search for final causes to be totally useless in physics; there is considerable rashness in thinking myself capable of investigating the {impenetrable} purposes of God."[130] It is worth noting that Descartes, who remains a devout Catholic, wishes to find a place for the action of God in the realm of efficient causality.[131] Yet he shares with his more sceptical contemporaries the narrowing of the scope of what is regarded as a possible or legitimate explanation.

The Roots of Modernity

The philosopher of religion Louis Dupré traces these developments back to late medieval nominalism, exemplified in the work of William of Ockham (ca. 1290–1349).[132] In the synthesis of Christian and Aristotelian thought that we find (for example) in Thomas Aquinas, words are united by a kind of natural bond with the reality which they make present (so that language possesses what we might call a "sacramental" value).[133] For the nominalist tradition, on the other hand, words are signs whose relationship to reality is merely conventional. Language now refers to reality "without participating in it";[134] its symbolic significance is reduced. It follows that the rise of nominalism promoted a voluntarist view of creation, which also has roots in Augustinian theology.[135] According to this view, "what is, is as it is, merely because God willed it so."[136] There is no meaning written into the very nature of things; in particular, the created order does not participate in the rationality of language. It follows that human beings are the only beings to whom purpose may be ascribed. While in such matters lines of influence are difficult to trace, nominalism seems to prepare the way for what I have described as the seventeenth century's narrowing of the scope of explanation. As Dupré writes, "Bacon tends to transfer the theoretical question: In what

[130]René Descartes, "Meditations on First Philosophy," in *The Philosophical Writings of Descartes,* translated by John Cottingham, Robert Stoothoff, and Dugald Murdoch (Cambridge: Cambridge University Press, 1984), 2:39. Here, too, the material within brackets ({ }) is taken from later translations approved by Descartes himself.
[131]Cf. Descartes, *Principles of Philosophy,* part 1, prop. 51 (pp. 22–23); part 2, prop. 36 (pp. 57–58).
[132]Cf. Louis Dupré, *Passage to Modernity: An Essay in the Hermeneutics of Nature and Culture* (New Haven, Conn.: Yale University Press, 1993), 39 et passim.
[133]Cf. ibid., 102–4.
[134]Ibid., 104.
[135]Cf. ibid., 124.
[136]Ibid., 72.

does a thing's nature consist? to the functional one: How does it work? and ultimately to the one: What human purpose does it serve?"[137]

We may assume that these developments also had an impact on biblical interpretation, although here, too, their influence is not easily documented. As we shall see, there is some trace of this in the work of Spinoza, who begins his discussion of biblical interpretation by insisting that the Bible is to be interpreted in the same way as the natural world, by careful observation, classification, and "logical inference."[138] As the seventeenth century began, the suspicion of allegorical interpretation had already narrowed the scope of biblical interpretation. In an age that was no longer prepared to take scriptural authority for granted and had developed a greater sense of the historical distance between ourselves and the text, the scope of biblical interpretation was narrowed still further. The meaning of the text was increasingly conceived of as related to the circumstances in which the text was produced (as "effect" to "cause"). The purpose of the human author, embodied in the text, would soon become the sole determinant of textual meaning.

Mechanistic Natural Philosophy
The narrowing of the scope of explanation went hand in hand with another development, also closely related to the rise of modern science. This was a new way of representing reality. The world was increasingly regarded as a vast, self-contained mechanism, the workings of which could be understood by the use of calculation and geometry.[139] If we limit ourselves to the period before Spinoza, we find that Galileo is once again a key figure. Galileo's insistence that nature is to be understood mathematically is one of the best-known aspects of his work. As he writes,

> philosophy is written in this grand book—I mean the universe—which stands continually open to our gaze, but it cannot be understood unless one first learns to comprehend the language and interpret the characters in which it is written. It is written in the language of mathematics, and its characters are triangles, circles, and other geometric figures, without

---

[137]Ibid.

[138]Baruch Spinoza, *Tractatus Theologico-Politicus,* translated by Samuel Shirley (Leiden: E. J. Brill, 1989), 141 (see also 145).

[139]Perhaps the clearest expression of the mechanistic view is to be found in Descartes's claim (*Principles of Philosophy,* part 4, prop. 188 [p. 276]) to have "described this Earth, and indeed this whole visible world, as a machine, considering nothing in it except figures and motions."

which it is humanly impossible to understand a single word of it; without these, one is wandering about in a dark labyrinth.[140]

It is important to note that Galileo arrived at this conclusion, not by way of sense observation (which in this respect he regarded as misleading), but by way of what we might describe as a metaphysical assumption.[141] This was the assumption "that the real world has a geometrical structure and can therefore be comprehended by geometrical methods."[142] In this respect Galileo's procedure offers us a vivid illustration of the formation of the modern scientific attitude. For Galileo did not simply see the world more clearly than his predecessors; he offered us a new way of looking at it.

Galileo's assumption that the world could be understood geometrically found expression in what would later be called the distinction between "primary and secondary qualities," a distinction that has remained central to modern science, at least until very recent times.[143] For Galileo the primary qualities of the world were shape, size, number, position, and motion[144] and he thought of these as characterizing objects "in themselves." Secondary qualities were qualities such as color, sound, taste, and odor, which were thought to characterize objects only in relation to us.[145] It is important to note that this distinction, too, was not based on Galileo's observations of the world. For in the everyday world of human experience secondary qualities seem at least as "real" as do

---

[140]Galileo Galilei, *The Assayer* (1623), in *The Controversy on the Comets of 1618,* translated by Stillman Drake and C. D. O'Malley (Philadelphia: University of Philadelphia Press, 1960), 183–84.

[141]Stillman Drake (introduction to *The Controversy on the Comets of 1618,* xxiv–xxv) argues against the idea that Galileo's reliance on mathematics represented a metaphysical assumption. It is true that Galileo's *method* is not metaphysical, for he seeks to derive knowledge of the world from observation, rather than by deduction from mathematical first principles. Nonetheless, insofar as his understanding of science was strongly realist, he does seem to have assumed that the world had a mathematical structure. For a more sophisticated understanding of these matters, which was of course unavailable to Galileo, see Karl R. Popper, *The Open Universe: An Argument for Indeterminism,* vol. 2 of *Postscript to the Logic of Scientific Discovery* (1956), edited by W. W. Bartley III (London: Hutchinson, 1982), 43.

[142]Alan Musgrave, *Common Sense, Science, and Scepticism: A Historical Introduction to the Philosophy of Knowledge* (Cambridge: Cambridge University Press, 1993), 110.

[143]Cf. Galilei, *The Assayer,* in *The Controversy on the Comets of 1618,* 151–336. An anticipation of this distinction may be found in the work of the ancient school of "atomism," as exemplified in the work of Democritus of Abdera (d. 404 B.C.E.). Cf. Felix M. Cleve, *The Giants of Pre-Socratic Greek Philosophy: An Attempt to Reconstruct Their Thoughts,* 3d ed. (The Hague: Martinus Nijhoff, 1973), 2:420.

[144]Cf. John Losee, *A Historical Introduction to the Philosophy of Science,* 3d edition (Oxford: Oxford University Press, 1993), 55.

[145]Cf. Galilei, *The Assayer,* 311–12.

primary qualities. Rather, the distinction may be regarded a corollary of Galileo's initial assumption regarding the geometrical structure of the world.

It was, once again, Descartes who shaped these assumptions into a philosophical system. Although he wished to maintain a sharp distinction between the material world and the mind, the material world at least was to be understood on the model of geometry. Thus when it came to scientific investigation, Descartes's fundamental principle was that "extension in length, breadth, and depth constitutes the nature of corporeal substance . . . for everything else which can be attributed to body presupposes extension."[146] Implicit in this claim was a similar distinction between primary and secondary qualities. This becomes clear later in the same work, where Descartes writes that the secondary qualities of bodies can be reduced to the impact upon our senses of their movement.[147] On the basis of this principle, Descartes could go on to spell out his physics in terms of certain laws of motion,[148] which could also be dealt with mathematically. Characteristically, he justifies these laws by reference to the immutability of God, who is "not only immutable in His nature, but also immutable and completely constant in the way He acts."[149] Despite this theological underpinning, the break with the cosmology of the ancient world is very clear: "henceforth, the only spectacle which presents itself to the enquiring eye of man is that of matter agitated by movements according to mathematical laws."[150]

To sum up these developments, we may say that over the course of the seventeenth century, the world was increasingly perceived as a mechanism "governed in accordance with natural law, conceived either prescriptively or descriptively."[151] Now it is important to note that this mechanistic worldview did not exclude reference to divine action. On the contrary! Many of its proponents saw it as most *favorable* to religion. For within this mechanistic worldview, matter—that out of which the world is composed—is not alive; it is inert. Like the levers and gears of a

---

[146]Descartes, *Principles of Philosophy,* part 1, prop. 53 (pp. 23–24). This principle is derived from his doctrine of the reliability of "clear and distinct ideas," as is evident from his "Third Meditation" (1641; see Descartes, "Meditations on First Philosophy," in *The Philosophical Writings of Descartes,* 2:29–30).

[147]Cf. Descartes, *Principles of Philosophy,* part 4, prop. 198 (p. 282).

[148]Cf. ibid., part 2, props. 37–40 (pp. 59–62).

[149]Ibid., part 2, props. 36–39 (pp. 58–59).

[150]Cf. F. E. Sutcliffe, introduction to *Discourse on Method and the Meditations,* by René Descartes, translated by F. E. Sutcliffe, Penguin Classics (Harmondsworth, Middlesex: Penguin, 1968), 21.

[151]Hans W. Frei, *The Eclipse of Biblical Narrative: A Study in Eighteenth and Nineteenth Century Hermeneutics* (New Haven, Conn.: Yale University Press, 1974), 53.

clock, the basic components of the world contain no *intrinsic* power of motion.[152] If they move, that motion must be imparted from outside the system. If they are arranged in ways that are functional, if they form (for instance) complex living organisms beautifully adapted to their environment, then this could not have happened spontaneously. There must exist a wise designer who has crafted this great machine. The mechanistic worldview, in other words, lent considerable support to theological arguments from design, arguments that were to endure until the Darwinian revolution of the nineteenth century. On the other hand, the deity to which these arguments pointed could appear to be an "absentee landlord"[153] who designed this great mechanism and set it in motion at the beginning of time before retiring from the scene. In other words, if a mechanistic worldview lent support to the existence of a god, it lent more support to the God of deism than that of Christian theism. Once the mechanism was running, it required little or no reference to divine action, except perhaps to provide the occasional correction. Its functioning was to a large degree self-explanatory.

It follows that, while *at first sight* the newly emerging mechanistic worldview appeared favorable to religion, *in practice* it was only one step away from making references to God redundant.[154] The newly emerging sciences were gradually eliminating the need for any appeal to divine activity. It is true that the banishing of God from our explanations of the world did not occur all at once. As I have just hinted, the final steps were taken only in the late nineteenth century.[155] But this outcome was foreshadowed even in the seventeenth century. We have already seen that—despite his advocacy of the mechanistic worldview—Descartes could still appeal to the action of God. Yet even the pious Descartes comes perilously close to threatening the biblical view of creation. In his *Discourse on Method* (1637) he remarks that, although he does not wish to call into question the traditional Christian view, his principles allow us to see how the world *could have* emerged from chaos, *without* any intervention of God.

> I did not wish to infer from all this that our world was created in the way I proposed, for it is much more likely that from the beginning, God made

[152]Cf. Steven Shapin, *The Scientific Revolution* (Chicago: University of Chicago Press, 1996), 30–46, 148; Brooke, *Science and Religion,* 13, 117–51.

[153]Cf. Shapin, *The Scientific Revolution,* 149.

[154]Cf. Brooke, *Science and Religion,* 118, 136, 148.

[155]For a discussion of the final triumph of what might be called the "positive episteme" in the work of Charles Darwin, see Neal C. Gillespie, *Charles Darwin and the Problem of Creation* (Chicago: University of Chicago Press, 1979).

it just as it had to be. But it is certain, and an opinion commonly accepted among theologians, that the act by which God now preserves it is the same as that by which he created it. So, even if in the beginning God had given the world only the form of a chaos, provided that he established the laws of nature and then lent his concurrence to enable nature to operate as it usually does, we may believe without impugning the miracle of creation that by this means alone all purely material things could in the course of time have come to be just as we now see them.[156]

Belief in the biblical account of creation is here accepted on authority, but it is no longer necessary. The development of the world (if not its conservation in being) could well be explained without any reference to divine activity.[157] It is only a small step to Spinoza's metaphysics, which (as we shall see) effectively identifies the action of God with the laws of nature. It is important to be clear about what is happening here. It is not so much that the newly emerging sciences "disproved" religious claims, although in some cases (as we have seen) that was the case. The problem was that when it came to talk of divine activity, the scientist increasingly "had no need of this hypothesis."[158] The most obvious result was a scepticism towards biblical accounts of divine action, particularly when these seemed to contravene the natural order (as in the case of miracles).

There seemed to be no limits to this challenge to traditional religious ideas. For instance, even when God was no longer needed to explain the *functioning* of the world, philosophers and theologians could continue to argue that he was needed to sustain its existence. The apparent contingency of the world seemed to require that one posit the existence of a necessary being. Once again, Descartes's philosophy provides an excellent illustration of this argument. For while his God sometimes seems to be reduced to the First Cause, who merely set the mechanism going at

[156]René Descartes, "Discourse on Method, Part Five," in *The Philosophical Writings of Descartes,* translated by John Cottingham, Robert Stoothoff, and Dugald Murdoch (Cambridge: Cambridge University Press, 1985), 1:133–34.

[157]See also Descartes's *Principles of Philosophy,* part 3, props. 43–47 (pp. 104–8), and part 4, props. 1–2 (pp. 181–82), where Descartes offers an account of how the universe could have been formed that again differs from the biblical. However, Descartes describes his view as only a hypothesis (in the sense discussed above), aspects of which must be judged to be false on theological grounds, even though they allow one to deduce the phenomena.

[158]The phrase is that of Pierre Simon de Laplace (1749–1827). In response to Napoleon's question about the place of God in his cosmology, Laplace is reported to have replied, *Je n'ai pas besoin de cet hypothèse* (I have no need of that hypothesis). This did not necessarily mean that he was an irreligious man; it meant merely that the idea of God no longer served any explanatory function.

the time of creation,[159] Descartes also argues that God's action is required to keep the world in existence.[160] As we shall see in chapter 1, Spinoza's philosophy broke down the walls of this last theological refuge. For Spinoza suggested that one can conceive of a world that requires nothing "outside of" itself for its continuation in being, indeed a world whose nonexistence is simply unthinkable.

It is this vision of a world functioning—and worse still existing—without reference to God that some Christian writers of our own time are inclined to dismiss as the "Enlightenment worldview."[161] It was a "worldview," insofar as it was a new way of representing reality, but it was also an enormously plausible one, whose reliability seemed to be vindicated by its success. Further discussion of these issues must await the chapters on Spinoza and Strauss. For the moment we should note that these developments were merely one of the factors influencing the rise of biblical criticism.

This chapter has attempted to describe some of the forces at work reshaping attitudes to the Bible in the early part of the century in which Spinoza wrote his *Tractatus*. They were not, of course, the last challenges to Christian faith. The eighteenth and nineteenth centuries would offer new criticisms of religion. One thinks, for instance, of the figure of Ludwig Feuerbach (1804–72), whose work haunts so much contemporary theology, or of Charles Darwin (1809–82). We will return to both figures in the chapters that follow. However, the seventeenth-century challenges to faith were those that made possible the historical criticism of the Bible. Without these changes, the question that forms the title of the present study would never have arisen. It is important, therefore, to look more closely at the effect of the seventeenth-century challenges to biblical authority. What were their consequences for Christian thought?

In one sense, the rest of this book will be spent answering that question. But a provisional answer will make the rest of the book intelligible.

---

[159]Cf. Descartes, *Principles of Philosophy,* part 2, prop. 36 (pp. 57–58).

[160]Cf. Descartes, "Meditations on First Philosophy, Third Meditation," in *The Philosophical Writings of Descartes,* 2:33.

[161]Dismissive references to an "Enlightenment worldview" are particularly common when contemporary theologians come to discuss miracles. For examples, see Ben F. Meyer, *The Aims of Jesus* (London: SCM, 1979), 101; N. T. Wright, *Christian Origins and the Question of God,* vol. 1, *The New Testament and the People of God* (Minneapolis: Fortress Press, 1992), 92; and Wolfhart Pannenberg, *Jesus—God and Man* (1964), translated by Lewis L. Wilkins and Duane A. Priebe (London: SCM, 1968), 109. As we will see in chapter 2, however, the decisive arguments against accepting reports of miracles are epistemological, not metaphysical. They do not, therefore, involve the acceptance of any particular worldview.

Traditionally, the Bible had been regarded as what one might call
the "metanarrative to end all metanarratives," embracing the whole of
nature and human history.[162] However, by the late seventeenth century
it was starting to become clear, to at least some of Europe's more per-
ceptive thinkers, that our knowledge of the world and of human history
would not longer fit within the biblical framework.[163] In other words, if
the sixteenth century had taken its stand on the Bible to challenge the
authority of the church, the seventeenth century began to call the Bible
itself into question.[164] No longer did the biblical narrative offer the
taken-for-granted starting point of human knowledge. Rather than
beginning with the Bible and fitting everything else into its picture of
the world, an increasing number of scholars were beginning with the
data of the natural sciences and of history. They were starting to understand the Bible within the framework provided by these secular disciplines.[165] The theologian Hans Frei has referred to this momentous shift
as "the great reversal." As he writes, biblical interpretation was now "a
matter of fitting the biblical story into another world with another story
rather than incorporating that world into the biblical story."[166]

It would be difficult to overestimate the significance of this Copernican revolution in the understanding of Christianity and its scriptures. As

[162]Cf. Erich Auerbach, *Mimesis: The Representation of Reality in Western Literature*
(1946), translated by Willard R. Trask (Princeton, N.J.: Princeton University Press, 1953),
15–16. As Auerbach notes, it is not just that Christians regarded the Bible as an all-
embracing narrative; rather, the Bible itself makes these claims.

[163]On this development, see also J. M. Creed, *The Divinity of Jesus Christ* (1938; London: Collins/Fontana, 1964), 109.

[164]See also Preus, *Explaining Religion,* xv et passim. Preus (8) relates his observations
to those of Hans Frei (see below) and traces the beginning of this shift in thought to the
age of Jean Bodin (1530–96). Yet, as Preus notes, for Bodin the biblical framework is "still
normative in that it provides the overall world-picture for both history (at least primal
history) and nature." There is no decisive break with that framework until the seventeenth
century (see ibid., 19), and it becomes widespread only in the eighteenth and nineteenth.

[165]Here one might call to mind Ernst Cassirer's description of the Enlightenment
attitude towards religious authority and reason in general (in *The Philosophy of the
Enlightenment,* translated by Fritz C. A. Koelln and James P. Pettegrove [1932; Princeton,
N.J.: Princeton University Press, 1951], 159). In the eighteenth century, he writes, "that
which formerly had established other concepts, now moves into the position of that
which is to be established, and that which hitherto had justified other concepts, now
finds itself in the position of a concept which requires justification."

[166]Frei, *The Eclipse of Biblical Narrative,* 130. I use Frei's illuminating phrase without
wishing to identify myself with either his theological project or that of the so-called
"post-liberal" theology that builds on it. In particular, I can make little sense of George
A. Lindbeck's attempt (*The Nature of Doctrine: Religion and Theology in a Postliberal Age*
[Philadelphia: Westminster Press, 1984], 112–38) to reduce biblical interpretation to an
"intratextual" affair. I cannot see how such a task could be carried through consistently.

Frei notes, for the first time in Jewish and Christian history the biblical narrative became distinguishable from that to which it claimed to refer.[167] In particular, our access to significant human history was no longer mediated by the Bible alone. The new knowledge of the world offered access to a much longer and broader view of human history, for our knowledge of which the biblical account was, at best, one source among many. In principle, there was nothing to prevent the historian from comparing the biblical account with other sources and finding it wanting. What had happened, in other words, was that a gap had been opened up between what the Bible said and the events to which it claimed to bear witness. Those wishing to uphold the biblical picture now had to defend it, for its truth could no longer be taken for granted. Only under these conditions could the modern "historical criticism" of the Bible develop. Only under these conditions could the question of the historical Jesus arise.

It follows that the question of the historical Jesus should not be viewed in isolation. It formed part of a wider process of religious change. Another way of describing this change would be to say that by the end of the seventeenth century, the burden of proof had shifted. At least in the context of public discourse about religion, it was no longer those who *opposed* biblical authority who had to prove their case, but those who *supported* it. It is true that theologians had always felt the need to offer arguments in support of biblical authority. But their arguments were shaped by the assumption that the evidence they adduced could not be seriously doubted by any person of good will.[168] If such a person were not persuaded by the fulfilment of Old Testament prophecies and by the New Testament miracles, then he ought to be persuaded by the worldwide spread of the Christian faith.[169] If a person resisted such arguments, it was almost certainly because of pride.[170] By the end of the

[167]Frei, *The Eclipse of Biblical Narrative*, 51.

[168]Cf. Anthony Kenny, *What is Faith? Essays in the Philosophy of Religion* (Oxford: Oxford University Press, 1992), 55.

[169]For examples, see Augustine, *The City of God*, 22.5 (p. 1113–15); *Epistle* 137.4.15–16, in *An Augustine Synthesis*, edited by Erich Przywara, S.J. (London: Sheed & Ward, 1945), 44–46; Thomas Aquinas, *Summa contra gentiles* 1.6,1.9. The Calvinist tradition, it is true, appeals primarily to the inner witness of the Holy Spirit, but even Calvin brings in these more general arguments by way of additional support. (See, for instance, John Calvin, *Institutes of the Christian Religion*, translated by Ford Lewis Battles, Library of Christian Classics, vol. 20 [London: SCM, 1961], I.vii.4–5 [pp. 78–81].)

[170]See, for instance, Augustine, *De vera religione* (Of true religion), 25.47, English translation by John H. S. Burleigh, in *Augustine: Earlier Writings*, Library of Christian Classics, vol. 4 (London: SCM, 1953), 248. This view—that there can be no innocent unbelief—is echoed in our own day by William Lane Craig in his work on Christian apologetics (*Reasonable Faith: Christian Truth and Apologetics*, revised edition [Wheaton, Ill.: Crossway Books, 1994], 35, 37).

seventeenth century, these assumptions could no longer be maintained. There were many who continued to believe in God, but—as my next chapter will demonstrate—one could no longer take it for granted that they were speaking of the *Christian* God. One could no longer assume that they would submit to the authority of the Bible. Indeed in an age in which the limits of biblical authority had been made clear, in which religious authority had been shown to lead to conflict, in which new modes of explanation made no appeal to divine action, one could no longer take *any* kind of religious faith for granted. For the first time since at least the age of Constantine, religion itself was on the defensive.

To clarify the focus of the present study, it may be helpful to make a distinction. I have spoken of the "historical Jesus question," which first arose as a result of these changes. But this phrase has a narrow sense and a broader sense. The narrow sense represents an *historical* question (in the strict sense of that word); the broader sense represents a *theological* question.[171] Some of the authors we are about to study dealt with the question of the historical Jesus in the narrow sense of that phrase. That is to say, they used the methods of enquiry that are characteristic of modern history in order to depict the figure of Jesus *as* a figure of his time and place. The problems to be dealt with here are largely empirical: they are questions of historical evidence. But behind this set of problems lies a larger question. This larger question was prompted by, but is not identical with, the historical question regarding the figure of Jesus. This larger set of problems has to do with the challenge of history to traditional notions of religious authority. This is a conceptual rather than an empirical problem.[172] As we will see, the challenge of history to religious authority was a twofold challenge. It arose first of all from the *content* of history: from the fact that the new knowledge of the age had split the biblical framework asunder. But the challenge was also *methodological,* for history was one of those new forms of critical enquiry that no longer relied on traditional forms of authoritative teaching. All of our authors were concerned with this broader challenge, which forms the focus of the present study.

Insofar as their work was shaped by this set of problems, the authors we are about to study may be regarded as forming a single "research

---

[171]These questions correspond almost exactly with what, almost a century ago, Ernst Troeltsch described as the two great problems facing modern Christian theology, to which I will return in chapter 4 (cf. Ernst Troeltsch, "Half a Century of Theology: A Review" [1908], translated by Robert Morgan, in *Writings on Theology and Religion,* translated and edited by Robert Morgan and Michael Pye [London: Duckworth, 1977], 69–71).

[172]For this distinction, see Larry Laudan, *Progress and Its Problems: Towards a Theory of Scientific Growth* (Berkeley, Calif.: University of California Press, 1977), 45–69.

tradition."[173] What do I mean by this term? In recent writing in the philosophy of science, a research tradition is thought of as a very broad intellectual entity, which may extend over many centuries of enquiry. It embraces a succession of individual theories, held together by a more or less common set of metaphysical and methodological assumptions. Within this framework, there exist a common set of problems, but the theories that make up the research tradition may well offer mutually exclusive solutions to those problems. While the term "research tradition" arose within the philosophy of science, it may certainly be applied to other forms of enquiry. For this reason there is nothing immediately incoherent about the idea of a *theological* research tradition (which is not, of course, to say that such a tradition will be successful).[174] The research tradition we are about to study focuses on the problem of religious authority in the Christian tradition.

Within this research tradition, broadly defined, a number of questions demanded an answer, questions that arose from the changes traced in the present chapter. If the Bible has to be judged against a wider framework of history, then what happens to its religious authority? Does the final authority in religious matters not rest with the historian rather than the theologian? One may wish to appeal to the figure of Jesus, but is the Bible an accurate record of what Jesus said and did? Was it not distorted by the limited knowledge and strong beliefs of its authors? Even if we *can* discover "the real Jesus," the Jesus of history, will he be anything more than a figure of his time and place, of no interest to a later age? More seriously, if the biblical *history* can no longer be taken as a reliable account of the past, why should the Bible's *religious* claims be taken any more seriously? In matters of doctrine, too, is it not merely another human and fallible document, whose statements must be tested before being accepted? If so, what happens to the great body of Christian belief, much of which rests not on its intrinsic plausibility but on the authority of the Bible? In the broader perspective of human history, can the Bible be seen as anything more than yet another example of "sacred scripture"? If it *is* a human document comparable to other documents, what happens to Christianity's claims to uniqueness? After all, human history is full of religious teachers and bodies of scripture. Why should this teacher and this body of scripture be regarded as any different in principle from the rest? Should they not all be judged by the same standards?

[173]For the idea of a research tradition, which is a more precise and more illuminating concept than that of the "paradigm" (Thomas Kuhn) or the "research programme" (Imre Lakatos), see Laudan, *Progress and Its Problems,* 78–119.
[174]Cf. ibid., 190.

These are the questions with which the authors we are about to study will grapple. I hope the reader will agree that they were important questions. I hope she will also agree that they were necessary questions, questions that could not be evaded, given the new horizons in European intellectual life that the seventeenth century had opened up. Nor has their importance diminished with the passage of time. However "postmodern" we may style ourselves, the questions of modernity have not simply disappeared. Indeed in a world in which competing faiths are brought into ever closer contact and in which all appeals to authority are deeply suspect, these questions are even more urgent. Can they be answered from the standpoint of faith? Have the leading theologians of the last two hundred years succeeded in doing so? That is the central question of this book.

Chapter One

The Divorce between History and Faith

Benedict Spinoza (1632–77)

> *The Ethics frightened them with its axioms and corollaries.*
> *[It] was like being in a balloon at night, in glacial coldness,*
> *carried on an endless voyage towards a bottomless abyss,*
> *and with nothing near but the unseizable, the motionless, the eternal.*
> *It was too much. They gave it up.*
>
> Gustave Flaubert

Baruch (or Benedict) Spinoza was certainly not the first seventeenth-century thinker to propose new ways of interpreting the Bible.[1] As our introductory chapter has shown, there were many who had begun to question biblical authority in the decades before he began to write.[2] Nonetheless, Spinoza's presentation of a new method of biblical interpretation stands out for its thoroughness, its consistency, and the degree to which its author is prepared to depart from traditional religious attitudes.[3] Even though later biblical interpreters rarely appealed to

---

[1]On the question of which of these earlier authors may have influenced Spinoza, see Brad Gregory, introduction to the *Tractatus*, 33–36; J. Samuel Preus, "The Bible and Religion in the Century of Genius," *Religion* 28 (1998): 119–22; Richard H. Popkin's two articles, "Spinoza and Biblical Scholarship," in *The Cambridge Companion to Spinoza*, edited by Don Garrett (Cambridge: Cambridge University Press, 1996), especially 386–94; and "New Light on the Roots of Spinoza's Science of the Bible," in *Spinoza and the Sciences*, edited by Marjorie Grene and Debra Nails, Boston Studies in the Philosophy of Science 91 (Dordrecht: D. Reidel, 1986), 171–88. On the particular question of the influence of Isaac de la Peyrère on Spinoza, see Richard Popkin's "Spinoza and La Peyrère," in *Spinoza: New Perspectives*, edited by Robert W. Shahan and J. I. Biro (Norman, Okla.: University of Oklahoma Press, 1978), 177–95.

[2]It is worth noting (with Scholder, *The Birth of Modern Critical Theology*, 4) that, while almost all the authors whose work we will study in the chapters that follow are German-speaking, these earliest developments took place almost entirely outside the world of German culture. In this respect, Spinoza, as a Jew of Portuguese background living in Amsterdam, is representative of the earliest developments.

[3]Even Richard Simon (1638–1712), who is rightly regarded as one of the pioneers of modern biblical criticism, seems appalled by what he describes as Spinoza's attack on biblical authority. (See the preface to his 1678 *Critical History of the Old Testament*.)

Spinoza,[4] his *Tractatus Theologico-Politicus* (Theological-political treatise) remains a foundational document. Not only does it outline what would become the established method of biblical criticism for the next three hundred years, but it couples this with a radical critique of biblical authority. Thus Spinoza both sums up and raises to a new level many of the developments that we have already seen to be characteristic of the seventeenth century.[5]

Spinoza's *Tractatus Theologico-Politicus,* as its name suggests, is an extended discussion of matters both religious and political.[6] Above all, it is a plea for freedom of thought and speech in all matters that do not undermine the very basis of a free society.[7] In the course of this plea Spinoza outlines a method of interpreting the Bible, a method that he claims will separate its true meaning from what he calls the "fabrications" foisted upon it by its authorized interpreters, Jewish and Christian.[8] Spinoza's method of interpretation involves a close study of the text, which is to take place in three stages. The first is a careful analysis of the language of the Bible.[9] Here Spinoza shows himself to be an heir to the humanistic tradition of classical philology, although he is, by his own admission, more at home with Old Testament Hebrew than New Testament Greek.[10] The second stage consists of a listing of biblical texts by topic, with a view to clarifying the biblical message.[11] Here, as we will see, Spinoza is anxious that we interpret the Bible on its own terms and do not import our modern standards of rationality into our reading of the text. Although in a very different way from that suggested by the Protestant

[4]Cassirer (*The Philosophy of the Enlightenment,* 187) notes that "Spinoza seems hardly to have had any direct influence on eighteenth-century thought." Cassirer traces the line of influence that gave birth to the historical criticism of the Bible back to the great sixteenth-century humanist Erasmus, and then down through his pupil Hugo Grotius (1583–1645) to Johann August Ernesti (1707–81) and Johann Salomo Semler (1725–91). For a discussion of the humanist influence on biblical criticism, see the introduction to the present work.

[5]Cf. Scholder, *The Birth of Modern Critical Theology,* 138.

[6]Edwin Curley ("Notes on a Neglected Masterpiece [II]: the *Theological-Political Treatise* as a Prolegomenon to the Ethics," in *Central Themes in Early Modern Philosophy: Essays Presented to Jonathan Bennett,* edited by J. A. Cover and Mark Kulstad [Indianapolis: Hackett, 1990], 111) notes that the *Tractatus* "is a work with multiple agendas" and suggests that in Spinoza's own mind the stated political goal of the work may have been subservient to the hermeneutical.

[7]Cf. Spinoza, *Tractatus,* 51, 299, et passim.

[8]Cf. ibid., 53.

[9]Spinoza, *Tractatus,* 142–43; reprinted in my anthology *The Historical Jesus Quest* (Leiden: Deo Publishing, 1999/Louisville, Ky.: Westminster John Knox Press, 2000), 8.

[10]Cf. Spinoza, *Tractatus,* 196.

[11]Cf. ibid., 143–44; *The Historical Jesus Quest,* 8–9.

Reformers, for Spinoza, too, the Bible is "its own interpreter" (*sui ipsius interpres*).[12] (We will return to this matter shortly.) The third stage of Spinoza's method would be familiar to any modern student who has ever taken a course in biblical interpretation. It involves first of all discovering the circumstances in which each biblical book was produced, including the life and character of its human author and the occasion on which it was written. It also involves tracing the history of the book's reception, canonization, and translation.[13] The purpose of this thoroughly historical study is not only the detection of errors that may have crept into the biblical text. It also involves distinguishing between those matters that are of eternal significance and those that are of relevance only to a particular people or age. Like Kepler and Galileo before him, Spinoza is concerned that proper limits should be placed on biblical authority.

Spinoza does not just outline this method of biblical interpretation; to a limited degree he seeks to exemplify it. A large part of the *Tractatus* is devoted to an historical analysis of the origins of the biblical writings. Here Spinoza anticipates in a number of ways the biblical scholarship of the nineteenth and twentieth centuries. He suggests, for example, that many of the Old Testament books received their present form only at the time of Ezra, or even later, and that the Old Testament canon dates (at the earliest) from the time of the Maccabees.[14] Even the materials that make up the Pentateuch appear to have been "collected indiscriminately" and only arranged at a much later date.[15] Spinoza makes similar comments about later biblical books, noting, for example, the discrepancies between the history found in the books of Chronicles and that found in the books of Kings.[16] Perhaps prudently, Spinoza does not carry this analysis through to the New Testament, citing his inadequate knowledge of Greek.[17] For this reason the *Tractatus* does not address the question of the historical Jesus, although one can see how easily it would have arisen, had Spinoza's analysis been continued. It is true that the details of his work are not particularly convincing, a fact hardly to be marveled at in one raising the questions for practically the first time. What is more interesting is why Spinoza felt compelled to ask these questions in the first place and the ways in which he deals with their religious implications.

---

[12]Cf. Preus, "The Bible and Religion in the Century of Genius," 119.
[13]Cf. Spinoza, *Tractatus,* 144–45; *The Historical Jesus Quest,* 9–10.
[14]Cf. ibid., 170, 191, 195, et passim.
[15]Cf. ibid., 175.
[16]Cf. ibid., 178.
[17]Cf. ibid., 196.

1. Spinoza and Religious Controversy

Religious Controversy

What motivated Spinoza's attempt to sketch so radically new an approach to biblical interpretation? Politically, his motivation seems clear. The *Tractatus* suggests that Spinoza, along with many of the thoughtful scholars of his age, was appalled by the bitterness and bloodshed associated with the European wars of religion and by the ongoing fact of religious controversy. As a citizen of the United Provinces of the Netherlands, Spinoza was in this respect fortunate: he could "live and work—though not publish—in a condition of freedom unique in seventeenth century Europe."[18] Even this freedom was not due to any particular virtue on the part of the Dutch. It was, as one commentator writes, something of an accident of history, "the outcome of a temporary stalemate in theological politics."[19] The *Tractatus* shows how aware Spinoza was of the evils that result from religious controversy. Towards the beginning of the work he writes:

> I have often wondered that men who make a boast of professing the Christian religion, which is a religion of love, joy, peace, temperance and honest dealing with all men, should quarrel so fiercely and display the bitterest hatred towards one another day by day, so that these latter characteristics make known a man's creed more readily than the former.[20]

Later in the work, while discussing the apostolic age, he writes that "many disputes and schisms" arose "to vex the Church continually right from the time of the Apostles, and they will assuredly continue to vex the Church until the day comes when religion shall be separated from philosophic speculation and reduced to the few simple doctrines that Christ taught his people."[21] This abhorrence of religious controversy is hardly surprising, given Spinoza's own Jewish and *marrano* background. After all, his grandfather had fled the Inquisition in Portugal and moved to France in order to escape religious persecution.[22] In his major philosophical work, the *Ethics,* Spinoza even offers a short but insightful

---

[18]Richard Mason, *The God of Spinoza: A Philosophical Study* (Cambridge: Cambridge University Press, 1997), 6.

[19]Ibid., 7.

[20]Spinoza, *Tractatus,* 52.

[21]Ibid., 203.

[22]Cf. Margaret Gullan-Whur, *Within Reason: A Life of Spinoza* (London: Jonathan Cape, 1998), 2.

analysis of the psychological roots of all forms of prejudice.[23] It follows that, while Spinoza's understanding of the Bible is (as we will see) influenced by his general philosophical stance, his attempts to find a new method of interpretation are motivated by the desire to counteract the effects of religious strife.

Religious Liberty

Since religious controversy is particularly destructive when religious authorities can invoke political power to enforce their decrees, the principal aim of the *Tractatus* is to ensure religious liberty. Spinoza insists that in religious matters "freedom of judgment" should be "fully granted to the individual citizen" so that "he may worship God as he pleases."[24] However, he argues for this liberty in what appears at first to be a paradoxical way. For in religious matters he first insists that complete power must be given to the ruler of the state.[25] As he writes,

> we cannot doubt that in modern times religion . . . belongs solely to the right of the sovereign. No one has the right and power to exercise control over it, to choose its ministers, to determine and establish the foundations of the church and its doctrine, to pass judgment on morality and acts of piety, to excommunicate or receive into the church, and to provide for the poor, except by the authority and permission of the sovereign.[26]

In the course of an argument for religious liberty, this seems an odd move. What lies behind it? Why does Spinoza insist on the right of the sovereign to control religious matters? There seem to be at least three reasons for this apparently self-defeating maneuver. The first is a very practical concern, namely, that religious disputes should not be permitted to disrupt the order of society. As Spinoza writes, "the practice of religion and piety must accord with the peace and welfare of the commonwealth."[27] To this extent Spinoza can be said to accept the compromise formula of *cuius regio, eius religio* (the religion follows the ruler), a principle which formed the basis of the peace of Augsburg in 1555 and was reapplied to bring to an end the Thirty Years War in 1648. The second reason why Spinoza holds to this position is more characteristic of

---

[23]Spinoza, *Ethics*, part 3, prop. 46; cf. *The Ethics and Selected Letters*, translated by Samuel Shirley (Indianapolis: Hackett, 1982), 131. All quotations from the *Ethics* in this chapter come from this translation.
[24]Spinoza, *Tractatus*, 51.
[25]Cf. ibid., 280–90.
[26]Ibid., 286.
[27]Ibid., 280.

his thought. In Spinoza's metaphysics, it makes no sense to speak of a "kingdom of God" or of "the laws of God" except insofar as these are expressed through the actions of earthly rulers. There *are* no "laws of God" until these are formulated by human beings. As he writes, "God has no special kingdom over men save through the medium of those who hold the sovereignty."[28] For this reason religion and the state are intimately linked. (Spinoza's reasoning here will become clearer when we come to examine his metaphysics.) A third and closely related line of reasoning is drawn from Spinoza's view of the origins of human society. In a way that is reminiscent of Thomas Hobbes (1588–1679),[29] Spinoza argues that "in a state of nature reason possesses no more right than does appetite."[30] In the state of nature it would make no sense to speak of either righteousness or transgression. Such concepts have meaning only when human beings have surrendered their sovereignty to a lawgiver. For this reason, too, religion and the state are inseparable.

This concentration of religious authority in the hands of the sovereign may be pragmatically desirable. It may even be consistent with Spinoza's metaphysics and political theory. Yet it remains, at first sight, an odd way of defending religious liberty. It takes on the character of such a defense when it is coupled with two restrictions. First of all, Spinoza makes it clear that the authority of the sovereign extends only to "acts of piety and the outward forms of religion."[31] It does *not* extend to the beliefs and attitudes of his subjects. For the existence of a state, it is necessary that human beings surrender their right to *act* as they think fit, but they cannot surrender their right "to reason and judge."[32] Only if political beliefs threaten to destroy society itself by undermining the "covenant" that lies at the very basis of the state should they be considered "seditious" and repressed.[33] Thus, Spinoza's ideal of political freedom is a freedom of thought and of speech; it is *not* an unlimited freedom of action. However, in matters of thought and speech he does insist that the state should allow for the greatest possible degree of liberty.

Spinoza's second restriction is one to which we will return, namely, a restriction of the scope of religious authority. He argues that the clear

[28]Spinoza, *Tractatus*, 281. We will return to Spinoza's idea of God in a later section of this chapter.

[29]Spinoza makes an explicit reference to Hobbes's work in a supplementary note to the *Tractatus* (307). Although he is there distancing himself from an aspect of Hobbes's thought, elsewhere a more positive influence may be discerned. On Spinoza's failure adequately to acknowledge his sources, see Gullan-Whur, *Within Reason*, 198.

[30]Spinoza, *Tractatus*, 281.

[31]Ibid., 280.

[32]Ibid., 293.

[33]Cf. ibid., 294.

teaching of the Bible consists of a number of "very simple doctrines easily comprehensible by all."[34] Those "very simple doctrines" are in fact reducible to certain basic ethical teachings, namely the call "to obey God with all one's heart by practicing justice and charity."[35] On the side of religious authority, there is nothing in this very simple vision of religion to serve as a basis for religious intolerance or warfare. More importantly, this restriction of the scope of religion has the effect of further limiting civil authority. For as Spinoza writes, "the state can pursue no safer course than to regard piety and religion as consisting *solely in the exercise of charity and just dealing.*"[36] The implication is that, provided their subjects live by these fundamental moral norms, there is no need for rulers to exercise any further religious compulsion. Elsewhere in the *Tractatus,* this argument is made explicit. For instance, in chapter 7 Spinoza writes that while the liberty of interpreting civil laws cannot safely be left in the hands of individuals, liberty in religious matters can. For since religion involves the cultivation of *internal virtues* rather than the performance of *external actions,* it does not belong to the sphere of public law.[37] It seems, then, that Spinoza's argument is a complex one. From an initial assertion of the authority of the sovereign in matters religious, Spinoza proceeds to restrict the scope of that authority to external practices and then to redefine religion in the simplest possible terms. The result of this process is an assertion of the religious liberty of the individual.

2. The Limits of Biblical Authority

Spinoza's Understanding of Revelation

In redefining religion as the cultivation of certain basic virtues Spinoza is, of course, already distancing himself from traditional Jewish and Christian attitudes. However, the novelty of Spinoza's approach to the Jewish and Christian scriptures is most evident in his analysis of biblical prophecy. This is a key issue, since for Spinoza prophecy is synonymous with revelation.[38] He first tackles this topic cautiously, using the relatively safe idea of the accommodation of scriptural language to the

[34]Ibid., 54.

[35]Ibid., 55.

[36]Ibid., 299 (emphasis my own).

[37]Cf. Spinoza, *Tractatus,* 159; *The Historical Jesus Quest,* 25.

[38]See the first line of the first chapter of the *Tractatus* (60), which reads: "Prophecy, or Revelation, is the sure knowledge of some matter revealed by God to man." On this equivalence, see Alan Donagan, "Spinoza's Theology," in *The Cambridge Companion to Spinoza,* ed. Don Garratt (Cambridge: Cambridge University Press, 1996), 357; and Mason, *The God of Spinoza,* 148, 150.

mentality of those to whom it is addressed.[39] This allows him to write
that the simple ethical message of the Bible was "adapted to the understanding and beliefs of those to whom the Prophets and Apostles were
wont to proclaim the Word of God."[40] However, in the opening chapters
of the *Tractatus,* where Spinoza undertakes an explicit analysis of prophecy,
he goes much further. First of all, he discusses the way in which the
prophets received their messages from God. He claims that biblical
prophecy was particularly related to the exercise of the imagination. It
came from God, but it was received (as Spinoza writes) "only with the
aid of the imaginative faculty," so that what was required of a prophet
was not intellectual insight but a lively imagination.[41] Now Spinoza
admits that a revelation conveyed by means of the imagination has a particular power, for imaginative knowledge can suggest things that are not
easily set out in propositional form. It follows that by the exercise of
their imagination the biblical prophets "may have perceived much that is
beyond the limits of intellect."[42] Yet we must not misunderstand Spinoza
at this point. In particular we should beware of reading his words in the
light of our more modern notions of language and thought. Philosophers of our own day may write appreciatively of the cognitive power
of metaphor and myth, but this was not Spinoza's position. For our
seventeenth-century thinker, a reliance on imaginative knowledge represented, on balance, not a strength but a weakness. For it implies that the
authority of the prophetic message is a limited authority, which compares poorly with that of other ways of accessing truth. To understand
this limitation, we may look briefly both at Spinoza's argument elsewhere in the *Tractatus* and at the epistemology (theory of knowledge)
found in his major work, the *Ethics.*

The Limits of Prophetic Authority
In the *Tractatus* itself, Spinoza argues that the role of imagination in biblical prophecy limits the *universality* of the prophetic message. For revelation received in this way was conditioned by the prophet's temperament,

---

[39]Cf. Preus, "The Bible and Religion in the Century of Genius," 128. For the use of
this idea by Kepler and Galileo, see the introductory chapter.
[40]Spinoza, *Tractatus,* 55 (see 66, 86). Unlike Preus ("The Bible and Religion in the
Century of Genius," 129) I do not think it is necessary to take Spinoza's language of
"accommodation" as ironic, but rather as a transposition into theological terms of the
limits of knowledge received through the imagination (see below). It is certainly not
accommodation in the traditional Christian sense, but then Spinoza habitually uses traditional theological terms in his own unique manner (cf. Mason, *The God of Spinoza,* 82).
[41]Spinoza, *Tractatus,* 65.
[42]Cf. ibid., 71.

his imagination, and his existing beliefs.[43] As Spinoza writes, "Solomon, Isaiah, Joshua and the others were indeed prophets: but they were also men, subject to human limitations."[44] It follows that the prophetic message was not only conditioned by its time and place and by the character of the prophet; it also suffered from the common misconceptions to which this kind of knowledge is subject. The result is that the prophetic writings can contain contradictory beliefs and errors that are due to prejudice.[45] As an example of such a prejudice, Spinoza cites the assumption of Joshua 10 that the sun moves around a motionless earth,[46] the text that had caused so much debate only a few decades before his time. Still more seriously, Spinoza suggests that biblical prophecy merely clothed existing ideas about the world in a new form. At least as far as factual knowledge is concerned, it provided nothing more than that which the prophets already have. In his own words, "the gift of prophecy did not render the prophets more learned, but left them with the beliefs they had previously held."[47]

The strictly limited value of biblical prophecy is even clearer when the *Tractatus* is read in the light of Spinoza's epistemology. They key text here is the discussion of the grades of knowledge in part 2 of Spinoza's *Ethics*.[48] There is, by the way, good reason for interpreting the *Tractatus* in the light of the *Ethics,* since Spinoza seems to have interrupted the writing of the latter work in order to complete the former. We may therefore assume that while writing the *Tractatus* "the philosophy of the *Ethics* was not far from his mind."[49] In the *Ethics* Spinoza divides knowledge (cognitio) into three categories.[50] There is a first kind of knowledge, which arises from encounters with those things that affect the human being "from outside" (as it were).[51] Such knowledge can itself be divided into

---

[43]Cf. ibid., 76.

[44]Ibid., 80.

[45]Cf ibid., 78.

[46]Ibid., 79.

[47]Ibid., 78.

[48]Spinoza, *Ethics,* part 2, prop. 40, schol. 2 (90).

[49]Gregory, introduction to Spinoza, *Tractatus,* 8–9. Edwin Curley ("Notes on a Neglected Masterpiece," 113) argues that the *Tractatus* is "an attempt to present, in a less forbidding, non-geometrical form, . . . many of the teachings of the *Ethics.* "

[50]A slightly different division is found in Spinoza's earlier *Tractatus de Intellectus Emendatione* (Treatise on the correction of the understanding), but that found in the *Ethics* is generally considered to represent Spinoza's developed thought (cf. Margaret D. Wilson, "Spinoza's Theory of Knowledge," in *The Cambridge Companion to Spinoza,* 91. My presentation of Spinoza's epistemology is heavily dependent on Wilson's essay.)

[51]For a slightly different interpretation, see Jonathan Bennett, *A Study of Spinoza's Ethics* (Cambridge: Cambridge University Press, 1984), § 6.2 (23–24).

two types. There is what Spinoza calls "knowledge from casual experience" (*cognitio ab experientia vaga*): this knowledge is drawn directly from the senses and offers what Spinoza calls knowledge of "individual objects . . . in a fragmentary and confused manner without any intellectual order." But it also includes knowledge drawn "from symbols" (*ex signis*): this emerges from the associations formed between ideas and those external signs by which they are represented to us.[52] Insofar as it emerges from that which is outside the human mind, this type of knowledge is the lowest form of knowing, which Spinoza designates as "imagination" or "opinion."

By way of contrast, knowledge "of the second kind" is what Spinoza calls "reason" (*ratio*). Such knowledge arises from the fact that "we have common notions and adequate ideas of the properties of things."[53] In other words, what distinguishes reason from the first grade of knowledge is that it consists of ideas of those qualities that the human body shares with other bodies (or of further ideas that can be deduced from these).[54] This kind of knowledge does not arise from outside oneself. For this reason it does not suffer from "the inherent limitations of sense and imagination."[55] The ideas characterizing this kind of knowledge include the attribute of extension and the states of motion and rest.[56] For Spinoza these are not abstractions, which would also suffer from the limitations of sense. Rather they are matters "directly accessible to the human mind" by virtue of the fact that—as he writes—the mind is "the idea of the body."[57]

The "third type of knowledge" is what Spinoza calls "intuitive knowledge" (*scientia intuitiva*). This knowledge, he writes, "proceeds from an adequate idea of the formal essence of certain attributes of God to an adequate knowledge of the essence of things." The distinction between this knowledge and that of the second type is not at all clear. Fortunately our present discussion does not require an extensive treatment. It seems that, while knowledge of the second type terminates in common notions, knowledge of the third type goes further to grasp what Margaret Wilson calls "the essences of singular things."[58] More precisely,

---

[52]Cf. Wilson, "Spinoza's Theory of Knowledge," 116.
[53]Cf. Spinoza, *Ethics,* part 2, prop. 40, schol. 2 (90).
[54]Cf. Wilson, "Spinoza's Theory of Knowledge," 111–16.
[55]Ibid., 112.
[56]Ibid.
[57]Ibid., 115; cf. Spinoza, *Ethics,* part 2, prop. 13 (71).
[58]Wilson, "Spinoza's Theory of Knowledge," 117 (see also 123). For a similar reading, see Frederick Copleston, *A History of Philosophy,* Image Books (Garden City, N.Y.: Doubleday, 1963), 4:241–42.

knowledge of the third kind is the insight that views these particular things *sub specie aeternitatis* ('in the light of eternity'), grasping their relationship to the necessary order of the universe and thus (for Spinoza) their relationship to God. In the following proposition of the *Ethics* Spinoza goes on to note that error arises only from the first kind of knowledge, whereas "knowledge of the second and third kind is necessarily true."[59]

The reader should not be disturbed if these distinctions are not immediately clear. They are not immediately clear even to many of Spinoza's learned commentators. What is important to note is that in the *Tractatus* Spinoza assigns prophetic knowledge (with the exception of that attained by Jesus[60]) to the category of the first and lowliest kind of knowledge, which is susceptible to error.[61] Prophetic knowledge is not what Spinoza calls "adequate knowledge," which would be of a more exalted kind, for the prophets "did not perceive God's decrees adequately, as eternal truths."[62] Moses, for example, pictured God as a ruler, a lawgiver, or a king, descriptions that are clearly incompatible with what the philosopher knows must be true of God. It follows that the prophetic knowledge is a limited knowledge. Yet Spinoza immediately qualifies this conclusion. For he argues that, while the prophets may have erred in what he calls their "philosophical speculation," they remain reliable guides in matters of "uprightness and morality."[63] It is easy to see the direction in which Spinoza is moving. He is suggesting that we *cannot* rely on the biblical writings for knowledge about the nature of the world (speculative knowledge, if you like). But we *can* rely on them for information about how we should behave and how best to manage human affairs (practical knowledge).[64] It is this practical knowledge that Spinoza sees as the core of the biblical message.

In this discussion of prophecy Spinoza goes well beyond the suggestions put forward by his predecessors (with perhaps the sole exception of Edward Herbert). For instance, Galileo and Kepler were also concerned to place limits on biblical authority. But they still wrote as though the

---

[59]Spinoza, *Ethics,* part 2, prop. 41 (91).

[60]Spinoza writes (*Tractatus,* 65) that God's ordinances were revealed to Jesus "not by words or visions, but directly." Indeed alone of all the prophets Jesus can be said "to have perceived things truly and adequately," and thus he "was not so much the prophet as the mouthpiece of God" (107). For a discussion of Spinoza's attitude to Jesus, see Mason, *The God of Spinoza,* 208–23.

[61]Cf. Donagan, "Spinoza's Theology," 365.

[62]Spinoza, *Tractatus,* 107.

[63]Ibid., 78.

[64]Cf. Donagan, "Spinoza's Theology," 365.

limitations found in the scriptures were the result of a conscious act of condescension on the part of the biblical writers.[65] Galileo makes this explicit. In a way that echoes Augustine,[66] he argues that it was not just the Holy Spirit who adapted the words of scripture to our human weakness. Rather, it was the choice of the human authors of the Bible, who were well aware of what they were doing. In Galileo's words, "the writers of Holy Scripture not only did not pretend to teach us about the structure and motion of the heavens . . . but they deliberately refrained from doing so, even though they knew all these things very well."[67] Now Spinoza also argues that the language of scripture is adapted "to the understanding of the common people."[68] But he does not attribute this act of condescension to the human authors of the Bible. In other words, Spinoza agrees with Kepler and Galileo that we should not expect to gain knowledge of scientific or philosophical matters from the Bible. This is not, however, because the biblical writers deliberately withheld the information they possessed; rather, for Spinoza, they never possessed this knowledge in the first place.[69] As far as Spinoza is concerned, ignorance on the part of the biblical writers is ignorance and is not to be disguised as a concession to human weakness. In fact, Spinoza's use of the traditional language of "accommodation" seems to be little more than a transposition into traditional theological terms of Spinoza's conviction that prophetic knowledge was primarily a matter of the imagination.

Natural and Revealed Knowledge
Another matter deserves at least a brief mention here, for it also relates to Spinoza's view of biblical authority. It is the fact that, although Spinoza uses the traditional Christian language of revelation, he effectively collapses any distinction between revealed and natural knowledge.[70] As we will see shortly, this is consistent with his understanding of God, for in Spinoza's theology traditional distinctions between the "natural" and the "supernatural" no longer apply. The natural *is* the supernatural, and vice versa. Thus for Spinoza the idea that biblical prophecy occurs by way of the prophets' imaginations does not mean that it is "merely" imaginative.

---

[65]Cf. McMullin, "Galileo on Science and Scripture," 303.

[66]Cf. Augustine, *De Genesi ad litteram* 2.9.20 (*The Literal Meaning of Genesis,* 1:59): "in the matter of the shape of the heavens the sacred writers knew the truth, but . . . the Spirit of God, who spoke through them, did not wish to teach men facts that would be of no avail for their salvation."

[67]Galileo, "Letter to the Grand Duchess Christina," in *GA,* 94.

[68]Cf. Spinoza, *Tractatus,* 120.

[69]Cf. ibid., 86.

[70]Cf. Donagan, "Spinoza's Theology," 357.

It was *both* a product of the human imagination *and* the revelation of God. As Spinoza writes, "the imaginative faculty of the prophets, in so far as it was the instrument for the revelation of God's decrees, could equally well be called the mind of God, and the prophets could be said to have possessed the mind of God."[71] Further discussions of these matters must await an exposition of Spinoza's idea of God. Before that is attempted, however, we should examine another way in which our author reinterprets scriptural authority.

3. Meaning and Truth

A Critical Distinction

We have yet to deal with the aspect of Spinoza's thought that represents perhaps his most radical break with traditional attitudes towards the Bible. This matter is easily overlooked, buried as it is deep within the argumentation of the *Tractatus*. Here, for what is possibly the first time in the history of Jewish and Christian biblical interpretation,[72] an interpreter makes a sharp distinction between the *meaning* and the *truth* of the biblical writings. Spinoza insists that the task of the interpreter is merely to understand what the biblical writers were attempting to say. The truth of their words is another matter entirely,[73] to be decided by other forms of investigation. In other words, our first task is to understand what the Bible is saying; our second task is to decide whether what it is saying is true.[74] Indeed, in interpreting the Bible, we should take care to *set aside* what we already know to be true, so that we can understand the biblical writings on their own terms.[75] For instance, if we find the Bible saying that "God is jealous" and if there is no evidence that this was intended to be understood metaphorically, then we must understand these words quite literally, even though we may know that they cannot be true.[76] In advocating this clear distinction between the question of meaning and that of truth, Spinoza is not only undermining the

[71]Spinoza, *Tractatus,* 70.

[72]J. Samuel Preus suggests (*Explaining Religion,* 35) that Spinoza's use of this distinction was anticipated by some thirty years in the work of Edward Herbert (see the introduction to the present work), who makes a similar point in his *De Religione Laici* (99). However, Spinoza's *Tractatus* still deserves our attention, since it utilizes this distinction in a clearer and more systematic way and in the context of spelling out a method of biblical interpretation.

[73]Cf. Spinoza, *Tractatus,* 143; *The Historical Jesus Quest,* 8.

[74]Cf. Spinoza, *Tractatus,* 210, 229.

[75]Cf. Spinoza, *Tractatus,* 143; *The Historical Jesus Quest,* 8.

[76]Cf. Spinoza, *Tractatus,* 144; *The Historical Jesus Quest,* 9.

assumption that the Bible is a reliable source of divine truth. He is also parting company with a long interpretive tradition. He is particularly opposed to the practice, found among both Jewish and Christian interpreters, of continuing the act of interpretation until there is found a meaning acceptable to both faith and reason.

The Example of Maimonides

To illustrate this practice, Spinoza chooses the medieval Jewish interpreter Moses Maimonides (1135–1204).[77] The passage on which Spinoza focuses his attention comes from Maimonides's *Guide of the Perplexed* (written in the year 1190),[78] in which the great Jewish scholar discusses the question of the eternity of the world. This was, of course, a lively issue for Jewish and Christian thinkers of the late Middle Ages, especially those who admired Aristotle but wished on religious grounds to distinguish themselves from the one whom they called simply "the Philosopher." In the passage from Maimonides to which Spinoza refers, the medieval Jewish scholar is rejecting the idea that the world is eternal. But, he argues, he does not reject this idea because there exist biblical texts that appear to contradict it, by stating that the world is created. For texts referring to the creation are no more numerous than the texts indicating that God has a body, and Maimonides has already established that those texts ought to be interpreted allegorically. But the reason such texts were interpreted allegorically was that it could be conclusively proven that God does *not* have a body. Since we already know that God does not have a body, the scriptural texts that appear to affirm that he does must be given another meaning. In the case of the eternity of the world, on the other hand, we are unable to give any conclusive proof that the world must have had a beginning. In the absence of a conclusive refutation of the doctrine of the eternity of the world, it would be wrong to interpret allegorically the scriptural texts that speak of creation. They must be taken in their literal sense. In any case, there are other reasons to reject the doctrine of the eternity of the world. For such a doctrine would destroy the Law of Moses and thus undermine the very foundations of religion.[79]

---

[77]Cf. Spinoza, *Tractatus,* 156–59; *The Historical Jesus Quest,* 22–25. Preus ("The Bible and Religion," 113, 116–17) suggests that Spinoza's real antagonist was not Maimonides, but rather his friend Ludwig Meyer (ca. 1629–81), who had put forward a comparable view in his *Philosophy the Interpreter of Sacred Scripture* of 1666.

[78]The work was originally written in Arabic as *Dalâlat al-hâ'irîn,* but Spinoza cites the title of the Hebrew version, *Môrê nebukhîm.*

[79]For the full text in a readable translation, see Moses Maimonides, *The Guide of the Perplexed: An Abridged Edition,* translated by Chaim Rabin (Indianapolis: Hackett, 1995), 2.25 (114–15).

This is a complex argument, in which at least two interpretative principles may be discerned. The first runs from rationality to text, as it were, judging the meaning of the text in the light of human reason. This principle states that passages of scripture must be interpreted figuratively if their literal sense is opposed to the certain judgments of reason. This leads Maimonides to reinterpret those passages that appear to speak of the corporeality of God. Spinoza rejects this interpretative principle. However, it is important to note the assumptions that underlie this principle, since they are rather different from our own. Maimonides is *not* arguing that the literal sense of the text is the intended meaning (as though the text *really* said that God had a body) and that to arrive at a true interpretation we should choose to read the text in another way, against the intention of its author. Rather, the figurative sense of the text *is* the intended meaning: it is this which embodies what we might call "the real intention of the text." This is clear from Maimonides' own practice: when discussing the incorporeality of God, for example, he does not argue from philosophical principles alone.[80] Rather, his starting point is the meaning of the phrase "image and likeness" in Genesis 1.[81] In other words, for Maimonides, interpretation is not simply a matter of deciding an issue philosophically and then reading this meaning, by any means possible, back into the text. Rather, our philosophical discussion will alert us to the fact that the literal meaning of the text cannot be the correct one, since reason and the divine word cannot be in conflict. Having realized this, we must seek to find out what the text really means. Moreover, in spelling out this first interpretative principle, Maimonides is cautious: one should not have recourse to figurative interpretation unless it is conclusively proved that the literal sense is contrary to reason. Since the eternity of the world is *not* conclusively proved, there is no need to reject the literal sense of those biblical passages that speak of the creation of the world.

Alongside this first interpretative principle one can discern a second, which from our modern point of view does not seem to be easily reconcilable with the first. This runs from text to reason, as it were, and states that what is contrary to the basic principles of the revealed faith cannot be true philosophically. In other words, if the meaning of the scriptures is clear, and it appears to contradict the findings of philosophy, this is a warning that something is probably wrong with one's philosophy. It is for this reason that Maimonides rejects the idea of the eternity

[80]Cf. Maimonides, *The Guide of the Perplexed,* translated by Schlomo Pines (Chicago: University of Chicago Press, 1963), 2.1–2 (243–54).
[81]Maimonides, *The Guide of the Perplexed: An Abridged Edition,* 1.1 (51–52).

of the world, not only because it is *not* conclusively proven, but also (and more importantly) because its acceptance would lead us into conflict with biblical passages that—as he says—"no sensible person" would read in anything other than their literal sense.[82] In setting out these principles, Maimonides is assuming the reliability of both scripture *and* reason. On the assumption that truth is one, a clear contradiction between scripture and reason can only mean that some mistake has been made, on one side or the other.[83] This assumption underlines both of his interpretative principles.[84]

Maimonides and Augustine

While Spinoza chooses a Jewish scholar to illustrate these principles, he could equally have chosen a Christian interpreter. Augustine, for example, in his major work on biblical interpretation, *On Christian Teaching* (*De doctrina christiana*), also discusses the question of how to decide between a literal and a figurative meaning of a biblical text. His rule is that if a literal reading cannot be reconciled with faith and morals, then a figurative interpretation should be chosen.[85] Augustine spells out this criterion in more detail by noting that "good morals [*morum honestas*] have to do with the our love of God and our neighbour" and "the true faith [*fidei veritas*] with our understanding of God and our neighbour."[86] A passage that does not conform to these specifications should be reinterpreted until it does.[87] The principles involved here are a little different from those held by Maimonides. Here it is not a matter of a conflict

[82]Ibid., 2.25 (116).

[83]It seems to me a mistake to interpret Maimonides as a latter-day rationalist, arguing that "if the eternity of the world could be demonstrated by strict philosophical proof, we should have to acknowledge it, although this would lead to the abandonment of the Torah" (Julius Guttmann, introduction and commentary to *The Guide of the Perplexed: An Abridged Edition,* by Maimonides, 217). Despite what he says at the end of 2.25, there is no reason to think that Maimonides ever conceived that one would be forced "to abandon the Torah." After all, in the introduction to the first part of his work (1.Preface to *The Guide of the Perplexed,* translated by Schlomo Pines, 5–6) he states that his aim is to remove "the heartache and great perplexity" of those who perceive a conflict between scripture and reason, and think they must choose between one and the other.

[84]It is, perhaps, the persistence of the second principle in Galileo's thought that leads him into the difficulties to which I alluded in the introductory chapter, for it leads him to compromise what I have called his principle of independence.

[85]Cf. Augustine, *De doctrina christiana,* translated by R. P. H. Green, Oxford Early Christian Texts (Oxford: Clarendon Press, 1995), 3.33 (146–47). The paragraph numbering given here is the same as that found in the more widely available paperback edition of Green's translation, although the page numbers will (of course) be different.

[86]Augustine, *De doctrina christiana,* 3.34 (147–49).

[87]Cf. ibid., 3.54 (156–57).

between scripture and reason, which Augustine deals with most explicitly in his commentary on the literal sense of Genesis. Here it is more a matter of a conflict between the basic principles of faith and morals and the literal sense of the Bible. However, the hermeneutical practice involved is the same: it means (to put it bluntly) that the interpreter of scripture must continue the work of interpretation until the meaning found is in conformity with what is already known to be true. While to the modern reader this may seem a questionable practice (as it did to Spinoza), to the interpreter of medieval or patristic times—Jewish or Christian—it must have seemed self-evident. Since the Bible was inspired by God, it could not be teaching obvious falsehoods or encouraging what was clearly immoral behavior. If your interpretation leads you to this conclusion, it must be false, or at least incomplete.[88]

Even when attempting to discover the *literal meaning* of the text, Augustine follows the same practice. Throughout his commentary on the literal sense of Genesis, he assumes that the literal meaning of the text will normally be identical with its truth. It is the literal sense of the text that he is seeking; he employs figurative interpretation only as a last resort. For instance, with regard to the interpretation of the description of paradise in Genesis 2, Augustine writes that the account is to be taken in its literal sense unless such an interpretation makes it "utterly impossible to safeguard the truth of the faith."[89] Only if there is *no* way of reading the literal sense in a way that is in conformity with the faith should that sense be abandoned and a figurative interpretation offered.[90] In any case, whether the reading offered is literal or figurative, the assumption is that it must conform with truths that are already well established. This applies to truths established by reason as well as truths of faith. For instance, in the passage to which Galileo would later make appeal,

[88]The last phrase is important, since Augustine's position is (as one would expect) both more sophisticated and more conservative than this description might lead one to expect. In various places (*De doctrina christiana* 3.48 [pp.152–53]; *Confessiones* 3.7) he argues that there were actions performed in the past that were permitted because of the particular needs of the time and were therefore without blame (polygamy is a clear example). Yet such actions are not permitted today. It follows that, while we may recognize the literal sense of the text as what we might call a "meaning for then," as far as its "meaning for now" is concerned, the text is to be interpreted figuratively. Therefore, it is not so much a matter of abandoning the literal meaning as of recognizing its limitations and adopting both a literal *and* a figurative interpretation. As Augustine writes (*De doctrina christiana* 3.73 [pp.164–65]), "all, or nearly all, of the deeds contained in the books of the Old Testament are to be interpreted not only literally but also figuratively [*non solum proprie, sed etiam figurate*]."

[89]Augustine, *De Genesi ad litteram* 8.1.4; *The Literal Sense of Genesis*, 2:34.

[90]See also Augustine, *De Genesi ad litteram* 11.1.2; *The Literal Sense of Genesis*, 2:134.

Augustine discusses the biblical passages that suggest that the heavens are "stretched out like a skin" (Ps. 103:2) or have the form of a vault (Genesis 1). He not only insists that there must be no contradiction between these two passages; he also argues that their interpretation should be in conformity with what we would call "scientific" knowledge. As he writes, our interpretation "should not contradict the theories that may be supported by true evidence, by which heaven is said to be curved on all sides in the shape of a sphere, provided only that this is proved."[91]

Augustine, no less than Maimonides, is here representative of premodern Jewish and Christian exegesis. In interpreting the Bible, he is attempting to uncover, not just the meaning of the text, but the truth of the matters of which it speaks. Indeed, he assumes that the two will be identical. For this reason there is no distinction in the work of a patristic or medieval commentator between what we would call exegesis and theology. Theology *was* the study of the *sacra pagina* ("the sacred page"); there is no question of the two operations being separated. In attacking the willingness of Maimonides to reinterpret the biblical text until a meaning in conformity with reason is found, Spinoza is certainly drawing on a suspicion of figurative interpretations of the Bible already to be found in Protestant Christianity.[92] However, his criticism goes much further than that of his Protestant predecessors. By insisting that the interpreter must restrict his task to that of discovering the meaning of the text, Spinoza drives a wedge between biblical interpretation and the task of theology. This is, of course, consistent with his overall purpose, the clearest possible distinction between the claims of religion and those of philosophy. However, its implications would become clear only in the centuries which followed.[93]

4. Spinoza and the New Sciences

Religion and Philosophy

While Spinoza's reinterpretation of biblical prophecy might seem to be destructive of traditional beliefs, he regarded it as part of a broader

[91] Augustine, *De Genesi ad litteram* 2.9.21; *The Literal Sense of Genesis,* 1:59.

[92] Cf. Preus, "The Bible and Religion in the Century of Genius," 16. In rejecting such interpretative strategies Spinoza, here in company with the Protestant Reformers, closes off what had been a useful escape route when dealing with morally repugnant biblical texts, thus creating a new set of problems for the devout interpreter.

[93] One thinks, for instance, of the title of James Barr's inaugural lecture at Oxford in 1977, which poses a question that would have been inconceivable to a medieval interpreter. See James Barr, *Does Biblical Study Still Belong to Theology? An Inaugural Lecture Delivered Before the University of Oxford on 26 May 1977* (Oxford: Clarendon Press, 1978).

project. As I have just noted, that broader project involved making a sharp distinction between religion and philosophy,[94] a distinction that would save what Spinoza saw as the essential claims of each. As one recent analysis puts it, while the nineteenth century was fond of describing the relationship between religion and science in terms of "warfare," what Spinoza sought was "an amicable divorce."[95] Spinoza argues that the aim of the biblical writings is to encourage obedience to God. Therefore the *only* religious claims to which the believer is obliged are those that are necessary to ensure obedience: namely, "that there is a Supreme Being who loves justice and charity, whom all must obey in order to be saved, and must worship by practising justice and charity to their neighbour."[96] For this reason there should be no conflict between biblical claims, rightly understood, and those of philosophy.[97] Summarizing his position at the beginning of the work, Spinoza writes that

> the object of knowledge by revelation is nothing other than obedience, and so it is completely distinct from natural knowledge in its purpose, its basis and its method, that these two having nothing in common, that they each have a separate province that does not intrude on the other, and that neither should be regarded as ancillary to the other.[98]

This is a very strong expression of what, in reference to the work of Galileo, I called the "principle of independence." The cognitive claims of philosophy and the ethical claims of religion are kept strictly apart. On this basis, there is no harm in the suggestion that in philosophical matters the biblical writers suffered from prejudices and errors. For they remain reliable guides in matters of morality.[99] In other words, since the purpose of revelation is merely the imparting of certain fundamental rules of behavior, these are the only matters in which biblical authority ought to be invoked. As Spinoza writes, in all other matters "one is free to believe as one will."[100]

---

[94]Spinoza (*Tractatus,* 221) describes this as "the main object of this entire treatise."

[95]Preus, "The Bible and Religion in the Century of Genius," 6.

[96]Spinoza, *Tractatus,* 224 (cf. 120, 212, 215, 223–26). Spinoza (cf. ibid., 224–25) goes on to develop this simple proposition into seven articles of faith, reminiscent of those produced by Edward Herbert (as discussed in my introductory chapter).

[97]In this context, "philosophy" should not be thought of in its narrow twentieth-century sense: it represents any knowledge of the world obtained by what Spinoza often calls "the natural light of reason."

[98]Spinoza, *Tractatus,* 55 (see also 232).

[99]Cf. ibid., 78.

[100]Ibid., 86.

Philosophy and the New Sciences
In insisting upon this separation of religion and philosophy, it is clear that
Spinoza has in mind a philosophy revised in the light of the new, mechanistic sciences.[101] Spinoza's interest in the new sciences is clear from his
correspondence with some of the leading scientists of the day. Indeed
current scholarship suggests that his famous lens grinding "may have
been more a matter of research in optics than of commercial manufac-
turing."[102] And the scientific knowledge with which Spinoza is attempting to accommodate religion is a mechanistic physics in the tradition
of Descartes. This is implied throughout the *Ethics*. It is also spelt out
in detail at one point in the same work,[103] where Spinoza defines the
human body as "a definite mode of extension actually existing, and
nothing else"[104] and goes on to discuss the behavior of bodies, both simple and compound. Although this anticipates a later discussion, I might
note immediately that Spinoza does much more than simply adapt religion to the new physics. He also expresses the assumptions underlying
the new physics in religious terms, something Descartes had been unable
to achieve.

One clear sign of the influence of the new sciences on Spinoza is that,
while he had little time for the empiricism of Francis Bacon,[105] he
shared with both Bacon and Descartes the seventeenth century's aver-
sion to teleology (explanations in terms of purpose). His discussion of
this matter is found in the appendix to part 1 of the *Ethics*. Spinoza
begins by identifying the belief to which he is opposed. It is, he writes,
"the widespread belief among men that all things in Nature are like
themselves in acting with an end in view."[106] Spinoza spends relatively
little space demonstrating the falsity of this belief; he is more interested
in how people come to embrace it. Insofar as he does argue against it, he
does so by referring back to the metaphysical claims put forward in the
first part of the *Ethics*. Of particular importance are what he calls the

[101]On Spinoza's ambivalent relationship to the new sciences, see Nancy Maull, "Spinoza in the Century of Science," in *Spinoza and the Sciences,* 3–13, and the other essays in
that same volume.

[102]Mason, *The God of Spinoza,* 8; see also Gullan-Whur, *Within Reason,* 88–90.

[103]David R. Lachterman ("The Physics of Spinoza's *Ethics*," in *Spinoza: New Perspectives,* 71–111) suggests that Spinoza's brief discussion of the principles of physics is not
only an attempt to clear up some of the anomalies in Cartesian physics, but also plays a
vital role in the *Ethics* as a whole.

[104]Cf. Spinoza, *Ethics,* part 2, prop. 13 (71).

[105]See, for instance, Spinoza's correspondence with Henry Oldenburg, soon to
become a secretary of the newly founded Royal Society (Letter 2, in Baruch Spinoza,
The Letters, translated by Samuel Shirley [Indianapolis: Hackett, 1995], 62–63).

[106]Spinoza, *Ethics,* part 1, appendix (57).

"proofs I have adduced to show that all things in Nature proceed from an eternal necessity and with supreme perfection."[107] Spinoza seems to be saying that it is meaningless to explain any event in terms of purpose if we have already decided that there could not have been any other result. The result was predetermined: that is all that can be said. (We will return to Spinoza's views on necessity and contingency shortly.) But there are further reasons to reject teleological explanations. Firstly, Spinoza asserts that teleological explanations put the cart before the horse (as it were): "this doctrine of Final Causes turns Nature completely upside down, for it regards as an effect that which is in fact a cause, and vice versa."[108] Secondly, he adds two arguments that rely on the idea that belief in final causes is contrary to belief in the perfection of God. The first is that such explanations imply a process of development, which in turns suggests that the immediate effects of God's action are less perfect than the more remote. The problem with this idea is that it runs contrary to the perfection of divine action. The second argument consists of the closely related idea that attributing purpose to God implies that something is lacking in the divinity, which he is attempting to supply. As commentators have noted, these are not strong arguments.[109] Along with so many of his contemporaries, Spinoza does not so much argue against teleological explanations; he simply assumes their absurdity.

More interesting is Spinoza's discussion of why people embrace teleological explanations. Here he suggests that the problem is what we might call anthropomorphism: human beings project onto the world and its assumed divine "governors" their own experience of what they believe to be free and purposeful action.[110] In other words, when human beings find that certain features of the natural world are useful to themselves, they jump to the false conclusion that there exists an agent who produced these things for human use. They go on to depict this agent in their own rather base image: they come to believe that "the gods" created the world so that human beings might hold them in honor and be bound to them in gratitude. From this error have evolved the different ways of worshiping God, which are in fact rather crude ways of trying to ensure that the divinity continues to serve human needs.[111] While the

---

[107]Ibid., part 1, appendix (59).

[108]Ibid.

[109]Cf. Mason, *The God of Spinoza*, 121–22, and Bennett, *A Study of Spinoza's* Ethics, 213–15.

[110]I say "*what they believe to be* free and purposeful action," for Spinoza wants to argue that even human actions cannot be accurately explained by reference to the "purposes" that we pursue (see Mason, *The God of Spinoza*, 123–27).

[111]Cf. Spinoza, *Ethics*, part 1: appendix (58).

worshiper of the true God will not strive to ensure that God will love him in return,[112] conventional religion turns the worship of God into the gratification of base human desires.

It is easy to see that Spinoza's rejection of teleological explanations will have a dramatic effect on traditional religious language and therefore a dramatic effect on his interpretation of the Bible. While Spinoza rejects teleological explanations in general, his particular target is language that attributes purpose to the universe as a whole or to its assumed divine ruler(s).[113] More particularly, his view leaves no room for claims that the world was created for the benefit of human beings, a view that Spinoza most firmly rejects. To talk of the purposes of God is merely a rather misleading way of talking about the natural laws by which the world is regulated, laws that operate by necessity. As Spinoza writes in the *Tractatus,* "by God's decrees and volitions, and consequently God's providence, Scripture means nothing other than Nature's order, which necessarily follows from her eternal laws."[114]

Spinoza's Religious Vision

Yet despite these sweeping attacks on traditional religious claims, Spinoza's philosophy is not materialist, nor does he separate religion and science so as to ignore religious concerns. Rather, Spinoza developed what can only be regarded as a deeply religious vision of reality, albeit one that bears little resemblance to traditional theism. It was certainly a worldview in which the metaphysical claims of the historical religions were reduced to a minimum, but it was equally one in which the claims of physics could be expressed in religious terms. Indeed, Spinoza deals with the emerging tension between natural and supernatural explanations of reality by simply denying that the two can be distinguished. This makes him infuriatingly difficult for interpreters for whom such distinctions are essential. As Richard Mason writes, "it is the desire to divide the natural from the divine and to read either in terms of the other that is the real anachronism in reading Spinoza."[115] How, then, does Spinoza turn his criticism of traditional religious claims into a religious vision of the world opened up by the new sciences?

Spinoza achieves his goal by radically revising our understanding of God, offering a new vision of God *and* the world in the opening sections of his major work, the *Ethics.* Yet despite Spinoza's ambition to achieve a clarity akin to that of geometry, the interpretation of his religious vision

---

[112]Cf. Spinoza, *Ethics,* part 5, prop. 19 (213).
[113]Cf. Bennett, *A Study of Spinoza's* Ethics, 213.
[114]Spinoza, *Tractatus,* 125.
[115]Mason, *The God of Spinoza,* 259.

is a notoriously difficult matter. As Edwin Curley writes, "we are about to plunge into waters that are very, very muddy. Many people talk with a great deal of confidence about Spinoza's philosophy. But among those who have studied it carefully, there is no general agreement on the meaning of even those doctrines that are the most central."[116] While I have tried to discuss these matters in very general terms, so as to avoid the disputed questions, one cannot expound Spinoza's thought without interpreting it. Yet the task cannot be evaded, for without some understanding of Spinoza's religious vision it is impossible to grasp his attitude to the biblical miracles. The best I can do is to offer a preliminary interpretation and then invite the reader to explore for herself the fascinating world of a thinker who in metaphysics as well as biblical interpretation was well ahead of his time.

(a) God, Substance, Nature

The easiest way into Spinoza's religious vision is by way of three of his most characteristic terms. When Spinoza describes what he regards as the fundamental reality of the world, he uses the terms "God," "Substance," and "Nature," the three terms being effectively equivalent.[117] The term "Substance" should not be taken here in a crassly material sense. In its classical usage, to which Spinoza continues to adhere, it could perhaps best be understood as "independent reality." However, Spinoza gives that classical usage a particular twist, so that his use of the term "Substance" approaches our contemporary use of the term "energy," insofar as energy is thought of as the fundamental reality of the universe.[118] More precisely, Spinoza defines Substance as "that which is in itself and is conceived through itself: that is, that the conception of which does not require the conception of another thing from which it has to be formed."[119] What does this definition tell us? It tells us immediately that Substance cannot have an external cause, since, if it did have an external cause, it would be known not through itself but by way of something else, namely, that which caused it.[120] Substance is, therefore, the "cause of itself" (*causa sui*), which is another way of saying that it cannot be thought of as *not* existing. Its existence is implied in its essence.[121]

[116]E. M. Curley, *Spinoza's Metaphysics: An Essay in Interpretation* (Cambridge, Mass.: Harvard University Press, 1969), 3.

[117]Mason, *The God of Spinoza,* 25.

[118]F. F. Hallett (*Benedict de Spinoza: The Elements of His Philosophy* [London: Athlone Press, 1957], 11) defines Spinoza's "Substance" as "potency-in-act."

[119]Spinoza, *Ethics* part 1, def. 3 (31).

[120]Cf. ibid., part 1, prop. 6 (33).

[121]Cf. ibid., part 1, prop. 7 (34).

Spinoza goes on to argue that Substance is also "necessarily infinite." For if Substance existed in a finite manner, it would be limited by something of the same nature as itself, something that would therefore have the same attribute.[122] Yet Spinoza argues that no two substances may have the same attribute (for reasons that would take us too far from our present discussion).[123] If this is accepted, it follows that Substance is infinite. As something infinite that exists in its own right and by necessity, "Substance" may be regarded as equivalent to "God."[124]

Some discussion of these dense propositions would seem to be called for. The term "Substance" is perhaps confusing, since we are inclined to think of it as representing some *thing*. But Spinoza's thought becomes clearer when we call to mind that he often takes traditional metaphysical terms and gives them a slightly different meaning. For one of the striking characteristics of Spinoza's "Substance" is its dynamism: it exists by acting, and that action is unlimited. As Spinoza writes, "from the necessity of the divine nature there must follow infinite things in infinite ways (*modis*)."[125] The key phrase here is "must follow": it is of the *very nature* of Substance to give rise to these "infinite things." Later, having identified Substance with God, Spinoza claims that "God's power *is* his very essence."[126] It is of the essence of God to act, and the first part of the *Ethics* is concerned with the nature of the divine activity. Thus while Spinoza continues to use a time-honored term, his "Substance" is, in the words of F. F. Hallett, "not a 'thing' but self-realizing and self-manifesting *agency*."[127] Bearing in mind that for Spinoza "Substance" or "God" is equivalent to "Nature" (a point to which we will return), I can perhaps recast Spinoza's thought in more accessible terms. What he seems to be saying is that "Substance" is equivalent to the universe viewed as "creative," as productive of apparently endless novelty. If this is correct, then the closest analogy in modern philosophy may well be the metaphysical vision of Alfred North Whitehead. Indeed, Whitehead notes the similarity, comparing Spinoza's "Substance" with his own vision of the fundamental reality of the world: "his one substance is for me the one underlying activity of realization individualising itself in an interlocked plurality of modes."[128]

[122]Cf. ibid., part 1, prop. 8 (34).

[123]Cf. ibid., part 1, prop. 5 (33).

[124]Cf. ibid., part 1, prop. 11 (37).

[125]Ibid., part 1, prop. 16 (43).

[126]Ibid., part 1, prop. 34 (56; emphasis mine).

[127]Hallett, *Benedict de Spinoza*, 12.

[128]Alfred North Whitehead, *Science and the Modern World*, The Lowell Lectures 1925 (New York: Mentor Books, 1948), 68.

(b) Natura naturans and Natura naturata

If it is true that in Spinoza's worldview to be *is* to act,[129] then Substance may be viewed as having a double aspect: one active and the other passive, one "producing" and the other "produced." In Hallet's words, "the primordial Real . . . is the duality in unity of cause or potency and effect or actuality."[130] This seems to be what Spinoza is attempting to say when he speaks of the distinction between *Natura naturans* and *Natura naturata,* two Latin phrases that defy elegant and accurate translation. The *naturans* of *Natura naturans* is a present, active participle, so that the phrase may be literally translated "Nature as naturing"; the *naturata* of *Natura naturata* is a past, passive participle, so that it may be rendered "Nature as natured."[131] These are also traditional terms,[132] but once again Spinoza uses them in his own manner. At least in the *Ethics,*[133] *Natura naturans* refers to "that which is in itself and is conceived through itself; that is, the attributes of Substance that express eternal and infinite essence; or . . . God in so far as he is considered a free cause."[134] Again, this requires some explanation. If Substance is thought of as agency, Spinoza's thought may be paraphrased by saying that *Natura naturans* is the world, insofar as the world is thought of in terms of its infinite potentiality. More precisely, it is the necessary order of the world's activity, but thought of actively, from the point of view of productivity. On the other hand, Spinoza defines *Natura naturata* as "all that follows from the necessity of God's nature, that is, from the necessity of each one of God's attributes; or all the modes of God's attributes in so far or as they are considered as things which are in God and can neither be nor be conceived without God."[135] In simpler terms, *Natura naturata* is the world, insofar as the world is thought of in terms of what follows from its infinite potentiality. More precisely, it is the necessary order of the world's activity regarded passively, from the point of view of product.

[129]Cf. Hallett, *Benedict de Spinoza,* 149 et passim.

[130]Ibid., 10–11.

[131]Mason (*The God of Spinoza,* 33–34) speaks of "nature-as-cause" and "nature-as-effect," although this is perhaps misleading insofar as we tend to think of a cause as external to its effect, whereas Spinoza's cause is what he calls "immanent" rather than "transitive" (*Ethics,* part 1, prop.18 [p.46]). Jonathan Bennett (*A Study of Spinoza's* Ethics, 119) regards the distinction between *Natura naturans* and *Natura naturata* as "quite without significance in the *Ethics*" and as "vexatious." Yet, while it may not be Spinoza's favored terminology, it does offer a helpful way into his thought.

[132]Cf. Hallett, *Benedictus de Spinoza,* 14.

[133]Mason (*The God of Spinoza,* 29–30) traces a certain development in Spinoza's use of this distinction.

[134]Spinoza, *Ethics,* part 1, prop. 29, schol. (52).

[135]Ibid., prop. 29, schol. (52).

We should note immediately that some caution is needed in interpreting this language. When Spinoza speaks of things "following from" the necessity of God's nature, he is not speaking of a temporal process. The verb "to follow" (*sequi*) here has a sense comparable to that found in logic or geometry. It is a "nonspatial, nontemporal" meaning.[136] Yet that does not mean that it is a purely logical relation, as though it yielded no information about the world "out there" (as it were).[137] Spinoza's vision *is* a vision of the world, but it is the world seen from the viewpoint of eternity. He is not interested in the (limited) process of the unfolding of the order of the world in time. Rather, he is interested in the order of the world's activity viewed 'in itself,' as necessarily following from the very nature of Substance. The unfolding of that order in time is ontologically insignificant once its timeless nature has been grasped. Similarly, by "the order of the world's activity" I do not mean the temporal sequence in which things actually occur. Spinoza refers to this as the "duration" of things, and claims we cannot have an adequate knowledge of this process, since we are unable to grasp the infinite chain of causality behind any particular event.[138] Rather by "the order of the world's activity" I mean the constitution of reality or—more precisely—its immanent causality, which determines the way in which events unfold. In a manner that we are inclined to find surprising, Spinoza insists the human mind *is* able to have "adequate knowledge" of this underlying order.[139]

It is important to note that for Spinoza *Natura naturata* is inseparable from *Natura naturans*. The distinction between the two is best understood as a distinction in thought, not in reality.[140] Once again, the reason for this may become clear if we think of Substance in terms of agency. For agency (or "action") always involves both potentiality and its actualization, "both a power of act*ing* and the expression of that power in something enact*ed*."[141] Thus *Natura naturans* and *Natura naturata* are the

---

[136]Samuel Shirley, translator's foreword to *The Ethics and Selected Letters,* 24 (see also Spinoza, *Ethics,* part 1, prop. 17, schol. [pp.44–46]).

[137]Compare Spinoza's claim (*Ethics*, part 2, prop. 7 and proof [p.6]) that "the order and connection of ideas is the same as the order and connection of things," since "the idea of what is caused depends on the knowledge of the cause of which it is the effect."

[138]Cf. Spinoza, *Ethics,* part 2, props. 30–31 and proofs (85).

[139]Cf. ibid., part 2, prop. 47 (94).

[140]Cf. Mason, *The God of Spinoza,* 34. While this statement is best left as it stands, it could be argued that in Spinoza's metaphysics a distinction in 'thought' and a distinction in 'reality' are (strictly) the same thing, understood in different ways (see Spinoza, *Ethics,* part 2, prop. 7, schol. [p.67]). As Hallett writes (*Benedict de Spinoza,* 17), for Spinoza "intellect is not extrinsic to Nature, like a spectator at the games, but is involved in it."

[141]Hallett, *Benedict de Spinoza,* 9.

one (and only) reality, but grasped in two different ways by the intellect. Substance itself is indivisible. Incidentally, this inseparability of *Natura naturans* and *Natura naturata* is one reason why Spinoza feels no need to "prove" the existence of God. The existence of God would need to be demonstrated only if God were a being separate from and "alongside" the world. But even when viewed as *Natura naturans,* Spinoza's God is distinct from the world only by an operation of the intellect. Therefore to ask if God exists is equivalent to asking if that which exists, exists. As Spinoza writes, "either nothing exists, or an absolutely infinite Entity necessarily exists, too. But we do exist. . . . Therefore an absolutely infinite Entity—that is . . . , God—necessarily exists."[142]

We should note that Spinoza regards this sort of *a posteriori* argument for the existence of God as a secondary argument, for (as we have seen when discussing Substance) God's existence can already be deduced from his essence. To define what you mean by God is to see that God cannot *not* exist. If you are inclined to deny the existence of God, Spinoza remarks curtly, then "conceive, if you can, that God does not exist. Therefore . . . his essence does not involve existence. But this is absurd . . . Therefore God necessarily exists."[143] The philosophically literate reader will recognize that this deduction of God's existence from his essence is another form of the famous ontological argument, first put forward by Anselm (1033–1109). Yet Spinoza has so radically redefined the idea of God that his argument functions in a rather different way. Since he is not wanting to demonstrate the existence of God as the existence of something *other* than the world, the usual objections to the ontological argument (and in particular Kant's insight that "existence is not a predicate") are simply beside the point.[144]

Before going on, I should warn the reader against a misunderstanding. Although in speaking of *Natura naturans* Spinoza describes God as a "free cause," by "free" he does not mean that God could "choose" (as it were) to act or not to act. He is using the word "free" here in a sense all his own,[145] for Spinoza's conception of God leaves no room for attributing intellect and will to the divinity.[146] By attributing 'freedom' to God, Spinoza is saying simply that "God alone exists solely from the necessity of his own nature . . . and acts solely from the necessity of his own

[142]Cf. Spinoza, *Ethics,* part 1, prop. 11, third proof (38); see also prop. 15 (40: "nothing can be or be conceived without God").

[143]Ibid., part 1, prop. 11 proof (37); see also part 1, props. 7, 20 (34, 46).

[144]For a similar argument, but expressed rather differently, see Hallett, *Benedictus de Spinoza,* 26–27.

[145]Cf. Spinoza, *Ethics,* part 1, def. 7 (31).

[146]Cf. ibid., part 1, prop. 17, schol. (44–46).

nature."[147] Paraphrasing Spinoza's thought, we might say that the actualization of the infinite potentiality of the world is determined by nothing other than the nature of the world. In other words, for Spinoza the order of the world's activity simply is as it is. It needs no other explanation. If we think it needs another explanation, we simply have not understood the nature of Substance, which *is* ordered activity. The world conceived as Substance, or Nature, is not passive matter, which needs to be shaped by some force from outside itself.

It follows from these ideas that Spinoza can only be a thoroughgoing determinist.[148] Since the order of the world's activity follows from the very nature of the world, it is a *necessary* order. It cannot take any other form than the form it actually takes. If it appears to us that particular beings and events could have been other than they are,[149] this is "for no other reason than the deficiency of our knowledge."[150] In more technical terms, the apparent contingency of the world is purely epistemic.[151] It is not that things could *in fact* have been other than they are; it is, rather, that *we cannot grasp* the long chain of causes that have led (necessarily) to the present state of affairs. In practice, we have to regard the order of the world as contingent; in fact it is shaped by necessity. As Spinoza writes in the *Tractatus,* "we plainly have no knowledge as to the actual coordination and interconnection of things—that is, the way in which things are in actual fact ordered and connected—so that for practical purposes it is better, indeed, it is essential, to consider things as contingent."[152]

(c) The Attributes of God

With regard to the attributes of God, Spinoza argues that only two are known to us,[153] namely, the familiar Cartesian attributes of thought and extension. Thought and extension together comprise the world as conceived from the point of view of the limited human intellect. Spinoza differs from Descartes in arguing that mind and body are not distinct

---

[147]Ibid., part 1, prop. 17, coroll. 2 (44).

[148]For a discussion of the way in which Spinoza's determinism does not undercut his ideal of the ethical life, see Hallett, *Benedict de Spinoza,* 148–58.

[149]I am using the phrase "beings and events," because both seem to be embraced by Spinoza's use of the Latin *res* (thing; cf. Samuel Shirley, translator's foreword to *The Ethics and Selected Letters,* 24).

[150]Spinoza, *Ethics,* part 1, prop. 33, schol. 1 (54).

[151]Cf. Mason, *The God of Spinoza,* 62–64; Curley, *Spinoza's Metaphysics,* 92.

[152]Spinoza, *Tractatus,* 102.

[153]Mason, *The God of Spinoza,* 44.

substances. "Mind and body," he writes, "are one and the same thing, conceived now under the attribute of Thought, now under the attribute of Extension."[154] Since extension and thought are attributes of God,[155] it follows that "finite minds are modes of God under the attribute of thought, and finite bodies are modes of God under the attribute of extension."[156] Once again we see that—for Spinoza—the natural world is "not ontologically distinct from God."[157] The world as we experience it is nothing less than the finite modes of the divine attributes. Moreover, there exists nothing other than the world, or God, for nothing can be conceived "apart from" Substance and its attributes. The infinity of the attributes of Substance does not allow us to conceive of any other being as existing independently of Substance or "outside of" Substance.[158]

Despite this apparent identity of God and nature, elsewhere expressed in his famous formula, *Deus sive Natura* (God, or Nature),[159] it is unhelpful to regard Spinoza's thought as a form of "pantheism." He certainly does identify "God" with the world, but he so radically revises our customary ideas of both God and the world that this term tells us very little. This seems to be the implication of Spinoza's remark in a letter of 1675 to Henry Oldenburg: "As to the view of certain people that the *Tractatus Theologico-Politicus* rests on the identification of God with Nature (by the latter of which they understand a kind of mass or corporeal matter) they are quite mistaken."[160] My suggestion is that in this remark Spinoza is *not* trying to distance himself from the identification of God with Nature, which is—as we have seen—at the very core of his thought. Rather, he is distancing himself from the identification of Nature with "a kind of mass or corporeal matter." While a closer discussion of this issue may seem to take us far from our topic, it is (once again) important if we are to understand Spinoza's attitude to the biblical miracles. It therefore deserves closer scrutiny.

(d) Was Spinoza a Pantheist?

We may begin by looking more closely at what Spinoza refers to as the "attributes" of God, or Substance. The attributes of Substance are

---

[154]Spinoza, *Ethics,* part 3, prop. 2, schol. (105–106).

[155]Cf. Spinoza, *Ethics,* part 1, prop. 14, coroll. 2 (40): "It follows that the thing extended and the thing thinking are either attributes of God or . . . affections of the attributes of God."

[156]Copleston, *A History of Philosophy,* 4:223.

[157]Ibid.

[158]Cf. Spinoza, *Ethics,* part 1, prop. 14 (39).

[159]For examples of Spinoza's use of this phrase, see his *Ethics* part 4, preface (154).

[160]Letter 73, in Spinoza, *The Letters,* 332.

nothing other than Substance *as known by the intellect.* In other words, the attributes of God *are* God as perceived by the power of reason. They are therefore not separable from Substance, nor are they qualities that Substance may be said to "possess," accidentally (as it were). In Hallett's words, "the attributes of Substance . . . are the essence of Substance as apprehended, and truly, by intellect: they do not *inhere* in it, but *constitute* its essence."[161] Or again, "the Attribute *is* the Substance under the determining scrutiny of intellect."[162] Spinoza himself is quite explicit about this matter, writing in a letter (probably of 1663) to Simon de Vries: "By substance I understand that which is in itself and is conceived through itself; that is, that whose conception does not involve the conception of another thing. *I understand the same by attribute,* except that attribute is so called in respect to the intellect, which attributes to substance a certain specific kind of nature."[163]

Now it is striking that Spinoza insists that the attributes of God are infinite and eternal.[164] He further insists that God (as 'Substance') is one and indivisible.[165] Yet this is not how we normally experience the world of particular beings and events. We customarily regard that world as finite, "temporal, multiplex, and divided."[166] Thus it seems that when Spinoza speaks of God, or Nature, he is speaking of the world *conceived in a particular manner.* As he writes,

> we conceive things as actual in two ways: either in so far as we conceive them as related to a fixed time and place, or in so far as we conceive them to be contained in God and to follow from the necessity of the divine nature. Now the things which are conceived as true or real in this second way, we conceive under a form of eternity, and their ideas involve the eternal and infinite essence of God.[167]

Thus when Spinoza speaks of "God, or Nature," he is speaking of the world conceived *sub specie aeternitatis* (from the point of view of eternity).[168] He is not speaking of the world as we experience it by way of

---

[161]Hallett, *Benedict de Spinoza,* 16.

[162]Ibid.

[163]Letter 9, in Spinoza, *The Letters,* 93 (emphasis mine); see also *Ethics,* part 1, def. 4 (31).

[164]Cf. Spinoza, *Ethics,* part 1, props. 11, 19, 21 (37, 46, 47).

[165]Cf. ibid., part 1, props. 12–13 (38–39).

[166]Hallett, *Benedict de Spinoza,* 15.

[167]Spinoza, *Ethics,* part 5, prop. 29, schol. (218).

[168]See also the *Ethics,* part 2, prop. 44, coroll. 2 (93: "It is in the nature of reason to perceive things in the light of eternity") and part 5, prop. 22 (215).

"casual experience," the lowest form of knowledge, which is able to grasp things only *sub specie temporis* (from the point of view of time).[169]

Once again, the question may be clarified by thinking of Spinoza's "Substance" in terms of agency. Seen as the necessary order by which things are actualized, the world is infinite and eternal, for that order *is* infinite and eternal. In still simpler terms, the world emerges in time as the product of its own inner nature, but the forms of that activity are timeless, since they are expressions of the eternal nature of the world.[170] Thus when Spinoza speaks of God as eternal and infinite, he is not talking about some other being, "alongside" (as it were) the changing, temporal world. As his phrase *Deus sive Natura* reminds us, he is asking us to think about the one world, the only world, in a new way. Indeed the highest degree of knowledge, intuitive knowledge (*scientia intuitiva*), consists in being able to see that what appears to be "finite, temporal, multiplex, and divided" is in fact but the actualization in time of the eternal and infinite agency which is the world (viewed *sub specie aeternitatis*).[171] It follows that Spinoza was right to insist that his God is not identified with "a kind of mass or corporeal matter,"[172] because in Spinoza's thought Nature is not understood in terms of "corporeal matter." In its deepest reality it is infinite, eternal, and indivisible; not finite, temporal, and divided. When Nature is seen in this light, the usual objections to the identification of God with Nature disappear.[173] Thus, while Spinoza does identify "God" with "the whole of reality" (and could therefore be described as a pantheist), he has also redefined both terms of the equation. What makes Spinoza's religious vision so difficult is that he asks us to rethink our conceptions of God and the world simultaneously.

The Question of Miracles

Much more could be said about Spinoza's understanding of God, but the present discussion should be enough to enable a proper grasp of Spinoza's attitude to the Bible. The key issue here is that of miracles, for

[169]As Hallett notes (*Benedict de Spinoza*, 44), Spinoza says very little about the distinction between Nature as eternal and infinite and the "durational beings" that emerge from Nature's activity. However, given his view of the indivisibility of Substance, the distinction must be a distinction in thought, and what he writes about the higher kinds of knowledge suggests that it corresponds to the difference between viewing the world *sub specie aeternitatis* and doing so *sub specie temporis.*

[170]See Spinoza's (somewhat circular) definition of eternity (*Ethics*, part 1, def. 8 [p.31]): "By eternity I mean existence itself insofar as it is conceived as necessarily following solely from the definition of an eternal thing."

[171]Cf. Spinoza, *Ethics*, part 5, prop. 29 (217–18).

[172]Letter 73, in Spinoza, *The Letters*, 332 (cited above).

[173]Cf. Hallett, *Benedict de Spinoza*, 15.

Spinoza's attitude to the miraculous is now readily comprehensible. Spinoza can find no room in his metaphysics for miracles in the sense of interventions of a personal God from "outside of" (as it were) the regular workings of nature. The reason is simple: there is no "outside of" nature. The natural world, in its two dimensions of "producing" and "produced," *is* all there is. Once again, this does not mean an elimination of the divine power, but it does mean the identification of this power with the necessary order of the activity of the world. In this matter, Spinoza is utterly explicit, writing in chapter 6 of the *Tractatus* (On miracles) that "nothing . . . can happen in Nature to contravene her own universal laws, nor yet anything that is not in agreement with these laws or that does not follow from them."[174] These laws *are* what the Bible speaks of as the divine purpose and action. As he writes, "the universal laws of Nature are merely God's decrees, following from the necessity and the perfection of the divine nature."[175] It follows that knowledge of God is equivalent to knowledge of the laws of nature: the more we understand the laws of nature, the more we understand the will of God.[176]

What does this imply about the biblical miracles? It can only mean that what the biblical authors regarded as a miracle is nothing more than a natural, albeit unusual, event of whose cause they were unaware.[177] For in the interests of piety it was the custom of ancient authors to attribute things directly to God that were in fact brought about by way of natural processes.[178] Whenever the biblical interpreter comes across reports of incidents for which no cause can be found and that appear to have happened contrary to the order of nature, this should not cause perplexity. The interpreter should have no hesitation in assuming a natural explanation. In Spinoza's words, we may take it for granted that "what truly happened, happened naturally."[179] Indeed, to attribute to God the capacity to work miracles is not only absurd; it is also a sign of impiety, calling into question the very existence of God. For since the laws of nature *are* the will of God, a miracle would imply that God was acting contrary to

---

[174]Spinoza, *Tractatus,* 126.

[175]Ibid. As Mason notes (*The God of Spinoza,* 168–69), the "merely" or "nothing but" in such expressions runs counter to the idea that Spinoza is "reducing" talk of divine activity to talk of the natural order of the world. If there is a "reduction" of one thing to another, in these instances it goes in the opposite direction: the existence of the natural order of the world is presented in religious terminology. Spinoza, of course, is not interested in the reduction of one term to another, but in their identification.

[176]Cf. Spinoza, *Tractatus,* 128.

[177]Cf. ibid., 126–27.

[178]Cf. ibid., 60.

[179]Ibid., 133.

his own nature.[180] It follows that, if reports of miracles are found in the Bible, we must assume that they were "inserted into Holy Scripture by sacrilegious men."[181] This argument must have seen disingenuous to Spinoza's contemporaries. But it was consistent with his overall religious vision. Since Spinoza has identified God (as active cause) with the regular and (for him) necessary principles by which the natural world operates, the discovery of a true miracle would in fact cast doubt on God's existence rather than proving it.[182]

A word or two on what Spinoza means by the "universal laws" of nature might be in order, since this is a misleading expression (as he would be the first to point out).[183] For Spinoza is not saying that nature is bound by some set of principles that have their origin outside of herself. In Spinoza's worldview there *is* nothing outside of nature. Therefore the laws of nature are not accurately described as regulations by which nature is bound.[184] Rather they are simply the way in which things exist and the way in which they (necessarily) act.[185] Despite his deployment of deeply religious language, there are no occult forces in Spinoza's world, which is radically stripped of anthropomorphism. The necessary "laws" by which things operate are simply another way of describing the nature of things. In another letter to Henry Oldenburg (dated 1665), Spinoza effectively identifies these two terms, speaking of the "laws or nature [*leges, sive natura*]" of the world.[186] In other words, the "laws" by which the world operates are not imposed from outside. (If they were, then a transcendent God could suspend these laws to perform miracles.) For such language is still anthropomorphic. The laws of nature are nothing other than the eternal and necessary order of the world's activity.

5. The Significance of History

Philosophy and History

What role, then, has history in Spinoza's understanding of the Bible? What would he have made of the historical Jesus question? As Ernst Cassirer notes, there is a certain irony in the fact that Spinoza became "the originator of the idea of the historicity of the Bible."[187] For Spinoza has

[180]Cf. ibid., 126.
[181]Ibid., 134.
[182]Cf. ibid., 128.
[183]Cf. Mason, *The God of Spinoza*, 76.
[184]Cf. ibid., 82.
[185]Cf. ibid., 61.
[186]Letter 32, in Spinoza, *The Letters*, 192.
[187]Cassirer, *The Philosophy of the Enlightenment*, 184–85.

little time for historical facts, or indeed for any recourse to merely empirical data,[188] seeking to ground knowledge first and foremost on those truths that are universal, eternal, and necessary. From this point of view, Spinoza stands much more in the tradition of René Descartes than that of Francis Bacon, although here, too, he has taken his own path. Certainly the idea that history is organized by some divine purpose is entirely foreign to Spinoza's thought: his criticism of teleological explanations applies as much to history as it does to the natural world. What is commonly called "divine providence," for example, is (as we have seen) "nothing other than Nature's order, which necessarily follows from her eternal laws."[189] For this reason Spinoza sees no *theological* value in the study of history. Why, then, does Spinoza subject the Bible to what we would call a 'historical' investigation? The answer can only be that he does so because he wishes the Bible to be treated in the same way as any other object of study.[190] Religion is a phenomenon of human history and must therefore be studied historically.[191] But this is not because history offers any particular insight into divine truth.

In other ways, too, Spinoza's approach to the Bible has little in common with that of the historian. For instance, his famous opposition to miracles has nothing to do with the historian's cautious weighing of his evidence. As we have seen, his opposition is not based on the unreliability of reports of the miraculous (as was David Hume's);[192] indeed he assumes that miracles *are* extraordinary events, albeit ones that can be explained naturally. Rather, his opposition to the miraculous is based on a particular understanding of divinity and (more precisely) of the inseparability of the divine and natural orders. For since Spinoza understands the natural world as nothing less than the modes of the divine being, "the chain of finite causality *is* the divine causality."[193] There can be no question of a transcendent God "intervening" in a natural world

[188]See Spinoza, *Ethics,* part 2, prop. 31 (85), as well as the discussion of Spinoza's epistemology above.

[189]Spinoza, *Tractatus,* 125. As Mason points out (*The God of Spinoza,* 179), this does not mean a secularizing of history, "because no contrast exists in his thinking by which the secular could be characterized." Yet, if there is divine activity in history, it is by way of the efficient causality of natural laws, rather than by way of an overarching purpose.

[190]See, for instance, Spinoza's insistence (*Tractatus,* 141; in *The Historical Jesus Quest,* 6) that the method of studying scripture ought to be identical to that employed in the study of nature.

[191]Cf. Mason, *The God of Spinoza,* 182: "His position was that the appropriate form of explanation for historical religions was history."

[192]Cf. Donagan, "Spinoza's Theology," 364. Hume's attitude to miracles is discussed in the following chapter, on the work of David Friedrich Strauss.

[193]Copleston, *A History of Philosophy,* 4:227.

that is distinct from him. In other words, for Spinoza the exclusion of the miraculous is an a priori, not an a posteriori, exclusion. He is a metaphysician for whom the idea of a divine "intervention" into the natural order of things is simply absurd. This does not mean that the biblical reports of extraordinary events are necessarily mistaken or fraudulent; it simply means that whatever happened must have had a natural cause.[194] In other words, Spinoza did not have the interest in history characteristic of the nineteenth century or the finely honed critical attitudes of the modern historian. As we have already seen, he had no particular interest in history as such. He was led into what we would call a historical study of the Bible simply by the desire to understand it on its own terms, in the way in which any other phenomenon should be understood.

The Historical Jesus

For this reason we may assume that Spinoza would have had little interest in the question of the historical Jesus. It is true that if his critical method had been carried through to a study of the New Testament, it would surely have resulted in the question being raised. Indeed, in writing to Henry Oldenburg in 1675, Spinoza offers an extraordinarily bold reinterpretation of the resurrection narratives. Spinoza first of all compares the stories of the appearances of the risen Christ to the story of God's appearance to Abraham in the person of the three messengers (in Genesis 18).[195] He notes that such stories were the result of accommodation: they were "adapted to the understanding and beliefs of those men to whom God wished to reveal his mind by these means."[196] The resurrection of Jesus was in fact a spiritual resurrection. As Spinoza writes,

> Christ's resurrection from the dead was in fact of a spiritual kind and was revealed only to the faithful according to their understanding, indicating that Christ was endowed with eternity and rose from the dead (I here understand "the dead" in the sense in which Christ said "Let the dead bury their dead"), and also by his life and death he provided an example of surpassing holiness, and that he raises his disciples from the dead in so far as they follow the example of his own life and death.[197]

[194]In other words, Spinoza favors what David Friedrich Strauss would later call "rationalist" accounts of biblical miracles, not doubting the report, but finding natural explanations for the reported phenomena. (See, for instance, his discussion of Joshua's miracle in the *Tractatus*, 79.)

[195]Letter 75, in Spinoza, *The Letters*, 338.

[196]Ibid.

[197]Ibid., 338–39.

While this leaves the exact nature of the resurrection appearances unclear, it certainly amounts to a denial of the literal truth of the Gospel reports. In response to Oldenburg's plea that the accounts of these appearances are "so lucidly recorded by the Evangelists" that "the narrative should be taken literally,"[198] Spinoza writes:

> The passion, death and burial of Christ I accept literally, but his resurrection I understand in an allegorical sense. I do indeed admit that this is related by the Evangelists with such detail that we cannot deny that the Evangelists themselves believed that the body of Christ rose again and ascended to heaven to sit at God's right hand, and that this could also have been seen by unbelievers if they had been present at the places where Christ appeared to the disciples. Nevertheless, without injury to the teaching of the Gospel, they could have been deceived, as was the case with other prophets.[199]

Spinoza is here making use of his distinction between the meaning and the truth of the biblical text. He does not deny that the evangelists, indeed the apostles themselves, believed in a bodily resurrection. That is the meaning of the text. He *does* deny that they were correct in their assertions, for he can make no sense of what they are saying. For this reason he can only assume they were deceived. That, as far as he is concerned, is the truth of the matter. The distinction between meaning and truth allows Spinoza to acknowledge the intended meaning of the text while simultaneously distancing himself from it. Unlike earlier Jewish and Christian commentators (of whom Maimonides and Augustine are examples), Spinoza does not reinterpret the text by arguing that the biblical authors were *writing* an allegory. No; the evangelists believed that the bodily resurrection actually occurred. Their intended meaning was literal, not allegorical. But Spinoza finds that he can only make sense of the text by *reading* it allegorically.

It is interesting that, when Spinoza does discuss biblical narratives in the *Tractatus,* it is only in passing that he calls into question their historical accuracy. For as we have seen, his inclination is to dismiss historical narratives as of little religious significance. As he writes, "belief in historical narratives of any kind whatsoever has nothing to do with the Divine Law, . . . it does not in itself make men blessed, . . . its only value lies in the lesson conveyed, in which respect alone some narratives can be superior to others."[200] It is true that the study of historical narratives "can be very

[198]Oldenburg, Letter 77, in Spinoza, *Letters,* 345.
[199]Letter 78, in Spinoza, *The Letters,* 348.
[200]Spinoza, *Tractatus,* 122.

profitable in the matter of social relations," enabling us to become "acquainted with the ways and manners of men" so that we may live among them more prudently.[201] Yet this is scarcely the traditional Jewish and Christian attitude to the Bible. In any case, such practical profit may be drawn from any historical narrative, not just the biblical. Spinoza's lack of interest in history is clearly grounded in his epistemology. History is simply incapable of yielding what Spinoza thinks of as the knowledge of God. As he writes, "nor can the belief in historical narratives, however certain, give us knowledge of God, nor, consequently, of the love of God. For the love of God arises from the knowledge of God, a knowledge deriving from general axioms that are certain and self-evident, and so belief in historical narratives is by no means essential to the attainment of our supreme good."[202]

The clearest hint as to what Spinoza would have made of the historical Jesus question comes in the 1675 letter to Henry Oldenburg that I have already cited.[203] With regard to the *Tractatus,* Oldenburg had asked for clarification of three matters, namely Spinoza's view of the relationship of God and nature, his understanding of miracles, and his view of Jesus.[204] In his reply Spinoza writes that for salvation it is not necessary to know Christ "according to the flesh." What is essential is that we grasp the eternal wisdom of God. This wisdom is revealed in the world, in the human mind, and "most of all in Christ Jesus."[205] Spinoza rejects, however, the church's traditional teachings about Jesus, such as the doctrine of the incarnation. Indeed he insists that he simply cannot make sense of such a doctrine, any more than he could make sense of the idea that "a circle has taken on the nature of a square."[206] Here Spinoza distances himself from both Christian orthodoxy and (by implication) from any idea that historical research could uncover an alternative portrait of Jesus that would be of religious significance. To know Jesus is to know the eternal truths revealed through him, but the historical particularities of Jesus' life are of no religious interest. It is true that Spinoza's view of Jesus is an exalted one. As we have seen, he even suggests that Jesus was the only biblical figure to have "adequate knowledge" of God.[207] Yet such claims must be read in the light of Spinoza's philosophy as a whole. In that philosophy, "the historical Jesus" could only ever play a very minor role.

[201]Ibid., 105.
[202]Ibid., 105.
[203]Letter 73, in Spinoza, *The Letters,* 332–34.
[204]Cf. Letter 71, in Spinoza, *The Letters,* 329.
[205]Letter 73, in Spinoza, *The Letters,* 333.
[206]Ibid.
[207]Cf. Spinoza, *Tractatus,* 107.

Chapter Two

History and Myth

David Friedrich Strauss (1808–74)

> *One must love the question Strauss raised, in order to understand it.*
> *It has been loved only by a few; most people have feared it.*
>
> Karl Barth

Up to this point I have discussed only the very earliest stages in the development of the historical criticism of the Bible. With this chapter we arrive at one of its greatest achievements, namely, the nineteenth-century work of David Friedrich Strauss. In the seventeenth century, Spinoza had outlined the program that a critical study of the Bible ought to follow. In the eighteenth, Hermann Samuel Reimarus (1694–1768) had applied that program to the Gospels, with scandalous results, in a work published only after his death and then anonymously and in fragments.[1] It fell to Strauss in the nineteenth century to moderate Reimarus's conclusions, but in a way that offered little consolation to believers. If, as Albert Schweitzer suggests,[2] Strauss's life was a tragic one, it could be said that he himself was the first victim of the critical method that his *Life of Jesus Critically Examined* so ably exemplified. While his first *Life of Jesus* made him immediately famous, it also ruined his chances of an academic career and alienated him from the very circles in which a man of his background could immediately have felt at home.[3]

While Spinoza was a philosopher, who only incidentally directed his attention to the interpretation of the Bible, David Friedrich Strauss was

---

[1]Reimarus's work was entitled *Apology or Defence of the Rational Worshippers of God,* fragments of which were published by Gotthold Ephraim Lessing (1729–81) between 1774 and 1778. For a translation of the key texts concerning Jesus, see *Reimarus: Fragments,* translated by Ralph S. Fraser and edited by Charles H. Talbot, Lives of Jesus Series (Philadelphia: Fortress Press, 1970), 61–269.

[2]Cf. Albert Schweitzer, *The Quest of the Historical Jesus,* 2d Edition (1913), translated by W. Montgomery, J. R. Coates, Susan Cupitt, and John Bowden (London: SCM, 2000), 65.

[3]Cf. Richard S. Cromwell, *David Friedrich Strauss and His Place in Modern Thought* (Fair Lawn, N.J.: R. E. Burdick, 1974), 111.

both a biblical scholar and (more generally) a religious thinker of some note.[4] It is primarily as a biblical scholar that he is remembered, but the careful reader of Strauss's studies of the Gospels soon becomes aware of his wider religious concerns. These are also evident from a quick glance at his published works,[5] for alongside Strauss's two books on Jesus and his biographical and literary studies we find several major theological works. The first is Strauss's dogmatic theology, published in 1840–41 under the title *Christian Theology Set Forth in Its Historical Development and in [Its] Struggle with Modern Knowledge.*[6] The second is an extended criticism of Schleiermacher's posthumously published lectures on the "Life of Jesus," which was published in 1865 as *The Christ of Faith and the Jesus of History.*[7] The third is a more popular presentation of Strauss's later religious position, published in 1872 and entitled *The Old Faith and the New: A Confession.* In other words, Strauss never restricted himself to strictly literary and historical studies of the Bible. He was always aware of the implications of such studies both for Christian faith and for the wider culture. Yet the lasting influence of Strauss's work stems, not from his theological reflections, but from his biblical criticism. Therefore my primary focus in the pages that follow will be on that criticism and on its implications for faith; I will make reference to those other works only when they shed light on his critical project.

1. Strauss's Lives of Jesus

The Life of Jesus Critically Examined

It may be that a Christian scholar can have the courage to undertake a critical examination of the Gospels only if there exists the hope of restoring what is thereby lost. This seems to have been what enabled the

---

[4]Cf. Horton Harris, *David Friedrich Strauss and His Theology,* Monograph Supplements to the Scottish Journal of Theology (Cambridge: Cambridge University Press, 1973), 276. Harris argues that, although Strauss was a theological thinker, he was not a "theologian" in the positive sense of one "who intends to formulate a constructive . . . exposition of the Christian faith."

[5]See Harris, *David Friedrich Strauss,* 287–95, for a complete list of Strauss's published works.

[6]*Die christliche Glaubenslehre in ihrer geschichtliche Entwicklung und im Kampfe mit der modernen Wissenschaft dargestellt.*

[7]David Friedrich Strauss, *The Christ of Faith and the Jesus of History: A Critique of Schleiermacher's "The Life of Jesus"* (1865), translated by Leander E. Keck, Life of Jesus Series (Philadelphia: Fortress Press, 1977). I have not dealt with this study of Schleiermacher, most of which consists of detailed criticisms of the latter's views. For a discussion of Strauss's deeply ambivalent attitude towards Schleiermacher, see Leander Keck's very helpful introduction to *The Christ of Faith and the Jesus of History* (l–lxxxii).

young Strauss to produce his first major work, The *Life of Jesus Critically Examined*. At the time Strauss undertook this work, he intended to balance his criticism with a more constructive reinterpretation of the significance of Jesus. In a letter to his friend Christian Märklin written some years before the publication of his first *Life of Jesus* Strauss writes:

> What engages me in the most lively way . . . is the plan for a course of lectures on the *Life of Jesus*. You will perhaps wonder about this choice, but you will see that this is actually the best preparatory work for the greater dogmatic plan which at present has been completely relegated to the back of my mind. . . . The whole thing would fall reasonably into three parts, a traditional, a critical, and a dogmatic part, or, into a directly positive, a negative, and a part which would recover the true positive. . . . In this way I would partly destroy, partly shake the infinite significance which faith attributes to this life—certainly only to restore it again in a higher way.[8]

However, the work that was finally published in 1835 embodies only a small part of this proposed project. The part it embodies was what Strauss himself described as "the negative," insofar as it is destructive of traditional attitudes to the Bible. Only in the final section of the book does Strauss allow himself to begin the task of reconstruction and to demonstrate his conviction that "the essence of the Christian faith is perfectly independent" of the criticism in which he has been engaged.[9] But as his opponents were quick to realize, Strauss's constructive theological work is far less convincing than his criticism.

The *Life of Jesus Critically Examined* is an extraordinarily meticulous study of the Gospel narratives, almost 1500 pages in the first German edition of 1835, spread over two volumes.[10] It is difficult to believe that it was written in little more than a year.[11] It is also a book that makes considerable demands on the reader.[12] Strauss's procedure is to take each incident from the Gospels in turn and to examine it from several different points of view. First of all, he takes the traditional, Christian "supernaturalistic" explanation, that is to say, one that assumes the divine origin

---

[8]Strauss to Märklin, cited in Harris, *David Friedrich Strauss,* 32–33.

[9]Strauss, *The Life of Jesus Critically Examined,* lii.

[10]David Friedrich Strauss, *Das Leben Jesu kritisch bearbeitet,* 2 vols. (Tübingen: C. F. Osiander,1835). Volume 2 is actually dated 1836, but Harris (*David Friedrich Strauss,* 64, n.7) notes that it, too, was published in 1835.

[11]Cf. Cromwell, *David Friedrich Strauss and His Place in Modern Thought,* 51.

[12]While I would like to say that I have defied George Eliot's prediction that no one would read the work right through (cf. Peter C. Hodgson, editor's introduction to *The Life of Jesus Critically Examined,* xlviii), I must confess I cannot.

and authority of the scriptures. He looks at the ways in which traditional interpreters have understood these stories, paying particular attention to their attempts to harmonize the inconsistencies that emerge when the different Gospel narratives of the same incident are set side by side. For example, there exist conflicting details in the genealogies of Jesus in the Gospels of Matthew and Luke; these were sometimes explained by suggesting that one Gospel offered the genealogy of Joseph, the other that of Mary.[13] In the same way, the differences in the accounts of the healing of a blind man at Jericho were sometimes explained by the suggestion that Jesus performed two healings, one on his entrance to the town and another on leaving.[14] In the case of miracle stories, Strauss also examines what he calls the "rationalist" explanations that had been so popular in the century or so before his time. The rationalist interpreters maintained that the Gospels were accurate insofar as they reported what actually happened, but also insisted that what actually happened could be explained naturally rather than supernaturally.[15] We might take as an example the Gospel report of an apparently miraculous feeding of 5000 people. Rationalist interpreters suggested that Jesus' willingness to share what he had with the crowd inspired them to share what they had with each other.[16] Similarly, they explained the apparently miraculous transfiguration of Jesus as a dream experienced by the disciples while asleep,[17] or perhaps as a trick of the light that made the apostles suppose that a perfectly ordinary meeting of Jesus with two strangers was in fact an encounter with Moses and Elijah.[18] Strauss's close analysis of the Gospels demonstrates that neither the traditional supernatural nor—in most cases—these more recent rationalist explanations can withstand close scrutiny. In their place he offers his own, "mythical" interpretation of much of the content of the Gospels. What Strauss means by a "mythical" interpretation is a question to which we will return shortly.

A New Life of Jesus
Strauss's second major study on the life of Jesus was published in 1864 and entitled *The Life of Jesus Examined, for the German People*.[19] The work

---

[13]Cf. Strauss, *The Life of Jesus Critically Examined,* §21 (115).

[14]Cf. ibid., §95 (442).

[15]In his major theological work, Strauss traces the essential features of the rationalistic explanation back to Spinoza. Cf. David Friedrich Strauss, *Die christliche Glaubenslehre in ihrer geschichtliche Entwicklung und im Kampfe mit der modernen Wissenschaft dargestellt* (Tübingen: C. F. Osiander, 1840), vol. 1, §17 (1:236).

[16]Cf. Strauss, *The Life of Jesus Critically Examined,* §102 (513).

[17]Cf. ibid., §106 (538).

[18]Cf. ibid., §106 (539–40).

[19]*Das Leben Jesu für das deutsche Volk bearbeitet.*

was translated a year later into English as *A New Life of Jesus*. As the original title suggests, Strauss intended this work as a popular study, the equivalent in German of Ernest Renan's famous *La Vie de Jésus* (The Life of Jesus), which had been published only a year previously.[20] However, it was also intended as a continuation of his earlier work: in the preface Strauss explains that he is taking the opportunity both to defend his general position against his critics and to amend his earlier conclusions in the light of new discoveries.[21] The book contains a lengthy introduction, in which Strauss surveys previous attempts at writing a life of Jesus and examines the nature of the Gospels as historical documents. This clears the way for a reassertion of his earlier argument regarding 'myth.' Strauss restates his conviction that neither the traditional supernatural nor the more recent rationalistic explanations are plausible ways of explaining much of the content of the Gospels. That content can only be understood as mythical. Indeed it is precisely the recognition of the presence of myth in the Gospels that allows the historian to begin to reconstruct the life of Jesus.[22] After some further remarks regarding miracle and myth, Strauss launches into the body of his work.

That work is divided into two parts. The first, comprising almost exactly half of the first volume of the English text, is a positive reconstruction, entitled "Historical Outline of the Life of Jesus." The second, comprising a second volume, does little more than rehearse the mythical interpretations of Strauss's earlier work. The first volume in particular is worthy of closer study. For in offering a historical reconstruction, Strauss goes beyond *The Life of Jesus Critically Examined*. The earlier work had been devoted to a refutation of the prevailing interpretations of the Gospels; it had given few glimpses of how Strauss himself regarded the historical figure of Jesus.[23] The portrait of Jesus found in the later work is less well known, perhaps because that work had a rather critical reception.[24] My own view is that at least some of this criticism is unjustified and that the work deserves more attention than it customarily receives. What is particularly notable is that in *A New Life of Jesus* Strauss affirms

---

[20]Cf. David Friedrich Strauss, *A New Life of Jesus* (London: Williams & Norgate, 1865), preface (1:xvii–xviii): "All I wish is to have written a book as suitable for Germany as Renan's is for France." Given Strauss's strongly pro-German and anti-French political views, later expressed in correspondence with Renan (cf. Harris, *David Friedrich Strauss,* 237), I am not quite sure how to read this remark.

[21]Cf. Strauss, *A New Life of Jesus,* preface (1:ix).

[22]Cf. ibid., §23 (1:195).

[23]Cf. ibid., §26 (1:215–16).

[24]See particularly Schweitzer's *The Quest of the Historical Jesus,* 168–70, and the defense of Strauss's work in Harris, *David Friedrich Strauss,* 212.

the existence of a historical core to the Gospels,[25] however much he may insist that "our historical knowledge of Jesus is defective and uncertain."[26] In trying to identify that historical core Strauss anticipates—to an extent which is seldom acknowledged—many of the conclusions of his successors.

At first sight the picture of Jesus that emerges from *A New Life of Jesus* is a sympathetic one. It echoes conclusions arrived at by the other liberal theologians of Strauss's time, conclusions that were apparently not incompatible with Christian faith. Strauss argues that Jesus had reached a particularly high level of religious development. This was what set him in opposition to aspects not only of the Judaism of his time but also of Old Testament religion. This new level of religious development was marked by an inward and spiritual ethic of love,[27] which led Jesus to place little importance on the observance of the Mosaic law. As Strauss writes, "the worthlessness of all this outward service contrasted with the inner" had become obvious to him.[28] Jesus' religious consciousness was marked by what Strauss calls "idealism," which he defines as a tendency towards separating religious concerns from political aspirations and a confidence that one can attain peace with God "in a purely spiritual way."[29] (The contrast here seems to be with external observances.) With regard to the messianic expectations of Judaism, Jesus came to recognize that he was the one of whom the scriptures of Israel had spoken. But he also aimed to purify the Jewish expectations from what Strauss calls their "worldly and political elements."[30] For this reason Jesus preferred the title "Son of Man," which Strauss argues was not yet in general messianic use, to "Son of God" or "Son of David."[31] For the title Son of Man implied an attitude of "meekness and humility," while Son of God suggested "miracle-seeking fanaticism" and Son of David conveyed a "spirit of exclusiveness and political expectations."[32] With regard to his future sufferings, Jesus may have gradually realized that the Son of Man was called to play the role of the suffering servant of the prophecies of Isaiah, even to the point of considering his death "an atoning sacrifice."[33]

Even though Strauss has stripped his portrait of Jesus of all supernatural elements, to this point it is not positively offensive to traditional

[25]Cf. Harris, *David Friedrich Strauss,* 211.
[26]Strauss, *A New Life of Jesus,* §99 (2:430).
[27]Cf. Strauss, *A New Life of Jesus,* §34 (1:278–80).
[28]Ibid., §35 (1:285).
[29]Ibid., §37 (1:303).
[30]Ibid., §37 (1:304).
[31]Cf. ibid., §37 (1:303–10).
[32]Ibid., §37 (1:310).
[33]Ibid., §38 (1:319).

Christians. Yet Strauss also boldly addresses what later scholars would refer to as the "apocalyptic" elements in the message of Jesus. These are the aspects of Jesus' teaching that refer to the future establishment of the kingdom of God and his own role in this supernatural and cosmic drama. While Strauss is prepared to relieve Jesus of responsibility for those extraordinary speeches in the Gospel of John in which he speaks of his pre-existence, he cannot relieve him of responsibility for those sayings, throughout the Gospels, in which he speaks of his return in glory.[34] It is clear that Jesus looked forward to the establishment of God's kingdom by way of some kind of supernatural divine action. It is true that some of Jesus' sayings suggest that the kingdom is already present and that it will develop in a perfectly natural manner.[35] Yet as Strauss writes, Jesus clearly distinguished this present "time of preparation" from the future time of the "perfection" of God's kingdom; the latter would come about only as "a change in the world to be brought about by God."[36] What is particularly distasteful to the modern reader, Strauss argues, is the way in which Jesus speaks of his own role in the supernatural inauguration of this new age. It cannot seriously be doubted that Jesus "declared himself the Being who will come with the clouds of Heaven, in the company of angels, in order to waken the dead and hold judgement."[37] Now it is one thing to expect that such events are about to occur; it is quite another to present yourself as the central actor in this divine drama. When Jesus makes such claims, he exalts himself above others in a way that is quite simply repugnant. The profundity of Jesus' moral teaching will lead us to reject the suspicion that he was "a braggart and an imposter,"[38] but it remains true that we would have to call Jesus a fanatic (or "enthusiast": *Schwärmer*). After all, even such a person can possess what Strauss calls "high spiritual gifts and moral endowments."[39]

Strauss accepts as historically plausible the basic outline of Jesus' trial and death as found in the synoptic Gospels, however much of the details may have been created out of Old Testament prophecies and passages in the Psalms.[40] With regard to the accounts of the resurrection, however, the situation is very different. It is sometimes suggested that the extraordinary rise of Christianity after the tragic death of its founder is explicable only if Jesus had indeed risen from the dead. But Strauss points out

[34]Cf. ibid., §39 (1:323).
[35]Cf. ibid., §39 (1:329–30).
[36]Ibid., §39 (1:330).
[37]Ibid., §39 (1:331).
[38]Cf. ibid., §39 (1:322–24).
[39]Ibid., §39 (1:324).
[40]Cf. ibid., §45 (1:387–96).

the fallacy in that argument, noting that the rise of Christianity proves only that the apostles *believed* Jesus had risen from the dead.[41] The key question for criticism concerns the *origins* of that belief. Now Strauss's position on this most delicate of issues needs to be correctly understood. He is certainly (as we will see) opposed to miracles, of which the resurrection is a most dramatic example. However, his opposition to belief in the resurrection is based above all on a weighing of the historical evidence. Even if we consider miracles to be possible (in principle), we will not accept a *report* of a miracle unless the falsity of that report were more difficult to conceive than the event that it relates.[42] Yet the evidence for the resurrection is far from sufficient for this purpose: it cannot outweigh the intrinsic improbability of such an event. For neither the Gospels nor the testimony of St. Paul represent *eyewitness accounts* of the original events.[43] Indeed if we turn to the Gospel narratives of the resurrection appearances, we find that they "contradict in many ways not only the accounts of the apostle Paul but also each other."[44] The popular rationalist idea that the resurrection of Jesus was a "natural revival"—that is to say, that Jesus was not really dead when taken down from the cross—is also historically implausible.[45]

What, then, may we suppose actually occurred? Strauss argues that some light may be shed on this question by looking at the later appearance of Jesus to the apostle Paul. For Paul himself ranks this experience alongside that of the other apostles. When we look at the New Testament accounts, we see that the appearance of Jesus to Paul is most easily understood as "a vision which Paul attributed indeed to an external cause, but which nevertheless took place in his own mind."[46] (The details of Luke's accounts of this event are clearly unreliable, and we know from Paul's own words that he was prone to such paranormal experiences.[47]) It may therefore be assumed that the appearances of Jesus to the disciples recounted in the Gospels were of a similar character. After the death of Jesus, the grieving disciples tried to reconcile their belief in his messianic dignity with the fate that had befallen him. The only possible reconciliation was to believe that God had raised Jesus to a position of heavenly authority. If Enoch and Elijah had been taken up to

---

[41]Cf. ibid., §46 (1:398–99).

[42]Cf. ibid., §46 (1:399). Strauss is here alluding to the argument against miracles put forward by David Hume (1711–76), which will be examined later in this chapter.

[43]Cf. Strauss, *A New Life of Jesus*, §46 (1:399–400).

[44]Ibid., §46 (1:402).

[45]Cf. ibid., §47 (1:408–12).

[46]Ibid., §48 (1:414).

[47]Cf. ibid., §48 (1:414–18).

heaven, so had Jesus, and—since "the soul without the body was a mere shadow"[48]—this meant his bodily resurrection. In the religious enthusiasm thus created, perhaps heightened by fasting, it was only a short step from this conviction to the experience of visions.[49] Strauss brings forward analogies from contemporary experience to demonstrate that visions can be induced in similar circumstances.[50] Even if it is true that such visions occurred in Jerusalem itself and very soon after Jesus' death, this explanation of their origin is not implausible. For Strauss argues that the development of belief in the resurrection could take place very quickly. While the apostles' claim could easily be refuted by the production of Jesus' body, Strauss suggests that the location of that body may well have been unknown. In any case, given the idea that bodies were unclean, even the opponents of the disciples would have been reluctant to search for it. In fact, however, Strauss considers it more likely that belief in the resurrection developed only after the disciples had returned to Galilee.[51]

What are we to make of this depiction of the life of Jesus? Aspects of Strauss's portrait of Jesus seem suspiciously well adapted to his own religious aims. For Strauss is attempting to achieve what he describes as a purification of religion. He wishes the religious sentiment to be set free from what he regards as arbitrary claims to authority and from dependence on external ceremonies.[52] Strauss clearly believes that this religious ideal, that of an ethical religion not dependent on external practices or a church hierarchy, corresponds to "the religion of Jesus."[53] It is belief in miracles, Strauss argues, that has turned this simple faith into "a supernatural religion of mysteries and sacramental graces."[54] For Strauss believes that Jesus worked no miracles (however naturally these might be understood), apart from those apparent cures that occurred almost against his will, as a result of people's faith.[55] Therefore to return to the religion of Jesus, we must banish such beliefs. As Strauss writes with emphasis, "*he who would banish priests from the Church must first banish miracles from religion.*"[56] The task before us today is that of continuing the process Jesus began. We must transform the religion of Christ into what

[48]Ibid., §49 (1:421–24).
[49]Cf. ibid., §49 (1:428).
[50]Cf. ibid., §49 (1:426–27).
[51]Cf. ibid., §50 (1:429–40).
[52]Cf. ibid., preface (1:xii, xiv).
[53]Ibid., preface (1:xv).
[54]Ibid., preface (1:xvi).
[55]Cf. ibid., §42 (1:360–70).
[56]Ibid., preface (1:xvi).

Strauss calls "the Religion of humanity," a purely ethical religion in which we will live by certain ideals of human perfection.[57] Jesus is important because of his contribution to our ethical ideals: despite the corruptions introduced by the church, Jesus' ideals of "patience, gentleness, and charity" have not been entirely lost.[58]

The hard-won reputation of this great critic of the Gospels is not well served by this particular religious vision. Those who admire Strauss's earlier work may well be discomforted by his lack of critical distance from the spirit of his own age and by his willingness to assume that this spirit was first exemplified in the figure of Jesus. Yet it is to Strauss's credit as a historian that he did not shy away from those aspects of Jesus' teaching that are incomprehensible or even repugnant from a modern standpoint. In this sense he avoids the failings associated with the liberal theology of Albrecht Ritschl. He also anticipates the "consistently eschatological" interpretations of Johannes Weiss and Albert Schweitzer, which we will examine in the following chapter. Strauss may not be sufficiently detached from the spirit of his own age, but he had achieved a degree of detachment from traditional religious attitudes.[59] It may be that it was this distance from traditional Christianity that enabled Strauss to confront what—from a modern perspective—can seem distressingly foreign elements in the teaching of Jesus. Similarly, it allowed him to set forth, in a frank manner, the problems surrounding belief in the resurrection, problems at which the theologians of his time had hinted but were reluctant openly to concede.[60]

2. Strauss's "Mythical Interpretation"

Strauss's Understanding of Myth

As we have seen, the term "myth" lies at the very heart of Strauss's critical study of the Gospels. Indeed in the preface to the first volume of *The Life of Jesus Critically Examined*, Strauss sets out the aim that will govern the whole work: to find an alternative to the outmoded forms of supernaturalism and (rationalistic) naturalism. Strauss's alternative is what he calls the mythical interpretation of the life of Jesus.[61] Yet, while the term is central to his thought, it is not easy to determine what Strauss understands by "myth." He admits that he is by no means the first to employ

[57]Strauss, *A New Life of Jesus,* §100 (2:436).
[58]Ibid., §100 (2:437).
[59]Cf. Strauss, *The Life of Jesus Critically Examined,* preface to the first edition (lii).
[60]Cf. Strauss, *A New Life of Jesus,* §46 (1:397–98).
[61]Cf. ibid., li; cf. *Das Leben Jesu kritisch bearbeitet,* v–vi.

the notion, whether in the study of the Bible as a whole or of the Gospels in particular.[62] Indeed he spends much of his introduction discussing the work of those who have employed the terms before him. However, rather than working our way through Strauss's predecessors,[63] it may be more helpful to look at his own descriptions of the nature of myth. Our starting point will be the introduction to the fourth edition of *The Life of Jesus Critically Examined*,[64] although we will also make use of Strauss's discussion of myth in *A New Life of Jesus*.

The first point to be made regarding Strauss's use of the term "myth" is that he understands "myth" in opposition to "history," that is to say, in opposition to a historically accurate account of events. Thus he writes that "the mythical mode of interpretation agrees with the allegorical, in relinquishing the historical reality of the sacred narratives."[65] To this extent Strauss's use of the term "myth" shares the negative connotations of the term in contemporary English. It is a narrative which is historical in *form*, but fictitious as regards its *content*. Yet Strauss insists that this represents only one side of what he understands by "myth." For if myth "relinquishes the historical reality" of the biblical stories, it does so only "in order to preserve to them an absolute inherent truth."[66] In other words, if myth is fictitious from the point of view of its apparent historical reference, it may still be taken to embody a truth. The truth, however, lies not in any historical claims the narratives may appear to make, but in the religious ideas that they embody.[67]

It follows that myth is representative of a primitive way of thinking, one which precedes our modern preoccupations with adequate documentation and historical accuracy. Even if some Greek and Roman writers

[62]Cf. Strauss, *The Life of Jesus Critically Examined*, §§8–9 (52–59).

[63]There is an excellent discussion of the background to Strauss's conception in Harris, *David Friedrich Strauss*, 259–73.

[64]I am making reference to the fourth (1840) edition of *The Life of Jesus Critically Examined*, since the George Eliot translation of this work is readily accessible and since it contains a more extensive introductory discussion of myth and miracle than was found in the earlier editions.

[65]Strauss, *The Life of Jesus Critically Examined*, §12 (65).

[66]Ibid.

[67]Strauss's conception of myth is probably influenced by "the common Hegelian distinction between the philosophical concept (*Begriff*)—the truth expressed in scientific thought—and the theological representation or conception (*Vorstellung*)—the popularised and [literally] erroneous form of the concept" (Harris, *David Friedrich Strauss*, 22). Yet it is also true that Strauss's mythical interpretation of the Gospels is not dependent on Hegel's philosophy. As Harris writes (ibid., 271), "Strauss was not concerned with the philosophical explanation for the origin of myths in general, but with the historical process by which the myths in the Gospel arose. . . . In the 1864 *Life of Jesus* the mythical principle remains substantially unchanged while the Hegelian viewpoint is abandoned."

of the first century exhibit the beginnings of a historical consciousness, the evangelists belonged to a very different mental world. For this reason Strauss can dismiss the objection that "such a mass of mythi" as he argues the Gospels represent could not have arisen "in an age so historical as that of the first Roman emperors."[68]

> We must not . . . be misled by too comprehensive a notion of an histori-
> cal age. The sun is not visible at the same instant to every place on the
> same meridian at the same time of year; it gleams upon the mountain
> summits and the high plains before it penetrates the lower valleys and the
> deep ravines. No less true is it that the historic age dawns not upon all
> people at the same period. The people of highly civilized Greece, and of
> Rome the capital of the world, stood on an eminence which had not
> been reached in Galilee and Judaea.[69]

More precisely, myth is not so much a literary technique as it is a mode of thought. It is a way of articulating religious insights in the absence of the more precise, philosophical conceptions of a later age. In Strauss's words, myth is "not a covering in which a clever man clothes an idea which arises in him for the use and benefit of the ignorant multitude"; rather, "it is only simultaneously with the narrative which he tells that he becomes conscious of the idea which he is not yet able to apprehend as such."[70]

This brings us to a third aspect of Strauss's understanding of myth. For he argues that myth is to be regarded as the product, not so much of the creative genius of an individual, but of the religious imagination of a community. Even if an individual writer can be said to have created particular expressions of myth, in so doing he is only giving voice to the sentiments of the community to which he belongs.[71] It follows that if the interpreter of myth is to understand its origins and meaning, he ought to seek out "the spirit and modes of thought of the people and of the age" in which it was produced.[72]

Out of which "spirit and modes of thought" were the New Testament myths woven? Strauss's answer is clear. They arose out of the Old Testament and out of the Jewish messianic expectations of the time immediately before the birth of Jesus. In *The Life of Jesus Critically Examined*,

---

[68]Strauss, *The Life of Jesus Critically Examined*, §13 (74).
[69]Ibid.
[70]Strauss, *A New Life of Jesus*, §25 (1:206).
[71]Cf. ibid., §14 (81); cf. Strauss, *A New Life of Jesus*, §25 (1:206).
[72]Strauss, *The Life of Jesus Critically Examined*, §12 (65).

Strauss assumes that these messianic expectations were clearly defined and that they need only to be transferred to the figure of Christ,[73] a process that could be achieved in the relatively short time between the death of Jesus and the writing of the Gospels.[74] In his later work, *A New Life of Jesus*, Strauss concedes that this Jewish messianic expectation was not "in all its features clear and defined."[75] Rather, the hope of a messiah combined "characteristics from many various sources," so that "there was a degree of uncertainty, the possibility of different modes of apprehension, and different combinations."[76] Yet he holds to his view that many of the stories in the Gospels arose by the transference of these notions to Jesus. Once Jesus' disciples had come to see him as Messiah, they simply assumed that everything that had been predicted about the Messiah *must have* happened to Jesus. Even if it were known that Jesus came from Nazareth, it was assumed that he must have been born in Bethlehem, for that accords with the prophecy of Micah. Even if Jesus had spoken against the desire for miracles, it was assumed that he must have worked miracles, since Moses worked miracles. As for the particular stories of miracles, these are simply woven out of the prophecy of Isaiah, which predicted that when the messianic age comes, the lame will walk and the blind will see.[77] It is important to remember, however, that Strauss did not argue that *all* the contents of the Gospels were "mythical." Rather he studied each incident on its own terms. As his later work shows, he rejected the position of the extreme sceptic, who would deny that we can know anything of Jesus.[78] However, he argued that where both the supernatural and the natural interpretations of certain incidents in the Gospels could be shown to be implausible, the mythical interpretation presented itself as the only reasonable alternative.

The Positive Role of Myth

Strauss's critical scholarship destroyed once and for all any remaining hopes that the Gospel narratives could be read as historically reliable reports. Yet, at least in the early stages of his career, Strauss did not regard his work as purely destructive. For he regarded myth as a positive category of religious history, which offered the basis of a more constructive approach to biblical interpretation. Interwoven with the new metaphysics of his age, the mythical interpretation of *The Life of Jesus Critically*

[73]Cf. ibid., §14 (83–84).
[74]Cf. ibid., §14 (86).
[75]Strauss, *A New Life of Jesus,* §25 (1:203).
[76]Ibid.
[77]Cf. ibid., 202.
[78]Cf. Strauss, *A New Life of Jesus,* §99 (2:434).

Examined would offer at least those Christians able to understand it a new interpretation of their faith.

Most importantly, the category of myth helped to rescue the Gospel writers from the crude charge of fraud with which Hermann Samuel Reimarus had burdened them. In the posthumously published fragments of his *Apologie*, Reimarus had written that Jesus had expected to be the messianic ruler of a temporal kingdom and that this expectation was shared by his disciples throughout his public ministry. However, after their hopes were dashed by his crucifixion, the disciples deliberately reformulated their teaching and began to speak of Jesus as a suffering savior who died for the sins of the world and was raised to life by God. Reimarus argued that the resurrection narratives in the Gospels are clearly unreliable as historical sources, and the story of the resurrection is a deliberate act of fraud, brought about by the disciples so as to ensure that they could maintain their positions of power and privilege. In his essay on Reimarus, published in 1877, Strauss rejects these accusations. It is true that Reimarus's assertion of fraud was a necessary stage in the development of biblical criticism. It was a position that was typical of the eighteenth century, insofar as it simply denied the church's point of view and offered a naturalistic alternative. But in the hands of Reimarus that alternative represents an extreme swing of the pendulum. Rather than regarding the Gospels as a divine work in the highest sense, it regards them as a human work in the worst sense. A more balanced position now needs to be found.[79]

What the eighteenth century lacked, Strauss argued, was a sense of the power and significance of the religious imagination. Once this is grasped, we no longer need to suppose that religions emerge from deliberate acts of deception. They may be—it is true—the result of a certain kind of self-deception,[80] but that does not necessarily imply bad faith.[81] What enables the nineteenth century to reach this more positive conclusion, Strauss argues, is its new appreciation of the power of imagination. Today we would attribute this sensitivity to what is often described as the Romantic reaction to Enlightenment rationality, exemplified, as Strauss himself notes, in the work of Johann Gottfried von Herder (1744–1803).[82] In any case, Strauss argues that the thinkers of the eighteenth century were too severely rational to appreciate what he calls "the

[79]Cf. David Friedrich Strauss, "Hermann Samuel Reimarus and His Apology" (1877), §§38–40, translated by Ralph S. Fraser, in *Reimarus: Fragments,* 44–45.

[80]Cf. ibid., 51.

[81]Cf. ibid., 49.

[82]Cf. ibid., 52.

fanciful spirit of the Orient" and its creative power.[83] For example, the disciples' conviction that they had encountered the risen Christ was technically a delusion, but "it was nonetheless a delusion that contained a great deal of truth."[84]

While Strauss uses his concept of myth to rule out deliberate fraud, he exhibits some ambivalence on a closely related question. This is the question as to whether the creation of the Gospels myths was a conscious or an unconscious process. In *The Life of Jesus Critically Examined,* Strauss suggests that the creation of myth out of the excited imagination of the earliest Christians was an unconscious matter. If we moderns would assume a deliberate act of deception, it may simply be that we are failing to appreciate how different was the world of the earliest Christians. As Strauss writes, "it is almost impossible, in a critical and enlightened age like our own, to carry ourselves back to a period of civilization in which the imagination worked so powerfully, that its illusions were believed as realities by the very minds that created them."[85] It is true that it is *difficult* to draw a sharp line between conscious and unconscious fiction.[86] When it is a matter of the invention of a story that has no historical basis at all, particularly when this is done by one person, one is forced to assume a conscious process.[87] On the other hand, even where we are speaking of conscious fiction, there is no need to assume a "fraudulent intention."[88] The evangelists, already convinced that Jesus was the awaited Messiah, could easily conclude that the Old Testament expectations must have been fulfilled in his lifetime. For them, we might say (although these are not Strauss's terms), the Old Testament *was* documentary evidence of the reality of the stories that they attributed to Jesus. In Strauss's own words, "such and such things must have happened to the Messiah; Jesus was the Messiah; therefore such and such things happened to him."[89]

In his later work *A New Life of Jesus,* Strauss takes this qualification further. For at least with regard to the Gospel of John, he posits a much more deliberate process of creation. For John's narratives are so carefully constructed that, if they are not historical, they can only be seen as deliberate inventions. As Strauss writes,

[83]Ibid., 52.
[84]Ibid., 53.
[85]Strauss, *The Life of Jesus Critically Examined,* §14 (83).
[86]Ibid., §14 (82).
[87]Cf. ibid., §14 (83).
[88]Ibid., §14 (83).
[89]Ibid., §14 (84).

in sketching the scene between Jesus and the Samaritan woman at Jacob's well, in the speeches and answers the interchange of which he describes, the author of the fourth Gospel must have been as much conscious that he was inventing freely, as Homer when he described the interview between Ulysses and Calypso, or between Achilles and his divine mother.[90]

However, just as Homer believed that his narrative reflected the very nature of the gods, so John may have believed that his narrative was true. For the truth in which John was interested was not a literal, historical truth, but the expression of a particular religious idea. Just as the author of Revelation projected his ideas onto an imagined future, so the author of John's Gospel projected his ideas onto an imagined past.[91] In any case, for the purposes of criticism the products of unconscious and conscious invention may both be described as "myth." The task of the interpreter is to determine which elements are history and which elements are fiction.[92]

We have seen that Strauss's conception of myth freed the evangelists from the charge of fraud. But it also had a more positive role. At least early in his career, mythical interpretation allowed Strauss to find ongoing religious significance in Christian claims about Jesus, even when the historical basis of those claims had been undermined. As I have suggested, this may be one reason why Strauss could be at ease with the destruction he wrought, for he believed that what he regarded as "the essence of the Christian faith" remained undisturbed.[93] In the same way as Spinoza regarded "the Jesus of history" as ultimately without significance, so the author of *The Life of Jesus Critically Examined* had discovered a way of transcending the consequences of his own criticism. However, to approach this topic is to raise the issue of Strauss's understanding of history, a matter of such importance that it will be dealt with in a separate section of this chapter.

Christianity and Other Religions

Strauss's motivations in adopting this mythical interpretation of the Gospels were complex. We may assume that he found it an attractive weapon with which to attack those traditional forms of faith which he considered no longer credible. However, Strauss's adoption of the category of myth was also motivated by one of the changes discussed in the introduction to the present work. The change to which I am referring is

[90]Strauss, *A New Life of Jesus*, §25 (1:208).
[91]Cf. ibid., §25 (1:209–10).
[92]Cf. ibid., §25 (1:210–11).
[93]Strauss, *The Life of Jesus Critically Examined*, lii.

a new awareness of the fact of religious diversity and (more particularly) of the existence of competing claims to religious authority. Indeed, Strauss must count as one of the first Christian thinkers openly to confront this fact of religious diversity and to draw out its implications in a consistent manner. We will shortly examine the way in which the existence of competing religious claims influenced Strauss's attitude to miracles. For the moment, we must note its influence on his mythical interpretation of the Gospels.

We may begin, once again, with the introductory remarks to *The Life of Jesus Critically Examined.* Strauss admits first of all that his mythical interpretation is opposed to the usual attitude of the believing Christian. But the problem here is that the average Christian inhabits a very narrow religious world, namely that of his own community.[94] The traditional attitude to the Gospels cannot be sustained when one gains a broader knowledge of religious history. For each of the religions of the world makes claims regarding the authority of its scriptures that are comparable to Christian claims regarding the Bible. Faced with such competing claims to authority, the historian can only regard all these religions as similar and judge them by the same criteria. If we judge that there are myths in the pagan histories, we cannot withhold this same judgment from the Jewish and Christian. It is true that Christian apologists try to demonstrate that their scriptures are different in principle from those of other religions. But Strauss attacks each of these arguments in turn. We cannot be confident that the Gospels are eyewitness reports.[95] Nor does their content distinguish them from pagan histories and scriptures.[96] The same processes that gave rise to myths outside of Christianity apply to the formation of the Gospels.[97] For this reason, as Strauss writes in his later study, only the mythical interpretation of the Gospels succeeds in treating all religions consistently. For only the mythical interpretation places "the original production of Christian myths . . . upon the same footing as that of those which we find in the history of the rise of other religions."[98]

3. The Question of Miracles

In the introduction to the present work I outlined the growth of a particular way of representing reality that was associated with the modern

[94]Cf. Strauss, *The Life of Jesus Critically Examined,* §13 (69).
[95]Cf. ibid., §13 (69–75).
[96]Cf. ibid., §14 (75–78).
[97]Cf. ibid., §14 (80–82).
[98]Strauss, *A New Life of Jesus,* 1:206.

sciences. This "mechanistic" depiction of the world not only made it unnecessary to speak of the activity of God; it also made it difficult to imagine just how such activity might occur, in a world apparently ruled by "the laws of nature." The question that focused these issues was, of course, that of miracles, and on this question Strauss displayed the full extent of his scepticism. At the risk of trying the reader's patience, I would like to attempt a careful examination of Strauss's attitude to the miraculous. For despite some praiseworthy attempts to rehabilitate Strauss's reputation,[99] this is a matter on which the subtlety of his critical approach continues to be misunderstood. It is also an issue that lies at the very heart of Strauss's method of interpreting the Gospels, for the presence of miracle stories constitutes one of the criteria by which the existence of myth is to be discerned.[100] It is therefore difficult to overestimate the importance of the question of miracles, which has returned to haunt New Testament studies in our own time. What was Strauss's position on miracles? And was he correct?

The most common objection to Strauss's position is one often made by apologists for traditional theism. Such writers argue that the rejection of miracles by eighteenth- and nineteenth-century critics was a foregone conclusion, since it stemmed from an a priori acceptance of a particular metaphysics.[101] Strauss too, it is said, came to his work already convinced that miracles were impossible. Two quotations, widely removed in time, will give a sense of this position. In 1837 the distinguished Tübingen theologian August Tholuck (1799–1877) published a defense of the reliability of the Gospels in which he said of Strauss:

> Had this latest critic been able to approach the Gospel miracles without prejudice, in the spirit of Augustine's declaration, *dandum est Deo, eum aliquid facere posse quod nos investigare non possumus* ("it has to be granted that God can do something that we cannot investigate"), he would certainly— since in addition to the acumen of the scholar possesses sound common sense—have come to a quite different conclusion in regard to these difficulties. As it is, however, he has approached the Gospels with the conviction that miracles are impossible; and on that assumption, it was certain

[99]Harris in particular (*David Friedrich Strauss*, 248, n.14, and 275) mounts a convincing defense of Strauss's reputation as a biblical critic and religious thinker, but on the matter of miracles I will argue that he, too, misunderstands Strauss's position.

[100]The close connection of the question of miracles with that of myth is also evidence in the introduction to Strauss's *A New Life of Jesus*, 194–95.

[101]I discuss this matter briefly in my introductory chapter, offering examples of this criticism. More examples will be offered in the course of the present discussion.

before the argument began that the evangelists were either deceivers or deceived.[102]

More than 130 years later, a biographer of our own time has written:

> Strauss meant his investigation to be without presuppositions—i.e., he refused to start with the supernatural presuppositions of orthodox theology, but his investigation was, in fact, simply based on the diametrically opposite presupposition—viz., that there was no supernatural activity in the world and independent of the world, apart from the laws of nature. If such a being as personal God actually existed, then he was not free to break into history. That meant there could be no incarnation, no supernatural, divine Christ, no miracles, and no resurrection of the dead.[103]

If this accusation is true, then it greatly weakens Strauss's position. In the pages that follow, however, I will argue that it is only partly justified. For there exist in Strauss's work at least three different types of argument against accepting reports of miracles.[104] However opposed to miracles Strauss may have been on metaphysical grounds, his other arguments are unable to be dismissed so easily.

The Metaphysical Argument

The first type of argument is precisely that which has been seized on by Strauss's opponents. I have described it as the *metaphysical* argument against miracles. It takes its stand on a particular understanding of God and the world, an understanding that either eliminates all talk of divine activity in the world or (more commonly) identifies the activity of God with the regular operation of the natural world. The second option is the more interesting for the student of religions and is most clearly exemplified in the work of Spinoza. For Spinoza—as we have seen—argued that

---

[102]August Tholuck, *Die Glaubwürdigkeit der evangelischen Geschichte, zugleich eine Kritik des Lebens Jesu von Strauss* (1837), cited in Schweitzer, *The Quest of the Historical Jesus,* 94.

[103]Horton Harris's *David Friedrich Strauss,* 43. Harris's otherwise excellent book is marred by his insistence—apparently motivated by a desire to defend traditional Christianity—that Strauss's mythical interpretation is entirely dependent upon such presuppositions. For other examples, see 89, 202, 204, 271 and especially his conclusion on 282–84.

[104]A fourth type of argument against acceptance of reports of miracles may be formulated, which takes its stand on the principle of ontological economy (*entia non sunt multiplicanda praeter necessitatem*: "entities should not be multiplied beyond necessity"), generally attributed to William of Ockham. If an event can be explained naturalistically, that is to say, without positing a supernatural cause, this explanation is to be preferred on the grounds of its simplicity. However, I have been unable to trace any explicit reference to this argument in Strauss's work, and it will not be further discussed here.

since "God" and "Nature" were effectively equivalent, the "laws of Nature" were nothing less than descriptions of the activity of God. To suggest that the regular order of Nature could be interrupted "from outside" (as it were) is simply absurd, for in Spinoza's metaphysics Nature is all there is, "outside" of which nothing can be conceived. Indeed a break in the order of Nature would cast doubt on the very existence of Spinoza's God.[105]

Does Strauss, like Spinoza, hold to a worldview that simply begs the question by excluding miracles from the realm of possibility? His earliest published reflections on these matters are, once again, his introduction to *The Life of Jesus Critically Examined*. When we look at this work, it would appear at first sight that the charge leveled by Strauss's opponents is justified. For Strauss *does* hold to a conception of both God and the world that would exclude the miraculous (in the sense of the production of certain effects by God apart from the regular order of nature). Already in section 13 of his introduction, Strauss writes that "no just notion of the true nature of history is possible, without a perception of the inviolability of the chain of finite causes, and of the impossibility of miracles."[106] Strauss's meaning becomes clearer in section 14, where he spells out what regards as the only defensible understanding of God's relationship to the world. Here he notes that in earlier generations people were much less conscious of the orderly operation of the natural world than we are today. They were therefore inclined to attribute important natural events directly to God. In our time, however, there exists "a conviction, that all things are linked together by a chain of cause and effects, which suffers no interruption."[107] This conviction has become so strong in our own time that it constitutes "a habit of thought,"[108] by which we instinctively (as it were) judge the credibility of narratives of extraordinary events.

Yet there is another side to Strauss's metaphysical argument that his opponents fail to notice. Strauss argues that it is not only our *conception of the world* that has changed since biblical times; the same is true of our *conception of God*. We have either removed divine causation from the world

---

[105]Incidentally, a similar understanding of divine activity seems to lie behind Albert Einstein's famous objection to indeterminacy in physics, namely that God "does not play dice." When asked about his religious convictions, Einstein professed belief in "Spinoza's God, who reveals himself in the orderly harmony of what exists, not in a God who concerns Himself with fates and actions of Human beings" (quoted in *The New York Times*, April 25, 1929, 60, col.4, and cited in Michel Paty, "Einstein and Spinoza" in *Spinoza and the Sciences*, 272).

[106]Strauss, *The Life of Jesus Critically Examined*, §13 (74–75).

[107]Ibid., §14 (78).

[108]Ibid.

or (in the manner of deism) we have restricted it to the original act of creation. At least at this point in his career, Strauss seems keen to distance himself from both these positions. He regards the view that restricts divine activity to the original act of creation as religiously inadequate. If the ancient world was so preoccupied with the idea of God that it overlooked the natural causality of the world, this modern view is so preoccupied by the natural causality of the world that it neglects the role of God. What Strauss calls "modern Supernaturalism" represents (in his mind) a kind of compromise position, whereby God is seen as *normally* acting through the regular order of nature, but *occasionally* directly, by way of miracles. Strauss finds this idea equally unacceptable, for it introduces "a changeableness, and therefore a temporal element,"[109] into the nature of divine activity. Strauss's argument here seems to be the same as that which he would put forward in 1864 in his second major study of the *Life of Jesus.* There he writes that

> the Theist cannot fail to see that a God who now at one time and then at another performs a miracle, consequently at one time exercises a certain kind of activity, at another time lets it rest, would be a Being subject to the conditions of time, and consequently not an absolute one; that, therefore, the action of God is to be understood as being an eternal act, as regards himself, simple and self-consistent, and only appearing on the side of the world as a series of individual, successive, divine operations.[110]

The only consistent way of thinking about divine activity, Strauss argues, is to accept that God does have an immediate relationship to the world as a whole, but that he exercises his influence on each individual part of the world "only by means of his action on every other part, that is to say, by the laws of nature."[111]

What may we conclude? It is true that Strauss was not prepared to concede the possibility of miracles and that his conviction of the impossibility of miracles was metaphysically grounded. Indeed, in the preface to *A New Life of Jesus,* Strauss states his own conviction very boldly: "everything that happens, or ever happened, happened naturally."[112] He insists that this is the presupposition of any truly historical inquiry. However, it is a serious misrepresentation of Strauss's position to argue—as does Horton Harris—that this assumption is derived from a "prior

---

[109]Ibid., §14 (79).
[110]Strauss, *A New Life of Jesus,* 1:198.
[111]Strauss, *The Life of Jesus Critically Examined,* §14 (79).
[112]Strauss, *A New Life of Jesus,* 1:x.

presupposition that there is no transcendent personal God."[113] While it may be true that Strauss's conception of God was always different from that of traditional Christianity, it is very significant that he offers an explicitly *theistic* argument against miracles.[114] Even granted the existence of what he himself calls a "personal God, separate from the world,"[115] one cannot conceive of such a God who sometimes acts in one manner, sometimes in another. It may be possible to give a satisfactory response to this argument, but it is not an accurate or an adequate response to accuse Strauss of denying theism. While his own religious position may not have been theistic, he is more than prepared to engage with theists on their own grounds. As we will see shortly, Strauss was very aware of the danger of tying his argument against miracles to a particular metaphysical position and took pains to ensure that his critical method could not be dismissed on those grounds alone.[116]

The Argument from Probability

While Strauss's acceptance of metaphysical arguments against miracles may be conceded, we must note immediately that his scepticism is more broadly based. In particular, Strauss makes reference to the arguments put forward in the eighteenth century by the Scottish philosopher David Hume (1711–76).[117] I will call this position the "argument *from probability*." Hume offers this argument in section 10 of his *Enquiry Concerning Human Understanding* (1748). To evaluate the charge that Strauss's opposition to miracles is based on nothing more than his own religious presuppositions, we must investigate the extent to which this second argument rests on metaphysical assumptions.

(a) David Hume's Argument

David Hume is far too suspicious of metaphysical claims to talk—as Strauss does—about "known and universal laws that govern the course of events."[118] Indeed Hume carefully avoids any "prescriptive" understanding

---

[113]Harris, *David Friedrich Strauss,* 283; see also 89, 271.

[114]Strauss had already referred to this argument in *Die christliche Glaubenslehre* (§17 [1:228]), in a passage to which we will return.

[115]Strauss, *A New Life of Jesus,* 1:198.

[116]Strauss's opposition to miracles on metaphysical grounds is evident also in *The Life of Jesus Critically Examined,* §16, where he outlines the criteria for distinguishing between history and myth. These criteria are not to be found in the first edition of the book, and merely allude to the arguments we have noted above. For this reason we will not examine them any further.

[117]Cf. Strauss, *A New Life of Jesus,* 1:197–99.

[118]Strauss, *The Life of Jesus Critically Examined,* §16 (88); reprinted in my anthology *The Historical Jesus Quest,* 97.

of the laws of nature. He does this not because he believes that these laws admit of exceptions, but because in his view the laws of nature are merely descriptions of our common experience. We are not in a position to say that such laws "govern" the course of events. Rather, they merely describe our *experience* of the course of events. Indeed, before he comes to discuss miracles, Hume has spent much of the *Enquiry* undermining metaphysical claims. Even so basic a conception as that of cause and effect is nothing more than a description of our experience of the regular association of certain events.[119] In Hume's words,

> when we look about us towards external objects, and consider the operation of causes, we are never able, in a single case, to discover any power or necessary connexion; and quality, which binds the effect to the cause, and renders the one an infallible consequence of the other. We only find, that the one does actually, in fact, follow the other.[120]

Thus the idea of cause is no more than "a customary connexion in the thought or imagination between one object and its usual attendant."[121] In other words, for Hume, we cannot say that the necessity that we perceive in both nature and human affairs is "built into" (as it were) the nature of things, for we have no insight into "the nature of things." It is an *epistemological*, not an ontological necessity: the human mind cannot help but form such associations as the result of continual experience.

This forms the basis of Hume's argument against miracles.[122] His famous principle, that "a wise man . . . proportions his belief to the evidence,"[123] is brought forward to illustrate the difference between what he calls "proof" and judgments of "probability." In what is generally regarded as proof, we have uniform experience of the association of one

---

[119]Cf. David Hume, "An Enquiry Concerning Human Understanding" (1748), in *Enquiries concerning the Human Understanding and Concerning the Principles of Morals,* edited by L. A. Selby-Bigge, 2d edition (Oxford: Clarendon Press, 1902), section 5, part 1, §38 (46) et passim.

[120]Ibid., section 7, part 1, §50 (63).

[121]Ibid., section 7, part 2, §61 (78).

[122]Pace C. S. Lewis (*Miracles* [1947; Glasgow: Collins/Fount, 1974], 106–7), it is not true that Hume's scepticism *undermines* his argument regarding miracles. It implies only that his argument rests on grounds that are epistemological, not metaphysical. According to Lewis, Hume first claims that nature is absolutely uniform and then, on this basis, opposes the possibility of miracles. In reality, however, Hume is merely saying that, although our assumption of the uniformity of nature is based on mere "custom," it is an assumption we cannot help but make, and it must be extended to our judgments about the past as well as the future.

[123]Hume, "An Enquiry concerning Human Understanding," section 10, part 1, §87 (110).

event with another. This uniform experience creates a firm conviction that this association will continue to occur. In judgments of probability, on the other hand, we are influenced by "which side is supported by the greater number of experiments."[124] We must weigh the evidence. Belief based on human testimony is no exception to this rule, for the agreement of testimony to the facts of the case is yet another example of the association of events. In the case of some witnesses (and—as we will see—some types of fact), this agreement may be so constant as to reach, practically, the level of proof. In other cases, it is merely a matter of probability. Common human experience tells us that the agreement is less constant and therefore less reliable when, for example, witnesses "contradict each other; when they are but few, or of a doubtful character; when they have an interest in what they affirm; when they deliver their testimony with hesitation, or on the contrary, with too violent asseverations."[125]

However, the reliability of testimony must also be judged from the side of that to which testimony is given. In other words, the *content* of the testimony will also be important. In particular, the agreement of witnesses with the facts will be felt to be less likely when their testimony "partakes of the extraordinary and the marvellous."[126] The reason for this is simple: where the witnesses testify to a sequence of events that falls *within* our usual experience of the world, we find it easy to believe their testimony. But if the sequence (or association) of events falls *outside of* our usual experience, we are less inclined to believe it. In this case, our customary faith in the reliability of witnesses must be weighed against our natural disinclination to believe such an extraordinary report. Even where we would normally consider a particular witness extremely reliable, when that witness testifies to an event which is—to say the least—unusual, our belief will be weakened to the extent that the event falls outside of our ordinary experience of the world.

Hume is ready to conceive that our ordinary experience of the world is not infallible, but may be limited by (for example) our own geographical and cultural context. This is clear from his example of "the Indian prince, who refused to believe the first relations concerning the nature of frost" because the freezing of water "arose from a state of nature, with which he was unacquainted, and which bore so little analogy to those events, of which he had had constant and uniform experience."[127] Such a person would be right to demand very strong testimony in support of

---

[124]Ibid., section 10, part 1, §87 (111).
[125]Ibid., section 10, part 1, §80 (112–13).
[126]Ibid., section 10, part 1, §89 (113).
[127]Ibid., section 10, part 1, §89 (113–14).

such an idea, but—given very strong testimony—he may eventually give his assent. Yet even in this case, the event narrated is not *contrary* to his experience. In other words, it is not that the Indian prince had had experience of a cold climate and had seen that in these circumstances water did *not* freeze.[128] He had *never experienced* the cold climate and was therefore in no position confidently to predict what might happen in these circumstances. If causality is regarded as the customary association of two events, he had never experienced the first and so had no basis on which to conclude that, given the first, the second would follow. The report of a miracle, however, *is* contrary to our experience, in the sense that we regularly observe the first event and know, from constant experience, that the second does *not* follow. After all, as Hume notes, the character of being contrary to constant experience is of the very essence of a miracle: "nothing is esteemed a miracle, if it ever happen in the common course of nature."[129] Therefore, when faced with a report of a miracle, I should immediately judge "whether it be more probable, that this person should either deceive or be deceived, or that the fact, which he relates, should really have happened."[130] Since (as mentioned above) the argument from constant experience amounts to a proof, a report of an event which contradicts constant experience could only be outweighed by a testimony, the falsehood of which would represent a still greater miracle. In practice, this will never occur. For given the likelihood that witnesses to miracles are either deceiving or being deceived, one cannot conceive that their testimony could ever outweigh the intrinsic improbability of the event.[131]

(b) Strauss's Appropriation of Hume

In *A New Life of Jesus*, Strauss makes it clear that, no matter how much he may accept the metaphysical arguments, his opposition to miracles requires nothing more than Hume's scepticism. Indeed he makes it clear that he does not want his argument against miracles to rest on metaphysical grounds alone. As he writes, every historical investigator will necessarily have "a philosophy," in the sense of a general view of "human and earthly things."[132] However, it would be foolish to base one's argument against miracles on these philosophical grounds alone. For, since

---

[128]Cf. ibid., section 10, part 1, §89, n.1 (114).

[129]Ibid., section 10, part 1, §90 (115).

[130]Ibid., section 10, part 1, §91 (116).

[131]This is the conclusion of part 2 of section 10, of which a detailed account need not be given here.

[132]Strauss, *A New Life of Jesus,* 1:197.

philosophical systems are disputed, such an argument could be easily disregarded by one who held a different philosophy. In Strauss's words, "he who rests his rejection of Miracle on philosophical grounds, destroys his chance of a general recognition of his process."[133] Strauss goes on to argue that all metaphysical systems are in fact opposed to belief in miracles, not only materialism and pantheism, but even (he argues) theism, when theists develop their position consistently.[134] But even apart from these metaphysical considerations, a sceptical and critical philosophy already rules out acceptance of reports of miracles. Here Strauss makes explicit reference to Hume, and writes that "Hume's Essay on Miracles in particular carries with it such general conviction, that the question may be regarded as having been by it virtually settled."[135]

To recapitulate, what is striking about the argument from probability is that its metaphysical commitments are exceedingly thin.[136] For Hume's argument is not an argument that miracles are impossible, or that such events have never occurred (even if most of its exponents believe this).[137] Rather, Hume is trying to demonstrate that, even if it is conceded that miracles *are* possible, we would never be justified in accepting a report of a miracle. Even more cautiously, this argument is attempting to demonstrate that (in Hume's own words) "a miracle can never be proved, *so as to be the foundation of a system of religion.*"[138] This qualification is worth noting. While much of Hume's argument is directed at reports of miracles in general, he is particularly keen to undermine the idea that reports of miracles might be used to support the claims of a particular religion.[139] This was, of course, a common use of the New

---

[133]Ibid.

[134]Cf. ibid., 1:197–98.

[135]Ibid., 1:199; see also Strauss, *Die christliche Glaubenslehre,* §17 (1:244).

[136]In dealing with the question, albeit as an "aside," John P. Meier (*A Marginal Jew: Rethinking the Historical Jesus,* Vol. 2, *Mentor, Message, and Miracles* [New York: Doubleday, 1994], 519) writes that "in varying ways, both Spinoza and Hume . . . reflect the Age of Reason's view of the universe as a closed mechanical system run by precise, eternal, and immutable laws." He cites Spinoza (as one can) in support of this contention, but wisely avoids citing Hume.

[137]Pace, for example, Craig, "The Problem of Miracles," 38. On Hume's own religious convictions at this time when he formulated this discussion, see Anthony Flew in his *Hume's Theory of Belief: A Study of His First Inquiry,* International Library of Philosophy and Scientific Method (London: Routledge & Kegan Paul, 1961), 192.

[138]Hume, "An Enquiry Concerning Human Understanding," section 10, part 2, §99 (127), emphasis mine. This is also Strauss's target in his *Die christliche Glaubenslehre* (cf. §17 [224]), where he names the topic of his discussion as "the teaching on miracles as a means of proving the divinity of Christianity" (*die Lehre von Wundern as Beweismitteln der Göttlichkeit des Christentums*).

[139]Cf. Flew, *Hume's Theory of Belief,* 188–90 et passim.

Testament miracle stories by Christian apologists in his day.[140] In any case, even at its strongest, Hume's argument is an epistemological, not an ontological one. Hume's argument assumes only that our present experience may be projected back into the past and that evidence for the past must be weighed critically in the light of that experience. Because the only assumptions behind this argument are epistemological, the objection often leveled at opponents of miracles—that they have accepted uncritically a particular "worldview"—has no force. Strauss's rejection of miracles may have been influenced by the mechanistic worldview of the modern sciences, but insofar as Strauss follows the lead of David Hume, his rejection of miracles is not metaphysically grounded.[141]

The Argument from Consistency

At one point in *The Life of Jesus Critically Examined,* Strauss explicitly addresses the issue of his presuppositions. In a footnote to section 14 (added in the second and later editions of the work), Strauss writes that his position is "free from presupposition."[142] What does he mean by this phrase? His enquiry, he writes, is free from presuppositions in the same sense that a person occupying a particular state of life might renounce the social privileges customarily associated with that state. The behavior of such a person has only "one presupposition, that of the natural equality of . . . citizens."[143] In the same way, Strauss takes for granted what he calls "the equal amenability to law of all events."[144] What Strauss has renounced, therefore, is the claim that the biblical history must be judged by some special standards that are not applied to events elsewhere.

---

[140]See the examples quoted by Flew (*Hume's Theory of Belief,* 214).

[141]The same point could be made by an examination of the section on miracles in Strauss's dogmatic theology, *Die christliche Glaubenslehre* (§17 [1:237–38]), where he distinguishes metaphysical arguments such as those offered by Spinoza from the historical argument offered by Hume: "To Spinoza's philosophical and exegetical critique of miracles Hume adds an historical. If the Bible-interpreting philosopher [i.e., Spinoza] asked: Can miracles happen, can they be perceived and prove something, and are the biblical stories necessarily to be understood as about miracles?—then the sceptical history-writer [i.e., Hume] posed the question: Can the biblical reports, indeed can any report in the world, make a miracle, a violation of the course of nature, worthy of belief?" (*Dieser philosophischen und exegetischen Wunderkritik des SPINOZA stellte HUME eine historische an die Seite. Hatte der bibelkundige Philosoph gefragt: Können Wunder geschehen, wahrgenommen werden und etwas beweisen, und sind die biblischen Erzählungen nothwendig von Wundern zu verstehen?—so stellte der skeptische Geschichtschreiber die Frage so: Können die biblischen Berichte, ja kann irgend ein Bericht in der Welt, ein Wunder, eine Abweichung vom Naturlaufe, glaublich machen?*).

[142]Strauss, *The Life of Jesus Critically Examined,* §14 (80, n.5).

[143]Ibid.

[144]Ibid.

Implicit in these words is a third major argument against acceptance of reports of miracles. This argument insists that the historian deal consistently with apparently similar reports, no matter what their source. In particular, it insists that the Christian reports of miracles should not be accorded a privileged status, a priori, but must be regarded as having no lesser or greater credibility than reports of miracles stemming from other religious traditions. Scepticism or credulity with regard to one set of miracles should be matched by an equal scepticism or credulity towards the other. More precisely, the same criteria should be applied when assessing the accuracy of such reports. I will describe this argument as the argument *from consistency.*

We find a clear statement of this principle in Strauss's later work on Jesus.[145] Christian faith, he writes, customarily recognizes those miracles associated with the foundation of Christianity, but rejects those of other religions. Orthodox commentators call on the scientific investigator of the New Testament to do the same: to allow that miracles may have occurred, at least at the time of the origins of Christianity. Strauss's response is to note that a scientific attitude cannot be so partisan. It must recognize miracles throughout the course of religious history, or nowhere at all. The concession here is purely hypothetical. For Strauss immediately notes that the critical investigator is *not,* in fact, prepared to concede the possibility of miracles throughout the course of religious history. Yet he goes on to argue that this rejection is not necessarily based on those "dogmatic" philosophical systems that would exclude miracles a priori (such as materialism or pantheism). Rather, it requires only a "sceptical and critical" philosophy such as that of Hume.[146] Once again, this brings us back to the second of our three types of arguments, that from a balance of probabilities. It follows that the third argument is also—in principle—independent of any particular metaphysical claims.

An Evaluation
In concluding this discussion, I would like to offer a few reflections on the strength of Strauss's arguments. Given the importance of the issue, we should not shy away from the question of whether his opposition to miracles was justified. Now Strauss's central argument, that from the balance of probabilities, may be regarded as a development of what Ernst Troeltsch would later describe as the principle of analogy. Long before Troeltsch, Hume had already articulated this principle, in part 2 of section 10 of his *Enquiry.* As he writes, "the maxim, by which we commonly

---

[145]Cf. Strauss, *A New Life of Jesus,* §24 (1:196).
[146]Cf. ibid., §24 (1:197–99).

conduct ourselves in our reasonings, is, that the objects, of which we have no experience, resemble those, of which we have" and "that what we have found to be most usual is always most probable."[147] In other words, the principle of analogy suggests that when reconstructing the past we must do so on the assumption of its similarity to the present. For in deciding between rival historical explanations, both of which may be supported by the documentary or archaeological evidence, the historian must employ some critical principle. There seems no safer principle than the assumption that as things occur now, so they must have occurred then. More precisely, if we have regular experience of a certain conjunction of events in the present, an experience that is apparently without exception, the burden of proof must fall on those who would assert that things were different in the past. Given the uniformity of our experience in the present, that burden of proof is so onerous that we may safely dismiss accounts of miracles in the past.

It is true that on the basis of this argument, at least as formulated by Hume,[148] there *are* circumstances in which a historian may be forced to take reports of miracles seriously. More precisely, there are *historians* who may be forced to do so. I am talking about historians who are already convinced not only that miracles are possible, but that we can observe them today in a regular and predictable way and in circumstances similar to those which prevailed in the past. For such historians, if they exist, no appeal to the principle of analogy could, by itself, settle the question. They would *not* have what the sceptical Hume assumes we *do* have, namely "constant experience" amounting to a proof that miracles do not occur. On the contrary, their experience would suggest that miracles, although by definition unusual, *can* occur. At the most, the principle of analogy would lead to the judgment that miracles are uncommon and therefore unlikely and that reports of miracles must be examined carefully. Not even Hume, it seems, could quibble with this conclusion, even if he were to argue that a belief in contemporary miracles must be mistaken.

While this concession must be granted, in practice it amounts to very little. Firstly, unless the historian who believes in miracles had witnessed such contemporary miracles herself, in circumstances in which she was utterly convinced she could not have been deceived, then Hume's scepticism regarding witnesses would also apply here. Witnesses to contemporary events may be as unreliable in this respect as witnesses to past

[147]Hume, "An Enquiry concerning Human Understanding," section 10, part 2, §93 (117).

[148]For a stricter reformulation of Hume's argument, which rests on a much stronger conception of natural law than that put forward by Hume, see Flew, *Hume's Theory of Belief,* 204–8.

events. Secondly, while a well-founded conviction that miracles occur today would allow for the *possibility* of miracles in the past, Hume could still demand that we assess the reliability of our historical testimony, and that we do so by weighing the balance of probabilities. We must still ask "whether it be more probable, that this person should either deceive or be deceived, or that the fact, which he relates, should really have happened."[149] In the context of religious claims, we may yet conclude, with Hume, that the possibility of deception or deceit is very high. Thirdly, insofar as the historian is writing a work of history and history is understood to be a public discipline, she is presumably intending to convince a public that consists of both believers and nonbelievers. While those who believe they have experience of miracles may be inclined to accept the New Testament reports, their experience does nothing to convince those who are sceptical. This is particularly important if miracles are to be used as evidence for particular religious claims (the resurrection of Jesus being the obvious example).[150] Last, but by no means least, there is the not insignificant problem of how we can *identify* events as miraculous.[151] In other words, how can we be certain that an event is both beyond the productive capacity of nature[152] and that it is performed by God (rather than some other supernatural power)? It is hard to see how this can be done outside of the framework of a particular set of religious beliefs, which tells us what we might expect from the action of God. Yet from the historian's viewpoint, the adoption of a particular religious framework is question-begging. Indeed, it is the willingness to set aside particular Christian claims and to regard the New Testament accounts with the same degree of scepticism as other historical documents which

[149]Hume, "An Enquiry concerning Human Understanding," section 10, part 1, §91 (116).

[150]The position being discussed here is not unlike the argument that, given belief in the Christian God, reports of miracles cannot be discounted, an argument put forward in (for example) William Lane Craig's "The Problem of Miracles: A Historical and Philosophical Perspective," in *Gospel Perspectives,* vol. 6, *The Miracles of Jesus,* edited by David Wenham and Craig Blomberg (Sheffield: JSOT Press, 1986), 31. This argument not only restricts acceptance of miracles to those who already share your religious position; it also abandons the claim made by the Christian apologists of Hume's day, namely, that miracles were a demonstration of the truth of the Christian faith.

[151]Spinoza raised this issue in a letter to Henry Oldenburg (Letter 75, 1675, in Spinoza, *Letters,* 339), to which Strauss makes reference in *Die christliche Glaubenslehre* (§17 [1:231]). Spinoza's argument is that, since we cannot know how far "the force and power" of nature extends, "we may . . . without presumption explain miracles through natural causes as far as possible," while suspending judgment regarding those events of whose causes we are still ignorant. Strauss also alludes to this argument against miracles in *The Life of Jesus Critically Examined,* §146 (766), where he again cites Spinoza.

[152]William Lane Craig's definition of a miracle (cf. "The Problem of Miracles," 29).

characterizes the rise of historical criticism. It is difficult to see how one can accept the New Testament accounts of miracles without abandoning that critical project in favor of a partial and tendentious use of one's sources. On these grounds alone Strauss was surely right to claim that miracles are "never recognised by historical investigation, in so far as it is allowed to follow its own laws."[153]

Finally, in defense of Strauss it should be noted that throughout his *Life of Jesus Critically Examined* he does not dismiss reports of miracles before a careful examination of the evidence. However much he may have been predisposed towards a sceptical conclusion, his procedure is essentially that of the historian. He does not, in practice, dismiss miracles a priori, but rather systematically undermines the credibility of the evangelical accounts, whether interpreted supernaturally or rationalistically, by showing their inconsistencies and implausibility. When showing their implausibility, he relies on nothing more than a tacit acceptance of arguments from analogy, as any historian would. As we have shown, such arguments do not necessarily depend on particular metaphysical claims; they ask only that the historian weigh the evidence. Only at the end of this process does Strauss offer his own, mythical interpretation, as a way of resolving these exegetical difficulties. One may choose to weigh the evidence differently, but that is a choice that would need to be defended on historical grounds. To say, as so many of his critics do, that Strauss merely takes for granted the impossibility of miracles and therefore refuses to take the Gospel miracle stories seriously is to overlook his 1400 pages of closely reasoned exegesis. There is much more that could be said about Strauss's attitude to miracles, and I will return to the topic when reflecting on Strauss's legacy.

4. The Significance of History

The "Speculative Christology"

As we have seen, the early Strauss seemed confident that, even after this process of criticism, the life of Jesus could be made to yield a religious meaning. In the final sections of *The Life of Jesus Critically Examined* Strauss outlines his positive doctrine. In a dramatic passage he remarks on the destructive consequences of his criticism for faith:

> The results of this inquiry which we have brought to a close, have apparently annihilated the greatest and most valuable part of that which the Christian has been wont to believe concerning his Saviour Jesus, have

---

[153]Strauss, *A New Life of Jesus,* §24 (1:196).

uprooted all the animating motives which he has gathered from his faith, and withered all his consolations. The boundless store of truth and life which for eighteen centuries has been the aliment of humanity, seems irretrievably dissipated; the most sublime levelled with the dust, God divested of his grace, man of his dignity, and the tie between heaven and earth broken.[154]

However content Strauss may be personally with this outcome, he does not want to leave the matter there. He certainly does not feel obliged to defend traditional Christianity on dogmatic grounds. Yet Strauss argues that *even as a critic* he is faced with the task of reestablishing doctrinally that which has been demolished critically. Why? Because the nineteenth century has arrived at a more positive attitude towards religion, which can now be seen to embody certain fundamental truths.[155] In any case, the task of criticism itself would be incomplete without extending that criticism to the doctrines of the church.[156] Only at the end of this process could Christian theology be regarded as what Strauss calls a "thoroughly tested and constituted science."[157] What, then *is* Strauss's doctrine of Christ? What remains after his criticism? Strauss sets forth his own position only after interacting with the views of others. It would therefore seem appropriate to summarize that interaction before examining his views.

Strauss begins by outlining the Christology of historic, orthodox Christianity and summarizing the objections to it raised by the theologians of his time, particularly Schleiermacher. In particular, he argues against the doctrine of the Council of Chalcedon (451 C.E.), that there exist two natures in Jesus, the divine and the human. This doctrine, Strauss argues, suffers from the fatal theological defect of placing divinity and humanity under one category. Worse still, the category under which it brings the two together—that of "nature"—is entirely inappropriate when applied to God, since it implies a limited being, which can be defined by reference to what it excludes. In any case, it is not at all clear how these two natures "could have but one centre," namely the "one person" of Chalcedonian faith.[158] For these reasons (and others) the traditional doctrine is no longer acceptable.

Strauss next looks at the doctrine of Christ offered by the rationalists, who regard Jesus as simply "the greatest man that ever trod the earth—a

---

[154]Strauss, *Critically Examined,* §144 (757).
[155]Cf. ibid., §144 (757–58).
[156]Cf. ibid., §144 (758).
[157]Ibid.
[158]Cf. ibid., §146 (765).

hero, in whose fate Providence is in the highest degree glorified."[159] For these thinkers, the greatness of Jesus lies in his religious teachings, namely, the fact that he taught an exalted ethical religion and lived a life that embodied those ideals. This rationalist doctrine may at first sight seem an attractive one, for it seems to offer a new way of attributing religious significance to Jesus. But Strauss argues that this rationalist position is theologically inadequate; it does not do justice to the historic Christian faith, which looks to the *person* of Jesus, not merely to his teachings. It thus fails to fulfill the requirements of a *Glaubenslehre* (doctrine of faith), which must accurately represent as well as reinterpret the faith of the church. In Strauss's own words, "a Christ who is only a distinguished man, creates indeed no difficulty for the understanding, but is not the Christ in whom the Church believes."[160]

Strauss passes on to an examination of what he called "the eclectic Christology of [Friedrich] Schleiermacher" (1768–1834).[161] Schleiermacher begins, Strauss writes, not with the developed doctrine of either the Bible or Christian tradition, but with the experience of contemporary believers. In particular, he focuses on the Christian experience of the forgiveness of sin and the imparting of holiness. This forgiveness and sanctification—Schleiermacher argues—cannot be attributed to the influence of one's fellow believers, who are equally sinners. Rather, it can only be attributed to an influence from outside, namely "a strengthening of our consciousness of God," so that the whole of our activities become directed by this "religious sentiment."[162] The source of this godly influence is the example of Christ; his ability to exercise this influence means that he must have possessed this consciousness of God in an absolute manner. In this sense Jesus can be seen as "the actualization of the ideal of humanity, which his church can only approach, never surpass."[163]

Strauss notes the power and attractiveness of Schleiermacher's position, before suggesting that it, too, is open to attack from the point of view of both history and theology. From the side of history, there is the difficulty of believing that the religious ideal of humanity could be fully manifested in a single, limited, historically conditioned human individual. This Christology involves, in effect, a readmission of the miraculous at this one point: to explain the origin of Jesus. For it would require a miracle for one man to transcend the limitations of history. From the side of theology, Schleiermacher's view of the resurrection is inadequate.

[159]Ibid., §147 (767).
[160]Ibid., §147 (768).
[161]Ibid., §148 (768).
[162]Ibid., §148 (769).
[163]Ibid., §148 (770).

For he relegates the resurrection and ascension of Jesus to the status of what we today might call "optional extras": for Schleiermacher these are not part of the core of Christian faith. Yet Christians have always understood the resurrection of Jesus to be "the foundation stone, without which the Christian church could not have been built."[164] As Strauss asks rhetorically, what *is* the Christian year without Easter?

The last position examined by Strauss is that which he calls "Christology reinterpreted symbolically."[165] This position, exemplified by Immanuel Kant (1724–1804), effectively abandons the attempt to reconcile eternal truths with historical facts. It regards the facts of history as no more than *symbols* of a religious truth. In particular, it holds that, while the moral ideal by which human beings are bound to live may be exemplified in a particular individual, that ideal can be known *independently* of this exemplification. This view, Strauss argues, is also inadequate. Religiously, it offers us only a collection of "empty ideas and ideals," ideals that replace the consolation of the gospel with an overwhelming sense of moral obligation.[166] There is no message of reconciliation in such a reinterpretation of Christianity. From the point of view of philosophy, there is also something empty about the notion of a religious idea "to which no reality corresponds."[167] If the infinite can be said to exist at all, it exists only through being manifested in finite realities. As Strauss writes, "the infinite has its existence in the alternate production and extinction of the finite; . . . the idea is realized only in the entire series of its manifestations."[168]

This last objection is already couched in language reminiscent of the philosophy of G. W. F. Hegel (1770–1831), and this allusion to Hegel brings the reader to what Strauss calls "the speculative Christology."[169] This Christology begins with Hegel's insight into the nature of God, or—as he preferred to say—"absolute spirit."[170] Hegel realized that God cannot be understood shut up (as it were) in his own infinity. Such a God is a mere ideal that has no reality. God as absolute spirit becomes real only when expressed in the finite world. In particular, Hegel's God arrives at self-consciousness only in the minds of human beings. As Strauss writes,

[164]Ibid., §148 (772).
[165]Ibid., §149 (773).
[166]Cf. ibid., §149 (776).
[167]Ibid., §149 (777).
[168]Ibid.
[169]Ibid., §150 (777); *The Historical Jesus Quest,* 104.
[170]To be borne in mind is the range of meanings possessed by the German word *Geist,* which can be translated as either "spirit" or "mind."

the true and real existence of spirit, therefore, is neither in God by himself, nor in man by himself, but in the God-man; neither in the infinite
alone, nor in the finite alone, but in the interchange of impartation and
withdrawal between the two, which on the part of God is revelation, on
the part of man religion.[171]

This philosophical insight is made known to human beings in religion,
"since religion is the form in which the truth presents itself to the popular mind."[172] It appears most clearly in the story of a particular human
being who is both human and divine, who unites in himself the infinite
and the finite. Hegel's philosophical teaching, in other words, finds its
most powerful symbolic expression in the Christian doctrine of the
incarnation. The story of the life, death, and resurrection of Jesus represents symbolically the fact that the infinite spirit enters into the lowest
depths of the finite world so as to bring that world to an awareness of its
identity with God.

It is important to note that, while this truth is *symbolized* in the story
of one, historic individual, the union of God and humanity cannot be
said to have really *occurred* in this one individual.[173] Such an idea would
be subject to the same objections as may be leveled at the traditional
Christology of the church. However, the rejection of the idea that God
and humanity were actually united in one historical individual does not
leave us with only Kant's empty ideal. God, the absolute spirit, *does* attain
reality by entering into this finite world, but he does so, not in one individual, but in the history of the human race. The union of the divine and
the human that the church attributes to Christ is nonsensical when
applied to a particular individual, but it makes complete sense when
applied to the race as a whole.[174] This is the new meaning that can be
given to the doctrine of Christ.

I do not need to address the question of the relationship of Strauss's
Christology to the religious thought of Hegel himself. All I wish to
underline here is the significance that Strauss's reinterpretation attributes
to history. Kant's position, Strauss had argued, effectively divorced eternal
truth and historical fact. At first sight, it is true, Strauss's Hegelian rein-

---

[171]Strauss, *The Life of Jesus Critically Examined,* §150 (777); *The Historical Jesus Quest,*
105.
[172]Strauss, *The Life of Jesus Critically Examined,* §150 (778); *The Historical Jesus Quest,*
105.
[173]Cf. Strauss, *The Life of Jesus Critically Examined,* §151 (779–81); *The Historical Jesus
Quest,* 107–11.
[174]Cf. Strauss, *The Life of Jesus Critically Examined,* §151 (780); *The Historical Jesus
Quest,* 109.

terpretation of the figure of Jesus might seem to do the same. For Strauss also attributes nothing more than a symbolic significance to the story of Jesus' life, death and resurrection. He has little interest in these events as *individual* historical facts, which remain nothing more than "a starting point for the mind."[175] On the other hand, what is symbolized by these facts is not simply a moral ideal; it is the meaning of human history *as a whole*. The individual facts may have little religious significance, but history as a whole certainly does, since for Hegel history is the realm in which the absolute Spirit (or God) comes to expression and achieves self-consciousness. Indeed, even if we cease to believe in the historical accuracy of the story of Jesus, this eternal truth remains unchanged. The religious value of the story of Jesus lies in what it represents. What it represents is the whole course of human history, in which the infinite but unconscious Spirit descends into the materiality of the world and then moves onwards and upwards into consciousness and personality in the minds of human beings. In this way, the Hegelian interpretation of Jesus reunites faith and history, but on a new and higher level.

The appropriation of Hegel's thought enabled Strauss to argue that his work was not merely destructive. It enabled him to suggest that he could restore the doctrines his criticism had destroyed. Strauss's reformulated Christology is scarcely the *traditional* Christian doctrine, but it *is* a way of giving new meaning to the old terms. As Strauss writes in a passage to which I have already alluded,

> the author is aware that the essence of the Christian faith is perfectly independent of his criticism. The supernatural birth of Christ, his miracles, his resurrection and ascension, remain eternal truths, whatever doubts may be cast on their reality as historical facts. The certainty of this can alone give calmness and dignity to our criticism, and distinguish it from the naturalistic criticism of the last century, the purpose of which was, with the historical fact, to subvert also the religious truth, and which thus necessarily became frivolous.[176]

The problem here is that everything depends on Hegel's reinterpretation of history. What happens if that interpretation can no longer be maintained? This is the problem with which Strauss was faced in his later works.

Strauss's Later Position

We might begin our discussion of Strauss's later thought by noting another feature of his "speculative Christology," namely, its teleological

[175]Ibid.
[176]Strauss, *The Life of Jesus Critically Examined,* preface (lii).

view of history. It is true that Hegel's thought gave rise to quite different interpretations.[177] But even in the "left-wing" form in which it is appropriated by Strauss, it implies that human history is, in a certain sense, preprogrammed: it has an immanent purpose. History is not a blind process, but one whose outcome is predetermined, as it were, by the very structure of reality. (This aspect of Hegel's thought seems to have persisted even in the ruthless materialism of Karl Marx, which would have such tragic consequences in the twentieth century.) Yet very soon after the publication of *The Life of Jesus,* Strauss abandons his belief in a Hegelian expression of Christianity. In Hegel's terms, he abandons the attempt to reconcile the religious *Vorstellung* (imaginative conception) with the philosophical *Begriff* (concept). As he writes in a letter of 1839 to his friend Christian Märklin,

> I now no longer hold to that Hegelian standpoint and would no longer care to speak of the virgin conception of Christ, his resurrection etc. as eternal truths. . . . And in this respect I stand by my opinion . . . that our cooperating with and giving philosophical support to the Christian dogmas is vain affectation, that no simple religious feeling that we have clothes itself naturally in a Christian form any more—indeed, that all the religious feelings may flee away from us rather than allow themselves to be forced into the old stinking cage of ecclesiastical doctrine—however nicely decorated it may be outwardly.[178]

The speed of this abandonment need not surprise us, since there is something forced and arbitrary about Strauss's attempt to reinterpret Christian doctrines speculatively. Strauss is much better as a critic than as a constructive thinker: his revised Christology seemed doomed to have a short life. What is perhaps more surprising is the fact that Strauss would soon distance himself, not just from the idea that Christian doctrines can be reinterpreted in Hegelian terms, but from Hegel's philosophy itself. In other words, he appears to have become alienated not just from the *Vorstellung* but also from the *Begriff.*[179] It may be that the later Strauss was

---

[177]Cf. Strauss, *The Old Faith and the New,* §37 (137–38).

[178]Cited in Harris, *David Friedrich Strauss,* 136.

[179]Cf. Harris, *David Friedrich Strauss,* 201. Frederick Gregory (*Nature Lost? Natural Science and the German Theological Traditions of the Nineteenth Century* [Cambridge, Mass.: Harvard University Press, 1992], 81) argues that Strauss continued to be influenced by Hegel throughout his career. In some respects this may be true, but it seems clear that the later Strauss had abandoned Hegel's idealist interpretation of history. Indeed, in *The Old Faith and the New* (§37 [137–38]) he seems to distance himself altogether from Hegel's philosophy.

influenced by the work of Ludwig Feuerbach (1804–72). He certainly makes reference to Feuerbach in discussing the idea of God.[180] But whatever the reason, by the time of *The Old Faith and the New* (1872), Strauss seems unable or unwilling to interpret history in these speculative terms. In Schweitzer's words, in this last work "the Hegelian system of thought, which served as a firm basis for the work of 1840, has fallen in ruins."[181]

This shift has enormous consequences. For the great advantage of Hegel's thought is that it offered a way of attributing religious significance to history. It may be that the *particular events* of the history of Jesus had little significance, but human history *as a whole* could be interpreted theologically. This idea enabled the theologian to reconcile what G. E. Lessing (1729–81) had called the eternal truths of reason with the accidental truths of history. For Hegel's philosophy enabled one to see these accidental truths as expressions of the eternal. It argued that history was nothing other than the unfolding of a divine rationality. The abandonment of Hegelian thought meant a return to a perspective much closer to that of Spinoza. For as we have seen, Spinoza had little interest in the historical figure of Jesus, looking instead to the eternal divine wisdom of which Jesus' life was an expression.[182] It is interesting to note that Strauss mentions Spinoza's attitude to history in both his early and his later work. In his earlier work he attributes Spinoza's attitude to Kant, from whose Christology he is wishing to distance himself.[183] In his later work he embraces Spinoza's position as his own,[184] citing Lessing's remark with approval in the same context.[185] It seems that for Strauss there is no longer any way of reconciling eternal truths with contingent historical facts. History no longer has a religious meaning.

For an interpretation of human history, Strauss now turns to the work of Charles Darwin. Yet Darwin's work offers little hope of anything resembling a religious interpretation of the past, and Strauss is well aware of this fact. One appreciates what Harris is attempting to say when he praises Strauss as "the first theologian to champion the evolutionary theory."[186] But it would be more accurate to say that Strauss is one of the first thinkers to appreciate how destructive of traditional religious attitudes Darwin's theory actually is. Indeed Strauss remarks that

---

[180]Cf. Strauss, *The Old Faith and the New*, §39 (153–55).
[181]Schweitzer, *The Quest of the Historical Jesus*, 71.
[182]Spinoza, Letter 73, in *The Letters*, 333.
[183]Strauss, *The Life of Jesus Critically Examined*, §149 (773).
[184]Strauss, *A New Life of Jesus*, §100 (2:435).
[185]Ibid., §99 (2:430).
[186]Harris, *David Friedrich Strauss*, 248.

conservative Christians are, by their own rights, perfectly correct to oppose it:

> That the orthodox, the believers in Revelation and in miracles, should brandish their repugnance and its accompanying weapon, ridicule, against Darwin's theory, is perfectly intelligible. They know what they are about, and have good reason, and right also, in combatting to the uttermost a principle inimical to them.[187]

Strauss champions Darwin, first of all, as the one who finally rids the world of miracles. Before Darwin, the attacks on miracles by philosophers and critical theologians were powerless. For they could offer no *natural* explanation of the order of the world to replace the theologian's appeal to divine action. Darwin's great achievement was to offer an entirely naturalistic explanation of the apparently miraculous structure and adaptation of living organisms. In this way he has finally succeeded in "casting out miracles, never to return."[188] Still more seriously for religion, Strauss sees Darwin's work as the last, fatal blow struck against teleological explanations of the world and of history.[189] To understand the origins and development of life, there is no need to posit some overarching or even immanent intelligence. For evolution by natural selection can produce beings that *appear* to be designed by a process that is mechanical and blind. The religious implications of this view are serious indeed, and Strauss was right to highlight them.

Once both the traditional Christian view of history and its Hegelian reinterpretation have been abandoned, what role is left for the historical figure of Jesus? At times Strauss seems to suggest that we can continue to be inspired by Jesus' exemplary moral teaching, for in this respect he remains one of the great figures of human history.[190] Yet Strauss also recognizes that appeal to Jesus' ethical teaching is not enough; it cannot undergird the role he has normally played in Christian faith. First of all, there is little in Jesus' ethics that is unique. He was not the only moral

---

[187]Strauss, *The Old Faith and the New,* §50 (203).

[188]Ibid., §50 (205); cf. ibid., §59 (230).

[189]Cf. ibid., §63–64 (245–52).

[190]See, for example, Strauss, *A New Life of Jesus,* §100 (2:437) and the other passages discussed in the first section of this chapter. The conclusion of Strauss's 1865 work on Schleiermacher (*The Christ of Faith and the Jesus of History,* 159–69) also suggests that some religious role remains for the figure of Jesus. But that role is limited to an appropriation of the ethical ideal which has traditionally been associated with Jesus. In *The Old Faith and the New* Strauss effectively abandons even this position.

teacher to inculcate ideals of gentleness and humility.[191] The same holds true of all the other Christian precepts: as Strauss writes, Christianity "neither introduced them into the world, nor will they disappear from the world along with it."[192] Secondly, a theology based on Jesus' ethical teaching would suffer from the same defects as does the Christology of the rationalists (which it would closely resemble).[193] It, too, would fail to be a *Glaubenslehre* (doctrine of faith), since it would bear little resemblance to historic Christianity. Thirdly and perhaps most significantly, Strauss is deeply aware of the problem that would later be raised—from a very different perspective—by Martin Kähler and the dialectical theologians. Religious devotion can hardly be directed towards a historical figure whose life we can reconstruct only with probability and at the cost of great scholarly efforts. In Strauss's words,

> a being of which I can only catch fitful glimpses, which remains obscure to me in essential respects, may, it is true, interest me as a problem for scientific investigation, but it must remain ineffectual as regards practical influence on my life. . . . the Jesus of history, of science, is only a problem; but a problem cannot be an object of worship, or a pattern by which to shape our lives.[194]

Or as he writes at the end of *A New Life of Jesus,*

> that the happiness of mankind is to depend upon belief in things of which it is in part certain that they did not take place, in part uncertain whether they did take place, and only to the smallest extent beyond doubt that they took place—that the happiness of mankind is to depend upon belief in such things as these is so absurd that the assertion of the principle does not, at the present day, require any further contradiction.[195]

Kähler and the dialectical theologians would agree with Strauss at this point, but would offer a very different response, reaffirming the traditional Christian faith and (in some cases) asserting its independence of historical inquiry. But Strauss regards such a faith as impossible, once its historical foundations have been cast into doubt. We will return to these matters shortly.

Left with no way of attributing any positive meaning to the Christian doctrines, Strauss does not hesitate to draw the obvious conclusion. In answer to the question as to whether we are still Christians, Strauss writes:

[191]Cf. Strauss, *The Old Faith and the New,* §30 (95).
[192]Ibid., §30 (98).
[193]Cf. Strauss, *The Life of Jesus Critically Examined,* §147 (767–68), as discussed above.
[194]Strauss, *The Old Faith and the New,* §28 (90).
[195]Strauss, *A New Life of Jesus,* §99 (2:434).

Our answer to the question with which we have headed this section of our account? Shall I still give a distinct statement, and place the sum-total of the foregoing in round numbers under the account? Most unnecessary, I should say; but I would not, on any consideration, appear to shirk even the most unpalatable word. My conviction, therefore, is, if we would not evade difficulties or put forced constructions upon them, if we would have our yea yea, and our nay nay,—in short, if we would speak as honest, upright men, we must acknowledge that we are no longer Christians.[196]

There is a sense, Strauss argues, in which those who accept the new knowledge of our time and draw the necessary conclusions *can* be said to be "religious." However, if they have a religious feeling, that feeling is directed no longer towards a personal God, but towards "the Cosmos" as a whole, on which we feel ourselves dependent and whose order and apparently infinite productivity we can admire.[197]

Strauss feels that these conclusions are inescapable. For this reason, his most trenchant criticism is reserved not for his orthodox critics but for the liberal theologians who accept so much of this new knowledge and yet refuse to face up to its implications. For example, with regard to the doctrine of creation, Strauss notes the incompatibility of the new sciences with the assertions of the author of Genesis 1. In the face of the new discoveries, he insists, those who truly hold to the old faith will *not* try to effect some compromise. On the contrary, they will stand firm on their belief in the inerrancy of the Bible, to the defiance of reason. "He . . . who is seriously convinced of the old Christian belief, ought . . . to say: 'A fig for science; thus it stands in the Bible, and the Bible is the word of God.'"[198] Strauss insists that one cannot have *both* the old faith, in some suitably modified form, *and* the new knowledge. Nor is Strauss impressed with the argument that we should continue to profess the traditional faith because we *need* it for the support that it gives to morality.[199] The problem here is that an alleged need for religion cannot bring about faith, and "we cannot make a prop of our action out of a faith which we no longer possess."[200] While the early Strauss was still grappling with the question of whether a biblical critic could continue to exercise the Christian ministry,[201] by the time of *The Old Faith and the New* he has become convinced that this is utterly impossible. Indeed one of Strauss's

---

[196]Strauss, *The Old Faith and the New,* §31 (107).
[197]Cf. ibid., §41 (161–64).
[198]Strauss, *The Old Faith and the New,* §6 (19).
[199]Ibid., §31 (98–99).
[200]Ibid.
[201]Cf. Strauss, *The Life of Jesus Critically Examined,* §152 (171–74).

most trenchant passages is his depiction of how a minister trained in the new criticism might preach on the feasts of Christmas, the Epiphany, Easter, and the Ascension, when he no longer believed in the historical events to which these feasts refer. More seriously, Strauss writes, how could such a minister justify praying to Jesus "as a mere man? for as such he regards Christ."[202] How could he continue to administer the sacraments? Even in our own day, it must be said, these questions have lost none of their force.

5. The Legacy of Strauss

"Myth" and the Principle of Analogy

According to Karl Barth, it was Strauss who clearly posed the question of whether historical research could deal adequately with the figure of Jesus.[203] There is much truth in this judgment, although it might be more accurate to say that Strauss posed the question of whether Christian faith could survive the results of historical research. But this is by no means Strauss's only contribution to modern religious thought, for his concept of "myth" is also of ongoing significance. Strauss's use of this category highlights the importance of what Ernst Troeltsch would call the principle of analogy. As we will see when examining Troeltsch's work, this principle states that the historian must rely on her knowledge of the present in order to reconstruct the past. Strauss invokes this principle when he judges as mythical any biblical account that contravenes the "known and universal laws which govern the course of events."[204] It is our knowledge of these laws in the present that enables us to make judgments about the past.

One can quibble with Strauss's *use* of this principle. The theologian Wolfhart Pannenberg, for example, has argued that what he calls a "negative analogy" is not a sufficient basis for historical judgments.[205] In

[202]Strauss, *The Old Faith and the New,* §31 (102).

[203]Karl Barth, *Protestant Theology in the Nineteenth Century: Its Background and History* (1952), translated by Brian Cozens and John Bowden (London: SCM, 1972), 541–68. While one can accept this particular comment, Barth's essay is an unreliable guide to Strauss's work. As Harris notes (*David Friedrich Strauss,* 248, n.14), "Barth's unsympathetic attitude towards Strauss is marked in many places by his failure to present Strauss's views truly, and a tendency to dismiss him all too lightly." For further criticisms, see Harris, ibid., 211 (note), 275.

[204]Strauss, *The Life of Jesus Critically Examined,* §16 (88); *The Historical Jesus Quest,* 97.

[205]A closer examination of Pannenberg's attitude to analogy will be found at the end of chapter 4 (on the work of Ernst Troeltsch), as well as in chapter 7, where Pannenberg's work will be studied more closely.

other words, the nonoccurrence of an event in the present may not *in itself* be sufficient reason for assuming that it could not have occurred in the past. Yet, as we will see in chapter 7, even Pannenberg admits the value of "positive analogies,"[206] a category that comes very close to Strauss's category of "myth." Positive analogies would consist of stories elsewhere that resemble those found in the Gospels, containing material we would normally judge to be factually unreliable. If such positive analogies exist, it is reasonable to assume that a similar process was at work in early Christianity. If we doubt the factual content of these stories when found *outside* the Bible, we can scarcely withhold doubt when they are found *within*. As Van Harvey wrote (once again on the issue of miracles),

> the [historian's] skepticism regarding miracles is not based merely on the conviction that they are incompatible with known laws. It is, rather, that the very existence of miracle stories has come to be regarded as a normal and expected occurrence. The contemporary historian expects to find miracle stories in certain kinds of literature, which is to say he has more reason for being puzzled when he does not find such stories than when he does. Not only is he aware of the fallibility of human testimony but also of the tendency of the human mind to create myths and legends, especially in the realm of the religious. Indeed, if anything has been learned from the comparative study of religion it is that myth and legend are the almost natural forms of expression for the veneration of extraordinary founders, teachers, and saints of religion.[207]

It is true that Strauss fails to make a distinction between negative and positive uses of analogy. But on at least some occasions he does seem to be using myth in the latter sense. This is certainly the case when he discusses the relationship of Christianity to other religions.[208] On these occasions he does not dismiss the Gospel stories simply because the events they describe are without analogy. He applies the same judgment to them that he would apply to similar tales in other religious traditions. His fundamental insight here concerns the creative power of the reli-

---

[206]Wolfhart Pannenberg, "Redemptive Event and History" (1959), translated by Shirley C. Guthrie Jr. and George H. Kehm, in *Basic Questions in Theology,* The Library of Philosophy and Theology (London: SCM, 1970), 1:49.

[207]Van A. Harvey, *The Historian and the Believer: The Morality of Historical Knowledge and Christian Belief* (1966; Urbana, Ill.: University of Illinois Press, 1996), 88. In Hume's terms, the prevalence of legend and myth in religious records *decreases* the probability of a reliable report of a miracle by *increasing* the probability that the witnesses "deceive or are deceived."

[208]Cf. Strauss, *The Life of Jesus Critically Examined,* §13 (69).

gious imagination. His category of "myth" reminds us that the religious imagination works in similar ways across religious traditions. This represents an important and enduring insight.

Strauss's Religious Position

I might conclude with some comments on Strauss's contribution to the central question of this book, namely, the question of religious authority. We might begin with his achievements. His greatest achievement was to identify in the clearest possible terms the key issues facing Christian faith. As Horton Harris writes,

> Strauss's *Life of Jesus* was the most intellectually reasoned attack which has ever been mounted against Christianity. . . . Strauss confronted theology with an either/or: either show that the Christian faith is historically and intellectually credible, or admit that it is based on myth and delusion. That was the alternative. Nothing less was and is at stake than the whole historical and intellectual basis of Christianity. If Strauss cannot be convincingly answered, then it would appear that Christianity must slowly but surely collapse.[209]

Harris believes that the challenge *can* be met by rejecting Strauss's metaphysical presuppositions. But our discussion of miracles has shown that the problems cannot be so easily resolved. The problems facing religious authority are, of course, heightened by the thoroughgoing naturalism of Darwin's work.[210] Strauss was surely correct to highlight this fact; in this respect, too, he was well ahead of his time. The challenge of Darwinism is much deeper than that of the reconciliation of evolutionary theory with the opening chapters of Genesis. For Darwin's work offers a view of the world that makes all talk of purposeful action simply redundant. This in turn offers a theological challenge that is rarely faced. In this respect, too, Strauss was surely right to point out how flimsy is the halfway house in which many theologians dwell.

On the other hand, a couple of criticisms are not out of place. Firstly, Strauss is a little too quick to assume that our world can easily survive its loss of faith. His rather glib approach to the serious issues involved can make his final work appear a little superficial. Shortly after the publication of *The Old Faith and the New*, the book was savagely reviewed by the philosopher Friedrich Nietzsche (1844–1900).[211] The dying Strauss

---

[209]Harris, *David Friedrich Strauss*, 282.

[210]Cf. Gillespie, *Charles Darwin and the Problem of Creation*, 1–18 et passim.

[211]Friedrich Nietzsche, "David Strauss, the Confessor and the Writer" (1873), in *Untimely Meditations*, translated by R. J. Hollingdale, Cambridge Texts in the History of Philosophy (Cambridge: Cambridge University Press, 1997), 1–55.

does not seem to have been particularly disturbed by this attack. Perhaps he realized that Nietzsche's views may have been due to envy of Strauss's popularity.[212] Yet there is some justice in Nietzsche's criticisms. To say that Strauss courageously faced up to his own loss of faith is true, but he is not beyond taking refuge in religious attitudes that, on his own grounds, can no longer be sustained. As Nietzsche writes, Strauss is certainly less cowardly than his contemporaries, which makes him a leader, but "there are very definite limits to his courage."[213] He pays little attention, for example, to the question of how one can account for—let alone advocate—the qualities of "compassion, love and self-abnegation" in a world shaped by the savage struggle for existence.[214] Does Darwin's view of the world not rather encourage what Nietzsche calls "the war of all against all and the privileges of the strong"?[215] Similarly, there is something deeply ambivalent about the cosmos toward which Strauss wishes us to maintain a religious attitude.[216] As Nietzsche writes, Strauss dares not tell his readers honestly: "I have liberated you from a helpful and merciful God, the universe is only a rigid machine, take care you are not mangled in its wheels!"[217] It may be unfair to accuse Strauss—as Nietzsche does—of being a "cultural philistine."[218] But one can surely ask if literature and music are enough to fill the gap left in the heart of Western culture by the death of God.[219]

Secondly, in his discussions of "the old faith," Strauss seems determined to put the worst possible construction on the doctrines of the early and medieval church. Indeed, in his disparagement of that faith he sometimes approaches the lack of seriousness for which he criticized his eighteenth-century predecessors.[220] The Christian doctrine of the atonement, for instance, deserves better than to be dismissed as "a perfect jumble of the crudest conceptions."[221] Similarly, even a sympathetic non-Christian might see more in the doctrine of the Eucharist than a "repulsive oriental metaphor of drinking the blood and eating the body

---

[212]Cf. Harris, *David Friedrich Strauss*, 254–55.
[213]Nietzsche, "David Strauss, the Confessor, and the Writer," §8 (39).
[214]Ibid., §7 (30).
[215]Ibid.
[216]Cf. ibid., §7 (31).
[217]Ibid., §7 (33).
[218]Ibid., §§2, 3 (7, 14), et passim.
[219]Cf. Strauss, *The Old Faith and the New*, §84 (343).
[220]Cf. Strauss, *The Life of Jesus Critically Examined*, lii.
[221]Strauss, *The Old Faith and the New*, §11 (31). In fairness to Strauss, a brief but more reasoned discussion is to be found in *The Life of Jesus Critically Examined*, §146 (764–67), as noted above.

of a man."[222] Such flippancy on doctrinal matters compares badly with the carefully argued case found in Strauss's exegetical works. It may be true that, at the end of the day, "the old faith" can no longer be defended. But the accused has the right to be more fairly represented before a final judgment is passed.

---

[222]Strauss, *The Old Faith and the New*, §31 (105).

Chapter Three

The Challenge of Apocalyptic

Albert Schweitzer (1875–1965)

> *It is of the highest importance to know*
> *whether we are not duped by morality.*
> Emmanuel Levinas

From David Friedrich Strauss, a great figure of the nineteenth century, we pass to Albert Schweitzer, whose work helped to shape the New Testament scholarship of the twentieth. Schweitzer's significance for our story lies in the fact that he was among the first to put forward what he himself called a "consistently eschatological" view of the life of Jesus. According to this view, Jesus' ministry was profoundly shaped by the apocalyptic beliefs of late second-Temple Judaism. In particular, his message and work were determined by his expectation that the end of history (the *eschaton*) was about to arrive, when God would establish his kingdom. Schweitzer can be described as "among the first" to adopt this position, because his eschatological portrait of Jesus was not entirely new. In the nineteenth century Johannes Weiss (1863–1914) had already sketched its outlines in a small but influential treatise entitled *Jesus' Proclamation of the Kingdom of God* (1892).[1] Yet it was Schweitzer who popularized this view of Jesus and was responsible for its dominance in New Testament studies, at least until very recent times.

Schweitzer's apocalyptic interpretation of Jesus is found in two works. The first, published in 1901 and entitled *The Secret of the Messiahship and Passion—A Sketch of the Life of Jesus,*[2] was translated into English as *The Mystery of the Kingdom of God.* The second, the much better-known work of 1906 entitled *From Reimarus to Wrede: A History of the Life of Jesus Research,*[3] was translated into English under the much more memorable title *The Quest of the Historical Jesus.* We will be looking closely at these two

---

[1]Johannes Weiss, *Jesus' Proclamation of the Kingdom of God,* translated by Richard H. Hiers and David L. Holland, Lives of Jesus Series (Philadelphia: Fortress Press, 1971).

[2]*Das Messianitäts-und Leidensgeheimnis. Eine Skizze des Lebens Jesu.*

[3]*Von Reimarus zu Wrede: Eine Geschichte der Leben-Jesu-Forschung.*

works in the pages that follow. I will also have reason to make reference
to a third work, unfinished at the time of Schweitzer's death, entitled
Reich Gottes und Christentum (The Kingdom of God and Christianity)
and translated into English as *The Kingdom of God and Primitive Christianity*.
It would be shortsighted to discuss Schweitzer's exegetical works in isolation. For alongside these studies Schweitzer produced a number of other
works dealing with broadly religious themes. These works are less well
known among students of the New Testament, presumably because they
are not works of biblical interpretation nor even (in any strict sense) works
of Christian theology. Yet they are important if we are to understand, not
just Schweitzer's historical conclusions, but what he believed to be their
implications for Christian faith. Of particular significance are the first two
volumes of Schweitzer's projected, but never completed, four-volume
series entitled *The Philosophy of Civilization* (German *Kulturphilosophie*).
Volume 1 is entitled *The Decay and Restoration of Civilization*. Volume 2 is
entitled *Kultur und Ethik,* which was translated as *Civilization and Ethics*.
Both works were published in 1923. A slightly more developed presentation of Schweitzer's thought is to be found in a work that came out some
twelve years later. This later book was originally entitled *The World-View of
Indian Thought*,[4] but it was translated into English as *Indian Thought and Its
Development*. In all of these works, Schweitzer's historical and exegetical
studies are taken up and incorporated into his broader philosophy. The
second part of this chapter will be devoted to an analysis of these books
and of their relationship to Schweitzer's work on the historical Jesus.[5]

1. The Apocalyptic Jesus

The Mystery of the Kingdom of God

The best place to begin examining Schweitzer's picture of Jesus is not
with his most famous work, *The Quest of the Historical Jesus,* but with his
earlier study *The Mystery of the Kingdom of God*. For *The Quest of the Historical Jesus* merely rehearses the arguments found in that earlier work,
but it was so popular that it continues to overshadow Schweitzer's other
achievements, and *The Mystery of the Kingdom of God* is unjustly neglected.[6] We may begin, then, by asking: What portrait of Jesus does
Schweitzer paint in this early work?

[4]*Die Weltanschauung der indischen Denken.*
[5]The present discussion will not examine Schweitzer's two books on the apostle
Paul. While these form an important contribution to New Testament studies, they touch
on questions of religious authority only in passing.
[6]James Brabazon, *Albert Schweitzer: A Biography* (New York: G. P. Putnam's Sons,
1975), 122–23.

Schweitzer begins the book by opposing what he calls the "modern-historical" representation of the life of Jesus. Exponents of this view argued that Jesus' mission was that of "the realisation of the Kingdom of God."[7] In other words, through his words and actions Jesus was to make that kingdom a reality. What was "the kingdom of God"? It was, such scholars argued, a new and internalized morality grounded in faith in God as a loving Father. For a start Jesus proclaimed this message in Galilee and gathered around him a community that strove to live by these teachings. This represented an initial period of success in Jesus' ministry. However, Jesus' inward ethic and detachment from the legal traditions of Judaism soon brought about the opposition of the Jewish leaders. In the face of this opposition, Jesus retired for a while to the northern parts of Palestine, before deciding that the conflict must be brought to a head by his journey to Jerusalem. Jesus foresaw that this might mean his death. However, he regarded such a death as the highest act of his messianic vocation, embodying in a dramatic way the moral ideals of the Kingdom, as an example to others.[8]

Schweitzer regards practically every aspect of this depiction as mistaken. He argues that there is no evidence in the Gospels of an early, successful period of ministry that is followed by one of conflict and failure. If anything, the order is reversed.[9] Nor does Jesus regard the kingdom of God as a community that attempts to live by his moral teaching. Indeed the Gospels clearly distinguish between the ethical behavior Jesus commands *right now,* and the advent of God's kingdom, which will occur only *in the future.* The ethical behavior that Jesus encourages does not *constitute* the kingdom of God. Rather, it is the way one must live in preparation for its advent. Jesus' ethical teaching is therefore an "*interim ethics,*" which has its force, Schweitzer writes, "*in expectation of the Kingdom of God.*"[10] Finally, Jesus does not regard his death as merely exemplary, the highest moral act of one who is already the Messiah. Rather, he regards his death as the means by which God will bring about the coming of the Messiah and therefore the arrival of the messianic kingdom.[11] Schweitzer notes that while the traditional Christian interpretation of the death of Jesus is no longer credible, it was correct in at least one respect. For it held that the death of Jesus brought about a new state of affairs. Jesus, too, believed that his death would bring about a new state

[7]Albert Schweitzer, *The Mystery of the Kingdom of God: The Secret of Jesus' Messiahship and Passion,* translated by Walter Lowrie (London: A. & C. Black, 1925), 61.
[8]Cf. ibid., 61–64.
[9]Cf. ibid., 64–69.
[10]Ibid., 76 (emphasis original).
[11]Cf. ibid., 73–80.

of affairs. That new state of affairs was the inauguration by God of his kingdom on earth. For "the coming of the Kingdom of God with power is dependent upon the atonement which Jesus performs."[12]

Schweitzer develops these points in the rest of the book, arguing throughout that the key to understanding the figure of Jesus is what he calls "eschatology." What does Schweitzer mean by this term? In both *The Mystery of the Kingdom of God* and *The Quest of the Historical Jesus* Schweitzer offers no extended explanation; he takes for granted that the reader is familiar with the Jewish expectations Jesus inherited. However, in his unfinished work *The Kingdom of God and Primitive Christianity,* Schweitzer offers a fuller discussion of the apocalyptic worldview that formed the context of Jesus' life and death.

Schweitzer insists that we must not assume that Jesus somehow "spiritualized" the expectations of Judaism. This is the error underlying what Schweitzer had earlier called the "modern-historical" view.[13] Echoing an argument already found in the work of Reimarus,[14] Schweitzer notes that there is no indication in the Gospels that Jesus was attempting to transform the views he inherited.[15] While it is true that Jesus is not interested in offering a *description* of the kingdom of God, it is clear that his understanding of that kingdom corresponds to that of his contemporaries. In particular, Jesus' eschatology resembles that of the books of Daniel and *Enoch*.[16] He believes that the Son of Man or Messiah is a "supernatural being," who will appear "on the clouds of heaven, surrounded by his angels, when the time for the Kingdom has come."[17] When that time arrives, the dead will be raised to life,[18] and those who inherit the kingdom will enjoy eternal life, along with the righteous of every generation and every nation. However, there must first be a universal judgment, not just of human beings, but also of the fallen angels, and this judgment is entrusted to the Son of Man.[19] It is this set of beliefs that governs not only Jesus' teaching but also his actions.

Jesus' teaching, however, is complex. In particular, Schweitzer writes, the combination of eschatological and ethical elements in that teaching

[12]Ibid., 83.
[13]Cf. Albert Schweitzer, *The Kingdom of God and Primitive Christianity* (1967), translated by L. A. Garrard (London: A. & C. Black, 1968), 89–90.
[14]Cf. Reimarus: Fragments, §30 (126–29).
[15]Cf. Schweitzer, *The Kingdom of God and Primitive Christianity,* 90.
[16]Cf. ibid., 92. For Schweitzer's description of Enoch's eschatology, see *The Kingdom of God and Primitive Christianity,* 44–50.
[17]Schweitzer, *The Kingdom of God and Primitive Christianity,* 91.
[18]Cf. Schweitzer, *The Mystery of the Kingdom of God,* 204.
[19]Cf. Schweitzer, *The Kingdom of God and Primitive Christianity,* 92.

poses a problem for historical research. Many scholars are tempted to eliminate the eschatology, but this is impossible, for "the eschatological sayings belong precisely to the best attested passages."[20] As already noted, Schweitzer insists we should not try to spiritualize the eschatology, which Jesus must have intended his hearers to take quite realistically. There is a compromise position, which holds that Jesus' teaching began as purely ethical and only later became eschatological. But this, too, seems unlikely. For it would represent not so much a development of Jesus' thought as its transformation, and there is no evidence of any event in the ministry of Jesus that would precipitate such a change.[21] The solution is to accept that Jesus' teaching is eschatological from beginning to end. It is shaped in all its aspects by the expectation of the coming kingdom of God. If we begin with Jesus' ethics, we can see no coherence in his teaching. But if we begin with his eschatology, we see that even his ethics was shaped by his eschatological view of the world.[22]

What, then, was "the secret" (or "mystery" [*Geheimnis*]) of the Kingdom of God? Schweitzer examines the parables to see what light they may shed on this issue. Of particular interest are those parables in which Jesus suggests that the advent of the kingdom can be compared to the processes of nature. Jesus' intention here is to indicate that his ministry, which appears to be only a tiny seed, is to be followed by events that are incalculably greater. For the establishment of the kingdom is not our work but God's work.[23] Later in the ministry of Jesus, Schweitzer argues, a new dimension of this secret emerges. This is the connection between repentance and the kingdom. By repentance and moral renewal human beings can, as it were, force the hand of God and compel the advent of his kingdom. This is the meaning of the mysterious saying about "men of violence" in Mark 11:12–14.[24] We will return to this idea shortly, when discussing the relationship of eschatology and ethics. In the last period of Jesus' life, the secret takes on a third dimension, highlighted by the German title of Schweitzer's book: it is the "the secret of the Messiahship and Passion."[25]

The new issue raised here is that of Jesus' messianic identity. Schweitzer argues that since Jesus proclaimed a future kingdom of God,

---

[20]Schweitzer, *The Mystery of the Kingdom of God,* 84; reprinted in my anthology *The Historical Jesus Quest,* 188.

[21]Cf. Schweitzer, *The Mystery of the Kingdom of God,* 86–87; *The Historical Jesus Quest,* 188–89.

[22]Cf. Schweitzer, *The Mystery of the Kingdom of God,* 92–93; *The Historical Jesus Quest,* 191–92.

[23]Cf. Schweitzer, *The Mystery of the Kingdom of God,* 106–10.

[24]Cf. ibid., 110–12.

[25]*Das Messianitäts-und Leidensgeheimnis.*

there was nothing in his proclamation that would lead people to suspect that he was the Messiah. Indeed Jesus himself customarily speaks of the Messiah in the third person and as a character of the future.[26] On the mountain of the transfiguration and at Caesarea Philippi he revealed to his disciples the secret of his messianic identity.[27] But that identity referred to a future state:[28] Jesus was the figure who *would come* in glory as the Son of Man. The people as a whole would never have expected this: they regarded Jesus as no more than Elijah (the Forerunner), the one who was to return before the inauguration of the messianic era. But what about Jesus' miracles? Would the crowds not have seen these as a sign of his messianic identity? Not at all, Schweitzer argues. They would have seen the miracles as evidence that Jesus was the Forerunner prophesied by Malachi (Mal. 3:23–24).[29] For the Messiah was expected to come not with miracles alone but with power and in glory, to inaugurate God's reign.

Jesus, however, knew what the crowds did not. He knew not only of his own future identity; he also knew that it was John the Baptist who was the Forerunner (cf. Mark 9:12–13; 11:14).[30] These facts constitute the secret that Jesus had to reveal to the disciples. It was so much a secret that even John the Baptist was not aware of it. His question about the "one who is to come" (Matt. 11:2–6) is not, as we normally understand it, a reference to the Messiah. There would be no doubt about the identity of the Messiah when he came in glory![31] It aims to establish whether Jesus is the Forerunner. Jesus' indirect answer is a way of avoiding the revelation of his future Messiahship, for he wished to reveal this only to his disciples. If John the Baptist suspected that Jesus might be the Forerunner, it is clear that he did not think of himself in that role. Rather he regarded himself as merely a prophet of repentance.[32] While John took Jesus' miracles as a sign that he was the Forerunner (cf. Mark 6:14; 8:28), Jesus knew that they had a deeper meaning. In particular, the casting out of demons was a first step in the overcoming of the power of Satan. These actions, too, would hasten the arrival of the kingdom of God.

When Jesus sends out the twelve disciples, he does so in the expectation

[26]Cf. Schweitzer, *The Mystery of the Kingdom of God,* 135–36. Schweitzer argues (199) that all references to "the Son of Man" that do not reflect the (future) apocalyptic figure of Daniel are unhistorical, having been added by Christian tradition.

[27]Cf. Schweitzer, *The Mystery of the Kingdom of God,* 127–28, 181–82.

[28]Cf. ibid., 185–90.

[29]Cf. ibid., 138–41.

[30]Cf. ibid., 147.

[31]Cf. ibid., 162.

[32]Cf. ibid., 147–56.

that the kingdom of God would shortly arrive in power (cf. Matt. 10:23). However, it does not appear as expected.[33] At this point Jesus comes to realize that he had misunderstood one aspect of the divine plan. Like his contemporaries, Jesus had expected the advent of the kingdom of God to be preceded by a period of general affliction (or trial: πειρασμός). It was this against which he had warned the disciples before sending them out: they were to expect suffering and to be prepared for it. (We misunderstand these warnings if we think of them as directed to the period after Jesus' death. Jesus expected this time of affliction not in some distant future, but immediately.[34]) Yet it also lay in God's power to shorten or even eliminate this period of trial, and it was this for which Jesus encouraged his disciples to pray.[35] When John the Baptist is executed and when the kingdom of God fails to appear, Jesus comes to a new understanding of the divine plan. He realizes that God has chosen him to bear the affliction *in his own person.* The others were to be spared: Jesus was to give his life as a ransom for many, in the way foretold by the prophet Isaiah.[36] As the one destined to be the Messiah, Jesus must suffer; it is this fact which he reveals to the disciples at Caesarea Philippi and against which Peter protests (Mark 8:31–33). The secret of Jesus' Messiahship is also the secret of his suffering. It is this belief that took Jesus to his death. The "betrayal" of Jesus by Judas was not the relatively insignificant matter of letting the authorities know where Jesus might be arrested. Rather, it was the betrayal of the secret of the Messiahship. Judas passed on to the authorities what Jesus had revealed to his disciples: that he was the one who was about to come in glory as "the Son of Man." It was through Judas that the high priest came to know of this secret. During the trial the high priest used this information to ask Jesus if he was indeed the Messiah, in order to elicit an admission that could be used to put him to death.[37]

The Quest of the Historical Jesus
Essentially the same view is to be found in the later chapters of Schweitzer's better-known work, *The Quest of the Historical Jesus,*[38]

---

[33]Cf. ibid., 261–64; *The Historical Jesus Quest,* 197–99.

[34]Cf. Schweitzer, *The Mystery of the Kingdom of God,* 219–20.

[35]Cf. ibid., 228–29.

[36]Cf. ibid., 232, 236–38.

[37]Cf. ibid., 214–18.

[38]The best-known English edition is the 1910 translation of the first German edition by W. Montgomery. However, there has recently been published a revised translation, based on the text of the second German edition, by John Bowden, incorporating the work of J. R. Coates and Susan Cupitt. I will be making reference to this translation, except as otherwise noted.

where he compares and contrasts his position with that of William
Wrede (1859–1906). He begins with the observation that the work of
both authors spells the death of the "modern historical" view of Jesus, so
widely utilized by the theologians of his day.[39] He goes on to note the
agreements between his view and that put forward by Wrede. Both
authors agree that there exist contradictions and inconsistencies in the
narrative of Mark's Gospel. Both agree that these are due to the juxtapo-
sition of two very different representations of Jesus, one natural and the
other supernatural. They also agree that the supernatural element in the
Gospel story has to do with the secret of Jesus' Messiahship.[40] However,
on the issue of the secret Wrede and Schweitzer part company. For here,
Schweitzer writes, there are two possibilities. The tension between the
natural and the supernatural elements in the story may be traced back
either to the figure of Jesus himself or to the creative work of the evangelist and the tradition that preceded him.[41] Schweitzer takes the first
path, while Wrede takes the second.

For Wrede the supernatural element in the Gospel story is the representation of Jesus as Messiah during the days of his ministry. Wrede traces
this representation back to the early Christian tradition. He suggests, at
least, that Jesus himself never made such a claim.[42] Wrede argues that the
earliest Christian tradition was that Jesus became Messiah only *after* his
resurrection. The idea that he was already Messiah during his public
ministry was a later development. The Gospel of Mark represents a transitional stage: it suggests that Jesus *was* already the Messiah during the
time of his public ministry, but that he tried to keep it a secret. In fact,
Wrede believes, this was merely a fiction that served to reconcile the
early belief with the later. After outlining this position, Schweitzer argues
against it, claiming that it leaves too many important aspects of the
Gospel without explanation. Firstly, if Mark had intended to represent
Jesus' Messiahship as a carefully kept secret, why would he suggest that
Jesus was condemned to death for his messianic claims?[43] There is an
inconsistency here that tells against Wrede's theory. More seriously,
Wrede's theory demands that the idea of the messianic secret be traced
not just to Mark but to the tradition which preceded him. But
Schweitzer argues that there is no reason why such a development would
have occurred so early. Why would the early Christians have wanted to
date back the Messiahship to the time of Jesus' public ministry? The

[39]Cf. Schweitzer, *The Quest of the Historical Jesus* (1913), 296–302.
[40]Cf. ibid., 301–2.
[41]Cf. ibid., 302.
[42]Cf. ibid., 303–5.
[43]Cf. ibid., 307–8.

apostle Paul, for instance, is quite indifferent to Jesus' earthly life, as are the speeches in Acts.[44] Still more seriously, if Jesus had *not* claimed to be the Messiah, what would have led his disciples to this conclusion? Wrede believes that it was the resurrection that produced the conviction that Jesus was the Messiah. But Schweitzer argues that the resurrection appearances would not, in themselves, have offered sufficient reason for such an extraordinary claim.[45] Finally, Schweitzer argues that Wrede places undue emphasis on the question of Jesus' identity, neglecting the much wider and more significant question of *Jesus' Proclamation of the Kingdom of God,* which can only be understood eschatologically.[46]

Schweitzer's alternative view is that—once again—the supernatural element in Jesus' teaching may be traced back to Jesus himself. It may be traced back to the apocalyptic worldview that shaped not just his teaching (as Johannes Weiss had pointed out) but the whole course of his public ministry.[47] Schweitzer's discussion here follows the same lines as I have already traced in discussing *The Mystery of the Kingdom of God.* The major difference is that in *The Quest of the Historical Jesus* Schweitzer emphasizes the "predestinarian" dimension of Jesus' teaching. While Jesus encourages people to live by a special "interim ethic" in preparation for God's kingdom, he is also convinced that it is *only those whom God has chosen* who will be saved.[48] Schweitzer admits that there is a certain tension between these two ideas but insists that the predestinarian idea is the dominant one. As he writes, for Jesus "the kingdom cannot be 'earned'; one is called to it and shows oneself to be called to it."[49] Appearances are generally a good guide as to who will be counted among the elect. (When Jesus proclaims that the poor, the meek, and the peacemakers to be blessed, he is not so much encouraging these attitudes as simply stating a fact. It is these whom God has chosen.) Yet appearances can be deceptive, for the final choice is in the hands of God. (Even the rich young man of Mark 10:17–27 may be among the elect, despite his unpromising response. In suggesting this possibility, Schweitzer argues, Jesus is not talking about the young man's possible "conversion," but about the fact that he may be among God's chosen ones.)

As in the earlier book, Schweitzer argues that the mystery of the kingdom of God is revealed in Jesus' parables. More precisely, Jesus reveals the mystery in a veiled way, so that it will be understood by "those who have

---

[44]Cf. ibid., 308.
[45] Cf. ibid., 309.
[46]Cf. ibid., 311–13.
[47]Cf. ibid., 315.
[48]Cf. ibid., 322–23.
[49]Ibid., 324.

ears to hear," that is to say, by God's elect. Of particular importance are those parables that depict the sowing of seed. Out of the tiny seed, which is the movement of repentance begun by John the Baptist and continued by Jesus, the kingdom of God is to come. But it will come by God's power, in a way that is entirely miraculous. Indeed, Jesus expected that the approaching harvest would be the last: "when the reapers are sent into the fields, the Lord in heaven will cause his harvest to be reaped by the holy angels."[50] He himself would be caught up into heaven before being revealed to the world as the promised Son of Man.[51] The disciples will not have completed their round of the towns of Israel before these great events occur (cf. Matt. 10:23). The great discourse of Matthew 10 speaks of the sufferings that will occur before that time, as well as of the expected supernatural revelation and empowerment of the elect. The view that this discourse is a mere "composite structure" is to be rejected. What would induce the evangelist to come up with what Schweitzer calls "the curious idea of making Jesus speak entirely of inopportune and unpractical matters, and of then going on to provide the evidence that they never happened"?[52] Rather, this extraordinary speech is to be regarded as historical *precisely because* by our modern standards it seems implausible.[53] The point is, of course, that Jesus did not think as we do. His standards of plausibility were not ours, caught up as he was in the belief that the ordinary course of history is to be brought to an end by the intervention of God. This "supernatural" expectation shapes his work.

The turning point in Jesus' ministry comes when this expectation of an immediate inauguration of God's kingdom is not fulfilled.[54] This causes him to withdraw for a time from public proclamation.[55] Jesus now comes to realize that the time of affliction, which was expected before the inauguration of God's kingdom, is to be concentrated on himself alone.[56] He is to go up to Jerusalem and die; this event would inaugurate the end of the age. His death is to be an atonement for the "many" predestined ones who await the manifestation of God's glory.[57] By dying for them, he can spare them the ordeal of undergoing the messianic affliction. For this reason Jesus goes up to Jerusalem, to bring about the circumstances that would result in his death. Right up to the end the

[50]Ibid., 325.
[51]Cf. ibid., 332.
[52] Ibid., 331.
[53]Cf. ibid., 330.
[54]Cf. ibid., 327–28.
[55]Cf. ibid., 331.
[56]Cf. ibid., 347.
[57]Cf. ibid., 348.

public know nothing of Jesus' messianic identity. If they hail him as a great figure, it is as the expected figure of Elijah, the Forerunner.[58] Because of this, the Jewish authorities, although informed of Jesus' claim by Judas, have trouble convicting him. They are unable to find the necessary witnesses. However, when the high priest puts the question explicitly, Jesus admits his identity and his condemnation is assured.[59]

The reader will recognize that Schweitzer's depiction of Jesus in *The Quest of the Historical Jesus* is essentially the same as that found in *The Mystery of the Kingdom of God*. Its special quality, as we have seen, lies in its emphasis on "predestinarian" teaching and in the fact that in the later book Schweitzer contrasts his "consistent eschatology" with the scepticism of Wrede. This disagreement between Wrede and Schweitzer remains a significant one. For these authors continue to represent the two different ways in which the Gospels may be regarded. Wrede looks at the Gospels with suspicion. He is convinced that the development of the Jesus traditions that occur *after* the writing of the Gospel of Mark had already begun to occur even *before* that Gospel was produced. It follows that not even Mark's Gospel can be taken at face value.[60] Schweitzer, on the other hand, is inclined to trust at least the basic outline of the Synoptic accounts. He argues that however inconsistent and contradictory they seem by our standards, they make perfect sense when viewed in the light of the extraordinary apocalyptic expectations of Jesus' time. Nothing that we would regard as a "natural explanation" can be given for the sequence of events found in the Gospel narrative. But this is not because it is unhistorical; it is because Jesus' behavior was governed by supernatural expectations, in the light of which normal behavior was no longer possible. Wrede is quick to attribute the shape of the Gospels to the theological creativity of the earliest Christians. But Schweitzer insists that the life of Jesus, too, was shaped by very definite theological ideas. As he writes, "[in Wrede's interpretation] the evangelist is supposed to have been compelled by 'community theology' to represent Jesus as thinking dogmatically and actively 'making history': if the poor evangelist can make him do it on paper, why should not Jesus have been quite capable of doing it himself?"[61]

2. Apocalyptic and Ethics

There is one aspect of Schweitzer's depiction of Jesus that I have left aside until now, for it is so central to Schweitzer's religious thought that

---

[58]Cf. ibid., 352–53.

[59]Cf. ibid., 353.

[60]Cf. William Wrede, *The Messianic Secret* (1901), translated by J. C. G. Greig, Library of Theological Translations (London: James Clarke & Co., 1971), 2.

[61]Cf. Schweitzer, *The Quest of the Historical Jesus* (1913), 315.

it merits separate treatment. This is the question of the relationship of Jesus' apocalyptic worldview to his ethical teaching.

An Interim Ethic

The first aspect of Schweitzer's discussion is one we have already encountered. It is the idea that Jesus' ethic is as an "interim ethic," an ethic of preparation for the kingdom of God. Strictly speaking, there is no ethics *of* the kingdom. When the kingdom of God is established, the conditions that make ethical instruction necessary will be abolished. In Jesus' view, Schweitzer writes,

> there is no place for a morality of the Kingdom of God or for a develop-
> ment of the Kingdom—it lies beyond the borders of good and evil; it will
> be brought about by a cosmic catastrophe through which evil is to be
> completely overcome. Hence all moral criteria are to be abolished. *The
> Kingdom of God is super-moral.*[62]

Schweitzer notes that our modern ethical consciousness sees ethics as unconditional and self-sufficient: ethical behaviour is an end in itself. But this view can be traced back to the influence of Greek thought on Christianity; it is foreign to Jesus' world. Jesus' ethical proclamation is conditional, in the sense that it is intimately related to the expected eschatological events. As Schweitzer writes, Jesus' ethic "stands in indis-soluble connection with the expectation of a state of perfection which is to be supernaturally brought about."[63]

This "indissoluble connection" with eschatology explains the strange mixture of life-affirmation and apparent life-negation in Jesus' ethical teaching. ("World-" and "life-affirmation" are key terms in Schweitzer's developed philosophy of civilization and we shall return to them shortly.) Jesus' ethic is an ethic of world- and life-affirmation because Jesus shares with the Old Testament prophets a belief in the fundamental goodness of God's creation.[64] Yet it is also an ethic of world- and life-negation, insofar as this present world order fades into insignificance in the face of the coming kingdom. In the light of this expectation of the kingdom, Jesus' ethical proclamation focuses on what Schweitzer calls "the attainment of inner perfection."[65] In other words, his ethics has nothing to do with altering the state of the world, but rather seeks to alter the state of the human heart in preparation for the coming events.

---

[62]Schweitzer, *The Mystery of the Kingdom of God,* 101–2; see also Schweitzer, *The Quest of the Historical Jesus* (1913), 332–33.

[63]Schweitzer, *The Mystery of the Kingdom of God,* 100.

[64]Cf. Schweitzer, *The Kingdom of God and Primitive Christianity,* 100.

[65]Ibid., 98.

This explains the radical nature of Jesus' ethics, the complete absence of considerations of prudence or practicality. He does not need to worry, for example, about whether "the command not to resist evil" might threaten the very basis of society.[66] The present world order is about to pass away, and there is no need to be concerned about its continuation. Rather, those who hear the proclamation of the kingdom of God must ensure that their hearts are purified so that they may show themselves worthy of being among God's elect.

Hastening the Kingdom

While Jesus shows no interest in the creation of a better world by human activity, it does not follow that human beings are entirely passive. It is true that the kingdom of God is precisely that, *God's* kingdom, and no amount of human activity can bring it about. Yet Schweitzer also argues that in Jesus' teaching human beings do have a role to play. Their repentance is not merely a matter of preparing themselves for the coming kingdom (although it is certainly that). It is also a force that may contribute to bringing the great day closer. In this respect Jesus shared the expectation of the Old Testament prophets. He, too, believed that righteous behavior will contribute to bringing about the intervention of God in Israel's history.[67] Yet he recast that belief in terms derived from the apocalyptic thought characteristic of the books of Daniel and *Enoch*.[68] As Schweitzer writes, for Jesus "repentance and moral renewal in prospect of the Kingdom of God are like a pressure which is exerted in order to compel its appearance."[69]

Suffering can play the same role as repentance; indeed, within Jesus' worldview the two are intimately linked. The coming of the kingdom requires not only repentance, but also the period of affliction that must precede the coming of the Son of Man. As Schweitzer writes, "the Affliction . . . represents in its extremest form the repentance requisite for the Kingdom."[70] It is for this reason that Jesus could see his own death as hastening the coming of the kingdom, for he came to believe that God had chosen to lay on him alone the burden of the messianic affliction. In *The Mystery of the Kingdom of God*, Schweitzer suggests that Jesus understands his death as an atonement for human guilt.[71] His suffering would not merely take the place of the affliction; it would hasten the arrival of

---

[66]Ibid., 99.
[67]Cf. Schweitzer, *The Mystery of the Kingdom of God*, 113.
[68]Cf. ibid., 114–15.
[69]Ibid., 112.
[70]Ibid., 229.
[71]Cf. ibid., 234–35.

God's kingdom by removing guilt. In his later work *The Kingdom of God and Primitive Christianity,* Schweitzer expresses some reservations about this idea. "Historical research must reckon with the possibility," he writes, that Jesus did *not* regard his death as an atonement for sins.[72] In this case, Jesus' death would hasten the coming of the kingdom of God by simply *taking the place of* the messianic affliction.[73] In any case, by both repentance and suffering, human beings can contribute to the process by which the kingdom of God would be established in power.

The Separability of Worldview and Ethics

While Schweitzer argues that in Jesus' teaching there was an "indissoluble connection" between ethics and eschatology, he also suggests that in later Christian history the two became separated. It is not clear at what point Schweitzer believes this separation occurred. In *The Philosophy of Civilization* Schweitzer suggests that it was the modern world, from the time of the Renaissance onward, that transformed Christianity from a world-denying to a world-affirming religion.[74] However, in *The Kingdom of God and Primitive Christianity* Schweitzer attributes the first stages of this transformation to the apostle Paul. Paul suggests that in a provisional way the kingdom has already come, and that its presence is expressed in ethical behavior: it consists of "righteousness and peace and joy in the Holy Spirit" (Rom. 14:17).[75] Schweitzer's earlier work even suggests that Jesus himself was—unwittingly—responsible for this transformation. When his apocalyptic expectations were not fulfilled, his followers were forced to reinterpret the message he preached. As Schweitzer writes, "with his death [Jesus] destroyed the form of his 'Weltanschauung' [worldview], rendering his own eschatology impossible."[76]

The Significance of History

This understanding of Jesus' teaching has radical implications. If Jesus' apocalyptic worldview—which shaped the whole of his teaching—must now be abandoned, then we can have little interest in Jesus as a figure of his time. Having discovered the historical Jesus, we are forced to go

---

[72]Schweitzer, *The Kingdom of God and Primitive Christianity,* 128.

[73]Cf. ibid., 123.

[74]Cf. Albert Schweitzer, *Civilization and Ethics,* The Philosophy of Civilization 2, translated by C. T. Campion (1923), 3d English edition, revised by Mrs. Charles E. B. Russell (London: A. & C. Black, 1946), 63.

[75]Cf. Schweitzer, *The Kingdom of God and Primitive Christianity,* 168.

[76]Schweitzer, *The Mystery of the Kingdom of God,* 251 (cf. 247–48).

beyond him.[77] This suggestion becomes very clear in the conclusion to *The Quest of the Historical Jesus,* where Schweitzer notes that the historical figure of Jesus can no longer serve as the foundation of a contemporary theology. Schweitzer couples this conclusion with a deep scepticism about the religious value of historical research: history, he argues, is unable to create a spiritual force for our own age.[78]

This scepticism is one side of Schweitzer's thought. Yet he cannot simply abandon the figure of Jesus. Schweitzer remains enough of a Christian and a theologian to believe that the figure of Jesus can still be of significance for our time. But how? One option presents itself immediately: the historian could simply distinguish between those elements in Jesus' teaching that are of abiding significance and those that are strictly relative to his age. We may no longer be able to appropriate the entirety of Jesus' teaching, but perhaps elements of his teaching could form the basis of a Christian theology. It is interesting to note that in the first edition of *The Quest of the Historical Jesus,* Schweitzer rejects the option outright. He argues that if we focus only on those elements in Jesus' teaching that seem to be of abiding significance, we will only destroy them by ripping them out of the context within which they originally made sense. In Schweitzer's words,

> it is not given to history to disengage that which is abiding and eternal in the being of Jesus from the historical forms in which it worked itself out, and to introduce it into our world as a living influence. . . . As a water-plant is beautiful so long as it is growing in the water, but once torn from its roots, withers and becomes unrecognisable, so it is with the historical Jesus when He is wrenched loose from the soil of eschatology, and the attempt is made to conceive Him 'historically' as a Being not subject to temporal conditions.[79]

Yet in the second edition Schweitzer retreats from this scepticism. At the very moment in which he insists that the historical Jesus can no longer be the foundation of a modern theology, he argues that an alternative foundation can be found. In one sense this alternative foundation is historical, but in another sense it is not dependent on historical knowledge.

---

[77]Cf. Erich Gräßer, *Albert Schweitzer als Theologe,* Beiträge zur historischen Theologie 60 (Tübingen: J. C. B. Mohr [Paul Siebeck], 1979), 244: "Schweitzer wishes to get to know the historical Jesus, so as to become free of him" (*Schweitzer will den historischen Jesus kennenlernen, um von ihm frei zu werden*).

[78]Cf. Schweitzer, *The Quest of the Historical Jesus* (1913), 479.

[79]Albert Schweitzer, *The Quest of the Historical Jesus,* 1st Edition (1906), translated by W. Montgomery (1910; London: SCM, 1981), 399.

What Schweitzer calls the fact of "the mighty spiritual force" that flows from Jesus "can neither be shaken nor confirmed by any historical discovery."[80]

What is this new "foundation" of Christianity? It has, Schweitzer writes, something to do with Jesus' personality, which "despite all that is strange and enigmatic in it, has great significance for us."[81] To grasp what is of abiding significance about the figure of Jesus requires no scholarly training. Nor does it require us to construct a "life of Jesus." What is of significance is precisely the eschatological *concern* in Jesus' teaching, which is immediately apparent from acquaintance with even a few of his sayings. What is timeless in the personality of Jesus is what Schweitzer calls his "will," in comparison with which his culturally-conditionally apocalyptic worldview fades into relative insignificance.[82] Schweitzer repeats the claim of the first edition: we cannot identify any *elements* in Jesus' teaching that would be of permanent significance. Rather, what we are faced with is a more radical task. We must attempt to express the will of Jesus "in the thought-forms available in our own age."[83] In this way we will create a new worldview that will have the same power in our own time as Jesus' worldview had in his.

What is of abiding significance is, therefore, the will of Jesus. But in what does this will consist? The answer is not entirely clear. Schweitzer does speak of Jesus' "natural and profound moral consciousness,"[84] while insisting that we must understand this consciousness eschatologically. Yet because we cannot accept Jesus' apocalyptic worldview, his teaching cannot be a source of doctrine for us. As Schweitzer writes, Jesus "cannot be an authority for us at the level of understanding, but only at the level of will."[85] All we can hope is that, in confrontation with his personality, our own thinking is reshaped, so that we can reproduce in our own time ideals that are the equivalents of his. Those ideals will have to do with what Schweitzer calls a "vigorous and purposeful desire for world-consummation,"[86] which will correspond to Jesus' expectation of the kingdom of God. While Jesus expected this consummation to be brought about supernaturally, we can only understand it as the result of our own efforts. There are other "alien and offensive" elements in the teaching of

[80]Schweitzer, *The Quest of the Historical Jesus* (1913), 479.
[81]Ibid., 480.
[82]Cf. ibid., 481.
[83]Ibid.
[84]Ibid., 482.
[85]Ibid.
[86]Ibid., 483.

the historical figure of Jesus, but these too will fade into insignificance when his spirit is translated into the categories of our time.[87]

While Schweitzer may appear to be redeeming the figure of Jesus for Christian use, there is a hint here that things are not quite so straightforward. The hint will be developed only in Schweitzer's later writings, which will cast doubt on the idea that the figure of Jesus is really the foundation of Schweitzer's thought. In *The Quest of the Historical Jesus,* however, these ideas are not developed. All we find is the claim that, while the historical figure of Jesus offers a challenge to our will, that challenge "has not come down to us from him through historical revelation. [Rather] it is inherent in us and is part of the moral will."[88] It is difficult to know what these words mean. They seem to suggest that the life and work of Jesus does not offer us any *new* revelation. If there is a truth conveyed to us by the figure of Jesus, then he is not the only means of access to that truth. The role of the historical Jesus is to remind us of something we could already find within ourselves, if only we chose to look. Schweitzer does say that there are heights of moral thinking that we would not reach without the influence of Jesus. But that influence consists of awakening within us forces that are apparently there already.[89] If this represents the ongoing significance of Jesus, then it falls far short of what Christians have traditionally claimed. Indeed, the teaching of Jesus becomes little more than a historically necessary catalyst in the formation of an ethic that in the end stands independent of him. In his more explicitly Christian works, Schweitzer seems reluctant to state things so baldly. But as we will see, in his other works this conclusion seems inescapable.

Is there any other way in which the historical Jesus might be of religious significance? As the last chapter showed, the young David Friedrich Strauss made an ultimately unsuccessful attempt to restore meaning to the old Christian beliefs. He did so by appealing to the idealist philosophy of history embodied in the work of G. W. F. Hegel. According to Strauss's reading of Hegel, the idea of the incarnation could function as a symbol of the union of the infinite and the finite, a union that takes place in the course of human history. According to this view, the story of Jesus embodies, in the form of myth, a philosophical truth about history as a whole. As the following chapter will show, this idealist philosophy of history continued to exercise a powerful influence on religious thinkers. In a less Hegelian form it would underlie the theology of Ernst Troeltsch

[87]Cf. ibid., 485.
[88]Ibid., 486.
[89]Cf. ibid., 482.

(1865–1923), who was for much of his life a contemporary of Schweitzer. Yet Schweitzer was never tempted to take this line. Indeed, in his more philosophical work he argued that, even if such an understanding of history were found plausible, it would be of little significance in the crisis facing the contemporary world. It could lend no support to our fundamental ethical convictions.[90] There is a deep dualism in Schweitzer's thought: history stands on the side of that which is ethically (and therefore religiously) without value. But these observations, too, anticipate our next topic, namely, Schweitzer's philosophy of "reverence for life." What is this philosophy and what relationship does it bear to the figure of Jesus?

3. Reverence for Life

It would offer a distorted picture of Schweitzer's thought to examine only his exegetical works and to leave aside his philosophy of "reverence for life."[91] That philosophy was closely related to what Schweitzer saw as the teaching of Jesus. It also sheds light on the implications of historical research for Christian faith. The key works dealing with this theme are those published under the series title *The Philosophy of Civilization*. The two published volumes of this series are in a sense complementary. The first, entitled *The Decay and Restoration of Civilization,* is a short and more popular work, discussing the crisis in which Western civilization found itself in the years following the First World War and hinting at a solution. The second, *Civilization and Ethics,* is a much more extensive discussion, which interacts with practically the entire history of philosophy and develops Schweitzer's own views in a more systematic way. The first volume is useful as an extended discussion of the problem, but the second develops Schweitzer's solution. Yet neither volume represents the best place to begin a discussion of Schweitzer's philosophy. A better starting point is a work published some years later, entitled *Indian Thought and Its Development* (1935). Although this work is devoted to the thought of India, Schweitzer believes it will shed light on the spiritual crisis of contemporary Western culture, and it provides him with the opportunity of presenting his earlier views in a more developed form.[92]

Ethics and Worldview
Schweitzer begins his study of Indian thought by setting out what he believed were the two great questions facing any serious thinker. The

---

[90]See Schweitzer's discussion of Hegel's philosophy in *Civilization and Ethics,* 144–47.

[91]*Ehrfurcht vor dem Leben.*

[92]Cf. Albert Schweitzer, *Indian Thought and Its Development,* translated by Mrs. Charles E. B. Russell (London: Hodder & Stoughton, 1936), 17.

first has to do with our fundamental orientation to life: whether we adopt an attitude of life-affirmation or one of life-negation. The second has to do with the relationship of that fundamental orientation to ethics.[93] The pursuit of these two questions is the central theme of Schweitzer's philosophical writings. From this point of view he examines the history of both Indian and—in *Civilization and Ethics*—Western religion and philosophy.

The terms that recur throughout these works are "world and life affirmation" and "world and life negation."[94] In *Indian Thought and Its Development* Schweitzer offers concise definitions of what he means by both expressions.

> World and life affirmation consists in this: that man regards existence as he experiences it in himself and as it has developed in the world as something of value *per se* and accordingly strives to let it reach perfection in himself, whilst within his own sphere of influence he endeavours to preserve and to further it.
>
> World and life negation on the other hand consists in his regarding existence as he experiences it in himself and as it is developed in the world as something meaningless and sorrowful, and he resolves accordingly (a) to bring life to a standstill in himself by mortifying his will-to-live, and (b) to renounce all activity which aims at improvement of conditions of life in this world.[95]

Although Schweitzer frequently speaks about "optimism" and "pessimism," he also makes it clear that world- and life-affirmation and negation are not to be identified with the natural dispositions that make individuals optimists or pessimists. A profound attitude of life-affirmation may conceivably exist in one naturally inclined to pessimism, while an attitude of life-negation may be developed in one naturally inclined to optimism. For Schweitzer is concerned with what shapes one's actions: this has to do with the will rather than with one's inherited personality. As he writes, "the question is not so much what man expects or does not expect from existence, but what use he aims at making of it."[96] These two attitudes to the world are at the heart of what Schweitzer sees as the crisis of contemporary Western culture.

Unfortunately Schweitzer does not offer a single, clear definition of the other key term in these discussions, namely, "ethics." His meaning

---

[93]Cf. ibid., vii.
[94]*Welt-und Lebensbejahung and Welt-und Lebensverneinung.*
[95]Schweitzer, *Indian Thought and Its Development,* 1–2.
[96]Ibid., 2.

must be picked up from hints throughout his work. In fact, Schweitzer uses this word in two quite distinct ways. The first is a relatively neutral sense, in which 'ethics' refers to a system of beliefs shaping human behavior. Particularly in *Civilization and Ethics* Schweitzer often speaks of different "ethics" in the sense of a variety of ethical systems. For instance, he laments the fact that the ethics of the early Stoic philosophers became what he calls "an ethics of decadence"; they were incapable of functioning as "an ethics of civilization."[97] He notes that for Spinoza altruism was not of the essence of ethics; his was an ethics of "self-perfection" rather than one of "self-devotion."[98] With regard to Arthur Schopenhauer (1788– 1860), Schweitzer writes that his ethics resembles that of Indian thought: it is an "ethics of resignation," of "universal pity," and of "world-renunciation."[99] In other places, however, Schweitzer uses the term "ethics" in a much narrower sense, with reference to only one *type* of ethical system. This is what he calls an ethics of "self-devotion" or an "ethics of civilization." For Schweitzer, this is the "true ethics." As he writes in *Indian Thought and Its Development,* "the maintenance of one's own life at the highest level by becoming more and more perfect in spirit, and the maintenance of the level of other life by sympathetic, helpful self-devotion to it—this is ethics."[100] Again, elsewhere in the same work he writes: "Ethics demand of man that he should interest himself in the world and in what goes on in it; and, what is more, simply compel him to action."[101] It is this *active* and *altruistic* ethic that Schweitzer greatly prefers and sometimes refers to, by a sort of shorthand, simply as "ethics." Indeed when Schweitzer speaks of "ethics" without qualification, it can generally be assumed that this is what he means: an ethics of "active love."[102] The reader will need to keep this in mind in the discussion that follows.

The Crisis of Western Civilization
Schweitzer begins both volumes of *The Philosophy of Civilization* by arguing that contemporary Western civilization has entered into a state of crisis. That crisis has to do with what Schweitzer considers to be the key ingredient of civilization, namely ethics.[103] Schweitzer argues that

---

[97]Schweitzer, *Civilization and Ethics,* 39.

[98]Cf. ibid., 117.

[99]Ibid., 166.

[100]Schweitzer, *Indian Thought and Its Development,* 260.

[101]Ibid., 8.

[102]Ibid., 9.

[103]Cf. Albert Schweitzer, *The Decay and Restoration of Civilization,* The Philosophy of Civilization 1, translated by C. T. Campion (1923; London: Unwin Books [in association with A. & C. Black], 1961), 41; *Civilization and Ethics,* 2–3, 7–8.

civilization requires a "life-affirming" and "world-affirming" worldview, for only an attitude of life-affirmation can encourage us to work for the betterment of the world.[104] Contemporary Western culture is in a state of crisis because it lacks such a worldview. It lacks, in other words, the foundations on which constructive human activity can be built. At first sight this claim may seem surprising, for at the very beginning of the modern period, we do find a strong affirmation of human potential. The age of the Enlightenment took it for granted that the world was developing towards a state of greater perfection, and this belief contributed to the material and spiritual progress of humankind.[105] Yet by the late nineteenth century, Schweitzer argues, this optimism had come to be shaken. More precisely, it had become clear that it was never firmly founded, for the world-affirming attitudes of the Enlightenment had shallow roots. They were based on little more than a confidence born of the material advances brought by science and by new technologies.[106] For this reason they were doomed eventually to wither. The demise of the optimistic worldview of the Enlightenment finally occurred in the mid-nineteenth century. The last stage in that process was the abandonment of the idealist interpretation of the universe found in the work of thinkers such as J. G. Fichte (1762–1814), F. W. J. von Schelling (1775–1854) and, of course, G. W. F. Hegel.[107] With the collapse of this life-affirming worldview we run the risk of the collapse of the civilization that rested on it, for that civilization is like a building erected on rotten foundations.[108]

Schweitzer argues that neither science nor contemporary philosophy has been able to fill the gap. Neither can provide the life-affirming worldview that we so desperately need. It is true that modern science gave rise to the optimism of the age of the Enlightenment, but it cannot of its own resources justify that optimism. Its ways of thought are simply too narrow, so that, in Schweitzer's words, "the newest scientific knowledge may be allied with an entirely unreflecting view of the universe."[109] Worse still, modern science is often—in practice—linked to materialism, a worldview that is ultimately hostile to the ethical affirmation of life. Nor has philosophy succeeded in supplying an ethical worldview.

[104]Cf. Schweitzer, *Civilization and Ethics,* 7.

[105]Cf. ibid., 6.

[106]In *The Development of Indian Thought* (5) Schweitzer is not quite so restrictive and traces the world affirmation of the modern West not only to science and technology, but also to the rediscovery of the philosophies of Aristotle and the Stoics and to the rediscovery of the Gospel ethic at the time of the Reformation.

[107]Cf. Schweitzer, *Indian Thought and Its Development,* 253.

[108]Cf. Schweitzer, *Civilization and Ethics,* 69–70.

[109]Schweitzer, *The Decay and Restoration of Civilization,* 67.

Indeed, contemporary philosophers have simply failed to address the question, for they have failed to reflect on the nature of civilization.[110] Hence the spiritual crisis of our times. That crisis consists in the fact that our contemporaries no longer really believe in what Schweitzer calls "the spiritual and ethical progress of men and of mankind."[111]

> By its belief in an optimistic-ethical philosophy the modern age became capable of a mighty advance towards civilization. But as its thought has not been able to show this philosophy to be founded in the nature of things, we have sunk, consciously or unconsciously, into a condition in which we have no worldview at all, a condition of pessimism, too, and of absence of all ethical conviction, so that we are on the point of complete ruin.[112]

This crisis was not created by the First World War, but it was spectacularly displayed in the barbarism which that war provoked.[113] Tragically for the cause of Christianity, the war also revealed the weakness of the churches, who (with the honorable exception of the Quakers) all too quickly conformed to the spirit of their age.[114]

Ethics and Life-View
While Schweitzer criticizes contemporary philosophy for failing to reflect on the nature of civilization, his criticism of philosophy goes much further. In *Civilization and Ethics* Schweitzer sets himself to review what he calls "the whole experience of mankind, in its search for the ethical,"[115] by looking at religious and philosophical views alike. The majority of Western thinkers—Schweitzer argues—have instinctively rejected those worldviews that are radically pessimistic and sceptical. For the tendency of Western thought is toward an affirmation of life and thus an activist ethic. (This is why Kant, for example, felt the need to struggle against the epistemological scepticism of Hume.[116]) The problem is that Western thinkers have been unable to offer a satisfactory *justification* of this choice. They have been unable to offer a convincing reason why one *should* adopt a life-affirming ethic.[117] Non-Western thought, on the

---

[110]Cf. ibid., 23.
[111]Schweitzer, *Civilization and Ethics*, 9.
[112]Ibid., 201.
[113]Cf. ibid., 1.
[114]Cf. ibid., 276.
[115]Schweitzer, *Civilization and Ethics*, 24.
[116]Cf. ibid, 13.
[117]Cf. ibid., 12.

other hand, does no better. It, too, fails to offer a firm foundation for an activist ethic. Indeed non-Western thought all too often abandons life-affirmation altogether. It leads its followers into a deeply pessimistic worldview and to a corresponding ethic of resignation, a fact that is particularly clear in the history of Indian philosophy. Schweitzer's conclusion is that, from the point of view of a life-affirming ethic, the history of human thought has been a history of failure.[118] Thinkers have either arrived at a world-*denying* ethic, which issues in an attitude of resignation (such as that of the early Stoics[119] or, more recently, that of Schopenhauer[120]), or they have insisted on a world-*affirming* ethic, but without being able to give this a convincing grounding. In our own day, for example, some thinkers have made what Schweitzer calls "touchingly naïve" efforts to relate their ethical affirmation of life to Darwin's views, without noticing that the worldview of Darwinism leads in quite a different direction.[121]

It follows that a "new way" is needed, one that frankly abandons the attempt to bring ethics and worldview into conformity. The history of thought shows that a truly life-affirming ethic cannot be constructed on the basis of any interpretation of the world.[122] In other words, we cannot arrive at a satisfactory ethic by raising what Schweitzer calls "being-like-the-world" to the status of a guide for human behavior. As Schweitzer admits candidly, "no motives to ethical activity are to be discovered in the course of nature."[123] Or, as he writes in his later work, "no ethics can be won from knowledge of the Universe. Nor can ethics be brought into harmony with what we know of the Universe."[124] A life-affirming ethic actually runs counter to the principles underlying the operations of the world.[125] It follows that any ethical position derived from a worldview is likely to be weak and inadequate. Either it is unable to explain the peculiar combination of life-affirmation with apparent life-negation that constitutes an ethics of altruism (or "self-devotion").[126] Or it ends up by subordinating the ethical to the nonethical, so that altruistic behavior becomes merely a means to an end, the

[118]A helpful summary of Schweitzer's argument is to be found in *Civilization and Ethics*, 217–20.
[119]Cf. Schweitzer, *Civilization and Ethics*, 39.
[120]Cf. ibid., 166–67.
[121]Cf. ibid., 13–14, 152–58.
[122]Cf. ibid., 221 et passim.
[123]Ibid., 233.
[124]Schweitzer, *Indian Thought and Its Development*, 12.
[125]Cf. Schweitzer, *Civilization and Ethics*, 112–13.
[126]Cf. ibid., 184.

end being, for example, the perfection of the individual (as in the case of Spinoza's ethics[127]). Schweitzer concludes that we cannot find any satisfactory basis for ethics by looking outside of ourselves.

His new way consists in finding support for such an ethics in our inner experience. He appeals in particular to the experience of the will to live that motivates all our activities.[128] For philosophy, this means a shift of focus from the human intellect to the human will. The intellect regards the world from a position of detachment, from outside the stream of life (as it were). The will, however, represents the human being as involved in that stream of life, engaged and committed.[129] The role of thought is to become aware of the affirmation of life that undergirds all the decisions of the human will and to bring us to a recognition that there exists an analogous will to live in all living beings.[130] When thought through consistently, reflection on one's own will to live leads to a reverence for all life. As Schweitzer writes,

> the problem of worldview, then, . . . may be put thus: "What is the relation of my will-to-live, when it begins to think, to itself and to the world?" And the answer is: "From an inner compulsion to be true to itself and to remain consistent with itself, our will-to-live enters into relations with our own individual being, and with all manifestations of the will-to-live which surround it, that are determined by the sentiment of reverence for life." Reverence for life, *veneratio vitae*, is the most direct and at the same time the profoundest achievement of my will-to-live.[131]

As this quotation suggests, Schweitzer's argument requires something more to be persuasive. It requires something like Kant's insistence that an ethics be consistent: I must want for others what I desire for myself.[132] Otherwise, his ethics would be nothing more than an unrestrained affirmation of the individual's will to live, an idea which is found in

---

[127]Cf. ibid., 117.

[128]Schweitzer's "will-to-live" resembles the *conatus essendi* (striving to exist), which Spinoza (cf. *Ethics,* part 3, props. 6–7, 21–22; part 4, props. 24–25) claims is characteristic of all beings. Schweitzer is certainly familiar with Spinoza's thought, and there may be some direct influence here. However, Schweitzer himself cites as antecedents of his concept a similar idea in the thought of Schopenhauer (cf. *Civilization and Ethics,* 163) and the ethical development of the idea in the work of Wilhelm Stern (cf. ibid., 190).

[129]Cf. Schweitzer, *The Decay and Restoration of Civilization,* 81; *Civilization and Ethics,* 213.

[130]Cf. Schweitzer, *Civilization and Ethics,* 241.

[131]Ibid., xvii.

[132]For a slightly different argument, see Schweitzer, *Indian Thought and Its Development,* 261.

the thought of Nietzsche.[133] In Schweitzer's words, "ethics consists . . . in my experiencing the compulsion to show to all will-to-live the same reverence as I do to my own."[134] Consistent reflection on my own will to live will lead me to work for the enhancement of all forms of life, even at the cost of self-sacrifice. For self-denial, with its apparent life-negation, also takes on a positive significance when put at the service of life-affirmation.[135]

An Ethical Mysticism

While Schweitzer's argument makes little reference to God, he insists that it is nonetheless deeply religious. It must be religious, since nothing less than a religious worldview will have the motivating power that is required. Only religion, he writes, can give human beings the "strength to suffer and to act."[136] He therefore describes his position as a kind of ethical mysticism. However, such language can easily be misunderstood. To appreciate Schweitzer's religious vision, we must look carefully at his use of the term "mysticism." In *Civilization and Ethics* Schweitzer argues against a particular *kind* of mysticism, namely, that which strives for an experience of union with some abstractly conceived world spirit. Such union, Schweitzer writes, can be described in various ways: "becoming one with the Absolute," "existence within the world-spirit," or "absorption into God."[137] The problem is that such a union is not in itself ethical; indeed, it is inclined to undermine ethics, insofar as it makes "absorption into the Absolute" into an end in itself.[138] More seriously, Schweitzer continues, terms such as the "Essence of Being," the "Absolute," or the "Spirit of the Universe" are in reality only empty abstractions. They represent nothing that actually exists, for all that exists is Being manifesting itself in individual phenomena.[139] As Schweitzer writes (in terms strikingly reminiscent of Spinoza), "there is no Essence of Being, but only infinite Being in infinite manifestations."[140] If I wish to enter into union with infinite Being, I can do so only by devoting myself to the individual manifestations of Being that lie within my reach. Such devotion represents an *ethical* mysticism.

---

[133]Cf. Schweitzer, *Civilization and Ethics,* 176–77.

[134]Ibid., 242.

[135]Cf. Schweitzer, *Civilization and Ethics,* 222–23; *Indian Thought and Its Development,* 6–7.

[136]Schweitzer, *Indian Thought and Its Development,* 11.

[137]Schweitzer, *Civilization and Ethics,* 234.

[138]Cf. ibid., 235.

[139]Cf. ibid., 237.

[140]Ibid., 238.

A very similar discussion is found at the end of Schweitzer's study of Indian thought. Here, too, he suggests that his ethic of "reverence for life" can be described as "mystical," for it brings one into union with the force that produces and sustains all forms of life.[141] Yet Schweitzer immediately qualifies this by noting that there are two types of mysticism. The first is what he calls "the mysticism of identity."[142] This holds that there exists an identity between the principles underlying the world and that which should govern human behavior. In Schweitzer's words, it assumes "that the World-Spirit and the spirit of man are identical."[143] But this view is untenable. It assumes that we are *able* to know the principles by which the world is shaped, when for the most part we cannot. More seriously, it offers no way of relating those principles to a world-affirming ethic.[144] However, Schweitzer argues that there exists a second type of mysticism, which derives, not from worldview, but from ethics. This position is resigned to agnosticism regarding the constitution of the world: it accepts that "the World-Spirit and world events remain to us incomprehensible."[145] It lives contentedly in the state of "learned ignorance" (*docta ignorantia*) spoken of by the medieval mystics. It therefore enters into no conflict with our knowledge of the world and of history. As Schweitzer writes succinctly, such an ethics "can let space and time go to the devil."[146] All it needs to know is the will to live that is within us. This alone offers an insight into the ethical nature of the world. Our own will to live teaches us, in Schweitzer's words, that "all Being is life, and that in loving self-devotion to other life we realise our spiritual union with infinite Being."[147]

[141]Cf. Schweitzer, *Indian Thought and Its Development*, 262. See also *Civilization and Ethics*, 236, and *The Decay and Restoration of Civilization*, 80–81.

[142]Schweitzer, *Indian Thought and Its Development*, 262.

[143]Ibid.

[144]In this respect, there is a certain ambiguity in Schweitzer's thought. In some places (e.g., *Indian Thought and Its Development*, 258) he suggests that we simply *cannot* know the principles underlying the order of the world. In other places (e.g., *Civilization and Ethics*, 245–46), he suggests that we *can* know those principles, but this knowledge is ethically useless. Throughout his work, however, Schweitzer insists we cannot understand the *relationship* of a life-affirming ethic to the order of the world at large. This is perhaps a more precise statement of his thought, and my summary of his position has reworded it in those terms.

[145]Schweitzer, *Indian Thought and Its Development*, 263. This seems to be a more deeply dualistic view than that hinted at in the conclusion to Schweitzer's *The Quest of the Historical Jesus* (1913), 486, where he can still speak of our becoming one with "the eternal moral will which governs the world."

[146]Schweitzer, *Civilization and Ethics*, 221.

[147]Schweitzer, *Indian Thought and Its Development*, 264.

4. Schweitzer and Christian Theology

Christianity and the History of Religions

In the introductory chapter I discussed the cultural shifts that reshaped attitudes to the Bible in the seventeenth century. One of these shifts was a sense of the diversity of human religions, which meant that Christianity came to be seen as merely one religion among others. It is a striking feature of Schweitzer's "philosophy of civilization" that this shift is everywhere taken for granted. Indeed in his *Civilization and Ethics,* Schweitzer insists that the reflection necessary for the development of a satisfactory worldview cannot limit itself to Western forms of thought. Rather, it requires a "world-philosophy," whose age is "just dawning."[148] True to this principle, he examines not just Western thought, but also (at least in passing) that of the religious thinkers of China and of India and that of the Persian Zarathustra (Zoroaster), the founder of Zoroastrianism.[149] As we will see shortly, this breadth of scope makes it impossible to classify Schweitzer's work in this field as "Christian theology" (in any usual sense of the word). While it makes reference to Jesus and develops an ethical position that it attributes to Jesus, it does so on grounds that are much broader than those offered by the Christian tradition. It is worth noting, too, that Schweitzer would later write an entire book on the history of Indian thought, to which we have already had reason to refer. Here, too, he develops his own ideas, not just on some assumed Christian basis, but in interaction with the ideas found in India.

Schweitzer addresses these matters more explicitly in his *Christianity and the Religions of the World,* a series of lectures delivered at the Selly Oak Colleges, Birmingham, England, in 1922. An exposition of this work lies beyond the scope of the present study. All we need to note here is Schweitzer's attitude. He begins the discussion with the remark that he will not defend Christianity by simply exempting its claims from rational enquiry. In particular, he will not take refuge in the argument that "Christianity contains truths which are above all reasoning, and which, therefore, do not have to enter into contest with philosophy."[150] Rather, he has always held that religious claims must be demonstrably rational: as he writes, "all religious truth must in the end be capable of being grasped as something that stands to reason."[151] Later in the lectures, he advises his Christian audience how to respond to the consistent and rational

---

[148]Schweitzer, *Civilization and Ethics,* 12. See also *Indian Thought and Its Development,* x.
[149]Schweitzer, *Civilization and Ethics,* 27–28.
[150]Albert Schweitzer, *Christianity and the Religions of the World,* translated by Johanna Powers (London: George Allen & Unwin, 1923), 18.
[151]Ibid.

philosophies of India and China. They should not appeal to the authority of Christianity's "historical revelation," for this would be "an unsafe defence."[152] Rather, they must be prepared to show that Christianity's apparent inconsistencies are precisely what is needed to sustain a life-affirming ethic. In any case, Schweitzer insists that Christianity must claim no special treatment in the contest with other religions. Rather, it must rely "solely on the power of its own inherent truth."[153]

It is true that, when it comes to the comparative study of religions, Schweitzer's theory is better than his practice. In practice, these lectures suffer from the common theological failing of dismissing other religious traditions for not conforming to Christian criteria. It is all too easy for Schweitzer to arrive at the conclusion that Christianity is "the deepest expression of the religious mind,"[154] since he has already defined "the religious mind" in Christian terms. (His 1935 work on Indian thought would exhibit a greater sophistication in this regard.) Yet the fact that he feels the need to set Christian claims in relationship to those of other religions indicates how thoroughly he has accepted the "great reversal" of the seventeenth century. But the question remains: Has Schweitzer managed to overcome the effects of this reversal? Has he found a new basis for Christian theology in an age of historical relativism?

Reverence for Life and Christian Theology

It is difficult to locate Schweitzer's thought within the theological spectrum of his time. In some respects, Schweitzer would seem to be working in the tradition of liberal theology. For he refuses to grant an a priori preference to Christianity over other religions. Neither does he take refuge in appeals to religious authority. On the contrary, he insists on finding rational grounds for religious claims. In these respects Schweitzer is at one with the liberal theology of the nineteenth century. It is true that as an exegete Schweitzer sets out to undermine at least one assumption held by his nineteenth-century predecessors. In company with Johannes Weiss, he insists that we cannot read our modern worldview back into the Gospels. We must interpret Jesus as a figure of *his* time rather than our own. Yet it could also be argued that Schweitzer rejoins the liberal theologians when articulating his own religious views. Like them he believes that, in a certain sense, it is Jesus' ethical teaching that should be at the heart of modern theology.

Yet before describing Schweitzer as yet another liberal theologian, in the tradition which would be opposed so vigorously by Karl Barth and

[152]Ibid., 83.
[153]Ibid., 19.
[154]Ibid., 18.

his followers,[155] we need to look more closely at his position. The key issue here relates to the basis on which Schweitzer constructs his philosophy of reverence for life. That philosophy certainly makes reference to the teaching of Jesus. It even claims to be a restatement of one element of that teaching. But is it *based* on the teaching of Jesus? Is it drawn from the Gospels? More importantly, does it continue to be dependent on them? Schweitzer displays great interest in discovering the teaching of Jesus. But what role does the teaching of Jesus play in his developed thought?

In the second volume of his *Philosophy of Civilization,* Schweitzer speaks of the role of Jesus' ethic in the development of Western civilization. He argues that Jesus' active and altruistic ethic enabled the transition from a world-denying to a world-affirming view of life. For while Jesus's worldview may have been a pessimistic and world-denying apocalypticism, his ethic was activist, for he encouraged an attitude of devotion to the needs of one's neighbor. This is what Schweitzer calls the "magnificent paradox" in the teaching of Jesus: it is the paradox of a world-affirming ethic embodied in a world-denying worldview.[156] As we have seen, Schweitzer maintains that in the history of Christianity Jesus' activist ethic becomes separated from his apocalyptic worldview. He insists that this process must be completed today.

It follows that the teaching of Jesus plays at best a *transitional* role in the development of an ethic for the modern world. The ongoing problem here is Jesus' pessimistic worldview, which cannot form the foundation of a world-affirming ethic. Liberal theology *could* use the Gospels in support of this ethic until historians uncovered the apocalyptic character of Jesus' teaching. At that point, Schweitzer writes, theology lost its innocence and reacted with horror, regarding Jesus as a mere enthusiast (or fanatic). In fact, however, it was only "putting to an end the false modernizing of his personality."[157] But the discovery of Jesus' apocalyptic worldview means that we can no longer appeal to this figure, at least in any simple, unself-conscious way, in support of our life-affirming ethic. The task before us now is to accept the world-affirmation implicit in Jesus' ethical teaching, while accepting that he speaks to us out of a worldview which we can no longer share. We cannot justify our life-affirming ethic in the way in which Jesus would have done. Rather, we must find a new basis for the same message.

If this is Schweitzer's position, then at least in his *Philosophy of Civilization,* he is not attempting to "do theology" in any traditional

---

[155]See chapters 5 and 6 below.
[156]Cf. Schweitzer, *Civilization and Ethics,* 65–67.
[157]Ibid., 67.

Christian sense. For he is not attempting to derive this world-affirming ethic from the teaching of Jesus, even if he insists that at least one element in Jesus' teaching corresponds to that ethic. Rather, he argues that Jesus' ethical teaching was a key factor in articulating an ethic that in the end has ceased to depend on it. The active and altruistic character of our ethical view owes much to what Schweitzer calls its "passage through Christianity."[158] But in the modern world ethics has become independent of any particular religion. Thus even those who have rejected traditional belief can come to share the ethical vision of "reverence for life."[159]

What, then, may we say about Schweitzer as theologian? There is a sense in which his work stands in continuity with the liberal theology of the nineteenth century. While he insisted that the "kingdom of God" did not originally refer to an ethical, this-worldly reality, he also admitted that only the ethical element of Jesus' teaching was of enduring religious significance.[160] Liberal theology's attribution of an optimistic worldview to Jesus was a "mistake," but it was a *felix culpa,* a happy mistake. Indeed, it may have been essential for the development of Western civilization, for the development of a modern, world-affirming ethic might never have taken place without what Schweitzer calls "the authority of the great personality of Jesus."[161] Nonetheless, the attribution of an optimistic worldview to Jesus *was* a mistake. Once the mistake has been discovered, the situation is changed. The life-affirming ethic of our time owes much to Jesus, but it can no longer be theologically grounded by attributing to Jesus a worldview he did not share. In affirming the ongoing significance of Jesus' ethic, Schweitzer is at one with the liberal theology of the nineteenth century. In noting that this ethic can no longer be justified by appealing to the religious worldview of Jesus, he parts company with theological liberalism. Indeed, in his insistence that this ethic is now independent of the Christian religion, it could be argued that Schweitzer parts company with theology altogether.

5. The Legacy of Schweitzer

Schweitzer's Portrait of Jesus

There have been many criticisms of Schweitzer's consistently apocalyptic interpretation of Jesus, and few scholars today would hold to his view

---

[158]Ibid., 64–65.
[159]Cf. ibid., 277.
[160]For Weiss's position, see his *Jesus's Proclamation of the Kingdom of God,* 131–36.
[161]Schweitzer, *Civilization and Ethics,* 67.

in its entirety.[162] It may be, for instance, that the world of late second-
Temple Judaism was much more diverse than Schweitzer believed.[163]
Certainly there is much material even in those sources which Schweitzer
favored, namely, the Gospels of Mark and Matthew, that cannot be successfully fitted into his relatively simple scheme. In a whimsical passage,
Schweitzer is critical of those who resort to psychological speculation in
their reconstructions of Jesus' life:

> Formerly it was possible to get through-tickets at the booking office of
> supplementary-psychological-knowledge . . . which enabled those writ-
> ing a Life of Jesus to use express trains, thus avoiding the inconvenience of
> having to stop at every little station, and run the risk of missing their con-
> nexion. This ticket office is now closed.[164]

However, he is not beyond resorting to such explanations himself in
order to form a coherent narrative out of the apparently inconsistent
Gospel accounts.[165] William Wrede's unflinching criticisms of such reconstructions would be a useful corrective in this regard.

Yet while Schweitzer's understanding of Jewish apocalyptic thought
needs some fine-tuning, there is a large measure of agreement between
his view and later interpretations of Jesus as an apocalyptic figure. Even
when later scholars would put forward what at first sight appear to be
very different views, these were often anticipated in Schweitzer's work.
The English scholar C. H. Dodd, for instance, would later argue for a
"realized eschatology," suggesting that Jesus proclaimed a kingdom of
God that was already present.[166] Schweitzer would not agree (and in this
he would not be alone), but his portrait of Jesus is sophisticated enough
to incorporate elements of Dodd's position. As we have seen, Schweitzer
insists that Jesus regarded both the repentance he proclaimed and his
own death as instrumental: they would *contribute to the process* of bringing
about the advent of God's kingdom. By his miracles, too, especially his
exorcisms, Jesus was conscious of hastening the approach of the kingdom.[167] Therefore, for Schweitzer Jesus was not simply a proclaimer of

[162]For a particularly severe criticism, see T. Francis Glasson, "Schweitzer's Influence—
Blessing or Bane?" *Journal of Theological Studies* NS 28 (1977): 289–302.
[163]In fairness, it should be noted that Schweitzer was not unaware of this complexity,
even if it is not always reflected, at least in his early work. (See, for instance, *The Kingdom
of God and Primitive Christianity,* 33–67.)
[164]Schweitzer, *The Quest of the Historical Jesus* (1913), 299.
[165]See, for instance, ibid, 332.
[166]See, for example, C. H. Dodd, *The Parables of the Kingdom* (1935; London:
Collins/Fontana, 1961), 29–61.
[167]Schweitzer, *The Mystery of the Kingdom of God,* 143.

the kingdom, but God's agent through whose work it was to be brought closer. As he writes, "for his contemporaries it was a question of *waiting for* the Kingdom, of excogitating and depicting every incident of the great catastrophe, and of preparing for the same; while for Jesus it was a question of *bringing to pass* the expected event through the moral renovation."[168] There are still, of course, differences between this view of Jesus' teaching and that put forward by C. H. Dodd. For Schweitzer, Jesus' activity represents the *preparatory work* that will hasten the coming of God's kingdom, while for Dodd it is that by which the kingdom *is being* established. But these two great scholars were perhaps not so far apart as is sometimes supposed.

What *is* clearly incompatible with Schweitzer's position is the recently floated idea that Jesus was not an apocalyptic prophet at all, but a teacher of ethical wisdom or perhaps a cynic-like disturber of conventional norms. This view is particularly associated with the work of the Jesus Seminar under the leadership of Robert W. Funk.[169] These suggestions may represent genuinely new historical insights, drawn from a reevaluation of documents such as the Gospel of Thomas and the hypothetical source Q, apparently used by both Matthew and Luke. Or they may turn out to be yet another way of avoiding the unpalatable implications of historical criticism, which would recognize Jesus as a man of his time, an apocalyptic prophet caught up in the deadly politics of late second-Temple Judaism. If one were to gamble on the outcome of this discussion, I would be prepared to wager that here, too, Schweitzer will be vindicated. But it is too soon to pass any final judgment on the future of this debate.

Schweitzer's Theological Significance
Even outside of his exegetical work, there are many aspects of Schweitzer's thought that may be regarded as prophetic. To see the contemporary relevance of his ideas, one need think only of the growing ecological movement of our time or our increasing concern that nonhuman life be treated with respect. Schweitzer was a "green" thinker long before that expression had been coined. Philosophically, too, many of Schweitzer's central ideas would be echoed by later thinkers. For instance, his emphasis on the need to integrate intellect and will anticipates the existentialist philosophy of the mid-twentieth century, which will be picked up and recast theologically by Rudolf Bultmann. When Schweitzer writes that

---

[168]Ibid., 115.

[169]A concise expression is to be found in Robert W. Funk's *Honest to Jesus: Jesus for a New Millennium* (London: Hodder & Stoughton, 1996), 166–69.

"every being who calls himself a man is meant to develop into a real personality within a reflective worldview which he has created for himself,"[170] this could be a paraphrase of the thought of his famous cousin,
Jean-Paul Sartre.[171] Similarly, Schweitzer's insistence that ethics should be
established independently of worldview is echoed in the thought of the
late Emmanuel Levinas, who sought to establish the priority of ethics over
ontology. Schweitzer's claim that ethics imposes a "responsibility without
limit"[172] is also strongly reminiscent of Levinas, although Schweitzer sees
this responsibility as directed to nonhuman as well as to human life. In
other words, whatever criticisms may be made of Schweitzer's thought,
there is no question as to its contemporary significance.

We should also note that Schweitzer takes with full seriousness the
challenge to traditional religion posed by the modern sciences. In particular, he realizes (in company with Bacon, Descartes, Spinoza, and Strauss)
that our modern worldview will not allow us to think teleologically. We
can no longer plausibly attribute some overall purpose to the workings
of the universe and establish an ethical view by relating human beings to
that purpose.[173] Hegel was perhaps the last to do so, but even he effectively reduced ethics to law.[174] To his credit, Schweitzer is also much
more aware than was Strauss of the cultural crisis that these developments create. To put it bluntly, Schweitzer shares with Strauss a great love
for music and literature. Indeed, his knowledge of music was surely more
profound than that of Strauss, on account of his not inconsiderable skills
as a musician. Yet he does not try to argue that music and literature can
fill the gap left in the heart of modern Western culture by the absence of
a satisfactory worldview.

A Critical Appraisal

What, then, may be said of Schweitzer's solution to this cultural crisis?
How satisfactory is his philosophy of "reverence for life"? Schweitzer
claims that in this philosophy he is thinking the issues through "from
scratch," as it were, as heir to the Enlightenment's demand that thinking
be without presuppositions. "I come forward . . . with confidence,"
Schweitzer writes, "as a restorer of that rational thought which refuses to
make assumptions."[175] Yet on closer examination his arguments turn out

---

[170]Schweitzer, *The Decay and Restoration of Civilization,* 82.

[171]More precisely, Sartre's grandfather was Albert Schweitzer's uncle (cf. Brabazon,
Albert Schweitzer, 28).

[172]Schweitzer, *Civilization and Ethics,* 244.

[173]Cf. Schweitzer, *Civilization and Ethics,* xiv; *Indian Thought and Its Development,* 257.

[174]Cf. Schweitzer, *Civilization and Ethics,* 145.

[175]Ibid., xix.

to be massively question-begging: they are shot through with assumptions. In other words, this is not a philosophy that goes boldly wherever the arguments may lead! It is clear that Schweitzer will allow the arguments to lead to only one position. It will not detract from an appreciation of Schweitzer's significance to note some of his assumptions and the difficulties they pose for his position.

First of all, Schweitzer simply takes for granted, from the very start of his argument, that we *must* arrive at an ethics that is both 'life-affirming' and 'world-affirming.' It is true that he at least appears to produce reasons for his stand, for he suggests that it is needed if "civilization" is to survive. But what does Schweitzer mean by "civilization"? Its distinguishing mark, he writes, is "material and spiritual progress."[176] The problem here is that Schweitzer has simply defined "civilization" in such a way that his conclusion is presupposed. This reduces his argument to something closely resembling a tautology: a society that is civilized—in the sense of making material and spiritual progress—will need to believe in the possibility of material and spiritual progress. Of course, few of Schweitzer's readers will be inclined to disagree. He writes for those who, like himself, are the heirs of the worldview of the modern West. Someone brought up in the civilization of the modern West will instinctively (as it were) prefer an activist ethic. To such a person, a world-affirming ethic will appear commendable, while an ethic of resignation will be perceived as an abdication of one's responsibilities. (Even modern Christians are inclined to admire those saints who work with the poor, while they are not so enthusiastic about those who retire to monasteries.) Yet this is to say no more than that someone brought up in a society that values an activist ethic will also value an activist ethic. It is not an argument for preferring one position over the other. However attractive and, indeed, self-evidently preferable Schweitzer's life-affirmation may be to his readers, it has hardly been arrived at by suspending all presuppositions.

Secondly and more seriously, Schweitzer presents his ethics as a necessity of thought, something that *must* be embraced once his argument is understood. He is not presenting a religious position that must be accepted on faith, but a religiosity that is arrived at rationally.[177] It is true that there will always be something irrational (or perhaps suprarational) about the idea of self-sacrifice, which is an essential component of his life-affirming ethic.[178] But Schweitzer wants to show that reflection on our will to live will *necessarily* lead one to adopt such an ethic. As he

[176]Schweitzer, *The Decay and Restoration of Civilization,* 40.
[177]Cf. Schweitzer, *Civilization and Ethics,* xx.
[178]Cf. ibid., 223.

writes, "if rational thought thinks itself out to a conclusion, it arrives at something non-rational which, nevertheless, is a necessity of thought."[179] We are therefore bound to ask: in what sense is "reverence for life" a *necessity* of thought? What argument would lead us to embrace Schweitzer's conclusions as inevitable?

At the heart of his argument is the claim that if I reflect on the implications of my own will to live, I will be obliged to live in a way that is respectful of other forms of life. But what necessity is there in this argument? There seems to be a missing link between the realization of my own will to live and the extension of that to others. As we have seen, this missing link *could* be supplied by the demand that my behavior be consistent—if I wish my life to be respected, I must respect that of others—but in *Civilization and Ethics* this new principle is merely hinted at and is not developed. Perhaps aware of the weakness of his case, in *Indian Thought and Its Development* Schweitzer resorts to another argument. We are led to act ethically, he writes, by reflection on "the physical fact that our life has sprung from other life and allows other life to proceed from it";[180] this shows that we cannot live for ourselves alone. This is, of course, an entirely different argument, and it is not immediately clear that it is any more successful. This gap, at a key point in Schweitzer's argumentation, is never entirely overcome.

A third and related criticism is that Schweitzer arrives at his ethic of reverence for life at considerable cost. He achieves his aim only after consigning to ethical insignificance all our knowledge of the world. His ethics must be based solely on our inner awareness of our own will to live. This is no innocent assertion. Despite his frequently professed agnosticism about the order of the world, Schweitzer is well aware that the natural world, at least, offers no support for his ethical position. In the natural world, one being asserts its will to live *against* another and often at the cost of the life of the other. In Schweitzer's own words, "the world is a ghastly drama of will to live divided against itself. One existence makes its way at the cost of another; one destroys the other."[181] Yet what is Schweitzer's response? He can only assert that human behavior must *not* be modeled on this "ghastly drama": once human beings become aware of this will to live, they must behave differently. They must not allow what happens elsewhere to influence their actions. But why? Why should human beings be different? Why should they *not* model

---

[179]Ibid., xx.

[180]Schweitzer, *Indian Thought and Its Development,* 261.

[181]Schweitzer, *Civilization and Ethics,* 245. Schweitzer presumably has in mind Darwin's dramatic portrayal of the struggle for existence.

their behavior on what seems to be the way of the world? "To these questions," Schweitzer responds, "there is no answer."[182]

It seems, then, that Schweitzer's thought suffers from a deep-seated dualism. Our knowledge of the world suggests one thing; our inner awareness of our will to live suggests something quite different. In one sense, this is hardly surprising, since Schweitzer is heir to what he himself describes as the dualistic tradition of Zoroastrian, Jewish prophetic, and Christian religious thought.[183] His separation of knowledge of the world and ethical claims is also reminiscent of the work of Immanuel Kant,[184] on which Schweitzer had written his first doctoral dissertation.[185] Indeed, it is not clear that Schweitzer would regard the charge of dualism as a criticism. For at times he suggests that such a dualism is the inevitable price to pay for an ethical view of life. In former ages, he writes in *Civilization and Ethics,* we hoped to be able to unite our ethics and our worldview. We hoped to find in our knowledge of the universe a basis for a life-affirming ethic. This is no longer possible. Our thinking now "finds itself involved in a dualism with which it can never be reconciled. It is the dualism of world-view and life-view, of knowing and willing."[186] At other times, however, Schweitzer expresses a preference for a monism. Indeed, in *Indian Thought and Its Development* he describes monism as the only worldview that is "in harmony with reality."[187] In other words, while Schweitzer sometimes admits that dualism is inescapable, at other times he suggests that he is at least *working toward* a single worldview which is both "true and valuable."[188]

If this second position represents Schweitzer's deepest intention, then it seems that his dualism ought to be a mere temporary expedient. Starting from ethics (rather than from observation of the world) he would like eventually to be able to construct a worldview consistent with that ethics. But this remains a desideratum; it is never achieved. To the very end of his work Schweitzer cannot provide any satisfactory account of the relationship between his life-affirming ethics and our wider worldview. He simply affirms that we must establish the first independently of the second. His philosophy is, by his own admission, a partially finished construction, and it is not at all clear that the building could ever be

[182]Schweitzer, *Civilization and Ethics,* 245.
[183]Cf. ibid., 27–28.
[184]Cf. Schweitzer, *Civilization and Ethics,* 106; *Indian Thought and Its Development,* 264.
[185]Cf. Brabazon, *Albert Schweitzer,* 83–89.
[186]Schweitzer, *Civilization and Ethics,* xv–xvi.
[187]Schweitzer, *Indian Thought and Its Development,* 14.
[188]Ibid., 261.

completed.[189] It seems that neither Christianity nor any other world-view can offer a satisfying explanation of both the universe *and* morality. Therefore, for the sake of morality, the cognitive claims of religion must be effectively abandoned, so that its ethical claim may be reasserted. In this respect, Schweitzer's philosophy has something else in common with the tradition of nineteenth-century liberal theology: it reestablishes religious claims by radically reducing their scope.[190] We have already noted this tendency in the work of Spinoza; it is even more striking in that of Schweitzer and will reach its climax in the work of Rudolf Bult-mann (which will be studied in chapter 6).

Finally, there exist some profound ambiguities in Schweitzer's references to God, for it is not at all clear what he means by this traditional religious term. We have seen that in discussing mysticism, Schweitzer argued that terms such as the "Essence of Being," the "Absolute," or the "Spirit of the Universe" are nothing more than empty abstractions. They represent the tendency to attribute reality to what are nothing more than "the symbols which have been coined by language."[191] Only indi-vidual "manifestations of being" can be said to really exist. Yet could not the same judgment be made of Schweitzer's religious language? When he writes, for instance, that our devotion to individual manifestations of being is a devotion to "infinite Being," what does this mean? Or when he claims that our will to live fulfils "its mysterious destiny by making a reality of its union with the infinite Will to live,"[192] we are surely entitled to ask what he means by "the infinite Will to live." Otherwise we might suspect that he, too, has fallen prey to the temptation to treat such abstractions as though they represented something real. Schweitzer's lan-guage is sometimes reminiscent of Spinoza. Yet, as we saw in chapter 1, Spinoza is quite clear that his "infinite Substance" is nothing other than the reality of the world, looked at sub specie aeternitatis (in the light of eternity). If this is what Schweitzer means, he has surely traveled a great distance from the God of traditional Christian theology. In the absence of a developed metaphysics, however, it is impossible to know if this is the case. Schweitzer's religious vision is undoubtedly attractive and has much to offer our age, but at key points it leaves the critical reader deeply dissatisfied.

[189]Cf. Schweitzer, *Civilization and Ethics,* 246.

[190]While Schweitzer (*Civilization and Ethics,* 206–7) criticizes the theologian Albrecht Ritschl and his followers for holding to "a modern doctrine of the two-fold nature of truth," he seems to have himself fallen into the same trap.

[191]Cf. Schweitzer, *Civilization and Ethics,* 237.

[192]Ibid., 216.

Chapter Four

The Historian's Theologian

Ernst Troeltsch (1865–1923)

> *At the most important junctures of our own intellectual*
> *enterprises we are disturbed to discover that we are wrestling*
> *with the same old issues, that the same questions*
> *have returned again in only a slightly different guise.*
> Van A. Harvey

Ernst Troeltsch is a theologian whose significance is being rediscovered in our own time. For a generation after his death, Troeltsch's work was widely dismissed. If he was referred to at all, it was as the foremost representative of a theological trend that could be regarded only as a tragic failure, a dead end from which theology had to liberate itself.[1] Yet even in the midst of this chorus of disapproval, there were some thinkers who recognized the significance of Troeltsch's achievement. More than thirty-five years ago, for example, J. M. Creed wrote that while some schools of modern theology seemed to bypass the problems raised by Troeltsch, those problems would assuredly recur.[2] His prophecy has proven to be abundantly justified. As the problems *have* recurred, a number of theologians have turned back to Troeltsch to see if his solutions could be reappropriated. Walter E. Wyman, for example, has suggested that "a post-Neo-Orthodox theology is in a position to appropriate Troeltsch's program and rectify its defects."[3] Garrett E. Paul, in the introduction to his translation of Troeltsch's *The Christian Faith*, writes: "The man once

---

[1] For a summary of these judgments, see B. A. Gerrish, "Ernst Troeltsch and the Possibility of a Historical Theology," in *Ernst Troeltsch and the Future of Theology*, edited by John Powell Clayton (Cambridge: Cambridge University Press, 1976), 111–12. As Sarah Coakley notes (*Christ without Absolutes: A Study of the Christology of Ernst Troeltsch* [Oxford: Clarendon, 1988], 189, n.1), it is disappointing to see this judgment repeated in so recent a work as Alister E. McGrath's *The Making of Modern German Christology: 1750–1990,* 2d edition (Grand Rapids: Zondervan, 1994), 115–22.

[2] Creed, *The Divinity of Jesus Christ,* 117.

[3] Walter E. Wyman, *The Concept of Glaubenslehre: Ernst Troeltsch and the Theological Heritage of Schleiermacher,* American Academy of Religion Academy Series 44 (Chico, Calif.: Scholars Press, 1983), 201.

thought to be the last theologian of the nineteenth century may yet turn
out to be the first theologian of the twentieth—or even the twenty-
first."[4] Even Roy Harrisville and Walter Sundberg (at first sight unlikely
sympathizers) have expressed similar sentiments:"There are signs everywhere that it may be Troeltsch, the romantic historicist, who speaks for
religion in the years ahead."[5] It is clear, then, that Troeltsch's work can no
longer be ignored. It is true that Troeltsch wrote relatively little on the
question of the historical Jesus, but much of his theological work is
devoted to the larger question of historical knowledge and its impact on
religious thought. He is therefore a key figure for the debate that is the
subject of this book. However, it should be noted that Troeltsch was not
only a theologian. He was also a philosopher, a historian, and one of the
first sociologists of religion. Indeed, he spent the last years of his academic life teaching, not in a theological faculty, but in the faculty of philosophy at the University of Berlin. His collected works (*Gesammelte
Schriften*) comprise four large volumes, and even these do not include all
his published writings.[6] For this reason the present study can make no
claim to do justice to Troeltsch's work in its entirety. Troeltsch *as theologian* is our subject here. Yet even when writing about Troeltsch as a
theologian, a further restriction is necessary. Troeltsch believed that
Christian theology, insofar as it was "scientific" at all, needed to be
founded on a broader "science of religion."[7] Such a science of religion
would begin with a psychological and epistemological study of religious
phenomena before moving on to a historical and metaphysical analysis.[8]
However, I have deliberately neglected Troeltsch's psychology and epistemology of religion,[9] in order to concentrate on his understanding of
history and its impact on religious authority.

---

[4]Garrett E. Paul, introduction to the English edition of *The Christian Faith,* by Ernst
Troeltsch, translated by Garrett E. Paul, Fortress Texts in Modern Theology (Minneapo-
lis: Fortress Press, 1991), xvi.
[5]Roy A. Harrisville and Walter Sundberg, *The Bible in Modern Culture: Theology and
Historical-Critical Method from Spinoza to Käsemann* (Grand Rapids: Eerdmans, 1995), 179.
[6]Ernst Troeltsch, *Gesammelte Schriften,* vols. 1–4 (Tübingen: J. C. B. Mohr [Paul
Siebeck], 1912–26). On the question of which material was included, see Hans-Georg
Drescher, *Ernst Troeltsch: His Life and Work* (1991), translated by John Bowden (London:
SCM, 1992), 359, n.65. The new *Kritische Gesamtausgabe* of Troeltsch's work, presently in
preparation, should eventually reach to twenty volumes.
[7]Cf. Ernst Troeltsch, "Religion and the Science of Religion" (1906), translated by
Michael Pye, in *Writings on Theology and Religion,* 88–89.
[8]Cf. ibid., 114–17.
[9]For a discussion, see Wyman, *The Concept of Glaubenslehre,* 26–36, which merely
reinforces a central claim of this chapter, namely, that Troeltsch's religious thought is
inextricably bound up with a type of metaphysical idealism.

Yet these restrictions do not represent a distortion of Troeltsch's thought.[10] At the very heart of Troeltsch's theological concerns is the question of "historicism" (*der Historismus*), which he defines as "the fundamental historicising of all our thinking about human beings, their culture and their values."[11] The meaning of this all too brief and rather circular definition will become clearer as our discussion unfolds. The following pages single out for comment four issues that are central to Troeltsch's theological achievement. The first issue concerns Troeltsch's understanding of historical research and its significance for faith. The second concerns Troeltsch's understanding of the course of history, which allowed him (as we will see) to reclaim historical research for theology. The third issue is closely related to the second: it concerns Troeltsch's understanding of the place of Christianity within the history of religions. The fourth has to do with the religious significance of the historical Jesus. We must examine each of these topics in turn before venturing any opinion on the significance of Troeltsch's thought for our own time. Can Christian theology survive the challenges of history by "appropriating Troeltsch's program and rectifying its defects"? Or are Troeltsch's solutions no longer available to the theologian of our time? Those are the questions to which the final section of this chapter will be devoted.

A word of warning: Troeltsch's work is not easily summarized. Not only did he spread his scholarly energies over a wide range of topics, but—by his own admission—he never developed a system of thought.[12] The nearest approach to a theological system is to be found in his work *The Christian Faith,* and we have this only in the form of a student's transcript of his lectures at Heidelberg in 1911–12.[13] For the most part

---

[10]In his 1913 essay "The Dogmatics of the History-of-Religions School" (translated by Walter E. Wyman Jr., in *Religion in History: Essays Translated by James Luther Adams and Walter F. Bense* [Edinburgh: T. & T. Clark, 1991], 95–99), Troeltsch leaves aside the question of the psychology and epistemology of religion and describes the "first task" of such a theology as comparative historical study.

[11]Ernst Troeltsch, *Der Historismus und seine Probleme—Erstes Buch: Das logische Problem der Geschichtsphilosophie,* Gesammelte Schriften 3 (Tübingen: J. C. B. Mohr [Paul Siebeck], 1922), 102: *[die] grundsätzliche Historisierung alles unseres Denkens über den Menschen, seine Kultur und seine Werte.*

[12]Ernst Troeltsch, "My Books" (1922), translated by Franklin H. Littell and revised by Walter F. Bense, in *Religion in History,* 365. See also Troeltsch's *Der Historismus und seine Probleme,* viii, where he suggests that any system he created would have to be "open and able to be modified" (*ein offenes modifikables System*).

[13]Ernst Troeltsch, *Glaubenslehre: Nach Heidelberger Vorlesungen aus den Jahren 1911 u. 1912* (Munich: Duncker & Humblot, 1925). Citations of the German text come from this edition, which will henceforth be cited as *Glaubenslehre.*

Troeltsch's writings are suggestive rather than conclusive: they attempt to open up questions from a variety of perspectives rather than to offer definitive solutions. Furthermore, Troeltsch was happy to change his mind over time. Indeed, he expected that his later writings would display different positions from those he had adopted earlier.[14] Even within a single work such as *The Absoluteness of Christianity,*[15] it is not clear that Troeltsch's thought is entirely consistent. In some ways these traits reflect his thoroughly historical attitude to truth, but they do not make it easy to summarize his ideas. In what follows I will attempt to systematize what Troeltsch himself so often left unsystematic, while indicating as far as possible the questions he left open and the developments and ambiguities in his thought.

1. Historical and Dogmatic Method

Ernst Troeltsch is perhaps best known today for his discussion of the principles of historical method, namely "criticism," "analogy," and "correlation." This discussion is found in an essay entitled "Historical and Dogmatic Method in Theology." The essay was first published in 1898 in response to criticisms of his work by Friedrich Niebergall (1866–1932), a disciple of the theologian Julius Kaftan (1848–1926).[16] These three principles of historical criticism are important, Troeltsch believes, because they summarize the intellectual challenge facing Christianity in the modern age. For this reason Troeltsch's discussion of these principles offers a helpful way into his religious thought.

Troeltsch begins by noting that contemporary theology has not yet grappled in a systematic way with the consequences of the new historical viewpoint of our time. It is true that theology deals with some of the *particular* problems raised by the historical criticism of the Bible, but it does so only in a piecemeal fashion. When Christianity is treated systematically, Troeltsch writes, theologians seize hold of whatever aspects of modern thought will enable them to shore up what Troeltsch calls "the

---

[14]Cf. Drescher, Ernst Troeltsch, 132.

[15]Ernst Troeltsch, *Die Absolutheit des Christentums und die Religionsgeschichte,* 2d edition (Tübingen: J. C. B. Mohr [Paul Siebeck], 1912). I have generally relied upon the English translation of the third edition: *The Absoluteness of Christianity and the History of Religions,* translated by David Reid, Library of Philosophy and Theology (London: SCM, 1972). On the inconsistencies in the second edition, see Coakley, *Christ without Absolutes,* 74–77.

[16]Ernst Troeltsch, "Historical and Dogmatic Method in Theology" (1898), translated by Ephraim Fischoff and revised by Walter Bense, in *Religion in History,* 11–32; reprinted in my anthology *The Historical Jesus Quest,* 29–53. For the circumstances of its composition, see Drescher, Ernst Troeltsch, 93.

old, authoritarian concept of revelation."[17] In this way they manage to "weave together a tolerable dogmatic system," while leaving exegetes and historians to grapple with the broader historical issues.[18] Exegetes and historians, for their part, do not attempt to deal with the larger theological problems raised by their research. What has yet to be undertaken, therefore, is a systematic reworking of theology on the basis of this new, historical mode of thought.

What is this new mode of thought? Troeltsch summarizes the new historical viewpoint under three principles. The first is the principle of "criticism," which holds that the source materials of the historian's work must be subject to evaluation. In other words, the historian must take a critical attitude towards his sources, which may be mistaken or deceptive. The results of this critical scrutiny can never be more than a matter of probability.[19] The second is the principle of "analogy," which holds that both in evaluating his materials and in constructing an account of the past, the historian must rely on the essential similarity of all historical occurrences. Our own experience of how accounts of events can be distorted leads us to recognize similar distortions in the material we are studying. The likelihood of certain events occurring in the past must be measured by the standards of the present.[20] Applied to the Bible, the principle of analogy means that Jewish and Christian history are regarded as comparable to other histories. In practice, Troeltsch writes, this equivalence is increasingly recognized. Only two aspects of the Gospel story, he suggests, are today exempted from the principle of analogy: namely "Jesus' moral character and the resurrection."[21] The third principle underlying the historical method is that of "correlation," which suggests that any historical event, however novel, must also be understood as shaped by the context in which it occurs. This means, for instance, that

[17]Troeltsch, "Historical and Dogmatic Method in Theology," 12; *The Historical Jesus Quest,* 31.

[18]Ibid.

[19]Troeltsch's point here is very close to what R. G. Collingwood (*The Idea of History* [1946; Oxford: Oxford University Press, 1961], 257–61, 274–82, et passim) intended when he contrasted "scissors and paste" with "critical" historiography. For Collingwood's disagreement with Troeltsch's principle of analogy, see the final section of this chapter.

[20]Cf. Troeltsch, "Historical and Dogmatic Method in Theology," 13–14; *The Historical Jesus Quest,* 32.

[21]Troeltsch, "Historical and Dogmatic Method in Theology," 14; *The Historical Jesus Quest,* 33. Troeltsch deals briefly with the resurrection appearances in *The Christian Faith* §18 (219). He expresses a preference for the view that these are explicable psychologically, as "visions" (an idea put forward—as we have seen—by D. F. Strauss and popularized in our own time by Gerd Lüdemann). In this way he brings the resurrection *appearances,* at least, under the principle of analogy.

the emergence of Christianity cannot be understood without a careful study of "the general political, social, and intellectual history of antiquity."[22] To put it bluntly, Christianity may be of divine origin (as in a certain sense even Troeltsch wishes to affirm), but it did not fall from heaven ready-made. It emerged only within a particular historical context and was decisively shaped by that context. For instance, the rise of Christianity has to be related to what Troeltsch calls "the disintegration of Judaism" and to "the political movements and apocalyptic ideas of the time."[23] The rest of Troeltsch's essay is devoted to a discussion of the implications of these principles, which are best discussed under the headings found below.

2. The Significance of History

Embracing the Great Reversal
It will already be clear that Troeltsch takes most seriously the challenges posed by the new knowledge of the seventeenth century.[24] In the introduction to the present work I outlined those challenges, which resulted in what Hans Frei has called "the great reversal," a major shift in attitude towards the Bible and Christianity. The old attitude, which held sway among Christian writers from the second century until about the mid-seventeenth, regarded Christianity as a unique phenomenon.[25] Christianity, along with its predecessor, biblical Judaism, was a "revealed religion," whose origin lay with the divinity himself. In the history of Israel and the life, death, and resurrection of Jesus, God had intervened in human history, with a series of actions that were without parallel, in order to establish the Christian dispensation. The Christian scriptures likewise possessed a divine origin. It is true that they were written by human beings, but only under the inspiration of the Holy Spirit. Therefore, while the scriptures had been "committed to" the church, they were in no sense "created" by it.[26] By way of contrast, the new mental-

---

[22]Troeltsch, "Historical and Dogmatic Method in Theology," 15; *The Historical Jesus Quest,* 34.

[23]Ibid.

[24]For a discussion of Troeltsch's gradual embrace of a thoroughly historical perspective, in opposition to the theology of Albrecht Ritschl and his school, see Coakley, *Christ without Absolutes,* 45–79.

[25]Karl Barth offers a helpful summary of this older view of Christianity among the "religions" in his *Church Dogmatics, vol. 1, part 2: The Doctrine of the Word of God,* translated by G. T. Thomson and Harold Knight (Edinburgh: T. & T. Clark, 1956), 284–88. I will examine Barth's rehabilitation of this position in chapter 5.

[26]Creed, *The Divinity of Jesus Christ,* 105–6.

ity regarded Christianity as first and foremost a fact of human history. Rather than an unparalleled phenomenon, Christianity became increasingly thought of as "a religion," one among many, the product of a particular history and culture. It may have emerged under special divine guidance; it may be the highest expression of the religious spirit. However, any such claim now needed proof; it could no longer be assumed.

This shift in attitude toward the Bible and the Christian faith is at the heart of Troeltsch's theological work. For the new perspective that followed this reversal is precisely that which Troeltsch described as "historicism." It is nothing less than "the fundamental historicising of our knowledge and thought,"[27] in the realm of religion. Indeed, the contrast I have drawn corresponds precisely to Troeltsch's distinction between the "dogmatic" and the "historical" method in theology. Troeltsch traces the development of this new attitude into at least five influences, which may be compared to those discussed in the introduction to the present work. There was the revival of humanist scholarship at the time of the Renaissance.[28] This was followed by the Reformation with its interest in history,[29] and the conflict between rival Christian groups which followed.[30] The seventeenth century saw the beginnings of the conflict between what Troeltsch calls "the autonomous rational philosophy of the late Renaissance" (i.e., early modern science) and a faith based on supernatural interventions of God into the natural order.[31] The Enlightenment thinkers of the eighteenth century undertook a criticism of established political and social institutions on historical grounds.[32] Finally, the period of European colonial expansion led to a new awareness of the diversity of human religions.[33]

The implications of these shifts in attitude are enormous. Indeed, Troeltsch argues that together they represent something new in the history of human thought. As he writes in *The Absoluteness of Christianity,* human horizons have been expanded, "both backward into the past and laterally across the entire breadth of the present."[34] As a result of this expansion, the authority of one's own culture can no longer be taken for

---

[27]Troeltsch, *Der Historismus und seine Probleme,* 9.

[28]Cf. Ernst Troeltsch, *The Absoluteness of Christianity and the History of Religions* (1st edition, 1902), 3d edition (1929), translated by David Reid, Library of Philosophy and Theology (London: SCM, 1972), 45.

[29]Cf. ibid.

[30]Cf. Ernst Troeltsch, "The Dogmatics of the History-of-Religions School," 88.

[31]Ibid.

[32]Troeltsch, *The Absoluteness of Christianity,* 45.

[33]Cf. Troeltsch, "The Dogmatics of the History-of-Religions School," 88.

[34]Troeltsch, *The Absoluteness of Christianity,* 46.

granted. One can no longer justify one's own religion simply by claiming, for example, that it (alone) is divinely revealed or that its truth is
obvious to any person of goodwill. As far as Christianity was concerned,
even when its opponents could produce no compelling arguments *against*
its claims, its uniqueness was called into question simply by being placed
in this new context. It looked different when viewed as *a religion*, comparable to others. Christianity, for example, might take its stand on
miracles and its opponents might not be able to deny the *possibility* of
miracles. But the historian must treat Christian and non-Christian claims
to miracles by the same criteria: "it is impossible for historical thought to
believe the Christian miracles but deny the non-Christian."[35] Thus the
Christian miracle stories lose plausibility, even if they cannot be—strictly
speaking—"disproven." In the area of theology, this new historical perspective is most clearly displayed in the "history of religions school" (*die
religionsgeschichtliche Schule*), which seeks to discern a history of human
religious development, and to locate Christianity within that history.
However, it is by no means restricted to those scholars who are generally
associated with this movement; it is the necessary presupposition of any
theology that claims to be in any sense "modern."[36] As Troeltsch writes,
"we are no longer able to think without this method or contrary to it."[37]

History as the Scene of Revelation
The idea that such a radically historical view should be the basis of a
new theology would have surprised many of Troeltsch's more sceptical
contemporaries. At first sight this radically "decentered" view of the
Christian religion would seem to put an end to Christian theology, with
its claims to uniqueness based on biblical authority. The most notable
nineteenth-century exponent of this sceptical view was Karl Marx
(1818–83), for whom this shift of attitude implied the overturning of
religious claims.[38] However, Troeltsch was clear that his work repre-

[35]Troeltsch, *The Absoluteness of Christianity,* 48. On miracles, see also *The Christian
Faith,* §18 (219); "The Place of Christianity among the World-Religions," translated by
Mary E. Clarke, in *Christian Thought: Its History and Application,* edited by F. von Hügel
(London: University of London Press, 1923), 12; "On the Question of the Religious A
Priori" (1909), in *Religion in History,* 43.
[36]Cf. Troeltsch, "The Dogmatics of the History-of-Religions School," 87–88; "Historical and Dogmatic Method in Theology," 19; *The Historical Jesus Quest,* 38.
[37]Troeltsch, "Historical and Dogmatic Method in Theology," 16; *The Historical Jesus
Quest,* 35.
[38]Cf. Karl Marx, "Contribution to the Critique of Hegel's Philosophy of Right"
(1844), in *Karl Marx: Early Writings,* translated by T. B. Bottomore (London: C. A. Watts,
1963), 43: "The basis of irreligious criticism is this: *man makes religion*; religion does not
make man."

sented an alternative to such (some would say "reductionist"[39]) views.[40] For Troeltsch was a firm believer in what he called "the independence of religion."[41] In a way that sets him in opposition to thinkers such as Marx and Feuerbach, Troeltsch argues that religion's claim to autonomy should be taken seriously. It should not be "reduced" to other manifestations of human spiritual life, such as the fear of natural forces or a projection of human needs onto the cosmos.[42] Religion is, of course, *related* to a variety of historical factors, but it has its own, independent reality. Religious judgments are no less "valid" than are our moral and aesthetic judgments.[43] It follows that religion is "independent" in the sense of being always more than the influences to which it is undoubtedly related.[44] As Troeltsch writes in his 1897 essay "Christianity and the History of Religion," "the deepest core of the religious history of humanity reveals itself as an experience that cannot be further analysed, an ultimate and original phenomenon that constitutes, like moral judgement and aesthetic perception and yet with characteristic differences, a simple fact of psychic life."[45] This belief in the independence of religion seems to be one of the few constants in Troeltsch's thought. Even in a lecture which he prepared for delivery at Oxford University in 1923, and in which he modified some of his earlier views, Troeltsch writes: "I have come more and more to regard the specific kernel of religion as a unique and independent source of power."[46]

It should now be clear that Troeltsch's position was a carefully nuanced one. On the one hand, he insisted that the theologian must accept the new, historical viewpoint, with all its implications. On the

[39]Troeltsch would undoubtedly approve of the term "reductionist," although it is in fact question-begging, as J. Samuel Preus points out (*Explaining Religion,* ix), preferring the term "naturalistic." On helpful and unhelpful uses of the term "reductionism," see Wayne Proudfoot, *Religious Experience* (Berkeley: University of California Press, 1985), 190–98.

[40]Cf. Troeltsch, "Religion and the Science of Religion," 83–84, 110–11.

[41]*Die Selbständigkeit der Religion*; cf. Drescher, *Ernst Troeltsch,* 75–85.

[42]Cf. Drescher, *Ernst Troeltsch,* 77; Wyman, *The Concept of Glaubenslehre,* 28–29.

[43]Cf. Wyman, *The Concept of Glaubenslehre,* 31. To support this claim, Troeltsch needs to postulate (in Kantian terms) a religious a priori, comparable to the structures of the mind which underlie moral and aesthetic judgments. See Troeltsch, "On the Question of the Religious A Priori," 33–45; "Religion and the Science of Religion," 116–17.

[44]Cf. Ernst Troeltsch, "Glaube und Ethos der hebräischen Propheten" (1916), in *Gesammelte Schriften* 4 (Tübingen: J. C. B. Mohr [Paul Siebeck], 1925), 34–38; translated by Joseph Mow as "Rival Methods for the Study of Religion," in *Religion in History,* 73–76.

[45]Ernst Troeltsch, "Christianity and the History of Religion" (1897), in *Religion in History,* 79.

[46]Troeltsch, "The Place of Christianity among the World-Religions," 31.

other, he remained a believer and a theologian, convinced that even if one rejected traditional, a priori claims to biblical authority, that did not mean that the Bible lost its religious significance. Certainly, one could no longer begin by privileging the biblical view of history as a scene of supernatural divine intervention. Christianity could only be understood as one phenomenon, comparable to others, among the diverse phenomena of human religious history. Yet its religious significance is not thereby undermined: Christianity continues to make binding demands on its adherents.

Of course, it is not easy to hold these two positions together. How could one reconcile regarding Christianity as a product of history with the continued assertion of its divine authority? A detailed answer to this question must await the next section; what will be noted here is the principle on which Troeltsch's solution was built. That principle was a simple one, which also remained remarkably consistent throughout his career: the principle of the theological significance of the course of human religious development. In other words, Troeltsch attributed a religious meaning, not only to the biblical story, but also to the wider sweep of history, within which the Bible now had to find its place. He held to a particular philosophy of history, which enabled him to see even the apparently secular past as a scene of divine activity. More precisely, for Troeltsch history is the place where divine revelation occurs, and this conviction makes theological reflection possible, even after the reversal of the seventeenth century. It follows that the difference between Troeltsch's theology and that of the patristic, medieval, and Reformation periods lay in its starting point. For the earlier theology, the starting point was the authority of the Bible as a repository of divinely revealed truth; for Troeltsch it was the religious development of humanity as a whole as uncovered by historical research. History was now the new *locus theologicus,* the source of the theologian's reflections, taking the place of the old dogmatic authorities.

Once again, Troeltsch's essay on "Historical and Dogmatic Method in Theology" offers evidence of these views, which are also found in his later work.[47] The first hint is to be found in Troeltsch's insistence—against his opponents—that the historical mode of thought need not give rise to what he calls "a nihilistic skepticism."[48] Judgments of value are still possible. The historical method means only that our judgments

---

[47]Cf. Troeltsch, *The Christian Faith,* §6 (82), *The Absoluteness of Christianity,* 126 et passim.

[48]Troeltsch, "Historical and Dogmatic Method in Theology," 18; *The Historical Jesus Quest,* 37.

must be based on the *whole* of history.[49] As he writes, "standards of values cannot be derived from isolated events but only from an overview of the historical totality."[50] Yet why *should* "an overview of the historical totality" yield an insight into lasting values? At first Troeltsch offers only a hint of an answer. A consistent application of the historical method, he writes, will enable us "to behold with greater detachment and freedom the glory of God in history."[51] But this only deepens the puzzle. What does it mean "to behold the glory of God in history"? It means, Troeltsch suggests, grasping the divine revelation that occurs through the influence of certain great religious personalities, a divine revelation that can also be described as a type of "religious intuition."[52]

What is reflected in these enigmatic sayings is Troeltsch's particular view of revelation, which is more clearly expressed in his work *The Christian Faith*.[53] Traditional orthodoxy, Troeltsch notes, restricted the field of revelation to the Bible. But this restriction proved to be scarcely tenable, even on orthodox grounds, for it is almost impossible to avoid talk of an ongoing revelation in post-biblical Christian history.[54] Yet even this is too narrow an idea. In our own time, the field of revelation cannot be limited even to the history of the Christian faith, although one can certainly defend the idea that Christianity is the highest revelation, which will not be surpassed, at least in the foreseeable future.[55] (We will return to this claim shortly.) It follows that the very idea of revelation needs to change: this idea, too, must be reworked in the light of our historical consciousness. Revelation can no longer be regarded as the transmission of certain changeless truths. It must be thought of as a particular development of human consciousness, a particular form of the

---

[49]As we will see shortly, Troeltsch will later qualify this view by noting that we cannot know the whole of history. We can only attempt to discern the direction in which it is moving.

[50]Troeltsch, "Historical and Dogmatic Method in Theology," 18; *The Historical Jesus Quest,* 37.

[51]Troeltsch, "Historical and Dogmatic Method in Theology," 19; *The Historical Jesus Quest,* 39.

[52]Troeltsch, "Historical and Dogmatic Method in Theology," 20; *The Historical Jesus Quest,* 39.

[53]Despite the controversy that has at times surrounded it, I have taken *The Christian Faith* as a faithful representation of Troeltsch's thought (cf. Wyman, *The Concept of Glaubenslehre,* xiv–xvii.) However, since no aspect of my argument rests on the *Glaubenslehre* alone, and since my presentation of Troeltsch's thought is relatively uncontroversial, I have not bothered to distinguish between the dictated text and Gertrud von le Fort's notes.

[54]Cf. Troeltsch, *The Christian Faith,* §3 (40).

[55]Cf. ibid., §3 (41; cf. *Glaubenslehre,* 41).

inner life. Troeltsch refers to this, somewhat enigmatically, as "an inner awareness [*eine . . . innere Erregung*] that issues from the mysterious connection of the divine and human spirits."[56] "Revelation" redefined in this way embraces what Troeltsch calls "the whole of the inner life, with its religious and ethical convictions and values."[57] It is this *inner life* that we find revealed in what Troeltsch calls "the great biblical personalities."[58] This accounts for the ongoing revelatory significance of the Bible, for it is through the biblical witness that we learn of these personalities.

What this means, we might note, is that the Bible is (strictly speaking) a "witness to revelation, not itself revelation."[59] More importantly, if this is how revelation is regarded, there is no reason to restrict it to the *biblical* personalities, nor (for that matter) to the past. As Troeltsch notes later in *The Christian Faith,*

> we must learn to see the light that shines from God, the revelation of God, in the whole of history [*im Ganzen des geschichtlichen Lebens*]. When we do, we will no longer view the profusion of religions as a hindrance. Revelation is not limited to Christianity; similar revelation and divine seizure [*göttliches Ergriffenwerden*] is to be found everywhere.[60]

It follows that for Troeltsch the new science of "the history of religions" was not merely the study of religion as a cultural phenomenon. Rather, it was a theological resource, indeed, the very foundation of any theology that wanted to do justice to the demands of modern knowledge. For Troeltsch, the testimony of secular history was not just a "fiery brook" through which theology must pass, and from which it might hope to emerge relatively unscathed. Rather, it was a positive resource, a new foundation for theology that functioned as an alternative to supernaturalist views of the Bible and the church.

The Influence of Idealism

Troeltsch's view of the theological significance of history was undergird by his adherence to the philosophical position known as idealism. (In chapter 2 I made reference to the idealist metaphysics of G. W. F. Hegel, which provided the young David Friedrich Strauss with an—admittedly

---

[56]Ibid.

[57]Ibid.

[58]Ibid.

[59]*Zeugnis der Offenbarung, nicht selbst Offenbarung.* (I have altered Garrett E. Paul's translation very slightly at this point.) The phrase is striking, since it calls to mind Karl Barth's position, to which I will return in chapter 5.

[60]Ibid., §6 (82); cf. *Glaubenslehre,* 94.

short-lived—way out of his theological difficulties.) "Idealism" is, of course, another notoriously vague term. We are therefore fortunate to have a discussion of its meaning written by Troeltsch himself, for the 1914 edition of James Hastings's *Encyclopedia of Religion and Ethics.* Troeltsch concedes that, even in its metaphysical sense, the term "ideal-ism" covers a wide variety of positions. What unites them all, however, is the idea that "the primary and most certain datum of experience" is "consciousness and its contents."[61] For the idealist, consciousness is not passive with regard to experience, as if it merely registered what was there. Rather, consciousness (or "mind") actively shapes our perception, so that the mind is in a very real sense "the formative principle of the real."[62] It follows that the mind (or "spirit")[63] cannot be regarded as derived from matter, since matter is only known insofar as it is shaped by the mind. Therefore, the mind is the source of meaning and is intelligi-ble to itself. In the same essay Troeltsch speaks of the "immense signifi-cance" of idealism for religious life and thought. Idealism stands opposed to all forms of "materialism and semi-materialism"[64] and is therefore "the metaphysical precondition of religious belief."[65]

In this brief article, Troeltsch does not discuss the implications of ide-alism for one's understanding of history. However, it is not difficult to see what these will be. Troeltsch notes that the goals that the mind pursues are revealed only "in the process of spiritual development."[66] By "the process of spiritual development" Troeltsch seems to mean something like what we would call the cultural history of humanity.[67] It follows that for the idealist, the history of human thought and belief will be of metaphysical interest, since it will reveal the nature of mind. This is of *metaphysical* interest because mind is (as just noted) "the formative prin-ciple of the real." It accounts for the shape of the world, at least *as we know it.*[68] The claims made in Troeltsch's "Historical and Dogmatic

[61]Ernst Troeltsch, "Idealism," in *Encyclopedia of Religion and Ethics,* edited by James Hastings (Edinburgh: T. & T. Clark, 1914), 7:90a.

[62]Ibid., 94b.

[63]As noted in chapter 2, in all discussions of idealism we should keep in mind the range of meanings possessed by the German term *Geist,* which can be translated as either "spirit" or "mind."

[64]Troeltsch, "Idealism," 94b.

[65]Ibid., 95a.

[66]Ibid., 94b.

[67]The German adjective *geistig,* generally translated as "spiritual," reflects the ambigu-ities of the term *Geist* and must be understood as embracing human cultural achieve-ments in the broadest sense.

[68]In post-Kantian idealism, this condition would tend to disappear; it would be sim-ply affirmed that mind (or spirit) was the formative principle of the real. Epistemology would quickly become metaphysics.

Method" become intelligible in the light of this view. Since the human mind stands in what Troeltsch calls "a mysterious connection" with the divine,[69] the cultural history of humankind becomes much more than the mere revelation of the potentialities of the human mind. It is nothing less than what Troeltsch calls "a disclosure of the divine reason."[70] Earlier in the nineteenth century such a view was often supported by appeal to Hegel's philosophy, with its understanding of human history as the progressive embodiment of the Absolute Spirit. (Here the divine mind and the human mind are regarded as identical.) Although Troeltsch continually distances himself from Hegel's scheme,[71] in his essay on "Historical and Dogmatic Method" he also acknowledges its "undeniable merits."[72] Troeltsch is clear (as we will see shortly) that the direction of human history cannot be deduced a priori from a knowledge of the nature of reason, as Hegel seemed to imagine. However, he is equally clear (in a way in which more recent historians are not) that the overall course of history is meaningful, since it is an expression of mind. As he writes,

> history is not a chaos but issues from unitary forces and aspires towards a unitary goal. For the believer in religion and ethics, history is an orderly sequence in which the essential truth and profundity of the human spirit rises from its transcendent ground. . . . With the great idealists, I believe that in this apparent chaos the divine depth of the human spirit reveals itself from different directions.[73]

Since there is an intimate relationship between human and divine reason, both being *Geist* or "spirit," the progressive revelation of the nature

---

[69]Cf. Troeltsch, *The Christian Faith*, §3 (41). The German text (*Glaubenslehre*, also 41) speaks of [*das*] *Geheimnis des Zusammenhangs des göttlichen und menschlichen Geistes*. The question of the relationship between the human mind and the divine mind is addressed more fully in Troeltsch's "On the Question of the Religious A Priori" (cf. 41) and in *Der Historismus und seine Probleme* (cf. 183–86; 677–79). A detailed study of this difficult matter would take us beyond the limits of the present work. For an attempt to piece together Troeltsch's metaphysical assumptions, which are nowhere spelt out systematically, see Wyman, *The Concept of Glaubenslehre*, 43–46.

[70]Troeltsch, "Historical and Dogmatic Method in Theology," 27; *The Historical Jesus Quest*, 47.

[71]James Luther Adams (introduction to Troeltsch, *The Absoluteness of Christianity*, 13) refers to Troeltsch's position as a "relativized Hegelianism." For the differences between Troeltsch's position and Hegel's, see particularly Troeltsch, "Modern Philosophy of History" (1904), in *Religion in History*, 292–93; "Religion and the Science of Religion," 117; *The Absoluteness of Christianity*, 63–83. For a discussion of some changes in Troeltsch's evaluation of Hegel, see Drescher, *Ernst Troeltsch*, 440, n.214.

[72]Troeltsch, "Historical and Dogmatic Method in Theology," 27; *The Historical Jesus Quest*, 47.

[73]Ibid.

of mind is also a revelation of God. In this way idealism enables Troeltsch to see history as the scene of revelation and thus as a theological resource.[74]

Throughout his life, Troeltsch continued to hold to philosophical idealism and to what he himself called "a religious interpretation of history."[75] We have just seen evidence of this view in his early essay on "Historical and Dogmatic Method in Theology." In the slightly later essay "Religion and the Science of Religion," Troeltsch remarks that only the adoption of an idealist metaphysics can ward off the danger of purely naturalist (or, if one prefers, "reductionist") theories of religion.[76] It is true that Troeltsch can spend an entire chapter of *The Absoluteness of Christianity* distancing himself from the evolutionary view of religion exemplified by Hegel. But in that work he also admits that his own solution has much in common with Hegel's. The commonality consists in a particular understanding of history.[77] Troeltsch's commitment to idealism is reiterated in his *The Christian Faith*. Here Troeltsch claims that something like an idealist metaphysics is indispensable if one wishes to maintain a religious point of view. The believer must reject materialism, positivism, pantheism (in its strict sense), and all forms of sceptical relativism.[78] The apparently a priori nature of this claim ("religion demands . . . ; therefore we must believe") does not bother Troeltsch in the least, since—like so many nineteenth-century thinkers—he regarded idealism as entirely defensible on purely philosophical grounds. In his words, "we must therefore not be misled by the pessimism and materialism that hover around us, for our highest and most civilized concepts point in the direction of idealism."[79] In his uncompleted study *Historicism and Its*

[74]It could be argued that German idealism was itself the product of a Christian culture (cf. Troeltsch, "The Common Spirit," translated by H. G. Atkins, in *Christian Thought: Its History and Application,* 104) and as such to have been the last expression of a publicly acceptable religious worldview. It certainly seems to have functioned in this way for D. F. Strauss, for whom a loss of confidence in idealism seems to have coincided with a loss of confidence in any traditional form of religion. If so, then there is an element of circularity in Troeltsch's philosophy of religion: something like the Christian vision of reality is assumed in order to demonstrate the superiority of the Christian vision of reality.

[75]Troeltsch, *The Christian Faith,* §6 (73). On the consistency of Troeltsch's search for a metaphysics of history, see the recent article by Peter De Mey, "Ernst Troeltsch: A Moderate Pluralist? An Evaluation of His Reflections on the Place of Christianity among the Other Religions," in *The Myriad Christ: Plurality and the Quest for Unity in Contemporary Christology,* edited by T. Merrigan and J. Haers, Bibliotheca Ephemeridum Theologicarum Lovaniensium 152 (Louvain: University Press, 2000), 364–76.

[76]Cf. Troeltsch, "Religion and the Science of Religion," 118.

[77]Cf. Troeltsch, *The Absoluteness of Christianity,* 61 (cf. 100).

[78]Cf. Troeltsch, *The Christian Faith,* §4 (54).

[79]Ibid., §4 (61).

Problems,[80] Troeltsch remains committed to what is still a recognizably idealist metaphysics, whatever alterations that may be undergoing. His solution to the problem of value judgment in history, for example, rests on an idealist assertion of what he calls "the fundamental and individual identity of finite spirits with the infinite spirit."[81] Even in a lecture that Troeltsch prepared shortly before his death we find language reminiscent of his idealist creed.[82] To understand the way Troeltsch builds on these idealist assumptions, we must turn to a closer study of his writings on Christianity.

3. Christianity among the Religions

We have seen that Troeltsch can attribute religious significance to history, in this way redeeming historical study for theological purposes. We have also seen that he does this on the basis of an idealist metaphysics. Yet the question remains as to how Troeltsch regarded *Christianity* in this context. What place, if any, remains for Christianity's apparently absolute claims to authority? If Christianity, like any other religion, can be understood only in terms of the principle of "correlation," that is to say, as the product of a particular time and place, how can it claim validity for *all* times and *all* places? The question is an important one, even for those outside the Christian fold, for it concerns the abiding value of *any* claim to ethical or religious truth.[83] Among all the thinkers studied in the course of this work, Troeltsch is the one to grapple most profoundly with these issues. He does not do so in the manner of Spinoza, by claiming certain truths to be timeless, beyond the reach of historical variability. Nor—in the manner of Schweitzer—does he attempt to isolate moral claims from metaphysical, claiming permanence only for the former. Rather, Troeltsch tries to argue that judgments of value can still be made, even though these judgments are also conditioned by the contexts in which they occur. Insofar as Troeltsch has difficulties maintaining this position, it is because his historical method is entirely consistent. He applied his method not only to the past, but also to the work of the

---

[80]*Der Historismus und seine Probleme.*

[81]Troeltsch, *Der Historismus und seine Probleme,* 677: *die wesenhafte und individuelle Identität der endlichen Geister mit dem unendlichen Geiste.* The quotation should not be taken out of context, since on the following page Troeltsch stresses the limits of this "identity."

[82]Cf. Troeltsch, "The Place of Christianity among the World-Religions," 32.

[83]A fact noted by Troeltsch himself; cf. Troeltsch, "Modern Philosophy of History," 275–76, and *The Absoluteness of Christianity,* 132–33. Indeed, his late work *Der Historismus und seine Probleme* is an attempt to grapple with the same issue in a larger cultural context, in which religious values are merely one set of values among others.

modern historian. Troeltsch recognizes that there is no standpoint that is itself immune from historical analysis, but he argues that recognition of this fact need not lead to a nihilistic relativism. We *can* make judgments of value, although we must also recognize that these are shaped by our own historical context. How does Troeltsch hold these two assertions together? What implications will this have for Christian theology?

The Absoluteness of Christianity

The evaluation of Christianity in the context of the history of religions is the central question of Troeltsch's major study *The Absoluteness of Christianity* (first published in 1902, but republished in a revised edition in 1912). If the title is taken as an indication of its author's intention, then it is misleading, as even Troeltsch at one point admits.[84] The book is more accurately described as an attempt to demonstrate what Troeltsch calls "the normative validity"[85] of Christianity. Can we still claim that Christianity has normative value while recognizing that this religion, too, is a product of human history, emerging and developing within particular social contexts, almost all of which are very different from our own?

Troeltsch rejects the two existing forms of Christian apologetic. The first is the old, supernaturalist and dogmatic view, which ultimately rests on the exclusive acceptance of the Christian miracles. We have already seen that Troeltsch regards this view as incompatible with a historical perspective; it requires no further discussion here. However, Troeltsch also rejects what he calls "the evolutionary apologetic," of whom Hegel and Schleiermacher were the foremost representatives. According to this view, Christianity is "the complete and exhaustive realization" of the religious principle,[86] the culminating point of the religious history of humanity. All the religious phenomena that preceded Christianity were but partial expressions of this principle. They were preparatory to the emergence of what could rightly be called the "absolute" religion. This absolute religion is Christianity, which is nothing less than the perfect expression of the religious idea and thus "the self-realization of God in the human consciousness."[87] As Troeltsch writes, this view was enormously popular in the nineteenth century. For it seemed to offer a way of reconciling a recognition of the historicity of Christian faith with the absolute nature of traditional religious claims.

Yet Troeltsch also rejects this "evolutionary" option. For he cannot

---

[84]Cf. Troeltsch, *The Absoluteness of Christianity,* 56–57.
[85]*Die normative Geltung;* cf. ibid., 57 et passim (cf. *Die Absolutheit,* 18 et passim).
[86]Cf. ibid., 49.
[87]Ibid., 55.

accept that we know in advance (as it were) the principle that underlies historical developments. We cannot discover some principle from which historical developments could be deduced. Rather, the realities of history are particular and contingent. They cannot be derived from some supposedly overarching developmental scheme.[88] Even if such a principle could be found, there are no phenomena in history that could be regarded as its "absolute realization." There are no "absolute realizations" in history, but only phenomena that are shaped and limited by the context in which they occur.[89] Christianity is certainly no exception to this rule. For instance, early Christianity was decisively shaped by what Troeltsch calls "the eschatological ideas which were a source of strength to Israel" in the historical situation in which it found itself.[90] These eschatological (or, as we would say, apocalyptic) conceptions gave early Christianity its distinctive ethic. (Here Troeltsch implicitly recognizes the insights of Johannes Weiss and Albert Schweitzer.[91]) Later on, Christianity was shaped by the ethics of Platonism and Stoicism. And so it continued, throughout Christian history. At no point could Christianity be regarded as the "absolute religion," the exhaustive and unchanging expression of some religious ideal.

What, then, can we do? Can value judgments be made on the basis of a thoroughly historical view of religion? If so, on what basis? Troeltsch argues that we can, and *must,* make judgments about what is normative in the history of religions. That is to say, we must judge between the different values expressed in the religions we study, and we must decide which values remain binding, even in our own time. The problem is that there is no historically unconditioned criterion by which such judgments can be made. Our criteria of judgment are also conditioned by the context in which they are embedded.[92] On what basis, then, may we judge between differing religions, without simply importing our own historically conditioned norms into another context? Do these insights not lead inevitably to a kind of relativism, which suggests that we cannot pass judgment on anything outside our own context?

Troeltsch certainly wants to avoid this conclusion. He does so by

[88]Cf. ibid., 66–67.
[89]Cf. ibid., 67.
[90]Ibid., 70.
[91]It seems that Troeltsch had read Schweitzer's *Von Reimarus zu Wrede* (translated as *The Quest of the Historical Jesus*) between the first and the second editions of *The Absoluteness of Christianity,* and Schweitzer's emphasis on Jesus' apocalyptic teaching made a considerable impact on his thought, as we will see below (cf. Coakley, *Christ without Absolutes,* 53, n.19).
[92]Cf. Troeltsch, "Modern Philosophy of History," 305.

arguing that certain historical values represent a "striving towards a future goal."[93] The diversity of religious history, he suggests, displays certain converging tendencies, that is to say, tendencies united by their convergence on a common ideal.[94] The ideal is never fully expressed in history, for it lies beyond it.[95] Nevertheless, it is recognizable in history as the point at which the major religious tendencies of humanity would eventually converge. In the sphere of religion, Troeltsch argues, it is not an impossible task to recognize these tendencies, since there exist only a limited number of major religious orientations. As he writes, "it is astonishing that man lives, in fact, by so few ideas."[96] It is this sense of an ideal towards which religions are converging that enables us to make judgments of value between them.[97]

Yet while "scientific" study may uncover the convergence point of the religious tendencies of human history, the application of this ideal to our own situation involves an element of personal decision. (There is something of the existentialist in Troeltsch, as Robert Morgan points out.[98]) A responsible judgment will involve entering into these major religious orientations and grasping the direction in which they are moving, before judging what is of value in our particular historical context.[99] The criteria we employ in making this judgment are admittedly the product of our own time and place. But the judgment should also be informed by a universal perspective, drawn from a study of the converging tendencies in major religious traditions. This universal perspective is what gives our judgment of value its objective dimension, insofar as it rests on an unprejudiced and empathetic study of the major religious traditions. Such a study prevents the discussion from breaking down into a mere cacophony of competing "opinions."[100] Despite these safeguards, such a judgment also has an unavoidably subjective dimension, insofar as it

[93]Troeltsch, *The Absoluteness of Christianity*, 90.

[94]Cf. ibid., 91.

[95]Cf. ibid., 98.

[96]Ibid., 92.

[97]Cf. ibid., 98–99. Cf. Troeltsch, "Historiography," in *Encyclopedia of Religion and Ethics*, edited by James Hastings (Edinburgh: T. & T. Clark, 1913), 6:722b: "The absolute *in* the relative, yet not fully and finally in it, but always pressing on towards fresh forms of self-expression, and so effecting the mutual criticism of it relative to individualization—such is the last word of the philosophy of history."

[98]Robert Morgan, "Troeltsch and the Dialectical Theology," in *Ernst Troeltsch and the Future of Theology*, 61–62.

[99]Walter Wyman (*The Concept of Glaubenslehre*, 189) sums up nicely the process that Troeltsch advocates: "A broad historical survey of the development of values through time is combined with an axiomatic deed in the present."

[100]Cf. Troeltsch, *The Absoluteness of Christianity*, 97–98.

remains a matter of personal decision.[101] Doing justice to both dimensions, the objective and the subjective, is a difficult matter. As Troeltsch writes, "not every theory-spinner who comes along is capable of this kind of work, but only thinkers who combine profound and extensive knowledge with serious ethical and religious concern."[102] We might describe Troeltsch's position here as the cultivation of a "disciplined subjectivity."

Troeltsch's own conviction is that such a judgment will come down on the side of Christianity. We need not outline his argument in detail; indeed, it would be difficult to do so, for when it comes to the point, his argument in favor of Christianity is remarkably brief. *The Absoluteness of Christianity* contains no extended study of any other religious tradition, and the superiority of Christianity is "demonstrated" in fewer than ten pages of argumentation. In these pages Troeltsch argues that only Christianity has made a complete break from the ideas of God and morality found in the nature religions.[103] Only in Christianity is the individual elevated above all "natural demands" and united with a truly morally transcendent God.[104] It follows that Christianity is what Troeltsch calls "the highest and most significantly developed form of religious life that we know."[105] It sums up in itself the positive tendencies found in the other major religious traditions of the world.[106] The reader must decide if this is an adequate application of the method Troeltsch has outlined in such detail or whether he has merely dismissed other religions for not measuring up to Christian criteria.

More interesting are the qualifications with which Troeltsch surrounds this conclusion. He notes that his verdict in favor of Christianity is—strictly speaking—a provisional one. We do not know *for certain* what direction the future religious development of humanity will take. (In this sense, we cannot know the totality of human history for the very simple reason that we cannot know the future.) For this reason, as Troeltsch writes, "it cannot be proved with absolute certainty that Christianity will always remain the final culmination point, that it will never be

---

[101]Cf. ibid., 96–97. See also Troeltsch, "Modern Philosophy of History," 305; "On the Question of the Religious A Priori," 38 (cf. Coakley, *Christ without Absolutes,* 57, n.27). In *The Christian Faith* (§2, 27) Troeltsch reworks this idea theologically, suggesting that the product of such a decision, namely, the personal appropriation of the religious elements of history, is equivalent to the inner "testimony of the Holy Spirit." See also Troeltsch, "What Does 'Essence of Christianity' Mean?" in *Writings on Theology and Religion,* 163.

[102]Troeltsch, *The Absoluteness of Christianity,* 97. See also Troeltsch, "What Does 'Essence of Christianity' Mean?," 167.

[103]See also *The Absoluteness of Christianity,* 140–45.

[104]Cf. Troeltsch, *The Absoluteness of Christianity,* 114.

[105]Cf. ibid., 117.

[106]Cf. ibid., 114.

surpassed."[107] A "higher revelation" may yet emerge. Yet if such a higher religion did emerge, it would emerge in a form analogous to that found in Christianity.[108] Christianity is—in all probability—the basis on which future religious developments will occur. It is unlikely to be simply surpassed.[109] But in these matters there is no question of proof. As Troeltsch writes, "here there is simply the self-confident faith that absolutely nothing can make a new and higher religion likely for us."[110] The absolute lies beyond history, but we can be confident that Christianity is the "embodiment" of that absolute "in our cultural context and our moment of history."[111]

The Place of Christianity among the World Religions

This qualification found in those final quotations is a significant one. It is developed in Troeltsch's lecture "The Place of Christianity among the World-Religions," prepared shortly before his death in 1923. Here Troeltsch admits that, while for all practical purposes he still holds to his earlier conclusions, in some matters his views have changed. Firstly, he now finds it much more difficult to reconcile the fact of historical particularity with an assertion of "supreme validity."[112] He has become much more aware of the unbreakable connection between Western Christianity and the historical contexts in which it emerged. As he writes, this Christianity "is a purely historical, individual, relative phenomenon, which could . . . only have arisen in the territory of classical culture, and among the Latin and Germanic races."[113] Secondly, Troeltsch writes, he can no longer affirm that Christianity is the only religion capable of appealing to what he calls "the inner certitude and devotion" of its followers.[114] In this respect he has become increasingly impressed with "Buddhism and Brahminism."[115] Finally, and perhaps most seriously, he has become aware that the diversity of human cultures extends right down to their very foundations. In his researches he found that "what was really common to mankind, and universally valid for it,

[107]Ibid., 114–15.
[108]Cf. ibid., 115–17. For the same arguments, see Ernst Troeltsch, "On the Possibility of a Liberal Christianity" (1910), translated by Walter F. Bense, in *Religion in History*, 349–50, and "The Significance of the Historical Existence of Jesus for Faith" (1911), in *Writings on Theology and Religion*, 205–6.
[109]Cf. Troeltsch, *The Absoluteness of Christianity*, 131.
[110]Ibid., 115.
[111]Ibid., 128–29.
[112]Troeltsch, "The Place of Christianity among the World-Religions," 22.
[113]Ibid.
[114]Ibid., 23.
[115]Ibid.

seemed . . . to be at bottom exceedingly little, and to belong more to the province of material goods than to the ideal values of civilisation."[116]

It follows that it is increasingly difficult to assert the normative value of Christianity outside of its European context. Within that context, Christianity is normative because it is inseparable from "our" European history and identity:

> Its primary claim to validity is . . . the fact that only through it have we become what we are, and that only in it can we preserve the religious forces that we need. . . . We cannot live without a religion, yet the only religion that we can endure is Christianity, for Christianity has grown up with us and has become a part of our very being.[117]

This assertion may seem a weak one, but it also has its theological implications. Christianity could hardly have been so important for the cultural history of Europe "if it did not possess a mighty spiritual power and truth."[118] Thus, *for those who belong to that culture,* Christianity is truly a revelation from God and must be recognized as normative. Other cultures, however, may receive divine revelation in quite different ways. They, too, may have religions that have become inseparable from their cultures and from which they cannot be expected to sever themselves without loss of their identity. In the case of the major world religions, religion and culture have become so intertwined that one cannot judge the religion without judging the culture as a whole.[119] But this is an impossible task, best left to God. In any case, this insight in no way undermines the normative character of Christianity for European culture.[120] As Troeltsch writes, "*a truth for us* does not cease, because of this, to be very Truth and Life."[121]

These last statements might seem to imply that Troeltsch has lapsed into relativism, a charge against which Sarah Coakley has ably defended him.[122] For Troeltsch, she argues, the impossibility of judging the relative merits of the major civilizations is a *practical* rather than a *theoretical*

---

[116]Ibid., 23–24.

[117]Ibid., 25.

[118]Ibid., 26.

[119]Cf. ibid., 27.

[120]One is reminded here of Edward Herbert's position (*De Religione Laici,* 99) that the Bible is in principle merely one sacred book among others, but that it holds a special position for the people of Europe because of its connection with their history. (For details, see my introductory chapter.)

[121]Troeltsch, "The Place of Christianity among the World-Religions," 34.

[122]Cf. Coakley, *Christ without Absolutes,* 38–39.

impossibility. Indeed, by expressing his admiration for "Buddhism and Brahminism," Troeltsch is in fact making such a value judgment, despite his reservations. In any case, we might add, Troeltsch certainly believes that value judgments are possible when it comes to the religions that are *not* embodied in major civilizations. In the same essay, for example, Troeltsch can speak without embarrassment of "the crude heathenism of smaller tribes" and of the missionary responsibility of the major religions towards such peoples.[123] Some value judgments *are* apparently still possible, and they presumably can be made in the ways indicated in Troeltsch's earlier work. In other words, while it is true that his 1923 lecture goes beyond at least the first edition of *The Absoluteness of Christianity*,[124] it is not necessarily a repudiation of its central thesis.

Nonetheless, it remains true that Troeltsch's later work embodies a heightened sense of what we might call cultural relativity. In his unfinished work *Der Historismus und seine Probleme,* Troeltsch admits that, because of the interrelatedness of all historical phenomena, the study of the development of particular phenomena must *in principle* embrace the whole of humanity.[125] In fact, of course, this is impossible, as Troeltsch notes elsewhere. The historical sources, as well as the facts they record, are too diverse for us to regard "humanity" as an object of historical study. For an object of historical study can only embrace phenomena that share common meanings.[126] But this cannot be said of humanity as a whole, either geographically or chronologically. Chronologically, the full extent of human history remains hidden to us.[127] Geographically, even the cultures of today, with which we are familiar, are too diverse to speak of a common realm of meaning.[128] As Troeltsch writes, "humanity as a whole has no spiritual unity and hence also no united development."[129] If one can no longer (in practice) write a unified world history, which would enable one to make judgments of relative value, then such judgments are effectively circumscribed by one's own culture. Only one's own culture can be known so thoroughly that its development can be traced and judgments made. In Troeltsch's own words, "we know in

[123]Troeltsch, "The Place of Christianity among the World-Religions," 29.
[124]On the differences between the first and the second editions, see Coakley, *Christ without Absolutes,* 46, 67–72, 74–77.
[125]Cf. Troeltsch, *Der Historismus und seine Probleme,* 62.
[126]Cf. ibid., 705: *Der historische Gegenstand kann nur durch einen ... einheitlichen oder zur Einheit zusammengewachsenen Sinngehalt zusammengehalten werden.*
[127]Cf. ibid., 186–87.
[128]Cf. ibid., 706–7.
[129]Ibid., 706: *Die Menschheit als Ganzes hat keine geistige Einheit und daher auch keine einheitliche Entwicklung.*

truth only ourselves and understand only our own being and hence also only our own development."[130]

It is hard to know what impact this new sense of cultural relativity would have had on Troeltsch's ongoing attempts to write a philosophy of history, had he lived to complete them. For the individual, of course, this restriction probably does not matter. In making ethical decisions, individuals can draw upon the resources of their own cultures and effectively ignore the very different cultural history of other peoples. Yet we live in a world grown ever smaller, in which not only individuals but nations and international bodies must find common norms against which behavior can be judged. Interestingly, Troeltsch recognizes this fact. As he says, "we have today grown into planetary horizons; politics and science must think in [terms of] continents."[131] He goes on to argue that, if there is ever to exist any spiritual unity across differing cultures,[132] it will only be created through political and social means. This in turn will call forth the creation of new ideals, which will be quite different from what we Westerners currently accept as truth.[133] This intriguing suggestion, that a new age might require new means of achieving unity among diverse cultures, also has implications for the future of Christianity. I will return to this issue in my concluding remarks.

History and Teleology

In his essay on the work of the philosopher Heinrich Rickert (1863–1936), Troeltsch argues that all historical judgments require a metaphysical

---

[130]Ibid., 709: *Wir kennen in Wahrheit nur uns selbst und verstehen nur unser eigenes Sein und deshalb auch nur unsere eigene Entwicklung.* Again, this does not necessarily mean that no cross-cultural understanding is possible, an idea that would be contradicted by everyday experience. Indeed, in the same context Troeltsch notes that "an understanding of other cultures may be of the greatest significance for self-knowledge, world-understanding and practical, mutual contact" (*Der Kenntnis der fremden Kulturen mag für Selbsterkenntnis, Weltverständnis und praktische gegenseitige Berührung von der größten Bedeutung sein*). He even notes that some knowledge of other cultures is needed to understand one's own (cf. 710; cf. 711). Rather, Troeltsch's point seems to be that this is not *the kind of knowledge* that enables one to make relative judgments of value or to build a cultural synthesis for humanity as a whole.

[131]Ibid., 187: *Wir sind heute in planetarische Horizonte hineingewachsen; Politik und Wissenschaft müssen in Kontinenten denken.*

[132]Troeltsch (ibid., 706) does not exclude the possibility that there will exist a common human history (*Menschheitsgeschichte*) in the future, but remarks that for the moment it lies "beyond any possibility of knowledge" (*außer aller Möglichkeit der Erkenntnis*).

[133]Cf. ibid., 186–87: *Sollte eine solche* [*Vernunft- und Menschheitseinheit*] *jemals eintreten, dann wird es durch politisch-soziale Ereignisse zuerst geschehen und dann eine neue Idealbildung hervorrufen, die sicher anders sein wird als alles, was heute für uns Abendländer ausgemachte Wahrheit ist.*

grounding.[134] It therefore seems reasonable to ask once again about the metaphysical grounding of his own work. The central argument of *The Absoluteness of Christianity* is based upon what Troeltsch himself calls a "teleological" understanding of history.[135] The course of religious history is guided by a goal that lies beyond it, but toward which different developments can be seen to converge. The presence of this teleological strain in Troeltsch's thought is revealing. For as we saw in the introduction to the present work, an understanding of the natural world that invoked "final causes" was one of the first targets of the pioneers of modern science. Neither the empiricist tradition of Bacon nor the rationalist tradition of Descartes would accept explanations that appealed to some purpose supposedly built into the structure of reality. Troeltsch admits this restriction when it comes to knowledge of the natural world, from which he concedes that teleology has been rightly banished.[136] But he cannot make the same admission about history. The reason is simple. A teleological view of history is simply another dimension of Troeltsch's metaphysical idealism and could not be abandoned without abandoning the idealism on which Troeltsch's philosophy and theology was based. Teleology and metaphysics go together, as Troeltsch himself notes. A teleological view of history requires what he calls "*a turn to the metaphysical, a retracing of all man's goals and aspirations to a transcendent force that actuates our deepest striving and is connected with the creative core of reality.*"[137] It is this, he continues, that constitutes the element of truth in the evolutionary (Hegelian) scheme.

To understand more clearly Troeltsch's teleological view of history we might turn again to his late work *Der Historismus und seine Probleme,* which can shed some light on his theological views. At one point in that work, while discussing the criteria to be used in making historical judgments, Troeltsch distinguishes between a deterministic teleology and what he calls "a teleology of the will."[138] Adherents of the deterministic view believe they can lay out the entire course of history as a series of

---

[134]Cf. Troeltsch, "Modern Philosophy of History," 315–17.

[135]Cf. Troeltsch, "Religion and the Science of Religion," 117; *The Absoluteness of Christianity,* 121. Sarah Coakley (*Christ without Absolutes,* 85–86) suggests that this teleological view of history is weakened in Troeltsch's 1923 lecture "The Place of Christianity among the World-Religions" (cf. 14), although it is certainly not abandoned. This may be true, but the point being made in this lecture—about the uniqueness of each manifestation of spirit in history—seems very similar to that made in Troeltsch's 1913 article on "Historiography" (cf. 722b).

[136]Cf. Troeltsch, "Historiography," 716b.

[137]Troeltsch, *The Absoluteness of Christianity,* 100.

[138][*Eine*] *Teleologie des . . . Willens;* cf. Troeltsch, *Der Historismus und seine Probleme,* 112.

steps that must inevitably be taken.[139] Such a teleology, they believe, once its principles are grasped, enables one to construct the course of world history objectively (as it were) from the point of view of its eternal goal. Troeltsch argues that such a strong view is untenable, for the point of view that would enable one to grasp the ultimate goal of history is available only to God.[140] Rather, what is required today is a teleology of the will. Such a teleology consists in a particular orientation of human activity, which needs to be re-formed at each moment, making use of the past in a way that is directed towards the future.[141]

At first sight, this might seem to take us beyond *The Absoluteness of Christianity,* where the impression is given that there is a goal towards which history is moving, even if it can be glimpsed only by way of the convergence of certain tendencies in different religions. To talk about a "teleology of the will" suggests that the goal is, as it were, created by human beings themselves, by using what resources are available to them at the particular historical moment in which they live. Yet the two positions are not irreconcilable. As we have seen, Troeltsch had always held that there was an element of decision in any ethical or religious position, and therefore an irreducible element of subjectivity. This seems to be what is at stake here. It is not that there *is* no goal transcending human ideals, but that ultimately it lies beyond our reach. It is never fully expressed within history, and our knowledge cannot reach beyond history. Therefore our judgment that certain ideals represent the expression of that goal in our particular context is never a matter of knowledge alone. It must be based on knowledge, but it always involves the will, in an act of decision that is suggested, but not necessitated, by the evidence.[142]

This insight seems closely related to another aspect of Troeltsch's thought, namely his distinction between religion and philosophy, out-

---

[139]Cf. ibid., 111.

[140]Elsewhere in *Der Historismus und seine Probleme* (cf. 183), Troeltsch generalizes this observation, noting that "no science can enable us to master the entire stream of life itself" (*Dem Gesamtflusse des Lebens selbst kann man mit keiner Wissenschaft beikommen*). We need to grasp the whole in some way, in order to understand particular events, but "the unity and sense of the whole can only be known as presentiment and feeling; it cannot be scientifically expressed and constructed" (*Aber Einheit und Sinn des Ganzen läßt sich nur ahnen und fühlen, nicht wissenschaftlich ausdrücken und konstruieren*). This resembles Troeltsch's insistence that the historian cannot study "humanity" as a whole: a knowledge of the spiritual history of humanity as a whole belongs only to God (cf. 709: *Etwas derartiges gibt es nur für Gott*).

[141]Cf. Troeltsch, *Der Historismus und seine Probleme,* 112.

[142]For a fuller statement of what is involved in such a decision, see Troeltsch's *Der Historismus und seine Probleme,* 221, which here, too, echoes the ideas found in *The Absoluteness of Christianity.*

lined most clearly in *The Christian Faith*. Troeltsch opposes the view, again put forward by Hegel, that "religious knowledge and philosophical knowledge are actually the same thing."[143] Troeltsch concedes that the *object* of piety is the same as that of philosophy, but insists that the *manner* in which that object is grasped is different.[144] For philosophy aims at attaining an "abstract unity" of thought, a unity that will always be provisional because of the limits of our knowledge. Religious piety, on the other hand, seeks to attain a "personal appropriation" of our knowledge, an appropriation that reshapes one's behavior.[145] "Religion," Troeltsch writes, "implies an inward turn and a specifically personal stance towards life, not the conclusion of a lengthy thought-process."[146] It is important to note that Troeltsch is *not* trying to separate religion and philosophy entirely, so that Christian faith can be protected from the corrosive effects of thought (a tendency that we will observe shortly in the thought of Rudolf Bultmann).[147] For Troeltsch also argues that since religion and philosophy have the same object, they must eventually converge, although we may never grasp the point of convergence.[148] As he writes, in the end our spiritual world cannot be split: "you cannot be a Spinozist with your head and a theist in your heart."[149] For the same reason, faith cannot coexist with just any philosophy but requires (as we have seen) some form of idealism.[150] Nonetheless, faith and philosophy—however closely related—remain distinct forms of thought. There is in faith (and therefore in Christian theology) an element of personal commitment that is absent from philosophy. For Troeltsch this element of personal commitment represents the expression, in the sphere of religion, of the subjective element in all religious and ethical judgments.

4. The Historical Jesus

We have seen that Troeltsch's philosophical idealism enables him to find a religious significance in the course of human history. This enables him to approach the phenomenon of Christianity from a thoroughly historical point of view, as one religion among many, confident that this will not lead to a nihilistic relativism. One question remains: what does this

[143]Troeltsch, *The Christian Faith*, §4 (59).
[144]Cf. ibid., §4 (60).
[145]Cf. ibid., §4 (54).
[146]Ibid., §4 (60).
[147]Cf. ibid., §1 (24).
[148]Cf. ibid., §4 (60–61).
[149]Cf. ibid., §4 (60).
[150]Cf. ibid., §4 (61).

mean for the question of the historical Jesus? What can the historian say about the figure of Jesus, and what significance has this figure for Christian faith?

Two Problems Facing Theology

The primary source for any discussion of Troeltsch's attitude to the historical Jesus is a small book published in 1911, *The Significance of the Historical Existence of Jesus for Faith.* But before we turn to this work, I might make a more general observation. Troeltsch's discussion of the historical Jesus ought to be seen in the context of his work as a whole. Within that context, it does not play a major role. Among the various challenges raised by historical research, Troeltsch did not consider the question of the historical Jesus to be the most serious. In an essay published in 1908, "Half a Century of Theology: A Review," Troeltsch spoke of two major problems facing the theology of his day. The first is what he calls the "historical critical uncertainty about our picture of Jesus,"[151] that is to say, the problem of the historical Jesus in its narrow sense. The second problem concerns the place of Christianity in the history of religions. For Troeltsch this second problem represents a much more serious issue, for a thoroughly historical study of Christianity calls into question its traditional claim to absolute authority.[152] The second question, of course, is the one to which the largest part of this chapter has been devoted. With regard to the first problem—that of the 'historical Jesus' in the narrow sense—Troeltsch believed this would eventually prove to be less of a challenge than many of his contemporaries believed. He was convinced that "the main traits" of the teaching of Jesus could be known with confidence. Moreover, he believed that this knowledge would vindicate the church's conviction that its teaching stood in a real continuity with that of its founder.[153] As he writes, "Christianity arose not through a misunderstanding or through some alien redeemer myth being attached to a certain 'Jesus,' but from the life and personality of its hero."[154] Despite the evident impossibility of writing a "life of Jesus" in the biographical sense,[155] the historical Jesus is by no means unknowable, and the knowledge gained from historical research is sufficient to form a basis for faith.[156]

---

[151]Ernst Troeltsch, "Half a Century of Theology: A Review," 69.

[152]Cf. ibid., 71.

[153]Cf. ibid., 72.

[154]Ibid.

[155]Cf. ibid., 69.

[156]This resembles Schweitzer's claim (*The Quest of the Historical Jesus* [1913], 480), noted in the last chapter, that we do not need to know "the details" of Jesus work in order to grasp his spirit.

The Historical Jesus and Faith

This confident judgment is reiterated in Troeltsch's essay on "The Significance of the Historical Existence of Jesus for Faith." First of all, Troeltsch rejects as merely "silly" the idea (that had recently been put forward by Arthur Drews) that there *was* no historical figure of Jesus.[157] He has no time for the idea that the very existence of Jesus was a creation of the early church. Secondly, Troeltsch reaffirms his conviction that enough can be known of the figure of Jesus to nourish Christian faith. The details of Jesus' life and work will certainly remain matters of dispute, but "the basic facts" are well known.[158] What are these basic facts? Troeltsch nowhere gives a clear answer to this question and for this he has been rightly criticized.[159] Troeltsch does speak of what he calls "the decisive significance of Jesus' personality for the origin and formation of faith in Christ."[160] He also speaks of "the basic ethical and religious character of Jesus' teaching and the transformation of his teaching in the earliest Christian congregations with their Christ cult."[161] Perhaps these are the basic facts on which Christianity rests. But these are broad categories. They leave unanswered the question of precisely *which facts* are essential for faith. Yet, however one may specify these basic facts, Troeltsch is confident they can be sufficiently known.[162]

Troeltsch's essay, then, is not devoted to the question of *what we can know* about the historical figure of Jesus. Troeltsch regards this as a purely historical and factual matter, of little interest to the philosopher and theologian. His essay is devoted to the question of the *religious significance* of that figure, which can be known only through an interpretation of the historical facts.[163] Troeltsch concedes that the significance of this question will depend on one's broader theological views. Those who hold to the traditional Christian understanding of redemption will be untroubled by the question of the historical Jesus. Such a theology simply takes for granted certain facts about Jesus, on which the believer can confidently rest. For Troeltsch, however, the traditional Christian theology of

---

[157]Cf. Troeltsch, "The Significance of the Historical Existence of Jesus for Faith," 182; *The Christian Faith,* §8 (88).

[158]Cf. Troeltsch, "The Significance of the Historical Existence of Jesus for Faith," 200.

[159]Cf. Coakley, *Christ without Absolutes,* 153–54.

[160]Troeltsch, "The Significance of the Historical Existence of Jesus for Faith," 200.

[161]Ibid.

[162]The same assertion is made in Troeltsch, "Half a Century of Theology," 72; "Faith and History" (1910), in *Religion in History,* 142; "On the Possibility of a Liberal Christianity," 349; as well as in the lectures of 1910–11 gathered together in *The Christian Faith,* §6 [84]).

[163]For this distinction, see Troeltsch, "The Significance of the Historical Existence of Jesus for Faith," 198; *The Christian Faith,* §8 (97).

redemption is no longer tenable.[164] This is not the place to ask why or to analyse the view of redemption that Troeltsch wishes to put in its place.[165] It will be sufficient to note that Troeltsch's view of redemption is centered on God rather than Christ. It sees redemption as achieved, not by a particular act in the past, but by a present-day revelation of God's saving will and readiness to forgive.[166]

This new understanding of redemption creates a problem for Troeltsch as theologian. For a "redemption" thus redefined scarcely requires the figure of Jesus. All that is required for redemption to occur is the proclamation of the grace of God. This message of forgiveness does not need to have originated in the life of a historic individual.[167] The origin of the message becomes a matter of purely contingent fact; it is of no significance for the present act of redemption. Even if one holds, as Troeltsch does, to the idea that divine revelation is mediated by powerful personalities,[168] it is by no means clear that such personalities need to have actually existed. Surely the *idea* of such an individual would suffice. A story can convey a message even if it is not historically true. The Gospel picture of Jesus would be a powerful symbol, even if it were admitted that it was a fiction.[169] Troeltsch's new view of redemption, in other words, raises in a particularly sharp way the question that constitutes the title of his essay. What is the significance of the historical Jesus for faith? Does this figure have a significance that is anything more than "pedagogical and symbolical"?[170] Does the historical existence of Jesus matter? If so, why?

The "Law of Social Psychology"
Troeltsch's answer to this question hinges on what he calls "a law of

[164]Cf. Troeltsch, "The Significance of the Historical Existence of Jesus for Faith," 184–86. For Troeltsch's criticisms of traditional Christian beliefs about Jesus, see Coakley, *Christ without Absolutes,* 103–35. It is also clear that Troeltsch regards the traditional depiction of Jesus as irreconcilable with what we now know to be the historical facts of his life. As he writes elsewhere ("On the Possibility of a Liberal Christianity," 348), "the attempt, associated particularly with liberal theology, to transfer to the human Jesus the role of a universal world-redeemer traditionally assigned by the Church to Christ, is wholly impossible and fraught with intolerable contradictions."

[165]For an analysis, see Coakley, *Christ without Absolutes,* 80–102.

[166]Cf. Troeltsch, "The Significance of the Historical Existence of Jesus for Faith," 185.

[167]Cf. ibid., 192–93.

[168]Cf. Troeltsch, *The Christian Faith,* §3 (41). See my discussion of "history as the scene of revelation" above.

[169]Troeltsch ("The Significance of the Historical Existence of Jesus for Faith," 186) notes that this was effectively the view held by D. F. Strauss "during his Christian period": the figure of Jesus was a useful symbol of the idea of the unity of the divine and the human that actually occurred only in the course of human history. (See chapter 2 of the present study.)

[170]Cf. Troeltsch, "The Significance of the Historical Existence of Jesus for Faith," 193.

social psychology."[171] He begins with the idea that the very core of religion is communal practice. This communal practice requires a "concrete focus," which dogmas and doctrines alone cannot provide.[172] Such a focus is customarily provided by a communal cult.[173] In more historically developed religions, this communal cult takes the form of the veneration of the founding figures. As Troeltsch writes, "in the religions of spirit it is the prophets and founder personalities who serve as archetypes, authorities, sources of power and rallying-points."[174] Troeltsch argues that the attraction of such veneration is easy to understand. The depiction of a concrete individual has what Troeltsch calls "a versatility and flexibility possessed by no mere doctrine or dogma."[175] The image of an individual also has an imaginative power far surpassing that of an abstract idea. Christianity is no exception to this rule. It, too, can survive only "by handing on and keeping alive the image of Christ, the adoration of God in Christ."[176]

In putting forward this argument, Troeltsch admits that one could—in principle—spell out the meaning of salvation without reference to Christ. In fact, much of the traditional language Christians have used to speak about Christ is no longer tenable. For instance, Troeltsch argues that it no longer makes sense to speak of "a real personal relationship" with Jesus.[177] Yet despite all this, the figure of Christ remains central to Christianity. It is central, not because of the doctrine of salvation, but because of our need for community and cult. In Troeltsch's words, "if . . . we need a cult and community then we need Christ as the head and rallying-point of the community too."[178] *In principle,* the Christian idea might exist without the figure of Jesus. But *in practice* Christianity requires this figure to act as the focus of our collective devotion.

What are we to make of this argument? We should note first of all that at least some of these claims are consistent with statements found elsewhere in Troeltsch's work. For instance, Troeltsch had always insisted that the distinctive characteristic of religion is cultic activity. In his earlier essay on "Religion and the Science of Religion," he argues that religions are to be distinguished from other forms of cultural life by precisely this

---

[171]Cf. ibid., 195 et passim.

[172]In both this essay (cf. ibid., 204–5) and in "On the Possibility of a Liberal Christianity" (355–59), Troeltsch laments the individualism of the age, which has led to a breakdown of a communal sense, particularly in the churches.

[173]Cf. Troeltsch, "The Significance of the Historical Existence of Jesus for Faith," 194.

[174]Ibid., 195.

[175]Ibid.

[176]Ibid., 196.

[177]Ibid., 197.

[178]Ibid.

feature: the presence of common forms of worship. For this reason not every instance of the personification of natural powers is to be taken as "religion";[179] it is a religion only when it involves worship. In insisting that the Christian church also needs common acts of worship, Troeltsch is merely extending these ideas to Christianity. But in insisting on the need for a *personal* focus of worship, Troeltsch is taking that argument further. He does so by invoking his "law of social psychology." The problem here is that there is something suspiciously ad hoc about this alleged "law." Troeltsch describes it as "a general law at work in all human affairs and applied to religion in particular,"[180] but it is not at all clear how far this law can be said to extend. If Troeltsch means merely that all religions require *some kind* of communal focus, then this seems a defensible claim. However, his argument requires him to go further. It requires him to argue that—at least in the higher religions—the focus of devotion is a figure of the past, normally the figure of the founder.[181] This is a much harder claim to defend.[182] As Sarah Coakley writes, the same role can be played in other religions by "a more general mythology, a book, or a whole pantheon of heroes."[183] Troeltsch's "law of social psychology" begins to look like an unwarranted generalization on the basis of Christianity alone.[184]

Implications

In any case, having discovered what he claims to be a "social-psychological" need for the figure of Jesus, Troeltsch goes on to reflect on its implications. The first implication is that the theologian cannot be indifferent to historical questions, for the believer cannot be satisfied with a figure who is merely mythical. As Troeltsch writes, the believer "will . . . insist upon standing with this symbol of his on the solid ground of real life. It is for him a truly significant fact that a real man thus lived, struggled, believed and conquered, and that from this real life a stream of strength and certainty flows down to him."[185] Christian faith therefore requires that we know *something* about the historical figure of Jesus. On the other hand, not a great deal of knowledge is required. All the Christian needs as a focus for her devotion is a fundamental outline of Jesus' personality

---

[179]Cf. Troeltsch, "Religion and the Science of Religion," 90.
[180]Troeltsch, "On the Significance of the Historical Existence of Jesus for Faith," 202.
[181]Cf. ibid., 195–96.
[182]Cf. Drescher, *Ernst Troeltsch,* 211; Coakley, *Christ without Absolutes,* 150–51.
[183]Coakley, *Christ without Absolutes,* 151.
[184]Cf. ibid.
[185]Troeltsch, "On the Significance of the Historical Existence of Jesus for Faith," 197.

and life.[186] As we have seen, Troeltsch is confident we can have such an outline, which offers a firm basis for Christian life.

Here too, it must be said, Troeltsch's argumentation is weak. Given Troeltsch's understanding of redemption, we may ask once again: Why *should* the Christian need to know that this central figure actually existed? Surely an admittedly mythical figure could act as an equally powerful symbol. For instance, Plato's depiction of the death of Socrates can continue to inspire us today, even though we may believe much of it to be fictional. It is the idea embodied in the story that is powerful, rather than the alleged facts it relates. If Christians *do* need the conviction "that a real man thus lived, struggled, believed and conquered,"[187] then there are plenty of Christian saints to whose example they could appeal. To be fair to Troeltsch, he does recognize that later Christian figures can play the same role as Jesus. As he writes, "Jesus will not be the only historical fact that is significant for our faith. Other historical personalities too can receive their due and be seen in some sense as visible symbols and guarantees of faith that sustain our strength."[188] Yet he also argues that "the Christian character" of our faith is maintained by relating our religious claims "to the rallying-point, the personality of Jesus."[189] A "unitary interpretation" of the Christian phenomenon requires the figure of Jesus.[190]

Troeltsch on Jesus—A Summary

It may help if I pause for a moment to summarize Troeltsch's position on the question of Jesus. With regard to the significance of the historical figure of Jesus, Troeltsch makes two points. First, there must be a connection between the historical Jesus and the Christ of faith. Christianity requires not just a figure who can be the focus of cult and community; it also requires the assurance that this figure actually existed. Therefore Christianity cannot escape "the historical problems of faith."[191] As Troeltsch notes in *The Christian Faith,* theology cannot establish facts, it can only interpret them, and its interpretation "cannot be an arbitrary exercise of the imagination; it must proceed from the historical meaning and spirit of the facts themselves."[192] Troeltsch's second point is a qualification of this claim, asserting that the significance of the historical Jesus for

[186]Cf. ibid., 198.
[187]Ibid., 197.
[188]Ibid., 201.
[189]Ibid.
[190]Cf. ibid., 203.
[191]Ibid., 199.
[192]Troeltsch, *The Christian Faith,* §8 (88).

faith is strictly limited. Only a few basic facts about Jesus must be known for faith to be sustained, and these are already,[193] or at least soon will be,[194] a matter of confident knowledge. It follows that the religious person can devote herself to Jesus undisturbed by the debates of the historians.[195]

In any case, it is not the isolated figure of Jesus that acts as a support for Christian faith, but Jesus viewed within both the history of Israel and the life of the church.[196] Within the history of Christianity, in particular, we see that the historical particularity of Jesus was soon transcended. As Troeltsch writes, "even the primitive church's faith freed the spirit of Christ from his appearance in history and saw it as a principle capable of development."[197] The implication seems to be that the particular facts about Jesus' life must be viewed in this larger context and that in this larger context some aspects of his life become less significant.

The Significance of Apocalyptic

The quotation with which that last section ended may well be a reference to Jesus' apocalyptic worldview. Sarah Coakley has indicated how reluctantly Troeltsch faced up to what we might call "the scandal of apocalyptic": the discovery that Jesus' life and message were deeply shaped by the expectation that God was about to effect a miraculous reversal of history.[198] Coakley cites, for instance, a letter Troeltsch wrote to his friend Wilhelm Bousset during the early 1890s, in which Troeltsch accuses Johannes Weiss of turning Jesus into "a ghastly enthusiast [or 'fanatic']."[199] She also traces alterations that Troeltsch made in his work as he gradually came to accept the insights of both Weiss and Schweitzer.[200] It is easy to understand Troeltsch's reluctance to embrace the apocalyptic portrait of Jesus. As we have seen, his understanding of divine revelation is based on the impact of the "personality" of the biblical figures. If the apocalyptic portrait is correct, some aspects of Jesus'

---

[193]Cf. Troeltsch, *The Christian Faith*, §6 (84).

[194]Cf. Troeltsch, "Half a Century of Theology," 72.

[195]See also the remarkable passage at the end of Troeltsch's The Absoluteness of Christianity (160–61), Sarah Coakley (*Christ without Absolutes*, 69–70) sees this as "a back-tracking towards 'Ritschlianism.'"

[196]Cf. Troeltsch, "On the Significance of the Historical Existence of Jesus for Faith," 200; *The Christian Faith*, §8 (88).

[197]Troeltsch, "On the Significance of the Historical Existence of Jesus for Faith," 203. This insistence that Jesus must be understood in the context of Christian history strongly resembles the views of Albrecht Ritschl, a fact that Troeltsch (cf. ibid., 201–2) readily admits.

[198]Cf. Coakley, *Christ without Absolutes*, 51, 53, 56, 57–58, 72.

[199]*Ein grauenhafter Schwärmer*, cited in Coakley, *Christ without Absolutes*, 53.

[200]Cf. Coakley, *Christ without Absolutes*, 51, n.16, 53, n.19.

personality are not only foreign to our own age (as Schweitzer noted) but also (as Strauss saw all too clearly) repugnant. To Troeltsch's credit as a thinker, he gradually came to accept the apocalyptic view of Jesus and incorporated it into his thinking.

The Essence of Christianity
There is, however, another aspect of Troeltsch's work that may have enabled him to live more easily with the scandal of apocalyptic. It is the fact—to which I alluded at the end of the previous section—that Troeltsch believed the teaching and personality of Jesus to be only *one* of the elements in a theology for our time. We see this expressed most clearly in Troeltsch's 1913 essay on "The Dogmatics of the History-of-Religions School," which itself picks up themes from his earlier work "What Does 'Essence of Christianity' Mean?"[201] The question to which the first essay is addressed is: What form would a Christian systematic theology take, if consistently erected on the basis of the history of religions? In response, Troeltsch speaks of three tasks such a theology must undertake. The first, which he himself undertook in *The Absoluteness of Christianity,* is that of "establishing, on the basis of a philosophy of the comparative study of religions, the fundamental and universal supremacy of Christianity for our own culture and civilization."[202] We have already examined the way in which Troeltsch attempted to do this. The second task is that of defining "the essence of Christianity." The third task is the "exposition" of that essence (which corresponds to what Troeltsch was attempting to do in *The Christian Faith*). Of these three tasks, it is the second that we must examine more closely. In pursuit of this aim, Troeltsch once again minimizes the significance of the historical Jesus by placing his life in a larger context.

Defining the essence of Christianity, Troeltsch writes, is not easy, because Christianity has always been a complex phenomenon. A historical study of Christianity, he notes, "reveals to us such a variety of interpretations, formulations, and syntheses that no single idea or impulse can dominate the whole."[203] Even the preaching of Jesus was an amalgam of various Jewish ideas.[204] The task is made more complicated by the fact

---

[201]The latter, it should be noted, was extensively revised before being incorporated into *Gesammelte Schriften* II (Tübingen: J. C. B. Mohr [Paul Siebeck], 1913), 386–451. These revisions enable the two works to be read together, despite the inconsistencies that they may have introduced (see S. W. Sykes's note in *Writings on Theology and Religion,* 180–81).

[202]Troeltsch, "The Dogmatics of the History-of-Religions School," 95.

[203]Ibid., 97.

[204]Cf. Troeltsch, "What Does 'Essence of Christianity' Mean?," 127, 134.

that—while Christianity begins with the impact of the personality of its founder—the essence of Christianity *cannot* be simply identified with the teaching of Jesus. For the impact of his personality on his followers created a new version of his gospel, found particularly in the preaching of Paul.[205] Not only in the New Testament period, but throughout the history of the church, the teaching of Jesus takes on new elements.[206] Our attempts to define the essence of Christianity, Troeltsch insists, must embrace all these developments.

The theologian's task, then, is to examine not only the life of Jesus but the whole history of Christianity. He must make a judgment as to which impulses and principles give continuity to Christian history. This judgment cannot be made by importing criteria from outside that history. Rather, it is a task of "immanent criticism,"[207] the kind of criticism that is employed in the analysis of any historical development. In a helpful analogy, Troeltsch compares this judgment to the act of interpretation involved in what he calls "the criticism of any book."[208] His point seems to be that one should criticize a book on its own terms, by grasping its central argument in all its developments and excluding those matters that are purely "accidental" (as it were). Once that argument is grasped, the book may be criticized from the point of view of the consistency or inconsistency with which that argument is developed. In a similar manner, one may define the essence of Christianity from a study, not just of the life of Jesus, but also of the whole history of the church.

Yet if we believe that religion is still a living force, then we must take our enquiry still further. If history is to be anything more than a matter of antiquarian concern, we must go beyond what a strictly scientific study of history can reveal. We must make judgments that pertain to the present and the future.[209] As is the case with any ethical decision or judgment of historical value, this will involve a decision, an act of the will.[210] A judgment of the essence of Christianity in this sense is not only an abstraction from history; it is also a new creation, which merges our knowledge of the past with that of the present in a personal act of synthesis.[211] As Troeltsch writes, "to define the essence is to shape it afresh. . . . The definition of the essence for a given time is the new

---

[205]Cf. ibid., 147–49.
[206]Cf. ibid., 150–51.
[207]Ibid., 142.
[208]Ibid., 143.
[209]Cf. ibid., 157–59.
[210]Cf. ibid., 161, 166, 179, et passim.
[211]Cf. ibid., 162.

historical formulation of Christianity for that time."[212] It follows that the definition of the essence of Christianity is not only a historical matter; it is a constructive, a properly *theological* task.[213]

Now if this is what the historian—or at least the historian as *theologian*—is bound to do, what will this mean for our study of the figure of Jesus? More precisely, what will it mean for our study of Jesus as an apocalyptic prophet? Troeltsch suggests that since Christianity was from the very beginning a complex phenomenon, different ages will appropriate different aspects of that complex reality. The worldview of Jewish apocalyptic was essential to the teaching of Jesus, but we must regard it as no longer essential for us.[214] What we can appropriate today is Jesus' ethical teaching. Yet we must also recognize that, because of its connection with apocalyptic, that ethic was itself "one-sided and abruptly transcendent."[215] This aspect of Jesus' teaching remains of significance insofar as it gives Christianity a continuous orientation toward what is "beyond history."[216] But Jesus' eschatological ethic should not be allowed to stand alone. Indeed, we can see from the history of Christianity that it was not allowed to stand alone. As a matter of historical fact, Christianity could survive only by a series of compromises.[217] These compromises themselves belong to the essence of Christianity and must become part of our own appropriation of that faith. In other words, in appropriating Jesus' ethical teaching for today, we must take into account, not only his apocalyptic ethic, but also the accommodation of that ethic to the ongoing needs of society, an accommodation that happened in the course of Christian history. Thus for Troeltsch the scandal of apocalyptic—the shocking historical particularity of the message of Jesus himself—is minimized. It is only one element in our contemporary judgment of the essence of Christianity, a judgment that must guide contemporary theological reflection.

5. The Legacy of Troeltsch

If the reader has persevered to this point, I hope she will agree that Ernst Troeltsch is a thinker of extraordinary contemporary significance. The current revival of interest in his work is amply justified and long

[212]Ibid.

[213]Cf. Troeltsch, "The Dogmatics of the History-of-Religions School," 99–100.

[214]Cf. Troeltsch, "What Does 'Essence of Christianity' Mean?," 153.

[215]Ibid., 155.

[216]Ibid.

[217]Cf. Ernst Troeltsch, *The Social Teaching of the Christian Churches,* translated by Olive Wyon (London: George Allen & Unwin, 1931), 2:999–1000 et passim.

overdue. Yet a question remains as to his *theological* significance. Does Troeltsch offer a workable solution to the ongoing challenge of history to religious authority? Two issues here deserve closer analysis. The first concerns the nature of that challenge, as spelt out in Troeltsch's three principles of "criticism," "analogy," and "correlation." The second concerns his answer to that challenge, in particular the religious interpretation of history on which his Christian theological work is built.

The Principle of Analogy
In my own judgment, Troeltsch's description of the work of the historian remains unrivaled. His principles of criticism and correlation are today utterly uncontroversial; only his principle of analogy remains subject to ongoing debate. I have already noted the positive role of analogy in the historical understanding of religious experience,[218] but some people would deny what we might call its negative role. Foremost among these is the theologian Wolfhart Pannenberg, whose views were briefly discussed at the end of chapter 2 and whose work will be examined in chapter 7. Pannenberg argues that insofar as history is concerned with the individual, the particular, and the contingent, it is concerned with phenomena "which cannot be contained without remainder in any analogy."[219] Analogies can help us to delimit this particularity by displaying what this event has in common with others. But they cannot do justice to the particularity of the event, which (by definition) exceeds all analogy. Therefore, while analogy can be used positively, to illustrate commonalities, it cannot be used negatively, to exclude the possibility of certain events.[220]

The argument is a good one, but it requires two qualifications. The first has to do with the role of what Pannenberg calls positive analogies. As I noted in chapter 2, even the critical use of analogy in historical research often begins with such positive analogies, that is to say, with patterns of behavior we can observe elsewhere. In these cases analogies are used, not to exclude the *possibility* of an event considered "in itself" (as it were), but to suggest why the *report* of that event may be unreliable. For instance, precisely because we witness the development of (historically unreliable) myths in other religious traditions—a positive analogy—we may assume their presence in early Christianity.[221] To take an example from Troeltsch's own work, the resurrection appearances may be regarded

---

[218]See the final section of chapter 2 (on the work of David Friedrich Strauss).
[219]Pannenberg, "Redemptive Event and History," 46.
[220]Cf. ibid., 48–49.
[221]Cf. ibid., 49.

as visions that are explicable psychologically,[222] not because we know of no other case of bodily resurrection (the negative use of analogy), but because we know that in similar circumstances visions do occur (the positive use of analogy).[223] In this way we may arrive at the same sceptical result, but in a way that simply bypasses Pannenberg's objection.

A second qualification has to do with the question of probability, which (as we saw in chapter 2) forms the basis of Hume's argument against miracles. Pannenberg would argue that the mere fact that we have no record of an alleged event (such as the resurrection of a dead man) does not, strictly speaking, *exclude* it from the range of possible historical explanations. Whatever one may think of this view (I will examine it in chapter 7), the lack of an analogy surely renders the alleged event *less probable*. Insofar as historical judgments are judgments of probability, they will be influenced by the presence or absence of analogies to the explanation being proposed. An explanation for which *no* analogy can be produced—however possible it may be in theory—will be unlikely to meet with acceptance.[224]

In a passing remark, the historian and philosopher R. G. Collingwood also takes exception to the principle of analogy. "That the Greeks and Romans exposed their new-born children in order to control the numbers of their population," he writes, "is no less true for being unlike anything that happens in the experience of contributors to the *Cambridge Ancient History*."[225] Once again, the objection has to do with what we might call the uniqueness or the particularity of historical phenomena, which (by definition) are without precise analogy. On reflection, however, we can see that Collingwood's objection has little force. Although there may be no *precise* parallel to infanticide in our experience, there are sufficient parallels to enable us to grasp this particular event. In other words, we can readily imagine, on the basis of our own experience, the circumstances under which infanticide may be practised. Indeed, loosely analogous decisions (such as those regarding abortion or euthanasia) *do* fall within the experience of Cambridge historians. In any case, analogy

---

[222]Cf. Troeltsch, *The Christian Faith* §18 (219).

[223]See, for instance, Gerd Lüdemann's examples in *The Resurrection of Jesus: History, Experience, Faith* (London: SCM, 1994), 106–7.

[224]This is, of course, the *epistemological* problem with attempts to speak of the resurrection of Jesus. With the best *metaphysical* will in the world, the historian finds it difficult to accept as an explanation of a phenomenon an event that is by definition unique. There is nothing to which it could be compared to make such an explanation plausible. I will return to this point when discussing Pannenberg's work in chapter 7, for its implications are more serious than the present discussion might suggest.

[225]Collingwood, *The Idea of History,* 240.

refers not just to the correspondence of past events with present experience but also to the correspondence of past events with each other. We certainly have records of infanticide outside of the Greek and Roman world, records that make the Greek and Roman reports credible.

Finally, those who reject the principle of analogy should reflect once again on Hume's point, namely, that a very similar assumption—that our present experience can be projected into the future—lies at the basis of *all* our knowledge. As Hume writes, "all our reasonings concerning matters of fact are founded on a species of Analogy, which leads us to expect from any cause the same events, which we have observed to result from similar causes."[226] To which we might add that, if any event were *utterly* unique, without any parallel with other events we have experienced or heard of, then it would be simply incomprehensible. For a further discussion of these issues, the reader is referred back to the final section of chapter 2, on the work of David Friedrich Strauss, and to my treatment of the resurrection of Jesus toward the end of chapter 7.

The Significance of History

A more serious objection to Troeltsch's theological position is raised by its dependence on an idealist philosophy of history. As we have seen throughout this analysis, Troeltsch's theological evaluation of history is based on a particular philosophy of history, which remains idealist even when it breaks with the specifically Hegelian form of idealism. If history cannot be regarded as having an overall goal, toward which the developments of human culture converge, then Troeltsch's method of deducing normative values collapses, as he himself readily admits.[227] Certainly Troeltsch believes that only something like an idealist metaphysics is compatible with Christian faith. Without such a philosophy, with its assertion of the close relationship between the human spirit and the divine, it would be impossible to link up talk of values in history with the "God-talk" of the Christian theologian. The key question here concerns teleology. Individual human beings may meaningfully be spoken of as acting purposefully, but does it make any sense to speak of *history* having a purpose or goal? Of course, it does make sense if this purpose is

[226]Hume, "An Enquiry concerning Human Understanding," section 9, §82 (104).
[227]Cf. Troeltsch, *The Absoluteness of Christianity,* 100; "Modern Philosophy of History," 316; cf. "Historical and Dogmatic Method in Theology," 26 (*The Historical Jesus Quest,* 46). In *Der Historismus und seine Probleme* (183–84), Troeltsch remarks that without the idea of God "or something analogous" (*oder irgendein Analogon*) there can be no construction of criteria of historical value. For the horrified reaction of his student Friedrich Gogarten to that phrase, to which we will return, see Coakley, *Christ without Absolutes,* 81, n.5.

attributed to a personal God. Yet to assert the existence of such a God is, of course, to beg some key questions. However defensible such an assertion may be, it cannot form the basis of the kind of thoroughly historical theology that Troeltsch is attempting to construct. One can hardly assume the existence of the Christian God in order to construct a philosophy of history that will enable one to deduce the truth of the Christian picture of God.

Troeltsch frequently suggests that adherence to an idealist view of history is itself a matter of personal decision.[228] More precisely, he concedes that the existence of an absolute value, toward which historical values converge, is not in any strict sense a matter of proof. Not only is there a personal act of faith involved in our judgments of value. A similar act of faith is required if we are to believe that such judgments are even possible. This is a metaphysical rather than a religious act of faith but it is an act of faith nonetheless. For example, in his 1904 essay "Modern Philosophy of History," Troeltsch writes that belief in the possibility of enduring value judgments is a kind of faith, albeit a necessary one, since it forms the presupposition of all our attempts to know.[229] In *The Absoluteness of Christianity,* Troeltsch insists that "absolute, unchanging value, conditioned by nothing temporal, exists not within but beyond history and can be perceived only in presentiment and faith."[230] In *Der Historismus und seine Probleme,* he concedes that the idea that there is an Absolute that comes to expression in the relative values of history could well be regarded as a "myth,"[231] although, of course, myths too can touch something very deep in the soul. Elsewhere in the same work, Troeltsch notes that we can only glimpse (*ahnen*) the meaning of reality as a whole and its connection with God. Any affirmations in this respect involve taking a risk, and it is always possible that we may be deceived. Here, too, there is a kind of "justification by faith."[232]

Now these are only hints, but their implications are quite serious. At the time Troeltsch wrote, the idealist act of faith may not, perhaps, have seemed too much of a risk. There seemed good reason to be an idealist, even apart from one's religious commitments. The idealist act of faith was apparently "confirmed" by the progress of humanity, by what

---

[228]Cf. Coakley, *Christ without Absolutes,* 36–37. (For examples, see below.)

[229]Troeltsch's argument here is that all our attempts to know *take for granted* both the value of truth and the value of knowledge for human culture (cf. Troeltsch, "Modern Philosophy of History, 301–2).

[230]Troeltsch, *The Absoluteness of Christianity,* 90.

[231]*Mag ein Mythos sein*; cf. Troeltsch, *Der Historismus und seine Probleme,* 212–13. See also Troeltsch, "Historiography," 722b.

[232]Cf. Troeltsch, *Der Historismus und seine Probleme,* 185.

Troeltsch calls "the deepening of personal life which is constantly taking place in history."[233] Indeed, the best thought of his age, Troeltsch insists, leads to the idealist conclusion.[234] In the age in which Troeltsch lived, therefore, one could make this metaphysical act of faith with some confidence. Yet even in Troeltsch's time, some had abandoned the idealist point of view. Many thinkers, for instance, were quick to build a materialist philosophy of history on the basis of the Darwinian evolutionary hypothesis, from which Troeltsch was (understandably) quick to distance himself.[235] In our own age, the problem has become much greater. The idealist view of history has now all but disappeared, yet another casualty of the great world wars of the twentieth century and of our disillusionment with the idea of progress. The dialectical theologians would express this disillusionment in the traditional Christian language of sin and grace, sometimes embellishing this with talk of "crisis" and "decision." As we have seen, Troeltsch also spoke of the need for personal decision, but—unlike the dialectical theologians—he never believed that the decision of faith had to be made *in opposition* to knowledge.[236] Rather, he was convinced that the decision of faith could be shown to be well founded. Faith and secular knowledge were different forms of knowledge, but they would eventually converge. For those who have lost that confidence, Troeltsch's theological scheme would be difficult to revive. More precisely, unless something resembling an idealist view of history can be defended and made plausible, any attempt to revive Troeltsch's solution to the theological problems of our age will be stillborn. *If* such a view of history could be defended, Troeltsch's theology would be a model for the theologian's task.[237] But this must be cold comfort to the contemporary theologian.

---

[233]Troeltsch, "Historical and Dogmatic Method in Theology," 26; *The Historical Jesus Quest,* 46 (German text from *Gesammelte Schriften* 2, 746).

[234]Cf. Troeltsch, *The Christian Faith,* §4 (61).

[235]Cf. ibid., §14 (178). See also Troeltsch's 1923 lecture "The Morality of the Personality and of the Conscience," translated by F. von Hügel, in *Christian Thought: Its History and Application,* 44, and *Der Historismus und seine Probleme,* 662–63.

[236]Cf. Troeltsch, "Half a Century of Theology," 57.

[237]Over against the judgment of Benjamin A. Reist (cf. *Towards a Theology of Involvement: A Study of Ernst Troeltsch,* Library of Philosophy and Theology [London: SCM, 1966], 154–201) that Troeltsch's theology was a tragic failure, Walter Wyman (*The Concept of Glaubenslehre,* 49) insists that aspects of that theology can be saved, even if Troeltsch's "philosophy of the history of religions" must be abandoned. Yet this is surely a desperate proposal. As Troeltsch's work continually reminds us, the place of Christianity in "the history of religions" is at the very core of the challenge of history to faith. If no answer can be given to that challenge, there is little future for Christian theology.

A Christian Theology?

Even with his idealist metaphysics, Troeltsch sometimes had trouble doing justice to traditional Christian claims. For example, the conclusion of *The Absoluteness of Christianity* falls far short of what Christians have generally believed, as its author readily admits.[238] The degree to which Troeltsch had moved away from traditional Christian views is even more evident in his 1923 lecture on "The Place of Christianity among the World-Religions," in which he admits that Christianity may be normative only for the peoples of Europe. As we have seen, his understanding of the role of Jesus also falls short of the authority that was traditionally granted to the founder of Christianity, although it may perhaps be compatible with some contemporary forms of liberal theology.[239] Indeed, it is not at all clear that the Christianity Troeltsch advocates has any need of the figure of Jesus. Toward the end of his life Troeltsch continues to use Christian language, but he seems increasingly reluctant to identify himself with any particular tradition of historic Christianity.[240] In one of his very last works he suggests that he has become what he calls "more and more radical and super-denominational."[241]

Finally, in another of Troeltsch's later works there is at least a hint that he is not optimistic about the future public role of Christianity. While our society badly needs a common, metaphysical and religious vision, Troeltsch writes, it is unlikely that such a vision will come from the churches. The churches served this role in the past, even if only by way of various kinds of compromise.[242] But they can do so no longer. A common metaphysical and religious vision for our time can develop only outside of and alongside the Christian communities of faith.[243] It is difficult to draw any firm conclusion from what is merely a passing remark, but it is at least possible that, at the time of his death, Troeltsch's thinking was approaching the view that we find in Albert Schweitzer's works. As we saw in the previous chapter, Schweitzer sees Jesus' teaching as *contributing* to the construction of a life-affirming ethic, but he no longer attempts to ground that ethic in an appeal to Christian authority. The Christian churches, it seems, can no longer provide the common vision we need. Troeltsch, too, may have been coming to a similar conclusion: that Christianity was now merely one of the historical resources out of

---

[238]Cf. Troeltsch, *The Absoluteness of Christianity*, 131.

[239]For some stimulating suggestions regarding one way in which Troeltsch's theology might be reappropriated, see Coakley, *Christ without Absolutes*, 191–97.

[240]Cf. Coakley, *Christ without Absolutes*, 75–76.

[241]Troeltsch, "The Place of Christianity among the World-Religions," 31.

[242]Cf. Ernst Troeltsch, "The Common Spirit," 117–18.

[243]Cf. ibid., 123–24.

which we might construct a common ethical philosophy for our time. If he had lived long enough to return to the philosophy of religion, as was his intention at the time of his death,[244] it would have been interesting to see what direction his thought would have taken.

This is not to say that Troeltsch has nothing to offer us at the beginning of the twenty-first century. If Troeltsch's religious philosophy falls short of being a satisfactory Christian theology, it may be the closest thing to theology that can be achieved, given our contemporary religious situation. Outside of the religious sphere, Troeltsch's work also seems prophetic. For instance, he may well be correct to insist that if we are to find any sort of answers to our ethical and religious questions, we can do so only by acts of personal judgment, informed but not determined by historical knowledge. He is also correct to point out how difficult such judgments are when we are faced with very different cultural and religious traditions.[245] As a thinker, Troeltsch has much to teach us. The questions he asked are the questions we are still grappling with today, questions of historical and cultural relativism and of the possibility of making binding ethical judgments.[246] His religious thought is exemplary for its willingness to face up to the critical questions and to renounce compromise solutions. However, from the point of view of Christian theology, Troeltsch offers no enduring answer to the challenge of history to religious authority.

---

[244]Cf. Troeltsch, *Der Historismus und seine Probleme,* viii.

[245]Troeltsch's work is here reminiscent of that of Alasdair MacIntyre, whose book *Whose Justice? Which Rationality?* (Notre Dame, Ind.: University of Notre Dame Press, 1988) discusses (inter alia) whether ethical debates can be successfully conducted across competing ethical traditions.

[246]From this point of view, Troeltsch's eloquent denunciation of what he calls "European arrogance" (*Europäerhochmut*), delivered at least fifty years before such attacks became fashionable, makes extraordinary reading (cf. *Der Historismus und seine Probleme,* 707–8).

Chapter Five

The Dialectical Theology (A)

Karl Barth (1886–1968)

> *Theology is thus the arbitrator and mistress of all,*
> *so that it judges by its own standards and is itself*
> *judged by no other science.*
>
> Friedrich Turretini (1623–87)

The early stages of the historical Jesus quest were followed by what appears to be a theological reaction against its assumptions. (In fact, as we will see, it is only a partial reaction.) The beginnings of this reaction may be traced to the figure of Martin Kähler (1835–1912), whose 1896 publication *The So-Called Historical Jesus and the Historic, Biblical Christ* reaffirmed the priority of the Christ of Christian preaching over the Jesus of the historian.[1] However, that protest reached a high point in the dialectical theology of Karl Barth.[2] Barth was not primarily a biblical scholar or an exegete but a systematic theologian. He was undoubtedly a great theologian.[3] Barth towers above his contemporaries, both in his sheer productivity and in the originality of his theological vision. For this reason, any discussion of Barth's theology is an audacious act. (One is uncomfortably reminded of Barth's habitual question to his critics, as to whether they had read *all* of his multivolume *Church Dogmatics*.[4]) Yet precisely because of

---

[1]Cf. Martin Kähler, *The So-Called Historical Jesus and the Historic, Biblical Christ* (1896), translated by Carl E. Braaten; Seminar Editions (Philadelphia: Fortress Press, 1964).

[2]The term "dialectical theology" remains a useful description of the thought of both Barth and Bultmann, despite the disagreements between them and despite developments in the thought of each. Bruce L. McCormack (*Karl Barth's Critically Realistic Dialectical Theology: Its Genesis and Development 1909–1936* [Oxford: Clarendon, 1995], 18, 274, et passim) argues convincingly that in important respects Barth remained a "dialectical theologian" even during the period of the *Church Dogmatics*.

[3]As unlikely an admirer as Pope Pius XII is said to have declared Barth the greatest theologian since St. Thomas Aquinas.

[4]For the record, the following study will focus on Barth's five major theological works, which enable one to trace his thought chronologically. These are the two commentaries on Romans (that of 1919 and that of 1921), the Göttingen lectures of 1924, the unfinished work entitled *Die christliche Dogmatik im Entwurf* (Christian dogmatics in outline) of 1927, which is the product of Barth's lectures in Münster, and the magnum opus of the *Church Dogmatics*, where our attention will be directed above all to the first volume (1932 and 1938).

Barth's influence on twentieth-century religious thought, no discussion of the challenge of history to religious authority would be complete without him.

At first sight, the scope of the present study might seem to make the task an easy one. Since Barth devoted comparatively little time to discussing the question of historical knowledge, what he did say could—on the face of it—be easily summarized. However, this initial impression would be deceptive. For Barth's apparent neglect of the question of history is eloquent. It was, in other words, a deliberate and studied neglect, and its significance can only be appreciated in the context of Barth's work as a whole. In that context we find that the issue of historical knowledge and its challenge to religious belief, while rarely addressed directly, is always in the background. As with much of Barth's theology, the really important questions lie beneath the surface, and some excavation is required to bring them to light.

To focus this study, I have chosen for closer examination four issues that are able to lead us gradually into the heart of Barth's theology. The first issue has to do with Barth's attitude towards biblical interpretation in general. As we will see, Barth is anxious to point out the strictly limited value of historical criticism, both as a general hermeneutical method and as a foundation for theology. The second issue has to do with the locus (or "place") of divine revelation. The key question here is: Where is the Word of God to be found? Is it to be found in the text of scripture or in the history to which it bears witness? The third issue, which brings us to the very heart of our topic, has to do with the relationship between divine action and human history: in what sense, if any, can it be said that God acts *in* human history? The fourth issue to be discussed is Barth's understanding of revelation and religion. Barth's attitude to religion and to the study of the history of religions says much about his attitude to the challenges of modernity. After examining these four issues, we will be better placed to appreciate the significance of Barth's work and the answer he gives to the challenge of history to faith.

1. The Task of Interpretation

Barth's first major theological work was his commentary on Paul's letter to the Romans, a commentary first published in 1919 and republished, in a totally revised edition, in 1921. It is here that the question of historical research and its relationship to faith first arises. The issues raised in *Romans* are picked up and developed in Barth's later works, most clearly in the first volume of the magisterial *Church Dogmatics,* published in 1932. We will therefore begin with the Romans commentary before moving on to the *Dogmatics.*

In itself, of course, the Romans commentary offers a living example of the way in which Barth believed the Bible ought to be interpreted. Its content and tone distinguished it immediately from the tradition of biblical commentary that dates from the seventeenth and eighteenth centuries, a tradition foreshadowed in the work of Spinoza. However, in the prefaces to Barth's commentary we also find an explicit discussion of historical criticism. This discussion will be the immediate focus of the following remarks.

The Limits of Historical Criticism

(a) The First Preface to Romans

Already in the opening lines of his preface to the first edition of *Romans* (1919), Barth sets out his hermeneutical manifesto. There could be no better place to begin.

> Paul, as a child of his age, addressed his contemporaries. It is however, far more important, that, as Prophet and Apostle of the Kingdom of God, he veritably speaks to all men [*zu allen Menschen*] of every age. The differences between then and now, there and here, no doubt require careful investigation and consideration. But the purpose of such investigation can only be to demonstrate that these differences are, in fact, purely trivial [keine *Bedeutung haben*].[5]

In the course of the present study we have examined the interpretative tradition that had its origins in the seventeenth century. This tradition highlighted the historical distance, the differences between the age of the biblical writers and our own. Barth begins his first major work by setting his face against that tradition, in an act of bold defiance,[6] and declaring these historical differences to be insignificant. Indeed, he argues that they

---

[5]Karl Barth, preface to the first edition, in *The Epistle to the Romans,* 6th edition (1928), translated by Edwyn C. Hoskyns (London: Oxford University Press, 1933), 1. For the German text, see Karl Barth, *Der Römerbrief (Erste Fassung), 1919,* Gesamtausgabe (Zurich: Theologischer Verlag, 1985), 3 (the emphasis, here and elsewhere in citations from Barth's work, is his own).

[6]As I have noted in the preface, the present study makes no attempt to situate Barth's defiance in its historical context, which ought to be done if it is to be properly understood. Of particular importance in this respect is Barth's disillusionment with the liberal theology in which he had been brought up, a disillusionment prompted particularly by the willingness of his former teachers to side with the German war policy in 1914. For a more complete discussion of Barth's theological conversion, see Eberhard Busch, *Karl Barth: His Life from Letters and Autobiographical Texts* (1975), translated by John Bowden (London: SCM, 1976), chap. 3 (60–126).

are so insignificant that they ought not to be the focus of the interpreter's attention. This act of defiance has often been misunderstood,
especially by those who claimed that Barth was "an enemy of historical
criticism."[7] If historical criticism is thought of as the attempt to understand the Bible in its historical context, then this criticism is entirely
unfounded, a fact which will become increasingly evident throughout
this chapter. Even in this opening statement of his earliest major work,
Barth does not deny that there exists a gap between the biblical world
and our own. Nor does he deny that the investigation of these matters is
one of the tasks of the interpreter. As he writes in the same context, "the
historical-critical method of Biblical investigation has its rightful place: it
is concerned with the preparation of the intelligence—and this can
never be superfluous."[8] Nonetheless, he insists that its results will be *comparatively* trivial. The discovery of historical differences counts for little
when set alongside those things that the biblical writers have *in common*
with our age. Barth goes on to suggest that this insight can be general-
ized. It is not a fact that applies to the Bible alone; it is equally valid for
any other kind of historical investigation.[9] "The understanding of history," Barth writes, "is an ongoing, ever more sincere and penetrating
conversation between the wisdom of yesterday and the wisdom of
tomorrow, which is one and the same."[10]

(b) The Second Preface to Romans

The second edition of *Romans* (1921) was a complete revision of the
earlier work, so much so that, as Barth wrote, "no stone remains in its old
place."[11] The revision occurred in the light of developments in Barth's
own thought as well as in response to criticism. Once again, our atten-

---

[7]Karl Barth, preface to the second edition, in *The Epistle to the Romans,* 6th edition, 6.
Where it is reliable, I will use the English translation of the later edition of *Romans.*
Unfortunately, it is not always reliable, and on occasions I will have recourse to the Ger-
man. On these occasions, the English references will also be given.

[8]Barth, preface to the first edition, in *The Epistle to the Romans,* 6th edition, 1.

[9]Cf. Barth's preface to the second edition, (*The Epistle to the Romans,* 6th edition, 12):
"I have . . . no desire to conceal the fact that my 'Biblicist' method . . . is applicable also to
the study of Lao-Tse and Goethe."

[10]Cf. Barth, preface to the first edition, in *The Epistle to the Romans,* 6th edition, 1;
Barth, *Der Römerbrief, 1919,* 3: *Geschichtsverständnis is ein fortgesetztes, immer aufrichtigeres
and eindringenderes Gespräch zwischen der Weisheit von gestern and der Weisheit von morgen, die
eine und dieselbe ist.* The wording here is interesting: not "the wisdom of *today,*" but "the
wisdom of *tomorrow.*" Barth is perhaps hinting at the ("eschatological") idea that it will
be the future action of God that reveals the deepest meaning of the Bible.

[11]Barth, preface to the second edition, in *The Epistle to the Romans,* 6th edition, 2.

tion here will be restricted to Barth's understanding of biblical interpretation. The preface to the second edition picks up the ideas of the preface to the first and carries them further. It also argues that the historical criticism of the Bible takes us only so far, for by itself such criticism falls short of the real purpose of a commentary. The leading biblical critics of the modern period claim to be offering an explanation of the text, but their comments amount to what Barth calls "no explanation at all, but only a first primitive attempt at such."[12] They do little more than to render the Greek text in the corresponding German words, with philological and archaeological comments, along with a more or less plausible reconstruction of its historical setting. The problem with such results, Barth argues—with reference to Romans—is that they do not attain "an understanding of Paul."[13] Such an understanding, he continues, must involve "more than a *repetition* in Greek or German of what Paul says: it involves the *reconsideration* of what is set out in the Epistle, until the actual meaning of it is disclosed."[14]

(c) Implications

Even from these introductory comments it is clear that Barth's attitude to the historical criticism of the Bible is ambivalent. On the one hand, he admits that historical criticism of the Bible remains necessary, since there are obvious differences between the age of the biblical writers and our own. For this reason, what they are saying can hardly be understood without *some* study of history. To this extent Barth remains within the research tradition that was established in the seventeenth century. On the other hand, he insists that, so long as such study remains on the level of historical description and a bare "repetition" of the message of the writer, it is not yet a commentary in the deepest sense of that word. For Barth, in other words, historical explanation represents a *necessary* but not a *sufficient* condition of a true commentary. As we continue our study, we will see this ambivalence reflected in Barth's later writings, up to and including the *Church Dogmatics*.

[12]Cf. Barth, preface to the second edition, in *The Epistle to the Romans,* 6th edition, 6; Karl Barth, *Der Römerbrief,* 6th edition (1928; Munich: Christian Kaiser, 1933), x: [*eine*] *Erklärung des Textes, die ich keine Erklärung nennen kann, sondern nur den ersten primitiven Versuch einer solchen.*

[13]Barth, *The Epistle to the Romans,* 6th edition, 6–7.

[14]Ibid. (emphasis mine). As we will see in a moment, the highlighted words correspond to two German terms, whose forms echo each other. A commentary, Barth insists, should not just *repeat* (*nachsprechen*), it should also *reconsider* (*nachdenken*) the thoughts found in the text.

Subject-Centered Criticism

If the work of the historical critics has fallen short of the true task of the commentator, then what *is* that task? What would Barth put in the place of the bare historical description that he rejects? As I have already noted, the text of the Romans commentary itself offers a living example of Barth's alternative. However, for a description of what that alternative involves, we may turn again to Barth's prefaces.

(a) The Second Preface to Romans

In the preface to the second edition of *Romans,* Barth not only criticizes the dominant school of biblical interpretation; he also spells out what he understands to be the true task of the commentator. He does so first of all by drawing attention to the contrast between modern historical criticism and the work of the great sixteenth-century Reformers. As Barth writes, a sixteenth-century figure like Calvin not only deals conscientiously with the text, but—moving beyond that preparatory work—he tries

> to *re*-think the text, that is to say, to wrestle with it at length, until the wall which separates the sixteenth century from the first becomes *transparent,* until Paul speaks and the person of the sixteenth century hears, until the conversation between the original document and the reader is entirely focused on the *subject-matter* (a subject matter which cannot be different from one age to the next!).[15]

It seems, then, that the deepest task of a commentary is what Barth calls (in German) *nachdenken* (consideration), a term that suggests a thinking of the author's thoughts "after" him. This process should be continued until the commentator has penetrated to the very subject matter of the text and has grasped the issues with which the author was grappling. Barth suggests that this *nachdenken* is distinguished from a mere *nachsprechen* (repetition): it is not a matter of merely repeating or even paraphrasing the author's words. It is a matter of pondering those words until our attention is no longer focused on the words, but on that of which

---

[15]Cf. Barth, preface to the second edition, in *The Epistle to the Romans,* 6th edition, 7; Barth, *Der Römerbrief,* 6th edition, xi: *Wie energisch geht [Calvin] zu Werk, seinen Text, nachdem auch er gewissenhaft festgestellt "was da steht", nachzudenken, d.h., sich solange mit ihm auseinander zu setzen, bis die Mauer zwischen dem 1. und 16. Jahrhundert* transparent *wird, bis Paulus dort redet und der Mensch des 16. Jahrhunderts hier hört, bis das Gespräch zwischen Urkunde und Leser ganz auf die* Sache *(die hier und dort keine verschiedene sein kann!) konzentriert ist.*

they speak. When the text is truly understood, it will have become practically invisible. At this point, which is the high point of the interpretative process, the interpreter will no longer be grappling with the problems of the text as a historical document. No less than the author, the interpreter will be grappling with the matters of which it speaks.

(b) The Third Preface to Romans

In his third preface to *Romans* (1922), Barth takes these ideas still further, arguing that a commentary in the deepest sense of the word requires an attitude of loyalty towards the author of the work studied. The interpreter, in other words, must be prepared to assume that the author has something to say and should be ready to follow his thought wherever that leads. Anything less than this loyalty will fall short of the deepest aims of interpretation. In the case of Romans, it will produce, at best, a commentary *on* Paul's letter, but not a commentary that thinks *with* its author.[16] For this reason an interpreter who is incapable of following the apostle's thought with this degree of loyalty would be better not to attempt a commentary. More precisely, he may attempt the more superficial task of a commentary *on* the work being studied, but he should not claim to have truly grappled with its thought.

Barth concedes that this loyalty towards the author's meaning does not exclude a criticism of the contents of his work. Yet he also insists that not *any* form of criticism is permissible. Insofar as he takes a stance towards the content of the work, the critic should do so on standards that are internal to it. In other words, criticism will be primarily a matter of assessing the degree to which the author has successfully carried through his intention; the extent to which the author has truly come to grips with the issue being addressed. As Barth writes in the preface to the second edition of his work, "criticism [κρίνειν] applied to an historical document means for me: the measuring of all the words and phrases contained therein against the subject-matter about which they openly speak—assuming that it is not entirely mistaken."[17] In this sense Barth can readily accept a criticism of the "letter" of the document by its "spirit."[18] Indeed, a real attitude of loyalty to the author will *demand* such criticism, since it is a loyalty not just to the author's words but to what

[16]Cf. Barth, preface to the third edition, in *The Epistle to the Romans*, 6th edition, 17.

[17]Cf. Barth, preface to the second edition, in *The Epistle to the Romans*, 6th edition, 8; Barth, *Der Römerbrief*, 6th edition, xii: κρίνειν *heißt für mich einer historischen Urkunde gegenüber: das Messen aller in ihr enthaltenen Wörter und Wörtergruppen an der Sache, von der sie, wenn nicht alles täuscht, offenbar reden.*

[18]Barth, *The Epistle to the Romans*, 6th edition, 18–19.

the author was trying to say. There is the even the possibility, Barth concedes, that we may eventually need to look "beyond" the biblical author.[19] But this takes for granted all that has already been said about the task of interpretation. In other words, we will be able to engage in this sort of criticism only if we have first endeavored, with an attitude of loyalty and with an uncompromising earnestness, to look *into* what he was trying to say.[20]

It would be easy to interpret this insistence on loyalty to the text as an implicit reference to the divine authority of the Bible, which demands the submission of the reader rather than a critical distance. However, at this point in his work, Barth is not yet basing this argument on divine authority. For Barth, this attitude of loyalty is simply a fundamental hermeneutical principle.[21] Not only when reading the Bible, but when reading any significant work, we must be prepared to assume that the author has something to say and that we should therefore attempt to follow his thought faithfully. As Barth writes, "I regard it as impossible to do justice to any author, to make any author speak once again, without risking this assumption, without entering into this relationship of loyalty."[22] For a theological discussion of the Bible and of the way it should be interpreted, we must move beyond the Romans commentary to the discussion of scripture in Barth's more systematic theological works.[23]

Human Witness to the Divine Word

(a) The Göttingen Lectures

The lectures Barth gave in Göttingen in 1924 are one of the most accessible sources for Barth's early theology. Only quite recently have these been published, under the title which Barth gave to his course, namely

[19]Ibid., 19.
[20]Ibid., cf. Barth, *Der Römerbrief,* 6th edition, xxii.
[21]On this topic, see also Karl Barth, *Church Dogmatics,* vol. I, part 2: *The Doctrine of the Word of God,* translated by G. T. Thomson and Harold Knight (Edinburgh: T. & T. Clark, 1956), §19.1 (464–65).
[22]Cf. Barth, preface to the third edition, in *The Epistle to the Romans,* 6th edition, 18; Barth, *Der Römerbrief,* 6th edition, xxi: *Ich halte es für ausgeschlossen, daß man irgend einem Schriftsteller gerecht werden, irgend einem Schriftsteller wirklich wieder zum Reden bringen kann, wenn man jene Hypothese nicht wagt, jenes Treuverhältnis zu ihm nicht eingeht.*
[23]For further comments on the way in which a historical document should be interpreted, the reader may wish to refer to Barth's introduction to his 1922 Göttingen lectures on Calvin (*Die Theologie Calvins,* edited by Hans Scholl, Gesamtausgabe [Zurich: Theologischer Verlag, 1993], 1–14) and to the *Church Dogmatics* I/2, §19.1 (466–68).

"Instruction in the Christian Religion."[24] These have in turn been translated into English as *The Göttingen Dogmatics.* For our purpose, what is of interest in these lectures is Barth's doctrine of the Word of God. What is striking about this doctrine is that Barth is anxious to make a clear distinction between the Word of God itself and the human words in which that divine Word comes to us. The divine Word comes to us only in historically conditioned human words, but the two are not to be confused. As Barth writes, "this means that I come up against a barrier. I do not hear God himself speak. I only hear from God and about God. His own Word comes to me only in this broken form."[25] In other words, God's Word "comes to us as an authority in history, and only thus."[26]

This distinction remains crucial to Barth's understanding of the Bible. It enables him to acknowledge the importance of an historical study of scripture, without identifying the Word of God with its results. We will return to these matters shortly. For the moment, we need only note once again Barth's readiness to accept the historical criticism of the Bible. As he writes in his *Göttingen Dogmatics,* "we do not have to withdraw the Bible from purely historical considerations. Naturally, like any other literature, the Bible has its place in the history of literature, culture, and religion."[27] Barth goes on to insist that no restriction should be placed on the historical study of the Bible, which must use the same methods as would be used in the study of any other ancient document. As we have seen, this acknowledgment keeps Barth within the "research tradition" of which I spoke at the end of my introductory chapter.

The insistence that God's Word comes to us only in human words is associated with another idea prominent in Barth's thought. This new idea has to do with the hiddenness of revelation. Just as the action of God lies hidden in history (an idea to which we will return), so the Word of God comes to us in the Bible, but not in a direct and unmediated manner. It comes concealed, hidden in the human words in which it is expressed. As Barth writes, "for the sake of the concealment of revelation, its communication must always be a human affair."[28] For this reason Barth opposes the traditional doctrine of the *verbal* inspiration of the

---

[24]*Unterricht in der christlichen Religion.* The title calls to mind not just John Calvin's famous work, but also the nineteenth-century work by Albrecht Ritschl. The latter allusion may well have been deliberate, an attempt to placate Barth's Lutheran colleagues at Göttingen.

[25]Karl Barth, *The Göttingen Dogmatics: Instruction in the Christian Religion* (1924), translated by Geoffrey W. Bromiley, vol. 1 (Grand Rapids: Eerdmans, 1991), §9.2 (230).

[26]Ibid., §9.2 (231).

[27]Ibid., §8.2 (216).

[28]Ibid., §8.2 (217).

Bible, the idea that "the biblical writers did not think and write on their own but simply took down heavenly dictation."[29] Such a doctrine overlooks the concealment, the hiddenness that Barth regards as an essential characteristic of revelation. Once again Barth insists that revelation does not come to us directly, but only as hidden in human words that are historically shaped and conditioned. For this reason the skills of the historian are needed for its interpretation.[30]

(b) The Church Dogmatics

Turning to the *Church Dogmatics,* we come across the same themes, but now expressed in a phrase that has become famous. The Bible is to be understood, Barth writes, as "a witness to divine revelation."[31] In fact, in the development of Barth's thought this phrase is not altogether new. It is already found in Barth's *Göttingen Dogmatics,*[32] as well as in the 1927 work *Christian Dogmatics in Outline,* which emerged from Barth's lectures at Münster.[33] However, its implications are fully developed only in the *Church Dogmatics,* in Barth's discussion of what he calls "Holy Scripture" as "the Word of God for the Church."[34]

Barth notes first of all that to describe the Bible as a "witness to divine revelation" implies a limitation, a restriction. As he writes, "a witness is not absolutely identical with that to which it witnesses."[35] However, this distinction needs to be stated carefully. Although Barth wants to make a *distinction* between the Bible and revelation, he certainly does not wish to imply that the two can be *separated.* As Barth writes, for us, who are not— like the apostles—witnesses of the resurrection and direct recipients of revelation, the Bible *is* revelation. It is nothing less than what Barth calls "revelation as it comes to us, mediating and therefore accommodating itself to us."[36] From our point of view, therefore, the biblical writings are indispensable. Revelation is inseparable from them: the Word of God

---

[29]Ibid. On Barth's doctrine of revelation, see section 2 of the present chapter ("The Locus of Revelation").

[30]Cf. Barth, *The Göttingen Dogmatics,* §10.3 (257).

[31]Barth, *Church Dogmatics* I/2, §19 (457).

[32]Cf. Barth, *The Göttingen Dogmatics,* §8.2 (216), §9.4 (249), et passim.

[33]Karl Barth, *Die christliche Dogmatik im Entwurf: Erster Band—Die Lehre vom Worte Gottes* (1927), Gesamtausgabe (Zurich: Theologischer Verlag, 1982), §20.1 (435, 438) et passim.

[34]As well as the passages cited below, see Karl Barth, *Church Dogmatics,* vol. I, part 1: *The Doctrine of the Word of God* (1932), translated by G. T. Thomson (Edinburgh: T. & T. Clark, 1936), §4.3 (124–26).

[35]Barth, *Church Dogmatics* I/2, §19.1 (463).

[36]Ibid.

cannot be heard apart from the Bible. Yet it remains true that the Bible and revelation should not be simply identified. There remains a distinction.

Wherein lies the distinction? It lies—once again—in the fact that the Bible consists of human words, *by means of which* the Word of God reaches us. What the church hears when it hears the Bible belongs, in the first instance, to the sphere of the merely human. It follows that, by referring to the Bible as a witness to revelation, Barth is able to recognize quite openly its human origin. As Barth writes, "we must not ignore the writtenness of Holy Writ for the sake of its holiness, its humanity for the sake of its divinity. We must not ignore it any more than we do the humanity of Jesus Christ Himself. We must study it, for it is here or nowhere that we shall find its divinity."[37] Yet again Barth implicitly acknowledges the importance of historical criticism.[38] As he writes, the humanity of the Bible means that we must take the Bible for what it is: human speech uttered at particular times, in particular situations, in particular languages, and with a particular intention. If the church recognizes the Word of God in the Bible, it recognizes it only *as* spoken at those times and in this situation, in this language, and with this intention. In this sense, revelation is conditioned by history, for it is expressed in forms that are a product of history. Yet—and the distinction is critical—it is *expressed* in these forms, not *identified* with them.

Barth's recognition of the humanity of the Bible can even extend so far as a recognition of its fallibility. Indeed, it is here that the full significance of Barth's distinction becomes clear, for it enables him to accept the apparently most destructive results of biblical criticism. The Bible's role as vehicle of divine revelation is not undermined by the fact that the biblical writers "shared the culture of their age and environment," a culture whose "form and content" can "appear debatable to us."[39] The Bible's reliability as a witness to revelation is unshaken by the fact that the biblical writers lacked our modern distinction between history and legend, so that at least parts of the Bible must be consigned to the category of the legendary.[40] The Bible's role in the life of the believer is unaffected by the fact that it seems to have so much in common with other documents of its time and place. It is unaffected by the fact that its authors must be recognized as "capable of error" even in religious and theological matters.[41] Barth can accept all of these limitations

[37]Ibid.
[38]Cf. ibid., §19.1, 464.
[39]Ibid., §19.2 (508).
[40]Cf. ibid., §19.2 (509).
[41]Cf. ibid., §19.2 (508–9).

because he has insisted that the Bible, as a document of history, is distinct from the revelation to which it bears witness. The marvel of God's self-communication to human beings is in no way lessened by the weakness and fallibility of the witnesses through whose work this miracle occurs.

Barth will later cite with approval Martin Luther's dictum that "God and the Word of God are two things, no less than the Creator and his creature are two things."[42] This saying hints at the deeper dimensions of Barth's distinction. Divine revelation is, for Barth, the revelation of nothing less than God himself.[43] It is not just a message about God, but God himself in his acts of revelation and redemption.[44] It follows that simply to *identify* human speech with divine revelation would be to create an idol, to break down the distinction between the divine and the human, to put the creature in the place of the Creator. Precisely because divine revelation is the revelation of God himself, God's Word can be described as God's Son, sharing his very nature.[45] Indeed, if one is to use the phrase "Word of God," then it must be admitted that the primary referent of this term is Christ, the incarnate Word.[46] Scripture deserves the name "Word of God" only because it witnesses to the incarnate Word. But it remains a human and even a fallible witness, even as it conveys that Word to us.

2. The Locus of Revelation

A brief look at Barth's understanding of the place (or locus) of revelation will bring us more deeply into his doctrine of scripture.

(a) The Göttingen Dogmatics

I should begin by saying a word or two about Barth's doctrine of *inspiration,* as found in his *Göttingen Dogmatics.* We have already seen that Barth opposes the traditional doctrine of the verbal inspiration of the Bible. His own doctrine of inspiration is a sophisticated one, which sees revelation as, above all, an *event.* The revelation of God is not to be thought of as something "contained" (as it were) in a document. Rather, it is an act of God. That act certainly occurs *by means of* the words contained in the Bible, but—once again—it cannot be simply identified with them. If

---

[42]Ibid., §19.2 (508): *Duae res sunt Deus et scriptura Dei, non minus quam duae res sunt creator et creatura Dei.*

[43]Cf. Barth, *Church Dogmatics* I/1, §5.2 (155–58).

[44]Cf. Barth, *The Göttingen Dogmatics,* §5.1 (88).

[45]Cf. Barth, *Church Dogmatics* I/1, §5.2 (155–56).

[46]Cf. Barth, *Church Dogmatics* I/2, §19.2 (512–13).

inspiration is thought of as the act of God that gives rise to revelation, then this act must be thought of as embracing past and present. It is not simply that the Holy Spirit inspired the biblical writers in the past. If the Bible is to be correctly understood, he must inspire its readers today. As Barth writes in his *Göttingen Dogmatics,* "we must view inspiration as a single, timeless—or rather, contemporary—act of God . . . in *both* the biblical authors *and* ourselves."[47]

A great deal could be said about this idea, which continues to be a major theme of Barth's work. Indeed, I will return to it when discussing the "Protestant Scripture-principle" in the final section of this chapter. All I need note here is one implication of this doctrine. Because inspiration is not simply an event in the past, but must occur again in our own time, the revelation of God is never delivered into our control. It is not as if the Bible were a document from which we could simply "read off" the Word of God (as it were), by the exercise of our own hermeneutical skills. Far from it! If the Word of God is to be heard, *as* the Word of God, then God must speak today as he did then. It follows that the act of revelation lies beyond the control of the historian or exegete. It is easy to see why Barth regards preaching as the model situation in which the Word is spoken—*through* the preacher rather than *by* him—and heard afresh in our own time.[48]

(b) The Christian Dogmatics in Outline

Despite his recognition of the humanity of the biblical writings, and despite his insistence that revelation involves a present-day act of God, Barth still has a strong sense of the authority of the biblical text.[49] As he writes in his *Christian Dogmatics in Outline,* it is true that the church's recognition of the Bible as the Word of God does not annul its status as human literature. It remains a collection of human words. But its canonical status implies that it is much more than this. What comes to us in the form of this human literature is nothing less than divine speech. It comes, to be sure, in a hidden form,[50] but it is no less God's Word for being hidden.

However, for Barth the hiddenness of revelation is a double-edged sword, and he is happy to wield this sword against two sets of enemies.

---

[47]Barth, *The Göttingen Dogmatics,* §8.3 (225).

[48]Cf. Barth, *The Göttingen Dogmatics,* §2.2 (30–36).

[49]Cf. McCormack, *Karl Barth's Critically Realistic Dialectical Theology,* 305–7.

[50]See, for instance, Barth, *Die christliche Dogmatik im Entwurf,* §20.1 (436), where he states that the Word comes to us "veiled as much as it is revealed, hidden as much as presented" (*ebenso verhüllt wie gezeigt, ebenso verborgen wie dargeboten*).

On the one hand, as we have seen, the hiddenness of revelation *legitimates* historical criticism: it gives it a theological grounding. The Word of God comes to us hidden in human words, and those human words are historically shaped and conditioned. On the other hand, the hiddenness of revelation *sets a limit* to the value of historical criticism. The Word of God is truly hidden in those words: it is not immediately evident that they are the vehicle of a divine message. It follows that the historian, *as historian,* cannot grasp the biblical revelation. A historical study of the Bible, however necessary, cannot reveal anything more than its status as human literature. It can inform us only of the frail human words in which the Word of God comes to us. It cannot bring us to a recognition of the Bible as divine speech. The historian as historian cannot *refute* the claim that the Bible is divine revelation, but neither can he *confirm* it.[51] It simply lies outside of his field of knowledge. That the Bible is a witness to the Word of God is a statement of faith, which can only be made by the believer and the theologian.

(c) The Church Dogmatics

We have just seen that Barth accepts the legitimacy of historical criticism, while simultaneously limiting its scope and its value. In the first volume of the *Church Dogmatics,* these same ideas are expressed in a new way. In this context, Barth is anxious to insist on the fact that divine revelation is inseparable from the particular form in which that revelation comes to us. It may be hidden in the words of the biblical witnesses, but it is nonetheless to be found *in* those words, and nowhere else. This particular form of words remains indispensable. Now this has an important implication. It means that revelation is *not* to be found in the historian's reconstructed account of "what actually occurred"; it is to be found, rather, in the *biblical witness* to those events. Once again, Barth's concern is clear: the content of revelation is not to be reduced to a matter of historical judgment.

Barth supports these claims by noting that when the Bible speaks of divine revelation, it also speaks of the divinely established role of the apostles and prophets. The witness of the apostles and prophets is part of the process by which divine revelation occurs. Their witness is the form in which divine revelation reaches us. Therefore, if we are to receive the Bible as a divine revelation, we may *distinguish,* but we may not *separate,* the content and the form of that revelation. In other words, biblical interpretation is not a matter of extracting a certain message from the

---

[51]Barth, *Die christliche Dogmatik im Entwurf,* §20.1 (436).

Bible, a message that can exist in other forms and that, once extracted, renders the biblical text superfluous. In particular, the Bible is not simply another historical source, which can be discarded once the "facts" lying behind the narrative have been recovered. Rather, revelation occurs only in and through the biblical witness, to which the church remains bound.[52]

Barth's principal target here is an idea that, he claims, "has tacitly developed in connection with modern theological historicism."[53] This is the idea that divine revelation is to be found in the events to which the Bible bears witness, but in a way that is *independent* of that witness. In Barth's words, it is the idea that "in the reading and understanding of the Bible the main concern can and must be to penetrate past the biblical texts to the facts which lie behind the texts. Revelation is then found in these facts as such (which in their factuality are independent of the text)."[54] There is nothing to prevent one's asking historical questions of the biblical text, in the sense of trying to understand the events that lie behind it. If one has an interest in antiquities, such questions might appear important. But when we attempt to read the Bible in this way, we risk missing "the real character" of these writings.[55] Divine revelation is not to be found in the events as such, but in the biblical witness to those events.

What does this mean for the work of the biblical scholar? It means a rethinking of the task of criticism. The scholar should not regard the Bible as an historical source, giving access to certain events. Rather, he should study and investigate the biblical texts "for their own sake."[56] Historical insights remain important, but the text itself should be the focus of study, not the events that the historian may suppose lie behind it.[57] For, once again, it is not the events *in themselves* (as it were) that are the locus of revelation, but the events *as they are conveyed to us by the biblical witnesses.*

(c) Implications

In this discussion Barth is not directly addressing the question of the historical Jesus. However, it is not difficult to spell out the implications of

[52]Cf. Barth, *Church Dogmatics* I/2, 19.2 (492), reprinted in my anthology *The Historical Jesus Quest,* 271.

[53]Ibid.

[54]Barth, *Church Dogmatics* I/2, 19.2 (492); *The Historical Jesus Quest,* 271–72.

[55]Cf. Barth, *Church Dogmatics* I/2, §19.2 (493); *The Historical Jesus Quest,* 273.

[56]Barth, *Church Dogmatics* I/2, §19.2 (494); *The Historical Jesus Quest,* 275.

[57]This, of course, brings Barth's hermeneutic into a close relationship with the "new criticism" that arose among literary theorists in the 1940s and 1950s, as well as with the move from a "diachronic" to a "synchronic" method of biblical interpretation. These similarities, however striking, should not be permitted to obscure Barth's specifically theological motives.

his position. What is the "historical Jesus" but the reconstruction of certain facts that are believed to lie "behind" the text? For Barth, even if such facts were to be discovered, they would be of little or no theological significance. To look for divine revelation in some reconstructed history is to overlook what the Bible itself tells us about that revelation. Revelation is mediated by the witness of the apostles. It is their picture of Jesus that we find in the Gospels. What is revelatory, therefore, is "the Christ of faith," the Christ to whom the New Testament writers bear witness. Any attempt to go behind that picture violates the way the Gospels are intended to be read. The quest for the historical Jesus could only be regarded as what Barth calls "a mistake from the very first."[58] We can begin to see why Barth is so uninterested in the historical Jesus question. To understand the deeper reasons for this lack of interest, we must turn to an issue more immediately related to the central topic of this book, namely, the relationship of divine action to human history.

3. God's History and Human History

On the key question of the relationship of divine action to human history, Barth's thought is not all of a piece: it develops over time. But it will come as no surprise to the reader to find that all these developments have a common aim. In a variety of ways, Barth is attempting to mark off the sphere of divine action from the field of "history" as it is known by the secular historian. To achieve this aim, Barth employs three strategies, which will be discussed more or less chronologically.[59] The first, found in the first edition of the Romans commentary, consists of a distinction between what Barth calls "real history" and "so-called history." The second, found in the second edition of the Romans commentary, consists of a distinction between history and "primal history." The third strategy, found in Barth's later works, involves rethinking the question of divine action and human history in terms drawn from early Christian discussions of the person of Christ.

[58]Barth, *Church Dogmatics* I/2, §19.2 (493); *The Historical Jesus Quest,* 272. In a fuller exposition of Barth's thought one could note the relationship of these criticisms to Barth's doctrine of the threefold Word of God, which comes to us as revelation, scripture, and preaching. Again, however, this would take us beyond the scope of the present work. Hermann Diem's criticisms of this doctrine (*Dogmatics* [1955], translated by Harold Knight [Edinburgh: Oliver & Boyd, 1959], 97) will be picked up—in effect—in the final section of this chapter.

[59]For the structure of the following discussion I am especially dependent on Bruce McCormack's recent study, *Karl Barth's Critically Realistic Dialectical Theology,* although the exegesis of Barth's work is my own.

Real History and So-Called History

(a) The Distinction

The first way in which Barth demarcates the action of God from ordinary human history is found in the first edition of his commentary on Romans. Here Barth makes a sharp distinction between what he calls "so-called history" (*sogenannte Geschichte*) and "real history" (*eigentliche Geschichte*).[60] "So-called history" is that which is made known to us by the usual means of historical study:[61] it is what we might call "empirical history." Barth first uses this term in the course of commenting on Romans 3:1–20. In this context he remarks that what is characteristic of "so-called" history is its alienation from the good, its split between ethical ideal and actual behavior. This split, Barth writes, is both "the essence and the tragedy of *so-called* history."[62] All that we see in empirical history is the fact of an unreachable ethical ideal set over against the actual behavior of human beings: ideal and life, in other words, have become detached.[63] As an expression of that ideal, the law given by God to Israel was the high point of "so-called" history. It was both the deepest sense of empirical history and a point of connection with the "real history" that is the history of the actions of God. Yet in practice the law of Moses could function as nothing more than a reminder of human sin, a reminder that what has been commanded by God has not in fact been performed.[64]

"Real history," on the other hand, is not world history (*Weltgeschichte*) but God's history (*Gottesgeschichte*).[65] It is, as Barth writes, "the history of history,"[66] a phrase suggesting that God's history is the reality that embraces and gives meaning to empirical history.[67] Yet, from the point of view of "so-called history," that meaning is hidden.[68] As Barth writes, the Jewish law, the high-point of so-called history, "hides" (or "disguises") the face of God.[69] (That is both its greatness and its weakness.) In "real history," God's history, there is *no* split between ideal and reality, no division between the righteousness of God and the deeds of the law. God's history is the history of the transformation of the human being, a

---

[60]Barth, *Der Römerbrief, 1919*, 66 et passim.
[61]Cf. ibid., 64.
[62]Ibid., 80: *das Wesen und die Tragik der* sogennanten *Geschichte.*
[63]Cf. ibid., 80–81.
[64]Cf. ibid., 75–76.
[65]Ibid., 46.
[66]Ibid., 64, 66: *die Geschichte der Geschichte.*
[67]Cf. ibid., 75: *Der Sinn der Geschichte ist Gottes Sinn.*
[68]Cf. ibid., 46.
[69]Ibid., 75: *Es verhüllt das Angesicht Gottes. Aber es verhüllt es auch.*

transformation that the law takes for granted but cannot achieve.[70] In the light of this history, empirical history appears unreal.[71] It has lost its validity;[72] its values have been abrogated by being subsumed into a new reality (*aufgehoben*) by the action of God.[73] It follows that the law of Moses has also lost its validity:[74] only God's standards of judgment are now in force.[75] Yet this action of God does not represent a mere cancellation of empirical history; it is also the fulfilment of its deepest tendencies.[76]

(b) Their Connection

How do these two histories relate? What connection, if any, has "real history" to "so-called history"? As Bruce McCormack notes, there is a certain tension in Barth's understanding of their relationship. On the one hand, Barth insists that "real history" has now broken into the empirical world. It is a reality within that world. As he writes,

> the ideas of God and the good no longer float as foreign bodies over a history which is estranged from them, but rather at *one* point in history that which was always intended, commanded, and prophesied in the law, the idea has taken place.[77] . . . In the stream of so-called history the new, opposing element of the real history becomes visible.[78]

On the other hand, if "real history" is *in* history as we know it, it is not *of* it.[79] To stress this independence of "real history" from empirical, "so-called history," Barth makes use of the distinction between time and eternity, which will play such an important role in the second edition of *Romans*.[80] With the breaking in of God's history, there is a new time (*eine*

[70]Cf. ibid., 85.

[71]Cf. ibid., 161.

[72]Ibid., 64: Dieser *Geschichte ist gegenstandslos geworden.*

[73]Cf. ibid., 66.

[74]Cf. ibid., 85.

[75]Cf. ibid., 64–65.

[76]Cf. ibid., 67, 85. For Barth, *aufheben* seems to have its double sense of "preserve" and "abrogate," a use familiar from the history of German philosophy.

[77]Barth seems to be alluding here, not only to the Jewish law, but to the "idea" that a metaphysical idealism takes to be the shaping force of reality.

[78]Barth, *Der Römerbrief, 1919,* 85: *Die Idee Gottes und des Guten schwebt nicht mehr als Fremdkörper über eine auch ihr fremdartigen Geschichte, sondern an einem Punkt der Geschichte ist das geschehen, was in der Idee, im Gesetz immer gemeint, geboten, geweissagt war. . . . Im Strom der sogennanten Geschichte wird das neue, entgegengesetzt strömende Element der eigentlichen Geschichte sichtbar.*

[79]Cf. McCormack, *Karl Barth's Critically Realistic Dialectical Theology,* 144.

[80]Cf. ibid., 144, 262–66.

neue Weltzeit), which (paradoxically) marks the end of all times.[81] Eternity brings time to a halt.[82] Time disappears into the eternal now.[83]

Indeed if "real history," God's history, is on the side of eternity, then in a sense it lies outside of history altogether. More precisely, its deepest reality lies outside of empirical history. As Barth writes in the first edition of the Romans commentary, "the revelation in Christ is not an 'historical' event."[84] Once again, however, the two histories are not entirely separate: they remain related. In an effort to grasp their relationship more clearly, we turn to Barth's response to a particular objection to Christian faith. It could be said, he writes, that the Christian's trust in God's promises is nothing less than a dangerous presumption, since the world as we know it is sinful, opposed to God. His response is to remind the reader that

> this age is not the last. There is . . . not only a truth on the other side but there are also events, a world-history in heaven, an inner movement in God. What we call history and events, are merely a confused reflection of changes on the other side. One such change of times on the other side is signalled in our "history" through the *cross of Christ*.[85]

On the one hand, this quotation reaffirms the point just made: that the deepest reality of "so-called history" lies outside of that history. The history we know is only a reflection of that reality. On the other hand, it asserts that what occurs in world history *is* a reflection of that deepest reality. The history "on the other side" of that great divide between time and eternity makes itself known on our side. The change in heaven gives rise to a new process on earth, on the level of empirical history.[86] We become caught up in the process that leads from heaven to earth. The process of redemption is not just heavenly; it also occurs on what Barth calls "the psychological and historical side of our existence."[87]

(c) Implications

We have seen that in Barth's earliest major work we find a striking disjunction between two types of history: "real history" and "so-called history."

---

[81]Barth, *Der Römerbrief, 1919*, 86.

[82]Ibid.: *die Zeit [wird] stillgestellt durch die Ewigkeit.*

[83]Ibid., 86: *die Zeit [verschwindet] im ewigen Jetzt.*

[84]Ibid., 106: *Die Offenbarung im Christus ist ja nicht ein "historisches" Ereignis.*

[85]Ibid., 161: *dieser Äon ist nicht der letzte. Es gibt . . . nicht nur eine jenseitige Wahrheit, sondern jenseitige Ereignisse, eine Weltgeschichte im Himmel, eine innere Bewegung in Gott. Was wir "Geschichte" und "Ereignisse" heißen, ist nur ein verworrener Widerschein jenseitiger Wendungen. Eine solche jenseitige Wendung der Zeiten wird in unserer "Geschichte" durch das Kreuz des Christus bezeichnet.*

[86]Cf. ibid., 167.

[87]Ibid., 167: *auf der seelisch-geschlichtlichen Seite unseres Daseins.*

The two are distinct, but they are also related, insofar as the "real history" of divine action is reflected in the history we know. What implications has this distinction for the historical criticism of the Bible? It is easy to see what the answer must be. This understanding of history can only devalue the historical study of the Bible. Indeed, in the first edition of his commentary on Romans this devaluation is explicit. For Barth argues that, when viewed in the context of "real history," the kind of truths that can be reached by historical investigation are of strictly limited value. As he writes, "alongside the great proof of the love of God towards us, all other *so-called* truths, namely, the merely historical and psychological truths, come to our attention as nothing more than provisional—or even additional—facts and apparent circumstances."[88] These merely historical matters are of little or no significance, since the great heavenly truths will both subsume and abrogate (*aufheben*) these lesser truths of empirical history.[89]

In some of these remarks Barth seems to be making yet another distinction, closely related to his idea that this-worldly historical events are merely a reflection of a heavenly history. This new distinction is between the *outward form* and the *inner reality* of God's actions in history. The inner reality of the events of redemption lies outside of "history," in the sense that it is not amenable to historical investigation. In particular, the cross of Jesus may be the reflection on earth of a heavenly event, but—as Barth writes—"the battle which Jesus fights upon the cross is only to the smallest, most superficial extent an individual, 'historical' event. Insofar as it is this, it is not our concern (2 Cor. 5:16)."[90] In particular, God's history, the inner meaning of history, does not become knowable in the categories of historical knowledge. In Barth's words, no "psychologically and historically knowable bridge leads over from the old to the new possibilities of life."[91] The implications are clear. The historical criticism of the Bible is not dealing with what we might call "the real thing." It is able to deal only with the "so-called truths" of "so-called history."[92]

---

[88]Ibid., 166: *Neben dem großen Beweis der Liebe Gottes gegen uns können all andern sogenannten Wahrheiten, nämlich die bloß historischen und psychologischen Wahrheiten, nur noch als vorläufige oder auch nachträgliche Umstände und Begleiterscheinungen in Betracht kommen . . .*

[89]Cf. ibid., 167.

[90]Ibid., 161: *Der Kampf, den Jesus am Kreuze kämpft, is nur zum kleinsten, äußerlichsten Teil, ein individueller, "historischer". Sofern er es ist, geht er uns nicht an (2. Kor. 5,16).*

[91]Ibid., 169: *Keine seelisch-geschichtlich erkennbare Brücke führt herüber und hinüber von den alten zu den neuen Lebensmöglichkeiten.*

[92]Worth noting in this context is Barth's refusal to identify what has traditionally been called "sacred history" with biblical history (cf. McCormack, *Karl Barth's Critically Realistic Dialectical Theology*, 305; Barth, *Die Theologie Calvins*, 1–3, 20). However much that history is the scene of divine revelation, the revelation itself remains distinct from it. The action of God may occur within history, but it is not itself able to be understood historically.

History and Primal History

In his later works, Barth develops these ideas in a new way. Here he uses yet another distinction, namely, that between history (*Geschichte*) and primal history (*Urgeschichte*).[93] Barth has drawn this distinction from the work of Franz Overbeck (1837–1905), where—as he himself admits—the term had a rather different meaning.[94] Although Barth first develops this distinction in his essay on Overbeck,[95] for our purpose that essay yields little of interest. To understand Barth's distinctive use of the term "primal history" we must turn first of all to the Romans commentary and then to Barth's 1927 work, *Christian Dogmatics in Outline.*

(a) The Second Edition of Romans

Romans 1:3–4

The first mention of "primal history" is to be found in the second edition of the Romans commentary, in the context of Barth's comments on Romans 1:3. To speak of the relationship of what he calls the "two worlds"—the divine and the human—Barth uses a series of geometrical images. These images are themselves an important indication of Barth's intention. Barth's most common geometrical metaphors are those of the point, the tangent, intersecting planes, and the perpendicular line. All of these metaphors are used to express the idea of a divine action that touches human history without becoming part of it. For instance, in relation to the phrase "Jesus Christ our Lord," Barth writes:

> In this name [Jesus] two worlds meet and go apart, two planes intersect, the one known and the other unknown. The known plane is God's creation, fallen out of its union with Him, and therefore of the world of "flesh" needing redemption, the world of men, and of time, and of things—our world. This known plane is intersected by another plane that is unknown— the world of the Father, of the Primal Creation, and of the final Redemption. . . . The point on the line of intersection at which the relation becomes observable and observed is Jesus, Jesus of Nazareth, the historical Jesus.[96]

[93]Bruce McCormack (*Karl Barth's Critically Realistic Dialectical Theology,* 163–64) argues that this development reflects Barth's move from a "process" eschatology to a "consistent" eschatology (cf. ibid., 184), a further discussion of which would take us beyond the limits of the present essay.

[94]Cf. McCormack, *Karl Barth's Critically Realistic Dialectical Theology,* 226–35. On the origin of the term, see Barth, *Die christliche Dogmatik im Entwurf,* §15.1 (309–10).

[95]Karl Barth, "Unsettled Questions for Theology Today" (1920), in *Theology and Church: Shorter Writings 1920–1928,* translated by Louise Pettibone Smith (London: SCM, 1962), 55–73.

[96]Barth, *The Epistle to the Romans,* 6th edition, 29.

The two worlds or—to use Barth's earlier terminology—the two histories touch in Jesus Christ, and they touch in Jesus *as* a figure of history.
Yet they only touch; they do not merge. Real history, the world of divine
action, does not become one with empirical history. As Barth writes,
there is "no marriage or fusion" of the divine and the human in this
encounter.[97] Like a geometrical point, the contact of the divine world
with empirical history has no dimensions, it is not "cut of the same
cloth" (as it were) as the history it touches. For this reason it cannot be
described in historical terms. It follows that the life of Jesus, historically
understood, has no positive religious significance. It is nothing more than
one of the craters, however "astounding," left in human history by the
force of the divine action. It is merely the hollow space that signals the
presence of the divine power, *at* that particular moment of history, but
not in any sense *within* it. "Within history," Barth writes, "Jesus as the
Christ can only be understood as Problem or Myth."[98] As the Christ,
Jesus cuts through the plane of history "vertically, from above."[99] He is
not a historical figure, but a figure of "primal history" (*Urgeschichte*).[100]

Barth goes on to discuss the resurrection of Jesus, which he regards as
the particular moment in which Jesus' identity is revealed (cf. Rom. 1:4).
The resurrection is what Barth calls "the establishment or *declaration* of
that point [of intersection] from above, and the corresponding discern-
ing of it from below," the point at which "the new world of the Holy
Spirit touches the old world of the flesh."[101] Once again, however, Barth
insists that this does not make the resurrection "an historical event." It is
certainly not an historical event in the sense that it could be subject to
the usual means of historical investigation. As Barth writes elsewhere in
Romans, "the raising of Jesus from the dead is not an event in history
elongated so as still to remain an event in the midst of other events. The
Resurrection is the non-historical . . . relating of the whole historical life
of Jesus to its origin in God."[102] In another place Barth redeploys his
geometrical metaphor. He insists that the resurrection is not an historical
event because the new world it reveals touches the old "as a tangent
touches a circle, that is, without touching it."[103] Therefore while the
resurrection *is* an event in history, insofar as it was discerned by people

[97]Cf. Barth, *The Epistle to the Romans*, 6th edition, 30; Barth, *Der Römerbrief*, 6th edition, 6: *keine Vermählung oder Verschmelzung*.
[98]Barth, *The Epistle to the Romans*, 6th edition, 30.
[99]Barth, *Der Römerbrief*, 6th edition, 6: *senkrecht von oben*.
[100]Ibid., 5–6.
[101]Barth, *The Epistle to the Romans*, 6th edition, 30.
[102]Ibid., 195.
[103]Ibid., 30.

living in history, in another sense "the Resurrection is not an event in history at all."[104] It does not have the usual characteristics of an historical event. As a divine action and revelation it was not "conditioned" (*bedingt*) by the events that surrounded it.[105]

Romans 4:17

It is clear from the geometrical metaphors with which it is surrounded that Barth understands "primal history" to be something utterly different from empirical history, even if at particular moments it "touches" our world. To understand more clearly what this means, we must turn to one of the later uses of the term "primal history" in *Romans*. In commenting on Romans 4:17, Barth cites a passage from Friedrich Nietzsche's "Untimely Meditations." The passage deals with what Nietzsche calls the "non-historical" (*das Unhistorische*),[106] which surrounds human activity and gives it its meaning. In a way that—as in the case of Overbeck—goes far beyond Nietzsche's intentions, Barth identifies this "nonhistorical" with the "non-historical radiance" of the human being's relationship with God. Interestingly, Barth seems to admit that this "light from above" falls not just on the biblical personalities (such as Abraham) but on history as a whole. As he writes, "at no time are history or historical personalities entirely without this unhistorical radiance."[107] This light, the light of God's relationship to the world, is the key to a proper understanding of history. It is for the sake of this "light from above," and *only* for its sake, that we pay attention to history.[108]

This idea also has some important consequences. When viewed in terms of God's relationship to the world, the particularities of history fade into insignificance. As Barth writes, this light "obliterates the isolation of personality, the remoteness of the past, the aloofness of peculiarity."[109] In

[104]Cf. Karl Barth, "Biblical Questions, Insights and Vistas" (1920), in *The Word of God and the Word of Man*, translated from *Das Wort Gottes und die Theologie* by Douglas Horton (New York: Harper & Row, 1957), 90: "the resurrection is not a historical event . . . our concern *here* is with an event which, though it is the only real happening *in* is not a real happening *of* history."

[105]Barth, *Der Römerbrief*, 6th edition, 6.

[106]Cf. Nietzsche, "On the Uses and Disadvantages of History for Life" (1874), in *Untimely Meditations*, 64–65. The title Barth gives to this section of his commentary (*Vom Nutzen der Historie*) seems a deliberate echo of Nietzsche's (*Vom Nutzen und Nachtheil der Historie*).

[107]Barth, *Der Römerbrief*, 6th edition, 116: *Nie ist die Geschichte, nie die geschichtliche Persönlichkeit des Menschen ganz ohne dieses ungeschichtliche Oberlicht.*

[108]Ibid.: *Um dieses Oberlichts willen, nur um seinetwillen, lauschen wir der Stimme der Geschichte.* (The German is here more emphatic than Hoskyns's English translation.)

[109]Barth, *The Epistle to the Romans*, 6th edition, 140.

the light of God's relationship to the world, the features common to all historical events appear. One is reminded here of Barth's remarks regarding the interpretation of the Bible. In the preface to the first edition of *Romans,* Barth had written that what is really important in history transcends historical particularity.[110] The same message is found here. If a person were able to grasp the "non-historical," he would be able to attain a standpoint above history. In this way he "would be absolved from the need to take history so seriously."[111] Now Barth goes on to identify Nietzsche's "unhistorical" with what he himself has called "primal history." It is "primal" because, as Nietzsche had already remarked, every great historical event has its origin in the "non-historical." The non-historical, which Barth has identified with God's relationship to the world, is thus "the primal-historical condition of all history."[112]

Implications

Once again, it is not difficult to see the implications of this series of distinctions. We have already seen that Barth uses the distinction between history and primal history to remove the resurrection of Jesus from historical scrutiny. Yet it is not just the resurrection that Barth withdraws from the historian's gaze. In the introduction to the present work, I discussed the difficulty raised by the seventeenth-century discovery of the length of human history. It became clear that this new knowledge would no longer fit into the biblical narrative of human origins, which began with the figure of Adam. Grappling with this problem led Isaac de la Peyrère to suggest that Adam was not the first human being, but merely the ancestor of the Jewish people. It will come as no surprise that here Barth's theology once again adopts a "supra-historical" viewpoint, which simply transcends any historical difficulties that the biblical story might raise. In commenting on Romans 5:12, Barth remarks that neither Adam nor the risen Christ can be regarded as "historical" figures. The sin that came into the world with Adam, along with the righteousness revealed in Christ, is a "timeless and transcendental disposition."[113] It follows that it does not matter what happened to the first human being,[114] for, whatever happened, it was only a matter of this transcendental disposition becoming actual. We should note what this means. Historical questions

---

[110]Barth, preface to the first edition, in *The Epistle to the Romans,* 6th edition, 1.

[111]Cf. Barth, *Der Römerbrief,* 6th edition, 116: *er wäre davon geheilt, die Historie von nun an noch übermäßig ernst zu nehmen.*

[112]Ibid., 117: *die ungeschichtliche, d.h. aber* urgeschichtliche *Bedingtheit aller Geschichte.*

[113]Barth, *Der Römerbrief,* 6th edition, 149: *die zeitlose, die transcendale Disposition der Menschenwelt.*

[114]Cf. ibid.: *Denn mag es sich mit dem ersten Menschen verhalten haben, wie es will.*

concerning the origins of humanity, whether—for example—human beings had one origin or many (a matter much debated by twentieth-century Catholic theologians[115]), are consigned to irrelevance. No new knowledge can threaten the Christian doctrine. The history of the human being's relationship to God is "timeless and transcendental."[116]

(b) The Christian Dogmatics in Outline

Barth makes use of the same distinction between history and primal history in his 1927 work *Christian Dogmatics in Outline*. After the treatment already given, an extensive discussion is not required. What *is* worth noting, however, is that at this point Barth begins to display a greater awareness of the historical character of revelation. Because of the importance of this development, the matter deserves some attention.

Barth's explicit discussion of the distinction comes late in the work, and it comes—appropriately—after his treatment of the incarnation. Describing the incarnation as "the revelation of God in Jesus Christ," Barth describes this revelation as a "primal-historical event."[117] It follows, he writes, that "revelation is primal-history."[118] What this means, as we have seen, is that revelation is not to be regarded as an historical event, in the usual sense of that term. Yet Barth now qualifies his position. We must also admit, he writes, that there is a sense in which "revelation is history."[119] For revelation has occurred *in time,* not merely in that timeless realm where God is God "in himself."[120] It is true, Barth continues, that there remains a certain sense in which revelation is "above history" (*Übergeschichte*). For the revelation of God reflects the eternal nature of the divine Trinity, the timeless relations between Father, Son, and Holy Spirit.[121] But these timeless relations are *not yet* revelation; revelation requires an action in time. Therefore revelation is not just above history; it *is* history.

These are important concessions, prompted by reflection on the incarnation. Yet there is a danger that they may be understood in the

---

[115]Pope Pius XII, for instance, in his 1950 encyclical *Humani Generis,* suggested that only a single origin for human beings could be reconciled with the doctrine of original sin.

[116]See also Barth's comment on Rom. 7:9 (*The Epistle to the Romans,* 6th edition, 248–49).

[117]Barth, *Die christliche Dogmatik im Entwurf,* §15.1 (309): [*ein*] *urgeschichtliches Ereignis.*

[118]Ibid., §15.1 (310): *Offenbarung ist Urgeschichte.*

[119]Ibid.: *Offenbarung ist Geschichte.*

[120]Worth noting is the contrast with the first edition of *Romans* (*Der Römerbrief, 1919,* 106), where Barth had stated bluntly that "revelation in Christ is not an 'historical' event" (*die Offenbarung im Christus ist ja nicht ein "historisches" Ereignis*).

[121]Cf. Barth, *Die christliche Dogmatik im Entwurf,* §15.1 (311).

manner of Ernst Troeltsch. Troeltsch saw history *in general* as the revelation of an immanent divine spirit. Barth distances himself immediately from this position. He does so by noting that, although it is true to say that "revelation is history," that sentence may not be reversed. One cannot say that "history is revelation."[122] As Barth writes, "history is a predicate of revelation, but revelation does not thereby become a predicate of history. God acts in history, but history is not thereby itself the revelatory action of God."[123] For revelation does not belong to history as such. It is always more than history, since it is the revelation of God himself. If it pleased God to set himself as a human being in time, this does not mean that history has become divine; it means rather that God has become historical.[124] The relationship thus established is not reversible. (As we will see shortly, Barth picks up this idea when he comes to deal with the traditional doctrine of Christ.)

Barth goes on to develop this distinction. He argues that the historical subject—the historical actor whose work is studied by the historian—is by definition not unique. It may be a particular subject and thus without *exact* parallel, but it remains broadly comparable to other historical subjects. (As we have seen, this is the implication of Troeltsch's principle of analogy, which Barth here implicitly accepts.) By way of contrast, the subject of primal history is God. He is the one who is acting in the events of revelation, and God is—also by definition—utterly unique, incomparable. No *historical* statement can be made about such a subject; to speak of this subject is the task of theology alone.[125] Indeed, Barth continues, it is "a disastrous ambiguity to claim that faith is grounded in history."[126] He notes that such a claim might be acceptable if by "history" one means a particular way of viewing and interpreting history. (One assumes Barth means "in the light of the Word of God.") But as he writes, "in history as such there is nothing, as far as the eye can see, which could be a grounding for faith."[127] On what then, we might ask, is faith grounded? Barth's answer can only be: on the authority of

[122]Ibid., §15.1 (311): *die Geschichte ist die Offenbarung.*
[123]Ibid., §15.1 (311–12): *Geschichte ist ein Prädikat der Offenbarung, aber Offenbarung wird darum kein Prädikat der Geschichte. Gott handelt in der Geschichte, aber die Geschichte ist darum nicht selbst das offenbarende Handeln Gottes.*
[124]Cf. ibid., §15.1 (312): *Nicht darum handelt es sich, daß die Geschichte göttlich, sondern daß Gott geschichtlich wird.*
[125]Cf. ibid., §15.1 (313).
[126]Ibid., §15.1 (317): *Es ist eine verhängnisvolle Zweideutigkeit, wenn mann sagt, der Glaube sei auf die Geschichte begründet.*
[127]Ibid., §51.1: *In der Geschichte an sich ist, soweit das Auge reicht, nichts, was den Glauben begründen könnte.*

the Word of God, in the light of which alone we can discern primal history within history, the action of God within this world.[128]

It should by now be clear that even in the *Christian Dogmatics in Outline,* Barth continues to make a clear distinction between history and primal history. The actions of God belong to the second realm, that of primal history. As Barth writes later in the same work, when discussing the "miracles" (*die Wunder*) of the virginal conception of Jesus and the resurrection, these are *history* only as *primal history.*[129] It follows that they are also removed from historical scrutiny, since they are the products of divine action, not of human action. Incidentally, Barth goes on to note that the historian has good reason to regard both stories as nothing more than "myths," comparable to similar stories found elsewhere. If they are regarded *simply* in historical terms, this is the only way they can be regarded. If we had not received the Word of God, we too would have to say that these reports fell into the category of myth.[130] If we are inclined to go further and to question the authority of the Word of God, then we are engaging in a discussion that for Barth is meaningless. That authority is self-authenticating, or—more precisely—it is revealed to us by the same Spirit by whose inspiration the Bible was written. This conviction, expressed in what Barth elsewhere calls "the Protestant Scripture-principle" (*das protestantische Schriftprinzip*), is the linchpin of his theology. It will be further discussed in the final section of the present chapter.

Anhypostatic–Enhypostatic Christology

As we have just seen, from about 1923 Barth begins to develop a more positive appreciation of the role of history as the scene of revelation. But in no way does he retract his earlier insistence that divine action must be *distinguished* from human history, even if that history takes the form of the life of Jesus.[131] Yet he does admit that, while divine action and human history can and must be *distinguished,* they cannot be *separated.* It is no accident that this formulation echoes the doctrinal definition of the Council of Chalcedon (451 C.E.), for this development reflects Barth's rediscovery of the traditional doctrine of Christ. To that matter we must now turn.

---

[128]Cf. ibid., §15.1 (314, 318–19).
[129]Ibid., §16.3 (368): *Geschichte nur als Urgeschichte.*
[130]Cf. ibid., §16.3 (366).
[131]Cf. Barth, *The Epistle to the Romans,* 6th edition, 29, 251.

(a) The Göttingen Lectures

Barth's new appreciation of the traditional Christological dogmas is already present in the Göttingen lectures of 1924, where he first reflects on the *anhypostatos-enhypostatos* doctrine.[132] This doctrine, developed during the Christological controversies of the fifth and sixth centuries, states that the human nature of Christ has no "personhood": it has (in more modern terms) no independent existence, outside of its union with the eternal Word of God.[133] It is therefore "without personhood" (*anhypostatos*). More positively, it exists only as caught up "in" (Greek *en*) the personhood of the eternal Word (being from this point of view *enhypostatos*). Barth suggests that—according to this doctrine—the human figure of Jesus "has never and nowhere existed *in itself*."[134] By this enigmatic statement Barth seems to mean that this figure does not sustain his own existence. As Barth writes in the following sentence, "the humanity of Christ, although it is body and soul, and an individual, is nothing subsistent or real in itself."[135]

Once again, it is not difficult to see the implications of this doctrine for interest in the historical Jesus. The historical Jesus is nothing other than Jesus as a human individual, and—according to the traditional doctrine—this individual is simply inconceivable apart from his union with the divine Word. It follows that the human figure of Jesus is of no theological interest, since he has no existence apart from the divine Word that is united to him and revealed in him. This Word is known only by faith. But the human figure of Jesus is the *only* figure whom the historian can grasp. It follows that the Jesus of history is not only of no theological interest, but in a certain (rather technical) sense, he does not exist. It is hard to imagine a more thoroughgoing theological victory! It may, of

[132]There is currently some controversy regarding the origin and various meanings of this doctrine. Barth's theology follows the interpretation customary in his time, and it could probably survive its more recent critics, but this is not a matter that can be pursued here. For a recent discussion, see U. M. Lang, "Anhypostatos-Enhypostatos: Church Fathers, Protestant Orthodoxy, and Karl Barth," in *The Journal of Theological Studies* NS 49 (1998): 630–57.

[133]As Barth himself notes (*Church Dogmatics* I/2, §15.2 [p.164]), we must not confuse "personhood" in this technical sense with our modern idea of "personality": "what Christ's human nature lacks according to the early doctrine is not what we call personality. This the early writers called *individualitas* . . . *Personalitas* was their name for what we call existence or being."

[134]Cf. Karl Barth, *"Unterricht in der christlichen Religion" Prolegomena* (1924), edited by Hannelotte Reiffen (Zurich: Theologischer Verlag, 1985), §6.4 (193): *Dieses die Natur des Menschen verkörperende Individuum hat* an sich *nie und nirgends existiert*. Unfortunately, the published English translation of this key phrase is even less clear than the German.

[135]Barth, *The Göttingen Dogmatics* §6.4 (157).

course, be a Pyrrhic victory, as the final section of this chapter will suggest, but it is a powerful response to the challenge of history to religious authority.

Barth had already made a similar point in his discussion of divine revelation. Here he insists (inter alia) that "the content of revelation is God *alone*."[136] It is therefore not "an object of . . . experience"; what we can experience is merely that which is the "mediator, bearer, instrument, or organ of revelation."[137] The mediators of revelation may be the indispensable *form* in which revelation reaches us, but they are to be distinguished from its *content,* which is God alone. The historical figure of Jesus is not excluded from these reflections. Taking a position directly contrary to that of Troeltsch, Barth states that divine revelation is not to be found in "the religious personality" of Jesus, "his inner life," "his view of God and the world and life," or indeed in any aspect of his humanity.[138] Revelation occurs through the historical fact of Jesus, particularly through his death and resurrection. But the historical figure of Jesus is not the content of the revelation, which must be God alone.

(b) The Church Dogmatics

These ideas are more fully expressed in the *Church Dogmatics.* Commenting on John 1:14 ("the Word became flesh"), Barth writes that in this statement it is the Word who is the subject. Since it is the Word who acts and since that Word is God, the becoming flesh is not "an element in the world process as such."[139] It might appear to be an event of history, but it is not necessitated or conditioned by the facts of history. The incarnation may be an event *in* history but it is most certainly not *of* history. It is not cut from the same cloth as ordinary, historical events. A few pages later Barth writes that, "strictly speaking," the relationship expressed by the doctrine of the incarnation is irreversible. For the eternal Word "can never become predicate or object in a sentence the subject of which is different from God."[140] In other words, one can say that Jesus is God become human, but to say that Jesus is a human become God is to misunderstand the relationship. The eternal Word exists in his own right, independent of this relationship, whereas the human being Jesus exists only as assumed by that Word. (This is, of course, a restatement of the

---

[136]Ibid., §5.1 (89).
[137]Ibid.
[138]Ibid., §5.1 (90).
[139]Barth, *Church Dogmatics,* I/2, §15.2 (134).
[140]Ibid., §15.2 (136).

traditional *anhypostatic-enhypostatic* doctrine.[141]) As Barth writes a little later, the "reality, existence and being" of the man Jesus "is wholly and absolutely that of God Himself, the God who acts in His Word. His manhood [i.e., humanity: *Menschheit*] is only the predicate of His Godhead, or better and more concretely, it is only the predicate . . . of the Word acting upon us, the Word who is the Lord."[142] Again, the implications of this discussion are clear. The acceptance of a traditional Christology implies the rejection of any theology that takes as its object the human nature of Christ, understood historically and psychologically.[143] Whatever else the historical Jesus may be, if indeed he can be said to "exist" at all, he is not a focus of faith. As Barth writes, "with this the 'historical Jesus' of modern Protestantism falls to the ground as the object of faith and proclamation."[144]

Once again, we may note the deep divide between the theology of Barth and that of Ernst Troeltsch. While Troeltsch, the metaphysical idealist, was convinced that history had theological significance as a revelation of the divine spirit, Barth insists that there is nothing revelatory about history as such. There is a sense in which revelation *is* history, but history in general is *not* revelation.[145] It is revelation only insofar as a particular portion of history becomes the scene of a divine act. Only to this extent is history of religious interest. Furthermore, that divine act remains inexplicable in historical terms. It does seem to be the case that reflection on the incarnation led Barth to a new appreciation of history, as the scene of a divine act. But in no sense does he allow the two to become confused. Throughout his work, Barth takes pains to insist that, however much it may be *in* history, revelation as a divine act is in no sense a product of historical forces. For this reason it simply lies beyond the historian's view; it cannot be grasped in historical terms.[146]

---

[141]Cf. ibid., §15.2 (163).

[142]Ibid., §15.2 (162).

[143]Cf. ibid., §15.2 (136).

[144]Ibid., §15.2 (137).

[145]Cf. Barth, *Die christliche Dogmatik im Entwurf*, §15.1 (311).

[146]This position remains constant throughout Barth's later work. See, for example, his insistence (*Church Dogmatics* III/1, translated by J. W. Edwards, O. Bussey, and Harold Knight [Edinburgh: T. & T. Clark, 1958], §41.1 [p.80]) that "in its immediacy to God every history is in fact 'non-historical,' i.e., it cannot be deduced and compared and therefore perceived and comprehended." Similarly, in a later volume (*Church Dogmatics* III/2, translated by Harold Knight, G. W. Bromiley, J. K. S. Reid, and R. H. Fuller [Edinburgh: T. & T. Clark, 1960], §47.1 [p.452]), Barth insists—in reaction to Bultmann—that the stories of the resurrection appearances are "about a real man of flesh and blood." But even here he argues that the event they describe lies "beyond the reach of historical research or depiction." It is difficult to see how these two claims can be reconciled, as Rudolf Bultmann points out (cf. "The Problem of Hermeneutics" [1950], translated by James C. G. Greig, in *Essays Philosophical and Theological* [London: SCM, 1955], 260–61).

4. Revelation and Religion

Barth's reaction against the liberal theology of the nineteenth and early twentieth centuries is nowhere more evident than in his discussion of the question of religion. Barth was well aware that the destructive effects of the historical criticism of the Bible were only one aspect of a wider phenomenon. That wider phenomenon was (as we have seen) the shift from a view of Christianity as the divinely given key to all human history to that of Christianity as a thoroughly historical phenomenon, simply another religion, one "world view" among many. If Barth has a single theological opponent, it is surely this one. This point was made by Rudolf Bultmann as early as 1922, in his review of Barth's *Romans* commentary, long before Barth developed his criticisms of "religion" in the *Church Dogmatics*. Noting that theological movements are best understood by reference to that which they are opposing, Bultmann writes:

> On what front is Barth fighting? Against the psychologizing and historicizing concept of religion, which not only plays a role in the historical (so-called) liberal theology, but in theology and modern intellectual life in general. He is fighting against all cults of "experience" (wherein experience is understood as a psychic factor or a psychic action), against every concept which sees in religion an interesting phenomenon of culture, which wishes to understand religion in the context of psychic historical life.[147]

Much later, in the *Church Dogmatics,* Barth would confirm Bultmann's judgment by expressing this concern quite unambiguously. The "more or less radical and destructive movements in the history of theology in the last two centuries," he writes, "are simply variations on one simple theme, that religion has not to be understood in the light of revelation, but revelation in the light of religion."[148] A better expression of what Hans Frei has called "the great reversal" would be difficult to find. To understand its impact on Barth's thought, we must turn to a closer examination of his attitude to religion.

(a) The Second Edition of Romans

To understand Barth's views on the subject of religion, we may turn first of all to the second edition of his commentary on Romans. We have

---

Be that as it may, Barth consistently maintains his distinction between matters accessible to the historian and those accessible to the believer.

[147]Rudolf Bultmann, "Karl Barth's *Epistle to the Romans* in its Second Edition" (1922), in *Rudolf Bultmann: Interpreting Faith for the Modern Era,* edited by Roger A. Johnson, The Making of Modern Theology: Nineteenth and Twentieth Century Texts (London: Collins, 1987), 55–56.

[148]Barth, *Church Dogmatics* I/2, §17.1 (290–91).

already seen that in this work Barth makes a distinction between "history" and "primal history." I will now argue that he uses this distinction to remove revelation not just from history in general, but from the history of religion in particular. The context in which Barth does so is his discussion of the Jewish law in Romans 7–8. In these chapters, Barth develops a strong contrast between religion and grace. Religion, Barth insists, is a human possibility, evoked by the memory of a lost relationship with God.[149] Yet it remains a *human* possibility, "a particular aspect of human behaviour."[150] It may be the "last and noblest" human possibility,[151] but it remains powerless to bring about union with God. (From this point of view, the Jewish law is simply the high point in the evolution of religion.[152]) Religion is the most exalted of what the apostle Paul called the "passions" of the flesh that bring about death: it is a "passion for eternity" that is no less dangerous than our other desires.[153] It follows that there is no bridge between religion and grace: the two are sharply contrasted. As Barth writes, "there is no stepping across the frontier by gradual advance or by laborious ascent, or by any human development whatsoever."[154]

The death of Jesus, who was condemned under the law, represents the end of religion. It represents a grace that is *not* "religion" because it is in no sense a human possibility. For this reason, those who rely on the grace of God revealed in Christ are removed from the realm of religion. They stand already on the other side of religion.[155] What does this mean? It means, Barth writes, that those who rely on the grace of God are "undisturbed by the relativity of our human religious experiences and histories, detached from their inner contradictions, and neither distressed nor contaminated by their ambiguous relationship with 'sinful passions.'"[156] It is worth looking more closely at what is implied in these words. While the history of religions suffers from the relativity and ambiguity of all human history, Christians need not be concerned, because they are removed from this history. Not altogether removed, it is true. Even Christians are still tossed here and there by the vagaries of religious

---

[149]Cf. Barth, *The Epistle to the Romans,* 6th edition, 230.
[150]Ibid., 233.
[151]Ibid.
[152]Cf. ibid., 243.
[153]Cf. ibid., 235–36.
[154]Ibid., 240.
[155]Cf. ibid., 237.
[156]Barth, *Der Römerbrief,* 6th edition, 219: *Unbeeinträcht durch die Relativität unsrer menschlichen religiösen Erlebnisse und Geschichten, unverflochten mit ihren inneren Widersprüchen, ungetrübt und unbetrübt durch ihre zweideutige Verwandtschaft mit den "Sündenleidenschaften"* . . .

experience; they are still tangled up in the network of things religious. But Barth insists that there is a real sense in which believers in Christ have gone beyond religion: they already stand "in the primal and ultimate history,"[157] detached from the uncertainties and ambiguities of religious experience. While Barth insists that such claims must be understood dialectically—so that freedom from religion is not turned into a new human possibility[158]—he nonetheless insists on the reality of this new state.

Elsewhere in *Romans,* Barth speaks of ambivalence with which one must speak about religion. Here his dialectical mode of thought becomes very clear. On the one hand, Barth insists not even the Christian can avoid religion altogether: religion is inescapable and cannot simply be rejected.[159] Even Christians live in the present world, the old order of sin, and cannot altogether escape its limitations. Indeed, in a sense we are *obliged* to be religious, to embrace what looks like "the best and the highest" in human achievement.[160] On the other hand, when we do all that religion demands, we will discover that our religious acts are valueless: they *cannot* bring about union with God. If history is regarded as the history of human possibilities, then in the history of religion it both reaches its high point and is shown to be a history of failure. But this failure is precisely what points us towards salvation. It shows that if we are to achieve union with God, it can only be through the grace of God, which must break into this history as something "wholly other."[161] In other words, we are saved by the grace of God, and the grace of God is something totally other than "religion." It is not subject to the conditions and limitations of human history. In one sense the grace of God is revealed *within* history, in the sending of the Son of God. But Barth argues that we have spoken rightly of the Son of God only if our manner of speech gives offence to "every possible human method of investigation."[162] In other words, if we have spoken of Jesus in historical terms, then we have yet not spoken of the Son of God, who is not able to be grasped in such terms.[163]

---

[157]Ibid.: [*wir stehen*] *schon in der* Urgeschichte *und* Endgeschichte.

[158]Cf. Barth, *The Epistle to the Romans,* 6th edition, 237–38.

[159]Cf. ibid., 254–55 (see also 182–86).

[160]Ibid., 251.

[161]Ibid., 249; *die schlechthinige Fremde* (Barth, *Der Römerbrief,* 6th edition, 232).

[162]Barth, *The Epistle to the Romans,* 6th edition, 277–78.

[163]See also ibid., 279–81, where Barth suggests that "the historical Jesus" is nothing other than "the likeness of sinful flesh" (Rom. 8:3) in which the Son of God appeared. As such, he is a figure entirely susceptible to all kinds of historical interpretations. There is nothing here that forces us to recognize his divine mission; this is "recognizable only by the revelation of God" (ibid., 279). In the light of revelation, Jesus' earthly existence has the character of a parable, but—paradoxically—the meaning of that parable becomes clear only with the dissolution of his earthly existence.

(b) The Göttingen Lectures

Barth does not deny, then, that from a certain perspective the Christian revelation can—and indeed must—be seen as one "religion" among others. Indeed in his Göttingen lectures, Barth can even speak with apparent equanimity of the kind of detached study of religions that we would today call "religious studies."[164] Barth's only qualification is that at some point the theologian cannot avoid making a judgment. At some point the question arises, "What are *you* going to say?," and at that point the task of dogmatics begins.[165] It is not that Christianity *cannot* be viewed as a religion. Of course it can. Indeed, from one point of view it cannot be viewed in any other way. But viewing Christianity as a religion overlooks its claim to be the vehicle of divine revelation, a revelation that makes a demand on us, rather than being something under our control.

Similarly, Barth's attitude to religions other than Christianity should not be oversimplified. Although he writes from the assumption that "divine revelation" is equivalent to "revelation in Christ," at least in his Göttingen lectures Barth does not exclude the possibility that other religions may also be vehicles of revelation. After discussing the Old Testament and New Testament "witnesses to revelation," Barth notes:

> The question arises whether there might not be a third group of witnesses to revelation, for example, prophets and apostles outside the canon, at a distance, but still worshippers of the one God. The figure of Socrates has constantly been for the church a paradigm of this problem. Today many might be more inclined to think of Lao-Tse or the Buddha.[166]

We cannot exclude this possibility. There is nothing absolute about Christianity; divine revelation alone is absolute, and we cannot exclude the possibility that this revelation has come to others.[167] Taking our stand on the revelation in Christ, all we can say is that these witnesses will also bear some relationship to the scandal of the incarnation.[168] What is Barth suggesting here? He seems to be saying that, if there is divine revelation outside the biblical canon, it will share in the character of the biblical revelation. It too will be the expression of a gracious act of God, which is clearly distinguished from religion as a human work. In any case, Barth argues that we can neither exclude the possibility that

[164]Cf. Barth, *The Göttingen Dogmatics,* §1.1 (5).
[165]Cf. ibid., §1.1 (5–6).
[166]Ibid., §6.3 (149).
[167]Cf. ibid., §6.3 (150).
[168]Cf. ibid., §6.3 (151).

there exist nonbiblical witnesses to revelation nor assume from the outset that this is the case.

(c) The Church Dogmatics

Given these qualifications, Barth continues to distinguish sharply between
revelation and religion, between divine grace and human possibility. He
picks up and develops these themes in the *Church Dogmatics*.[169] Once
again, Barth defines religion from the outset as "man's reality and possibility,"[170] a human work rather than a divine gift. If this is what religion
represents, then it is clear that to subsume the Christian revelation under
this category is radically to misunderstand it. From one point of view the
Christian revelation takes the form of a religion, and from this point of
view it is by no means unique.[171] Yet just as Barth had earlier argued that
"real history" and "primal history" are hidden in the course of empirical
history, so he now insists that the revelation of God is hidden in the form
of "Christianity," which appears to be merely one religion among others.[172] It follows that to regard Christianity *as* a religion is to overlook
the revelation hidden within it and to abandon the true theme of theology. A theology that does this, that takes as its basis the history of
religions rather than the revelation of God, will become "hollow and
empty," a "mere shadow" of itself.[173] Indeed, such a theology is nothing
other than an expression of "unbelief."[174]

For Barth, a theology that takes as its basis the history of religions not
only overlooks the fact of divine revelation; it also overlooks its content.
For divine revelation is nothing less than the revelation of the incapacity
of human beings to know anything of God.[175] Revelation may come to
us in the form of a religion, but the grace of God of which it speaks does
not affirm the value of religion. Quite the contrary! It speaks of the incapacity of religion. Barth is strongly opposed to any suggestion that the

---

[169]The issue of "Grace and Religion" is also discussed in Barth's *Die christliche Dogmatik im Entwurf*, §18 (396–416), but in terms similar to those found elsewhere.

[170]Barth, *Church Dogmatics* I/2, §17.1 (283).

[171]Cf. ibid., §17.1 (281).

[172]Cf. ibid., §17.1 (282).

[173]Ibid., §17.1 (283).

[174]Cf. ibid., §17.1 (293–94).

[175]It could, of course, be argued that even this idea finds its parallels in the history of
religions. Barth accepts this (cf. *Church Dogmatics* I/2, §17.3 [340–41]), referring to a parallel development in Japanese Buddhism. However, despite his openness in *The Göttingen
Dogmatics* (§6.3 [149–51]), on this occasion Barth seems reluctant to concede that this
might be also an expression of divine grace. For Christian faith, he says, not just a "religion of grace" but "the one name of Jesus Christ is decisive" (ibid., §17.3 [p.343]).

grace of God meets human beings in their religious striving, "as though religion were a kind of outstretched hand which is filled by God in His revelation."[176] As he writes, "Jesus Christ does not fill out and improve all the different attempts of man to think of God and to represent him according to his own standard."[177] Rather, revelation in the Christian sense stands opposed to all such attempts, because it is a final judgment on religion.[178] Insofar as the Bible speaks of God's totally unmerited grace given to a sinful humanity, it is simultaneously the revelation that human religions, no matter how exalted, are nothing other than the expression of sinful self-assertion. They represent nothing other than unbelief, the attempt to reach God by one's own efforts, instead of receiving his salvation by faith.[179]

What, then, may we say about the Christian faith? Christian faith must be understood as nothing less than an expression, however entangled in matters religious, of the grace of God. While the unique act of God that is revelation has assumed certain aspects of human history, and these (inevitably) have the characteristics of a religion, by being assumed they have been transformed. Barth's analogy here is the incarnation, in which the humanity of Jesus exists *only as* it has been assumed by the eternal Word, with which it forms a unity and apart from which it has no independent existence.[180] In the same way, Christianity can now be properly understood only from God's side, from the point of view of revelation. And that revelation comes as a judgment upon religion.

It will be evident that Barth is here applying to the question of religion what I earlier described as his "Christological" solution to the question of history. For the question of religion is only a particular instance of the question of history. As we saw when discussing the question of history, Barth insists that in the act of revelation God has assumed a certain portion of history, without becoming identified with it. The two remain distinct. We now see that this distinction is not abrogated when the history assumed is *religious* history. As we saw then, Barth argued that revelation falls outside the purview of the historian. He now insists that it does not fall within the grasp of the historian just because she may happen to be a historian of religions. The grace of God can only be expressed historically, in the form of a particular religion, but it is not to be identified with that religion. The history of religions can never be a

---

[176]Barth, *Church Dogmatics* I/2, §17.2 (308).
[177]Ibid.
[178]Cf. ibid., §17.2 (303).
[179]Cf. Barth, *Church Dogmatics* I/2, §17.2 (303).
[180]Ibid., 17.1 (297).

basis for Christian theology, and from the very moment that Christianity is regarded as one religion among others, the theologian's attention is wrongly focused.

5. The Legacy of Barth

Thinking "From God Out"

The influence of Karl Barth continues to be felt in contemporary theology. He is, therefore, a figure with whom we must continue to grapple. The question facing us here concerns his solution to the challenge of history to religious authority. Is this a theology for our time, one that overcomes the relativity of historical knowledge? One could take issue with particular aspects of Karl Barth's theology, but there is little point in such a piecemeal approach. Barth's grand scheme stands or falls as a whole. If the fundamental direction of his theological project is the correct one, then the details could be debated and, if necessary, altered. Barth's rethinking of theology was a radical rethinking, and any response to Barth must be equally radical.

The present brief study is, of course, selective and one-sided. It gives little sense of the magnificence of Barth's achievement. One cannot help but be deeply impressed by both the audacity with which he overturned the assumptions of his predecessors and the power of his religious vision. I remarked in the previous chapter that Ernst Troeltsch's religious philosophy may be the closest thing to theology that can be achieved, given our contemporary religious situation. Surveying Barth's achievement, I am tempted to say that, if our religious situation were different and Christian theology (in the fullest sense of that word) were still possible, then this is what it would look like. However, such a judgment would be hasty and would beg some important questions. The most important question is this: can a bold and uncompromising Christian theology, such as is offered by Barth, still be defended?

In an attempt to answer this question, I would like to take over a phrase found in the first edition of the commentary on Romans, a phrase that—for these purposes—may be taken as a summary of Barth's theological project. Barth's theology was an endeavor, in his own words, "to think from God out."[181] From the moment he began his magisterial commentary on Romans, Barth was engaged in what Bruce McCormack calls "the (seemingly impossible) attempt to think from a standpoint lying in God Himself."[182] While profoundly traditional, this is very

---

[181] *Denken von Gott aus*; cf. Barth, *Der Römerbrief, 1919*, 71.
[182] McCormack, *Karl Barth's Critically Realistic Dialectical Theology*, 129.

different from the starting point of, for example, Ernst Troeltsch, who began with human beings and their experience of the world. Does Barth's radical reversal of the direction of theological thought offer an answer to the challenges of history to faith?

In one sense, it does. What Barth has shown is that, if we *do* learn to think "from God out," the problems of history become insignificant or disappear. With regard to the Bible, Barth's theology allows for a recognition of its human origin, while affirming its theological role as a witness to revelation. With regard to the act of interpretation, Barth was right to insist that the interpreter should go beyond historical questions and grapple with *die Sache* (the subject matter) of the text. Indeed, this idea anticipates some recent trends in the secular discipline of hermeneutics.[183] With regard to revelation, Barth is right to insist that a divine revelation in history must be inseparable from the words in which it first came to speech. History by itself is mute; it needs to be interpreted. Only an interpreted history could be regarded as revelatory. Finally, Barth deploys the resources of Christian tradition to make a clear distinction between the action of God and human history. The result is that talk of divine action is protected from the leveling effect of historical research: it falls outside all canons of historical analogy. From the point of view of the questions that have dominated this study, Barth's theology is an impressive tour de force.

The problem—for there is a problem—is that Barth assumes from the outset that we already know what it means to think "from God out." It means to think in the terms laid down by the Bible and Christian tradition. From this starting point, the challenges of history can indeed be overcome. This is Barth's great achievement. But the challenges of history are nothing less than challenges to the authority of the Bible and Christian tradition. The seventeenth-century critics and their successors demonstrated that the Bible's claim to represent a divine standpoint is questionable. It is not necessarily false, but it is certainly questionable. Once the question has been raised, it deserves an answer. Barth's insistence that we think "from God out" represents a demand that we make a leap of faith—despite these questions—to a standpoint from which the questions disappear. For those who can make this leap, Barth's theology offers a powerful Christian vision. But what of those who have internalized (rather than merely learned about) the challenges of the seventeenth century? What of those who can no longer confidently assume the

---

[183]See especially Hans-Georg Gadamer, *Truth and Method* (2d ed. 1965; London: Sheed & Ward, 1979), 463, 473; and—more recently—Dominick La Capra, introduction to *Rethinking Intellectual History: Texts, Contexts, Language* (Ithaca, N.Y.: Cornell University Press, 1983), 13–69.

Christian perspective? Such people can make little sense of Barth's insistence that we take our stand on the biblical viewpoint, in order to make objections to that viewpoint disappear. Indeed, to these people his theology can only appear as massively question-begging. In a word, Barth's theology is a living theology only for those people who have never seriously faced the challenges of the seventeenth century. For the rest of us, it can only be admired from a distance.

The Protestant Scripture Principle

If that reads like a final judgment on Barth's work, then from one point of view it is. Yet we have yet to uncover the most significant fact about Barth's theology, a dimension of Barth's thought, which, if accepted, simply makes such criticisms redundant. To understand this dimension, we must turn to what he calls "the Protestant scripture principle." This principle enables us to understand the ease with which Barth can brush off what seem like obvious criticisms of his project. Therefore, we must turn our attention to this principle, as it is found first in the Göttingen lectures and then in the *Church Dogmatics.*

(a) The Göttingen Lectures

The "Protestant scripture principle" can be summed up in what Barth calls the "childishly simple statement" that "the Bible cannot come to be God's Word if it is not this already."[184] Scripture, in other words, authenticates itself. It is, in Calvin's words, αὐτόπιστος (to be believed of itself):[185] "we are forbidden to submit it to any argument or proof."[186] More precisely, this principle holds that the Bible bears witness to its own authority by the power of the Holy Spirit. The "inner testimony of the Spirit,"[187] on which the Reformers laid so much emphasis, is nothing other than the joint testimony of what Barth calls the Spirit *in words* and the Spirit *in us*. Barth insists that both of these are important. If one focuses only on the Spirit in words, one ends up with the (untenable and unedifying) doctrine of verbal inspiration. If one focuses only on the Spirit in us, one ends up with a pietist or a liberal appeal to inner experience. This is why the two manifestations of the Spirit must always be understood together.[188] But if they are understood together, the Bible needs no other proof.

[184]Barth, *The Göttingen Dogmatics,* §8.3 (219).
[185]Calvin, *Institutes of the Christian Religion,* I.vii.5 (80).
[186]Barth, *The Göttingen Dogmatics,* §8.3 (222).
[187]Cf. Calvin, *Institutes of the Christian Religion,* I.vii.4 (78–80).
[188]Cf. Barth, *The Göttingen Dogmatics,* §8.3 (223–25).

Barth notes that the Protestant Reformers themselves held firmly to this principle. But he concedes that both they and their successors buttressed this principle with arguments. These arguments were designed to demonstrate the authority of scripture from the point of view of human reason.[189] It is true that the Reformers did not regard such arguments as decisive, since they believed the Bible ultimately *requires* no arguments in support of its authority. Yet Barth argues that even to spell out such arguments was a dangerous and regrettable move. It was regrettable since, as Barth writes, it "brings us into a sphere in which the pros and cons are secretly or openly set out alongside one another, in which we cannot do more than advance probabilities, and in which it is not impossible that one day the opposite might be stated and proved."[190] It is worth pondering these words. What Barth is saying is that it is dangerous to adduce arguments in favor of the authority of scripture, since the very fact of employing arguments opens one to refutation. In other words, one's fundamental commitment to the authority of the Bible should be kept removed from any realm in which either proof or disproof is possible. As Barth writes, "if the thesis that Scripture is God's Word is seriously doubted or seriously proved, it may be all kinds of things but it is not any longer the Protestant scripture principle. That thesis is the Protestant scripture principle only to the extent that it stands firm, that it can be neither seriously doubted nor seriously proved."[191]

(b) The Church Dogmatics

A more developed presentation of this argument is found in the *Church Dogmatics,* toward the end of Barth's discussion of "Scripture as the Word of God." Here Barth remarks that "the statement that the Bible is the Word of God is an analytical statement, a statement which is grounded only in its repetition, description and interpretation, and not in its derivation from any major propositions."[192] This claim makes use of the famous philosophical distinction between analytic and synthetic propositions. The first are propositions that are true in virtue of the words they contain; the second are propositions whose truth is dependent on something outside of themselves. "The Bible is the Word of God," he argues, is a statement of the first type, comparable (in this respect only) to the statement that "all brothers are male siblings." It justifies itself insofar as it needs no other proof. The doctrine of the Word of God is thus—in the

---

[189]Cf. Calvin, *Institutes of the Christian Religion,* I.viii (81–92).
[190]Barth, *The Göttingen Dogmatics,* §8.3 (220–21).
[191]Ibid., §8.3 (221).
[192]Barth, *Church Dogmatics* I/2, §19.2 (535).

final analysis—what Barth calls "a logical circle . . . of self-asserting, self-attesting truth into which it is equally impossible to enter as it is to emerge from it."[193] The truth of the authority of the Bible is "either already known and acknowledged or it is not accepted."[194] Any other grounds on which the authority of the Bible might be accepted are secondary to, and dependent upon, this assertion of its self-evidence.

In his *Glaubenslehre,* David Friedrich Strauss had already criticized this principle, arguing that it was ultimately untenable. Strauss arrives at this conclusion after tracing the development of the doctrine of biblical authority, with particular attention to Protestant theology. He notes that the Reformers were faced with the task of establishing the authority of the Bible without appealing either to the church (in the manner of Catholicism) or to human reason (the results of which were always open to doubt).[195] One could claim, as Calvin did, that the divinity of scripture impressed itself upon the mind in the same manner as external sensations, so that we recognize this authority in the same manner that we recognize colors or tastes.[196] By itself this was not a satisfactory answer, for it reduced the authority of the Bible to a matter of human judgment. The solution was to argue that the self-evidence of scripture was nothing less than the inner testimony of the Holy Spirit, so that, in assenting to its self-evidence, one was obeying, not one's own human reason, but the infallible voice of God.[197] This seemed a firm resting place, but over time it crumbled on both sides. On one side, the so-called "fanatics" were able to argue that if the recognition of the authority of the Bible rested on an inner testimony of the Spirit, then the highest Christian authority was not the Bible but this inner testimony.[198] On the other side, there was an even more dangerous argument, raised by the rationalists. If the divinity of the Bible is confirmed by an inner testimony of the Spirit, who can confirm in turn that this "inner testimony" is truly the Holy Spirit? Who can witness to the divinity of this witness? As Strauss writes, there are only two possible answers.[199] Either the assurance is

[193]Ibid.

[194]Ibid., §19.2 (536).

[195]Cf. Strauss, *Die christliche Glaubenslehre,* §12 (1:131–33).

[196]Cf. ibid., §12 (134); Calvin, *Institutes of the Christian Religion,* I.vii.5 (76).

[197]Cf. Strauss, *Die christliche Glaubenslehre,* §12 (1:134–35).

[198]This, of course, is why Barth does not want to separate "the Spirit *in us*" from "the Spirit *in words,*" in which respect he stands within the orthodox Calvinist tradition.

[199]In fairness it should be noted that Calvin (*Institutes of the Christian Religion,* I.ix.2–3 [94–95]) offers an alternative, namely, that we know this is the Spirit because of its conformity with scripture. Of course, this creates a circular argument, whereby the Spirit authenticates the Word and the Word authenticates the Spirit. Calvin seems aware of this fact but apparently does not consider it a serious objection to his doctrine.

provided by the "inner testimony" itself, which amounts to no assurance at all, or it is provided by something—perhaps a feeling or thought—in the human spirit (in which case one is falling back upon human testimony). As Strauss writes, "here we find the Achilles" heel of the Protestant system."[200]

What is most stunning about Barth's position is that he accepts this criticism. As he says, "Strauss was right to criticise this rule. . . . Indeed, who does attest the divinity of this witness?"[201] Yet Barth is not disturbed by what Strauss saw as a fatal flaw in the Protestant scripture principle. He responds merely by noting that Strauss expected too much of the principle and did not appreciate that—paradoxically—the weakness of the principle is its strength. As he writes, "what Strauss failed to see is that there is no Protestant "system", but that the Protestant Church and Protestant doctrine has had necessarily and gladly to leave this question unanswered, because there at its weakest point, where it can only acknowledge and confess, it has all its indestructible strength."[202] In other words, Barth continues to assert this fundamental theological principle, even after accepting the strength of the arguments against it. He has no reply to make to these arguments and apparently feels no need to make a reply. The confession of faith here stands without support; worse still, it is reaffirmed in defiance of the arguments against it. At a key point in Barth's theology, all pretense of rational argument is abandoned.[203]

An Evaluation

Faced with such extraordinary claims, I am tempted to say that one either stands within this charmed circle of faith or one does not. Within that circle, the Bible's authority will be self-authenticating and that self-authentication will be attributed to the work of the Holy Spirit.[204]

---

[200]Strauss, *Die christliche Glaubenslehre,* §12 (136): *hier ist die Achillesferse des protestantischen Systems.*

[201]Barth, *Church Dogmatics* I/2 (537). One is reminded of Barth's recognition (*The Göttingen Dogmatics,* §8.2 [p.217] = *"Unterricht in der christlichen Religion",* §8.2 [p.265]) that a purely historical and (if one likes) "reductionist" approach to Christianity "seems, and more than seems, to be the only possible one," but that—despite everything—the theologian should simply "laugh in the face" of such an approach.

[202]Barth, *Church Dogmatics* I/2, §19.2 (537).

[203]In one sense, of course, this should not surprise us, since Barth (*Church Dogmatics* I/1, §1.1 [p.8]) has declared in advance his unwillingness to be strictly bound even by the principle of noncontradiction. Yet it is surprising *in this context.* For Barth is not trying to describe some profound mystery (such as the nature of God), which one could argue lies beyond the grasp of reason. He is attempting to describe the principles underlying his theological claims. If these cannot be articulated and defended before the tribunal of reason, something is surely wrong!

[204]I might note that at least the early Barth (e.g., *Der Römerbrief, 1919,* 170) can describe Christian faith as a risk (*ein Wagnis*). But he goes on to note immediately that

Outside the circle, there is no response to that claim.[205] The believer can only call on the unbeliever to submit to biblical authority, so as to enter into this process of self-authentication.[206] While this would be an accurate description of the problem facing Barthian theology, Barth's position ought to be placed in a larger context. Barth's theology reflects a general tendency—found in some branches of contemporary Christian theology—to reject what is sometimes called "evidentialism."[207] The "evidentialist" holds that religious commitment, even if it goes *beyond* reason, must nevertheless not be *contrary* to reason. For this tradition, religious commitment is not "self-authenticating" but is a matter of evidence and therefore, at best, a matter of probability. Its reasonableness can be demonstrated and—precisely for this reason—it is open to refutation. One can maintain a reasonable faith, in other words, only at the risk of losing one's faith. It follows that theology is subject to at least certain fundamental rational norms. These are public norms, so that religious claims are open to intersubjective criticism. It is true that Christian theology does have a distinct object of knowledge and thus a relative and provisional independence. Its ways of thought do not have to be identical to those of other disciplines. Yet since religious belief rests upon a reasoned foundation, theology remains bound to the rules under which all rational discussions are conducted.[208] For those who belong to this

---

"this risk can be neither explained nor justified on religious or historical grounds," since it "explains and justifies itself" (*Dieses Wagnis kann seelisch-geschichtlich weder erklärt noch gerechtfertigt warden. Es erklärt und rechtfertigt sich selber.*) Or, as he writes in the same context, "only God explains and justifies faith, but he does do it" (*Nur Gott erklärt und rechtfertigt den Glauben, aber er tut es*). Thus Barth's attitude to faith sometimes resembles the idea of a groundless commitment urged by Blaise Pascal (1623–62) and Søren Kierkegaard (1813–55), but it more often picks up Calvin's idea that the biblical revelation is self-authenticating.

[205] As Wolfhart Pannenberg points out (*Theology and the Philosophy of Science,* translated by Francis McDonagh [London: Darton, Longman & Todd, 1976], 266 n.537) Barth does on one occasion ("The Principles of Dogmatics according to Wilhelm Herrmann" [1925], in *Theology and Church,* 258) offer something like a justification of his position, although he himself would insist that it needs no justification.

[206] This does seem to require a submission to biblical authority, as Paul Helm points out in his helpful discussion of "self-authentication" (cf. *The Varieties of Belief,* Muirhead Library of Philosophy [London: George Allen and Unwin, 1973], 106–7, 115).

[207] Cf. William Alston, "Plantinga's Epistemology of Religious Belief," in *Alvin Plantinga,* edited by James E. Tomberlin and Peter van Inwagen, Profiles (Dordrecht: D. Reidel, 1985), 292–93.

[208] I might add that theology remains bound to common norms of rationality for another reason, namely, because such norms underlie *any* form of discussion. They are not (pace Barth) norms external to theology, for theologians cannot engage in a discussion, even among themselves, without adhering to such norms. To insist that at one point in the discussion—generally a fundamental one—the norms no longer apply is an entirely arbitrary act. This is an argument that applies to any understanding of theology, not just an "evidentialist" one. For a developed form of this argument, see Bartley, *The Retreat to Commitment,* 158–75.

tradition, among whom I must number myself, Barth's attitude is ultimately incomprehensible.

However, over against "evidentialism" there stands another tradition of religious thought, which holds that religious belief is what we might call "properly basic."[209] According to this view, there are circumstances in which I may be justified in holding such beliefs, even in the absence of independent evidence. A statement such as "God is speaking to me" is from this point of view comparable to the statement "I see a tree."[210] Such beliefs *are* justified, since they are not groundless. But the grounding of such a belief consists of nothing more than a set of conditions under which this truth is presented to me. It does not consist of a reference to other beliefs, a reference that would form some kind of inductive or deductive argument.[211] Argument is not required, because the belief is already justified by the context in which I accept it.

This is, of course, a philosopher's description of this alternative tradition, drawn from the work of Alvin Plantinga (b. 1932). But Plantinga's work is, by his own admission, deeply rooted in the Reformed tradition, so much so that he can call his view a "Calvinist epistemology."[212] It thus bears a close resemblance to what Barth is describing as "the Protestant scripture principle."[213] Its usefulness in this context is that it is perhaps the only way in which an "evidentialist" can regard Barth's "Scripture-principle" as anything more than a piece of irrationalism. It is an interesting question as to whether Barth would accept such a defense of his view. It may be that he would regard Plantinga's epistemology as yet another external principle to which theology should not be subject. But if any sense is to be made of this linchpin of Barth's theology, at least by those who stand outside his charmed circle, it may be by way of Plantinga's idea of "properly basic" truths.

A more lengthy discussion of Plantinga's work would take us far beyond the boundaries of the present study. I will note only that there exists a lingering suspicion that Plantinga's view may not take us very far. It may be that his "properly basic" truths are accurately described as such, but only *for* a particular person or *for* a particular community.[214]

---

[209]For a concise presentation, see Alvin Plantinga, "Is Belief in God Properly Basic?" *Noûs* 15 (1981): 41–51.

[210]Cf. ibid., 47.

[211]Cf. ibid., 44–45.

[212]Cf. Alvin Plantinga, "Self-Profile," in *Alvin Plantinga,* 55–64.

[213]On the similarity, see especially Plantinga, "Is Belief in God Properly Basic?," 46–47.

[214]Cf. James E. Tomberlin, "Is Belief in God Justified?" in *Journal of Philosophy* 67 (1970): 36–37. For similar suggestions from Plantinga himself, see his article "Is Belief in

For another person or community, quite different beliefs might be "properly basic." An atheist, for example, might describe belief in the *non*existence of God as "properly basic," that is to say, as justified by the context in which she comes to accept it.[215] If no way is to be found of adjudicating between these two perceptions, then the question of truth is no further advanced. The individual who submits herself to the authority of the Bible may experience this authority as self-authenticating. But such an experience is of its very nature incommunicable: it cannot form the basis of a *public* discussion of religious claims, one that would be meaningful to believers and unbelievers alike.[216] Plantinga's more recent work grapples with this issue by focusing on the "proper functioning" of what we might call the human "cognitive equipment,"[217] but this is an argument that quickly falls into circularity.[218] All I can remark on here is the relationship of Plantinga's ideas to Barth's work and the fact that these discussions are far from over.

God Properly Basic?," 44, 50. Wolfhart Pannenberg (*Systematic Theology,* vol. 1 [1988], translated by Geoffrey W. Bromiley [Grand Rapids: Eerdmans, 1991], §4 [44–45]; *Theology and the Philosophy of Science,* 273–74, 276–77, 319–20) suggests that Barth's theology remains—despite his intentions—grounded in the subjectivism of modern Protestant thought. The same criticism could be made of Plantinga's project.

[215]Cf. James E. Tomberlin, "Is Belief in God Justified?" in *Journal of Philosophy* 67 (1970): 38.

[216]Taking a slightly different line, Helm (*The Varieties of Belief,* 116) writes that, on this view, the grounds of faith are communicable, in the sense that they can be described, "but they are not such as will inevitably bring any other reasonable man to believe." The disagreement with my own position is verbal, not substantial.

[217]Cf. Alvin Plantinga, *Warrant and Proper Function* (New York: Oxford University Press, 1993), viii–ix et passim.

[218]The problem is that Plantinga explains "proper functioning" by reference to the notion of a "design plan," a notion that seems inseparable from theism. With considerable chutzpah, Plantinga turns this apparent circularity into an argument against naturalism and for theism.

Chapter Six

The Dialectical Theology (B)

Rudolf Bultmann (1884–1976)

> *No contemporary theologian known to me speaks so much about understanding,*
> *and none has as much reason to complain that he himself has been misunderstood.*
> Karl Barth

It is one of the ironies of modern Christian theology that many students have regarded Rudolf Bultmann as the consummate theological liberal. It is true that some aspects of his work might give that impression. His most widely quoted remark, for example, may well be that which he made about the world of the New Testament:

> It is impossible to use electric light and the wireless and to avail ourselves of modern medical and surgical discoveries, and at the same time to believe in the New Testament world of spirits and miracles. We may think we can manage it in our own lives, but to expect others to do so is to make the Christian faith unintelligible and unacceptable to the modern world.[1]

Similarly, Bultmann is best remembered for his program of what he called "demythologizing" (*Entmythologisierung*), the translation of the ("mythical") categories of the New Testament into new forms, forms shaped by the existentialist philosophy of continental European thought.[2]

---

[1]Rudolf Bultmann, "The New Testament and Mythology," in *Kerygma and Myth: A Theological Debate*, edited by Hans Werner Bartsch (1948), translated by Reginald H. Fuller, 2d edition (London: SPCK, 1964), 5.

[2]It has been customary to attribute Bultmann's theological categories to the influence of Martin Heidegger (1889–1976). While Heidegger was undoubtedly an influence, as we will see, more recent studies have suggested a broader background in continental philosophy. For a useful summary, see Roger A. Johnson, *The Origins of Demythologizing: Philosophy and Historiography in the Theology of Rudolf Bultmann*, Studies in the History of Religions (Supplements to *Numen*) 28 (Leiden: E. J. Brill, 1974), especially 18–29 and 188–93. It should also be noted that Bultmann is above all a theologian, who stands within a certain tradition of Christian thought (on which, see both note 5 below and the later discussion of Bultmann's Lutheran roots).

248

As we will see, this was only a small part of Bultmann's overall project. But it *was* a part. Insofar as he was attempting to recast Christian doctrine in terms more accessible to a modern audience, Bultmann did have something in common with the liberal theologians of the nineteenth and early twentieth centuries.

However, Bultmann's theology is radically misunderstood if it is thought of primarily in those terms. Especially in the early part of his career, Bultmann joined Karl Barth in a vehement protest against the liberal theology of their time.[3] In fact, Bultmann distinguished his work from liberal theology at the very moment when he was spelling out his famous program of "demythologizing."[4] For this reason Bultmann and Barth belong together, as (very different) representatives of the dialectical theology. But it is not only in his opposition to liberal theology that Bultmann belongs with Barth. In some respects Bultmann was a deeply traditional theologian, who was attempting to preserve what he saw as the fundamentals of Christian faith. He believed, for example, that his theology stood in continuity with that of the great sixteenth-century Protestant Reformers, presenting at least one of their central concerns in modern guise.[5]

In the essay that follows, I will tackle four aspects of Bultmann's thought. The first is Bultmann's understanding of the relationship of religious and secular knowledge, a topic that will take us into the very heart of his theology. Here I will suggest that Bultmann's varied work is marked by one central theological concern: his battle against what he calls "objectification" in matters of faith. (What this means will—I hope—become clear.) The second issue, following closely from the first, is the nature of historical knowledge and its relationship to Christian faith. The third issue is that which forms the title of this study, namely, the issue of the historical Jesus. Under this same heading, we will also examine Bultmann's reinterpretation of the world view of Jewish apocalyptic, which he believes to be characteristic of Jesus' teaching. The

[3]Cf. Rudolf Bultmann, "Liberal Theology and the Latest Theological Movement" (1924), in *Faith and Understanding,* translated by Louise Pettibone Smith, Library of Philosophy and Theology (London: SCM, 1969), 38–39; reprinted in my anthology *The Historical Jesus Quest,* 242–68.

[4]Bultmann, "The New Testament and Mythology," 13–15; see also Rudolph Bultmann, "Theology as Science" (1941), in *New Testament and Mythology and Other Basic Writings,* translated by Schubert M. Ogden (London: SCM, 1985), 51–52.

[5]Karl Barth once remarked ("Rudolf Bultmann—An Attempt to Understand Him," in *Kerygma and Myth: A Theological Debate,* edited by Hans-Werner Bartsch and translated by Reginald H. Fuller [London: SPCK, 1962], 2:123) that "those who throw stones at Bultmann should be careful lest they accidentally hit Luther, who is hovering somewhere in the background."

fourth aspect of Bultmann's work to be studied, in which he perhaps comes closest to Karl Barth, is his discussion of revelation and religion, and of the place of Christianity among the religions of the world. A study of these four topics will enable us to assess Bultmann's response to the challenge of history to religious authority.

1. Faith and Knowledge

As I have already suggested, Bultmann's theological career may appear paradoxical to many contemporary readers. This is hardly surprising, since his many-faceted writings are not entirely consistent. One commentator, for instance, compares Bultmann's theology to a medieval cathedral. The visitor knows that the cathedral has evolved through a series of additions and alterations and that "some of these innovations should seem incongruous," but nonetheless "the final form of the building gives the impression of an esthetic whole."[6] There is, in other words, an overriding concern behind much of Bultmann's writing that lends his work a certain unity. That concern may be described as an opposition to what Bultmann calls the "objectification" (*Objectivierung*) of the human being and his relationship to the world. What does Bultmann mean by this term?[7]

Objectification Defined

To understand Bultmann's use of "objectification," we may turn first of all to an essay of 1925 entitled "What does it mean to speak of God?" Bultmann begins his discussion by noting that the phrase "to speak of God" (*von Gott zu reden*), which forms the title of his essay, is ambiguous. It could be understood in the sense of speaking "about God" (*über Gott*).[8] But from the theologian's point of view this would be a mistake: it would be to misunderstand what is involved in the religious affirmation of God. Indeed, Bultmann argues that to speak *about* God implies that one has no comprehension of the reality of God, for one can speak

---

[6]Johnson, *The Origins of Demythologizing,* 250.

[7]While I follow Johnson in suggesting that an opposition to "objectifying" thought is the unifying factor in Bultmann's theology, Johnson also argues (cf. ibid., 255) that this term does not have a single precise meaning in Bultmann's work. It has, rather, the character of a symbol. What follows is an attempt to describe the various realities embraced by that symbol.

[8]Cf. Rudolf Bultmann, "What Does It Mean to Speak of God?" (1925), in *Faith and Understanding,* 53; cf. Bultmann, "Welchen Sinn hat es, von Gott zu reden?" (1925), in *Glauben und Verstehen: Gesammelte Aufsätze* (Tübingen: J. C. B. Mohr [Paul Siebeck], 1933), 1:26.

about something only from "a standpoint external to that which is being talked about."[9] To speak about God in this way would be comparable to speaking *about* "love" or about the relation of "fatherhood and sonship."[10] To discuss these realities from a standpoint outside of them is to dissolve them, for they exist only as enacted by the speaker. As Bultmann writes, they have "no existence alongside me or behind me."[11]

What is being said here? There is an obvious, if trivial, sense in which these assertions are false. The relationship between father and son, for example, *can* be regarded as a matter of sheer biological fact. In this sense, it *does* exist, even apart from the actions of the people involved. Bultmann, however, insists that this biological fact is not what is "essential" about this relationship.[12] At this point his concerns become clear. To speak about fatherhood in purely biological terms (or to speak about love only in psychological terms) is to overlook its meaning for the people involved. And when it comes to such fundamental human experiences, we are all "the people involved." These are the important realities with which we are all faced. In the light of these realities we must make the key decisions that shape our existence as human beings. Of course, an opponent of Bultmann might continue to maintain that these two aspects of human reality should not be set in opposition. The lived reality of, say, fatherhood or of love builds on certain facts, "about" which one may surely speak. The *experienced* relationship between father and son, for instance, clearly presupposes the *biological* reality, without which there would be no lived experience. Even love has its roots in certain psychological realities, which can be described, even perhaps by one who has not shared in the experience. In this sense, one could concede the legitimacy of Bultmann's concern, while taking issue with the manner of its expression. (We will come back to this idea shortly.)

Bultmann goes on to apply these considerations to language about God. In a striking manner he speaks first of all about the denial of God, arguing that only the more obvious forms of denial take the form of atheism. The denial of God can also take the form of affirmations *about* God. This is a more subtle form of denial, which has the outward appearance of faith. The problem here is that there is a certain way of speaking about God that *effectively* denies his reality, despite all protestations to the contrary. This denial occurs when we speak of God as an object of our

[9]Bultmann, "What Does It Mean to Speak of God?" 53.
[10]Ibid., 53–54.
[11]Ibid., 54.
[12]Sein *eigentliches Wesen*; cf. Bultmann, "What Does It Mean to Speak of God?" 54 ("Welchen Sinn hat es, von Gott zu reden?" 27).

knowledge, something "out there" (as it were), to be subsumed under the general laws of human knowledge. This involves a fundamental mistake. It overlooks the fact that "God" is the reality that determines my existence, "outside" of which I cannot step. To speak of God in general propositions, claiming universal validity, is therefore to speak of something other than God.

More precisely, to speak of God "in scientific propositions" is to remain under the influence of a particular view of reality. This way of regarding reality, Bultmann claims, "has dominated our thinking since the Renaissance and the Enlightenment,"[13] but it has its origins in Greek thought. If we remain under the influence of this way of regarding the world, it does not matter which metaphysics we adopt. We can equally well be idealists or materialists. In either case, we will conceive of the world in a way that is "objectifying." This is the fundamental error, compared to which the question of the particular metaphysics we adopt is unimportant.

What, then, is this particular way of regarding reality, which Bultmann describes as "objectification"? An objectifying view of the world is one that involves "a picture of the world conceived without reference to our own existence,"[14] in which we are thought of as objects alongside other objects. The problem here is the assumption that we can understand human existence in the same way as the natural world: as something "out there," to be studied "scientifically" by reference to general principles derived from observation. This objectification, whether in matters religious or secular, is what Bultmann calls "the primary falsity ($\pi\rho\hat{\omega}\tau o\nu$ $\psi\epsilon\hat{\upsilon}\delta o\varsigma$)."[15] It is a falsity because it overlooks my involvement in the world, as an individual and as a subject, which is prior to all forms of analytic thought.[16] In particular it enables me to escape the demand for decision and commitment that I encounter in my lived experience by fleeing into a world of abstract and general ideas.

It follows, Bultmann argues, that this modern worldview is godless. It is godless in its vision of the world as governed by law. It remains godless

---

[13]Ibid., 58.

[14]Ibid.

[15]Ibid., 59.

[16]This seems to be what Bultmann is saying, although in this context his underlying conception of the human being is not made explicit. The reader may wish to compare Bultmann's thought at this point with that of Martin Heidegger; see particularly the latter's *Being and Time* (7th edition, 1927), translated by John Macquarrie and Edward Robinson (London: SCM, 1962), 78–90. As will become clear, however, a more immediate influence is that of Bultmann's teacher Wilhelm Herrmann (1846–1922) and the Marburg neo-Kantian philosophy by which his thought was shaped.

even when the lawlike operation of the world is attributed to a divinity.[17] For the work of God—rightly understood—cannot be spoken of apart from its determination of my existence. To illustrate this fact, Bultmann again makes reference to some everyday human realities, namely "love, gratitude, and reverence." In our everyday life, he argues, these are not subsumed under the scientific way of regarding the world. As he writes, no one considers love, gratitude, and reverence "to be functions of law—at least not when he is truly living in them."[18] In the same way the reality of God is misunderstood if it is thought of as "objectively given," as a reality "*in respect of which* we could establish an attitude of one kind or another."[19] For this, too, is to look from the outside at (in a word, to "objectify") a reality that can be affirmed and understood only from the standpoint of my own existence.

Once again, it is tempting to accuse Bultmann of a kind of rhetorical overstatement. One could readily agree that certain realities can only be *fully* understood from within, from the standpoint of those who experience them. But one could also argue that, in striving to make this point, Bultmann has set in opposition realities that ought to be viewed as complementary. We have already noted that "fatherhood," for instance, is *both* a biological reality *and* a lived experience. Similarly, a traditional theologian might want to say that God is *both* the creator of the world of natural law *and* the one whose demands confront me "existentially" (as it were). From this point of view, one could simply acknowledge Bultmann's concerns, while disagreeing with the manner in which they are expressed. But this would be an unsatisfactory response. It would be to underestimate the power of Bultmann's thought and to misunderstand his intentions. For the manner in which Bultmann's concerns are expressed is not accidental; it takes us to the very heart of his theology. Bultmann is not merely employing an antithetical mode of expression, as if for rhetorical effect. Rather, his antithetical mode of expression may be traced to a deeply rooted dualism in his thought. A closer analysis is therefore needed.

To understand this dualism, we may look first of all at Bultmann's conception of the sphere of religion. Here we will see that Bultmann carves out a sphere of operation for the religious sensibility *in opposition to* all forms of objectifying knowledge. This opposition is then reinforced by the Lutheran flavor of his thought, which leads him to identify objectification with unbelief and sin. It is further reinforced by Bultmann's understanding of history. If (as he believes) human history is concerned

[17]Cf. Bultmann, "What Does It Mean to Speak of God?" 59.
[18]Ibid.
[19]Ibid., 60.

with the struggle to create an authentic existence, then the understanding of history should be radically different from our understanding of the natural world. These topics, therefore, will lead us more deeply into Bultmann's theology.

The Sphere of Religion

A useful place to begin is with Bultmann's discussion of "Religion and Culture," first published in the journal *Christliche Welt* in 1920. Bultmann begins this essay by noting that, at first sight, religion and culture might seem to be intimately related. For the origins of human culture seem inextricably entangled with a religious worldview. The sciences, the arts, and ethics all seem to have developed on religious grounds. But a closer examination shows that there has also occurred a gradual emancipation of culture from religion, an emancipation that suggests the two ought *not* to be identified. Culture enjoys a certain autonomy. One can understand this autonomy, Bultmann argues, by a closer examination of the nature of both culture and religion.

Bultmann argues that "culture" in the broadest sense of that word is closely related to human reason. Indeed, it is nothing less than what he calls "the methodical unfolding of human reason in its three fields, the theoretical, the practical and the aesthetic."[20] The rationality characterizing culture has the character of a rationality that is necessary and generally valid.[21] What is merely incidental and personal is of little interest. For this reason culture deals with that which can be reduced to general principles and laws. It has the character of that which surpasses the individual person.[22] The knowledge and the thought forms of religion, by way of contrast, do *not* have the character of the necessary and the generally valid. In this sense they are not lawlike. On the contrary, they have a purely individual validity.[23] The general principle may thus be established: "Religion does not exist in objective forms, as does culture, but rather in the process of realization, that is to say, in that which happens to the individual."[24]

It follows that religion is neutral with regard to the forms of human

[20]Rudolf Bultmann, "Religion und Kultur" (1920), in *Anfänge der dialektischen Theologie,* edited by Jürgen Moltmann (Munich: Christian Kaiser, 1963), 2:17: *Die Kultur ist die methodische Entfaltung der menschlichen Vernunft in ihren drei Gebieten, dem theoretischen, dem praktischen und dem ästhetischen.*

[21]Ibid.: *[der] Charakter der Notwendigkeit und Allgemeingültigkeit.*

[22]*Des* Überindividuellen; cf. Bultmann, "Religion und Kultur," 17.

[23]*Nur individuelle Geltung*; cf. ibid., 18.

[24]Ibid., 19: *Die Religion ist nicht in objektiven Gestaltungen vorhanden wie die Kultur, sondern im Verwirklichtwerden, d.h. in dem, was dem Individuum geschieht.*

culture: it can live with any particular cultural forms.[25] Religion is neutral first of all with regard to *knowledge*.[26] A philosophy of religion, for example, can deal only with "objectifications of the religious experience,"[27] but these are by no means identical with religion itself. Religion is neutral with regard to *art,* for the artist's productions are also lawlike. That is to say, the forms of art must also correspond to certain laws, in this case the laws of aesthetics. Strikingly, Bultmann argues that religion is neutral with regard to *morality*.[28] Even a person who lacks morality (*der "unmoralische" Mensch*) can be a religious hero. Finally, religion is a private matter and has nothing to do with civil society or the state.[29]

Most interestingly, Bultmann goes on to extend this comparison to the question of cultural history (*Geistesgeschichte*). Cultural history, he argues, exists only as the history of science, morality, and art. "By way of contrast," he writes, "there is no history of religion. There cannot be any such, since the life of religion exists not in objective forms, but rather in the individual life. The moments of this lived experience form no lawlike interrelations, whether of causality or of teleology."[30] Similarly, religious experience does not undergo development through history. It is either there or not there; it is, in principle, always the same. Once again, Bultmann makes the comparison with everyday realities such as trust,

---

[25]Bultmann's dualism here is rooted in, but not identical to, that espoused by his teacher Wilhelm Herrmann. Both share the desire to find a distinct sphere of activity for religion, removed from the claims of law-bound human knowledge. Both find that sphere in the existence of the individual. For some comparisons, see the following notes.

[26]Bultmann, "Religion und Kultur," 19. Compare Wilhelm Herrmann, *Systematic Theology* (Dogmatik), translated by Nathaniel Micklem and Kenneth A. Saunders (London: George Allen & Unwin, 1927), 31–32: "Science is something quite different from religion. Science sets out to prove the reality of things as a system of natural law; religion makes no such attempt. Religion, on the contrary, posits a reality which to the man who sees it seems a miracle—a miracle that he himself can experience but can demonstrate to no one else."

[27]Bultmann, "Religion und Kultur," 19: *Objektivierungen des religiösen Erlebnisses.*

[28]Ibid., 19–20. Compare Herrmann, *Systematic Theology,* 31: "No less clear is the distinction between morality and religion. In morality man must not obey an alien will, but his own sense of absolute obligation, which is the moral end of volition. Morality means independence, whereas in religion man feels himself in the power of a Being to whom he surrenders himself. It means sheer dependence."

[29]Throughout this discussion, Bultmann appeals to the early work of Friedrich Schleiermacher, *On Religion: Speeches to Its Cultured Despisers* (1799), as does his teacher Herrmann (*Systematic Theology,* 31–33).

[30]Bultmann, "Religion und Kultur," 22: *Dagegen gibt es keine Geschichte der Religion. Es kann sie nicht geben, wenn das Leben der Religion nicht in objektiven Gestaltungen, sondern im individuellen Leben vorhanden ist. Die Momente dieses Erlebens bilden keinen gesetzlichen Zusammenhang weder der Kausalität noch der Teleologie.*

friendship, and love. No one, he writes, would think of writing a history of trust! The reason that a history of religion *appears* possible is that religious experience, like all experience, gives rise to thoughts, institutions, and works of art, whose history can be written. But once again "these objectifications" (*diese Objektivierungen*) are not religion; they only "witness to it."[31] They form part of the history of culture, which (as already demonstrated) is distinct from religion.

If religion is entirely distinct from the different forms of human culture, we might ask: What *is* the sphere of religion? Where is it to be found? To answer this question, we may turn to some observations that Bultmann makes later in the same essay. Here he notes that the key question facing us as individuals concerns our fate (*Schicksal*).[32] Certain events happen to us in the course of our existence. The key question is whether we can take hold of these events and make them our own. If we cannot, then they remain meaningless. We can only struggle against them. In this way we close ourselves off from these experiences, before which we are passive and helpless. The capacity to embrace and make sense of the events that befall us is itself a gift. It is a new experience of life that comes to us from outside. At such moments we become aware of our dependence on something greater than ourselves. For Bultmann this experience of sheer dependence is the moment in which religion is born.

Bultmann argues that this religious experience of dependence is a renewed experience of life. It is an experience of a life that comes to us from beyond ourselves, when we have abandoned all attempts to rely on our own resources. For this reason, it is an experience that *cannot* be understood by reference to either the natural world or the world of human culture. It follows that the religious person does not and cannot understand her experience in scientific, lawlike terms. For religion is born from an experience of something *beyond* the world of the scientifically comprehensible. In Bultmann's own words, in religious experience reality is not grasped "as a system of rationally envisaged lawfulness. Rather, on the other side of the world of experience a point is reached from which all reality appears as a meaningful unity."[33]

We can now begin to glimpse the roots of Bultmann's deeply dualistic thought. What he is doing here is marking off a sphere for religion, a sphere quite distinct from that of human culture, whether in the form of

---

[31]Ibid., 23.

[32]Cf. ibid., 25.

[33]Ibid., 25–26: *Das Wirkliche wird nicht etwa als ein System verstandesmäßig gedachter Gesetzmässigkeit erfaßt, sondern jenseits der Welt der Erfahrung ist ein Punkt gewonnen, von dem aus alles Wirkliche als sinnvolle Einheit erscheint.*

knowledge or in the form of moral and aesthetic experience. As he writes, because the experience of an inner power that is at the heart of religion is an experience of something "from the other side" (*Jenseits*), then religion lies "on the other side of nature and culture."[34] More importantly, because culture is the sphere of the regular and lawlike (the realm of *Gesetzmässigkeit*),[35] then religion falls outside of the realm that can be measured by law, whether that law be a "natural law" of science or a norm of historical judgment. What is happening here? Bultmann has distinguished the realms of science and history from those of religion not by way of a theology (in the manner of Barth) but by way of an anthropology. Science and history deal with the regular and lawlike, viewed "from outside" (as it were). Religion deals with the individual, as subject, not determined by natural laws but free to choose her destiny. But the distinction is just as clear as it is in the work of Barth, the demarcation equally sharp. We will return to these matters shortly.

A Lutheran Theology

The second factor giving a strongly antithetical form to Bultmann's thought is more directly theological. Bultmann's theology has a strongly Lutheran flavor, being rooted in at least two influential Reformation themes. The first is the idea that I truly know God only insofar as I acknowledge God's claim on my life. The second is the idea that I am unable to make this acknowledgment by my own power, since I am held captive by sin. I must be rescued by the grace of God.

The first view is reflected in, for instance, the saying of Philip Melanchthon (1497–1560): "to know Christ is to know his benefits, not to contemplate his natures or the mode of his incarnation."[36] In support of his project of "demythologizing," Bultmann would later cite this saying with evident approval.[37] In the same context he also cites a saying attributed to his teacher, Wilhelm Herrmann. Hermann had taken Melanchthon's principle one step further, arguing that "we cannot say of

---

[34]Ibid., 26: *als Jenseits im Verhältnis zur Natur wie zur Kultur.*

[35]On the influence here of the Marburg Neo-Kantian philosophy of Hermann Cohen (1842–1918) and Paul Natorp (1854–1924), see Roger Johnson, *The Origins of Demythologizing,* 42–86.

[36]For a similar sentiment from John Calvin, see his *Institutes* III.ii.33 (*Institutes of the Christian Religion,* 580–81): "It will not be enough for the mind to be illumined by the Spirit of God unless the heart is also strengthened and supported by his power. In this matter the Schoolmen go completely astray, who in considering faith identify it with a bare and simple assent arising out of knowledge, and leave out confidence and assurance of heart."

[37]Cf. Rudolf Bultmann, "On the Problem of Demythologizing" (1952), in *New Testament and Mythology and Other Basic Writings,* 99.

God how he is in himself but only what he does to us."[38] Both sayings express a concern that closely resembles Bultmann's opposition to "objectification." It is the Lutheran concern that knowledge of God should not be divorced from the claim which that knowledge makes on my life.

The second Lutheran emphasis is reflected in Bultmann's insistence that objectification is not only misguided but represents unbelief and sin. In the essay "What Does It Mean to Speak of God?" Bultmann cites with approval Luther's exegesis of Adam's fall. According to Luther, this fall was not so much a matter of eating the forbidden fruit. As Bultmann writes, Adam's sin "was that he raised the question, 'Ought God to have said?' He began to 'argue about God' (*disputare de deo*) and so set himself outside God and made God's claim upon men a debatable question."[39] It may be objected that our current situation demands that we speak about God in this way. We *must* ask questions about God, because the truth of God's claim on us can no longer be taken for granted. Bultmann's response is that this merely shows how deeply we are immersed in sin. As he writes, if we are incapable of speaking other than *about* God, this only demonstrates that "of ourselves we can do nothing to escape from sin."[40] The solution is not to try to cease speaking about God, for that is not something we can do of ourselves. Even if we were to cease speaking about God, our silence would be no more than another useless human "work." Here, too, the influence of Bultmann's Lutheran roots is evident. For he insists that in this matter, too, we are incapable of saving ourselves. We can speak rightly of God only through God's grace.

In later writings, Bultmann takes this idea further and identifies an "objective" knowledge of human beings with "inauthentic" existence.[41] His earlier claim that objective knowledge represents unbelief is here recast in terms apparently derived from the phenomenological philosophy of Martin Heidegger. Objectification is now equated not only with unbelief but also with inauthentic existence. To understand this new twist to Bultmann's thought we must turn to his understanding of history.

2. History and Existence

History and Objectification

Bultmann's understanding of history is shaped by the idea that the usual methods of historical study tend towards objectification. Thus the usual

[38]Cited by Bultmann (ibid.).
[39]Bultmann, "What Does It Mean to Speak of God?" 54.
[40]Ibid., 55.
[41]Cf. Rudolf Bultmann, "On the Problem of Demythologizing" (1961), 158.

methods of history are unable to lead us to a true understanding of the human condition. As he writes in a later essay, in "a positivistic historicism . . . the historian stands over against history as a subject observing an object, thereby becoming a spectator outside of the historical process as it follows its course in time."[42] Today, Bultmann continues, we have become aware that such a position is impossible. We now realize that "the act of perceiving a historical process is itself a historical act."[43] (This insight parallels Ernst Troeltsch's observation that our historical judgments are themselves historical, shaped by the context in which they arise.[44]) We also need to be aware that human beings are qualitatively different from other beings in the natural world. As Bultmann writes, "we do not simply take our place in the causal continuum of natural processes but must ourselves each take over our own being and are responsible for it."[45] Human existence is created by the decisions we make, decisions that involve an appropriation of the past in light of the future. (Here again there are striking similarities to Troeltsch's work, despite Bultmann's anxiety to distance himself from the work of his predecessor.[46]) Only someone prepared to shoulder this responsibility can be said to be living an "authentic" existence.[47]

Despite these facts, the possibility remains of regarding history in an objectifying manner, as something that stands over against us. Indeed, Bultmann admits that this is not only a possibility; it is a necessity—an admission that leads him into some difficulties. For the history that becomes the basis of my personal decisions is accessible only *through* a study of history as object. We human beings exist only within concrete situations, and an understanding of these situations requires an objectifying form of study.[48] In addition to this, we must admit that even our free decisions are not simply free. We *are* part of the natural world, and our decisions are shaped by forces which—like the rest of the natural world—can be understood in terms of what Bultmann calls "the sequence of cause and effect."[49]

---

[42]Rudolf Bultmann, "On the Problem of Demythologizing" (1961), 156.

[43]Ibid.

[44]Cf. Troeltsch, "Modern Philosophy of History," 305.

[45]Bultmann, "On the Problem of Demythologizing" (1961), 156.

[46]See, for example, Bultmann, "Liberal Theology and the Latest Theological Movement," 29, 30, 31–32; *The Historical Jesus Quest*, 243, 244–45, 246.

[47]Cf. Bultmann, "On the Problem of Demythologizing" (1961), 157.

[48]Cf. ibid., 158. See also Rudolf Bultmann, *Das Verhältnis der urchristlichen Christusbotschaft zum historischen Jesus*, 2d edition, Sitzungsberichte der Heidelberger Akademie der Wissenschaften (Heidelberg: Carl Winter, Universitätsverlag, 1961), 15.

[49]Bultmann, "On the Problem of Demythologizing" (1961). 158.

The question then becomes one of the relationship between the existentialist interpretation of history and the objectifying view of history. Are these simply contradictory, so that one would have to speak of what Bultmann calls "two realms of reality or even of a double truth?"[50] Bultmann denies that this is the case, but his solution seems characterized by a profound ambiguity. There is, he insists, only one reality. This reality, he writes, can be seen in two ways, which correspond to the two modes of human existence, namely, authentic and inauthentic existence. The relationship between these two ways of viewing reality is " 'dialectical', insofar as one is never given without the other."[51] It follows that there is no existentialist interpretation without an objectifying view. The reason for this is itself rooted in the nature of human existence. The human being whose authentic life is realized in decisions is an *embodied* being. This means—once again—that our "existential" decisions can be made only in concrete situations. Because of our embodiment in these concrete situations we are part of the world and its history. We must therefore take responsibility for that world. Yet we can understand that world only through objectification. From this argument it would seem that an objectifying view of history is inescapable; it is simply a consequence of the fact that we have bodies and are part of the physical world. But in the very same context Bultmann suggests that objectification remains a temptation we must resist. It represents a form of inauthentic existence. More precisely, the world of objective knowledge, the world that stands at our disposal, is not our "authentic reality."[52]

The obscurity of these claims arises from the tension between two views of objectification, both of which are found in Bultmann's work. On the one hand, Bultmann argues that we *need* to view history as an object. Objectification is an inevitable consequence of our human nature, embodied as it is in concrete situations that can be understood only in terms of cause and effect. On the other hand, he insists that to view history as an object is to overlook the fact that it is a field of personal decision and to fall into inauthentic existence. If this second line of argument is followed, it appears that, while objectification is inescapable, it is also godless and sinful.

This tension in Bultmann's thought cannot easily be resolved. It certainly cannot be resolved, as Bultmann attempts to do, by labeling this relationship "dialectical." This merely begs the question. Nor can one argue that to view history as an object is perfectly acceptable, provided we do not *forget* its meaning for our existence. On this view, inauthentic

[50]Ibid.
[51]Ibid., 158–59.
[52]Ibid., 159.

existence would reside, not in objectification *as such,* but in allowing ourselves to be dominated by it. In a later essay, Bultmann attempts to take this line, while speaking of the relationship between "faith" and "worldliness." Of this relationship he writes:

> *The relation of faith and worldliness is a dialectical relationship.* ...The loving look into an eye which is loved and loving is fundamentally different from the objectivizing look with which the ophthalmologist examines the eyes of a patient. But when the doctor who has to treat the diseased eye is also the one who loves, the two ways of seeing stand in a dialectical relationship; he has to examine the eye of the other in an objectivizing way precisely in his love. The objectivizing way of seeing enters into the service of those who love. [53]

Bultmann is here suggesting that objectification may stand in the service of faith, as a form of knowledge that is adequate, good, and indeed necessary in its own sphere. The problem is that this "moderate" view of objectification stands in stark contrast to views found elsewhere, particularly in Bultmann's earlier work. Bultmann elsewhere argues that an objectifying view of the world is the consequence of sin. The fact that we cannot avoid it is merely evidence of our godlessness. According to this view, what we are faced with is *not* a choice between a good and a better, between two things that are both good in their own sphere. It is a choice between a good and an evil, even if objectification is an evil from which we are unable to liberate ourselves. Once again, it is difficult to see how these two views can be reconciled.

This tension becomes very clear in Bultmann's essay on miracles, "The Question of Wonder." We will examine this essay shortly, when we seek to understand how Bultmann speaks of the action of God. In the meantime, I would like to draw attention to this one aspect of his work. In this essay, Bultmann also speaks of objectification, not (admittedly) in the realm of history, but in that of natural science. [54] We have already seen that Bultmann identifies objectification with a view of the world as governed by law (*gesetzmässig*). [55] In his essay on miracles, Bultmann picks up this idea. Indeed, he argues that the idea that the world is bound by law

---

[53]Rudolf Bultmann, "The Idea of God and Modern Man" (1963), translated by Robert W. Funk, in *Translating Theology into the Modern Age,* Journal for Theology and the Church 2 (Tübingen: J. C. B. Mohr [Paul Siebeck], 1965), 91.

[54]We have already seen that for Bultmann these two types of knowledge cannot be clearly distinguished. Both belong to the realm of culture and are fields in which objectification is both possible and (in a certain sense) inevitable.

[55]Cf. Bultmann, "What does it mean to speak of God?" 59; cf. "Welchen Sinn hat es, von Gott zu reden?" 32: "Anyone who holds to the modern view of the world as a world governed by law (*das durch den Gedanken des Gesetzes konstituiert wird*) has a godless conception of the world."

is inescapable. As he writes, this idea "underlies explicitly or implicitly all of our ideas and actions which relate to this world."[56] It cannot, therefore, be regarded as merely an interpretation of the world or a judgment about it. It is not just a matter of a worldview that we would be free to adopt or reject. The idea that the world is governed by law did not first arise with the growth of the modern sciences, however much these may have heightened our perception of this fact. It is, rather, quite primitive. Indeed, Bultmann argues that the very idea of a miracle—as a *violation* of the laws of nature—takes for granted the idea of a world governed by law. It merely introduces another actor into this world, namely, God. It follows that objectification is, as Bultmann writes, "given with our existence in the world" (*mit unserem Dasein in der Welt gegeben*).[57] We may note immediately that this argument is consistent with Bultmann's 1961 essay, where he argues that objectification is rooted in our bodily existence.[58]

The problem arises a few pages later, where Bultmann addresses the question of why we do *not* in fact see the world as the scene of divine activity. Why are we so blind to the actions of God? The reason is that we see the world as governed by law, and this view of the world leaves no room for divine action. To speak of the action of God is to speak of something that *contradicts* our experience of the world. Bultmann goes on to argue this blindness has its roots in human sin. As he writes,

> the impossibility of seeing world events as wonders must obviously have its cause in my godlessness. My inability to see world events as wonders has been developed and formulated in the *idea of nature* as a sequence governed by law; therefore this idea must obviously be adjudged *godless*. But that does not mean that I simply abandon it. I cannot do that. It merely becomes clear to me that godlessness is not something which man can discard by a strong act of will; on the contrary, godlessness is a mode of my being, my existence is determined by sin.[59]

It appears here that objectification is not a simple fact of our "existence-in-the-world," an inevitable consequence of our existence as embodied creatures. Rather, it is the result of sin, a sign of the godlessness that marks our existence, from which we can be liberated only by God himself.

[56]Rudolf Bultmann, "The Question of Wonder," in *Faith and Understanding,* 248; cf. Bultmann, "Zur Frage des Wunders," in *Glauben und Verstehen: Gesammelte Aufsätze* 1, 215.
[57]Bultmann, "Zur Frage des Wunders," 215.
[58]Cf. Bultmann, "On the Problem of Demythologizing" (1961), 158–59.
[59]Bultmann, "The Question of Wonder," 253.

A few pages later Bultmann will try to adopt the mediating position that I have already identified. Once again, he argues that the concept of nature—as something governed by law—is a necessary concept. We cannot do without it.[60] The theological problem arises only when we allow ourselves to be dominated by this view, when we allow it to become our "master."[61] This attempt at mediation is manifestly a failure. To be blunt, Bultmann cannot consistently have it both ways. He cannot insist that objectification is inseparable from our existence as embodied creatures, something that as human beings we cannot escape, while simultaneously arguing that objectification is by its very nature sinful. That is to say, Bultmann cannot maintain both ideas without also holding to a deep anthropological dualism that regards the fact of embodiment as the root of sin. (I am assuming that this is not his intention!) In the absence of a consistent—but from a Christian perspective deeply heretical—anthropology, it can only be said that Bultmann's thought is marked and marred by this unresolved tension. For the moment, we can only note the tension and try to understand the rest of his thought on this basis.

A Redefinition of the Historical

In opposition to the objectification of human existence that characterizes a positivist historiography, Bultmann proposes a redefinition of the term "historical" (*geschichtlich*). This becomes clear in Bultmann's 1928 essay "The Significance of 'Dialectical Theology' for the Scientific Study of the New Testament." Here he repeats his objections to the objectification of religious language. He insists that one can utter a "theological" statement (in the true sense of that word) only when one speaks of the significance of God *for the speaker*, at this particular time and place.[62] As he writes, "a theological statement is not true because its content expresses something which is timelessly valid. It is true when it gives the answer to the question posed by the concrete situation in time to which the sentence itself belongs when it is being spoken."[63] However, he then takes his argument further by insisting that such a statement is what is meant by a *historical* statement. What does he mean by this? In what way is such an "existential" statement properly "historical"?

Bultmann's point here is that a theological statement must not only speak of God; it must also speak of the human being to whom the Word

[60]Cf. ibid., 258.

[61]Ibid.

[62]See also Bultmann, "Science and Existence" (1955), in *New Testament and Mythology and Other Basic Writings,* 131–44.

[63]Bultmann, "The Significance of 'Dialectical Theology' for the Scientific Study of the New Testament" (1928), in *Faith and Understanding,* 147.

of God is addressed. This position assumes a particular understanding of human existence. It assumes that a human being is not so much a being as "a potentiality to be" (*ein Sein-Können*).[64] For human nature is (as it were) "open," not determined in advance. It is shaped by the concrete decisions of life, in circumstances over which the individual has little control. This characteristic of human existence—its openness to being reshaped in the light of my own deliberate choices—Bultmann calls "the historical nature of man's being."[65]

This has its implications for the study, not just of the New Testament, but of any document of human history, for such documents speak of the possibilities of human existence. But this means we should approach our study of such documents with the readiness to allow them to speak to our existence. It will also mean that the process of interpretation must continue until this occurs. We will not have truly understood the text until we have understood the possibilities of human existence. This in turn means understanding the possibilities of my own existence. This is why the exegete is always personally involved in the work of exegesis. He is, as Bultmann writes, always "realizing his own potentiality-to-be, grasping his own possibility in the exegesis."[66] This is the deepest reason why an objectifying form of historical study is unacceptable.[67] (It is also, of course, why objectifying *theological* statements are not worthy of the name.) For the topics with which the Bible deals cannot be approached on the assumption that they are objects accessible to our gaze. As Bultmann writes, "no one 'knows' what death is, or happiness, or love, or hate, in the way one knows that $2 \times 2 = 4$, or that the Council of Nicea met in 325."[68]

Incidentally, it is at this point that the true import of Bultmann's famous project of "demythologizing" becomes clear. Bultmann argues that the problem with the mythological language of the New Testament is not just that it embodies an outmoded worldview. It is a still more serious matter. The problem with mythological language is the fact that—when read in our contemporary context—it presents as a matter of objective "fact" what can be understood only in terms of the realities

---

[64]Bultmann, "The Significance of 'Dialectical Theology' for the Scientific Study of the New Testament," 149; cf. Bultmann, "Die Bedeutung der «dialektischen Theologie» für die neutestamentliche Wissenschaft" (1928), in *Glauben und Verstehen: Gesammelte Aufsätze* 1, 118.

[65]*Die Geschichtlichkeit des menschlichen Seins* (ibid.).

[66]Cf. Bultmann, "The Significance of 'Dialectical Theology' for the Scientific Study of the New Testament," 150.

[67]Cf. ibid., 150–51.

[68]Ibid., 152.

that shape my existence. It follows that for Bultmann the program of demythologizing is *not* a matter of anachronistically reading modern existentialist philosophy back into the pages of the New Testament (as some of his critics have suggested). On the contrary, Bultmann insists that such a reading corresponds to the nature of ancient mythological thought.[69] "The real purpose of myth," he writes elsewhere, "is not to express an objective picture of the world as it is, but to express man's understanding of the world in which he lives."[70] For this reason "myth should be interpreted not cosmologically, but anthropologically, or better still, existentially."[71] For instance, faced with the concept of *mana* in so-called "primitive" religions, the interpreter should not simply dismiss the idea as the relic of a prescientific worldview. Rather, she should seek to discover "what understanding of human existence finds expression in the concept of *mana*."[72] We may find, Bultmann continues, that "a much truer conception of human existence is expressed here than in the Stoic view of the world or in that of modern science."[73]

It follows that the "scientific" (*wissenschaftlich*) reconstruction of the past is (at best) only the first step in the historian's work. It is certainly not to be regarded as the goal of historical study. Such a study merely identifies the views expressed in the text and assigns it to the context of its time and place.[74] In this kind of historical investigation the text is merely what Bultmann calls a "source" for our knowledge of the past. But this "scientific" investigation of the past does not yet achieve *understanding,* in the proper sense of that word. For it does not call the interpreter's own existence into question. It does not allow the text to confront the interpreter with new possibilities for his own life. "Historical understanding," in the proper sense of that word, "is not achieved as an appropriation of knowledge, an acquiring of unknown 'facts'."[75] Rather, it involves a decision about oneself.

It is against this background that the much debated question of the

---

[69]This contention is, of course, highly debatable, but Bultmann's conception of "myth" need not detain us here. Roger Johnson (*The Origins of Demythologizing,* 30 et passim) distinguishes three conceptions of mythology in Bultmann's work: the "history of religions" formulation of myth, the Enlightenment formulation, and the existentialist formulation. The first two of these are related to D. F. Strauss's use of the term, which is similarly ill-defined.

[70]Bultmann, "The New Testament and Mythology," 10.

[71]Ibid.

[72]Bultmann, "The Significance of 'Dialectical Theology' for the Scientific Study of the New Testament," 152.

[73]Ibid., 152–53.

[74]Cf. ibid., 155.

[75]Ibid., 158.

"presuppositions" of the interpreter must be understood. When an ancient text deals with what Bultmann calls "natural objects or with events in the world of space-time," then we can readily understand the subject matter, since we inhabit the same world.[76] However, when the text speaks of human existence, the situation is more complex. In these cases I will understand what it is saying only if I have a certain "preknowledge" of the possibilities of human existence.[77] That knowledge should be open-ended; it is, at best, a kind of preliminary knowledge. Bultmann refers to it as an "unknowing knowledge, a knowledge which has the characteristic of a question," for "an individual existence never knows itself conclusively; it is always coming to know itself afresh and differently, because it is never finished."[78] Therefore, what is required of the exegete is not a preknowledge of the *results* of his or her exegetical work.[79] What is required is a certain set of questions, a certain preliminary understanding of the subject matter, and (above all) a living relationship to that subject matter.[80] This living relationship is "the fundamental presupposition for understanding history."[81] History is never truly understood unless its subject matter is of concern for us and represents a challenge to us.

We have seen that Ernst Troeltsch saw history—rather than dogma or scripture—as a new starting point for theological reflection. He was confident that the study of history would yield theologically constructive results. It should by now be clear that Bultmann rejects the idea that historical study *by itself* can form the starting point of theological reflection. He finds no meaning in history as such; meaning can be found only in the present, in the responsible decisions of the individual.[82] History is of value only insofar as it confronts the individual with material that forces her to make such decisions. Bultmann's problem is not just—as

[76]Ibid., 156.

[77]Ibid., 156–57.

[78]Ibid., 159.

[79]Rudolf Bultmann, "Is Exegesis without Presuppositions Possible?" (1957), in *Existence and Faith*, 289.

[80]Cf. ibid. 292–94. See also Bultmann's *Jesus Christ and Mythology* (1951; New York: Charles Scribner's Sons, 1958), 49–51; "The Problem of Hermeneutics" (1950), in *Essays: Philosophical and Theological*, Library of Philosophy and Theology (London: SCM, 1955), 246: "Only those understand Plato who philosophize with him."

[81]Bultmann, "Is Exegesis without Presuppositions Possible?" 294.

[82]This is the conclusion of Bultmann's 1955 Gifford Lectures, the last of which provides a helpful summary of his understanding of history. See Rudolf Bultmann, *History and Eschatology: The Gifford Lectures 1955* (Edinburgh: Edinburgh University Press, 1957), 138–55.

Robert Morgan writes—that he doubts "the capacity of a historical reconstruction to bear the positive theological weight of presenting the Christian message" (although this is certainly true).[83] Rather, he sees at least our normal practice of history writing as yet another objectivizing discipline whose results simply bypass the existential challenge and consolation of faith. It is true that Bultmann later admits that an "existentialist interpretation of history has need of objectifying observation of the historical past."[84] Yet he is also strongly disposed to disparage objectifying knowledge, on theological as well as anthropological grounds. Indeed, he is inclined to suggest that our reliance on such an objectifying view of history is nothing less than "inauthentic" existence.[85] In theological terms, it is merely a sign that we cannot liberate ourselves from our sin.

Miracles and the Action of God

It is time to return to Bultmann's essay on miracles, to see how he envisages the action of God. Is the divine action an action *in* history? If so, in what sense of the word "history"? More specifically, is the action of God accessible to the historian?

Bultmann begins his essay on miracles by distinguishing two senses of the German term *Wunder.* This term, he writes, can mean either an act of God (as distinct from a human act) or an event contrary to the laws of nature (a "miracle" in our usual sense). The second sense, that of a miracle, has become impossible for us today, because it violates our sense of the natural world as a world governed by law.[86] In any case, Bultmann argues, it is not a properly religious notion.[87] For the idea of a miracle assumes what Bultmann has already described as the "godless" idea of a world governed by law.[88] A further problem arises from the fact that in the biblical world miracles can be performed by demons as well as by God. Therefore, one could not recognize a miracle without already knowing God and knowing what would constitute an act of God.[89] For all these reasons, the Christian will wish to exclude the idea of a miracle. It is true that miracles are reported in the Bible. But this is only because

---

[83]Robert Morgan, "Troeltsch and the Dialectical Theology," 38.

[84]Bultmann, "On the Problem of Demythologizing" (1961), 159; cf. "The Significance of 'Dialectical Theology' for the Scientific Study of the New Testament," 157, n.9.

[85]Cf. Bultmann, "On the Problem of Demythologizing" (1961), 158.

[86]Cf. Bultmann, "The Question of Wonder," 247–48.

[87]Cf. ibid., 249.

[88]Cf. ibid., 248–49.

[89]As I noted in chapter 2, this is an old argument, used by Spinoza (cf. Letter 75, 1675, in Spinoza, *Letters,* 339), to which Strauss also makes reference in *Die christliche Glaubenslehre* (vol.1, §17 [p.231]) and in *The Life of Jesus Critically Examined,* §146 (766).

the biblical writers did not realize that belief in miracles was incompatible with true religion.[90] (Bultmann's actual words are a little more circumspect, but this seems to be their meaning. "The biblical writers," he says, "in accordance with the presuppositions of their thinking, had not yet fully apprehended the idea of miracle and its implications."[91])

What remains is the idea of *Wunder* in the more general sense of "an act of God." This idea certainly cannot be abandoned without abandoning Christian faith altogether. But what can it mean? A favored option in our time, Bultmann writes, is that of identifying the actions of God with the workings of nature. (We saw in chapter 1 that this view was consistently developed by Spinoza.) Against this "pantheistic" idea Bultmann brings two closely related objections.[92] The first will by now be familiar. It is that such an understanding of divine action puts theological statements on the same level as statements of science, which speak about the world in general. But a theological statement in the proper sense of this term does not speak about the world in general. It speaks about my own existence. The second objection is a closely related one. It is the fact that this understanding of divine action embodies a mistaken view of the world, a view of the world as governed by law, rather than "the specific reality in which I live and act, *my* world."[93]

What, then, does Bultmann understand by the action of God? First of all, he insists that the action of God is hidden. (This was, of course, also a prominent idea in the theology of Karl Barth, albeit for slightly different reasons.) As Bultmann writes,

> in no sense whatever is wonder as wonder an observable event in the world, not in any place nor at any time. To claim an event as an observable wonder would be to separate it from God and understand it as world. God is not provable by observation. *Wonder is hidden as wonder,* hidden from him who does not see God in it[94]

Indeed faith in God's action can only take the form of a "contradiction of all that I see in the world."[95] As we have already seen, I inevitably see the world as self-explanatory, as governed by its own laws. This way of regarding the world is a sign of my godlessness, but it cannot be escaped.

---

[90]Presumably, one is tempted to say, the evangelists had not yet read Heidegger or even Kant.

[91]Bultmann, "The Question of Wonder," 249.

[92]Cf. ibid., 251–52.

[93]Ibid., 252.

[94]Ibid.

[95]Ibid., 253.

As Bultmann writes, "I cannot free myself from that view of it by deciding that it ought to look otherwise."[96] The action of God is therefore hidden and accessible only to faith.

It follows that the action of God is not accessible to the historian. This conclusion becomes explicit in Bultmann's 1961 essay on demythologizing, to which we may turn for a moment. Bultmann first repeats his contention that the historian "views the historical process in an objectifying way and thus understands it as a closed continuum of causes and effects."[97] Indeed, he argues that on one level this way of viewing reality is quite appropriate. Indeed, it is essential. As he writes, "the historian cannot proceed otherwise if he or she wants to achieve reliable knowledge of some particular fact—for example, by determining whether some traditional account is really a valid testimony to a certain fact of the past."[98] But this necessary reliance on objectifying knowledge means that the historian must exclude miracles. Indeed, she must exclude any talk about the actions of God, whether miraculous or not. As Bultmann writes,

> the historian cannot allow that the continuum of historical happenings is broken by the interference of spiritual powers, nor can he or she acknowledge any wonders in the sense of events whose causes do not lie within history. Unlike the biblical writings, the science of history cannot talk about an act of God that intervenes in the historical process. What it can perceive as a historical phenomenon is not God's act but only faith in God's act. Whether there is any reality corresponding to such faith it cannot know, since any reality that lies beyond the reality visible to an objectifying view is for it invisible.[99]

The action of God must be excluded from the writing of history because such action is inaccessible to objectifying knowledge. It is a reality only in relation to the individual and her existence. As Bultmann writes, the action of God "can be talked about only if we at the same time talk about our existence as affected by God's act."[100] It therefore lies outside the historian's view.

Returning to Bultmann's essay on miracles, we find that here too he discusses the hiddenness of God's actions. On this occasion, however, he takes a slightly different line. The reason why we cannot see the actions of God, he suggests, is that we think of the world as "the working world

[96]Ibid.
[97]Bultmann, "On the Problem of Demythologizing" (1961), 159.
[98]Ibid., 159–60.
[99]Ibid., 160.
[100]Ibid., 161–62.

amenable to . . . [our] control."[101] In doing this, we show ourselves to be dominated by a particular view of human activity. Within this view, we estimate ourselves by our work and try to make ourselves secure through our work. (Once again, Bultmann's anthropology shows itself to be deeply Lutheran: objectification turns out to be another instance of "justification by works.") Rather than regarding our actions as obedience, we regard them as achievement. We look back at what has been accomplished, rather than looking forward in obedience to God's call. The only way we can be freed from this backward-looking, achievement-oriented way of thinking is through forgiveness. It is true that the past is always with us. The key question is, as Bultmann writes, whether the past is with us "as sinful or as forgiven. If the sin is forgiven, that means that we have freedom for the future; that we are really hearing God's claim and can yield ourselves to him as 'his instruments' (Rom 6.12ff)."[102]

It follows that the revelation of the forgiveness of God is *the* wonder, the *only* wonder.[103] Through this revelation, Bultmann writes, "God takes away (*aufhebt*) our understanding of ourselves as achievers who as such are continually relapsing into the past."[104] By doing this, God has "abolished (*aufhebt*) the character of the world as the working world under our control."[105] To see the action of God as an event that has occurred within the world (*ein geschehenes Weltereignis*) is to fall back into the perspective of the unbeliever. For the believer, the action of God can never be an event *in* the world. The action of God has nothing to do with the world of cause and effect. It abrogates the idea of a world governed by law. It is true that the idea of natural law remains part of our understanding of the world. We cannot live without it; it cannot simply disappear. It follows, as Bultmann writes, that "in our actual living, conceptions belonging to work and those belonging to faith are interchanged."[106] But they are interchanged in such a way that "the former are always delimited by the latter."[107] We must not allow the objectifying view to become our master, but must allow our behavior to be shaped by faith. From this point of view, it is significant that Bultmann, like Barth,[108] uses the term *aufheben,* with its double sense of preservation

---

[101]Bultmann, "The Question of Wonder," 255.
[102]Ibid., 257.
[103]Cf. ibid., 254.
[104]Ibid., 257; cf. "Zur Frage des Wunders," 224.
[105]Ibid.
[106]Bultmann, "The Question of Wonder," 258; "Zur Frage des Wunders," 259.
[107]Ibid.
[108]Cf. Barth, *Der Römerbrief, 1919,* 67, 85, 167 (with regard to "real history" and "so-called history").

and abrogation.[109] The objectifying view is preserved, but it is also abrogated.

By itself, of course, such language is paradoxical. It does not so much resolve the problem as heighten it. The question of the relationship of faith and objectifying knowledge remains unsolved.[110] All Bultmann has done is to assert that objectifying knowledge cannot be escaped, while the faith is what allows us to speak of the action of God. The same tension emerges from Bultmann's 1961 essay on demythologizing. Here, too, he argues that statements about God have "a legitimate basis only in our existential self-understanding."[111] Yet he also admits that what faith calls acts of God can also be seen "as processes within the continuum of natural and historical happenings."[112] Indeed, Christian faith "sees an utterly special act of God in a certain historical event, which as such can be objectively established."[113] This event is the appearance of Jesus Christ. While this appearance is an "eschatological event" which "put an end to history," it is also a historical event.[114] Bultmann concedes that this involves an inescapable paradox, which he calls "the paradoxical identity of an occurrence within the world with the act of the God who stands beyond the world."[115]

What, then, have we discovered? Bultmann begins his career by attempting to distinguish between the world of religious claims and the world of secular knowledge. The world of secular knowledge is that of "culture" in all its forms: cognitive, aesthetic, and moral. As such, it is the product of the objectifying human intellect, which sees the world as governed by law (as *gesetzmässig*). The sphere of religion, by way of contrast, is the world of the individual's existence, the world of freedom and decision. At least in Bultmann's early work, the two are quite clearly separated. Religious claims have nothing to do with objectifying knowledge.

---

[109]Schubert Ogden in his translation of "On the Problem of Demythologizing" ([1961], 162) uses the more technical term "sublate."

[110]Neither can it be resolved by another stratagem, namely that of arguing that objectification is a legitimate way of regarding the world; it should simply not be used in our language about God. Bultmann insists that all our statements about God are also statements about human existence and for this reason statements about a "being in the world." He is therefore right to argue ("On the Problem of Demythologizing" [1961], 158) that there is only one reality, but it is precisely this fact that leads him into difficulties.

[111]Bultmann, "On the Problem of Demythologizing" (1961), 162.

[112]Ibid.

[113]Ibid.

[114]Ibid., 163; cf. Bultmann, *History and Eschatology*, 151–53.

[115]Bultmann, "On the Problem of Demythologizing" (1961), 162.

However, Bultmann later retreats from this position, admitting that there is only one reality, which can be regarded in two ways. This forces Bultmann to clarify the relationship of these two forms of knowledge.

But the clarification leads Bultmann into apparently contradictory claims. On the one hand, an objectifying view of the world is a necessity. We cannot do without it. On these grounds, for instance, the historian is quite correct to exclude "miracles" (in the popular sense) from her descriptions of the world. Bultmann even suggests that objectification may stand in the service of faith.[116] We need only ensure that we are not dominated by it. On the other hand, Bultmann elsewhere suggests that an objectifying view of the world stands in the way of faith. It is nothing less than sinful, insofar as it is the reason we do not see the world as the sphere of divine action. Objectifying knowledge is therefore godless. If we cannot avoid it, it is because we are so immersed in sin that we cannot escape other than through the grace of God.[117] The wonder of divine forgiveness is that it abrogates this way of viewing the world, releasing us from the idea that the world is a world under our control, a sphere of human achievement. It follows that the objectifying view of the world that is so inseparable from our bodily existence is also that from which the grace of God releases us.[118]

In the light of these apparent contradictions, as we have seen, Bultmann resorts to describing the relationship of faith and objectifying knowledge as "dialectical" or even "paradoxical." He can even compare it to the traditional Lutheran formula of *simul justus et peccator* (at the one time justified and a sinner), which suggests that, even after the declaration of God's forgiveness, the Christian remains a sinner.[119] But such language merely highlights the tension in his thought. I began this essay by observing the antithetical nature of Bultmann's language. We can now see that Bultmann's antitheses are no rhetorical ornament, which may be stripped away at will. Rather, his thought is antithetical "all the way down," being rooted in a deep dualism between objectifying and existential knowledge. The sharp distinction between the two—heightened by a Lutheran theology—allows Bultmann to shield religious claims from the challenge of secular knowledge. The historian (or the scientist) may

[116]Cf. ibid., 159.

[117]Cf. Bultmann, "The Question of Wonder," 253.

[118]I am reminded of Barth's criticism ("Rudolf Bultmann—An Attempt to Understand Him," 93) that Bultmann's description of the consequences of sin is "remarkably reminiscent of Platonism."

[119]Cf. Bultmann, *History and Eschatology,* 154. More precisely, Bultmann sees this formula as a reflection of what he calls "the paradox that Christian existence is at the same time an eschatological, unworldly being and an historical being."

do her worst, but she will be unable to touch the claims of faith. But the cost of this protection is great, for Bultmann is forced to admit that both types of knowledge are necessary. In the terms of our present study, we need both history and faith. This admission leads Bultmann into unresolved conflicts and threatens to undermine the protective walls he has erected. It seems that the historical challenge to religious authority cannot be answered so easily.

3. The Historical Jesus

Jesus and the Gospels

With regard to historical research into the figure of Jesus, Bultmann is sceptical about both its possibility and its theological value. On historical grounds alone, Bultmann is sceptical about our ability to know the Jesus of history. In the introduction to his own study of Jesus he writes: "I . . . think that we can now know almost nothing concerning the life and personality of Jesus, since the early Christian sources show no interest in either, are moreover fragmentary and often legendary; and other sources about Jesus do not exist."[120] For Bultmann, the Gospels do not have this character by accident. He believes that the Gospels have their origin in the Hellenistic churches and therefore reflect the form which the preaching of Christianity took in that environment. In his 1921 *History of the Synoptic Tradition* Bultmann expands on this argument, arguing that the Hellenistic churches were interested, not in the historic Jesus, but in what he calls "the Christ of faith and the cult."[121] For this reason their proclamation focused on "the death and resurrection of Jesus Christ as the saving acts which are known by faith and become effective for the believer in Baptism and the Lord's Supper."[122] In terms derived from the history of religions, Bultmann describes this Hellenistic proclamation (or *kerygma*) as "cultic legend" and the Gospels as "expanded cult legends."[123] Therefore the Gospels differ from (for example) Greek biographies in that they embody "no historical-biographical interest."[124] As he writes, "they have nothing to say about Jesus' human personality, his appearance and character, his origin, education and development."[125]

---

[120]Rudolf Bultmann, *Jesus and the Word,* translated from *Jesus* (1926) by Louise Pettibone Smith and Erminie Huntress Lantero (London: Collins/Fontana, 1958), 14.

[121]Rudolf Bultmann, *The History of the Synoptic Tradition* (1921), translated by John Marsh (Oxford: Basil Blackwell, 1963), 370.

[122]Ibid.

[123]Ibid., 371.

[124]Ibid., 372.

[125]Ibid.

The Gospels "do not tell of a much admired human personality, but of
Jesus Christ, the Son of God, the Lord of the Church, and do so because
they have grown out of Christian worship and remain tied to it."[126]
Because of this exclusive interest in the Christ of faith, as encountered in
worship, the Gospels are not documents that may be used to construct a
"life of Jesus." In a way that is consistent with this scepticism, Bultmann's
own study of Jesus claims to be no more than an approximation to that
picture of Jesus to be found in what he calls "the oldest layer of the synoptic tradition."[127]

Jesus and the Kerygma

A more detailed discussion of these issues is to be found in a later study
entitled *The Relationship of the Early-Christian Proclamation of Christ to
the Historical Jesus,* in which Bultmann replies to his critics. Here he
approaches the same matters from a slightly different point of view. He
does so by addressing the question of whether there existed some continuity between the Jesus of history and the Christ of the early Christian
proclamation (*kerygma*). While Bultmann had been accused of denying
the existence of such a continuity, he here denies this accusation. Indeed,
he insists that the *kerygma* itself takes this continuity for granted. As he
writes, the early Christian *kerygma* "contains the paradoxical assertion
that an historical event—even the historical Jesus and his history—is
the eschatological event (the turn of the ages and its accompanying
events)."[128] Therefore we cannot deny that the *kerygma* presupposes the
historical existence of Jesus. The important question is whether the
kerygma presupposes anything more than Jesus' existence. Does it include
the assertion of certain *facts* about this figure of history?

(a) Jesus' Word and Actions in the Kerygma

The attempts to answer this question, Bultmann argues, have generally
approached it in two ways. The first is to ask whether a depiction of the
historical Jesus and his work is *implicit* in the *kerygma*. If this were the
case, then it could be argued that Christian faith depends on the accuracy of certain reported historical facts. The church's proclamation could
not be believed unless the depiction of Jesus found in the *kerygma* could

---

[126]Ibid., 373.
[127]Bultmann, *Jesus and the Word,* 18.
[128]Bultmann, *Das Verhältnis der urchristlichen Christusbotschaft zum historischen Jesus,* 8:
*Das Kerygma enthält die paradoxe Behauptung, daß ein historisches Ereignis—eben der historische
Jesus und seine Geschichte—das eschatologische Ereignis (die Wende der Äonen und was damit
gegeben ist) sei.*

be shown to be well-grounded.[129] Bultmann, however, argues that this is not the case. He notes first of all that even the Synoptic Gospels are *not* written in order to serve as historical reports. Although Luke's Gospel presents itself not only as a work of proclamation but also as a historical report, it is no exception to this rule. Here, too, the work of proclamation takes priority: the historical Jesus and the Christ of the *kerygma* are inseparable. It follows that the primary concern of the Gospel writers is not to convey historical facts. For this reason, the Gospels do not provide any *direct* evidence for a historical reconstruction of the life of Jesus.

The question remains as to whether they offer any *indirect* evidence of the character of this historical figure. In other words, may such a depiction be drawn from them, even *against* the intention of their writers? Here Bultmann concedes that by way of historical research we can indeed know something about Jesus. As he writes,

> even when the synoptics cannot be used as sources for a reconstruction of the life of Jesus, nor for a sketch of his person in the proper sense (since they allow us to know nothing of his inner development), they still allow us to know so much about the work of Jesus that some characteristics of his nature become visible.[130]

Nonetheless, there are strict limits to this knowledge. Indeed we cannot even know how Jesus regarded his death, the event the New Testament regards as the most important fact of his life. All we know for sure is that Jesus died at the hands of the Romans as a political criminal. The historical Jesus could hardly have seen this death as the natural climax and fulfilment of his mission. Rather, his death as a political criminal appears to be the result of a misunderstanding of his mission. Historically speaking, Jesus' death would therefore appear to be a meaningless fate (*ein sinnloses Schicksal*). We cannot tell whether Jesus himself found some significance in it. Indeed, the historian cannot exclude the unpalatable possibility that he died in despair.[131]

Even if we can know something about Jesus, does this knowledge serve as the foundation of early Christian faith? For instance, if historical research could affirm that Jesus went willingly to his death, would this

---

[129]Cf. ibid., 10.

[130]Ibid., 11: *Denn wenn die Synoptiker auch nicht als Quellen für eine Reconstruktion des Lebens Jesu ausreichen, und wenn sie nicht ausreichen, ein Personbild im eigentlichen Sinn zu zeichen, da sie von Jesu innerer Entwicklung nichts erkennen lassen, so lassen sie doch vom Wirken Jesu so viel erkennen, daß indirect einige Züge seines Wesens sichtbar werden.*

[131]Cf. ibid., 12: *Die Möglichkeit, daß er [Jesus] zusammengebrochen ist, darf man sich nicht verschleiern.*

represent a legitimation of the *kerygma*? Far from it! For—once again—
the Gospels make no attempt to ground that faith in historical facts.
Quite the contrary. The Gospels set out to present the history in the light
of the *kerygma,* not vice versa. To try to validate the early church's proclamation through research into the historical Jesus is to impose a modern
concern on the Gospel writers, who understood the historical Jesus only
in the light of their faith in him as the crucified and risen one. At this
point Bultmann makes two further points. Firstly, he suggests that what
was true for the Gospel writers is also true for the modern researcher. In
neither case does faith arise from the perception (*die Wahrnehmung*) of
certain historical facts.[132] Rather, the *kerygma*—the proclamation that
Jesus died for us—demands faith of those who hear it, who encounter its
demand in the depths of their conscience. Secondly, Bultmann suggests
that, while historical research can affirm the existence of the figure of
Jesus and can make certain more or less probable claims about him, it
cannot assert a correspondence in content ([*eine*] *sachliche Übereinstim-
mung*) between the work of Jesus and the message of the early church.[133]

What is very evident in these remarks is Bultmann's scepticism about
the idea that the *kerygma* presupposes certain facts about Jesus. It may
presuppose his existence, but the proclamation of the Christian message
was in no way dependent on a historical knowledge of what Jesus said
and did. The evangelists were not interested in conveying such knowledge: proclamation was much more important to them than historiography. Bultmann admits that today we can make certain historical claims
about Jesus. But he also insists that these cannot form the basis of Christian faith. Faith is not based on history or legitimated by it.

(b) The Kerygma in Jesus' Words and Actions

Having dealt with the question of whether a depiction of the historical
Jesus and his work is *implicit* in the *kerygma,* Bultmann moves on to the
second way in which one may approach the historical Jesus debate. This
is to ask whether the early Christian faith was already present "in kernel"
(*in nuce*) in Jesus' words and works. Can we say that Jesus' proclamation
already had a "kerygmatic character"?[134] Bultmann argues that in this
respect we may affirm at least one fact with confidence: that Jesus understood his own work and teaching "eschatologically," as marking the end
of the present age. In this conviction, at least, Jesus was at one with the

[132]Cf. ibid., 13.
[133]Cf. ibid., 14.
[134]Cf. ibid., 10, 15.

early church.[135] Starting from this observation, one may also affirm that Jesus' proclamation carried with it an implicit Christology. In particular, Jesus' teaching and actions carried with them a claim to plenipotentiary authority (*Vollmachtsanspruch*). This, too, forms a point of contact with the later *kerygma*.[136]

Once again, however, Bultmann draws back from developing these ideas, for he argues that even this line of enquiry does not take us very far. It may demonstrate a point of contact between Jesus and the *kerygma*, but it falls short of demonstrating that the two had the same content (*die sachliche Einheit*).[137] More importantly, the early church was right to pay no attention to such historical facts, for they are of little *religious* use. The early Christian *kerygma* seeks to transmit an eschatological self-understanding to its hearers. But a claim to authority on the part of the historical Jesus is of little relevance here. It is limited to its own time and place; it does not reach out to later generations. It does not allow the present-day hearer to be addressed directly, as the early Christian proclamation clearly intends to address every generation. As Bultmann writes, for this purpose "the Christ of the *kerygma* has displaced the historical Jesus and now addresses the hearer—any hearer—in power."[138]

Jesus and Faith

These critical observations lead Bultmann to a more positive conclusion, which by now will come as no surprise to the reader. It is the suggestion that historical research is of limited value, since it needs to be at least supplemented by an existential understanding of the realities it studies. As Bultmann writes,

> the way towards a solution appears to open up, when the objectifying, historical-critical consideration of the activity of Jesus is replaced or—better still—completed or carried further through *an interpretation of history, that rests on the historical, that is to say, existential encounter with history.*[139]

This existential encounter with history, and this alone, enables us to understand the early Christian faith in Jesus.

[135]Cf. ibid., 16.

[136]Cf. ibid., 16–17.

[137]Cf. ibid., 17.

[138]Ibid.: *Der Christus des Kerygmas hat den historischen Jesus sozusagen verdrängt und redet jetzt in Vollmacht den Hörer—jeden Hörer—an.*

[139]Ibid., 18: *Der Weg zu einer Antwort scheint sich zu eröffnen, wenn die objektivierende historische-kritische Betrachtung des Wirkens Jesu ersetzt, oder besser: ergänzt oder weitergeführt wird durch eine* Interpretation der Geschichte, die auf der geschichtlichen d.h. existentiellen Begegnung mit der Geschichte beruht.

It enables us to understand, for example, why "the proclaimer had to become the proclaimed."[140] It enables us to see, in other words, why the figure of Jesus had to become the object of the church's faith. The earliest community saw that the history of Jesus was nothing less than "the decisive eschatological event."[141] If it was that, then this event could not remain *simply* past. It had to become present. As Bultmann writes, the first Christians were obliged to transform the "one time" (*Einmal*) of Jesus' life and work into a "once for all times" (*Ein-für-allemal*).[142] It became present, an event for all times, through the church's proclamation of Jesus. Through the church's proclamation of Jesus as Lord the message of Jesus offers a new possibility of existence to the people of every age.

It follows that the *kerygma,* the church's proclamation of Jesus, effectively *takes the place* of the historical Jesus. It both represents and (in a certain sense) replaces him.[143] Interestingly, Bultmann draws a further conclusion: there can be no faith in Christ that is not simultaneously faith in the church as bearer of the *kerygma* (and therefore faith in the Holy Spirit, who sustains and guides the church). With this conclusion, we might note, the historical Jesus quest has come full circle. It first emerged, in the seventeenth century, from an implicit faith in the church as bearer of the true message of Jesus. It emerged through criticism of the authority of both church and Bible. With Bultmann and—we might add—the later Barth, the historical Jesus debate returns to a reaffirmation of faith in the church's authority, however much that word "church" may be qualified.[144]

However, this return to a reaffirmation of the early church's *kerygma* is no simple return to the past. Rather, it follows from Bultmann's conviction that only the *proclaimed* Christ can open up new possibilities of human existence. It stems from his conviction that even if we did know Jesus in the way in which the historian customarily knows figures of the past, such knowledge would have little to do with Christian faith.[145]

---

[140]Ibid., 23. *warum mußte der Verkündiger zum Verkündigen werden.*

[141]Ibid., 25: *die älteste Gemeinde . . . die Geschichte Jesu als das entscheidende eschatologische Ereignis verstanden hat.*

[142]Cf. ibid., 25.

[143]Cf. ibid., 26: *so hat es [das Kerygma] sich an die Stelle des historischen Jesus gesetzt; es vertritt ihn.*

[144]In good Lutheran manner, Bultmann (ibid., 26, n.80) is insistent that the word "church" must not be taken as a reference to a particular human institution. The church is, rather, in this sense an "eschatological event" (*eschatologisches Geschehen*).

[145]One is reminded here of Martin Heidegger's remark in *An Introduction to Metaphysics* (1953), translated by Ralph Mannheim (New Haven, Conn.: Yale University Press, 1959), 44: "All relations to history cannot be scientifically objectified and given a place in science, and it is precisely the essential ones that cannot."

Such a picture of Jesus would offer only a false objectivity, false because when we view any historical phenomenon as something "out there," to be understood without reference to our own existence, we fail to grasp its deepest meaning.[146] In other words, Bultmann would have us deal with the New Testament in the same way as any other historical source; "as a genuine historical phenomenon, that is, with the presupposition that in it a possibility of human existence has been grasped and ex-pressed."[147] As has just been noted, for Bultmann those possibilities of human existence can be known only in the course of grappling with the demands of one's own life, that is to say, in a "living relationship" with the text. For this reason the exegete is always personally involved in such an act of interpretation. As Bultmann writes, "it must be recognized in relation to exegesis, as in relation to any historical phenomenon, that the exegete is always realizing his own potentiality-to-be, grasping his own possibility in the exegesis."[148] In a word, it is not history as an "object" for study that yields theologically interesting results, but only history grasped as a challenge to decision and commitment.

The Teaching of Jesus and Religion
For Bultmann, this conclusion is merely reinforced by an examination of the Jesus traditions. We have just seen that Bultmann's examination of the early Christian message leads him toward an existentialist interpretation. But a closer examination of what we *do* know of the historical Jesus leads him to the same conclusion. Bultmann argues that the earliest tra-ditions about Jesus are of little theological interest, since they contain little that truly belongs to the sphere of religion. They, too, are in need of existential reinterpretation.

We find this extraordinary claim in another 1920 article for *Christliche Welt*, entitled "Ethical and Mystical Religion in Early Christianity." Here Bultmann writes that Jesus' sayings fall into two categories. The first category of sayings is characterized by the "child-like belief in provi-dence and naïve optimism"[149] that we find in the Old Testament psalms and wisdom literature, as well as in the naïve popular religion of other cultures. A second group of sayings belongs to the category of apocalyp-tic. In these sayings Jesus' picture of God is "the mythical [picture] of

[146]Bultmann, *Jesus and the Word*, 12.
[147]Bultmann, "The Significance of 'Dialectical Theology' for the Scientific Study of the New Testament," 151.
[148]Ibid.
[149]*Kindlicher Vorsehungsglaube und naiver Optimismus;* Rudolf Bultmann, "Ethische und mystische Religion im Urchristentum" (1920), in *Anfänge der dialektischen Theologie,* 2:44.

eschatology."[150] (We will return to this point shortly.) What is important to note is that, for Bultmann, neither set of sayings represents a *religious* claim in the true sense of that word.[151] The salvation for which Jesus hoped (i.e., the kingdom of God) was merely a combination of ethical ideals with worldly hopes and pious reverence. It was not, in the strict sense of the word, a properly "religious" good. This kind of expectation becomes religious, Bultmann continues, only when the individual senses the *existential demand* of these moral ideals and worldly hopes. In other words, even Jesus' own teaching becomes truly religious only through its transformation into existential proclamation. It becomes religious only when—in Bultmann's own words—"the human being, who submits to the demands of the good, experiences thereby an inner history, in which he grasps a reality which is not that of the moral ideal, but of life."[152]

This statement could hardly be understood if one had not already grasped Bultmann's delimitation of the sphere of the religious. (See the first section of the present chapter.) As we have seen, for Bultmann the religious sphere is not about anything "objective"; it does not deal with realities that can be subjected to a lawlike rationality. Religion is not even to be identified with our highest ethical ideals, for these, too, are the product of reason. Rather, religion has to do with the transforming power that an individual experiences in her own existence. It is about the "wholly other" of which Rudolf Otto spoke in his *The Idea of the Holy.*[153] The ethical idea of the good, on the other hand, is not "wholly other," since it is the product of human reason. The realm of religion, by way of contrast, is that of the inner history of the individual, an inner history which may be provoked by the individual's encounter with the rational law of morality, but which is not identical with it.

It should by now be clear why for Bultmann the historical figure of Jesus was of little importance. It is of little importance for the same reason that any other type of "objectifying" knowledge is of little significance for faith. Not even the historical Jesus can be the locus of revelation. As Bultmann writes in his essay on miracles, "to apply the conception of revelation to the historically demonstrable personality of Jesus is as senseless as to apply the conception of creation and of wonder to the world seen as nature."[154] It follows that the historian's scepticism

---

[150]Ibid.: *In anderen Aussagen ist seine Gottesvorstellung die mythische der Eschatologie.*

[151]Cf. ibid.: *Beide Vorstellungen wird man kaum als eigentlich religiös bezeichnen können.*

[152]*Wenn der Mensch, der sich der Forderung des Guten beugt, dabei eine innere Geschichte erlebt, in der er eine Wirklichkeit erfaßt, die nicht die des sittlichen Ideals ist, sondern eine Lebenswirklichkeit* (ibid.).

[153]Cf. ibid., 45.

[154]Bultmann, "The Question of Wonder," 261.

can in no way threaten Christian claims. For that scepticism concerns nothing more than the "Christ after the flesh" of 2 Corinthians 5:16. In his 1927 essay on Christology, Bultmann writes that he has no reason to engage in "salvage operations," in the manner of so many conservative New Testament scholars, seeing what can be rescued from the fires of criticism. Rather, as he writes, "I calmly let the fire burn, for I see that what is consumed is only the fanciful portraits of Life-of-Jesus theology, and that means nothing other than 'Christ after the flesh' (χριστὸς κατὰ σάρκα)."[155] What is important is the Jesus of the early Christian proclamation (or *kerygma*), for through this proclamation the revelation of God's forgiveness reaches us, with its call to decision. Bultmann's indifference to the results of historical research extends to the resurrection of Jesus. He is not interested in speculations about the mode of existence of the risen Christ, about the empty grave or the Easter stories. Bultmann's critics had alleged that he reduced the resurrection of Jesus to the idea that "Jesus has risen in the proclamation of the church."[156] Bultmann's response is to argue that—rightly understood—this statement is entirely correct. As he writes, "to believe in the Christ present in the *kerygma*, that is the meaning of Easter faith."[157]

The Meaning of Apocalyptic

Despite his radical reinterpretation of the significance of history, Bultmann's break with the tradition of nineteenth and early twentieth-century theology was never as radical and uncompromising as that of Barth. He remained, after all, not only a theologian but also an exegete of some note. In his autobiographical sketch, Bultmann makes the point that his criticisms of liberal theology never lead him to a blanket condemnation of the movement. "On the contrary," he writes, "I have endeavoured throughout my entire work to carry further the tradition of historical-critical research as it was practiced [*sic*] by the 'liberal' theology and to make our more recent theological knowledge fruitful for it."[158] Indeed, he elsewhere hints at the need, not to reject historical research, but to "modify, enrich or clarify the method of historical investigation."[159]

[155]Rudolf Bultmann, "On the Question of Christology" (1927) in *Faith and Understanding*, 132.
[156]Cf. Bultmann, *Das Verhältnis der urchristlichen Christusbotschaft zum historischen Jesus*, 27.
[157]*An dem im Kerygma präsenten Christus glauben, ist der Sinn des Osterglaubens* (ibid.).
[158]Rudolf Bultmann, "Autobiographical Reflections" (1956), in *Existence and Faith*, 288.
[159]Bultmann, "The Significance of 'Dialectical Theology' for the Scientific Study of the New Testament," 146.

Furthermore, while he describes as misguided any attempt to write a biography of Jesus or a study of his personality, his own study of Jesus offers a substantial reconstruction of what he himself calls Jesus' "purpose."[160]

(a) Jesus' Proclamation of the Kingdom

Bultmann's reconstruction of Jesus' purpose owes much to the historical work of (among others) Johannes Weiss and Albert Schweitzer. As will already be clear, Bultmann's Jesus is above all an eschatological prophet. His life and death can be understood only in the context of his expectation of the imminent arrival of God's kingdom. Bultmann entirely rejects the idea—which has been revived in our own time—that Jesus was merely a moral teacher, a teacher of some kind of ethical wisdom. He considers the possibility that the eschatological elements in Jesus' reported teaching could have been added by the early church, but he believes this suggestion to be implausible.[161] Indeed, he argues that Jesus "was probably far more an eschatological prophet than is apparent from the tradition."[162] It follows that Jesus' teaching cannot be identified with our modern idea of a "highest good," as is found (for instance) in the theology of the great nineteenth-century figure of Albrecht Ritschl.[163] Nor has Jesus' conception of the kingdom of God anything to do with the ideal of a community living by his moral teaching.[164] For Jesus the kingdom of God is in no way a matter of human achievement; it is not within our control. In this respect Bultmann is in agreement with Weiss and Schweitzer. Yet in describing Jesus' adaptation of the apocalyptic teaching of his time, Bultmann also gives that teaching a new slant. This transformation lies at the heart of Bultmann's reinterpretation of apocalyptic, and it deserves a closer examination.

In Bultmann's reconstruction of Jesus' purpose, he focuses on what he calls the "real meaning" of Jesus' eschatological message.[165] This real meaning no longer has to do with a coming age or a coming world order. It is true that both Jesus and his contemporaries expected some kind of "tremendous eschatological drama."[166] They expected the coming

---

[160]Cf. Bultmann, *Jesus and the Word*, 14.

[161]Cf. ibid., 91–92.

[162]Ibid., 92.

[163]Cf. ibid., 33–34. For Ritschl's view, see (for example) his *Instruction in the Christian Religion*, §5, in Albrecht Ritschl, *Three Essays,* translated by Philip Hefner (Philadelphia: Fortress Press, 1972), 222; see also my anthology *The Historical Jesus Quest,* 154–55.

[164]Cf. Bultmann, *Jesus and the Word*, 90.

[165]Cf. ibid., 47.

[166]Ibid., 35.

of a messianic figure (the "Son of Man" of Daniel 7), the resurrection of the dead, a heavenly judgment and a fiery punishment. However, while Jesus undoubtedly shared these expectations, he shows no interest in *describing* these future events. For Jesus the coming kingdom of God represents merely what Bultmann calls "the transcendent event, which signifies for man the ultimate Either-Or, which constrains him to decision."[167] In other words, Jesus' attention is focused not on the future events themselves but on their implications for present behavior. (What those implications are is a question we will examine shortly.) For Jesus the important thing about the kingdom of God is that it is a future act of God that demands a certain response in the present. More generally, we may say that the kingdom of God represents the demand of the future on human existence, the demand that one make a decision, a decision that will shape one's identity. It is understandable that Jesus should believe that the coming of the kingdom is imminent, because at every hour human beings are faced with this "crisis of decision."[168] In a sense "every hour is the last hour."[169] In Jesus' teaching this idea comes to expression in mythological terms, namely, in the apocalyptic images of future glory.[170] What has contemporary value in Jesus' teaching is not, therefore, the mythological imagery of apocalyptic thought. (Here, too, a "demythologizing" is needed.) What has lasting value is the particular "conception of human existence" that underlies Jesus' teaching,[171] namely the "conception of man as forced to a decision through a future act of God."[172]

Clearly Bultmann is here going beyond a simple historical description of Jesus' teaching. This is entirely consistent with Bultmann's understanding of the hermeneutical task. As we saw earlier in this chapter, Bultmann believed that—when dealing with the records of human culture—it is not enough simply to describe the past. Such a description would fail to reveal the significance of the past *for us*. It would fail to bring to light the possibilities of human existence contained in those records. Accordingly, Bultmann makes it clear that he has little interest in Jesus' purpose "as a part of history."[173] Rather, his focus is that element in his purpose "which makes a present demand on us."[174] He therefore

---

[167]Ibid., 37.
[168]Ibid., 44.
[169]Ibid.
[170]Cf. ibid., 47.
[171]Ibid., 45.
[172]Ibid., 47.
[173]Ibid., 14.
[174]Ibid.

grapples with Jesus' teaching until he finds what from this point of view appears to be its essential element: the proclamation of a future act of God that calls one to decision in the present. This constitutes the aspect of Jesus' teaching that can be appropriated for today.

We should not underestimate the theological achievement in Bultmann's re-appropriation of Jesus' apocalyptic message. As we saw in chapter 3, Albert Schweitzer despaired of being able to find any positive meaning in this aspect of Jesus' life. Jesus' apocalyptic teaching was so shaped by a worldview we can no longer accept that it remained—for Schweitzer—irretrievably foreign. Schweitzer could only hold onto Jesus' moral teaching and suggest that for Jesus such behavior might hasten the coming of God's kingdom. By way of contrast, Bultmann has succeeded in appropriating that message for the contemporary reader. He has done so by reading this teaching "existentially," in terms of what it demands of the individual faced with its challenge. But this reappropriation has come at a cost, for Bultmann has made Jesus' message of significance to the later reader only by emptying it of almost all its positive content. It is reduced to nothing more than the ("mythological") proclamation of a future act of God that summons human beings to an act of obedience.

(b) Jesus' Ethics

Bultmann's reinterpretation of Jesus' ethical teaching is equally bold, and it also comes at a cost. He first of all rejects the idea that Jesus' ethical teachings were merely an interim ethic, a set of "practical rules for the last, short span of time which remained before the end" (as Schweitzer had suggested).[175] Bultmann argues that this view underestimates the radical character of Jesus' teaching. But he also insists that Jesus offers no ethical system and no positive view of the future. As he writes, Jesus "knows no ends for our conduct, only God's purpose; no human future, only God's future."[176] The one concern in Jesus' teaching, Bultmann writes, "was that man should conceive his immediate concrete situation as the decision to which he is constrained, and should decide in this moment for God and surrender his natural will."[177] It follows that for Jesus the demands of God are mediated neither by the Law of Moses nor by some kind of ethical theory. These demands arise "quite simply from the crisis of decision in which man stands before God."[178] In this

---

[175]Ibid., 93.
[176]Ibid., 96.
[177]Ibid.
[178]Ibid., 67.

moment, Bultmann insists, "no standard whatsoever from the past or the present is available"; rather, "*now* man must know what to do and leave undone."[179] More precisely, the only thing Jesus commands is love. For Jesus the will of God insofar as it concerns human behavior *is* the commandment of love (love being understood here as "an act of will").[180] "If a man really loves," Bultmann writes, "he knows already what he has to do."[181] But even this command is not to be understood as an ethical ideal, but as a spelling out of the meaning of radical obedience. It follows that Jesus' ethical teaching may also be reduced to a call to radical obedience in the light of a future act of God, an act whose content cannot be described except "mythologically."

4. Revelation and Religion

Bultmann was quick to recognize that the challenge of history to religious authority was not just in the field of biblical interpretation. The historical consciousness of our age affects one's view of Christianity *as a whole*. Indeed, Bultmann has given us a concise statement of the various dimensions of this problem. In a 1931 essay entitled "The Crisis in Belief," Bultmann writes:

> Have we still something to say about the crisis in which belief is placed by the *science of history*—in that this science deals critically with the New Testament, and casts doubt on our knowledge of the historical Jesus— and, further, places the Christian religion in the context of the history of religions as a whole, thus giving it a relative status as one phenomenon among others?[182]

I have examined Bultmann's general understanding of history (insofar as that lends itself to a clear exposition), as well as his understanding of the historical Jesus. I must now turn briefly to his understanding of the other dimension of that crisis: the question of the place of Christianity among the history of religions.

I might begin by recalling a fact that I have already highlighted, namely, that from Bultmann's point of view, there cannot be—strictly speaking—a history of *religion*.[183] There can, of course, be a history of *religions,* but for Bultmann such a history would be (at best) a history of the

---

[179]Ibid., 68.
[180]Ibid., 88.
[181]Ibid., 72.
[182]Rudolf Bultmann, "The Crisis in Belief" (1931), in *Essays Philosophical and Theological,* 18.
[183]Cf. Bultmann, "Religion und Kultur," 22.

cultural forms of religious life, not a history of religious life itself. Religious life has little to do with the forms of cultural life, for these are always objectifying and lawlike (*gesetzmässig*). Rather, religion has to do with the sphere of the individual's existence. We have already seen that this is a key distinction in Bultmann's thought. In principle, we might note, there is nothing to prevent one who accepts this distinction from generalizing it. One could regard it as applicable to any religious tradition. Any religion, it could be argued, may be viewed either from the point of view of the cultural forms that sustain it or from the point of view of its existential meaning.[184] By itself, therefore, this observation leaves unanswered the question of Christianity's relationship to other religious traditions.

To answer that question we may turn to Bultmann's essay on "The Problem of 'Natural Theology,'" published in 1933. (Later essays merely reinforce the points made here, as my footnotes will suggest.) Bultmann begins this work by noting that "for Protestantism," a natural theology is impossible. For the Protestant understanding of faith does not admit that any knowledge of God is possible apart from revelation. It holds, as Bultmann writes, that "God becomes manifest only through his revelation and that in the light of that revelation everything which was previously called God is not God."[185] On the basis of this principle Bultmann argues that traditional forms of natural theology are unthinkable. But equally unacceptable is the new form of natural theology that seeks to base its claims on the philosophy of religion. Such a theology must regard Christianity as merely one instance of the phenomenon called "religion." (As we have seen, the clearest representative of this new style of natural theology is Ernst Troeltsch, to whose work Bultmann alludes.) The problem with such a theology, Bultmann argues, is that it reduces the object of faith to something within this world. As he writes, it transforms "faith . . . into a human attitude" and results in "the elimination of God as the 'Beyond,' as the Other in relation to man."[186] Instead of revelation and faith, Bultmann writes, this theology can only speak of "processes of the soul or of consciousness."[187]

Yet, while rejecting any form of natural theology, Bultmann concedes that the questions it raises remain important. They remain important for three reasons. Firstly, the Christian gospel can (and must) be understood

---

[184]This seems to be the position adopted some years ago by Wilfred Cantwell Smith in his book *The Meaning and End of Religion* (1962; London: SPCK, 1978).

[185]Bultmann, "The Problem of 'Natural Theology'" in *Faith and Understanding,* 314.

[186]Ibid.

[187]Ibid.

even by one who is not a believer. This raises the question of how such an understanding is possible. Secondly, the existence of *other* religions raises the question as to whether they, too, are speaking of God. Thirdly, the discipline of philosophy also claims to understand human existence. For this reason the claims of philosophy overlap those of theology, and their relationship must be clarified. I will leave aside Bultmann's treatment of the first question and the third, and focus on the second, for this is the issue with which I am concerned here.

"What does it mean," Bultmann asks, "*when other religions or when men in general outside the Christian faith speak of God or to God?*"[188] In the light of the principle that we know God only through revelation, Bultmann can assert only that they are mistaken. Other religions "are not really speaking of and to God, because they are not speaking of and to the true God."[189] The followers of other religions may *appear* to speak of God, but in fact they are speaking of an idol, a mere human invention. As Bultmann writes, "all religions, apart from faith, remain fixed in unbelief, in idol worship. Faith rejects the idea that God is revealed everywhere in religions and in religious people."[190] Of what, then, do these other religions speak, if they do not speak of the true God? Bultmann responds that they are speaking (at best) of the world. It may be the world understood as the abode of elemental spirits, it may be the world "in its unity and conformity to law (*Gesetzlichkeit*). . . regarded as God,"[191] or it may be the world of human consciousness, which is regarded as in some sense divine. In any case, these other religions are speaking only about the world; they are not speaking about the true God.

What all religions have in common—Bultmann continues—is that they speak of God as a "supreme being." Bultmann concedes that this supreme being may easily be conceived as nothing other than the projection of man's desires. Echoing Feuerbach, Bultmann writes that "*man speaks of God because he knows himself beset by his own desires and fears, because he knows himself helpless before the unknown, before the enigma. He hypostasizes his dream-wishes and his fears into a being who can bring fulfilment or annihilation to his life.*"[192] But Bultmann adds immediately that this fictitious being, a being created out of human hopes and fears, is not the biblical God. Therefore, a belief in this fictitious being cannot act as a foundation for Christian faith: it does not constitute what was traditionally called a *preparatio evangelica* (a preparation for the Gospel), except

[188]Ibid., 318.
[189]Ibid.
[190]Ibid.
[191]Ibid.
[192]Ibid., 319.

in a negative sense.[193] The God spoken of outside of Christianity is quite simply *not the biblical God.* The revelation of the true God comes as the denial of this created deity: it contradicts what Bultmann calls "the purpose (*intentio*) of the natural man,"[194] who seeks to make himself secure by possessing divine power. Revelation does not build on our natural concept of God; rather, it subjects that concept to judgment.

It is true that both Christian revelation and human religion use the word ("God") for the object of their worship. But this does not mean that religion and revelation actually *have* the same object. All religions may represent a search for God, but that does not mean that the God who is sought is the true God. The true God becomes known only through revelation.[195] Bultmann therefore rejects the idea that Christianity should be seen as the high point of a history of religions. It is true—Bultmann concedes elsewhere—that in a certain sense Christianity can be viewed in this way.[196] It has the *outward form* of a high point in religious history. But this is to regard Christianity as what Bultmann calls "a phenomenon of the history of the human mind, or of religion."[197] It is to lose sight of its claim to be a divine revelation. All attempts to demonstrate the truth of Christianity by viewing it as a phenomenon of religious history are therefore misguided. Bultmann entirely rejects the possibility of a "theology of the history of religions," exemplified by the work of Troeltsch and picked up in our own time (as we will see) by Wolfhart Pannenberg. The best one can say about human religion is that it has grasped the *question* to which the revelation of God is the *answer.* There does exist a point of contact between revelation and the unbeliever. That point of contact is the question posed by human existence.[198] But even this point of contact is a negative one, since existence outside of faith can only be inauthentic existence. In any case, even if human religion has grasped the question of human existence, the question is *not* the answer.[199] The God worshiped outside of Christianity may therefore be rightly described as nothing more than "the devil."[200]

---

[193]See also Rudolf Bultmann, "The Question of Natural Revelation" (1941), in *Essays Philosophical and Theological,* 113, and "Points of Contact and Conflict" (1946), in *Essays Philosophical and Theological,* 135, where Bultmann asserts that "*God's action conflicts with man,* and with man in his religion at that."

[194]Bultmann, "The Problem of 'Natural Theology,'" 319.

[195]Cf. ibid., 321.

[196]Cf. Bultmann, "Points of Contact and Conflict," 133.

[197]Ibid., 134.

[198]Cf. Bultmann, "Points of Contact and Conflict," 137.

[199]Cf. Bultmann, "The Problem of 'Natural Theology,'" 323.

[200]Ibid., 322.

It is clear that with such remarks Bultmann is not discussing the place of Christianity among the religions. Rather, he is refusing to admit that Christianity belongs there. More precisely, while *Christianity* as a phenomenon of cultural history might belong in the history of religions, *Christian faith* surely does not. For Christian faith is a response to divine revelation. Interestingly, Bultmann seems even less prepared than Barth to concede that such revelation may occur outside of the Christian dispensation. He simply rejects the idea of what he calls "other revelations besides that in Christ."[201] Yet Bultmann and Barth are at one in rejecting the idea that Christian revelation falls into the historical category of religion. In his "Autobiographical Reflections" of 1956, Bultmann writes of the dialectical theology:

> It seemed to me that in this new theological movement it was rightly recognized, as over against the "liberal" theology out of which I had come, that the Christian faith is not a phenomenon of the history of religion, that it does not rest upon a "religious *a priori* " (Troeltsch), and that therefore theology does not have to look upon it as the phenomenon of a religious or cultural history. It seemed to me that, as over against such a view, the new theology had correctly seen that Christian faith is the answer to the word of the transcendent God that encounters man.[202]

This clear distinction between (Christian) faith and religion enables both Bultmann and Barth to accept the worst that modern critics of religion have been able to assert.[203] They are able to accept these criticisms, because they have withdrawn Christian faith from the sphere to which such criticisms apply. The God of whom Christian faith speaks is entirely different from the God attacked by the modern criticism of religion. This strategy naturally infuriates latter-day critics of religion.[204] But it is not entirely arbitrary. It is not, as many critics suspect, a mere ad hoc response to the criticism of religion. Bultmann is here drawing upon important elements of his traditional Lutheran faith, just as Barth is drawing on aspects of the Calvinist tradition. For those who can bring themselves to accept its assumptions, the effectiveness of this strategy cannot be denied.

[201]Bultmann, "The Question of Natural Revelation," 114.

[202]Bultmann, "Autobiographical Reflections," 287–88.

[203]For Barth's attitude, which parallels Bultmann's, see his "Ludwig Feuerbach" (1920), in *Theology and Church: Shorter Writings 1920–1928,* translated by Louise Pettibone Smith (London: SCM, 1962), 217–37.

[204]See, for instance, Preus (*Explaining Religion,* 54), who regards this exemption of Christian faith from the criticism of religion as "quite arbitrary."

5. The Legacy of Bultmann

The Success of Bultmann's Theology

If we wish to list the strengths of Bultmann's theology, we may begin with his hermeneutical principles. Bultmann is surely right to insist that a historical text has not been fully understood until we have grasped its significance for our time. In this respect he is at one with Barth, although Barth would distance himself from Bultmann's adoption of certain philosophical categories. These hermeneutical insights have implications that go well beyond the field of theology. They are echoed, for example, in the work of the philosopher Hans-Georg Gadamer. Indeed Gadamer's major study, *Truth and Method,* praises both Barth and Bultmann,[205] while noting that Bultmann's work is "too much bound up with dogmatic tensions to be conducive to methodological reflection."[206]

With regard to the larger question of history and religious authority, Bultmann's theology is a powerful response to the challenges that first emerged in the seventeenth century. By insisting that the sphere of religion (rightly understood) is entirely different from that of human culture, Bultmann has shielded Christian faith from the challenges of both the natural sciences and history. The action of God is accessible to neither the scientist nor the historian, whose forms of "objectifying" knowledge are helpless before the claims of faith. With regard to the question of the historical Jesus, Bultmann can accept the most sceptical results of biblical criticism without concern. For the focus of his faith is not the historical figure of Jesus, but the Christ of the early Christian proclamation. It is this figure through whom the existential challenge of faith reaches the contemporary believer. If attention is drawn to the apocalyptic element in both Jesus' teaching and the early church's proclamation, Bultmann is quick to insist that this, too, can and ought to be interpreted existentially. For what apocalyptic represents is a call to radical obedience in the light of a future action of God. If historical research might seem to relegate Christianity to the place of one religion among others, Bultmann can simply insist that—rightly understood—Christian faith is not a matter of "religion" at all. It cannot be understood in the historian's categories. Bultmann's much-vaunted liberalism is thus a painless liberalism, for he has created a storm-free area within which the believer may continue to sail smoothly, untouched by the waves of criticism.

Finally, one should not overlook the strength of the philosophical traditions from which Bultmann's work draws. Of particular importance is

---

[205]Hans-Georg Gadamer, *Truth and Method,* 463, 473.
[206]Ibid., 473. My own judgment will echo Gadamer's (see below).

the tradition that dates from the time of Søren Kierkegaard (1813–55) and was developed in the phenomenological philosophy of Martin Heidegger (1889–1976). That tradition reminds us—in the words of Bryan Magee—that "all real existence is individual and therefore not to be captured in generalizing systems of abstract thinking."[207] Human beings in particular cannot be adequately understood "as material objects governed by scientific laws."[208] The problem is that Bultmann, as theologian, tries to smuggle the Christian God into the gaps he has created in our "law-governed" (*gesetzmässig*) view of the world. (In our own day, some theologically inclined readers of Emmanuel Levinas seem to be engaged in a similar project.) The theologian may, of course, choose to use the word "God" when speaking of this realm of subjectivity. But as soon as the theologian assigns a *content* to that word, as she must if she is to speak of the *biblical* God, she lapses back into objectifying thought. The attempt to enlist phenomenological analyses of consciousness in the service of religious claims seems doomed to fall into the antinomies that were Bultmann's downfall.[209]

Unresolved and Unresolvable Tensions

A defining characteristic of Bultmann's thought is precisely this: his tendency to think in antitheses. This characteristic not only marks the entirety of Bultmann's writing; it may be regarded as its fatal flaw. It is fatal, because it is inseparable from his theological project, being rooted in both a particular philosophical position and Bultmann's strongly Lutheran theology. It follows that one cannot rescue Bultmann's theology by recasting it in some nonantithetical form. This tendency to think in antitheses is a flaw, because it sets in opposition matters that cannot be regarded as strictly opposed. The falsity of such oppositions is already evident in the examples which Bultmann draws from everyday life, where the "lived reality" of, say, fatherhood or love presupposes a certain biological foundation, which *can* be described "objectively." More seriously, the same tendency to false antitheses marks Bultmann's theology, which sets faith and objectifying knowledge in opposition, the latter being a form of godlessness from which we need to be liberated. The problem here is that Bultmann also admits that objectifying knowledge is rooted in the

---

[207]Bryan Magee, *Confessions of a Philosopher* (New York: Modern Library, 1997), 431.
[208]Ibid., 452.
[209]The deeper problem here may be the inability of the phenomenological tradition to deal adequately with the relationship between the "first-person" world of consciousness and the "third-person" world of the sciences (cf. ibid., 428, 455–56). The most it can do is to set these in an unfruitful opposition. But further exploration of this question lies beyond the scope of the present work.

fact of our being in the world, a simple and inescapable consequence of our being embodied creatures. Furthermore, objectifying knowledge remains the foundation for the claims of faith. Only through such knowledge can we come to know—"existentially"—of the demands of God on our existence. Therefore, the opposition between these two forms of knowledge cannot be maintained. No appeal to the Lutheran principle of *simul justus et peccator,* no talk of "dialectic" or "paradox" can preserve Bultmann's theology from incoherence at this critical point.

Even if successful, Bultmann's careful demarcation of the realm of religion from that of "objectifying" knowledge would come at a considerable cost. For it would mean consigning to religious insignificance our ordinary knowledge of the natural world and of human history. Such knowledge is at its best "godless." Our knowledge of the world is thus divided into an "objectifying" knowledge that is inauthentic and godless and an existential knowledge that alone has meaning. (I have noted a similar weakness in the thought of Albert Schweitzer, who asserts his ethic of "reverence for life" in the face of a world order that in practically every respect seems to contradict it.) Religious claims have been saved, but at the expense of radically reducing the sphere within which they may be said to apply. Bultmann is not alone in this respect. In a recent study Frederick Gregory has traced the process by which a tradition of modern theology simply abandoned claims regarding the natural world. Bultmann's theology may be regarded as the culmination of this trend. The loss to theology of the natural world, Gregory argues, is not only out of step with what Christians have traditionally believed and—at grassroots level—continue to assert. It also has undesirable consequences, since it risks abandoning the natural world to unbridled technical manipulation.[210]

Still more seriously, we have seen that Bultmann locates the sphere of religion beyond the realm of *Gesetzmässigkeit,* of that which is bound and measured by law. But if one moves beyond that realm, then in a certain sense one has moved beyond the bounds of rationality. The Marburg neo-Kantians, for all their desire to find a place for religion, were very aware of this fact. For instance, in his posthumously published work *Religion of Reason out of the Sources of Judaism,* Hermann Cohen wrote that, however much religion goes beyond ethics in its focus on the individual in relationship to God, it "cannot violate the unifying method" of reason.[211] Since reason is the realm of law, then "the religion of reason

[210]Cf. Gregory, *Nature Lost?,* 261–64.

[211]Cf. Hermann Cohen, *Religion of Reason out of the Sources of Judaism* (1919), translated by Simon Kaplan (New York: Frederick Ungar, 1972), 16.

comes under the light of lawfulness."[212] By way of contrast, Bultmann insists that the voice of reason *cannot* be the voice of God. As he writes, "the pious man may trace his rational abilities . . . back to God, but this does not alter the fact that *in the use of his reason it is not God who speaks to him.*"[213] If not in the realm of reason, then in what realm does God speak? More seriously, how may we distinguish the voice of God from other voices, if not by the use of reason? By setting the realm of religion in opposition to that of reason, Bultmann opens up a space for Christian faith, but that same faith could equally be filled with any kind of irrationality.

A Nonevidentialist View of Faith
It follows that the difficulty facing Bultmann's theology is closely related to the difficulties I have identified with the theology of Karl Barth. That is to say, such a theology soon becomes untenable, at least for one who holds to what I there called an "evidentialist" view of faith. According to this view, Christian faith may perhaps take us *beyond* what can be rationally demonstrated, but it should not be held *in defiance of* reason. More than that, it should have some *rational grounds,* in the sense of being defensible over against alternative religious and metaphysical commitments. It could be argued that this understanding of faith is itself the result of an arbitrary commitment, namely, a commitment to certain norms of rationality. In fact, I would regard such norms as simply inseparable from the discussion in which we are all engaged. (There is no obligation to continue the tradition of reasoned discussion, but the person who raises this question has already accepted its rules.) Within that discussion, the obligation to subject faith commitments to rational scrutiny is a simple consequence of the intellectual revolution of the seventeenth century. For better or for worse, that revolution reduced Christianity to one religion among others, obliged to demonstrate its claims at the tribunal of secular reason. By calling into question biblical authority, the thinkers of the seventeenth century made an evidentialist view of faith compulsory. (Even Alvin Plantinga, its most powerful recent opponent, must develop his alternative understanding of faith on the basis of general philosophical considerations. He is engaged in the apparently paradoxical operation of bringing a different kind of evidence *against* an evidentialist view of faith.[214]) Ernst Troeltsch, in particular, fully accepted

[212]Ibid., 10.
[213]Bultmann, "Religion und Kultur," 16: *Der fromme Mensch mag seine Vernunftbegabung . . . auf Gott zurückführen; das ändert nichts an der Tatsache, daß im Gebrauch seiner Vernunft nicht Gott zu ihm spricht* (emphasis mine).
[214]On these matters, see the final section of chapter 5.

this "great reversal," and set out to demonstrate—without complete success—that Christian authority could still be defended. Troeltsch was, therefore, the evidentialist theologian *par excellence.*

Bultmann, like Barth before him, simply rejects this requirement outright. This becomes particularly clear in his 1952 essay "On the Problem of Demythologizing," where he writes that the demythologizing project

> is the parallel to the Pauline-Lutheran doctrine of justification through faith alone without the works of the law. Or, rather, it is the consistent application of this doctrine to the field of knowledge. Like the doctrine of justification, it destroys every false security and every false demand for security, whether it is grounded on our good action or on our certain knowledge. Those who would believe in God as their God need to know that they have nothing in hand on the basis of which they could believe, that they are poised, so to speak, in midair and cannot ask for any proof of the word that addresses them. For the ground and the object of faith are identical.[215]

The Lutheran doctrine of justification by faith is here given an epistemological twist, or—more precisely—Bultmann's epistemology is given a Lutheran twist. To ask for evidence that would support Christian faith is equivalent to seeking to be justified before God by one's works. Bultmann does not say as much—at least not in this context—but the implication would seem to be that to ask for evidence is merely an expression of unbelief and of sin.

On the one hand, therefore, Bultmann's theology approaches that of Barth, in its simple rejection of the demand for justification. In a closely related move—since any justification of faith would be a matter of fallible human judgment—Bultmann also insists that the knowledge appropriate to faith must be *certain* knowledge, beyond the reach of doubt. For instance, in his 1924 essay, Bultmann writes that

> historical research can never lead to any result which could serve as a basis for faith, for *all its results have only relative validity.* How widely the pictures of Jesus presented by liberal theologians differ from one another! How uncertain is all knowledge of "the historical Jesus"! Is he really within the scope of our knowledge? Here research ends with a large question mark—and here it *ought* to end. [216]

---

[215]Bultmann, "On the Problem of Demythologizing" (1952), 122.

[216]Bultmann, "Liberal Theology and the Latest Theological Movement," 30; *The Historical Jesus Quest,* 244.

By implication, Bultmann accepts Troeltsch's principle of criticism, which insists that all historical knowledge is only probable, but insists that this principle is not applicable to the knowledge on which faith is based. Similarly, Bultmann rejects the idea that theology should be subject to Troeltsch's principle of correlation. Troeltsch was right to argue that historical entities can only be understood as "relative," existing "within an immense inter-related complex" and therefore unable to claim absolute value.[217] But when this conception is applied to Jesus it can only run "exactly counter to the Christian view."[218] Similarly, in his 1928 essay Bultmann writes that human science (*Wissenschaft*) can produce only relative certainty, and for this reason it is unusable (*unbrauchbar*) for theology and the church, which demand "absolutely certain pronouncements."[219]

Insofar as it has its roots in a particular anthropology, Bultmann's theology is more open to rational discussion than is the theology of Barth. One could at least imagine recasting it in a more defensible form. For instance, it could perhaps be argued that, while historical research remains fallible, the realization of its meaning for me (as an individual, a subject) is indisputable. Because this meaning is personal and individual, it would not be open to public discussion. It would resemble, in this respect, statements describing one's inner life, such as "I experience pain." Such statements, assuming they are uttered honestly, may be regarded as incorrigible. But even this argument—the only defense of Bultmann's theology that I can muster—does not take us far. Firstly, the realization of the meaning of a historical event "for me" can only rest upon a certain "objectification," as even Bultmann concedes.[220] I must know something about the history I am studying before I can judge its existential significance. Faith cannot be completely shielded from historical fact. (As we have seen, at this point Bultmann's antitheses—so essential to his theology—break down.) Secondly, religious claims are generally thought to be claims about the world, not just about my inner state. They may be *grounded* in my inner state—insofar as their truth is revealed by

[217]Bultmann, "Liberal Theology and the Latest Theological Movement," 31; *The Historical Jesus Quest,* 246.

[218]Bultmann, "Liberal Theology and the Latest Theological Movement," 32; *The Historical Jesus Quest,* 246.

[219]Bultmann, "The Significance of 'Dialectical Theology' for the Scientific Study of the New Testament," 154; cf. "Die Bedeutung der «dialektischen Theologie» für die neutestamentliche Wissenschaft," 123. Compare Rudolf Bultmann, "Faith as Venture" (1928), in *Existence and Faith,* 57: "For man is not asked whether he will accept a theory about God that may possibly be false, but whether he is willing to obey God's will."

[220]Cf. Bultmann, "On the Problem of Demythologizing" (1961), 158–59.

way of some state of consciousness—but they claim to make reference to something outside of myself. For this reason they involve an inescapable element of interpretation and, with that, the possibility of error.[221] While no one else may be able to question the statement "I feel pain," others may legitimately question the statement "God speaks to me here." My consciousness of God may turn out to be a "false consciousness." At this point the sceptical criticism of religion—the criticism voiced, in different ways, by Marx, Nietzsche, and Freud—comes into play.

It seems, then, that there exists no invulnerable area for Christian theology, no peaceful haven sheltered from the winds of criticism, unless it be carved out by a sheer, willful assertion. But if it be carved out by sheer assertion, then it has no way of opposing those who would make contrary assertions. It steps outside the realm of discussion. We might even say that, to be successful, Bultmann's theology would need more closely to resemble that of Barth. But, in doing so, it would be subject to the same criticisms. Like the theology of Barth, it would be unable to defend itself against charges of irrationality.

---

[221]For arguments against the idea of an immediate, that is to say, uninterpreted and therefore incorrigible, religious experience, see Proudfoot, *Religious Experience,* 75–102.

Chapter Seven

In the Shadow of Bultmann

Ernst Käsemann and Wolfhart Pannenberg

> *True faith is not a state of blissful gullibility.*
> Wolfhart Pannenberg

The dialectical theology of Barth and Bultmann cast a long shadow, from which twentieth-century theology has only slowly emerged. Some theologians, of course, have been happy to continue their project. But many others came to recognize its limitations, particularly in relation to the question of history. A key moment in this development was a lecture given in 1953 by a former pupil of Bultmann, namely Ernst Käsemann. This lecture reopened the historical Jesus question and initiated what is generally described as the period of the "new quest." This work, therefore, will form the starting point of this chapter. Some twelve years later Käsemann would take up the theme again, in an essay entitled "Blind Alleys in the 'Jesus of History' controversy."[1] Since this essay deals with some of the developments since 1953, it should also receive a brief analysis.

While the anthology on which this work is based ends with the work of Käsemann, the present work takes the discussion one step further. For there is another figure whose contribution to the question of religious authority cannot be ignored: the theologian Wolfhart Pannenberg. As we will see, Pannenberg has revived the project first undertaken by Ernst Troeltsch: to rebuild Christian theology on the basis of a wholehearted acceptance of the historical consciousness of our age. Yet Pannenberg's theology differs in important respects from the theology of Troeltsch. It therefore deserves at least a brief treatment in its own right. Pannenberg believes that Christian theology can survive the challenges of history. But if his bold solution can be shown to be untenable, we may conclude that the questions first raised in the seventeenth century remain unanswered even today.

---

[1]No attempt will be made to discuss Käsemann's theology in its entirety, for it is these two works that mark his contribution to the historical Jesus debate.

1. Ernst Käsemann (1906–1998)

"The Problem of the Historical Jesus"

Ernst Käsemann's essay "The Problem of the Historical Jesus" was first presented in 1953 as a lecture to a reunion of former students of the Marburg theological faculty. In its renewed recognition of the theological significance of historical questions, it marks a break with the dialectical theology of Barth and Bultmann. Yet within this break, there is a considerable degree of continuity. For Käsemann shares many of the theological concerns of his teacher Bultmann. Following the outline of the lecture itself, I will deal first of all with what they have in common before looking at the novelty of Käsemann's position.

(a) A Continuation of the Dialectical Theology

The first point of continuity between Käsemann and Bultmann has to do with Käsemann's attitude to the liberal theology of the nineteenth century. The dialectical theologians had criticized the liberal theology from at least two points of view. Both Barth and Bultmann argued—for various reasons—that the question of the historical Jesus could not be decisive for Christian faith. Christian faith could not be built on the evidence of any particular historical facts; faith was, in principle, independent of historical knowledge. To this objection *in principle,* Bultmann added an objection *in practice.* The Gospels were such, he argued, that it was difficult or even impossible to uncover the facts about Jesus' life. This strictly historical difficulty was highlighted by the work of the form critics, who had focused attention on the way in which the Jesus traditions had been reshaped, even before they were recorded in the Gospels. It had become increasingly clear that the Gospels are records of the proclamation of the earliest Christians rather than materials for a biography of Jesus.

Käsemann endorses these criticisms, which he insists remain valid even today.[2] However, he also notes that the question of the historical Jesus has not gone away. It is being raised once again, but by rather a different group of thinkers. As Käsemann argues, there is some irony in this development. For the question of the historical Jesus was first raised by the liberal critics of traditional Christianity. They were delighted to find that the Jesus of history was *different* from the Christ of faith proclaimed by the church, for this enabled them to use their historical research to

---

[2]Cf. Ernst Käsemann, "The Problem of the Historical Jesus" (1953), translated by W. J. Montague, in *Essays on New Testament Themes,* Studies in Biblical Theology 41 (London: SCM, 1964), 15–16; reprinted in my anthology *The Historical Jesus Quest,* 279–81.

criticize the church's dogmatic formulations. In more recent times, how-ever, those who raise the historical Jesus question are doing so from a more conservative position. In reaction to the radical separation insisted upon by Bultmann (and—to a lesser degree—by Barth), they are anxious to find a *continuity* between the Jesus of history and the Christ of faith. In any case, since these matters are being discussed once again, it is important to look more closely at the theological significance of the his-torical Jesus.[3]

Käsemann's starting point is a general observation about history. He argues that the past is of no interest to us "in itself" (as it were); it is of interest only as transmitted and interpreted. It is the ongoing process of interpretation that makes the past both accessible and meaningful.[4] For the believer, too, the mere fact that certain events occurred in the past is—in itself—of little significance. What is important is *the meaning* of those events for us. Even if one could prove that certain extraordinary things happened in the past, a mere report of extraordinary events can-not serve as a basis for faith. Extraordinary events by themselves prove nothing. In some cases, such events can be shown to resemble similar events that occurred elsewhere (one assumes that Käsemann is here alluding to the comparative study of religions), in which case they are not unique. In other cases, these reported events may remain unique, but as historically unique events they represent mere "curiosities" that "can convey no certainty of revelation."[5] In general terms, then, historical facts as such are of no interest except insofar as they can be shown to be meaningful for us. It is in the meaning of the facts that we find the con-tinuity between past and present.

Now it is clear that the early Christians were at least tacitly aware of this fact. They realized that the facts of history are significant only when they are retold in a way that addresses the needs of a later audience. In Käsemann's words, the early Christians knew that "mere history only takes on genuine historical significance in so far as it can address both a question and an answer to our contemporary situation."[6] For this reason, the earliest Christian records of Jesus are already overlaid with interpre-tation. We can now see that this development was entirely appropriate. The adaptation of the message of Jesus should not be regarded as a

[3]Cf. Käsemann, "The Problem of the Historical Jesus," 17–18; *The Historical Jesus Quest,* 281–83.
[4]Cf. Käsemann, "The Problem of the Historical Jesus," 18; *The Historical Jesus Quest,* 283.
[5]Käsemann, "The Problem of the Historical Jesus," 19; *The Historical Jesus Quest,* 284.
[6]Käsemann, "The Problem of the Historical Jesus," 21; *The Historical Jesus Quest,* 286.

distortion of that message, but as the only way it could be made relevant to a later age. A genuine historical continuity demands nothing less than change and adaptation. There is, admittedly, a paradox here, but it is inescapable. As Käsemann writes, "to state the paradox as sharply as possible: the community takes so much trouble to maintain historical continuity with him who once trod this earth that it allows the historical events of this earthly life to pass for the most part into oblivion and replaces them by its own message."[7] This is why the New Testament contains history only in the form of the *kerygma,* the early Christian proclamation of Jesus as the Christ. In the New Testament documents, that history is already reinterpreted in the light of the early church's faith.

Given that this is the way in which the New Testament documents were written—with scant interest in history "as such"—scholarship has rightly abandoned any attempt to write a life of Jesus. The Jesus portrayed in the New Testament is portrayed, "*not* as he was in himself, *not* as an isolated individual, but as the Lord of the community which believes in him."[8] Any aspects of Jesus' life that do not relate to this fact are entirely overshadowed. It follows that—in Käsemann's words—"we are no longer in a position to delineate with even approximate accuracy and completeness his portrait, his development, the actual course of his life."[9] For this reason the road of theological liberalism—which sought to uncover Jesus' life story and correct the church's faith accordingly—was rightly abandoned. Even if one raises again the question of the historical Jesus, Käsemann insists, it cannot be done with a view to reviving this liberal project.

(b) A Break with the Dialectical Theology

With these qualifications firmly established, Käsemann can now turn his attention to the other side of the historical Jesus debate. For while he accepts these criticisms of the liberal theological project, he also insists that liberal theology embodied some legitimate concerns. One of these concerns is represented by the historical Jesus question. This question remains important, not simply because secular historians continue to pose questions about the founder of Christianity, but because it is at the heart of the New Testament witness.[10] No matter how deeply the

---

[7]Käsemann, "The Problem of the Historical Jesus," 20; *The Historical Jesus Quest,* 285.
[8]Käsemann, "The Problem of the Historical Jesus," 23; *The Historical Jesus Quest,* 288.
[9]Ibid.
[10]Cf. Käsemann, "The Problem of the Historical Jesus," 24; *The Historical Jesus Quest,* 289.

earliest Christians buried the historical Jesus under layers of reinterpretation, they clearly understood their proclamation of the Gospel to be
grounded in the events of his life, death, and resurrection. In other
words, while early Christian faith is based on belief in the resurrected
and exalted Christ, it will not allow what Käsemann calls "myth to take
the place of history nor a heavenly being to take the place of the Man of
Nazareth."[11]

The early Christians, then, for all their reinterpretation of the message
of Jesus, are also concerned that their message be based upon historical
events. Paradoxically, this fact is most clearly revealed in those parts of the
Gospel that we would regard as historically unreliable. Käsemann takes as
an example the infancy narrative of Matthew's Gospel. He describes
these chapters as nothing less than the "historification" [*Historisierung*] of
Old Testament legends. Matthew assumes that the early life of Jesus must
have taken the same form as that of Moses, and "records" the stories of
his birth accordingly. (As we saw in chapter 2, this is essentially D. F.
Strauss's understanding of "myth.") What does this fact tell us? It shows
that the early Christians were so keen to demonstrate that the *kerygma*
had a historical grounding that, where necessary, they were prepared to
invent an appropriate history. This process seems to have occurred very
early in Christian history. As Käsemann writes, "Matthew no longer has
any doubt that he is recapitulating genuine history."[12] By handing on
what we would judge to be a fictitious history, Matthew unwittingly
bears witness to how much he valued historical facts.

(c) History and Eschatology

Yet Käsemann immediately qualifies his conclusion. It is not entirely
accurate to describe what Matthew is doing as the invention of "history,"
for Matthew's claims are rooted in an eschatological interpretation of
Jesus' life. (Here, too, Käsemann's theology converges with that of his
teacher Bultmann.) Indeed, the general pattern of the early Christian
proclamation is to see the life of Jesus, not so much as an event *within*
history (comparable to other, similar events), but as the *end* of history. It
is the point at which God breaks into history, at which God acts in a way
that sets this life apart from other historical events. Luke's two-volume
work (the Gospel and the Acts of the Apostles) constitutes what Käsemann regards as an unfortunate exception to this trend. For Luke
replaces the eschatology that dominates the other Gospels with what

---

[11]Käsemann, "The Problem of the Historical Jesus," 25; *The Historical Jesus Quest,* 290.
[12]Käsemann, "The Problem of the Historical Jesus," 26; *The Historical Jesus Quest,* 291.

Käsemann calls a kind of "salvation history."[13] He depicts the events of Jesus' life in such a way that they are both rooted in the history of Israel and extended forward into the life of the early church. For Luke, the life of Jesus is precisely that, a human life: it has both a "before" and an "after" to which it is linked in terms that are recognizably historical. The Gospel of Luke is thus what Käsemann calls "the first 'life of Jesus.'"[14] This development is an unfortunate one, since it turns the story of Jesus into what Käsemann describes as "something absolutely in the past, namely *initium Christianismi* [the beginning of the Christian religion]— mere history indeed."[15]

Fortunately, however, Luke's work is the exception to the general New Testament trend. The other evangelists are not interested in writing a biography of Jesus; his life has interest for them only insofar as it is the "point at which the eschatological events intersect."[16] The other evangelists take for granted Jesus' historical existence, but they do not portray his life in historical terms, that is to say, in terms that could be applicable to any other human being. Rather, they depict Jesus' life as what Käsemann calls "an unbroken series of divine revelations and mighty acts, which has no common basis of comparison with any other human life and thus can no longer be comprehended within the category of the historical."[17] What Käsemann seems to be arguing is that, for the Gospel writers, there is *no* analogy (in Troeltsch's sense) between Jesus' life and any other human life. Nor can the life of Jesus be adequately understood as the product of a complex of historical causes (Troeltsch's principle of correlation).

At this point Käsemann breaks into theological mode. No longer merely describing the attitude of the Gospel writers, he endorses it. By way of their eschatological treatment of the life of Jesus, the New Testament writers present his life as an ἐφ᾽ ἅπαξ (a Greek phrase meaning both 'once' and 'once for all'), that is to say, as an event that is unique.[18] This is as it should be, for divine revelation cannot be understood as the culmination of some process of historical development. As soon as it is brought within the nexus of cause and effect, it "ceases to be God's revelation."[19] It is not immediately clear what Käsemann is saying here. He seems to be insisting that, as soon as an event is understood as historically

[13]Käsemann, "The Problem of the Historical Jesus," 28; *The Historical Jesus Quest,* 293.
[14]Käsemann, "The Problem of the Historical Jesus," 29; *The Historical Jesus Quest,* 294.
[15]Ibid.
[16]Käsemann, "The Problem of the Historical Jesus," 30; *The Historical Jesus Quest,* 295.
[17]Ibid.
[18]Cf. Käsemann, "The Problem of the Historical Jesus," 30; *The Historical Jesus Quest,* 296.
[19]Käsemann, "The Problem of the Historical Jesus," 31; *The Historical Jesus Quest,* 296.

conditioned, it cannot *also* be seen as revelatory. As he writes, revelation "is what it is only when it is seen as an unconditioned happening."[20]

Now it is not immediately clear why Käsemann holds to this view. After all, Troeltsch's theology wished to argue that certain events could be seen as *both* historically conditioned *and* as divine revelation. But Käsemann rejects this option. One can only assume that he is here under the influence of Bultmann's insistence that the sphere of faith be marked off from that of lawlike (*gesetzmässig*) historical reality. In any case, Käsemann develops his argument in strongly antithetical terms, which are very reminiscent of Bultmann's work. Revelation, he writes, does not convey an idea, nor is it a matter of my coming to know certain facts; rather "it is an act which lays hold of me."[21] For this reason revelation can be rejected, since one cannot meaningfully speak of rejecting a fact. (We will return to these antitheses shortly.)

(d) The Objectivity of Faith

However eschatological the New Testament's depiction of Jesus, the Gospel writers assume that there exists a continuity between the exalted Lord and the earthly Jesus. The New Testament writers had no desire to separate the Christ of faith from the historical Jesus. History was important to them, Käsemann argues, and for this reason it should be important to us. It was important to them because it gave what we might call a degree of objectivity to their message. The New Testament writers wanted to make it clear that the call to decision with which we are faced comes from outside of ourselves. It was grounded, not just in some present experience, but in the life and death of a particular historical individual. For this reason they insisted that the Christ of faith was also the Jesus of history. It follows that Käsemann cannot accept Bultmann's attitude towards the question of the historical Jesus. Insofar as this question has to do with the continuity between the Christ of faith and the Jesus of history, it represents a matter that was important to the New Testament writers themselves. It follows that the historical Jesus question cannot be dismissed as theologically irrelevant. It remains what Käsemann calls "a genuine theological problem."[22]

(e) The Historical Jesus

Only at this point does Käsemann begin to sketch his own view of the historical figure of Jesus. He begins by reminding us once again of the

[20]Ibid.
[21]Ibid.
[22]Käsemann, "The Problem of the Historical Jesus," 34; *The Historical Jesus Quest,* 299.

difficulty of the task. He notes first of all that we can no longer doubt the legitimacy of a critical approach to the Gospels. Indeed, the key question is no longer whether criticism is permitted; it is, rather, where such criticism should stop. The burden of proof now rests, not on those who would affirm the need for criticism, but on their opponents, on those who insist that the Gospels *are* a reliable record of Jesus' words and deeds.[23] How, then, are we to go about the work of criticism? How can we identify the historical Jesus beneath these layers of interpretation? The task is made more difficult by the fact that we possess "no formal criteria" by which historically authentic material about Jesus may be recognized.[24] If we are to identify the early Christian reshaping of the Jesus traditions, then we must make some assumptions about the development of earliest Christianity. For that development would have affected this reshaping. The problem is that we simply do not know what form that development took, so that any assumptions we make in this regard are highly speculative.[25] Käsemann concludes that the only firm criterion we have is that which later became known as the criterion of "double dissimilarity." We may confidently attribute material to Jesus, he writes, "when there are no grounds either for deriving a tradition from Judaism or for ascribing it to primitive Christianity."[26] In other words, where the depiction of Jesus differs from *both* the Jewish norm *and* the Christian norm, we may be confident that it represents Jesus himself. The authenticity of such material is particularly clear when we see that the early Christian community has modified the tradition, "having found it too bold for its taste."[27]

On this basis Käsemann attempts to discern what is distinctive about the message of Jesus. He begins with the striking sayings contained in Matthew's "Sermon on the Mount" (Matthew 5–7), in which Jesus contrasts his teachings with those of Jewish tradition. At least some of these sayings appear to be genuine. If they are, then they indicate that Jesus made a truly extraordinary claim to authority. His claim to authority goes beyond that of a rabbi or a prophet, whose authority could never exceed the authority of Moses.[28] The only biblical role that could make

[23]Cf. Käsemann, "The Problem of the Historical Jesus," 34; *The Historical Jesus Quest,* 300.

[24]Cf. Käsemann, "The Problem of the Historical Jesus," 35; *The Historical Jesus Quest,* 301.

[25]Cf. Käsemann, "The Problem of the Historical Jesus," 36; *The Historical Jesus Quest,* 301–2.

[26]Käsemann, "The Problem of the Historical Jesus," 37; *The Historical Jesus Quest,* 302.
[27]Ibid.

[28]According to Käsemann ("The Problem of the Historical Jesus," 40–42; *The Historical Jesus Quest,* 306–8), the fact that Jesus acted as a teacher of wisdom is also incompatible with the role of a rabbi.

sense of such a claim is that of the Messiah. It matters little whether Jesus used this title of himself or whether (as Käsemann himself believes [29]) it was used of him only after his death.[30] Jesus' messianic claim may not have been explicit, but it was certainly implicit in his words and deeds. The same extraordinary claim to authority may be seen in Jesus' attitude to the ceremonial law and to issues of ritual purity. As Käsemann writes,

> Jesus felt himself in a position to override, with an unparalleled and sover-
> eign freedom, the words of the Torah and the authority of Moses. This
> sovereign freedom not merely shakes the very foundations of Judaism and
> causes his death, but, further, it cuts the ground from under the feet of the
> ancient world-view with its antithesis of sacred and profane and its
> demonology.[31]

This is the first conclusion of Käsemann's enquiry.[32]

The second is that Jesus' claim to authority makes most sense when viewed in the light of his eschatological (or "apocalyptic") teaching. Jesus clearly believed "that, in his word, the *basileia* [kingdom] was coming to his hearers."[33] Käsemann opposes the "realized eschatology" advocated by the English scholar C. H. Dodd: the idea that Jesus believed the kingdom of God had already come. Rather, Käsemann believes that Jesus spoke of a future kingdom, in line with the apocalyptic expectations of his time. But he modifies this idea by claiming that in the word of Jesus the kingdom of God was in a certain sense already "breaking through," presenting its hearers with the choice between obedience and disobedience.[34] (Here, too, one hears the echoes of Bultmann.) It follows that Jesus' eschatology was neither simply future nor simply present; it was an "inaugurated eschatology."[35] Convinced of the eschatological dimension of Jesus' teaching, Käsemann ends his discussion by rejecting the idea that Jesus should be regarded as primarily a moral teacher. As he writes, "Jesus did not come to proclaim general religious or moral truths, but to

[29]Cf. Käsemann, "The Problem of the Historical Jesus," 43; *The Historical Jesus Quest*, 309.

[30]Cf. Käsemann, "The Problem of the Historical Jesus," 37–38; *The Historical Jesus Quest*, 302–3.

[31]Käsemann, "The Problem of the Historical Jesus," 40; *The Historical Jesus Quest*, 305.

[32]A similar argument is put forward by Bultmann in his 1961 work *Das Verhältnis der urchristlichen Christusbotschaft zum historischen Jesus*, 16–17 (see chapter 6), to which Käsemann's 1965 essay will respond.

[33]Käsemann, "The Problem of the Historical Jesus," 43; *The Historical Jesus Quest*, 309.

[34]Cf. Käsemann, "The Problem of the Historical Jesus," 44; *The Historical Jesus Quest*, 310.

[35]Ibid.

tell of the *basileia* that had dawned and of how God was come near to man in grace and demand."[36]

What has this sketch achieved? Käsemann argues that it has achieved no more than an outline, which later research would need to fill in. But he also insists that it is *not* an outline of a "life of Jesus." For a life of Jesus would need to include an account of both his inner development and the outer course of his life, and the Gospels do not provide that sort of information. All one can show is that certain features were characteristic of the message and work of Jesus and that early Christianity "united its own message with these."[37] The discovery of this *relationship* between the Jesus of history and the Christ of faith can be said to be the one valuable result to emerge from the nineteenth-century "life of Jesus" research. Käsemann ends his discussion by reaffirming his theological continuity with the dialectical theologians under whom he was trained. He affirms that the figure of Jesus himself escapes the categories of psychology, comparative religion, and general history. The problem of the historical Jesus is "a riddle," the existence of which may be established by the historian, but that cannot be resolved by historical research alone.[38] It can be grasped only by those who accept Jesus as their Lord, and who allow his proclamation to be today, as it was then, a challenge to faith.

(f) An Evaluation

The contribution of Ernst Käsemann's 1953 essay to this debate is very clear: it raised once again the question that the dialectical theologians had done their best to set aside. Yet to raise a question is not to answer it. Indeed, Käsemann himself does not pretend to have done anything more than sketch some possible lines of enquiry. We might note that, in doing so, he begins to experience the same kinds of theological difficulties that Bultmann experienced. Käsemann insists that revelation is no longer revelation if it is reduced to a matter of historical knowledge. Indeed, he reinterprets the apocalyptic message of the New Testament as a statement that the life of Jesus cannot be understood in this way. There is a uniqueness, an ἐφ' ἅπαξ, about the life of Jesus, that eludes historical understanding. Yet Käsemann also argues that this eschatological understanding of Jesus does not *exclude* historical claims, for even the New Testament writers take for granted the continuity between the

[36]Käsemann, "The Problem of the Historical Jesus," 45; *The Historical Jesus Quest,* 311.
[37]Käsemann, "The Problem of the Historical Jesus," 46; *The Historical Jesus Quest,* 312.
[38]Cf. Käsemann, "The Problem of the Historical Jesus," 46–47; *The Historical Jesus Quest,* 312–13.

Jesus of history and the Christ of faith. These two ideas remain in an uneasy tension.

This tension may be explored by looking more closely at two other passages from Käsemann's work. The first is a passage to which I have just alluded, within the 1953 essay that has been the focus of our discussion. Käsemann here argues that revelation is "not primarily" a matter of knowing some fact; rather, it is a matter of a personal encounter with the One who reveals himself. As Käsemann writes, "in revelation, I do not primarily encounter some *thing* or other, but my ultimate Lord."[39] For this reason, Käsemann continues, revelation ceases to be revelation when it is thought about historically, in terms of cause and effect. Here we have a strongly antithetical mode of thought—revelation is not a matter of historical facts, but of personal encounter—but one that is softened by the words *"not primarily."* For Käsemann cannot exclude the idea that *some* facts may be involved. The difficulty here is that if facts *are* involved, they should be accessible to the historian. If they are, then Käsemann cannot continue to set revelation and historical fact in opposition. This admission brings us back to the question of the relationship between historical knowledge and Christian faith, a question to which Käsemann gives no answer.

The same tension is found in another paper given in 1953, this time on the relationship between science and faith. In this paper Käsemann addresses the question of miracles, which—here as elsewhere—proves to be a key issue in the debate over religious authority. Käsemann argues that a miracle, properly understood, is "an encounter with the divinity and its power."[40] As he writes, "it is not merely that *something* extraordinary is happening but that I encounter *someone,* be it deity or demon."[41] Therefore, its meaning can be understood only by one involved in this encounter. It is not accessible to what we might call the "objective and detached" gaze of the outsider. There is undoubtedly some truth in this claim. Indeed, it represents an important insight into the New Testament idea of a miracle. The difficulty is that Käsemann also concedes that this divine encounter *takes for granted* the occurrence of some earthly event. For a divine epiphany (or manifestation) is—as he writes—"always the irruption of the heavenly into the sphere of earth."[42] Once again, Käsemann is thinking in antitheses, but these antitheses cannot be consistently

---

[39]Käsemann, "The Problem of the Historical Jesus," 31; *The Historical Jesus Quest,* 296.

[40]Ernst Käsemann, "Is the Gospel Objective?" (1953), translated by W. J. Montague, in *Essays on New Testament Themes,* Studies in Biblical Theology 41 (London: SCM, 1964), 52.

[41]Ibid.

[42]Ibid., 53.

maintained. The miracle story tells *not only* of an encounter, *but also* of an earthly event. It would be difficult to find a better expression of the difficulty in which the dialectical theologians and their disciples found themselves. They wished to remove Christian claims from historical scrutiny but were forced to concede that, since Christianity speaks of an earthly encounter with God, it also speaks of something that falls within the historian's ambit. But if this concession is made, we are back with the question of how historical knowledge and Christian claims may be related. We saw this tension in the work of Bultmann. It is unresolved in the work of his disciple.

In this same essay, Käsemann shows his closeness to the dialectical theologians in yet another respect. He is anxious to insist that Christian faith cannot be grounded on any kind of objective proof. Indeed, the German title of the essay gives a better sense of its flavor: "On the Theme of Non-Objectifiability."[43] In the course of discussing the biblical canon, Käsemann concedes that our choice of this particular religious authority can seem quite arbitrary. After all, Christianity is not the only religion there is, nor is the Bible the only set of sacred scriptures. Yet no reason can be given for our choice. As Käsemann writes, "there is no objective reason which we can give to the neutral observer or the neutral spectator why we shall not give [the Bible] up altogether and replace it by other organs of tradition. That is a decision of faith and as such must appear quite arbitrary to any outsider."[44]

More generally, Käsemann argues that divine revelation is not susceptible to objective proof. As he writes, revelation "has no existence in the realm of the objective—that is, outside our act of decision."[45] It follows that even if we *are* able to make some historically defensible claims about the historical Jesus, these do not and cannot form the basis of our act of faith.[46] In fact, there *is* no objective basis for faith. The authority of the Bible is grounded on nothing more than our own act of decision, which is made under the influence of the Holy Spirit.[47] We are here faced with the same difficulties that were raised by the theologies of Barth and Bultmann. One stands either inside the charmed circle of Christian faith or outside of it. If one stands on the outside, then no reason can be given why one should step within. For further comment on this position, which is essentially that of the dialectical theologians, the reader may refer to the final sections of chapters 5 and 6.

---

[43] *Zum Thema der Nichtobjektivierbarkeit.*
[44] Ibid., 57.
[45] Ibid., 58.
[46] Cf. ibid., 61.
[47] Cf. ibid., 62.

"Blind Alleys in the 'Jesus of History' Controversy"

Käsemann's second major contribution to this debate came in a study first published in 1965 in a work entitled *Exegetical Essays and Reflections,*[48] part of which was translated into English as *New Testament Questions of Today.* This study takes the form of some reflections on what had occurred in the years since the 1953 essay. In particular, Käsemann attacks what he sees as errors on either side of his own position. The first error is represented by the work of the New Testament scholar Joachim Jeremias, which Käsemann sees as a continuation of the liberal theological program.[49] The second error—at the other end of the theological spectrum—is represented by Rudolf Bultmann's response to those who, like Käsemann, had distanced themselves from his position. We will look briefly at each of these in turn. Once again we will see that—despite his distancing of himself from Bultmann—Käsemann's attitude to religious authority is not far removed from that of his great teacher.

(a) Joachim Jeremias

Käsemann's response to the work of Joachim Jeremias takes the form of a critique of an essay entitled "The Present Position in the Controversy concerning the Problem of the Historical Jesus."[50] It is not necessary to examine Jeremias's work here or to describe Käsemann's response in any detail. The value of that response is that it highlights the continuity between Käsemann's thought and that of the dialectical theologians.

Käsemann argues first of all that in focusing on the historical figure of Jesus, Jeremias is "swimming against the stream" of the New Testament itself.[51] His own work witnesses to the fact that the New Testament writers absorbed any "historical" information about Jesus into their testimony concerning the Christ. Any historical information we may find in the New Testament tradition is already reshaped by the early Christian testimony to Jesus as the Christ. Jeremias argues that the fact of the incarnation—the idea that God entered human history—demands historical research into the figure of Jesus, even if this means allowing Christian faith to be dependent on the results of historical scholarship.[52] But Käsemann responds that this approach risks repeating all the errors that

---

[48] *Exegetische Versuche und Besinnungen.*

[49] Cf. Ernst Käsemann, "Blind Alleys in the 'Jesus of History' Controversy" (1965), translated by W. J. Montague, in *New Testament Questions for Today,* New Testament Library (London: SCM, 1969), 24.

[50] An English version of Jeremias's essay is found in *The Expository Times* 69 (1958): 333–39. As the editor of Käsemann's response notes, it is not identical with the German text on which Käsemann is commenting.

[51] Käsemann, "Blind Alleys in the 'Jesus of History' Controversy," 26.

[52] Cf. ibid., 27–28.

Schweitzer had so severely criticized in his *The Quest of the Historical Jesus.*[53] More seriously, a renewed attempt to write a life of Jesus leads the scholar back into what Käsemann describes as "the world of religion."[54] Historical study, Käsemann suggests, cannot do justice to Christian faith, for "the historian never uncovers anything but relative claims."[55] Moreover, while Jesus' claim to sovereignty finds no *precise* parallel in the history of religions, the same cannot be said of other aspects of the Gospels. There is, for instance, nothing unique about either the miracle stories or Jesus' ethical teaching. In the light of historical research, even Jesus' unparalleled claim to sovereignty must be set alongside competing claims to authority, however differently these may be worded. When described historically, Jesus inevitably becomes one religious teacher among others. For all these reasons, Käsemann insists, historical study can never lead to that which is the object of faith, namely God.

These remarks demonstrate the gulf separating the work of Käsemann from that of the liberal theologians, of which the foremost representative was Ernst Troeltsch. While Troeltsch insisted that an intellectually respectable theology must accept the "great reversal" of the seventeenth century, Käsemann is equally insistent that it must not. While Troeltsch argued that a responsible faith can only be built on the foundation of historical research, Käsemann argues that history can provide no basis for religious claims. While Troeltsch argued that we cannot avoid regarding Christianity as one religion among others, Käsemann—in company with the dialectical theologians—insists that this is precisely what we must *not* do. Käsemann may be prepared to enlist the historian in a demonstration of the continuity of Jesus' teaching with that of the early church. But this is far from a wholehearted endorsement of what Troeltsch described as the "historical" rather than the "dogmatic" method in theology. On the contrary, Käsemann opposes any idea that "the historian has an access road to God himself" or that historical criticism can decide "the content and the limits of the Gospel."[56]

(b) Rudolf Bultmann

Käsemann's response to Bultmann, on the other hand, allows him to reiterate the central arguments of his 1953 essay. The work to which

---

[53]It is perhaps unfair of Käsemann to enlist Schweitzer at this point. For what Schweitzer criticized was not the historical Jesus quest as such—after all, he produced his own portrayal of Jesus—but the anachronistic way in which it had so often been conducted.

[54]Käsemann, "Blind Alleys in the 'Jesus of History' Controversy," 30.

[55]Ibid.

[56]Cf. ibid., 34.

Käsemann is responding is Bultmann's 1961 study *The Relationship of the Early-Christian Proclamation of Christ to the Historical Jesus,* the content of which was summarized in chapter 6. Again, a detailed discussion is not required. It will be enough to note Käsemann's deeply ambivalent relationship to the work of his teacher.

First of all, Käsemann agrees with Bultmann that there can be no question of *grounding* Christian faith in a knowledge of the historical figure of Jesus.[57] But this, of course, is not what Käsemann's 1953 essay was suggesting. What Käsemann was concerned about there was another question altogether: the relationship between the early Christian *kerygma* and the historical figure of Jesus. Käsemann had argued that the early Christian *kerygma* takes for granted the historical figure of Jesus and understands itself to be grounded in the events of his life and work.[58] Indeed, precisely for this reason the early Christians eventually wrote Gospels, a literary form that highlights the way in which they valued historical facts.[59] (The fact that the Gospels do not appear to us to recount *reliable* facts in no way undermines the force of this observation.)

Why *did* the early church recount the historical facts of Jesus' life (as they saw them)? Why did they come to believe that the earthly life of Jesus was important? It was because reports of what Jesus had said and done enabled them to oppose those "enthusiasts" who would effectively invent a new message from purported revelations of the Spirit.[60] In later history, too, this grounding of the message in the life of Jesus was important. It enabled the sixteenth-century Reformers to engage in the distinctively "Protestant" act of criticizing ecclesiastical tradition.[61] By effectively subsuming Christology into ecclesiology or anthropology, Käsemann argues, Bultmann cuts off the possibility of such criticism.[62] In other words, by allowing the historical Jesus to disappear into either the early Christian *kerygma* or the "existentialist" challenge to decision, Bultmann makes it impossible to appeal to Jesus against either church tradition or the limitations of our present-day self-understanding. For all these reasons we cannot simply ignore the question of the historical Jesus. We cannot accept Bultmann's "radical antithesis" between the earthly Jesus and the faith of the early church.[63]

---

[57]Cf. ibid., 47.
[58]Cf. ibid., 48.
[59]Cf. ibid., 40–41, 56–57, 62–63.
[60]Cf. ibid., 50, 52, 63.
[61]Cf. ibid., 58.
[62]Cf. ibid., 60.
[63]Cf. ibid., 36.

(c) An Evaluation

Once again, we may pause for a moment to evaluate these claims. While Käsemann's exegetical and theological observations have some force, he fails to see how serious the theological problem is. It is true that Bultmann's antitheses could not finally be maintained, a fact which Käsemann himself notes.[64] But the shielding of biblical authority from the corrosive effects of history depends on nothing other than the maintenance of such antitheses. This marked the very essence of the dialectical theology. If Christian faith was to be saved from historical relativism, religious claims and historical knowledge had to be kept very clearly apart. However much one may disagree with Barth and Bultmann, it does seem that they were more deeply aware of the problem facing the theologian. Their responses are correspondingly more radical than that of Käsemann. Indeed, while Käsemann may express some dismay at the revival of the liberal theological project, he was perhaps a little naïve in believing that this could be avoided. Once he admits that historical methods may—and indeed should—be employed in the investigation of the continuity between Jesus and the *kerygma,* he can hardly complain if historians broaden their study to locate both Jesus and the *kerygma* within the history of religions. Once he admits that the historical Jesus can be a standpoint from which one may oppose both spiritual enthusiasts and church tradition, then he cannot prevent the sceptical historian from opposing the very authority that the church claims for Jesus. Once the genie is out of the bottle, there is no limit to the havoc it can wreak. Both Barth and Bultmann tried very hard to keep the bottle firmly closed. For better or for worse, Käsemann reopened it.

The Value of Käsemann's Work
It follows that, despite Käsemann's attempt to carve out a middle ground between the liberal and the dialectical theologies, his work fails to answer the challenge of history to religious authority. With regard to this question, Käsemann wishes to align himself with the dialectical theologians. Paradoxically, however, his work effectively revives the very project that they so vigorously opposed. We may conclude that the importance of Käsemann's work lies not so much in the answers it gives as in the questions it raises, the lines of enquiry it opened up.

    There are at least two such lines of enquiry, which correspond to the two dimensions of the historical Jesus discussion identified in my opening chapter. The first is the strictly historical question. What can we know, using the critical methods of modern historical research, about the

[64]Cf. ibid., 51–53.

person of Jesus? In the intervening years this discussion has, of course, flourished. The most immediate consequence of Käsemann's essay was what has become known as the "new quest" of the historical Jesus, in which theological and historical concerns remained united. In more recent years, this new quest has turned into the "third quest," in which theological concerns were largely set aside and a greater effort was made to relate Jesus to his Jewish environment. Still more recently, a group of scholars have moved from acceptance of Jesus as an apocalyptic prophet to suggestions that he was an ethical teacher or a subversive disturber of the status quo. No attempt will be made to summarize the course of that discussion here, for it lies outside the scope of this book and (in any case) useful summaries are not difficult to find.[65]

The second line of enquiry is that which forms the focus of the present study. It is the more strictly theological question, which has to do with the relationship of Christian faith to our modern historical consciousness. This is the deeper issue with which all our authors have been grappling. As we have seen, the difficulties facing Christian theology in the modern age were most clearly outlined by Ernst Troeltsch: they are helpfully summarized in his essay on "Historical and Dogmatic Method in Theology." A quick glance at the work done in the decades following Käsemann's 1953 essay reveals a striking characteristic: a very significant imbalance between attempts to answer the first question and attempts to answer the second. While the literature on the strictly historical question of the figure of Jesus has abounded, few attempts have been made to explore the deeper theological issues. The imbalance is partly due to a fact to which I have already alluded: the fact that historians writing on Jesus within the last thirty years—the so-called "third quest"—have deliberately avoided theological concerns. While the discussion of what we can know about Jesus has flourished, little attention has been paid to the challenge of history to religious authority. How can traditional religious claims to universality be maintained when they can be shown to be the products of a particular time and place? What happens when historical knowledge and faith assertion come into conflict? More generally still, what is the relationship between biblical authority and historical

[65]See, for instance, Ben Witherington III, *The Jesus Quest: The Third Search for the Jew of Nazareth* (Downers Grove, Ill.: InterVarsity, 1995); *Studying the Historical Jesus: Evaluations of the State of Current Research,* edited by Bruce Chilton and Craig A. Evans, New Testament Tools and Studies 19 (Leiden: E. J. Brill, 1994); and the more recent work *Whose Historical Jesus?* edited by William E. Arnal and Michel Desjardins, Studies in Christianity and Judaism/Études sur le christianisme et le judaisme 7 (Waterloo, Ontario: Wilfred Laurier University Press, 1997).

knowledge?[66] Must the two be coordinated, or do they belong to entirely different spheres? If they must be related, in what ways may their sometimes conflicting claims be reconciled?[67]

2. Wolfhart Pannenberg (b. 1928)

Among the few attempts to answer these questions in recent decades, the work of one figure stands out. This figure is Wolfhart Pannenberg, the contemporary theologian to whose work I have already had occasion to refer. Pannenberg's theological career cannot yet be discussed in its entirety, since he continues to write. (Indeed, Pannenberg would be the first to insist that the meaning of any life can be known only once it is over.) Yet the present study would be incomplete without some attention to his contribution.

Revelation as History

Pannenberg's theological revolution began with two works, both of which challenged the theological consensus of his day. The first was a lecture given in 1959 and published as "Redemptive Event and History."

[66]There is yet another strategy employed by those who wish to limit historical claims to make room for religious authority. This involves drawing a sharp distinction between "history" in the sense of the past *in itself* (*an sich,* if you prefer) and "history" in the sense of the past *as known to us.* Thus the phrase "the historical Jesus" may be understood to refer to Jesus as he was *in himself* or it may be understood as referring to Jesus *as he is known by the historian.* It is then suggested that the historian works under certain limitations, certain assumptions built into her knowledge of the past (derived from the use of analogy) and that faith enables us to go beyond these limits. But this argument does nothing to lessen the tensions between history and faith. For—as Pannenberg argues ("Redemptive Event and History," 50)—the limits of historical knowledge *are* the limits of our knowledge of the past. Faith cannot supply what history is unable to deliver. Even if it could, the question would remain of how one may coordinate these two ways of accessing the figure of Jesus. The historical Jesus problem would lose nothing of its force.

[67]James M. Robinson ("A New Quest of the Historical Jesus" in *A New Quest of the Historical Jesus and Other Essays* [1959; Philadelphia: Fortress Press, 1983], 29) deploys a further strategy. He also argues that historical study cannot "exhaust the reality of Jesus of Nazareth," not because (as Barth sometimes suggests) there exist facts about the past inaccessible to the historian, but rather because there is more to history than facts about the past. This extra element has to do with what Robinson (ibid., 28) calls "the dimension in which man actually exists, his 'world,' the stance or outlook from which he acts, his understanding of his existence behind what he does." This enables Robinson to argue for the legitimacy of a "new quest," which is justified precisely by this new understanding of history. Now Robinson's argument, while interesting and important, also does nothing to lessen the tension between the claims of history and those of faith. As Bultmann's work shows, an "existentialist" interpretation of Jesus cannot be completely divorced from the historian's attempts to understand the "facts" of his life.

The second was a jointly authored series of essays published in 1961 under the title *Revelation as History*. In these works Pannenberg attempted to overcome the divorce between history and faith that had so dominated the theology of the previous generation. The easiest place to begin a study of Pannenberg's theology is with one of those essays, a programmatic work entitled "Dogmatic Theses on the Doctrine of Revelation."

Pannenberg begins this study by examining what he regards as the dominant biblical conception of revelation. The Bible, he argues, speaks above all of an *indirect* revelation of God. God makes himself known to Israel, not so much by direct appearances (theophanies), but rather by way of his action in Israel's history. This idea is found throughout the Bible, Pannenberg continues, but it took on an important new form after the Babylonian exile. This new development is found in the work of the anonymous prophet known to scholars as Deutero-Isaiah (the author of Isaiah 40–55), who directed Israel's attention to a salvation yet to come. The apocalyptic writings then build on this idea, looking forward to a decisive manifestation of God's glory in the future. With the teaching of Jesus, Pannenberg writes, "the sharp distinction between the times vanishes."[68] The future, we might say, becomes present. This merging of present and future also finds expression in the writings of the apostle Paul, for whom the fate of Jesus manifests the glory and the judgment of God. For Paul the judgment that was expected at the end time has already occurred.[69]

Pannenberg identifies this "eschatological" tradition of thought as the proper basis for a contemporary Christian theology. Theologically speaking, the history of Israel may be regarded as a history of revelation, and that revelation was continually being revised as Israel's history continued. The apocalyptic tradition took this idea to its logical conclusion. The apocalyptic writers argued that it would be only *at the end of history* that revelation would be complete. Only then would the meaning of history become clear. Without this revelation of the end times, even our own time remains obscure to us: the meaning of the present also becomes clear only in the light of God's future act.[70] (We will come back to this idea shortly.) The key insight characteristic of the New Testament is that this future act of God is anticipated in the life, death and—most clearly—the resurrection of Jesus. In these events, the *eschaton*, the end of history, is finally revealed.

[68]Wolfhart Pannenberg, "Dogmatic Theses on the Doctrine of Revelation," in *Revelation as History*, edited by Wolfhart Pannenberg (1961), translated by David Granskou (New York: Macmillan, 1968), 127.

[69]Cf. ibid., 129.

[70]Cf. ibid., 132.

Pannenberg is most insistent that this revelation of God, a revelation that finds its high point in the resurrection of Jesus, is accessible to "anyone who has eyes to see."[71] It is not a secret knowledge, accessible only (as it were) to the eyes of faith. Rather, it is a truth in principle open to all.[72] The idea that divine revelation can be recognized only by faith, Pannenberg argues, is in fact a gnostic idea, a distortion of what the Bible understands by revelation. As Pannenberg writes, "God has proved his deity in this language of facts"[73] and these facts can—in principle—be independently verified. It is true that these facts are transmitted to us by way of a tradition of interpretation, of which the Bible is an expression. This tradition is important, indeed indispensable, since it tells us *in what way* these events are revelatory. (To this extent Pannenberg would agree with Barth.[74]) But this tradition of interpretation must not invent or distort the facts; it must be true to them.[75] The special character of the history of Israel and the life of Jesus lies in the nature of the events themselves, not in some special way of regarding them.[76] As Pannenberg writes,

> a person does not bring faith with him to the event as though faith were the basis for finding the revelation of God in the history of Israel and of Jesus Christ. Rather, it is through an open appropriation of these events that true faith is sparked. . . . Thus a person does not come to faith blindly, but by means of an event that can be appropriated. True faith is not a state of blissful gullibility.[77]

[71]Ibid., 135.

[72]Cf. ibid., 137.

[73]Ibid.

[74]Cf. ibid., 152–53; cf. Barth, *Church Dogmatics* I/2, §19.4 (492–95).

[75]Cf. Wolfhart Pannenberg, "On Historical and Theological Hermeneutic" (1964), in *Basic Questions in Theology* (1967), translated by George H. Keim, Library of Philosophy and Theology (London: SCM, 1970), 1:139. One is reminded of Troeltsch's insistence (*The Christian Faith*, §8 [88]) that theology cannot establish facts, it can only interpret them, and that its interpretation "cannot be an arbitrary exercise of the imagination; it must proceed from the historical meaning and spirit of the facts themselves."

[76]Pannenberg makes the same point regarding the *kerygma*, the early Christian proclamation. It must accompany the events, but it merely explicates their meaning; it adds nothing to them. The events are, in principle, self-evidently revelation. As Pannenberg writes ("Dogmatic Theses on the Doctrine of Revelation," 155), "the kerygma is not to be thought of as bringing something to the event. The events in which God demonstrates his deity are self-evident as they stand within the framework of their own history. It does not require any kind of inspired interpretation to make these events recognizable as revelation."

[77]Pannenberg, "Dogmatic Theses on the Doctrine of Revelation," 137–38.

For Pannenberg, then, there is a very close link between Christian faith and historical knowledge, since faith can only be built on the basis of the demonstrable character of certain historical events.

An opponent might ask whether Pannenberg's position does not do away with faith altogether. If the events of God's revelation in history are in principle accessible to all, why do we need faith? In response to this objection, Pannenberg argues that faith *is* still required, but that it is *not* required to fill some gap in our knowledge of the past.[78] As Pannenberg writes, "the proclamation of the gospel cannot assert that the facts are in doubt and that the leap of faith must be made in order to achieve certainty. If this sort of assertion were allowed to stand, one would have to cease being a theologian and a Christian."[79] Faith certainly goes beyond knowledge, but it goes beyond knowledge, not by filling up its gaps, but by being directed in trust towards the future.[80] In the last analysis faith has to do with the future: it is a matter of confidence in the future actions of God. It is this confidence that brings salvation. But that confidence must be securely based on a knowledge of the past. Our trust in God must be based upon what Pannenberg calls the "fact (taken to be reasonably and reliably true) that in the fate of Jesus of Nazareth, God has been revealed to all men."[81]

These are striking claims, which mark a clear break with the theologies of Karl Barth and Rudolf Bultmann. As we have seen, both Barth and Bultmann insisted that the knowledge of divine revelation was to be distinguished from secular knowledge. It was a knowledge stemming from faith, which alone could penetrate behind the veil (as it were) to discover the action of God hidden in human history. Pannenberg turns this position upside down.[82] He does, however, qualify his own view.

[78]See also Wolfhart Pannenberg, "The Revelation of God in Jesus of Nazareth," in *Theology as History*, edited by James M. Robinson and John B. Cobb Jr., New Frontiers in Theology 3 (New York: Harper & Row, 1967), 128: "Faith does not take the place of knowledge. On the contrary, it has its basis in an event which is a matter for knowing and which becomes known to us only by more or less adequate information." As Pannenberg writes in the same essay (129–30), "without such well-founded knowledge faith would be blind gullibility, credulity, or even superstition."

[79]Pannenberg, "Dogmatic Theses on the Doctrine of Revelation," 138.

[80]Using the traditional distinction between faith as *fiducia* (trust) and faith as *fides* (the acceptance of certain facts), we might say that Pannenberg comes down heavily on the side of *fiducia*. For Pannenberg, faith as *fides* is directed not towards the past but towards the future. (Cf. Pannenberg, "Redemptive Event and History," 65.) The astute reader may recall that in the seventeenth century Edward Herbert (*De Religione Laici*, 91) made a not dissimilar distinction (as noted in my introductory chapter).

[81]Pannenberg, "Dogmatic Theses on the Doctrine of Revelation," 138.

[82]For Pannenberg's opposition to Barth and Bultmann, see especially his "Redemptive Event and History," 14–15. (We will return to this essay shortly.)

First of all, while faith stems from historical knowledge, it remains independent of the *details* of historical knowledge. All that is required is that we have sufficient knowledge of the past to assess and to participate in the events in which revelation has occurred.[83] (This seems to resemble Ernst Troeltsch's claim that all the believer needs to know about the historical Jesus are "the basic facts" of his life.[84]) Secondly, while the Christian's act of faith is based on a knowledge of the past, it also transcends this knowledge. History can take us so far, but faith takes us further. As Pannenberg writes, faith leads the believer to "new and better understandings of history, which are the basis for his life."[85]

History and Eschatology

As we have already seen, for Pannenberg the biblical idea of revelation reaches a high point in the worldview of the later biblical writers. In the period following the Babylonian exile (586–538 B.C.E.), the biblical writers reenvisaged Israel's God as the God of all humanity. This led them to broaden the history of salvation until it included all human history.[86] The apocalyptic writers, in turn, built on this conception by looking to a final revelation that would occur only at the end of time. It is this revelation that enables us to understand even our own age.

Pannenberg goes on to argue that this biblical view of history has shaped our Western understanding of history right up to the time of Hegel and Marx. The histories written by Marx and Hegel are also universal histories, which take their orientation from what they see as the end of history. Like the biblical writers, they believed that history receives its meaning from its goal. Pannenberg endorses this basic insight, however much he may argue that the Hegelian and Marxist visions of the end of history were tragically flawed. He insists that there can be no meaningful writing of history without a vision of the whole sweep of human activity. Even an understanding of the present requires an idea of the totality to which it belongs. Since the totality of history includes the future, any vision of history as a whole requires a viewpoint akin to that of the apocalyptic writers. This idea—the idea of a necessary connection between history and eschatology—represents a major pillar of Pannenberg's theology. It therefore deserves closer attention.

We may begin our closer examination with Pannenberg's 1959 essay on "Redemptive Event and History." Pannenberg begins this work by

---

[83]Cf. Pannenberg, "Dogmatic Theses on the Doctrine of Revelation," 138.
[84]Troeltsch, "The Significance of the Historical Existence of Jesus for Faith," 200.
[85]Cf. Pannenberg, "Dogmatic Theses on the Doctrine of Revelation," 139.
[86]Ibid., 133.

pointing out the importance of history for the biblical concept of revelation (his particular opponent here being Bultmann).[87] He goes on to discuss the modern concept of history in its relationship to the biblical,[88] while also affirming that our only access to the past is by way of historical knowledge. (If the past is not accessible to the historian, it is equally inaccessible to the theologian. Faith may not claim some independent means of access to the past.[89]) After insisting that faith must therefore be based on historical knowledge (in terms reminiscent of the discussion summarized above),[90] Pannenberg arrives at the question of history and revelation. This section of his essay is of particular significance for our present discussion.

If revelation is to be found in certain past events, as known by the historian, then in what way may this revelation be discerned? Pannenberg argues that if divine revelation does occur in history, then it will be visible only to one whose historical vision is universal. For practical reasons, the secular historian normally studies only a small portion of human history. But this is too narrow a vision for the theologian. As Pannenberg writes,

> a small segment of history such as the historian usually has in view because of the need to limit his material, does not in any case provide sufficient basis for meaningfully raising the question of whether a God has revealed himself here. . . . In order to raise this question it is obviously requisite that one should have history as a whole in view, corresponding to the universality of God, whose revelation is the object of inquiry. Only on the assumption of a universal-historical horizon can there be such an inquiry.[91]

Yet this raises a serious question: Is this "assumption of a universal-historical horizon" realistic? Can one conceive of "history as a whole"?

Pannenberg's answer is unequivocal. The historian is not only *able* to conceive of history as a whole; at a certain point he cannot *avoid* doing so. For the writing of history takes for granted the idea that history has a certain unity.[92] This unity enables us to relate sometimes distant events

---

[87]Cf. Pannenberg, "Redemptive Event and History," 16–38.

[88]Cf. ibid., 39–50. I have discussed Pannenberg's comments on the principle of analogy in the final sections of chapter 2 (on D. F. Strauss) and chapter 4 (on Ernst Troeltsch) and will return to them when discussing the resurrection of Jesus later in this chapter.

[89]Cf. Pannenberg, "Redemptive Event and History," 50–53.

[90]Cf. ibid., 53–66.

[91]Ibid., 66–67.

[92]Cf. ibid., 68–69.

320 The Historical Jesus Question

to one another.[93] But the idea of the unity of history assumes, in turn, a certain vision of history in its entirety. (Pannenberg's reasoning here seems to be that without some vision of the whole of history we cannot be confident about the unity of history, for that unity must embrace the future as well as the past and the present.) It follows that for the historian, too, the study of particular historical events is meaningful only against this universal horizon. As Pannenberg writes, "without world history there is no meaning of history."[94] Pannenberg concedes that in speaking of the meaning of history as a whole, the historian must take care to preserve the contingency of historical events. He must not imply that the events of history unfold by some kind of immanent necessity.[95] But this in no way undermines the historian's obligation to form a vision of history as a whole.

In other essays, Pannenberg arrives at the same conclusion by way of some more general considerations. He argues, for instance, that anything which is merely a *part*—in the field of history and elsewhere—can be understood only in relation to the *whole* to which it belongs.[96] It follows that we can know the meaning of any particular experience only by way of a vision of the totality to which it contributes.[97] Since the totality of history includes the future, we can know the meaning of any particular historical event only by anticipating the end of history.[98] Pannenberg goes on to suggest that it is *religion* that offers such a vision. For religion offers us a glimpse of the "infinity" (in Schleiermacher's words) out of which we carve our understanding of finite realities.[99]

Returning to "Redemptive Event and History," we find that Pannenberg takes this argument one step further. In this context he argues that it is not *religion in general* that offers us this vision; it is *Christianity*. Christian faith has a vital role to play in our understanding of history, because

---

[93]It is not entirely clear what Pannenberg means by "the unity of history," and I will return to this phrase in the final section of the present chapter.

[94]Pannenberg, "Redemptive Event and History," 69.

[95]Cf. ibid., 72.

[96]Cf. Wolfhart Pannenberg, "On Historical and Theological Hermeneutic," 162–63 (on the work of Wilhelm Dilthey [1833–1911]).

[97]Cf. Pannenberg, *Theology and the Philosophy of Science,* 206–24. Here Pannenberg argues on the basis of contextual theories of verbal meaning that "every specialised meaning depends on a final, all-embracing totality of meaning in which all individual meanings are linked to form a semantic whole" (ibid., 216).

[98]Cf. Wolfhart Pannenberg, "Faith and Reason" (1965), in *Basic Questions in Theology* (London: SCM, 1971), 2:61–62.

[99]Cf. Pannenberg, *Systematic Theology,* 1:165, 167; *Theology and the Philosophy of Science,* 333. For a parallel line of argumentation, with regard to truth in general, see Pannenberg's essay "What Is Truth?" in *Basic Questions in Theology* 2:1–27.

only this faith allows us to see history as a unity.[100] What advantage has Christianity over other religions? Its advantage lies in the particular conception of God found within the biblical tradition. The Bible speaks of a God who works *within* history but who is not bound by it. The biblical God, in other words, transcends history. Because he transcends history, he can be related to history without compromising the contingency of historical events.[101] It follows, Pannenberg writes, that the Christian view of history is "the only appropriate view of historical reality."[102] In other words, if history is to be intelligible at all, it must be understood in its relationship to the biblical God. This relationship gives history its unity.

The apocalyptic doctrine of the New Testament takes on a particular significance in this context. As Pannenberg writes in his "Dogmatic Theses on the Doctrine of Revelation," it is "through an extraordinary vision" that "the apocalyptic writer sees ahead to the end of all things."[103] This extraordinary vision of the end of history enables us to glimpse the meaning of history as a whole, for (once again) "the history of the whole is only visible when one stands at its end."[104] The resurrection of Jesus confirms this apocalyptic revelation of the end of history, for that resurrection achieves for one human being *here and now* what is promised for everyone *at the end of time*. Because it is a revelation of the end of history, the revelation of God in Jesus remains unsurpassable.[105] There can be nothing more to be revealed, since Jesus' resurrection is "a proleptic unveiling of the eschatological event."[106] In a word, the resurrection of Jesus is nothing less than the indispensable key to an understanding of human history.

It is worth noting what Pannenberg has achieved here, for this is an impressive theological tour de force. Firstly, he has found a basis on which a religious meaning may be attributed to history. We have already seen that Troeltsch finds meaning in human history by way of an idealist metaphysics. But Pannenberg rejects this option.[107] If he wishes to give a religious meaning to history, he must do so by another route. He achieves this goal by arguing that there exists a convergence between the needs of historical knowledge and the nature of apocalyptic thought. The problem of historical knowledge is that we can understand the

---

[100]Pannenberg, "Redemptive Event and History, 74–75.
[101]Cf. ibid., 75–76.
[102]Ibid., 78.
[103]Pannenberg, "Dogmatic Theses on the Doctrine of Revelation," 141.
[104]Ibid., 142.
[105]Cf. ibid., 143–44.
[106]Ibid., 145.
[107]Cf. Pannenberg, "Redemptive Event and History," 72.

meaning of history only by reference to its goal. Apocalyptic thought offers an answer to this problem, for the apocalyptic writers offer nothing less than a vision of the end time. Secondly, Pannenberg is able to argue that the revelation of God in Jesus is final and definitive. (As we saw, this was one of the points at which Troeltsch's theological project fell short.[108]) The revelation of God in the resurrection of Jesus is final and definitive *precisely because* it is an anticipation of the end of history. If the end of history has been revealed in these events, then that revelation is by definition unsurpassable. Thirdly, Pannenberg—like Bultmann before him—has found a positive meaning that could be attached to the puzzling and sometimes scandalous apocalyptic language of the New Testament. Indeed, in this respect he goes much further than Bultmann. For Bultmann, the apocalyptic "kingdom of God" represents the demand of the future on human existence, the crisis of decision that faces each individual.[109] Unlike Pannenberg, Bultmann was *not* prepared to claim that we could know the goal of history; his aims were deliberately modest. As he wrote,

> the historical meaning of an event can be understood only from the standpoint of its future. . . . Therefore, the meaning of historical processes is to be definitively understood only from the end of history. Since, however, such a view from the end of history is not possible for human seeing, a philosophy that endeavors to understand the meaning of history is likewise impossible. The meaning of history can be talked about only as the meaning of the moment, which is meaningful as the moment of decision.[110]

In his desire to vindicate the universal claims of biblical faith, Pannenberg takes issue with this position. He does not want to restrict the meaning of apocalyptic to the question of the individual human existence, but this leads him to a very bold statement about our understanding of history. History, he argues, can properly be understood only in light of the resurrection of Jesus. Whether that bold statement can be supported is a question to which we will return.

---

[108]Compare Troeltsch's remark (*The Absoluteness of Christianity*, 114–15) that "it cannot be proved with absolute certainty that Christianity will always remain the final culmination point, that it will never be surpassed" with Pannenberg's claim ("The Revelation of God in Jesus of Nazareth," 124) that "the history of Jesus has the character of ultimacy in the midst of our perishing time."

[109]Cf. Bultmann, *Jesus and the Word*, 37 et passim.

[110]Bultmann, "On the Problem of Demythologizing" (1961), 157–58. For the same idea, see also Bultmann, *History and Eschatology*, 138.

A Theology of the History of Religions

I have just alluded to another important dimension of Pannenberg's thought: his insistence that—in speaking about the Creator God—theology can, and must, make universal claims. The same conviction underlies Pannenberg's understanding of the history of religions. From the beginning of his work, this has been an important issue. As early as his "Dogmatic Theses on the Doctrine of Revelation," Pannenberg reflects on what he calls "the relation to theology to the science of religion (*Religionswissenschaft*)."[111] He argues that the science of religion is important for theology for at least two reasons. First of all, Israel cannot be isolated from its religious environment. Not just at the beginning of its history, but throughout its development, Israel's faith was shaped by its interaction with surrounding cultures. Secondly, the idea that Israel's God is the God of humanity *as a whole*—an idea expressed most clearly by the later Old Testament prophets—demands reflection on the entirety of religious history.[112] If God is the God of all human beings, we cannot assume that his revelation will be restricted to the history of any one people.[113]

(a) Christianity and the Religions

Pannenberg picks up and develops these ideas in his 1962 essay "Toward a Theology of the History of Religions."[114] What is remarkable about this essay is that it so closely resembles the project undertaken by Ernst Troeltsch, a project that the dialectical theology had brought to an untimely end. Indeed, Pannenberg begins his essay by referring to a similar proposal by the theologian Paul Tillich and noting *its* dependence on the questions raised by Troeltsch.[115] Pannenberg argues that if Christian theology is to maintain its credibility, it is urgent that it face these questions again. Making reference to the unconditional adherence of Barth and Bultmann to the early Christian proclamation (or *kerygma*), Pannenberg writes:

[111]Pannenberg, "Dogmatic Theses on the Doctrine of Revelation," 134.

[112]Cf. ibid., 134–35. Pannenberg, unlike so many modern Protestant theologians, also approves of the appropriation of Greek philosophy by Christian thinkers (cf. ibid., 135). On this matter, see also Wolfhart Pannenberg, *Metaphysics and the Idea of God* (1988), translated by Philip Clayton (Grand Rapids: Eerdmans, 1990), 3–6 et passim.

[113]On these themes, see also Pannenberg, "Redemptive Event and History," 76–77.

[114]For a restatement of essentially the same view, see Pannenberg, *Systematic Theology,* 1:151–71.

[115]Cf. Wolfhart Pannenberg, "Toward a Theology of the History of Religions" (1962), in *Basic Questions in Theology,* translated by George H. Keim (London: SCM, 1971), 2:65–66.

the longer theology persists in a kerygmatic approach that permits no questioning of the truth of the kerygma itself, the longer the urgent questions concerning Christianity as a religion among the religions, first brought to light in a comprehensive way by Troeltsch, are put off, the greater will be the devastation that will occur when it awakens from its kerygmatic dreaming.[116]

Christian faith cannot simply detach itself from the world of religion; on the contrary, it must face up to the question of its relationship to the other religions of human history. In raising this question, Pannenberg argues, Troeltsch was entirely in the right.

Pannenberg's proposal is that Christian theology must base itself on what he calls (in the title of his essay) "a theology of the history of religions." In other words, Christian theology must have the broadest possible base; it must be able to defend itself in the context of religion as a universal human phenomenon. Such a theology cannot afford to base itself on what Pannenberg calls "specifically Christian beliefs."[117] If it does this, it will renounce all claim to be taken seriously outside of its own community of faith. It need not *deny* its Christian perspective, but it must "appeal . . . to observable states of affairs" rather than simply resting its claims on Christian presuppositions.[118] But how can this be done? In an attempt to answer this question, Pannenberg examines a number of options. He reflects first of all on the "phenomenological method" in the study of religions, which was the dominant approach in religious studies at the time in which he wrote.[119] While recognizing the contribution of such methods, Pannenberg repeats two frequently made criticisms. The first is that phenomenological study plucks particular features of religious traditions out of their context in order to identify analogous features across a range of religions. (Pannenberg's example is the Christian doctrine of incarnation, which some phenomenologists had wrongly subsumed under the general category of "manifestations of divinity."[120]) The second is that phenomenologists of religion tend to regard religious structures as unchanging across time. In this way they neglect the element of development in any religious tradition. In both cases, Pannenberg argues, the "historical particularity" of the religions is neglected.[121]

---

[116]Ibid., 66–67.

[117]Ibid., 70.

[118]Ibid.

[119]For a helpful discussion of the "phenomenological school" in religious studies, outlining its history as well as its strengths and its weaknesses, see Eric J. Sharpe, *Comparative Religion: A History* (London: Duckworth, 1975), 220–250.

[120]Cf. Pannenberg, "Toward a Theology of the History of Religions," 74.

[121]Ibid., 76.

More seriously, the radically historical nature of human existence is overlooked.[122]

Pannenberg next examines what he calls "evolutionary" interpretations of human religious history. Such interpretations would include the proposal (which Pannenberg attributes to Hegel) that particular religions may be regarded as "stages" in human religious development, with Christianity seen as the highest stage. But it would also include the more subtle idea that within *each* religion a similar process of development may be discerned. One thinks, for instance, of the suggestion that religions have developed "from chaotic demonism to monotheism."[123] Here, too, Pannenberg notes some obvious objections. First of all, evolutionary approaches assume that we can know about the earliest stages of human religion. In practice, scholars have often assumed that these earliest stages of religion were reflected in the so-called "primitive" religions of our own time. But in the absence of clear evidence from ancient cultures, this assumption remains doubtful. The earliest stages of human religiosity remain hidden to us. Secondly, insofar as "primitive" religions *do* offer any evidence to this effect, they do *not* in fact support any kind of simple evolutionary view.

Pannenberg also concedes that the evolutionary view is not entirely wrong. In particular, evolutionary theorists are right insofar as they try to understand religious history as a whole. The major religions of human history grew up in interaction with each other. For this reason, no one of them can be fully understood in isolation from the rest. As Pannenberg notes, "the growth of the biblical figure of God" is no exception to this rule; it, too, "has the form of a syncretistic process."[124] The biblical picture of God, in other words, incorporates elements derived from the surrounding cultures. Indeed, it owes much of its power to this process of assimilation. It follows that there does exist a certain unity in religious affairs, a unity that is the product of a long history of interaction and mutual influence.[125] This process of interaction continues today. Sometimes it takes the form of conflict between competing religious claims, but even this conflict has a shaping effect, since it eventually forces some kind of readjustment in each religion's beliefs. Each religion is forced to give an account of the others. The evolutionary view of religions was right to highlight the interaction of religions. But it was wrong to assume that the outcome of such interaction can be predicted or that it

---

[122]Cf. ibid., 78.
[123]Ibid., 82.
[124]Ibid., 87.
[125]Cf. ibid., 88.

can be "deduced from some kind of principle."[126] Rather, the outcome of this interaction can "be understood only by reflecting on the way it actually took place."[127]

Can we then discover *any* kind of unity in the history of religions? The question is an important one. For if we cannot discover some unity in this diverse history, it will be impossible to arrive at a theological interpretation. We will be unable to view the history of religions as a history of revelation. Pannenberg concludes that we cannot discern any unity in the *origin* of religions. Rather, one can begin to speak of a unified history only when one or two religions begin to expand over the face of the earth. Indeed, the unity of human religious history first becomes manifest in "the history of Christian missions and in the Islamic conquests."[128] In our own time, this process has continued. The political and economic expansion of the Christian West has forced the religions of the world into a new period of interaction, even when that interaction involves conflict. It follows, Pannenberg argues, that "the unity of the history of religions is . . . not to be found in their beginnings, but rather in their end."[129] One can trace the process by which this gradual integration has occurred. One can even interpret it theologically, for this integration—Pannenberg suggests—is a necessary consequence of the unity of God.[130] But such affirmations presuppose that there is a divine reality lying behind the religions of history. It is to this more properly theological matter than Pannenberg now turns.

Before we pass on, one comment may perhaps be permitted. There is something more than a little ominous about Pannenberg's argument at this point. We have just noted his suggestion that the increasing integration of the religious history of humanity may be related to the unity of God himself. The suggestion sounds harmless enough. It even sounds benign, insofar as it assumes that this interaction of religions is ultimately a force for good, rather than merely a cause of conflict. However, a closer analysis shows its less attractive implications. For Pannenberg notes that in the modern period this integration has been brought about by "the expansion of Western civilization and technology in the last century."[131] When Pannenberg then suggests that "the unity of the divine reality" is "operative" in this process,[132] what is he saying? Is he suggesting that the

[126]Ibid., 91.

[127]Ibid. These criticisms, the reader may recall, closely resemble Troeltsch's criticisms of evolutionary views of religion (cf. *The Absoluteness of Christianity*, 49 et passim).

[128]Cf. Pannenberg, "Toward a Theology of the History of Religions," 93.

[129]Ibid., 94.

[130]Cf. ibid., 95.

[131]Ibid., 93.

[132]Ibid., 95.

Western colonization of the Americas, Asia, and Africa was in some sense the work of God? Is he arguing that the ongoing expansion of Western culture in our own time is also the work of God?[133] Such a suggestion would be—to put it mildly—surprising. It is, however, not inconsistent with Pannenberg's conviction that God works "through the experience, plans, and deeds of men, despite and in their sinful perversion."[134] The danger here is that the theologian will give her blessing to all kinds of human wickedness, on the grounds that "somehow" the actual course of history must reflect the will of God. (It is perhaps this danger against which Karl Barth was reacting, when he rebelled against the theological acceptance of the German war policy of 1914.)

(b) The Reality Reference of Religious Experience

In the final section of the essay, Pannenberg addresses what he calls "the reality-reference (*Wirklichkeitsbezug*) of religious experience."[135] The first challenge to be faced here, Pannenberg writes, is that of Ludwig Feuerbach. For Feuerbach argued that religious phenomena are *nothing but* "projections of subjective human states."[136] Pannenberg notes that not even Troeltsch could offer a satisfactory answer to this charge, although he attempted to do so by postulating the existence of a religious a priori, a religious dimension to human knowledge. While Troeltsch's solution is less than satisfactory, Pannenberg argues, it does raise a question that continues to be of importance: does there exist an irreducibly religious element in human experience?[137] Any defense of religion would need to show that there does exist such an element, which cannot be understood as simply the projection of human needs.

Pannenberg notes that this is only a first stage in the modern defense of religion. It is true that the theologian must first of all counter Feuerbach's charge. He must show that religion has a certain independence (as Troeltsch insisted). The theologian must demonstrate that religion is not *merely* a product of psychic forces, such as fear or hope. But even if this defense were successful, Pannenberg argues, it would not go far enough. If religion cannot be exhaustively explained as a product of human hopes and fears, then religious claims must be taken seriously. But we have not yet demonstrated that any particular religious claims are true.

---

[133]Pannenberg (ibid., 93) puts forward the debatable view that this secular culture is itself "a product of Christianity."

[134]Pannenberg, "Redemptive Event and History," 79.

[135]Pannenberg, "Toward a Theology of the History of Religions," 96.

[136]Ibid., 98.

[137]Cf. Troeltsch, "On the Question of the Religious A Priori," 33–45; "Religion and the Science of Religion," 116–17.

The theologian must show that human existence actually *presupposes* and *demands* the recognition of a particular divine reality. In this context, Pannenberg notes, we must not think of God as one object of experience alongside others. Rather, the infinite God must be thought of as *a dimension* of our experience of finite reality.[138] If human beings encounter God at all, it is in the course of their dealings with worldly realities. As Pannenberg writes, it is precisely *in* its "experience of finite reality" that human existence "reaches beyond its finitude."[139]

How can this encounter with God be demonstrated? In other words, how can one know that one encounters *God* in these experiences? Pannenberg's answer to this question is not at all clear. It is therefore best approached by quoting his very words: "The reality of God or of divine power can be proven only in its happening [*Widerfarnis*], namely, in that it proves itself powerful within the horizon of the current experience of existence [*Daseinserfahrung*]."[140] What does this mean? We know the Christian God exists—Pannenberg appears to be saying—when we have an overwhelming experience of his significance for our existence.[141] For Pannenberg, this experience is apparently self-authenticating: it needs no further evidence of its veracity. His only qualification is that it ought to relate to the *whole* of reality. It ought to embrace not just our inner life (as Bultmann argued) but also our knowledge of the external world. If the religious claims in question shed light on that experience as a whole, Pannenberg seems to be arguing, we may regard them as justified.

While these comments do not relate directly to the central issue of our

---

[138]In another work (*Theology and the Philosophy of Science,* 301–2) Pannenberg notes that we cannot exclude the possibility of a direct experience of God. But such an experience has the "intersubjective validity" that theology seeks only when it reshapes our common, "indirect" experience of God.

[139]Pannenberg, "Toward a Theology of the History of Religions," 104.

[140]Pannenberg, "Toward a Theology of the History of Religions," 104; cf. Wolfhart Pannenberg, "Erwägungen zur einer Theologie der Religionsgeschichte" (1962), in *Grundfragen systematischer Theologie: Gesammelte Aufsätze* (Göttingen: Vandenhoeck & Ruprecht, 1967), 284.

[141]At least, this seems to be what Pannenberg means. The key sentence reads ("Toward a Theology of the History of Religions," 105): "Where the god transmitted by tradition from earlier generations, or remembered from one's own previous experience, or even as never before so conceived—or even the impersonal hidden mystery of human existence—suddenly becomes relevant for the experience of human existence in a concrete situation, at that point there takes place a happening of *the* reality to which religious language and, implicitly, all human behavior is related in its transcending fore-conception beyond itself and everything finite. This is what in Christian terms is called an act of God." Recourse to the original sheds no further light: Pannenberg's translator has here faithfully rendered the obscurity of his German (cf. Pannenberg, "Erwägungen zur einer Theologie der Religionsgeschichte," 284).

study, they nonetheless deserve closer scrutiny. If I have understood Pannenberg right, he seems to be offering something akin to an "inference
to the best explanation" justification of religious belief. The only difference from traditional arguments of this form is that he begins with the
historical reality of religious traditions rather than with our knowledge of
the world. If, in a moment of insight, we find that a particular religious
tradition makes sense of our current experience, then its truth may be
taken as demonstrated. If this is what Pannenberg is saying, then there are
clearly some difficulties to be faced. Given the existence of competing
religious traditions, how are we to decide which has the greater degree of
explanatory power? A personal decision that this tradition "makes sense
of" my existence is scarcely adequate, for members of competing religious traditions would presumably arrive at different conclusions. What
publicly accessible criteria might be offered for making such judgments?
In any case, a truly critical theology would presumably want to measure
the claims of *religious* traditions against those of *nonreligious* bodies of
thought. Christianity would need to justify itself over against the competing traditions of secular explanation so characteristic of modernity, traditions that see appeal to the actions of God as simply redundant.

However, for the moment we may leave these matters aside. We may
grant—for the sake of the argument—that these difficulties can be overcome and that a religious tradition could be vindicated by the experience of its explanatory power. Pannenberg continues his argument by
identifying this experience with "what in Christian terms is called an act
of God."[142] More precisely, he identifies it with the act of divine revelation.[143] The act of divine revelation occurs when the God of religious
history becomes the one who demonstrates his reality by shedding light
on the whole of human experience. If one accepts the argument to this
point, it follows that the question of the *existence* of God is closely bound
up with the question of his *appearance*, that is to say, with the question of
revelation.[144]

(c) Revelation and the History of Religions

If the question of the religious truth can only be answered by reference
to such experiences of revelation, then we are brought back to the *history
of religions*. For these experiences of revelation only occur within particular

[142]Pannenberg, "Toward a Theology of the History of Religions," 105.

[143]Cf. Pannenberg, *Systematic Theology,* 1:171: "The manifestation of divine reality
even within the unresolved conflicts of religious and ideological truth claims is called
revelation."

[144]Cf. Pannenberg, "Toward a Theology of the History of Religions," 105.

religious traditions, which have their own interacting histories. It follows that if divine revelation is to be found anywhere, it will be found in the history of religions. But there exists another reason why divine revelation is to be sought in history. It is the fact that only a historical revelation corresponds to the infinity of God.[145] (Pannenberg's reasoning here seems to be that an infinite God cannot be disclosed in any particular finite reality. The revelation of the infinite God requires a still open history, within which any particular divine appearance is provisional.) Israel's religion has an advantage over other religions in this respect, for it is preeminently historical, being directed to a still undisclosed future. But in the development of other religions, too, we can see that each *particular* revelation is provisional. Each revelation is in fact directed to a future fulfilment. (This fact may be evident only to the historian, since the religions themselves are reluctant to acknowledge it.[146]) It follows that we can view the history of religions as nothing less than a history of divine revelation. As Pannenberg writes, "the history of religions is the unending path along which the infinite destination of man for the infinite God moves towards its appropriate realization," even if this movement sometimes happens "contrary to the self-consciousness of the religions" in question.[147]

Pannenberg goes on to face a theological objection to the idea of revelation in history, one that is reminiscent of Karl Barth's insistence on the "infinite qualitative distinction between time and eternity."[148] If God represents an *infinite* reality, it would seem impossible that he should be made manifest in any particular, *finite* event. Pannenberg's response is that such a manifestation *is* possible, *if* the revelation of God in a particular event is simultaneously a revelation of what he calls "the openness of the future."[149] If the revelation of God involves an essential reference to the future, then this reference to the still open future serves as a reminder that our knowledge of God is never complete. Such a revelation would respect the infinity of God. It is not hard to see where Pannenberg's argument is leading. It is the nation of Israel who came to understand

---

[145]In his *Theology and the Philosophy of Science* Pannenberg arrives at the same conclusion by a different route, arguing (cf. 302) that, if God is to be thought of as "the all-determining reality," then evidence for his existence and action is to be sought in the totality of reality. But since the totality of reality includes the future, evidence for God must be sought in our anticipations of the future that give meaning to history (cf. 309–10).

[146]Cf. Pannenberg, "Toward a Theology of the History of Religions," 108–9.

[147]Ibid., 109.

[148]Barth, preface to the second edition, in *The Epistle to the Romans,* 6th edition, 10.

[149]Pannenberg, "Toward a Theology of the History of Religions," 109.

history as directed to the future. And it is Jesus who insisted that this future was truly new, that it could not be understood on the model of the past.[150] In this way Pannenberg returns his reader to the world of apocalyptic, with its vision of the future. Jesus' apocalyptic vision of the coming kingdom of God offers a revelation that is definitive and unsurpassable, while not contradicting the idea of God's infinity.[151] Once again, Pannenberg has found a way of attributing theological significance to the strange world of Jewish apocalyptic. More importantly, it has enabled him to affirm the superiority of the Christian revelation to any other event in the history of religions, for only this "eschatological" revelation can correspond to the infinity of God.

(d) Pannenberg and Troeltsch

Before looking more closely at these ideas, I would like to note some differences between Pannenberg's work and that of Ernst Troeltsch. While Pannenberg's proposal for a "theology of the history of religions" appears to be a revival of Troeltsch's work—both insist that history is the scene of divine revelation—it should be clear that the two proposals are by no means identical. Troeltsch believed that one could *not* know the goal of history, at least in any "scientific" way.[152] But Pannenberg believes that this goal has been made known to us in the resurrection of Jesus. The resurrection is nothing less than an anticipation of the end of history; it is the clue that allows us to deduce the meaning of history as a whole. For Troeltsch, on the other hand, the goal of history lies outside of history; it is never fully expressed within the flow of historical events.[153] At best, we can attempt to identify the point outside history at which the developments of human culture would converge.[154] Even this identification involves a certain risk and remains a matter of personal decision. For this reason we are unable to know for certain that Christianity will never be surpassed, although we can be confident that its positive insights will never be lost.[155] Pannenberg, by way of contrast, argues that since we *do* know the goal of history, we can state quite confidently that the Christian revelation *will* never be surpassed.[156] In this respect, Pannenberg's theology arrives at a much more traditional conclusion.

[150]Cf. ibid., 113.

[151]Cf. ibid., 114.

[152]Cf. Troeltsch, *Der Historismus und seine Probleme,* 111, 183.

[153]Cf. Troeltsch, *The Absoluteness of Christianity,* 67, 98, et passim.

[154]Cf. ibid., 98 et passim.

[155]Cf. ibid., 115–17, 131.

[156]Cf. Pannenberg, "Dogmatic Theses on the Doctrine of Revelation," 144–45; "The Revelation of God in Jesus of Nazareth," 124.

The Resurrection of Jesus

As we have seen, Pannenberg has in common with Troeltsch the desire to develop a theology that is responsive to the demands of history. With regard to the "history of religions," Pannenberg outlines what such a theology might involve, but he leaves its completion to others.[157] He assumes that, if such a project were carried through, it would result in an interpretation favorable to Christian claims.[158] This assumption seems to be based on his understanding of eschatology and its relationship to the resurrection of Jesus. Since he is convinced that the future has been revealed in the resurrection of Jesus, Pannenberg can take it for granted that Christianity represents something unsurpassable in the history of religions. For only the Christian revelation corresponds to the infinity of God, and only the Christian revelation provides the much needed answer to the meaning of history. Much rests, therefore, on Pannenberg's claims regarding the resurrection.[159] He must not only show that the resurrection of Jesus really occurred. He must also demonstrate that this event represents a vision of the goal and hence the meaning of history. Since Pannenberg argues that a rationally defensible theology must avoid tendentious presuppositions, he must argue that the resurrection of Jesus is a historically verifiable event, accessible not just to the believer but to any unprejudiced observer.[160] To these remarkable claims we must now turn.

Pannenberg addresses these issues most directly in his christological work, *Jesus—God and Man,* where he offers a lengthy argument in support of the historical reality of the resurrection of Jesus.[161] Against Barth

---

[157]Cf. Pannenberg, "Toward a Theology of the History of Religions," 116–18.

[158]Despite his professed belief (*Systematic Theology,* 1:171) that revelation occurs "within the unresolved conflicts of religious and ideological truth claims," in his systematic theology Pannenberg is content to expound Christian truth claims in isolation, confident that they will thereby vindicate themselves.

[159]For Pannenberg, it not just that Christian faith rests on belief in the resurrection; that belief must also be *historically defensible.* As he writes (*Jesus—God and Man,* 28), "only on the basis of what happened in the past . . . do we know that Jesus lives as the exalted Lord. Only in trust in the reliability of the report of Jesus' resurrection and exaltation are we able to turn in prayer to the one who is exalted and now lives, and thus to associate with him in the present."

[160]Cf. Pannenberg, *Jesus—God and Man,* 109: "If . . . historical study declares itself unable to establish what 'really' happened on Easter, then all the more, faith is not able to do so; for faith cannot ascertain anything certain about events of the past that would perhaps be inaccessible to the historian."

[161]A similar discussion is found in Wolfhart Pannenberg, *Systematic Theology,* (1991), translated by Geoffrey W. Bromiley (Grand Rapids: Eerdmans, 1994), 2:343–63. With regard to the evidence for the resurrection, this treatment adds little that is new, other than interacting with more recent scholarship. I will discuss shortly the ways in which it subtly modifies Pannenberg's earlier conclusion.

and Bultmann, Pannenberg insists that, while the resurrected Lord may belong to a new sphere of reality, which eludes historical grasp, he did make himself known to us in historically verifiable events.[162] It is true that the resurrection itself can only be described "metaphorically," just as it could be made known to the disciples by way of extraordinary, "visionary" experiences. But these experiences were nonetheless events that "actually happened at a definite time in the past,"[163] and they provide evidence for the resurrection. The resurrection, in other words, *is* a historical event insofar as it has historical consequences. At least in this sense, the resurrection of Jesus is open to historical scrutiny. As Pannenberg writes, "there is not justification for affirming Jesus' resurrection as an event that really happened, if it is not to be affirmed as a historical event as such."[164] He therefore sets himself to examine the New Testament traditions, to see if the resurrection of Jesus is indeed accessible to the historian.

(a) The Resurrection Appearances

Pannenberg first of all examines the New Testament reports of the appearances of the risen Christ. He argues that 1 Corinthians 15:1–11 strongly suggests that these reports have some historical foundation. The first letter of Paul to the Corinthians is so early a work that it is difficult to believe that these stories of Jesus' appearances were simply invented.[165] (It is of course true that some of the *details* of these reports may be legendary, such as the idea that the risen Christ appeared in bodily form and could be touched.[166]) It therefore seems likely that a number of early Christians had an experience that they *interpreted* as an encounter with the risen Christ. But it leaves open the question of the nature of that experience. What actually occurred?

In 1 Corinthians, the apostle Paul lists his own experience of the risen Christ alongside that of the other witnesses. This implies that the experience of the other apostles was comparable to that of Paul. The apostle elsewhere describes his own experience in terms that seem to fall into the category of a "vision."[167] It was clearly a unique kind of vision (visionary experiences in early Christianity were apparently common),

---

[162]Pannenberg, *Jesus—God and Man*, 99.
[163]Ibid.
[164]Ibid.
[165]Cf. ibid., 91.
[166]Cf. ibid., 89.
[167]Cf. ibid., 93.

although it is difficult to specify in what way it was unique. But the designation of Paul's experience as a "vision" does not necessarily imply that it was without objective reality. It is true that many attempts have been made to explain these visionary experiences without reference to "the reality of the resurrection."[168] Pannenberg classes all these attempts together under the heading of "the subjective vision hypothesis."[169] In the present study, we have seen this hypothesis exemplified in the work of David Friedrich Strauss. Strauss argues that, after the death of Jesus, the disciples tried to reconcile their belief in his messianic dignity with the fact of his death. Their solution was the conviction that God had raised Jesus to a position of heavenly authority. If Enoch and Elijah had been taken up to heaven, so had Jesus, and—since "the soul without the body was a mere shadow"—this meant his bodily resurrection.[170] In the religious enthusiasm thus created, perhaps heightened by fasting, it was only a short step to the experience of visions.[171] Ernst Troeltsch held to a similar view but did so with a little more discretion, so as not to cause scandal.[172]

Pannenberg, however, argues that all such attempts have failed. Firstly, the subjective vision hypothesis implies something like the psychiatric concept of a hallucination.[173] But this concept cannot immediately be applied the apostles' experience; we cannot simply assume without further evidence that these experiences were pathological.[174] Secondly, it cannot be said that these visions were created by the faith of the disciples, since that faith would hardly have survived Jesus' death. In any case, the apocalyptic imagination of the disciples would not have led them to think that Jesus *alone* had been raised; they would have expected a *general*

---

[168]Cf. ibid., 95–96.

[169]Cf. ibid., 96.

[170]Strauss, *A New Life of Jesus,* §49 (1:421–24).

[171]Cf. ibid., §49 (1:428).

[172]Cf. Troeltsch, *The Christian Faith* §18 (219).

[173]In fact, it does not. Both here and in his *Systematic Theology* (2:354) Pannenberg assumes there is no middle position between seeing visions as objectively grounded and seeing visions as signs of mental illness. Since there is no reason for ascribing mental illness to the disciples, their experience must have been objectively grounded. But this is a false antithesis. There is abundant evidence that people can have the kind of visionary experience that we would normally judge to be without objective referent, while displaying no other signs of mental illness. On this matter, see (for instance) Mike Jackson and K. W. M. Fulford, "Spiritual Experience and Psychopathology," in *Philosophy, Psychiatry, and Psychology* 4:1 (March 1997): 41–65; or (for a slightly different view) Erikur Líndal, Jon G. Stefánsson, and Sigurjón B. Stefánsson, "The Qualitative Difference of Visions and Visual Hallucinations: A Comparison of a General-Population and Clinical Sample," in *Comprehensive Psychiatry* 35:5 (September/October 1994): 405–8.

[174]Cf. Pannenberg, *Jesus—God and Man,* 95.

resurrection. Thirdly, the number of visions and what Pannenberg calls "their temporal distribution" also tells against this hypothesis.[175] For instance, the assumption of a certain "chain reaction" seems implausible, since the visions did not (apparently) follow each other as rapidly as this hypothesis would require. For all these reasons, the subjective vision hypothesis lacks support. We must therefore assume that the apostles' visionary experiences did have an objective referent. In other words, if the only way these events can be explained is by invoking the apocalyptic idea of the resurrection of the dead, then this is the explanation we must choose.

(b) The Empty Tomb Traditions

Pannenberg moves on to examine the traditions of the empty tomb. He notes first of all that if the grave of Jesus had not been empty, it would have made the proclamation of the resurrection impossible.[176] The disciples' claim could easily have been disproven. The Jewish authorities, for example, could simply have produced Jesus' body. Some scholars have suggested that they would have been reluctant to go near the body for fear of ritual impurity. But Pannenberg argues that this suggestion is implausible, for the Gospels assume that the women who go to the tomb have no such scruples. In fact, even the first opponents of Christianity seem to have accepted that the tomb was empty. The empty tomb is, for example, taken for granted by early Jewish anti-Christian polemic.[177] Other scholars have suggested that Jesus' burial place may have been unknown, but Pannenberg notes that there is no evidence at all for such an idea. On the contrary, there is reason to believe that the tradition of Jesus' burial is an ancient one.[178] Indeed, there is reason to believe that the empty tomb traditions came into existence independently of the reports of the appearances. If so, this would makes the subjective vision hypothesis even less likely. It follows that the empty tomb traditions merely confirm Pannenberg's earlier conclusion that Jesus was indeed raised from the dead.[179]

(c) Apocalyptic Assumptions

To evaluate these arguments, we need to uncover their assumptions.

[175]Cf. ibid., 96–97.
[176]Cf. ibid., 100.
[177]Cf. ibid., 101.
[178]Cf. ibid., 103–4.
[179]Cf. ibid., 105–6.

Reduced to its barest outline, Pannenberg's argument is that, in the absence of a more plausible explanation of the New Testament traditions, we should accept the claim that Jesus was raised from the dead. In his later work, Pannenberg does not overturn this judgment, although he does qualify it. His later qualifications are of interest, since they reveal both the assumptions on which this argument is built and the difficulties it soon experiences.

In the second volume of his *Systematic Theology* (1991), Pannenberg at first appears to be maintaining his earlier position. For instance, he insists that the New Testament witness to the resurrection is not to be accepted on blind faith; it is to be tested in the same way as any other historical event.[180] But he also makes at least three revealing concessions. Firstly, he admits that the Christian judgment regarding the resurrection will always be disputed, at least until its truth is confirmed by the general resurrection at the end of time.[181] Secondly, he suggests that he is trying only to affirm that belief in the resurrection "will stand up to historical investigation."[182] He is not trying to say that it is "historically provable," in the sense that it can be established beyond debate. Thirdly, Pannenberg admits that his arguments depends on a certain conception of reality, which assumes the *possibility* of a resurrection of the dead.[183] But he also argues that there is no reason to exclude such a possibility, except secular prejudice. That prejudice is called into question by the biblical idea that God acts in the world.[184] For this reason, Pannenberg argues, it is not those who *affirm* the resurrection but those who *deny* it whose judgment "rests on a prior dogmatic decision."[185]

These are extraordinary claims. What is Pannenberg saying? He is admitting, in effect, that before his argument regarding the resurrection becomes plausible, his readers must accept certain assumptions. They must accept a particular understanding of divine action, and they must accept the possibility of resurrection from the dead. More precisely, Pannenberg's readers must accept both the biblical conception of God and the specifically apocalyptic vision of the end time.[186] Yet Pannenberg insists that it is not those who *believe* in the resurrection but those

---

[180]Cf. Pannenberg, *Systematic Theology,* 2:353.

[181]Cf. ibid., 2:351, 361.

[182]Ibid., 2:361, n.115.

[183]Cf. ibid., 2:362; *Systematic Theology,* 1:56.

[184]Cf. Pannenberg, *Systematic Theology,* 2:362.

[185]Ibid.

[186]For a similar criticism, see Jürgen Moltmann, *Theology of Hope: On the Ground and the Implications of a Christian Eschatology* (1965), translated by James W. Leitch (London: SCM, 1967), 82.

who *deny* it who are dogmatists! What are we to make of these ideas? Is this a tenable position? Do these concessions not undermine his claim that the resurrection of Jesus is a publicly accessible event?

There is another way of approaching this topic, which may shed some light on Pannenberg's argument. It is to reexamine his criticisms of Troeltsch's principle of analogy (which I discussed in the final sections of chapters 2 and 4). In his *Systematic Theology*, Pannenberg repeats his earlier claims about the positive and the negative uses of analogy. He insists—once again—that the absence of an analogy does not *by itself* disqualify a proposed explanation.[187] The fact that such an event does not happen today does not mean that it could not have happened then. Yet Pannenberg has already accepted that analogy marks the limits of our knowledge of the past and that positive analogies are an essential part of any historical explanation.[188] It seems, then, that Pannenberg does not want *to do away with* the principle of analogy. Rather, he wants to expand it, to allow the historian to speak about the resurrection of Jesus. As he writes in *Jesus—God and Man*, "as long as historiography does not begin dogmatically with a narrow concept of reality according to which 'dead men do not rise,' it is not clear why historiography should not in principle be able to speak about Jesus' resurrection."[189]

But on what basis *could* we expand our historiographical assumptions? In the absence of positive analogies (for, after all, the resurrection of Jesus is a unique event), on what basis could we agree that "dead men do rise"? Only, it seems, by accepting what Pannenberg calls "the biblical concept of reality as a field of divine action, including its eschatological consummation."[190] These ideas provide the analogy that the historian needs. (The analogy would, admittedly, be drawn from a depiction of the future, rather than from the present or the past, but it *would* be an analogy.) In other places, Pannenberg makes much the same point, but with more explicit reference to the world of Jewish apocalyptic. In both his earlier and his later work he insists that the resurrection of Jesus is intelligible only against the backdrop of apocalyptic thought. This was certainly true for the disciples: "resurrection" was nothing less than the apocalyptic concept that they used to interpret their experiences.[191]

---

[187]Cf. Pannenberg, *Systematic Theology*, 2:360–61; "Redemptive Event and History," 48–49. (For a discussion of this matter, see the final sections of chapters 2 and 4.)

[188]Pannenberg, "Redemptive Event and History," 50: "The limits of the cognitive power of historical analogy are the limits of possible knowledge of the past generally."

[189]Pannenberg, *Jesus—God and Man*, 109.

[190]Pannenberg, *Systematic Theology*, 2:362.

[191]Cf. Pannenberg, "Dogmatic Theses on the Doctrine of Revelation," 146; *Systematic Theology*, 2:348–49.

Indeed, the apostle Paul himself suggests that belief in the general resurrection is a precondition for belief in the resurrection of Jesus. (Pannenberg here cites 1 Corinthians 15:16: "If the dead are not raised, then Christ has not been raised."[192]) For us, too, the resurrection makes sense and becomes plausible only in the light of apocalyptic thought. As Pannenberg writes in his *Systematic Theology*, "the proclamation of the resurrection of Jesus . . . presupposes the possibility of maintaining with sufficient plausibility the universal validity of Jewish expectation of a general resurrection of the dead, at least in its basic features."[193] Even in the midst of arguing for the reality of Jesus' resurrection in *Jesus—God and Man*, Pannenberg admits that his argument functions only "if an element of truth is to be granted to the apocalyptic expectation."[194] But what does this mean for his argument regarding the resurrection? It means that those who wish to affirm the resurrection must also demonstrate the truth of the apocalyptic worldview. For it is only in the light of this apocalyptic worldview that belief in the resurrection becomes intelligible.

(d) The Truth of Apocalyptic

Can this be done? Can one demonstrate the plausibility of the resurrection of Jesus by demonstrating the truth of the apocalyptic worldview? If one could, then Pannenberg might expect his arguments regarding the resurrection to carry some weight. But we should note what this involves. As Pannenberg himself admits, the apocalyptic worldview embodies a whole range of assumptions regarding God and his relationship to the world.[195] To make this worldview plausible to the non-Christian enquirer will be a difficult task. To be fair, we should note that Pannenberg does make some gestures in this direction. But a quick glance at these gestures show that they do not lead very far.

In *Jesus—God and Man*, Pannenberg supports the apocalyptic conception of the end times by arguing—on phenomenological grounds—that "it belongs to the essence of conscious human existence to hope beyond death."[196] (By itself, of course, an argument from the *phenomenon* of hope in the face of death proves little. This hope could be merely a widespread and persistent delusion, as Feuerbach would have argued.) Pannenberg then notes that our contemporary understanding of human

---

[192]Pannenberg, *Jesus—God and Man*, 81.

[193]Pannenberg, *Systematic Theology*, 2:351.

[194]Pannenberg, *Jesus—God and Man*, 97–98.

[195]Cf. Wolfhart Pannenberg, *Systematic Theology* (1993), translated by Geoffrey W. Bromiley (Grand Rapids: Eerdmans, 1998), 3:532.

[196]Pannenberg, *Jesus—God and Man*, 85.

beings has made belief in the immortality of the soul unacceptable, for "the idea of a soul existing without a body is no longer possible."[197] These two facts together, he argues, lend support to belief in a bodily "resurrection of the dead." Yet even if one accepts the argument to this point, Pannenberg admits, we do not yet have satisfactory evidence for the apocalyptic worldview *in its entirety*. For the apocalyptic vision of the end-times consists of much more than belief in the resurrection of the dead. Pannenberg begins his further argument for the apocalyptic vision by making two points. He argues first of all that the unity of humanity suggests that, if resurrection occurs, it may be assumed to be a universal event. This lends support to the idea of a *general* resurrection. He then suggests that this resurrection must occur at the *end* of history, since it cannot be thought of as happening within this world.[198] At this point, he breaks off his argument, noting only that a fuller discussion belongs to what he calls "a systematic anthropology."[199] These considerations, he writes, are enough to show that "the expectation of a resurrection of the dead need not appear meaningless from the presuppositions of modern thought."[200]

In his *Systematic Theology*, Pannenberg reaffirms his earlier position: he admits that belief in the resurrection of Jesus depends on belief in the general resurrection. He also notes that this latter belief requires the support of some kind of argument.[201] But in this context he is content to take the possibility of such an argument for granted. As he writes, "fuller discussion of this theme belongs to the whole sphere of eschatological problems and hence will have to come later. For the moment we may provisionally presuppose the possibility of this type of argument."[202] Yet in the third volume of his *Systematic Theology* (1993), where Pannenberg comes to deal with eschatology, the matter is not substantially advanced. Pannenberg traces the decline and revival of eschatological thought in modern theology. He notes that, while Christian hope is rightly based on the promises of God, those promises need to be given some kind of anthropological grounding.[203] He refers to Kant's argument in favor of immortality, while noting that it "cannot yield rational certainty" and is "always exposed to the suspicion" that it rests on "subjective projections"

[197]Ibid., 87.
[198]Cf. ibid., 87–88.
[199]Ibid., 88.
[200]Ibid.
[201]Cf. Pannenberg, *Systematic Theology*, 2:351.
[202]Ibid., 2:352.
[203]Cf. Pannenberg, *Systematic Theology*, 3:539–41.

(that is to say, mere wishful thinking).[204] Pannenberg looks with more favor on the work of the Roman Catholic theologian Karl Rahner, while noting that even his arguments "can offer no certainty" regarding a future hope.[205] In a word, no argument one can adduce in favor of Christian hope amounts to a "final proof" of its content.[206] It shows, at most, that the Christian hope *corresponds to* human aspirations and needs. It is not even clear that one can produce a definitive argument in support of the idea that our world will eventually end.[207]

On what, then, is the Christian's confidence based? It is based, not on the strength of such arguments, but on the life, death, and resurrection of Jesus, which confirms the apocalyptic vision.[208] (In the earlier volume of his *Systematic Theology,* Pannenberg notes that precisely this argument is put forward by the apostle Paul, who can argue from Jesus' resurrection to the general resurrection *as well as* vice versa.[209]) As Pannenberg writes, "in the work of Jesus the future of the kingdom is already present, and the same is true of the Easter event as regards his person. . . . Precisely for this reason Jesus Christ is the basis of the hope of his community as it looks ahead to the consummation that has yet to come."[210] It may well be true that the resurrection of Jesus confirms the truth of the apocalyptic vision, as Pannenberg argues, but it is the resurrection of Jesus whose reality is under dispute. If this argument is then taken to support belief in the resurrection of Jesus, it can only be described as hopelessly circular.

The problem with this argument may be clarified by reference, yet again, to the principle of analogy. In his earlier work, Pannenberg argues that historical phenomena are characterized by their particularity. For this reason they "cannot be contained without remainder in any analogy."[211] This is, of course, true and is a good reason for caution. One should not be too quick to exclude a possible explanation simply because the event it postulates is without precise analogy. Yet it is an entirely different matter when an event is without *any* analogy. In this case, the explanation will be without historical plausibility. Indeed, it is not clear how one could even *begin* to speak about the event concerned, if there is nothing else in our experience to which it could be con-

---

[204]Ibid., 3:542.

[205]Ibid., 3:543.

[206]Cf. ibid., 3:541–42.

[207]Cf. ibid., 3:589–93.

[208]Cf. ibid., 3:544–45, 550, 593. See also Pannenberg, "On Historical and Theological Hermeneutic," 178–79; "Dogmatic Theses on the Doctrine of Revelation," 141.

[209]Cf. Pannenberg, *Systematic Theology,* 2:351.

[210]Pannenberg, *Systematic Theology,* 3:545.

[211]Pannenberg, "Redemptive Event and History," 46.

nected. As Pannenberg indicates, much Christian apologetic has focused on finding parallels to the resurrection in our own experience,[212] which is the only way the event can be described, let alone made plausible. (Hence the popularity of seeds falling into the ground, the myth of the phoenix or—in our own day—caterpillars turning into butterflies.) At a popular level, the resurrection is often imagined as resembling the resuscitation of one *apparently* dead, which is about the closest analogy we can find from our ordinary experience. However, as theologians often and rightly insist, "resurrection" does not mean resuscitation.[213] Again, this is true, but it merely raises the question, What then *does* it mean? If one no longer inhabits the world of the apocalyptic imagination, there remains no analogy that would make the term intelligible, let alone a plausible explanation of a historical event. Pannenberg rightly insists that to understand the resurrection we must occupy the world of apocalyptic thought. But he can give the unbelieving historian no convincing reason why he should do so.

What follows? By the end of his *Systematic Theology,* Pannenberg's claim that the resurrection of Jesus can be established historically—a claim that he modifies but never openly abandons[214]—lies in ruins. A history that requires one to accept from the outset the apocalyptic view of the world is no history at all, but a highly tendentious theology. Insofar as history is a public discipline, which does not involve a prior commitment to particular religious views, there is no sense in which Pannenberg's argument could be presented as "historical." For one would need to be a believer (that is to say, to have already accepted belief in the resurrection of the dead) before this argument would become convincing. In other words, just as Troeltsch's position loses credibility once his idealist and hence teleological view of history becomes no longer plausible, so Pannenberg's loses credibility once one steps outside the framework of apocalyptic thought that the theologian has inherited from the Jewish and Christian scriptures. Pannenberg may insist that apocalyptic thought has much to recommend it, but as he readily admits, this is not yet a convincing argument for its truth. If its truth cannot be demonstrated—and in this context there is no point demonstrating it by reference to the resurrection of Jesus!—then Pannenberg's argument that the resurrection is a historically accessible event collapses. If that argument collapses, it is hard to see on what basis Pannenberg's theology rests, if not on some otherwise ungrounded appeal to "the promises of God."

[212]Cf. Pannenberg, *Systematic Theology,* 2:352.
[213]Cf. ibid., 2:348.
[214]Cf. ibid., 2:353.

An Evaluation

There is no doubt that Pannenberg is one of the few theologians of our time to take seriously the challenge of history to Christian faith. His recovery of the role of reason in relation to faith is a relief to those of us who cannot accept arbitrary appeals to religious authority. Pannenberg's theology has therefore been welcomed by those who are repelled by Barth's exemption of faith from critical scrutiny,[215] or by Bultmann's insistence that faith can achieve a certainty that is immune to doubt.[216] Over against such views, there is something profoundly humane and reasonable about Pannenberg's position. He is prepared to concede that theological claims are "hypothetical," not—admittedly—from the point of view of the assertion of faith, but certainly from the point of view of the hearer or reader.[217] One can only admire at least the early Pannenberg's willingness to admit that, if the resurrection is not historically demonstrable, it is all over with Christianity.[218] Here at last is something that can be meaningfully discussed by believers and nonbelievers alike. Indeed, I would not be doing justice to Pannenberg's theology if I did not take up his invitation and subject it to criticism. Some fairly severe criticisms have been offered already. Here I wish to offer some further reflections, beginning with another pillar of Pannenberg's theology, namely, his understanding of the work of the historian.

(a) The Unity of History

As we have seen, Pannenberg argues that the historian must take for granted the unity of history.[219] Surely this claim deserves closer examination. It may be true that the historian must assume a certain unity in human affairs. It may also be true that if we are interested in the meaning of history *as a whole,* then this can only be known only by reference to the end of history.[220] But at this point the question may be asked: Do we *need* to know the meaning of history "as a whole" in order to write

[215]Cf. Barth, *The Göttingen Dogmatics,* §8.3 (220–21); *Church Dogmatics* I/2, §19.2 (535).

[216]Cf. Bultmann, "Liberal Theology and the Latest Theological Movement," 32.

[217]Cf. Pannenberg, *Theology and the Philosophy of Science,* 332–33; *Systematic Theology,* 1:56–58.

[218]Cf. Pannenberg, *Jesus—God and Man,* 28, 108–14.

[219]Cf. Pannenberg, "Redemptive Event and History," 68–69.

[220]Cf. Pannenberg, "Dogmatic Theses on the Doctrine of Revelation," 142; "On Historical and Theological Hermeneutic," 163 et passim.

meaningful history?[221] In other words, can one assume a certain unity in history (so that its study is meaningful) without claiming to know in advance history's goal?[222]

The answer to this question depends upon what one means by "the unity of history." At least two meanings may be attributed to this phrase. First of all, the historian must assume a certain unity to history in the sense that she must assume that human beings have something in common—across time and space—that makes the study of other cultures and other ages possible. (It is this commonality that Troeltsch assumed for most of his life but that his final work begins to call into question.[223]) It does seem that *without* such a unity, there can *be* no history, a fact that makes the recent "postmodern" challenges to this idea particularly serious.[224] This is an important matter, but it does not seem to be the sense in which Pannenberg is using the phrase "the unity of history." In any case, this first meaning of the phrase "the unity of history" does not imply that one requires a vision of history in its totality.

There is, however, a second, more pragmatic sense in which one can speak of the unity of history. It is the fact that in the study of history the local and the universal are interrelated. Troeltsch gives expression to an

---

[221]Arthur Danto (*Narration and Knowledge,* 353) suggests that if we did know the future (which we must do if we are to know the meaning of history as a whole), this would make the writing of history impossible. The predestination implied in such knowledge would dissolve any sense of a link between present and future and would reduce "history" to a chronicle of independent events.

[222]Hans-Georg Gadamer (*Truth and Method,* 174) notes that Dilthey's insistence that there is no history without world history is drawn from "the application to history of the hermeneutical principle that we can understand a detail only in terms of the whole text" (a fact that Pannenberg acknowledges [cf. "On Historical and Theological Hermeneutic," 162]). But while Dilthey's successors (including von Ranke) agreed that the historian needed a sense of world history, they also argued that this did not necessarily mean knowing the *goal* of history. Their view of history was teleological, but it was (Gadamer argues [ibid., 179]) a teleology "without a telos." As I pointed out in the case of Troeltsch, this view depends on a certain kind of philosophical idealism, as Gadamer also notes (cf. ibid., 185). But it does suggest that there exist ways of assuming a certain unity within history—at least as a "regulative idea" (ibid., 183) of historical research—without claiming to know its goal.

[223]Troeltsch, "The Place of Christianity among the World-Religions," 23–24. "What was really common to mankind, and universally valid for it, seemed . . . to be at bottom exceedingly little, and to belong more to the province of material goods than to the ideal values of civilisation."

[224]Cf. Peter Novick, *That Noble Dream: The "Objectivity Question" and the American Historical Association,* Ideas in Context (Cambridge: Cambridge University Press, 1988), chap. 14 (469–521). Novick's chapter is entitled "Every group its own historian."

extreme form of this idea when he writes that "all historical happening is knit together in a permanent relationship of correlation"; in this sense "every single event is related to all others."[225] The historian may choose to study a small section of the flow of human history: her subject may be apparently local. But she will very often find that these local events cannot be *fully* understood without reference to what was happening (or had happened) elsewhere. It is true that in practice the historian is not obliged to—and indeed cannot—trace all these relationships. The historian abstracts from the complexity of the historical process certain aspects of the past that are of interest for various reasons. There is nothing final or definitive about the resulting historical narrative, which will need to be revised as our interests change and as new events occur to which the past must then be related. Nor does the historian ever claim that this is a *complete* depiction of the past.[226] Nonetheless, the historian's scope is *in principle* unlimited. In this sense local history and world history are inseparable.

Yet even these reflections do not imply that we must know the *whole* of history. In particular, they do not imply that we must know the goal of the historical process. At least, they do not carry this implication *if* we are prepared to accept that the historian's knowledge is provisional and open to revision. Based on her knowledge of world history, a bold (or perhaps foolish) historian might speculate as to the direction in which history might move in the future. But such speculation is by no means essential to the study of history; indeed many historians would argue that it is entirely out of place.[227] Pannenberg's desire to know the meaning of history as a whole, and his assertion that we cannot understand particular events without this knowledge, seems to assume that unless our knowledge is complete and definitive, it is not knowledge at all. (Pannenberg perhaps has this in common with Hegel and his disciples.) If the historian is content—as she must be—with a more modest but more achievable aim, the historical side of Pannenberg's theological project collapses.

(b) The Reappropriation of Apocalyptic

The other side of Pannenberg's theology, namely his reappropriation of apocalyptic thought, also has its difficulties. In particular, there exists a

---

[225]Troeltsch, "Historical and Dogmatic Method," 14; *The Historical Jesus Quest,* 33.

[226]Danto (cf. *Narration and Knowledge,* 17–18) argues that the very idea of a complete depiction of the past is incoherent, since the historian's depiction of the past includes its relationship to later events, and at least some of these are unknown to us. In a word, we cannot completely describe the past, since we cannot know the future.

[227]Pannenberg's appeal to Collingwood ("Redemptive Event and History," 72) is odd, since the latter insists (*The Idea of History,* 54) that "eschatology is always an intrusive element into history. The historian's business is to know the past, not to know the future."

tension between the idea that the future is still open and the idea that the future has been revealed in the resurrection of Jesus. As we have seen, Pannenberg is quick to insist on the contingency of historical events: he opposes any suggestion that the course of history is predetermined. Indeed, he argues that the openness of history is preserved by belief in a God whose decisive self-revelation is still to occur.[228] But this wholly admirable insistence on the openness of history must be reconciled with Pannenberg's further suggestion that the goal of history has already been revealed in the resurrection of Jesus. Admittedly, Pannenberg insists that this revelation is a provisional revelation.[229] For the resurrection of Jesus is "only an anticipation of the end, not the end itself,"[230] since we still await the general resurrection of the dead. But the difference between the two is "quantitative," not "qualitative": in the resurrection of Jesus we experience what Pannenberg calls *"the eschatological reality itself."*[231] This fact raises the question of the openness of history. For if we truly know the future, then the future must be predetermined: a real knowledge of the future must undermine the idea of human freedom.[232] On the face of it, therefore, one cannot have *both* a knowledge of the future *and* a history that is truly contingent and in which human freedom is preserved. Admittedly, Pannenberg could escape from this dilemma. He could argue, for instance, that the future is known *only in general terms,* so that its details are still open. (We might know, for instance, that there will be a resurrection of the dead, but we do not know the fate of individuals.) But these are questions that still have to be answered.[233]

Even if answers could be found, Pannenberg's theology—along with any philosophy that claims to know the goal of history—may have some undesirable consequences. The fact that Pannenberg identifies Karl Marx's understanding of history with the biblical view should be warning

[228]Cf. Pannenberg, "Redemptive Event and History," 75–76.

[229]Cf. Wolfhart Pannenberg, "Hermeneutic and Universal History" (1963), in *Basic Questions in Theology,* 1:135; "On Historical and Theological Hermeneutic," 171.

[230]Pannenberg, "On Historical and Theological Hermeneutic," 179.

[231]Ibid. (emphasis mine; cf. ibid., 181).

[232]Cf. Danto, *Narration and Knowledge,* 352–53.

[233]The same problem attends Pannenberg's insistence (cf. "Toward a Theology of the History of Religions," 110) that no completed event can be a definitive divine revelation since this would contradict the infinity of God. The problem here is that he also wants to argue that the resurrection of Jesus *is* a definitive and unsurpassable revelation. He can hold these two together only by arguing that the infinity of God is reflected in the openness of the future and that Jesus' teaching and resurrection point toward this still open future. However, we may ask once again, if the resurrection is a truly foretaste of the eschatological events, in what sense is that future still open?

enough.[234] (One is reminded of Sir Karl Popper's protest against the totalitarianism of those who claim to know the goal of human history.[235]) It is true that there is a kind of "eschatological reserve" in Pannenberg's theology. He would argue that, although the goal of history has been revealed in Jesus, only *God* can finally inaugurate his kingdom, and our knowledge of God's future remains always provisional.[236] Yet, however provisional our knowledge of God's future may be, it *is* knowledge, a knowledge revealed to us in the resurrection of Jesus. Herein lies the problem, for as the history of Jewish apocalyptic makes clear, human beings are all too inclined to take these matters into their own hands. Either they try to set in motion the sequence of events by which history will be brought to an end (the utopian temptation), or they exalt their own age as the high point and goal of human development (the ideological trend).[237] If Schweitzer is correct, Jesus himself may have succumbed to the first of these temptations, accepting death in the hope that it would initiate the arrival of God's kingdom. In any case, apocalyptic thought led to tragedy in the history of biblical Judaism. It has led to still greater tragedies when embodied in the secularized forms of apocalyptic thought so characteristic of our own time.

(c) The Christian View of History

Finally, we have seen that Pannenberg argues from the nature of historiography to the Christian view of history, since only belief in the Christian God enables us to attribute unity to history without sacrificing its contingency.[238] If (as I have suggested) the historian does not need to attribute unity to history *as a whole,* this argument carries no weight. In

[234]Cf. Pannenberg, "Dogmatic Theses on the Doctrine of Revelation," 133.

[235]Karl Popper, *The Poverty of Historicism* (1957; London: Ark Paperbacks/Routledge, 1986), 3 et passim.

[236]Cf. Pannenberg, "Dogmatic Theses on the Doctrine of Revelation," 144: "The church is always tempted to play down the still-impending future of the eschatological life and to forget that all forms of Christian life in this world are provisional." (See also Pannenberg's "Toward a Theology of the History of Religions," 110; "Redemptive Event and History," 37; "Hermeneutic and Universal History," 135; "On Historical and Theological Hermeneutic," 171.)

[237]One thinks not only of the various forms of Marxist and Fascist utopianism, against which Popper fought, but also of the more recent (ideological) position which holds that, with the triumph of global capitalism and—less obviously—liberal democracy, history has indeed come to an end. There is nowhere else to go; nothing more to hope for. This seems to be a secularized form of what theologians call "realized eschatology." "If you wish to know the goal of history, look around you!"

[238]Cf. Pannenberg, "Redemptive Event and History," 74–78.

any case, by itself it hardly proves what Pannenberg wants it to prove. To suggest that the unity of history must be sought in something outside of history is to argue in favor of some kind of theism, but Christian theism is by no means the only option. To argue in favor of the Christian view of history, Pannenberg needs an additional argument. He finds this in the idea that one can demonstrate historically that Jesus was raised from the dead, his resurrection being the anticipation of the goal of history. Yet Pannenberg's attempt to demonstrate that the resurrection *is* a matter of public knowledge fails, since at the crucial moment it must presuppose that which it is seeking to demonstrate. In a word, while Pannenberg is surely right to seek a reasonable solution to the question of history and faith, his attempts to do so cannot be said to have been a success.

3. The Present Situation

These few reflections are scarcely an adequate response to these more recent developments. Yet they suggest that neither Ernst Käsemann nor Wolfhart Pannenberg have come any closer to answering the questions posed by the development of the seventeenth century. It may be worth calling to mind what those questions were. In the introductory chapter I traced the process whereby the knowledge of the seventeenth century broke out of the framework which the Bible had provided. The result was an unprecedented challenge to biblical authority. If the Bible can no longer be taken as a reliable account of the past, can we believe what it says about Jesus? Is the biblical Jesus the "real Jesus"? Is the real Jesus, the Jesus of history, of any interest to our own time? More seriously, if the Bible's *historical* authority is under threat, then what of its *doctrinal* authority? What happens to the great body of beliefs that were tradition-ally justified (and can only be justified) by appeal to the Bible? In the broader sweep of human history, does the Bible not become merely one religious authority among others? Should they not all be treated in the same way? Can Christianity hold its own in this contest of competing religions?

If we look at the attempts to answer these questions in the years since Barth and Bultmann, the most honest and straightforward attempt has undoubtedly been that of Pannenberg. The merit of Pannenberg's work is that it picks up Käsemann's claim that history *is* important to faith and that a bridge must be found between religious and historical claims if Christianity is to regain its plausibility. Yet he himself has been unable to build this bridge. He *affirms* that faith must be based on claims about the past that can be independently verified, but he himself has been unable to live up to this ideal. While Ernst Troeltsch remained faithful to his historical method, with the result that his theology is barely Christian, Pannenberg does produce a thoroughly Christian theology (in three volumes!), but by effectively abandoning the rational ideals he himself put forward. By the end of his work, it is difficult to see that his theology is based on anything more than the same ungrounded appeal to faith that Pannenberg so strongly rejected in the work of Barth and Bultmann.

As I have just noted, the key issue to emerge from the revolution of the seventeenth century was that of biblical authority. It was not only a matter of reconciling particular Christian claims with historical knowledge and the methods of historical scholarship. (Could one, for instance, talk about miracles or about the greatest miracle of all, the resurrection?) It was also a question of whether one could still appeal to biblical authority in support of one's religious claims. How, if at all, could appeals to biblical authority be justified? If they cannot be justified, it is hard to see what would become of the great body of Christian doctrine, a body of doctrine traditionally deduced from biblical authority. The theological research tradition we have been studying attempted to find an answer to this question. Has it been successful? Can historical knowledge and religious authority be reconciled? This is the issue to which I will turn in my final chapter.

Conclusion

The Lessons of History

In the last analysis we are concerned not with Christianity but with the truth.
Ernst Troeltsch

This survey of the historical Jesus question has taken us from the mid-seventeenth century to the late twentieth. It has spanned a period of extraordinary change in European intellectual life, from the emergence of the modern world with its challenges to an age that often thinks of itself as "postmodern." It has not, of course, been an exhaustive survey: many other authors have contributed to this debate. In particular, I have not attempted to survey the more recent attempts by historians to depict the figure of Jesus. I have said very little about the "new quest" of the historical Jesus initiated by Käsemann; I have entirely neglected the so-called "third quest," which continues to the present day. For the focus of this book has been on the larger question of the challenge of history to religious authority. As I noted in chapter 7, in recent years this question has been largely neglected (Wolfhart Pannenberg is here the honorable exception), and it is surely time it was revisited. While—for better or for worse—the debate will undoubtedly continue, it does seem reasonable to draw some conclusions. Is there anything we can learn from the authors studied? What are the strengths and weaknesses of the answers they gave? What may we learn from their successes and their failures?

The Challenge Summarized

In the introduction to the present work, I suggested that the authors we have studied form part of a single research tradition. That research tradition emerged as a result of the religious challenges that began in the seventeenth century. One of those challenges was that of the development of a secular sense of history, a change that—following Hans Frei—I have described as "the great reversal." The new knowledge which that century provided could no longer be "shoehorned" (as it were) into the framework provided by the Bible.[1] Rather, that knowledge provided a new, nonreligious framework into which the Bible could be fitted and against

---

[1] For this image, see Preus, *Explaining Religion,* 82.

which it could be judged. The result was a radical and unprecedented challenge to religious authority, a challenge reinforced by the growth of the new natural sciences and by disillusionment with religious conflict.

If we were to sum up that challenge in two rather ugly words, we could say that its effect was both to "relativize" and to "level." The new historical consciousness "relativized" historical phenomena, insofar as it suggested that certain aspects of cultural life may be of significance only to the people of a particular time and place. It could no longer be assumed that they were of significance for us. This challenge had particular implications for our understanding of Jesus, since it raised the question of whether he could be a religious leader for our time. More seriously, the new historical consciousness "leveled" all the phenomena that fell within its scope. It did so in two senses. Firstly, it insisted that we could understand the past only by way of the principle of analogy. In the field of religion, for instance, the Christian miracle stories must be understood by reference to similar reports from our own time and from other religious traditions. Secondly, the new historical consciousness refused to grant an a priori authority to any particular cultural phenomenon. In the sphere of religion, the Bible was reduced to being one alleged authority among others. Its reliability—whether in historical or religious matters—could no longer be taken for granted. Still more seriously, Christianity was reduced to one religion among others. Even if aspects of the biblical message or of the work of the historical Jesus could be shown to be (relatively) unique, even if their relevance to our own time could be demonstrated, this was no reason for privileging them theologically. One could not take it for granted that they represented a uniquely authoritative revelation of God. For similar claims could be made for the foundational documents and events of other religious traditions. They could also be seen as relatively unique and capable of addressing our age. At least in the public forum, the burden of proof now fell on those who would affirm the religious authority of the Bible rather than on those who would deny it.

Before summarizing the varied responses to this crisis, I should note that there does exist an alternative. There is a way of dealing with the challenge of history that the present study has not yet mentioned, for it falls outside the research tradition that is the subject of this book. It involves simply continuing to believe and practise one's faith, as Christians had done for so many centuries before these fateful questions arose. Outside the world of the academic study of religion, this attitude is widespread. Insofar as they assume that all believers are (or perhaps should be) concerned with these matters, theologians perhaps overestimate the importance of their work. When adopted in a self-conscious way, this attitude of indifference can be described as "fundamentalism." Yet there are also those who continue to practice their faith in an *un*self-conscious way, since (as D. F. Strauss once remarked) not everyone adopts at one time the characteristic thought forms of a particular age.[2] In our own age, however, it has become increasingly difficult to maintain this state of innocence, as religious questions are debated on television and blazoned forth in popular books and magazines. Once one begins to discuss these matters, whether sympathetically or in a self-conscious act of defiance, one is engaged in the theological task, and the state of innocence has been lost.

A Theological Problem

The theological response to this loss of innocence has been the subject of this book. I should note, too, that it is the *theological* response in which I am interested. While these questions may have serious personal implications—as we saw in the case of David Friedrich Strauss—I am not concerned with those implications here. The individual's choice to belong to a particular religious tradition is one matter; theology as a public discussion of religious claims is another. One could argue that the two should not be separated, but for the purpose of discussion they may be distinguished. Indeed some of the murkiness that accompanies these discussions arises from a failure to make this distinction. A brief discussion of this matter may help to clarify the limits of the present study.

The theological question, properly so-called, is that of the truth—or, more precisely, the defensibility—of certain religious claims. Traditionally, Christians have based their claims to truth not merely on rational arguments but also on the authority of the Bible and of the events and people of which it speaks.[3] It is true that a purely "natural theology," relying on reason alone, was a popular option among the deists. It remains a possible option today. But it scarcely corresponds to Christianity as traditionally understood. Traditionally it has been the Bible, and not reason alone, that is the source of Christian faith. Even today it is hard to see how Christianity could continue without some form of dependence—however qualified—on biblical authority. If there is to be anything distinctive about Christian belief, it will surely be drawn from

---

[2]Cf. Strauss, *The Life of Jesus Critically Examined*, §13 (74).

[3]See, for instance, Thomas Aquinas, *Summa Contra Gentiles*, I.3. While Protestant Christianity casts doubt on the possibility of a "natural theology," this merely strengthens the traditional idea that we know certain truths only through an authoritative revelation. For a helpful description of this understanding of faith, see Anthony Kenny's *What Is Faith? Essays in the Philosophy of Religion*, 46–60.

the biblical witness. It follows that the Christian theologian must be able to argue that the authority of the Bible is in some sense reliable. In addition to this, Christian theology customarily claims to have its own integrity: it makes little reference to other religions once its basic claims are established. For this reason the theologian must argue, not only that the Bible is a reliable authority, but that it is a uniquely reliable authority. It is only on the basis of a uniquely reliable source of religious claims that something resembling the traditional shape of Christian theology can be maintained. If Christian theology is to continue, if it is to present itself as a respectable form of public discussion, it is faced with this fundamental question: What publicly contestable arguments may be put forward for the idea that either the Bible or the historical figure of Jesus are uniquely reliable religious authorities?

That is the theological question around which the present study has been centered. The question of individual religious practice is another matter. It is the question as to whether I should commit myself to this particular religious tradition or, more commonly, remain within it. While theological considerations will surely enter into such a decision, the two issues are by no means identical. There are at least two reasons for this. Firstly, the maintenance of religious practice may still be defensible even in the absence of a satisfactory theology. The existence of unresolved theological difficulties does not exclude the possibility that a solution may yet be found, any more than the existence of unresolved problems disqualifies a set of scientific theories.[4] If there are other good reasons to hold the beliefs in question, one may reasonably continue to do so, at least for a time, in the hope that they may yet be vindicated. (In any case, a religious commitment, if it is to have any force, must be a relatively stable matter. It should not be immune to criticism, but neither can it be undone by every argument that can be brought against it.) Secondly, the factors influencing religious practice go far beyond the arguments that may be mustered for and against belief. To speak bluntly, one can go to church for a variety of reasons, not all of which have to do with the credibility of Christian faith. Some of these reasons may be perfectly respectable. However much theological arguments ought to be a contributing factor—perhaps in the end a decisive factor—in determining one's religious practice, they are by no means all that is involved.

I am all too aware that these matters require a more extensive treatment. But enough has been said to indicate why I wish to distinguish the question of religious practice from the question of theology. There is

---

[4]Cf. Laudan, *Progress and Its Problems,* 26–30.

something intensely personal and indeed incommunicable about the individual's commitment to a particular religious tradition. But theology has at least traditionally aspired to be a public discipline, whose "rules of engagement" are (in principle) comprehensible to all. More importantly, theologians have traditionally claimed to be dealing with truths that are public, not merely private. The object of theology has normally been understood to be a reality that makes demands on us all. In this context, therefore, what I am interested in is the theological question. More precisely, I am interested in the success or failure of the theological research tradition that attempts to reconcile claims to biblical authority with the historical consciousness of the modern age.

The Options Summarized

The theological options the present study has identified are three in number. The first is what we might call an acceptance of the challenges of history followed by the abandonment of theology as traditionally understood. This is the path exemplified, in both a Jewish and a Christian context, by Benedict Spinoza and David Friedrich Strauss. This option is often, although not always, associated with the abandonment of religion *tout court*. A second option consists of the attempt to reformulate Christian claims in the light of these challenges. This is the path taken, again in very different ways, by Albert Schweitzer, Ernst Troeltsch, Rudolf Bultmann (in at least one aspect of his work), Ernst Käsemann, and Wolfhart Pannenberg. The third option is that of attempting to shield traditional Christian claims from the corrosive effect of historical criticism by creating a "safe area" within which the faith may flourish. This was the path taken by both Karl Barth and Rudolf Bultmann (insofar as Bultmann may be classified as a dialectical theologian). The task that remains is that of assessing the viability of each of these options.

1. The Rejection of Traditional Theology

The first option is the rejection of theology as traditionally understood. Since theology as traditionally understood takes its stand on the acceptance of the authority of the Bible, this option involves the abandonment of biblical authority. It was illustrated first of all by the work of Benedict Spinoza, who—after rejecting the authoritative traditions of Judaism—developed his own deeply rational religious vision. It was illustrated very differently by David Friedrich Strauss, who not only rejected traditional Christian theology, but also abandoned its Hegelian reinterpretation. Indeed, toward the end of his life Strauss arrived at a position that scarcely counts as religious at all, at least in any traditional sense. In his case the theological crisis precipitated a personal crisis of faith and a movement beyond the bounds of Christianity.

There is much to be said for this option, which has the virtue of being honest and straightforward. The key figure here is surely Strauss. His work raised in the starkest possible terms the central question of the historical Jesus debate. Can the distinctive claims of the Christian tradition still be defended after the reliability of the documents in which they are embodied has been called into question? For as we have just seen, the authority of the Christian faith has traditionally rested on the reliability of the witnesses to its foundational events. Once "the great reversal" has occurred, once the Bible is no longer the taken-for-granted framework of knowledge, what role is left for the theologian? If the Bible can no longer function as "the metanarrative to end all metanarratives," what function *can* it play? Strauss's final answer to this question was a simple one. The Bible no longer has a role to play. A theology that can no longer make its traditional claims is not worth attempting to preserve, and we must honestly face the consequences of what is effectively a loss of faith.

Many believers argue that those consequences are so serious that biblical authority must be preserved, however desperate the strategies by which this is achieved. This, too, is a serious argument. (One is reminded of the anguished admission of Ivan in Dostoevsky's *The Brothers Karamazov* that without faith in God, "everything is permitted."[5]) As I noted at the end of chapter 2, Strauss is perhaps not fully aware of the strength of this position: he is not sufficiently conscious of the cultural crisis created by "the death of God." His contemporary, Friedrich Nietzsche, who was perhaps his fiercest critic, had a deeper grasp of these issues.[6] Ernst Troeltsch defended the Christian faith in a similar way, by arguing that the consequences of its abandonment are too awful to be borne. For he argued that, without the idea of God ("or something analogous" to this), we are simply unable to make binding ethical judgments.[7] He also argued that—for this purpose—the distant God of deism is of no use to us: historical value judgments require belief in a God who is involved

---

[5]Cf. Fyodor Dostoevsky, *The Brothers Karamazov,* translated by Ignat Avsey, World's Classics (Oxford: Oxford University Press, 1994), 87, 330 (book 2, chap. 6; book 5, chap. 5). Ivan, interestingly enough, does not deny the *existence* of God, but rejects as morally repugnant the world which that God has apparently created. His attitude, as the pious Alyosha realizes with horror, is one of rebellion, not simply unbelief (cf. ibid., 308).

[6]Cf. Nietzsche, "David Strauss, the Confessor and the Writer," in *Untimely Meditations,* 3–55.

[7]Cf. Troeltsch, *Der Historismus und seine Probleme,* 183–84.

with the world. If history is to be the source of our judgments of value, Troeltsch argues, then we need *something like* the prophetic and Christian view of God. Once again, this is a serious and a powerful argument. It does not, we should note, necessarily lend support to the *Christian* view of God in all its specificity. It does lend support to something like an idealist view of history, one that sees history as the gradual manifestation of a divine spirit. Such a view is all that is required to support our judgments of value. We have seen that an idealist view of history was characteristic of Troeltsch's work and undergird his philosophy of religion. Whether an idealist view of history, in turn, lends support to traditional Christian claims is a question to which we will return shortly.

One can therefore attempt to buttress biblical authority by appeal to its ethical utility. But there are problems with such an argument. The first has to do with the alleged dependence of morality on religion. Are the two really inseparable? Bultmann, for instance, saw the history of ethical thought as the history of its *emancipation* from religion, an emancipation that finds its high point in Kant's insistence on the autonomy of ethical judgments.[8] David Friedrich Strauss also opposes the idea that morality is dependent on religion. Indeed, Strauss highlights a second problem with this position. For the postulation of a religious foundation for ethics takes for granted the reliability of religious authority, and it is the reliability of religious authority which is in question. As Strauss remarks curtly, "we cannot make a prop of our action out of a faith which we no longer possess."[9] In other words, the assertion of the human *need* for faith cannot by itself *produce* faith. It certainly cannot produce the kind of faith that could once again undergird the moral order of society. (As we have seen, in practice Schweitzer seems to have accepted this fact, and Troeltsch comes very close to holding a similar view.[10]) This objection applies to any argument in favor of religion that begins with the words "we need." It *is* tempting to invoke religion as the ultimate guarantor of morality, as did many of the deists of the eighteenth century. Yet, in a world in which religious authority has already been called into question, it is hard to see how one could convincingly base an ethics on religious claims. For such a strategy amounts to defending the doubtful by the more doubtful. In other words, if moral claims can be called into question, religious claims are even more questionable,

---

[8]Cf. Bultmann, "Religion und Kultur," 15–16.
[9]Strauss, *The Old Faith and the New,* §31 (98–99).
[10]Cf. Troeltsch, "The Common Spirit," 123–24.

and the attempt to defend the first by reference to the second is surely doomed to failure.[11]

Faced with what he saw as the indefensibility of traditional religious views, Spinoza set about the task of radically rethinking the nature of God, so as to preserve a religious attitude towards a world radically stripped of anthropomorphism. Strauss, too, in his last work, set himself to work out the consequences of living in a world that was no longer shaped by religious faith. If those consequences were more horrifying than he was able to see, that is no reason for shying away from the question or for taking refuge, by various stratagems, in a faith that can no longer be defended. As Horton Harris writes—in a passage already cited but that bears repeating—Strauss is right to remind us of the seriousness of the challenge:

> Strauss's *Life of Jesus* was the most intellectually reasoned attack which has ever been mounted against Christianity. . . . Strauss confronted theology with an either/or: either show that the Christian faith is historically and intellectually credible, or admit that it is based on myth and delusion. That was the alternative. Nothing less was and is at stake than the whole historical and intellectual basis of Christianity. If Strauss cannot be convincingly answered, then it would appear that Christianity must slowly but surely collapse.[12]

Strauss's great merit was to ask unflinchingly the questions posed by the intellectual developments of the seventeenth century and to follow the consequences courageously. That led him outside of the world of Christian theology and therefore outside the research tradition that is the subject of this book. For he no longer believed that tradition could be maintained. Yet there were many who believed those questions *could* be "convincingly answered." We must now ask whether they were correct.

---

[11]Of course, it could be argued that the very existence of a sense of moral obligation demands that we postulate the existence of a God, at least as a regulative idea shaping our actions. (This observation represents the "axiological" or moral argument for belief in God.) But this is an entirely different matter from arguing that we need religion in order to act morally. As Kant wrote (*Dreams of a Spirit-Seer* [1766], translated by E. F. Goerwitz, Key Texts: Classic Studies in the History of Ideas [Bristol: Thoemmes Press, 1900/1992], 121), it is "more in accordance with human nature and the purity of morals to ground the expectation of a future world upon the sentiment of a good, than, conversely, to base the soul's good conduct upon the hope of another world."

[12]Harris, *David Friedrich Strauss,* 282.

2. The Rethinking of Christian Claims

The second theological option we have examined is that of embracing the new worldview of the seventeenth century and attempting to reformulate Christian claims in the light of this knowledge. This was the path chosen by those "liberal" theologians who wished to bring about a reconciliation between faith and history. The theological options here are two in number. The first *broadens* the field of divine revelation by looking to history as a whole; the second *narrows* its scope by looking to Jesus' ethical teaching alone. By way of a summary, we may examine each of these in turn.

The Revelation of God in History

The first strategy is exemplified by (a) the Hegelian reinterpretation of Christianity attempted by the early Strauss, (b) the less strongly idealist view of history put forward by Ernst Troeltsch, and (c) the eschatological understanding of history put forward by Wolfhart Pannenberg. In all three cases, the "relativizing" effect of historical knowledge was countered by dramatically broadening the field of divine activity. (In my introductory chapter, the reader may recall, we saw this option already exemplified by Edward Herbert.) If it must be accepted that Christianity is merely one religion among others, and that Jesus is one religious teacher among others, then perhaps the whole of human history can be given a religious interpretation. Strauss, in his Hegelian phase, holds that Christian doctrine represents the deepest truth about history as a whole, while Troeltsch argues that Christianity is in some sense the pinnacle of human religious development,[13] and Pannenberg suggests that it is of the very nature of the Christian apocalyptic vision to be unsurpassable.

Strauss soon abandoned his Hegelian reinterpretation of Christianity. Its abandonment went hand in hand with his acceptance of Charles Darwin's view of the world and of human origins. The significance of Darwinian theory for Strauss was that it dealt a final blow, not just to miracles, but to any sense of a purpose built into the very nature of things. A teleological view of history, Strauss believed, was no longer possible. Once again, Strauss's work was prophetic, since the religious

---

[13]Interestingly Peter Byrne ("The Foundations of the Study of Religion in the British Context," in *Religion in the Making: The Emergence of the Sciences of Religion,* edited by Arie L. Molendijk and Peter Pels, Studies in the History of Religions [*Numen* Book Series] 80 [Leiden: E. J. Brill, 1998], 57) argues that the great scholar of religions Max Müller (1823–1900) arrived at the same solution to the same theological difficulty. This is a reminder of the close relationship that originally existed between liberal Christian theology and what we now call "Religious Studies."

challenge of evolutionary theory has merely intensified since his time. Ernst Troeltsch, on the other hand, continued to hold to his idealist faith—with its teleological view of history—well into the twentieth century. Perhaps tragically, his idealist view of history became increasingly implausible as the twentieth century continued. Pannenberg does not attempt to defend an idealist understanding of history, but his own "theology of the history of religions" rests heavily on his claims regarding the resurrection of Jesus. With regard to this issue, Pannenberg takes the historical method much less seriously than did Troeltsch. In particular, his attempt to expand the principle of analogy to include the resurrection is far from convincing.

Of the three options, the most attractive is surely that of Ernst Troeltsch. For one could argue that an idealist metaphysics, or something resembling it, may yet prove to be a plausible philosophical option. In commenting on the work of Troeltsch, Robert Morgan has written that "the whole question of contemporary theology's relation to the German idealist tradition remains open. . . . Empiricist philosophy may despise metaphysics, but it is difficult to see how Christian theology can afford to do so."[14] This is surely correct. Nor is nineteenth-century German idealism the only option. In developing his own metaphysical vision, Alfred North Whitehead (1861–1947) noted its similarity to the idealist philosophy of F. H. Bradley (1846–1922), despite their many disagreements.[15] Indeed Whitehead could even suggest (very cautiously) that his own cosmology may be regarded as "a transformation of some main doctrines of Absolute Idealism onto a realistic basis."[16] Yet Troeltsch's religious thought requires a philosophy of *history,* and it is not clear how one could develop a philosophy of history on the basis of Whitehead's metaphysics.[17] It seems, then, a revival of Christian theology in the manner of Troeltsch remains—at best—a possibility. In the absence of a suitable metaphysics, it is difficult to see how that possibility could be brought to realization.

Of course, even if a suitable metaphysics were to be revived, it would be no more than a basis on which one could *begin* to mount an argument for Christianity. Troeltsch was confident that a study of European history would lead to the conclusion that Christianity was the highest

[14]Robert Morgan, "Troeltsch and Christian Theology," in *Writings on Theology and Religion,* 226.
[15]Cf. Alfred North Whitehead, *Process and Reality* (1929), corrected edition, edited by David Ray Griffin and Donald W. Sherburne (New York: Macmillan/Free Press, 1978), xii–xiii.
[16]Ibid., xiii.
[17]Cf. ibid., 46–48.

spiritual power we know and therefore binding "on us." After a second world war and more than fifty years later, it is not at all clear that we would reach the same conclusion. Here again, I can offer no more than a hint. But if—in the manner of Troeltsch—one were to trace the important cultural movements of our own age in order to find their point of convergence, would Christianity even feature among them? The privatization of religion, already well underway in Troeltsch's time, has accelerated its pace in our own. While religion remains an important factor in the personal lives of many individuals,[18] its public role continues to decline. It could certainly be argued that there have been constructive cultural developments since Troeltsch's time. One thinks, for example, of the legal recognition of human rights or efforts (however halfhearted) to establish a more just and peaceful international order. On this basis, one could once again suggest that the course of human history displays signs of development. Yet it could also be argued that what progress has been made, has been made on purely secular grounds. Few if any of our international agencies or popular movements of social change claim religious inspiration. Since Troeltsch mounted his argument for the normative force of Christianity on the grounds of its cultural significance, the cultural significance of Christianity has continued to decline, and his argument looks even less convincing now than it did then.

We also need to keep in mind how cautious Troeltsch's conclusions were. To many theologians, Troeltsch's work has seemed a flimsy basis on which to erect a Christian theology. Troeltsch himself seems to have been aware of this problem. For he spent an entire chapter of *The Absoluteness of Christianity* arguing that even his modest religious claims were enough to sustain a lively faith.[19] Yet this claim is questionable: one does not need to be a Barthian to understand Barth's protest. One can appreciate Troeltsch's religious philosophy, while questioning whether it really qualifies as a Christian theology. In particular, while Troeltsch offers us a religious interpretation of history in general, he seems unable to provide a satisfactory interpretation of the figure of Jesus. Troeltsch's doctrine of Christ remains the weak point in his theological scheme, despite recent attempts to rehabilitate it. Although there is much talk of a revival of Troeltsch's theology, it seems—to be blunt—unable to get beyond what Troeltsch himself called "the empty braggadocio of announcing programmes."[20] There are many assertions that Troeltsch's

[18]See, for instance, Peter L. Berger, "Secularism in Retreat," *The National Interest* (Winter 1996/97): 3–8.
[19]Cf. Troeltsch, *The Absoluteness of Christianity*, 117–29.
[20]Troeltsch, "My Books," 370.

work *could* form the basis of a contemporary theology, but few attempts actually to produce one. In the absence of a developed theology, one is entitled to doubt that it is actually possible. Troeltsch's work may be the closest thing to theology that can be achieved, given our contemporary religious situation. But it not clear that we can go even as far as Troeltsch.

Jesus as Ethical Teacher

A second strategy is exemplified by the work of Albert Schweitzer: to continue to maintain the validity of Jesus's ethical teaching, even if many other aspects of his message must be rejected. This option looks behind the Bible to the historical Jesus, but it focuses on Jesus as a moral teacher. It argues that even if his own apocalyptic worldview cannot be accepted, and even if the claims made about him by the church can no longer be defended, his ethics can still be appropriated for our time. In other words, even if we can no longer describe Jesus as a supernatural being or as a spiritual savior, we *can* see him as one who exemplifies the highest moral ideals of which human beings are capable. As an ethical teacher, Jesus may still form the foundation of a Christian theology.

Yet the theological shortcomings of this strategy are clear. For what does a Christian theology built on this foundation require? It needs to argue that Jesus' ethical teaching justifies the claim that he is *in some unique sense* the revelation of God. There are at least three problems here, all of which were pointed out by David Friedrich Strauss. First of all, there is little which is unique about the ethics of this particular Jewish teacher.[21] Why appeal to the authority of Jesus when there exist other equally profound moral teachers in history? We may choose to regard Jesus' ethic as in some sense authoritative, but it is hard to see how it could be regarded as *uniquely* authoritative. Second, any appeal to Jesus' ethical teaching must utilize the results of historical criticism, since it is an appeal to Jesus *as a historical figure*. But the results of criticism are simply too uncertain to function as a basis for theological reflection.[22] Finally, the specifically religious difficulty with this proposal is also worth noting. While the historical Jesus is an interesting intellectual problem, it is hard to see how he could be an object of religious devotion, at least in any meaningful sense of this term.[23]

For these reasons there seems little future in this option. Despite continued attempts to do so, one cannot build a substantial Christian

---

[21]Cf. Strauss, *The Old Faith and the New,* §30 (98).
[22]Cf. Strauss, *A New Life of Jesus,* vol. 2, §99 (434).
[23]Cf. Strauss, *The Old Faith and the New,* §28 (90).

theology on the basis of Jesus' ethical teaching alone. For even if Jesus' ethics could be divorced from his apocalyptic claims—even if the historical Jesus proves to be a cynic sage, a believer in radical justice, or a mere disturber of the status quo—why should we ascribe divine authority to *this* ethical teacher rather than another? Jesus' ethical teaching, along with the teachings of other great religious figures, may continue to be a source of inspiration. But this scarcely justifies making the historical Jesus the focus of one's faith or the authoritative foundation of a system of theology.

Indeed, the greatness of Albert Schweitzer's work lay in the fact that he thought this option through in the most consistent way possible. In doing so, Schweitzer argues for two ideas. First, the ethics of Jesus represents the only aspect of his teaching that we could appropriate today, for his apocalyptic worldview is simply unintelligible. Second, Jesus' ethical teaching is nothing less than an "interim-ethics," which is inseparable from his apocalyptic worldview. Together, these two ideas are fatal to any sense of Christian authority. For if Jesus' ethic is inseparable from his worldview, and if we cannot accept his worldview, then we cannot accept his ethic, at least not in the way in which he proposed it. While Schweitzer at first seems reluctant to draw this conclusion, he acknowledges its truth in the course of his work. For in his "philosophy of civilization," Schweitzer attempts to work out an ethic that is independent of both Jesus' worldview and the metaphysical claims associated with traditional Christianity. He himself never felt the need to make a formal break with the Christian faith, but—despite his admiration for the ethics of Jesus—his final *Lebensanschauung* (life-view) was entirely separable from the religious tradition from which he had come.

In fact, Schweitzer goes further. He insists that his "ethical mysticism" cannot be derived from *any* view of the world: it rests entirely on our own experience of the "will-to-live" that is within us. In this respect his strategy begins to resemble that of the dialectical theologians, from whom he would certainly want to distance himself.[24] For Schweitzer, too, wishes to create a "safe area," not—admittedly—for traditional Christian affirmations of faith, but for his ethics of "reverence for life." Faced with the impossibility of deriving such an ethics from our knowledge of the world, Schweitzer boldly asserts that our ethics need have nothing to do with our knowledge of the world. As he writes, his ethical vision "engages in no conflict with the knowledge gained from experience."[25] Yet the question must be asked: is this a plausible option, at least

---

[24]Cf. Ice, *Schweitzer: Prophet of Radical Theology,* 39.
[25]Schweitzer, *Indian Thought and Its Development,* 263.

for one who wishes to think consistently? In effect, Schweitzer is asking us to base our ethics on a single fact about the world, albeit one we know intimately, while ignoring all other facts that seem to fly in the face of this conviction.[26]

3. Revelation and History Distinguished

The Achievement of the Dialectical Theology

The dialectical theologians represent the most theologically successful response to the rise of historical criticism. By reaching back into the resources of Christian history, they discovered ways of consigning historical claims to theological irrelevance. In this way they forged a faith that was immune to historical criticism. Despite the accusations of some of their critics, theirs was not the "fundamentalist" response of denying that there exists a problem. Rather, they crafted theological responses to that problem, responses that rendered the challenges of history theologically insignificant. It could be argued that Barth's theology is in this respect more consistent and successful than that of Bultmann. But both thinkers share this common strategy.

Barth creates a safe zone for theological claims by sharply distinguishing between two types of history: the history of God's actions and the history of human deeds. Only the second is accessible to the historian. The history of God's actions is a hidden history, accessible only to faith. The role of the historian is therefore a limited one. While historical research is needed to uncover the meaning of the biblical text, the Word of God can be heard only by submitting oneself to the witness of the text. It cannot be heard by attempting to reconstruct the history to which the text bears witness. No wedge can be driven between the Bible and divine revelation: the two are inseparable. It follows that the truth about revelation rests entirely in the hands of the theologian; it cannot be judged by the historian. While the Christian revelation occurs in history, it is not part of history. The Christian revelation is not to be seen as one "religion" among others; it is of an entirely different order. By simply removing the Christian faith (and the revelation of which it speaks) from the history of religions, Barth is able to preserve it from the relativizing and leveling effects of historical knowledge.

---

[26]Troeltsch, we might note, could reconcile Christian morality with nature's "struggle for survival" by suggesting that the latter belongs to an earlier stage in the development of morality (cf. "On the Possibility of a Liberal Christianity," 353–54). However, this again depends on an idealist and teleological view of history.

Bultmann's response resembles that of Barth, insofar as he affirms that divine revelation transcends history and cannot be grasped in historical terms. But he backs up these theological assertions with an anthropological argument. Drawing not just on his own Lutheran theological tradition, but also on the neo-Kantian and existentialist philosophies of his time, Bultmann carves out a sphere for religious claims, beyond the reach of the scientist or historian. He does so by setting up sharp antitheses, to the point that he identifies the objectifying knowledge of science and history with inauthentic existence and with sin. Our attempts to control the world through knowledge, he argues, are nothing less than the sin of attempting to justify oneself by one's works. Religion, properly understood, is concerned not with objectifying knowledge but with the sphere of the individual. It has to do with the individual human being, confronted by circumstances over which she has little control and forced to make the decisions that will shape her very being. Even the teaching of Jesus must be reinterpreted in this way. While Jesus spoke about a coming kingdom of God, to be manifested by cosmic signs, Bultmann insists that his apocalyptic message must be recast in existentialist terms. The historical Jesus, as a man of his time, proclaiming a message shaped by his historical context, is of no importance. What matters is the Christ proclaimed by the church, for in this proclamation I am faced with the radical call to decision that is the heart of the gospel.

The Failure of the Dialectical Theology

Even when these strategies appear to succeed, they do so at a terrible price. This is most evident in the work of Barth; it is particularly clear in his discussion of "the Protestant scripture principle." For Barth's strategy succeeds only if one is prepared to submit oneself, in an apparently arbitrary manner, to the authority of the Christian Bible. On this basis one can indeed construct a new kind of history—a "real" or "primal" history that is the history of God's actions—immune to historical criticism. But in demanding this submission, Barth's theology simply begs the question which the seventeenth century posed.[27] If one can defend biblical authority only by assuming biblical authority, then this is no defense at all. In any case, while Barth's scripture principle is the linchpin of his theology, that principle faces—as Strauss argued—some serious

---

[27]Troeltsch ("Historical and Dogmatic Method," 21) had already complained about the strategy of constructing another history, a salvation history (*Heilsgeschichte*), alongside that dealt with by the theologian, so that one could simply bypass the historian's questions. On Barth's acceptance of the term "salvation history," see his *Church Dogmatics* III/1, §41.1 (59).

objections. As we saw, Alvin Plantinga's epistemology might be used to provide a justification of Barth's position (a position that Barth himself would insist needs no justification). It is too soon to tell whether Plantinga's project will be ultimately successful, but the initial signs are not hopeful. His proposal has certainly failed to meet with widespread acceptance.

In any case, neither Barth's Protestant scripture principle nor Plantinga's epistemology can offer a satisfactory basis for a *public* discussion of religious claims. The problem here may be glimpsed by comparing the work of the dialectical theologians with that of their great Calvinist forebears. The Calvinist tradition held that there existed both external and internal reasons for believing in the authority of the Bible.[28] One could, in other words, produce reasoned arguments for biblical authority *as well as* appealing to the inner testimony of the Spirit.[29] In the eyes of the Reformers, these arguments may have been only supplementary, but they provided a publicly accessible way into the question, a common ground that could be occupied by believers and nonbelievers alike. Barth and Bultmann were well aware that the force of these external arguments had faded over time. (In this respect they were more sophisticated than many of their liberal opponents, who continued to believe that Christian claims could be publicly supported.) Their response was to abandon external arguments altogether—Barth rejects them vigorously, while Bultmann relegates them to the realm of objectifying knowledge—and to rely on the inner testimony of the Holy Spirit alone, albeit (in Bultmann's case) dressed up in existentialist guise. But from the moment they made this choice, they condemned Christian theology to the ghetto. For the sense of certitude to which their theology appeals is accessible only to those who submit themselves to biblical authority. However "self-authenticating" the Bible might appear to be to those within the community of faith, such claims mean nothing to those outside.[30]

It is true that the work of Bultmann is more philosophically interesting and—at first sight—more plausible. It has some of the strengths of Barth's theology, with the added attractiveness of Bultmann's interaction with contemporary continental philosophy. But on its theological side it

[28]Cf. Helm, *The Varieties of Belief,* 107–8.

[29]Cf. Calvin, *Institutes of the Christian Religion,* I.viii (81–92).

[30]If, as Paul Helm suggests (*The Varieties of Belief,* 108–9), the "inner testimony of the Holy Spirit" is best regarded as a kind of intuition, then the dialectical theology faces even more serious problems. For recent psychological studies of intuition both enable us to explain the subjective sense of certitude to which it gives rise and warn us against mistaking this for certainty. See, for example, Tony Bastick, *Intuition: How We Think and Act* (Chichester: John Wiley & Sons, 1982), 150, 153, 334.

falls into the same difficulties as the work of Barth. For Bultmann, too, can give no reason why the Christian faith, rather than any other religious system, should be exempted from the limitations of human history. His own leap of faith seems equally arbitrary, at least to those outside its self-authenticating circle. On its anthropological side, Bultmann's problem is that his sharp antitheses between faith and objectifying knowledge cannot ultimately be maintained. As he himself admits, objectifying knowledge is inseparable from our being in the world. It is therefore indispensable for faith and cannot be dismissed as nothing more than an expression of sin. It follows that theology must work out its relationship with the objectifying knowledge of the historian. Bultmann has been unable to do this. While Bultmann's disciple Ernst Käsemann raises again the question of history, he, too, is unable to solve it. His theology runs into the same difficulties as that of his erstwhile teacher.

It follows that, while assuming nothing but good faith in either Barth or Bultmann, we cannot say their strategies have succeeded. Barth's theology is apparently the more successful. For if one can bring oneself to accept Barth's reformulation of the Christian faith, if we are prepared to think "from God out,"[31] then the challenges of history may be made to disappear. But for those who are not prepared to make what can only be a blind leap of faith, for those who have internalized the challenges of the seventeenth century and can no longer confidently assume the Christian perspective, the problems remain. In its assertions regarding the nature of revelation, Bultmann's work shares the strengths and the weaknesses of the theology of Barth. But Bultmann's anthropological arguments also lead him into difficulties. For insofar as he concedes that we cannot dispense with historical knowledge, his theology falls back into the very difficulties it sought to escape. As the work of Ernst Käsemann and (more positively) Wolfhart Pannenberg reminds us, you may drive historical questions out with a pitchfork, but they cannot be kept at bay forever. As I remarked earlier, if a fully Christian theology were possible today, it would look something like the dialectical theology of Barth and Bultmann. But even at its best, such a theology seems to lack public plausibility. Insofar as the dialectical theology aspired to be a public discipline, it is difficult to see how it could be defended.

4. The Research Tradition Evaluated

Throughout this work, I have suggested that the thinkers we have studied form a single research tradition. But given the diversity of their

---

[31]Barth, *Der Römerbrief, 1919,* 71.

solutions, can this claim be substantiated? I contend that it can. The dialectical theologians might appear, at first sight, to be offering a radical alternative to the liberal theology of the nineteenth and early twentieth centuries. And in one sense they were: it would be foolish to overlook their degree of disagreement with their predecessors. But insofar as their theology may be seen as a response to the same set of problems with which the liberal theologians had grappled, it would be equally foolish to overlook the degree of continuity. While there are many ways in which these currents of thought could be grouped and classified, it is helpful to regard them all as forming a common tradition of enquiry. The question we must now face is: Was this tradition of enquiry successful? Might it still have a future?

Contemporary philosophers of science are inclined to regard a successful research tradition as one that enables us to solve an increasing number of problems.[32] More precisely, a successful tradition may be judged, not just by the adequacy of its individual theories, but by its ability to make progress over time.[33] If it solves a greater number of problems than do its rivals without thereby creating further problems or a larger number of anomalies, then it would be reasonable to regard it as a success.[34] On this basis, how does the research tradition we have been studying rate? While the individual chapters of this book have attempted to assess the adequacy of *individual* solutions, it is time to look at the explanatory power of this research tradition *as a whole,* in its progress over time.

There has certainly been no consistent pattern of progress. The earliest of our authors, Benedict Spinoza, developed a notion of religious authority so much at odds with his own Jewish tradition and with Christian theology that it has found few followers from within the household of faith. David Friedrich Strauss began hopefully enough but found the problems intractable and quite self-consciously abandoned his earlier religious positions. Ernst Troeltsch's work was enormously suggestive, but this, too, led to conclusions that many believed to be scarcely Christian. Albert Schweitzer, in turn, developed a humanitarian ethic built on foundations that were scarcely religious. All of these authors arrived at more or less adequate solutions to the problem of religious (and ethical) authority, but none of the solutions was distinctively Christian. If the problem of religious authority is thought of as the problem of vindicating biblical authority, that is to say, of showing biblical authority

[32]Cf. Laudan, *Progress and Its Problems,* 82.
[33]Cf. ibid., 106–8.
[34]Cf. ibid., 111, 124, et passim.

to be in some sense reliable, then none of these solutions seems *theologically* adequate.

Karl Barth and Rudolf Bultmann were among the first to realize the inadequacy of these solutions. Their own radical rethinking of the theological task may therefore be regarded as a last-ditch effort to save this research tradition from failure. Yet if the dialectical theology did resolve the conceptual problems with which liberal theology was faced, it did so only by creating new anomalies (in the case of Barth) or by building a system that was internally incoherent (in the case of Bultmann). It is not surprising that the next generation of theologians, represented by Ernst Käsemann and Wolfhart Pannenberg, abandoned much of what their teachers had stood for. Indeed, Käsemann and Pannenberg sought cautiously to recover the best insights of the thinkers against whom Barth and Bultmann had reacted. But Käsemann could not quite escape the deeply dualistic thought in which he had been brought up, while Pannenberg's theology ultimately fails to take seriously the challenge of history.

5. Conclusion

This rather unhappy record invites a sceptical conclusion. It is true that such a conclusion might seem premature. For the evaluation of a research tradition normally requires one to make a comparison: we ought to compare the research tradition with its rivals.[35] It makes little sense to reject a research tradition until one has an alternative, one that has proved itself better able to address the same issues. This is borne out by the history of science: a research tradition is not normally abandoned before a more satisfactory alternative has been developed.[36] But an alternative research tradition must either address the same problem or be able to show that the problem as previously formulated is no longer important. What does this mean for the present study? The tradition of enquiry that has been the focus of this work revolves around a set of problems that are *conceptual* rather than *empirical*.[37] They have to do with the reconciliation of claims to biblical authority with the findings and the

[35]Cf. ibid., 109, 120, et passim.

[36]Cf. Imre Lakatos, "Falsification and the Methodology of Scientific Research Programmes," in *Criticism and the Growth of Knowledge,* edited by Imre Lakatos and Alan Musgrave (Cambridge: Cambridge University Press, 1970), 155. For a qualified response, see Alan Musgrave, "Method or Madness? Can the Methodology of Research Programmes Be Rescued from Epistemological Anarchism?" in *Essays in Memory of Imre Lakatos,* edited by R. S. Cohen et al. (Dordrecht: D. Reidel, 1976), 464–65.

[37]For this distinction, see Laudan, *Progress and Its Problems,* 45–69, and the final section of the introduction to the present work.

methods of the historian. It may be that a more satisfactory solution to
this problem will one day be forthcoming. But this long history of failure offers few grounds for confidence. It leads one to suspect that the
problem is wrongly posed or (more probably) that it is a pseudoproblem,
one based on false assumptions.

It may be that the false assumptions in question are those underlying
the modern discipline of history. In this case, the problem would be the
historian's rather than the believer's. It would be up to the historian to
adopt a more satisfactory way of approaching her data. Interestingly,
none of the authors we have studied has adopted this line of argument.
Barth and Bultmann came close, by insisting that the assumptions of the
historian are simply not applicable to the object of Christian faith. But
even they admitted that those assumptions were entirely reasonable in
other fields, an admission that made it necessary to justify what looked
like special treatment for Christian claims. This, of course, is what their
theologies attempt to do. The introduction to the present study suggests
that Barth and Bultmann were right, for the questions raised by the
"great reversal" of the seventeenth century do seem inescapable. It is not
the historian who has a problem; it is the believer.[38]

If one accepts this argument, then one seems forced to adopt an alternative interpretation. If the assumptions underlying historical criticism
are justified, if the questions asked by the historian are right and proper
and the theologian can give no satisfactory answer, then what follows? It
seems that there is something wrong with the believer's claim to religious
authority. If this is the case, then the problem with which our authors
have been dealing is a pseudoproblem, not because of the historian's
assumptions, but because of the theologian's. The simplest explanation
would seem to be the sceptical one. There *is* no way of reconciling Christian claims to religious authority with the knowledge and methods of
the discipline of history. The historical viewpoint of our age undermines
claims to biblical authority, while the Jesus of history is not a figure who

[38]Much contemporary theology draws on the work of such thinkers as Michael
Polanyi and Alasdair MacIntyre to argue that all forms of knowledge involve some type
of "faith-commitment" and that there exist competing traditions of rationality. (See, for
instance, Trevor Hart, *Faith Thinking: The Dynamics of Christian Theology,* Gospel and Culture [London: SPCK, 1995], 11–106.) Others draw on the work of the later Ludwig
Wittgenstein to argue that such traditions are comprehensible only by reference to particular forms of life. Such arguments are, of course, deeply contestable, but even if one
accepts them (as I would not), they provide no way of avoiding the challenge of history
to religious authority. If the theologian is to avoid the relativism of thinkers such as
George Lindbeck (cf. Hart, *Faith Thinking,* 86–89), the question remains how these competing traditions are to be brought into relationship with one another. For all their
apparent fideism, Barth and Bultmann were well aware of this fact.

can be reappropriated for our own time. Of the authors we have studied, only two, namely, Spinoza and the later Strauss, have been willing to take this step, and even Spinoza dressed up his conclusions in language that to the casual observer might appear conventionally pious.

I have no wish to shy away from this conclusion, which—to me at least—seems inescapable. (The reader of chapter 2 will already have sensed my admiration for the honesty of David Friedrich Strauss.) However, even if one accepts this sceptical view, there is much we can learn from the research tradition we have studied. Of all our thinkers, Ernst Troeltsch seems to have been most aware of this fact. Troeltsch reminds us that it is not just *religious* authority that comes under threat when the historian sets to work.[39] The challenge of history to religious authority is simultaneously a challenge to traditional *ethical* claims. (As we have seen, Albert Schweitzer's work was largely motivated by this same concern.) While our ethical traditions are not necessarily dependent on religious beliefs, they do have some features in common with religious traditions. They also make claims that are not easily reconciled with the viewpoint of the historian. They too appear, at first sight, to be nothing more than products of particular times and places, bound to the norms and conventions of the societies out of which they arose. How can they claim any universal validity? It follows that, even if one set aside this *theological* research tradition as a relic of past patterns of thought, analogous questions would arise in an *ethical* context.

In making this observation, I am not attempting to smuggle theology back in under the guise of ethics, a temptation to which theologians are particularly exposed. I have already rejected the idea that moral obligations require religious backing. Neither am I convinced by the Kantian idea that the existence of moral obligations requires us to postulate the existence of God. My own view is that it may well be possible to answer our ethical questions in a thoroughly naturalistic way, without any reference to religious beliefs.[40] Indeed, given the difficulties facing religious belief, I rather hope this is the case. A secular ethic has surely a much better chance of being accepted in our diverse and deeply divided world than one that needs religious backing. I wish only to point out that the questions with which our thinkers were faced have implications outside the field of religion. For this reason they are questions of interest, not just to theologians, but to us all.

[39]See, for instance, Troeltsch, "Modern Philosophy of History," 275–76; *The Absoluteness of Christianity*, 132–33; and the whole of *Der Historismus und seine Probleme*.

[40]J. L. Mackie, for example, in his *Ethics: Inventing Right and Wrong* (London: Pelikan, 1977), vigorously defends a thoroughly naturalistic point of view, arguing that it takes nothing away from the seriousness of our ethical traditions.

List of Works Cited

Adams, James Luther. Introduction to *The Absoluteness of Christianity and the History of Religions,* by Ernst Troeltsch, translated by David Reid. Library of Philosophy and Theology. London: SCM, 1972.

Alston, William P. "Plantinga's Epistemology of Religious Belief." In *Alvin Plantinga,* edited by James E. Tomberlin and Peter van Inwagen. Profiles. Dordrecht: D. Reidel, 1985.

Aquinas Thomas. *Summa Theologica.* Turin: Marietti, 1915.

———. *Summa Contra Gentiles.* Turin: Marietti, 1914.

Aristotle. *The Complete Works of Aristotle: The Revised Oxford Translation.* Edited by Jonathan Barnes. Vols. 1 and 2. Bollingen Series 71, 2. Princeton, N.J.: Princeton University Press, 1984.

Arnal, William E., and Michel Desjardins, eds. *Whose Historical Jesus?* Studies in Christianity and Judaism/Études sur le christianisme et le judaisme 7. Waterloo, Ontario: Wilfred Laurier University Press, 1997.

Auerbach, Erich. *Mimesis: The Representation of Reality in Western Literature* (1946). Translated by Willard R. Trask. Princeton, N.J.: Princeton University Press, 1953.

Augustine. *The City of God Against the Pagans.* Translated by R. W. Dyson. Cambridge Texts in the History of Political Thought. Cambridge: Cambridge University Press, 1998.

———. *De doctrina christiana* (On Christian teaching). Edited and translated by R. P. H. Green. Oxford Early Christian Texts. Oxford: Clarendon Press, 1995.

———. *Epistle* 137. In *An Augustine Synthesis,* edited by Erich Przywara, S.J. London: Sheed & Ward, 1945.

———. *De Genesi ad litteram libri duodecim.* English text: *The Literal Meaning of Genesis.* Translated by John Hammond Taylor, S.J. Ancient Christian Writers 41. New York: Newman, 1982.

———. *De vera religione* (Of true religion). Translated by John H. S. Burleigh. In *Augustine: Earlier Writings.* Library of Christian Classics, vol. 6. London: SCM, 1953.

Bacon, Francis. *The Works of Francis Bacon.* Edited by James Spedding, Robert Leslie Ellis, and Douglas Denon Heath. Vol. 4. London: Longmans & Co., 1875.

Barr, James. *The Bible in the Modern World.* London: SCM, 1973.

———. *Does Biblical Study Still Belong to Theology? An Inaugural Lecture Delivered before the University of Oxford on 26 May 1977.* Oxford: Clarendon Press, 1978.

Barth, Karl. "Biblical Questions, Insights and Vistas" (1920). In *The Word of God and the Word of Man.* Translated from *Das Wort Gottes und die Theologie* by Douglas Horton. New York: Harper & Row, 1957.

370

———. *Die christliche Dogmatik im Entwurf: Erster Band—Die Lehre vom Worte Gottes* (1927). Gesamtausgabe. Zurich: Theologischer Verlag, 1982.

———. *Church Dogmatics*, vol. I, part 1: *The Doctrine of the Word of God*. Translated by G. T. Thomson. Edinburgh: T. & T. Clark, 1936.

———. *Church Dogmatics*, vol. I, part 2: *The Doctrine of the Word of God*. Translated by G. T. Thomson and Harold Knight. Edinburgh: T. & T. Clark, 1956.

———. *Church Dogmatics*, vol. III, part 1: *The Doctrine of Creation*. Translated by J. W. Edwards, O. Bussey, and Harold Knight. Edinburgh: T. & T. Clark, 1958.

———. *Church Dogmatics*, vol. III, part 2: *The Doctrine of Creation*. Translated by Harold Knight, G. W. Bromiley, J. K. S. Reid, and R. H. Fuller. Edinburgh: T. & T. Clark, 1960.

———. *Church Dogmatics*, vol. IV, part 1: *The Doctrine of Reconciliation*. Translated by G. W. Bromiley. Edinburgh: T. & T. Clark, 1956.

———. *The Epistle to the Romans*. 6th edition (1928). Translated by Edwyn C. Hoskyns. London: Oxford University Press, 1933.

———. *The Göttingen Dogmatics: Instruction in the Christian Religion* (1924). Translated by Geoffrey W. Bromiley. Vol. 1. Grand Rapids: Eerdmans, 1991.

———. "Ludwig Feuerbach" (1920). In *Theology and Church: Shorter Writings 1920–1928*, translated by Louise Pettibone Smith. London: SCM, 1962.

———. "The Principles of Dogmatics according to Wilhelm Herrmann" (1925). In *Theology and Church: Shorter Writings 1920–1928*, translated by Louise Pettibone Smith. London: SCM, 1962.

———. *Protestant Theology in the Nineteenth Century: Its Background and History* (1952). Translated by Brian Cozens and John Bowden. London: SCM, 1972.

———. *Der Römerbrief (Erste Fassung), 1919*. Gesamtausgabe. Zurich: Theologischer Verlag, 1985.

———. *Der Römerbrief*. 6th edition (1928). Munich: Christian Kaiser, 1933.

———. "Rudolf Bultmann—An Attempt to Understand Him." In *Kerygma and Myth: A Theological Debate*, edited by Hans-Werner Bartsch and translated by Reginald H. Fuller. London: SPCK, 1962.

———. *Die Theologie Calvins* (1922). Edited by Hans Scholl. Gesamtausgabe. Zurich: Theologischer Verlag, 1993.

———. "Unsettled Questions for Theology Today" (1920). In *Theology and Church: Shorter Writings 1920–1928*, translated by Louise Pettibone Smith. London: SCM, 1962.

———. "*Unterricht in der christlichen Religion*" *Prolegomena* (1924). Edited by Hannelotte Reiffen. Zurich: Theologischer Verlag, 1985.

Bartley, William Warren III. *The Retreat to Commitment*. New York: Alfred A. Knopf, 1962.

Bastick, Tony. *Intuition: How We Think and Act*. Chichester: John Wiley & Sons, 1982.

Bennett, Jonathan. *A Study of Spinoza's Ethics*. Cambridge: Cambridge University Press, 1984.

Bentley, Jerry H. *Humanists and Holy Writ: New Testament Scholarship in the Renaissance*. Princeton, N.J.: Princeton University Press, 1983.

Berger, Peter L. "Secularism in Retreat." *The National Interest*, Winter 1996/97:3–8.

Blackwell, Richard J. *Galileo, Bellarmine, and the Bible*. Notre Dame, Ind.: University of Notre Dame Press, 1991.

Brabazon, James. *Albert Schweitzer: A Biography.* New York: G. P. Putnam's Sons, 1975.

Brooke, John Hedley. *Science and Religion: Some Historical Perspectives.* Cambridge History of Science. Cambridge: Cambridge University Press, 1991.

Bultmann, Rudolf. "Autobiographical Reflections." In *Existence and Faith: Shorter Writings of Rudolf Bultmann,* translated by Schubert M. Ogden from *Lebenslauf* (1956). London: Hodder & Stoughton. 1961.

———. "Die Bedeutung der 'dialektischen Theologie' für die neutestamentliche Wissenschaft" (1928). In *Glauben und Verstehen: Gesammelte Aufsätze.* Vol. I. Tübingen: J. C. B. Mohr (Paul Siebeck), 1933.

———. "The Crisis in Belief" (1931). Translated by James C. G. Greig. In *Essays: Philosophical and Theological.* London: SCM, 1955.

———. "Ethische und mystische Religion im Urchristentum" (1920). In *Anfänge der dialektischen Theologie.* Edited by Jürgen Moltmann. Vol. 2. Munich: Christian Kaiser, 1963.

———. "Faith as Venture" (1928). In *Existence and Faith: Shorter Writings of Rudolf Bultmann,* translated and edited by Schubert M. Ogden. London: Hodder & Stoughton, 1961.

———. *History and Eschatology: The Gifford Lectures 1955.* Edinburgh: Edinburgh University Press, 1957.

———. *The History of the Synoptic Tradition* (1921). Translated by John Marsh. Oxford: Basil Blackwell, 1963.

———. "The Idea of God and Modern Man" (1963). Translated by Robert W. Funk. In *Translating Theology into the Modern Age.* Journal for Theology and the Church 2. Tübingen: J. C. B. Mohr (Paul Siebeck), 1965.

———. "Is Exegesis without Presuppositions Possible?" In *Existence and Faith: Shorter Writings of Rudolf Bultmann,* translated and edited by Schubert M. Ogden. London: Hodder & Stoughton, 1961.

———. *Jesus and the Word* (1926). Translated by Louise Pettibone Smith and Erminie Huntress Lantero. London: Collins/Fontana, 1958.

———. *Jesus Christ and Mythology* (1951). New York: Charles Scribner's Sons, 1958.

———. "Karl Barth's *Epistle to the Romans* in its Second Edition" (1922). In. *Rudolf Bultmann: Interpreting Faith for the Modern Era,* edited by Roger A. Johnson. The Making of Modern Theology: Nineteenth and Twentieth Century Texts. London: Collins, 1987.

———. "Liberal Theology and the Latest Theological Movement" (1924). In *Faith and Understanding,* translated by Louise Pettibone Smith. Library of Philosophy and Theology. London: SCM, 1969.

———. "The New Testament and Mythology." In *Kerygma and Myth: A Theological Debate,* edited by Hans Werner Bartsch (1948) and translated by Reginald H. Fuller. 2d edition. London: SPCK: 1964.

———. "On the Problem of Demythologizing" (1952). In *New Testament and Mythology and Other Basic Writings,* translated by Schubert M. Ogden. London: SCM, 1985.

———. "On the Problem of Demythologizing" (1961). In *New Testament and Mythology and Other Basic Writings,* translated by Schubert M. Ogden. London: SCM, 1985.

———. "On the Question of Christology" (1927). In *Faith and Understanding,* translated by Louise Pettibone Smith. Library of Philosophy and Theology.

London: SCM, 1969.

————. "Points of Contact and Conflict" (1946). In *Essays Philosophical and Theological*, translated by James C. G. Greig. Library of Philosophy and Theology. London: SCM, 1955.

————. "The Problem of Hermeneutics" (1950). In *Essays Philosophical and Theological*, translated by James C. G. Greig. Library of Philosophy and Theology. London: SCM, 1955.

————. "The Problem of 'Natural Theology' " (1933). In *Faith and Understanding*, translated by Louise Pettibone Smith. Library of Philosophy and Theology. London: SCM, 1969.

————. "The Question of Natural Revelation" (1941). In *Essays Philosophical and Theological*, translated by James C. G. Greig. Library of Philosophy and Theology. London: SCM, 1955.

————. "The Question of Wonder" (1933). In *Faith and Understanding*, translated by Louise Pettibone Smith. Library of Philosophy and Theology. London: SCM, 1969.

————. "Religion und Kultur" (1920). In *Anfänge der dialektischen Theologie*, edited by Jürgen Moltmann. Vol. 2. Munich: Christian Kaiser, 1963.

————. "Science and Existence" (1955). In *New Testament and Mythology and Other Basic Writings*, translated by Schubert M. Ogden. London: SCM, 1985.

————. "The Significance of 'Dialectical Theology' for the Scientific Study of the New Testament" (1928). In *Faith and Understanding*, translated by Louise Pettibone Smith. Library of Philosophy and Theology. London: SCM, 1969.

————. "Theology as Science" (1941). In *New Testament and Mythology and Other Basic Writings*, translated by Schubert M. Ogden. London: SCM, 1985.

————. *Das Verhältnis der urchristlichen Christusbotschaft zum historischen Jesus*. 2d edition. Sitzungsberichte der Heidelberger Akademie der Wissenschaften. Heidelberg: Carl Winter, Universitätsverlag, 1961.

————. "Welchen Sinn hat es, von Gott zu reden?" (1925). In *Glauben und Verstehen: Gesammelte Aufsätze*. Vol. 1. Tübingen: J. C. B. Mohr (Paul Siebeck), 1933.

————. "What Does It Mean to Speak of God?" (1925). In *Faith and Understanding*, translated by Louise Pettibone Smith. Library of Philosophy and Theology. London: SCM, 1969.

————. "Zur Frage des Wunders." In *Glauben und Verstehen: Gesammelte Aufsätze*. Vol. 1. Tübingen: J. C. B. Mohr (Paul Siebeck), 1933.

Burke, Peter. *The Renaissance Sense of the Past*. London: Edward Arnold, 1969.

Busch, Eberhard. *Karl Barth: His Life from Letters and Autobiographical Texts* (1975). Translated by John Bowden. London: SCM, 1976.

Byrne, Peter. "The Foundations of the Study of Religion in the British Context." In *Religion in the Making: The Emergence of the Sciences of Religion*, edited by Arie L. Molendijk and Peter Pels. Studies in the History of Religions (*Numen* Book Series) 80. Leiden: E. J. Brill, 1998.

Calvin, John. *Institutes of the Christian Religion*. Translated by Ford Lewis Battles. Library of Christian Classics, vol. 20. London: SCM, 1961.

Cassirer, Ernst. *The Philosophy of the Enlightenment*. Translated by Fritz C. A. Koelln and James P. Pettergrove. Princeton, N.J.: Princeton University Press, 1951.

Chilton, Bruce, and Craig A. Evans, eds. *Studying the Historical Jesus: Evaluations of the State of Current Research*. New Testament Tools and Studies 19. Leiden: E. J. Brill, 1994.

Cleve, Felix M. *The Giants of Pre-Socratic Greek Philosophy: An Attempt to Reconstruct Their Thoughts*. 3d edition. Vol. 2. The Hague: Martinus Nijhoff, 1973.

Coakley, Sarah. *Christ without Absolutes: A Study of the Christology of Ernst Troeltsch*. Oxford: Clarendon Press, 1988.

Cohen, Hermann. *Religion of Reason out of the Sources of Judaism* (1919). Translated by Simon Kaplan. New York: Frederick Ungar, 1972.

Collingwood, R. G. *The Idea of History* (1946). Oxford: Oxford University Press, 1961.

Copenhaver, Brian P., and Charles B. Schmitt. *Renaissance Philosophy*. A History of Western Philosophy 3. Opus. Oxford: Oxford University Press, 1992.

Copleston, Frederick. *A History of Philosophy*. Vol. 3, part 2. Image Books. Garden City, N.Y.: Doubleday, 1963.

Craig, William Lane. *A History of Philosophy*. Vol. 4. Image Books. Garden City, N.Y.: Doubleday, 1963.

———. "The Problem of Miracles: A Historical and Philosophical Perspective." In *Gospel Perspectives*. Vol. 6, *The Miracles of Jesus*, edited by David Wenham and Craig Blomberg. Sheffield: JSOT Press, 1986.

———. *Reasonable Faith: Christian Truth and Apologetics*. Revised edition. Wheaton, Ill.: Crossway Books, 1994.

Creed, J. M. *The Divinity of Jesus Christ* (1938). London: Collins/Fontana, 1964.

Cromwell, Richard S. *David Friedrich Strauss and His Place in Modern Thought*. Fair Lawn, N.J.: R. E. Burdick, 1974.

Curley, E. M. *Spinoza's Metaphysics: An Essay in Interpretation*. Cambridge, Mass.: Harvard University Press, 1969.

———. "Notes on a Neglected Masterpiece (II): The *Theological-Political Treatise* as a Prolegomenon to the *Ethics*." In *Central Themes in Early Modern Philosophy: Essays Presented to Jonathan Bennett*, edited by J. A. Cover and Mark Kulstad. Indianapolis: Hackett, 1990.

Daniel, Norman. *Islam and the West: The Making of an Image* (1960). Oxford: Oneworld, 1993.

Danto, Arthur C. *Narration and Knowledge*. New York: Columbia University Press (Morningside Edition), 1985.

Dawes, Gregory W., ed. *The Historical Jesus Quest: A Foundational Anthology*. Leiden: Deo Publishing, 1999/Louisville, Ky.: Westminster John Knox, 2000.

de Lubac, Henri. *Medieval Exegesis*. Vol. 1, *The Four Senses of Scripture* (1959). Translated by Mark Sebanc. Grand Rapids: Eerdmans, 1998.

De Mey, Peter. "Ernst Troeltsch: A Moderate Pluralist? An Evaluation of His Reflections on the Place of Christianity among the Other Religions." In *The Myriad Christ: Plurality and the Quest for Unity in Contemporary Christology*, edited by T. Merrigan and J. Haers. Bibliotheca Ephemeridum Theologicarum Lovaniensium 152. Louvain: University Press, 2000.

Descartes, René. "Discourse on Method." In *The Philosophical Writings of Descartes*, translated by John Cottingham, Robert Stoothoff, and Dugald Murdoch. Vol. 1. Cambridge: Cambridge University Press, 1985.

———. "Meditations on First Philosophy." In *The Philosophical Writings of Descartes*, translated by John Cottingham, Robert Stoothoff, and Dugald Murdoch. Vol. 2. Cambridge: Cambridge University Press, 1984.

———. *Principles of Philosophy*. Translated by Valentine Rodger Miller and

Reese P. Miller. Synthese Historical Library 24. Dordrecht: D. Reidel, 1983.

Diem, Hermann. *Dogmatics* (1955). Translated by Harold Knight. Edinburgh: Oliver & Boyd, 1955.

Dodd, C. H. *The Parables of the Kingdom* (1935). London: Collins/Fontana, 1961.

Donagan, Alan. "Spinoza's Theology." In *The Cambridge Companion to Spinoza*, edited by Don Garratt. Cambridge: Cambridge University Press, 1996.

Donahue, William H. Translator's introduction to *New Astronomy*, by Johannes Kepler. Cambridge: Cambridge University Press, 1992.

Dostoevsky, Fyodor. *The Brothers Karamazov*. Translated by Ignat Avsey. World's Classics. Oxford: Oxford University Press, 1994.

Drake, Stillman. Introduction to Galileo's *Letter to the Grand Duchess Christina*. In *Discoveries and Opinions of Galileo*, translated by Stillman Drake. Garden City, N.Y.: Doubleday, 1957.

――――. Introduction to *The Controversy on the Comets of 1618*. Translated by Stillman Drake and C. D. O'Malley. Philadelphia: University of Philadelphia Press, 1960.

Drescher, Hans-Georg. *Ernst Troeltsch: His Life and Work* (1991). Translated by John Bowden. London: SCM, 1992.

Dupré, Louis. *Passage to Modernity: An Essay in the Hermeneutics of Nature and Culture*. New Haven, Conn.: Yale University Press, 1993.

Flew, Anthony. *Hume's Theory of Belief: A Study of His First* Inquiry. International Library of Philosophy and Scientific Method. London: Routledge & Kegan Paul, 1961.

Frei, Hans W. *The Eclipse of Biblical Narrative: A Study in Eighteenth and Nineteenth Century Hermeneutics*. New Haven, Conn.: Yale University Press, 1974.

Funk, Robert W. *Honest to Jesus: Jesus for a New Millennium*. London: Hodder & Stoughton, 1996.

Gadamer, Hans-Georg *Truth and Method*. 2d ed. (1965). London: Sheed & Ward, 1979.

Galilei, Galileo. *The Assayer* (1623). In *The Controversy on the Comets of 1618*, translated by Stillman Drake and C. D. O'Malley. Philadelphia: University of Philadelphia Press, 1960.

――――. "Letter to Castelli" (1613). In *The Galileo Affair: A Documentary History*, translated and edited by Maurice A. Finocchiaro. California Studies in the History of Science. Berkeley, Calif.: University of California Press, 1989.

――――. "Letter to the Grand Duchess Christina" (1615). In *The Galileo Affair: A Documentary History*, translated and edited by Maurice A. Finocchiaro. California Studies in the History of Science. Berkeley, Calif.: University of California Press, 1989.

Gerrish, B. A. "Ernst Troeltsch and the Possibility of a Historical Theology." In *Ernst Troeltsch and the Future of Theology*, edited by John Powell Clayton. Cambridge: Cambridge University Press, 1976.

Gillespie, Neal C. *Charles Darwin and the Problem of Creation*. Chicago: University of Chicago Press, 1979.

Glasson, T. Francis. "Schweitzer's Influence—Blessing or Bane?" *Journal of Theological Studies* NS 28 (1977): 289–302.

Gräßer, Erich. *Albert Schweitzer als Theologe*. Beiträge zur historischen Theologie 60. Tübingen: J. C. B. Mohr (Paul Siebeck), 1979.

Gregory, Brad. Introduction to *Tractatus theologico-politicus,* by Benedictus Spinoza, translated by Samuel Shirley. Leiden: E. J. Brill, 1989.

Gregory, Frederick. *Nature Lost? Natural Science and the German Theological Traditions of the Nineteenth Century.* Cambridge, Mass.: Harvard University Press, 1992.

Gullan-Whur, Margaret. *Within Reason: A Life of Spinoza.* London: Jonathan Cape, 1998.

Guttmann, Julius. Introduction and Commentary in *The Guide of the Perplexed: An Abridged Edition,* by Moses Maimonides, translated by Chaim Rabin. Indianapolis: Hackett, 1995.

Hallett, F. F. *Benedict de Spinoza: The Elements of His Philosophy.* London: Athlone Press, 1957.

Harris, Horton. *David Friedrich Strauss and His Theology.* Monograph Supplements to the Scottish Journal of Theology. Cambridge: Cambridge University Press, 1973.

Harrison, Peter. *"Religion" and the Religions in the English Enlightenment.* Cambridge: Cambridge University Press, 1990.

Harrisville, Roy A., and Walter Sundberg. *The Bible in Modern Culture: Theology and Historical-Critical Method from Spinoza to Käsemann.* Grand Rapids: Eerdmans, 1995.

Hart, Trevor. *Faith Thinking: The Dynamics of Christian Theology.* Gospel and Culture. London: SPCK, 1995.

Harvey, Van A. *The Historian and the Believer: The Morality of Historical Knowledge and Christian Belief* (1966). Urbana, Ill: University of Illinois Press, 1996.

Heidegger, Martin. *Being and Time.* 7th edition (1927). Translated by John Macquarrie and Edward Robinson. London: SCM, 1962.

———. *An Introduction to Metaphysics* (1953). Translated by Ralph Mannheim. New Haven, Conn.: Yale University Press, 1959.

Helm, Paul. *The Varieties of Belief.* Muirhead Library of Philosophy. London: George Allen & Unwin, 1973.

Herbert, Edward. *De Religione Laici* (1645). In Harold R. Hutcheson, *Lord Herbert of Cherbury's* De Religione Laici. New Haven, Conn.: Yale University Press, 1944.

Herrmann, Wilhelm. *Systematic Theology (Dogmatik).* Translated by Nathaniel Micklem and Kenneth A. Saunders. London: George Allen & Unwin, 1927.

Hodgen, Margaret T. *Early Anthropology in the Sixteenth and Seventeenth Centuries.* Philadelphia: University of Pennsylvania Press, 1964.

Hodgson, Peter C. Editor's Introduction to *The Life of Jesus Critically Examined,* by David Friedrich Strauss. 4th German edition (1840). Translated by George Eliot and edited by Peter C. Hodgson. Lives of Jesus Series. Philadelphia: Fortress Press, 1972.

Hume, David. "An Enquiry concerning Human Understanding" (1748). In *Enquiries concerning the Human Understanding and concerning the Principles of Morals,* edited by L. A. Selby-Bigge. 2d edition. Oxford: Clarendon Press, 1902.

———. "The Natural History of Religion" (1757). In *Principal Writings on Religion.* Oxford World's Classics. Oxford: Oxford University Press, 1993.

Hutcheson Harold R. *Lord Herbert of Cherbury's* De Religione Laici. New Haven, Conn.: Yale University Press, 1944.

Ice, Jackson Lee. *Schweitzer: Prophet of Radical Theology*. Philadelphia: Westminster Press, 1971.

Jackson, Mike, and K. W. M. Fulford. "Spiritual Experience and Psychopathology." *Philosophy, Psychiatry, and Psychology* 4:1 (March 1997): 41–65.

Jeremias, Joachim. "The Present Position in the Controversy concerning the Problem of the Historical Jesus." *Expository Times* 69 (1958): 333–39.

Johnson, Roger A. *The Origins of Demythologizing: Philosophy and Historiography in the Theology of Rudolf Bultmann*. Studies in the History of Religions (Supplements to *Numen*) 28. Leiden: E. J. Brill, 1974.

Kähler, Martin. *The So-Called Historical Jesus and the Historic, Biblical Christ* (1896). Translated by Carl E. Braaten. Seminar Editions. Philadelphia: Fortress Press, 1964.

Kant, Immanuel. *Dreams of a Spirit-Seer*. Translated by E. F. Goerwitz. Key Texts: Classic Studies in the History of Ideas. Bristol: Thoemmes Press, 1900/ 1992.

Käsemann, Ernst. "Blind Alleys in the 'Jesus of History' Controversy" (1965). Translated by W. J. Montague. In *New Testament Questions for Today*. New Testament Library. London: SCM, 1969.

―――. "Is the Gospel Objective?" (1953). Translated by W. J. Montague. In *Essays on New Testament Themes*. London: SCM, 1964.

―――. "The Problem of the Historical Jesus" (1953). Translated by W. J. Montague. In *Essays on New Testament Themes*. London: SCM, 1964.

Kelley, Donald R. *Foundations of Modern Historical Scholarship: Language, Law, and History in the French Renaissance*. New York: Columbia University Press, 1970.

―――. "The Theory of History." In *Cambridge History of Renaissance Philosophy*, edited by Charles B. Schmitt and Quentin Skinner. Cambridge: Cambridge University Press, 1988.

Kenny, Anthony. *What Is Faith? Essays in the Philosophy of Religion*. Oxford: Oxford University Press, 1992.

Kepler, Johannes. *Defence of Tycho against Ursus*. In *The Birth of History and Philosophy of Science: Kepler's* A Defence of Tycho against Ursus *with Essays on Its Provenance and Significance,* by N. Jardine. Cambridge: Cambridge University Press, 1984.

―――. *New Astronomy*. Translated by William H. Donoghue. Cambridge: Cambridge University Press, 1992.

La Capra, Dominick. Introduction to *Rethinking Intellectual History: Texts, Contexts, Language*. Ithaca, N.Y.: Cornell University Press, 1983.

Lachterman, David R. "The Physics of Spinoza's *Ethics*." In *Spinoza: New Perspectives*, edited by Robert W. Shahan and J. I. Biro. Norman, Okla.: University of Oklahoma Press, 1978.

Lakatos, Imre. "Falsification and the Methodology of Scientific Research Programmes." In *Criticism and the Growth of Knowledge*, edited by Imre Lakatos and Alan Musgrave. Cambridge: Cambridge University Press, 1970.

Lang, U. M. "Anhypostatos-Enhypostatos: Church Fathers, Protestant Orthodoxy and Karl Barth." *Journal of Theological Studies* NS 49 (1998): 630–57.

la Peyrère, Isaac de. *Praeadamitae sive Exercitatio super versibus duodecimo, decimotertio et decimoquarto capitis quinti Epistolae D. Pauli ad Romanos quibus inducuntur Primi Homines ante Adamum conditi*. Amsterdam: Louis & Daniel Elzevier, 1655.

Laudan, Larry. *Progress and Its Problems: Towards a Theory of Scientific Growth.* Berkeley, Calif.: University of California Press, 1977.

Lewis, C. S. *Miracles* (1947). Glasgow: Collins/Fount, 1974.

Líndal, Erikur, Jon G. Stefánsson, and Sigurjón B. Stefánsson. "The Qualitative Difference of Visions and Visual Hallucinations: A Comparison of a General-Population and Clinical Sample." *Comprehensive Psychiatry* 35 (Sept./ Oct. 1994): 405–8.

Lindbeck, George A. *The Nature of Doctrine: Religion and Theology in a Postliberal Age.* Philadelphia: Westminster, 1984.

Losee, John. *A Historical Introduction to the Philosophy of Science.* 3d edition. Oxford: Oxford University Press, 1993.

Lüdemann, Gerd. *The Resurrection of Jesus: History, Experience, Faith.* London: SCM, 1994.

Luther, Martin. "Lectures on Genesis, Chapters 1–5." In *Luther's Works,* vol. 1, edited by Jaroslav Pelikan. St. Louis, Miss.: Concordia, 1958.

———. *Tischreden,* vol. 4. In *D. Martin Luthers Werke kritische Gesamtausgabe.* Weimarer Ausgabe. Weimar: Hermann Böhlaus Nachfolger, 1916.

MacIntyre, Alasdair. *Whose Justice? Which Rationality?* Notre Dame, Ind.: University of Notre Dame Press, 1988.

Mack, Burton L. *The Lost Gospel: The Book of Q and Christian Origins.* Rockport, Mass.: Element, 1993.

Mackie, J. L. *Ethics: Inventing Right and Wrong.* London: Pelikan, 1977.

Magee, Bryan. *Confessions of a Philosopher.* New York: Modern Library, 1997.

Maimonides, Moses. *The Guide of the Perplexed* (1190 C.E.). Translated by Schlomo Pines. Chicago: University of Chicago Press, 1963.

———. *The Guide of the Perplexed: An Abridged Edition.* Translated by Chaim Rabin. Indianapolis: Hackett, 1995.

Marx, Karl. "Contribution to the Critique of Hegel's Philosophy of Right" (1844). In *Karl Marx: Early Writings,* translated by T. B. Bottomore. London: C. A. Watts, 1963.

Mason, Richard. *The God of Spinoza: A Philosophical Study.* Cambridge: Cambridge University Press, 1997.

Maull, Nancy. "Spinoza in the Century of Science." In *Spinoza and the Sciences,* edited by Marjorie Grene and Debra Nails. Boston Studies in the Philosophy of Science 91. Dordrecht: D. Reidel, 1986.

McCormack, Bruce L. *Karl Barth's Critically Realistic Dialectical Theology: Its Genesis and Development 1909–1936.* Oxford: Clarendon Press, 1995.

McGrath, Alister E. *The Making of Modern German Christology: 1750–1990.* 2d edition. Grand Rapids: Zondervan, 1994.

McKee, David Rice. "Isaac de la Peyrère, a Precursor of Eighteenth-Century Critical Deists." *Publications of the Modern Language Association of America* 59 (1944): 456–85.

McKim, Donald K., ed. *Historical Handbook of Major Biblical Interpreters.* Downers Grove, Ill.: InterVarsity, 1998.

McMullin, Ernan. "Galileo on Science and Scripture." In *The Cambridge Companion to Galileo,* edited by Peter Machamer. Cambridge: Cambridge University Press, 1998.

———. "How Should Cosmology Relate to Theology?" In *The Sciences and Theology in the Twentieth Century,* edited by A. R. Peacocke. Stocksfield: Oriel Press (Routledge & Kegan Paul), 1981.

Meier, John P. *A Marginal Jew: Rethinking the Historical Jesus.* Vol. 2, *Mentor, Message and Miracles.* New York: Doubleday, 1994.

Metzger, Bruce M. *The Text of the New Testament.* 2d edition. Oxford: Clarendon Press, 1968.

Meyer, Ben F. *The Aims of Jesus.* London: SCM, 1979.

Moltmann, Jürgen. *Theology of Hope: On the Ground and the Implications of a Christian Eschatology* (1965). Translated by James W. Leitch. London: SCM, 1967.

Morgan, Robert. "Introduction: Ernst Troeltsch on Theology and Religion." In *Writings on Theology and Religion*, translated and edited by Robert Morgan and Michael Pye. London: Duckworth, 1977.

————. "Troeltsch and Christian Theology." In *Writings on Theology and Religion*, translated and edited by Robert Morgan and Michael Pye. London: Duckworth, 1977.

————. "Troeltsch and the Dialectical Theology." In *Ernst Troeltsch and the Future of Theology*, edited by John Powell Clayton. Cambridge: Cambridge University Press, 1976.

Musgrave, Alan. *Common Sense, Science, and Scepticism: A Historical Introduction to the Philosophy of Knowledge.* Cambridge: Cambridge University Press, 1993.

————. "Method or Madness? Can the Methodology of Research Programmes Be Rescued from Epistemological Anarchism?" In *Essays in Memory of Imre Lakatos*, edited by R. S. Cohen et al. Dordrecht: D. Reidel, 1976.

Nietzsche, Friedrich. "David Strauss, the Confessor and the Writer" (1873). In *Untimely Meditations*, translated by R. J. Hollingdale. Cambridge Texts in the History of Philosophy. Cambridge: Cambridge University Press, 1997.

————. "On the Uses and Disadvantages of History for Life" (1874). In *Untimely Meditations*, translated by R. J. Hollingdale. Cambridge Texts in the History of Philosophy. Cambridge: Cambridge University Press, 1997.

Novick, Peter. *That Noble Dream: The "Objectivity Question" and the American Historical Association.* Ideas in Context. Cambridge: Cambridge University Press, 1988.

Pannenberg, Wolfhart. "Dogmatic Theses on the Doctrine of Revelation." In *Revelation as History* (1961), edited by Wolfhart Pannenberg and translated by David Granskou. New York: Macmillan, 1968.

————. "Erwägungen zur einer Theologie der Religionsgeschichte" (1962). In *Grundfragen systematischer Theologie: Gesammelte Aufsätze.* Göttingen: Vandenhoeck & Ruprecht, 1967.

————. "Faith and Reason" (1965). In *Basic Questions in Theology.* Translated by George H. Keim. Vol. 2. Library of Philosophy and Theology. London: SCM, 1971.

————. "Hermeneutic and Universal History" (1963). In *Basic Questions in Theology* (1967), translated by George H. Keim. Vol. 1. Library of Philosophy and Theology. London: SCM, 1970.

————. *Jesus—God and Man* (1964). Translated by Lewis L. Wilkins and Duane A. Priebe. London: SCM, 1968.

————. *Metaphysics and the Idea of God* (1988). Translated by Philip Clayton. Grand Rapids: Eerdmans, 1990.

————. "On Historical and Theological Hermeneutic" (1964). In *Basic Questions in Theology* (1967), translated by George H. Keim. Vol. 1. Library of Philosophy and Theology. London: SCM, 1970.

————. "Redemptive Event and History" (1959). Translated by Shirley C.

Guthrie Jr. and George H. Keim. In *Basic Questions in Theology*. Vol. 1. Library of Philosophy and Theology. London: SCM, 1970.

———. "The Revelation of God in Jesus of Nazareth." In *Theology as History*, edited by James M. Robinson and John B. Cobb Jr. New Frontiers in Theology 3. New York: Harper & Row, 1967.

———. *Systematic Theology*. Vol. 1 (1988). Translated by Geoffrey W. Bromiley. Grand Rapids: Eerdmans, 1991.

———. *Systematic Theology*. Vol. 2 (1991). Translated by Geoffrey W. Bromiley. Grand Rapids: Eerdmans, 1994.

———. *Systematic Theology*. Vol. 3 (1993). Translated by Geoffrey W. Bromiley. Grand Rapids: Eerdmans, 1998.

———. *Theology and the Philosophy of Science*. Translated by Francis McDonagh. London: Darton, Longman & Todd, 1976.

———. "Towards a Theology of the History of Religions" (1962). In *Basic Questions in Theology*, translated by George H. Keim. Vol. 2. London: SCM, 1971.

———. "What is Truth?" In *Basic Questions in Theology*, translated by George H. Keim. Vol. 2. London: SCM, 1971.

Parker, T. H. L. *Calvin's Old Testament Commentaries*. Edinburgh: T. & T. Clark, 1986.

Paul, Garrett E. Introduction to the English edition of *The Christian Faith*, by Ernst Troeltsch, translated by Garrett E. Paul. Fortress Texts in Modern Theology. Minneapolis: Fortress Press, 1991.

Pera, Marcello. "The God of Theologians and the God of Astronomers: An Apology of Bellarmine." In *The Cambridge Companion to Galileo*, edited by Peter Machamer. Cambridge: Cambridge University Press, 1998.

Plantinga, Alvin. "Is Belief in God Properly Basic?" *Noûs* 15 (1981): 41–51.

———. "Self-Profile." In *Alvin Plantinga*, edited by James E. Tomberlin and Peter van Inwagen. Profiles. Dordrecht: D. Reidel, 1985.

———. *Warrant and Proper Function*. New York: Oxford University Press, 1993.

Popkin, Richard H. "The Development of Religious Scepticism and the Influence of Isaac la Peyrère's Pre-Adamism and Bible Criticism." In *Classical Influences on European Culture A.D. 1500–1700: Proceedings of an International Conference Held at King's College, Cambridge, April 1974*, edited by R. R. Bolgar. Cambridge: Cambridge University Press, 1976.

———. "New Light on the Roots of Spinoza's Science of the Bible." In *Spinoza and the Sciences*, edited by Marjorie Grene and Debra Nails. Boston Studies in the Philosophy of Science 91. Dordrecht: D. Reidel, 1986.

———. "Spinoza and Biblical Scholarship." In *The Cambridge Companion to Spinoza*, edited by Don Garrett. Cambridge: Cambridge University Press, 1996.

———. "Spinoza and La Peyrère." In *Spinoza: New Perspectives*, edited by Robert W. Shahan and J. I. Biro. Norman, Okla.: University of Oklahoma Press, 1978.

Popper, Karl R. *The Open Universe: An Argument for Indeterminism*. Vol. 2 of *Postscript to the Logic of Scientific Discovery* (1956). Edited by W. W. Bartley III. London: Hutchinson, 1982.

———. *The Poverty of Historicism* (1957). London: Ark Paperbacks/Routledge, 1986.

Preus, J. Samuel. "The Bible and Religion in the Century of Genius." *Religion* 28 (1998): 3–27, 111–124.

———. *Explaining Religion: Criticism and Theory from Bodin to Freud.* New Haven, Conn.: Yale University Press, 1987.

Proudfoot, Wayne. *Religious Experience.* Berkeley, Calif.: University of California Press, 1985.

Ptolemy, Claudius. *Almagest.* English text: *Ptolemy's Almagest.* Translated by G. J. Toomer. London: Duckworth, 1984.

Quine, W.V., and J. S. Ullian. *The Web of Belief.* 2d edition. New York: Random House, 1978.

Quinton, Anthony. *Bacon.* Past Masters. Oxford: Oxford University Press, 1980.

Reimarus, Hermann Samuel. "Concerning the Intention of Jesus and His Teaching." In *Reimarus: Fragments,* translated by Ralph S. Fraser and edited by Charles H. Talbot. Lives of Jesus Series. Philadelphia: Fortress Press, 1970.

Reist, Benjamin A. *Towards a Theology of Involvement: A Study of Ernst Troeltsch.* Library of Philosophy and Theology. London: SCM, 1966.

Reventlow, Henning Graf. *The Authority of the Bible and the Rise of the Modern World* (1980). Translated by John Bowden. London: SCM, 1984.

Robinson, James M. "A New Quest of the Historical Jesus" In *A New Quest of the Historical Jesus and Other Essays* (1959). Philadelphia: Fortress Press, 1983.

Schleiermacher, Friedrich. *The Christian Faith* (1830). Edited by H. R. Mackintosh and J. S. Stewart. Edinburgh: T. & T. Clark, 1928.

Scholder, Klaus. *The Birth of Modern Critical Theology: Origins and Problems of Biblical Criticism in the Seventeenth Century* (1966). Translated by John Bowden. London: SCM, 1990.

Schweitzer, Albert. *Christianity and the Religions of the World.* Translated by Johanna Powers. London: George Allen & Unwin, 1923.

———. *Civilization and Ethics.* The Philosophy of Civilization 2. Translated by C. T. Campion (1923). 3d English edition revised by Mrs. Charles E. B. Russell. London: A. & C. Black, 1946.

———. *The Decay and Restoration of Civilization.* The Philosophy of Civilization 1. Translated by C. T. Campion (1923). London: Unwin Books/A. & C. Black, 1961.

———. *Indian Thought and Its Development* (1935). Translated by Mrs. Charles E. B. Russell. London: Hodder & Stoughton, 1936.

———. *The Kingdom of God and Primitive Christianity* (1967). Translated by L. A. Garrard. London: A. & C. Black. 1968.

———. *The Mystery of the Kingdom of God: The Secret of Jesus' Messiahship and Passion* (1901). Translated by Walter Lowrie. London: A. & C. Black, 1925.

———. *The Quest of the Historical Jesus.* 1st edition (1906). Translated by W. Montgomery (1910). London: SCM, 1981.

———. *The Quest of the Historical Jesus.* 2d edition (1913). Translated by W. Montgomery, J. R. Coates, Susan Cupitt, and John Bowden. London: SCM, 2000.

Shapin, Steven. *The Scientific Revolution.* Chicago: University of Chicago Press, 1996.

Sharpe, Eric J. *Comparative Religion: A History.* London: Duckworth, 1975.

Shirley, Samuel. Translator's foreword to *The Ethics and Selected Letters,* by Baruch Spinoza, edited by Seymour Feldman. Indianapolis: Hackett, 1982.

Smith, Wilfred Cantwell. *The Meaning and End of Religion* (1962). London: SPCK, 1978.

Spinoza, Benedict. *The Ethics and Selected Letters.* Translated by Samuel Shirley and edited by Seymour Feldman. Indianapolis: Hackett, 1982.

———. *The Letters.* Translated by Samuel Shirley. Indianapolis: Hackett, 1995.

———. *Tractatus Theologico-Politicus.* Translated by Samuel Shirley. Leiden: E. J. Brill, 1989.

Strauss, David Friedrich. *Die christliche Glaubenslehre in ihrer geschichtliche Entwicklung und im Kampfe mit der modernen Wissenschaft dargestellt.* Tübingen: C. F. Osiander, 1840.

———. *The Christ of Faith and the Jesus of History: A Critique of Schleiermacher's "The Life of Jesus"* (1865). Translated by Leander E. Keck. Life of Jesus Series. Philadelphia: Fortress Press, 1977.

———. "Hermann Samuel Reimarus and His Apology" (1877). Translated by Ralph S. Fraser. In *Reimarus: Fragments,* edited by Charles H. Talbot. Lives of Jesus Series. Philadelphia: Fortress Press, 1970.

———. *Das Leben Jesu kritisch bearbeitet.* 2 vols. Tübingen: C. F. Osiander, 1835.

———. *The Life of Jesus Critically Examined.* 4th German edition (1840). Translated by George Eliot and edited by Peter C. Hodgson. Lives of Jesus Series. Philadelphia: Fortress Press, 1972.

———. *A New Life of Jesus* (1864). Vols. 1 and 2. London: Williams & Norgate, 1865.

———. *The Old Faith and the New: A Confession.* 6th edition (1872). Translated by Mathilde Blind. London: Asher & Co., 1873.

Sutcliffe, F. E. Introduction to *Discourse on Method and the Meditations,* by René Descartes. Translated by F. E. Sutcliffe. Penguin Classics. Harmondsworth, Middlesex: Penguin, 1968.

Tomberlin, James E. "Is Belief in God Justified?" *Journal of Philosophy* 67 (1970): 31–38.

Toomer, G. J. Introduction to *Ptolemy's Almagest.* London: Duckworth, 1984.

Troeltsch, Ernst. *The Absoluteness of Christianity and the History of Religions.* 3d edition (1929). Translated by David Reid. Library of Philosophy and Theology. London: SCM, 1972.

———. *Die Absolutheit des Christentums und die Religionsgeschichte.* 2d edition. Tübingen: J. C. B. Mohr (Paul Siebeck), 1912.

———. *The Christian Faith* (1925). Translated by Garrett E. Paul. Fortress Texts in Modern Theology. Minneapolis: Fortress Press. 1991.

———. "The Common Spirit." Translated by H. G. Atkins. In *Christian Thought: Its History and Application,* edited by F. von Hügel. London: University of London Press, 1923.

———. "The Dogmatics of the History-of-Religions School" (1913). Translated by Walter E. Wyman Jr. In *Religion in History—Ernst Troeltsch: Essays Translated by James Luther Adams and Walter F. Bense.* Edinburgh: T & T. Clark. 1991.

———. "Faith and History" (1910). In *Religion in History—Ernst Troeltsch: Essays Translated by James Luther Adams and Walter F. Bense.* Edinburgh: T & T. Clark, 1991.

————. *Glaubenslehre: Nach Heidelberger Vorlesungen aus den Jahren 1911 u. 1912.* Munich: Duncker & Humblot, 1925.

————. "Glaube und Ethos der hebräischen Propheten" (1916). In Gesammelte Schriften 4. Tübingen: J. C. B. Mohr (Paul Siebeck), 1925.

————. "Half a Century of Theology: A Review" (1908). Translated by Robert Morgan. In *Ernst Troeltsch: Writings on Theology and Religion*, translated and edited by Robert Morgan and Michael Pye. London: Duckworth, 1977.

————. "Historical and Dogmatic Method in Theology" (1898). Translated by Ephraim Fischoff and revised by Walter Bense. In *Religion in History—Ernst Troeltsch: Essays Translated by James Luther Adams and Walter F. Bense.* Edinburgh: T & T. Clark, 1991.

————. "Historiography." In *Encyclopedia of Religion and Ethics*, edited by James Hastings. Vol. 6. Edinburgh: T. & T. Clark, 1913.

————. *Der Historismus und seine Probleme—Erstes Buch: Das logische Problem der Geschichtsphilosophie.* Gesammelte Schriften 3. Tübingen: J. C. B. Mohr (Paul Siebeck), 1922.

————. "Idealism." In *Encyclopedia of Religion and Ethics*, edited by James Hastings. Vol. 7. Edinburgh: T. & T. Clark, 1914.

————. "Modern Philosophy of History" (1904). In *Religion in History—Ernst Troeltsch: Essays Translated by James Luther Adams and Walter F. Bense.* Edinburgh: T. & T. Clark, 1991.

————. "The Morality of the Personality and of the Conscience." Translated by F. von Hügel. In *Christian Thought: Its History and Application*, edited by F. von Hügel. London: University of London Press, 1923.

————. "My Books" (1922). Translated by Franklin H. Littell and revised by Walter F. Bense. In *Religion in History—Ernst Troeltsch: Essays Translated by James Luther Adams and Walter F. Bense.* Edinburgh: T. & T. Clark, 1991.

————. "On the Possibility of a Liberal Christianity" (1910). Translated by Walter F. Bense. In *Religion in History—Ernst Troeltsch: Essays Translated by James Luther Adams and Walter F. Bense.* Edinburgh: T & T. Clark. 1991.

————. "On the Question of the Religious A Priori" (1909). In *Religion in History—Ernst Troeltsch: Essays Translated by James Luther Adams and Walter F. Bense.* Edinburgh: T & T. Clark. 1991.

————. "The Place of Christianity among the World-Religions." Translated by Mary E. Clarke. In *Christian Thought: Its History and Application*, edited by F. von Hügel. London: University of London Press, 1923.

————. "Religion and the Science of Religion" (1906). Translated by Michael Pye. In *Ernst Troeltsch: Writings on Theology and Religion*, translated and edited by Robert Morgan and Michael Pye. London: Duckworth, 1977.

————. *The Social Teaching of the Christian Churches.* Translated by Olive Wyon. London: George Allen & Unwin, 1931.

Weiss, Johannes. *Jesus' Proclamation of the Kingdom of God* (1892). Translated by Richard H. Hiers and David L. Holland. Lives of Jesus Series. Philadelphia: Fortress Press, 1971.

Whitehead, Alfred North. *Process and Reality* (1929). Corrected Edition. Edited by David Ray Griffin and Donald W. Sherburne. New York: Macmillan/Free Press, 1978.

————. *Science and the Modern World.* Lowell Lectures 1925. New York: Mentor Books, 1948.

Wilson, Margaret D. "Spinoza's Theory of Knowledge." In *The Cambridge Companion to Spinoza*, edited by Don Garratt. Cambridge: Cambridge University Press, 1996.

Witherington, Ben. *The Jesus Quest: The Third Search for the Jew of Nazareth.* Downers Grove, Ill.: InterVarsity, 1995.

Woodfield, Andrew. *Teleology.* Cambridge: Cambridge University Press, 1976.

Wrede, William. *The Messianic Secret* (1901). Translated by J. C. G. Greig. Library of Theological Translations. London: James Clarke & Co., 1971.

Wright, N. T. *Jesus and the Victory of God.* Christian Origins and the Question of God, vol.2. Minneapolis: Fortress Press, 1996.

———. "Jesus, Quest for the Historical." In *Anchor Bible Dictionary*, edited by David Noel Freedman. Vol 3. New York: Doubleday, 1992.

———. *The New Testament and the People of God.* Christian Origins and the Question of God, vol. 1. Minneapolis: Fortress Press, 1992.

Wyman, Walter E. *The Concept of Glaubenslehre: Ernst Troeltsch and the Theological Heritage of Schleiermacher.* American Academy of Religion Academy Series 44. Chico, Calif.: Scholars Press, 1983.

Index of Names

Note: Page numbers refer only to substantive discussions of an author's work, whether in the text or in footnotes.

Adams, James Luther,   172 n.71
Anselm, St., 65
Aquinas, Thomas   *See* Thomas Aquinas
Aristotle,   10, 24, 27, 52, 142 n.106
Arnal, William E.,   313 n.65
Auerbach, Erich,   34 n.162
Augustine, St.,   15, 16, 21, 27, 35 nn.169, 70; 50, 54–56, 74

Bacon, Francis,   25–26, 27–28, 58, 72, 183
Barr, James,   56 n.93
Barth, Karl
    analogy,   228
    authority of Bible,   210, 215
    biblical hermeneutics,   204–10, 240
    Christology,   228, 229–32, 238
    context of theology,   xii, 205 n.6, 327
    eschatology,   223 n.93
    historical criticism,   205–7, 211, 213, 215–17, 222
    historical Jesus,   217–18, 230–32, 235, 235 n.163
    history,   204, 218–32
    history of religions,   234, 235, 238
    inspiration,   211–12, 214–15, 241
    liberal theology,   217, 233
    miracles,   229
    naturalistic explanation,   244 n.201
    Protestant scripture principle,   229, 241–44, 363–64
    religion,   233–39
    resurrection,   224–25, 226, 229, 232 n.146
    revelation,   210–14, 215–17, 227–29, 233–39
    time and eternity,   220–21
    Word of God,   211–12, 214, 218 n.58
Bartley, William Warren III,   245 n.208
Bastick, Tony,   364 n.30
Bellarmine, Robert Cardinal,   14 n.68, 16 n.78
Bennett, Jonathan,   47 n.51, 63 n.131
Bentley, Jerry H.,   4–5

Berger, Peter,   359 n.18
Blackwell, Richard J.,   14 n.69, 16 n.78
Bodin, Jean,   34 n.164
Bradley, F. H.,   358
Bultmann, Rudolf
    apocalyptic,   276–77, 279–80, 281–85
    biblical hermeneutics,   264–66, 279, 283–84, 290
    context of theology,   xii
    demythologizing,   248–49, 264–65, 283
    dualism,   253, 255 n.25, 256–57, 263, 272
    historical criticism,   281–82
    historical Jesus,   273–79, 282–85
    history,   258–71, 279, 280–81
    history of religions,   255, 285–86, 288–89
    liberal theology,   233, 248–49, 281–82
    Lutheranism,   249 n.5, 253, 257–58, 270, 272, 278 n.144, 289, 294
    miracles,   262, 267–71, 272
    objectification,   249, 250–54, 258–63, 270–71, 272
    religion,   254–57, 279–81, 285–89
    resurrection,   281
    revelation,   285–89
Burke, Peter,   3
Busch, Eberhard,   205 n.6
Byrne, Peter,   357 n.13

Calvin, John,   15, 35 n.169, 208, 211 n.24, 243, 243 n.199, 244 n.204, 257 n.36
Capra, Dominick La   *See* La Capra, Dominick
Cassirer, Ernst,   34 n.165, 40 n.4, 71
Chilton, Bruce,   313 n.65
Coakley, Sarah,   159 n.1, 164 n.24, 180–81, 181 n.124, 183 n.135, 190, 192, 201 n.239
Cohen, Hermann,   257 n.35, 292–93
Collingwood, R. G,   163 n.19, 197–98, 344 n.227
Copenhaver, Brian P.,   2 n.3
Copernicus, Nicolaus,   10–11

388 *Index of Names*

Index of Subjects

Note: Some subjects are also listed after major authors in the Index of Names.

accommodation *See* Bible, accommodation of message
affliction, the messianic *See* messianic affliction
allegory *See* Bible, allegorical interpretation
analogy, principle of, 103–4, 117–19, 163, 196–98, 228, 337–38, 340–41
anthropomorphism, 59–60, 71, 356
apocalyptic thought *See also* ethics
   appropriation of, 195, 281–84, 301–3, 318–22, 331, 344–46
   ethics and, 125–26, 132–35, 195, 284–85, 360–62
   kingdom of God and, 82, 85, 122, 130, 176, 192–93, 276–77, 279–80
   scandal of, 82, 85, 135, 150, 192–93, 195, 284, 322
   truth of, 338–41
a priori, religious, 167 n.43, 289, 327
astronomy, 2, 10–16
authority, religious *See* religious authority
axiological argument, 356 n.11, 369

Bible *See also* historical criticism
   accommodation of message, 11, 13–14, 15 n.70, 45–46, 49–50, 73
   allegorical interpretation, 4, 24, 55–56, 74, 86
   authority *See* religious authority
   biblical personalities *See* revelation
   fallibility, 8–10, 11, 46–50, 51–52, 74, 213–14
   historical knowledge, 21 n.101, 21–22, 34–35 *See also* faith, historical facts and
   inspiration *See* inspiration, doctrine of
   its own interpreter, 40–41
   mythical interpretation, 79, 80, 85–91, 106, 117–19 *See also* myth
   rationalist interpretation, 73 n.194, 79, 80, 106
   scientific knowledge, 11–16, 31–32 *See also* science and religion
   supernaturalist interpretation, 78–79, 80, 96, 106

witness to revelation, 170, 210–14
Word of God, 211–12, 214, 215, 218 n.58

causality, 24, 63 n.131 *See also* teleology
Christianity and other religions *See* religious diversity
Christology, 106–11, 187–95, 228, 229–32, 238, 277, 311
contingency and necessity, 59, 66, 176, 183–84, 320–21, 344–46
controversy, religious, 2, 5–10
correlation, principle of, 163–64, 295, 344
creation, 31–32, 116
criticism, principle of, 163, 295

deism, 1 n.1, 6–10, 31, 96, 351, 354
demythologizing, 248–49, 264–65, 283
design, argument from, 114
determinism *See* contingency and necessity
dialectical theology, 115, 149–50, 200, 203 n.2, 249, 289, 298–301, 312, 353, 362–65
dogmatic method, 162–64, 310
dualism, 139, 157–58, 253, 255 n.25, 256–57, 263, 272

Enlightenment, 33 n.161, 89, 142, 154, 165, 252
eschatology *See* apocalyptic thought; realized eschatology
ethics
   competing traditions of, 174, 202 n.245, 369
   eschatology and, 125–26, 132–34, 195, 360–62
   interim ethics, 124, 130, 133–34, 284, 361
   law and, 154
   religion and, 255, 354–56
   teaching of Jesus, 114–15, 195, 284–85, 305–6, 310, 360–62
   worldview and, 135, 139–41, 144–45, 147, 150, 156–58
Eurocentrism, 202 n.246

389